The Play

A CRITICAL ANTHOLOGY

SUPPLEMENTARY TO THIS VOLUME

another critical anthology of the drama edited by Eric Bentley

FROM THE MODERN REPERTOIRE

First Series 1949 · *Second Series (in preparation)*

UNIVERSITY OF DENVER PRESS

EDMOND ROSTAND · *Cyrano de Bergerac* · OSCAR WILDE · *The Importance of Being Earnest* · MOLIÈRE · *The Miser* · WILLIAM SHAKESPEARE · *Twelfth Night* · *Othello* · SOPHOCLES · *Antigone* · HENRIK IBSEN · *Ghosts* · AUGUST STRINDBERG · *The Ghost Sonata* · ARTHUR MILLER · *Death of a Salesman*

The Play

A CRITICAL ANTHOLOGY

edited by
Eric Bentley

New York · Prentice-Hall, Inc. · 1951

PRENTICE-HALL ENGLISH COMPOSITION AND
INTRODUCTION TO LITERATURE SERIES

Thomas Clark Pollock, Editor

COPYRIGHT 1951 BY PRENTICE-HALL, INC. ALL RIGHTS RESERVED.
PRINTED IN THE UNITED STATES OF AMERICA.

To

STARK YOUNG

from whom I have tried to learn

Le théâtre, c'est une géométrie vivante.
—FRANCISQUE SARCEY

ACKNOWLEDGMENT

IN WRITING the commentary for this book I tried to draw on my experience—however limited—as theater-goer and director. I also learned a good deal from students at the University of Minnesota and the Kenyon School of English. I compiled the present table of contents while presenting a general course on drama at the latter institution. Among the Kenyon students whose brains I am aware of having picked are Miss Beatrice Gottlieb and Mr. Henry Popkin. (The latter's unpublished essay on *Cyrano* I found especially suggestive.) The work of another Kenyon student, Mr. Lloyd Parks, is acknowledged in the text where his translation of *The Miser* appears.

I should like to thank the owners of the copyright in the plays and articles appearing in this book for their permission to reprint them here. Specific acknowledgment of this permission is given at the appropriate place in the text. I should also acknowledge the courtesy of Harcourt, Brace & Co. in granting me permission to adapt two passages from *The Playwright as Thinker* to a new context in this volume.

Last but not least, the Guggenheim Foundation should be thanked for allowing me to devote a year to setting down my thoughts on dramatic art: an enterprise which included the compilation of this book.

TABLE OF CONTENTS

A LETTER TO THE READER   1

1. CYRANO DE BERGERAC, *by Edmond Rostand*
   TR. HUMBERT WOLFE   10
   The problem of translation : This version and others : CYRANO as melodrama : Problem of judging : Begin with standard terms—plot, character, theme, spectacle, dialogue : Primacy of plot : Rostand's "artificial" characters : Special artifice of his CYRANO : Theme —life as a performance : But theatricality more important than theme—as witness plot, character, theme, spectacle and, especially, dialogue : The collaboration of Wolfe and Laughton

2. THE IMPORTANCE OF BEING EARNEST,
   by Oscar Wilde   148
   As CYRANO is a "complication" of melodrama, IMPORTANCE is "complication" of farce : The ridiculous story, the stream of comment on serious topics : How these two elements interact to their mutual advantage : The plot, having to counterbalance all the rest, gains importance : The comment, as defined by the plot, comes to be effectively true

3. THE MISER, *by Molière*   TR. LLOYD PARKS   214
   Demands made by a play written long before our time :

x   THE PLAY

   The two historical backgrounds—social and theatrical : Louis XIV and the *commedia dell'arte* : Desirability of knowing France and French : Difficulty of Molière for the foreigner : Chief point of contact between him and us—our comedians : Help needed from descriptive critics (e.g., Bergson, Stoll) : Comic repetition : Comic coincidence : Molière's acceptance of artifice (cf. modern distaste for) : His use of artifice to make points, to note traits : Yet plot, not character, is basic : Plot "unrealistic" but used for presentation of reality : Plot a machine for definition of subject : Parallelism and contrast : Molière's special genius

4. TWELFTH NIGHT, *by William Shakespeare*   285
   Shakespeare easier for us to approach : Can and should be seen on stage : Elementary tips on reading him (vocabulary, scene division) : Two components of TWELFTH NIGHT (romance and low comedy) alternate : To define Shakespeare's subject : Shakespeare's themes not always easy to locate, therefore procedure recommended to novice —take any important idea involved and trace its treatment through a play : *Love* in TWELFTH NIGHT : Love at different levels : Love true and false : A story as "education" of one character by another—Viola as teacher of Olivia and Orsino : Feste—a convention humanized : His place in an action where appearance mocks reality : Total pattern of play—conventionality of main plot, realism of subplot : Topic for further investigation— language and symbolism

5. OTHELLO, *by William Shakespeare*   372
   Is the difference between a comedy and a tragedy (for Shakespeare) more than one of degree? : OTHELLO treats same contrast of appearance and reality as TWELFTH NIGHT but pushes it further : Tips for reading: (1) read with sense of musical organization (though beware of "just listening"), (2) keep the sense of plot as basis acquired

from reading melodrama, farce, and comedy, (3) be on guard for anachronisms in your "natural" responses to (e.g.) Shakespeare's version of marriage : conventions again—how we are to take (1) a conventional plot, (2) conventional characters (Iago, Desdemona) : Difference of opinion as to Othello

6. ANTIGONE, *by Sophocles*
ADAP. JEAN COCTEAU—TR. CARL WILDMAN   489
How far can we understand authors so far removed in time? And read in translation? : Need for adaptation : Cocteau's bird's-eye view : The story of KING OEDIPUS and OEDIPUS AT COLONUS : The categories of Aristotle— *Antigone* an "action," not a portrait : Is Creon the villain? : Greek attitude to law : To Unwritten Laws : The meaning of the play now : The idea of humanity : Edmund Wilson's view—Antigone as neurotic : Form—alternation of episode and chorus : Role of latter : Merits and shortcomings of Cocteau version

7. GHOSTS, *by Henrik Ibsen*   TR. EVA LE GALLIENNE   518
Again realism : So-called realistic works have unrealistic elements and vice versa : *Ghosts* famous for its realism but not without artifice : Ibsen's technique—the retrospective method : Ibsen's subject-matter (but is syphilis what the play is about?) : Triple symbolism of its title : Double tragedy of Mrs. Alving : Drama of ideas? : Ibsen's attitude to ideas : What view of life does the play present—that "society is to blame"? : Important to work over all the details for oneself : Samples—ironical contrast of rain and sun, ironical parallel of Engstrand and Manders : Ibsen's notes for the play

8. THE GHOST SONATA, *by August Strindberg*
TR. ELIZABETH SPRIGGE   588
An allegedly nonrealistic play, a fantasy : Difficult because of (1) abstruse ideas, (2) heavy use of nonverbal

arts of theater : Scene by scene analysis : The main lines of the action : The leitmotif of guilt : Repeated images—creditors and vampires : The idea of the play : Does it grow out of the action or is it wishfully imposed? : Form: a visual myth : Technical originality but produced by moral-ideological energy : Musical in structure yet a realistic study of life : Similar to *Ghosts* : Middle-class civilization haunted by guilt

9. DEATH OF A SALESMAN, *by Arthur Miller*   629
The reader his own drama critic : Reviews of the play —Brooks Atkinson, Ivor Brown, John Mason Brown, Eleanor Clark, Frederick Morgan

APPENDIX   755
Style and Medium in the Motion Pictures, by Erwin Panofsky

SUGGESTIONS FOR READING   777

A LETTER TO THE READER

DEAR READER: This anthology provides the basic material for some elementary lessons on the drama. It is designed to be used either privately or in classes. The idea behind it is simply that if you want to know something of drama, you may as well begin by reading plays. Here are nine. Arranged in their present order and accompanied by the present Notes they are intended to call your attention to one feature after another of dramatic art.

The main thing is to read the plays, passing from superior melodrama (*Cyrano de Bergerac*) and superior farce (*The Importance of Being Earnest*) to high comedy of two kinds (*The Miser* and *Twelfth Night*) and thence to tragedy of two kinds (*Othello* and *Antigone*) and finally to modern drama of two kinds, the realistic and the fantastic (*Ghosts* and *A Ghost Sonata*). After this quick journey back to the Greeks and forward again to the moderns, it is time to take breath and ask: "How much the wiser am I? When I go to the theater now, am I a better judge of a play than I was before?" At this point is set before you a recent American play. No editorial notes: only a sketch of the New York production and the hopelessly conflicting opinions of its critics. Do you feel capable of arriving at an opinion of your own? An opinion that is more than one "personal impression" among many? If not, you have been wasting your time with this book.

But be warned. The book will not provide you with the answers. There are the plays, and there is an amount of commentary which is far from doing them justice. Critical notes (the editor thinks) should be incomplete. They should lead away from themselves and towards:

(1) the writings of critics who on this subject or that are more expert or more intelligent;

(2) discussion on your part (is what the editor says true?); and

(3) re-reading of the plays.

Suggestions for (1) are provided in the Notes themselves. (2) is justified at any point in the text whatsoever. (Is the theme of *Cyrano* really what the editor says? Does *Antigone* really mean that?) (3) takes place as a matter of course: you return to the text to check a critic's comment or your own recollection, to see what the truth is. You thus become pretty well acquainted with some plays and are in a position to become acquainted with others.

You may have very few opinions on the "true nature of tragedy." You may not be able to give a generalized account of dramatic technique. Do not be perturbed. The discussion of what tragedy is can begin too early. It is best to begin with makeshift definitions, read some plays that have been called tragedies in some sense or other, and discover what these plays contain—one can scarcely speak for the others. The aim is not to talk about drama in general but to understand particular plays.

Thus it should not disturb you that this or that technical feature is not discussed within the bounds of the present course, that this or that technical term is not used. We have nine plays before us. The discussion can be limited to what they seem to demand. It is true that from any one play you *could* derive any discussion you wanted and any number of technical terms. But *should* you? Surely most musicians would agree that a little technical analysis of music should be preceded by a lot of listening. In fact technical analysis need only be made at all if it helps you to listen better; analysis is made for art not art for analysis. In our time too little attention has been paid to artistic experience itself, too much to more tangible outward tokens of Culture. There are many people who can rattle on about Sonata Form, just as there are many people who can rattle on about the life and loves of Beethoven. It would be better if some of them had forgotten to learn who Beethoven was and had simply been quiet and listened. When you have "listened" to some plays, you will reach after terms which enable you to discuss and comprehend them; you may even begin to speculate on the nature of certain groups of plays (tragedies, comedies, or what not). But the listening comes first.

It is as well to have no prior opinions as to what drama should be and do. Such opinions prevent your accepting anything that stands outside your categories. Even professional critics are perpetually prevented by their view of what drama should be from accepting genuine originality—because originality, by definition, implies something not already formulated and known. Read plays, see plays, and observe for yourself what playwrights have done; whether they conform to Mr. A's definition of drama is neither here nor there. The more you can make your mind a blank for dramatists to write on, the better.

But here we come to a problem. The editor's mind has already been written on by dramatists and for some years. He is therefore full of opinions about drama which for him seem to spring from experience but which, taken over by you, would be precisely the kind of ready-made formula just condemned. Rather than make a ridiculous attempt at keeping all these opinions in abeyance, he prefers to state some of the principal ones here. If there is no concealment there can be no deception. What for the editor are convictions can for you be hypotheses.

If this anthology was planned with some disrespect to certain established principles, it could hardly be planned without recourse to counter-principles. Some of these have already been hinted at. To proceed: we are prepared to start listening to music out of mere curiosity, but we are prepared to continue listening only if we enjoy it. Pleasure is the first return we expect from any art. If one does not begin by finding Mozart enjoyable one cannot end by finding him great. One may end *saying* he is great—reporting that he is *considered* great—but such sayings and reportings are second-hand goods, do not touch your experience, are worthless to you. If your initial curiosity about an art is not followed by pleasure you are foiled at the start. If you have never enjoyed a play, and do not, let us say, enjoy reading—or seeing—the first play in this volume or the second you are . . . . an exceptional case and, in relation to the drama, a lost soul. If on the other hand you have found certain plays amusing, though ever so little, you have made a beginning. Through pleasure you can come to experience an art, to know it from the inside. To know it from the outside is not to know it at all. To know names and dates without having had the pleasure is to know the words on the jar without ever tasting the jam.

Courses on how to enjoy jam are not offered in the schools because it doesn't matter if you do not enjoy it and, if you do, the pleasure is simply there and needs no study. In taking up this book, however, you have assumed that the art of drama matters; you have placed yourself among those who believe that the arts are part of a full human life. If you do not as yet feel competent to judge drama, it is because you sense that one does not understand it without learning to do so. It is the assumption of liberal education that learning to understand it will not only exercise your faculties (which is true also of crossword puzzles) but will further your development as a human being.

The editor's method in this book would be called by some "the purely critical approach." His assumption here (since we are uncovering as many editorial assumptions as possible) is that sheer knowledge of facts is not your primary need. You need to learn how to apprehend works of art, how to be properly sensitive to them, how to respond finely, accurately, and adequately. However, it is not assumed that the responses of an ignoramus are fine, accurate, and adequate. The aim (limiting ourselves to the art of literature for the moment) is to understand an author's words. Three centuries have passed since Molière—let us say—wrote. Whereas we can rest easy and imagine ourselves contemporaries of Rostand and Wilde, who were our grandfathers' contemporaries, we can come into the company of Molière only by deliberate effort. The meaning of his words has changed. Even where the dictionary would record no change, since the dictionary deals almost exclusively with denotation, the associations of words have changed, their whole emotional, connotative value. Hence, historical knowledge that will help us recapture the original denotations and, still more, *con*notations of the words is extremely valuable, and it must not be imagined that the "purely critical" approach of a volume like the present one supplies any substitute for historical scholarship. Rather, it invites you to discover the original meanings of words, and it particularly warns you against anachronism: we have to see how both the mores and the arts, both ideas and dramatic conventions, have changed. Many of the Notes below are designed to prevent you from relying on your "natural" (i.e., modern) response when an understanding of an older idea or convention is required.

Admittedly one can spend a lifetime studying the times of Molière. Yet when those who *have* spent a lifetime so doing contest the right

TO THE READER 5

of the rest of us to have an opinion on their special subject, one begins to wonder. If the claims of the specialist be justified, how can there ever be a civilized community? How can the great writers and any conceivable public ever meet? No one would ever know more than a single period, and not many would be regarded as masters of even so much! The following counter-ideas seem called for. One never understands everything about anything. What the expert gains by concentration he loses by narrowness. In the understanding of a great poet knowledge gained in other literary fields, or even outside literature altogether, is often as useful as the specialist's erudition. And what we need today is not more and more specialization but the re-creation of cultural community.

The common reader of even the most successful cultural community could not be expected to know everything. As one who is forced to live economically, he has the right to ask: What knowledge can I do without? What (in the present instance) *must* I know to read Molière with pleasure and fair understanding? Such a question can receive only an improvised answer. A teacher's tendency is to accumulate the *musts* till they reach infinity. But at some point the pupil shrugs his shoulders. If the one who shrugs them first is the cynic, the one who never shrugs them at all is an impossibilist. Time is scarce; there are other things to do besides read plays.

Well and good. The editor has to accept you with your ignorance on your head. But also with your self-respect: you are not a child. Discussing an anthology with abundant explanatory Notes, Jacques Barzun complains:

> As for those emerging from respectable ignorance and finding names they do not know, they are entitled to the important service of *not* being told, for the very absence of explanation would inform them that here is something which, given their aspirations, they should know and set about acquiring.

You have just as easy access to dictionary and encyclopedia as the editor.

Editors also must live economically, and ask: What questions need I not ask? What *must* I mention to help someone enjoy and understand Molière? The present editor has found that, though an infinite number of questions *can* be asked about a play, two are enough to prompt a thorough investigation of it. The traditional wording of these two questions is: What is the form? and, What is the content? Modern critics have pointed out that form and content become one in a successful work of art. Not only can this be granted. One can go even further and admit that form and content are abstractions from the concrete reality, not having any real, separate existence but invented for the convenience of the analyst. When, however, you *are* the analyst it is only the latter part of this proposition that interests you. Form and content *are* very convenient terms, and whenever banished from criticism they re-appear in disguise. In the present anthology, when questions are asked about *structure,* it is the form we are after. When questions are asked about *theme,* it is the content—or part of the content—that we are after.

Undue preoccupation with content, with theme, has been characteristic in our time of Marxist critics; they tend—and they are not the only ones—simply to approve of plays with themes they agree with, simply to disapprove of plays with themes they disagree with. Undue preoccupation with form has been characteristic of many who have wanted to show antagonism to Marxism and also of simple souls who will talk only of a play's theatrical effectiveness and not of its meaning—but would it not be the merest pedantry to discuss the structure of *Antigone* and not its significance? To talk of chorus and episode and not of law and rebellion?

Yet it is not enough to be interested in content. You have to be interested in it in a particular way, namely, morally. It is not enough to talk of law and rebellion historically. If you need to know what the play must have meant for the Greeks, this is only because you want to know what it can legitimately mean for you. All living art touches *us,* and the theater in particular is an art of the actual, the topical, the immediate. Thus the editor makes no apology for mentioning totalitarianism in his Note on *Antigone.* What he says about it may be wrong; but it is not irrelevant.

An author, as well as an editor, may proffer an opinion, a theme, a moral philosophy that is unacceptable to you. At the same time, it is characteristic of the dramatic poet to discover and present much that people of different philosophies can accept as true. In *Othello* and *Ghosts,* ideas of marriage are involved which you or another reader may reject; but it seems doubtful whether the plays stand or fall on these ideas. Rather, it seems that the dramatic poet's profoundest attachment is to the truly human, the essentially pure; and this in the midst of inhumanity and impurity. In *The Miser, Twelfth Night, Othello, Ghosts*. . . . (I find myself listing all the plays in the book), it is a corruption of the human being, not dependent on the particular mores of the poet, that is depicted.

As to form, much of what you know or learn about poetry or the novel * will apply also to drama. But since theatrical writing has some special qualities, you should be especially on the look-out for them. And then there are the other arts of the theater, which are not simply additional to a text, but constitute, together with a text, another, if composite, art with its own identity. It is an art which, like music but unlike painting and unlike other kinds of literature, is transmitted to its audience through performers. Writing for performance presents special problems. The playwright must visualize his characters not only in their natural surroundings, as the novelist does. He must visualize them on the stage. The same is true of the reader: he must see Viola not only as a girl on the sea coast of Illyria but as an actress on a stage, standing before an audience and even speaking directly to it. A novelist's characters are characters and nothing else. A playwright's are also rôles.

At this point the scholar may add that Shakespeare wrote, not for "the stage" in general, but for a particular kind of stage, considerably different in design from the stages of today, and that we should imagine his plays on his own sort of stage. Again, one is bound to say: Yes, if you have time to study it. But Shakespeare can be impressively performed on a modern stage, and no great harm is done if (for the time being) the theater in your mind is of the modern sort. The main thing is to visualize actors, appropriately dressed, going through the movements which the text suggests.

An actual director of a play must visualize more than this. Since Shakespeare's scripts do not contain his stage directions in anything like full form, the director has to invent a good deal of stage action which the text itself does *not* directly imply; Shakespeare production is a challenge to directorial genius. If therefore *you* are advised to consider yourself a director of Shakespeare, you probably will not

* See *The Story*, by Mark Schorer (Prentice-Hall, 1950), a companion to the present volume. *The Poem*, by John Crowe Ransome, is in preparation.

wish to take the advice literally. No reader can create in his mind's eye a complete stage performance. It is a matter of degree.

One does what one can, and one can at least give a play two readings. It is a commonplace that one gets more out of a good novel at a second reading; a play has to be read twice whether it is good or not, because it presents to the reader special difficulties which arise from the fact that it is designed for performance. Thus, where a novelist prepares not only his dialogue but all that is not dialogue specifically for a reader, the playwright simply throws the "not-dialogue" at him in the form of stage directions. Even if the stage directions are novelistically written (as by Bernard Shaw), there is still a great difference between reading about a stage setting and actually seeing it. It is the generic difference between an art (fiction) that addresses only the mind's eye and an art (theater) which addresses the physical eye as well. To be given visual and auditory imagery by a writer is one thing; to be given pictures by a painter and sounds by a musician is another. The novelist does the first; the playwright does the first *and* the second.

It is hard to figure from the printed page just what a playwright is doing. During opening scenes, for example, it is often hard to realize who is who. Whereas on the stage you are confronted by this man and that, their identity established by their whole appearance and manner, in the book you are given only a name and speeches: what kind of a person is speaking you discover as you go along. Hence the second reading is your first proper experience of a play. Only now do you start seeing who is who, as in the theater.

A painter can show things side by side. A writer can *mention* that things are side by side, but since his words come out one after the other, in effect he shows things one after the other. The playwright is, in this regard, both painter and writer. When you meet him in a book—that is, when you meet him as a writer—you must make a conscious effort not to forget the "painter" in him. One of the commonest stage effects is *simultaneity*—more than one thing happening on stage at the same time. Someone at the left of the stage is talking, but what somebody at the right is *doing* may be equally—or even more—important. Thus one may read what Richard II *says* in Shakespeare's text and simply think: "This is quite eloquent but nothing more" because one has not visualized the silent person to whom

Richard is addressing his remarks: the usurper Bolingbroke whose taciturnity is half the drama of the scene.

Molière said: "It is well-known that comedies are made only to be acted. And the only people I advise to read this play [one of his own] are those whose eyes can, while reading, uncover all the stage action." Having uncovered the visual stage action, the *spectacle,* you are in a position to uncover the drama as a whole: plot, character, theme, dialogue. At first it is a useful exercise to jot down in a notebook what a playwright is doing with each. You are recommended to do so in the Notes to the first play in the present collection, and a mode of study is suggested by a number of queries; thereafter you are left more and more to ask your own questions. Plot, character, and so forth come up only as required by each play. We shall see, for example, how several playwrights used *plot* as the very basis of their work. We shall see how all our playwrights tried, by various conventions and devices, structures and forms, to "define"—or give contour to—their ideas or their conception of a dramatic action, a "subject."

In analyzing form, a good starting point is the logical proposition that things must be either like or unlike each other. The technique of a playwright may be seen in the way he uses parallelism (likeness) and contrast (unlikeness). Through words and through the other arts of the theater he devises situations and incidents which bring out the similarity or the difference. He creates all possible ironies, relationships, interactions. Repetition, juxtaposition, inversion, alternation, "counterpoint" are his stock in trade. It sounds rather formidable, perhaps, this language of analysis; and there is danger in it. "The theater is a living geometry," said a great theater critic; when you feel you have learnt the geometry of the theater, make sure you have not forgotten that it is living. If our experience of art must begin with pleasure, it must end there too. Analysis comes in between.

THE EDITOR

1. CYRANO DE BERGERAC · 1897

This is a book for people who wish to know something of dramatic art. Of course, everyone knows something about it already: for everyone has been to the movies. The habit of theater-going (if we may follow American usage and call a cinema a theater) was never more widespread than today. Can one, then, take cinematics as something already understood, and proceed to the question: what is the relation of the art of the screen to that of the stage? One would have to be very optimistic to think so. People indeed see the movies; but are they conscious of the art that goes into them (art, good or bad)? On the contrary we—the modern public—are more passive and imperceptive during the hours we spend in the movie-theater than at any other time during our day except when we are actually asleep. Nobody can be alert and observant all the time; we need to set aside certain hours for inactivity, for laziness; and many of us pass these hours—and these hours only—at the "theater."

Some say that the Hollywood movie-makers are responsible for this situation, in that they direct their movies to the sluggish, unthinking, half-conscious mind. Others say that the public itself is to blame, since it *demands* what the movie-makers provide. It's a vicious circle. The upshot, insofar as it concerns us here, is that people are no more conscious of film, which they have seen so much of, than they are of stage drama, which they have seen so little of. Often, indeed, their notion of stage drama is clearer and more to the point. What little they know, they know. If they have put on a bit of a play at school or have seen a famous actor on tour they know the phenomenon Drama and in all likelihood they have gone to meet it in a more active spirit than that in which they go to the movies. Putting on a play yourself is an exacting experience. The visit of a star to your town is a special event that arouses a good deal of inquisitiveness. And though inquisitiveness is not always a virtue it is the least passive of mental attitudes.

Since we live in the age of the camera, a comparison of stage and screen must certainly be made, sooner or later, by any student of the former. Since one cannot, however, take the screen as "known" in any critical sense, it will be better to undertake the comparison later rather than sooner. Some pointers towards a systematic comparison will be provided, not in the body of this book, but in an appendix. Here, instead of the popular art of the screen, we can occupy ourselves with the more popular kinds of drama. However, it has not seemed necessary to the editor to begin with the kind of play which is already well within everybody's capacity to enjoy and understand. Our reader we have already defined as a learner. If the level of his understanding is to be raised, we can, even at the outset, stand at a slightly higher level. It is like giving a piano student pieces just a little too hard for him to rattle right off. Now, if we want to start out on our study of drama with something popular yet not merely of the moment, something that has pleased masses of men for a certain period of time, not excluding the present, and yet which is not so crude that all its effects are immediately understood, if in short we are looking for a play which most readers will at once enjoy yet which they can learn something from, perhaps we have what we want in *Cyrano de Bergerac*.

Cyrano de Bergerac is a play which one can read, or see on the stage, without knowing anything of the author (Rostand) or much of his time and milieu (the eighteen-nineties and Paris). As for the subject of the play, the storybook notion we all have of French courtiers in more or less remote centuries is in some ways more relevant than a knowledge of the seventeenth century would be. There was a historical Cyrano de Bergerac; but a portrait of him would probably tell you less about Rostand's Cyrano than, say, portraits of the actors who have played the rôle since 1897, beginning with the great Coquelin, for whom the part was conceived. What about the present English version?

Anyone who knows languages knows how much a work of literature changes by being translated. Opinions differ as to what should be done about it. Humbert Wolfe's solution was a discreet one. He stays as close to the original as other translators, yet contrives to use the English language with an air of freedom. If he inevitably misses the rhetorical effect of the French twelve-syllable line, he makes up for it, in some measure, by his English gift for witticism and comic rhyming. Those who are interested in the question of translation and adaptation can compare the present Wolfe version with other versions of the same play. Does rhyming verse have a different effect from prose and, if so, how? The Wolfe version might be compared with the more famous Brian Hooker version by those who want to answer this query with examples rather than with generalities.

But the query is rather too special for our present purpose—which is the "sheer reading" of *Cyrano* for pleasure. Our understanding of works of art can never run ahead of our enjoyment of them. To try to make it do so is to produce a hideous double standard: there will be works we like and don't respect and works we respect and don't like. No artist makes light of pleasure; it may be that, in the end, his work exists mainly for the sake of pleasure; but it does not necessarily exist for pleasure alone, or pleasure may not all be as simple as we think, or we may learn to take pleasure in what we began by regarding as unpleasurable. But these too are matters we can leave in abeyance. Here is *Cyrano*.

CYRANO DE BERGERAC

by Edmond Rostand

TRANSLATED BY HUMBERT WOLFE

✷

Reprinted by permission of Ann Wolfe. All rights whatsoever in this play are strictly reserved, and applications for performances, etc., should be made to A. D. Peters, 10 Buckingham Street, London, WC 2, England.

Cyrano de Bergerac

Characters

CYRANO DE BERGERAC	ANOTHER MUSKETEER
CHRISTIAN DE NEUVILLETTE	A SPANISH OFFICER
COMTE DE GUICHE	A TROOPER
RAGUENEAU	A PICKPOCKET
LE BRET	A SPECTATOR
THE OFFICERS	A GUARDSMAN
CARBON DE CASTEL-JALOUX	BERTRANDOT THE PIPER
LIGNIÈRE	THE CAPUCHIN
DE VALVERT	TWO MUSICIANS
A MARQUIS	THE POETS
SECOND MARQUIS	THE PASTRYCOOKS
THIRD MARQUIS	
MONTFLEURY	ROXANE
BELLEROSE	SISTER MARTHE
JODELET	LISE
CUIGY	THE BARMAID
BRISSAILLE	MOTHER MARGUERITE
A BORE	THE DUENNA
THE PORTER	SISTER CLAIRE
A CITIZEN	AN ACTRESS
A MUSKETEER	SECOND ACTRESS

Pages, Citizens, Pickpockets, Guards of Gascony, Actors, Violinists, Children, Spanish Soldiers, Spectators, Nuns, Women, etc., etc.

Act I

A PLAY AT THE
HOTEL DE BOURGOGNE

The hall of the Hotel de Bourgogne, 1640. It resembles a tennis-court which has been decorated for theatrical purposes.

The hall is an oblong. It is seen obliquely, so that one of its sides forms an angle with the stage, which is partly visible.

There are seats at both sides of the stage. The curtain consists of two hangings to be drawn. Over a harlequin's cloak are the Royal arms. There are steps from the stage to the floor of the theatre. The orchestra takes its place at the two sides of the staircase. Footlights. There are two rows of side galleries, the higher divided into boxes. No seats in the pit, which is in fact the stage of the real theatre. At the back of the pit there are a few seats, making a stand, and under a staircase, which gives access to the upper seats, a sort of buffet decorated with small candelabra, flowers, glasses, dishes of cakes, bottles, etc.

The entrance to the theatre is in the background under the boxes. The main door is half open to admit the audience. There are red bills printed with "La Clorise" on the panels of this door, in various corners of the theatre, and above the buffet.

As the curtains rise the hall is in semi-darkness, still empty. The candelabra are lowered into the middle of the pit ready to be lighted.

THE *public trickling in.* SOLDIERS, CITIZENS, LACKEYS, PAGES, *a* PICK-POCKET, BARMAID, *the* PORTER, *and followed by the* MARQUISES OF CUIGY, BRISSAILLE, VIOLINS, *etc.*

Confused voices without. A trooper stamps in.

THE PORTER, *following him.* Where is your money?
TROOPER. I'm on the free list.
THE PORTER. Whose?
TROOPER. Yours. Don't you know a trooper in the Blues!
THE PORTER, *to a second trooper entering.* What about you?
2ND TROOPER. Free!
PORTER. Why?

ACT I] CYRANO DE BERGERAC 17

2ND TROOPER. A musketeer!

1ST TROOPER. They don't begin till two. Nobody's here.
Let's take a turn with the foils. *They start a practice bout.*

1ST LACKEY. You Flanquin—Catch!

2ND LACKEY. Champagne!

1ST LACKEY, *showing cards and dice.* And these—a game?

2ND LACKEY, *sits.* You bet, old Scratch!

1ST LACKEY, *lights a candle-end and sticks it on the ground.*
I borrowed this. The boss would be delighted.

GUARDSMAN, *to a flower-girl.*
Charming to come before the lamps are lighted.

A FENCER, *being hit.* A hit.

A CARD-PLAYER. It's Clubs!

THE GUARDSMAN, *following the girl.* A kiss.

THE FLOWER-GIRL, *shaking herself free.* They'll see.

THE GUARDSMAN, *drawing her away.* Not they!

A MAN, *sitting on the ground with others who have brought their own food.* First come, first served!

A CITIZEN, *with his son.* Sit down, my child. This way!

A PLAYER. Nap?

A MAN, *taking a bottle from under his coat, and sitting.*
When a man is drunk what better sign
than a Burgundy pub for the Burgundy wine.

THE CITIZEN, *to his son.*
Is this a theatre or a stews—this place full—
Points to the drunkard with his cane—of drunks—*A trooper jostles him*—louts—*He stumbles among the card-players*—gamblers!

THE GUARDSMAN, *behind him, still badgering the flower-girl.*
Kiss me, sweet!

THE CITIZEN, *taking his son away.* Disgraceful!
Who would believe this bagnio housed the play
of Rotrou, child?

THE SON. Yes, and the great Corneille!

A COMPANY OF PAGES, *arm-in-arm dancing and singing.*
With a hey and a ho, and a hey nonny no!

THE PORTER, *sharply, to the pages.*
None of your nonsense, boys!

1ST PAGE, *deeply grieved.* We're angels, look!

To 2nd page, eagerly, as the porter turns. Got any string?
>2ND PAGE. Not half—and here's a hook!
>1ST PAGE. Upstairs, my lads. We'll maybe land a wig!
>PICKPOCKET, *to a group of young toughs.*

Now, you young filchers, if you want to prig,
watch uncle—and make fortunes as you please!
>2ND PAGE, *shouting to others seated in the gallery.*

Hi! got your peashooters?
>3RD PAGE, *from the gallery.* You bet—and peas.

He peppers him with peas.
>SON, *to his father.* What is the play?
>CITIZEN. Clorise.
>SON. The author's name?
>CITIZEN. Balthazar Baro—who deserves his fame.

He walks up stage arm-in-arm with his son.
>THE PICKPOCKET, *to his pupils.*

Knee-ruffles—for example—snip 'em neat!
>A SPECTATOR, *pointing to the gallery.*

At the first night of "The Cid" that was my seat.
>THE PICKPOCKET, *making the appropriate gestures.*

Watches like this!
>THE CITIZEN, *coming back with his son.*

You'll see some stars!
>THE PICKPOCKET. One handles handkerchiefs so.
>THE CITIZEN. Montfleury.
>VOICE, *from the gallery.* Light the candles!
>THE CITIZEN. Bellerose, l'Epy, La Beaupré, Jodelet!
>A PAGE, *in the pit.* Refreshments?
>BARMAID. Milk or oranges to-day?

Grenadine, bitters——
Noise without.
>A FALSETTO VOICE. You filthy fellows, quit!
>1ST LACKEY, *surprised.* Marquises?
>2ND LACKEY. For a moment—in the pit.

Enter a troupe of young Marquises.
>A MARQUIS, *seeing the theatre half empty.*

God! We might be a pack of haberdashers.

No one to hustle, no toes to feel our smashers!
But look who's here! *He recognizes his friends.*
Cuigy! Brissaille! *Salutations.*
 CUIGY. That's right!
True to our word, more punctual than the light.
 THE MARQUIS. The lamplighter be blasted. May he scorch—
 2ND MARQUIS. Why worry? Here he is complete with torch.
The audience cheering the lamplighter.
Hurrah!

Crowds round the candelabra. A few seated in the gallery. Enter LIGNIÈRE *in the pit, arm-in-arm with* CHRISTIAN DE NEUVILLETTE. LIGNIÈRE, *a dissipated but distinguished rake;* CHRISTIAN, *well dressed but not in the latest fashion, quizzes the boxes with a preoccupied air.*

 CUIGY. Lignière.
 BRISSAILLE, *smiling.* Still sober?
 LIGNIÈRE, *whispers to* CHRISTIAN. I'll present you—
De Neuvillette!
 THE CROWD. Hip!
 CUIGY, *to* BRISSAILLE, *looking at* CHRISTIAN.
Don't his head content you!
 1ST MARQUIS, *who has overheard.* Nonsense!
 LIGNIÈRE, *introducing.* De Cuigy, De Brissaille!
 CHRISTIAN. Enchanted!
 1ST MARQUIS, *to* 2ND.
Handsome enough, but there is something wanted
in the way of fashion!
 LIGNIÈRE, *to* CUIGY. Monsieur is from Touraine.
 CHRISTIAN. Three weeks in Paris, but everything's in train.
I join the Guards to-morrow!
 1ST MARQUIS. Really! Ha!
The Lord Chief's wife.
 BARMAID. Milk, oranges.
 VIOLINS, *tuning up.* La—La!
 CUIGY, *to* CHRISTIAN, *showing the theatre filling.*
They're coming now!
 CHRISTIAN. In scores!

1ST MARQUIS. The cream of fashion! *They point to smart women, taking their seats in the boxes. There is an exchange of greetings and of smiles.*

2ND MARQUIS. De Guéménée.

CUIGY. Bois-Dauphin.

1ST MARQUIS. All our passion!

BRISSAILLE. De Chavigny—

2ND MARQUIS. Who dices with our hearts.

LIGNIÈRE. Look! Corneille back from Rouen!

SON, *to father.* Now it starts!

Is the Academy here?

CITIZEN. Yes, quite a number.

Look! Boudu, Boissat, Cureau of the Chamber;
Porchères, Colomby, Bourdon and Arbaud—
and those are names no years can overthrow!

1ST MARQUIS. Attention, boys! Here are the Souls en masse.

Barthenoide, another, Cassandace,
Urimedonte——

2ND MARQUIS. Nicknames; God save the mark! Is this group all your acquaintance?

1ST MARQUIS. Yes, dear Marquis.

LIGNIÈRE, *taking* CHRISTIAN *on one side.*

I only came on your account. I think,
since she's not here, I'll vanish for a drink.

CHRISTIAN. No, stay and tell me, poet of Court and City,
her name for whom I die, the unknown pretty.

1ST FIDDLE, *tapping with his bow.* Gentlemen!

REFRESHMENT-GIRL. Macaroons and lemonade!

Violins begin.

CHRISTIAN. I fear me she's no simple country-maid.
If I accosted her I'd die of fright.
It's quite beyond me—the way you speak and write.
I'm only a poor speechless soldier—
—That empty box is always kept for her!

LIGNIÈRE, *moving.* I'm off.

CHRISTIAN. I beg you stay.

LIGNIÈRE. No, first things first!
The tavern calls me and a noble thirst!

BARMAID, *passing with a tray.* Orangeade, milk!

LIGNIÈRE. Good God! Here, woman, halt!

Pour me a glass of the right Rivesalte. *He sits down at the buffet, where the barmaid pours out Rivesalte.*

Cries without as a plump, cheerful little man enters.

Cheers! 'Tis mine host—the famous Ragueneau.

RAGUENEAU, *in a pastrycook's Sunday clothes, walks over to* LIGNIÈRE.

Has anybody seen our Cyrano?

LIGNIÈRE, *introducing* RAGUENEAU *to* CHRISTIAN.

The pastrycook of actors and the Muse!

RAGUENEAU. You are too kind.

LIGNIÈRE. Maecenas, it's no use!

RAGUENEAU. It's true they are my customers.

LIGNIÈRE. On credit!

And no mean poet yourself.

RAGUENEAU. Sir! You have said it!

LIGNIÈRE. He's mad for odes!

RAGUENEAU. 'Tis true that for a runlet

of verse

LIGNIÈRE. You'd swap a bun?

RAGUENEAU. Well, say a bunlet!

LIGNIÈRE. No, you do better than that. What is the dole

for a good triolet?

RAGUENEAU. A penny roll!

LIGNIÈRE. What of the stage? D'you like it?

RAGUENEAU. She's my mistress

who grants her favours in return for pastries!

LIGNIÈRE. Your seat to-night—as between friends, how much?

RAGUENEAU. Four custard pies and fifteen puffs and such.

He looks round about him. Cyrano not here: That's odd!

LIGNIÈRE. And why, I ask?

RAGUENEAU. Montfleury's acting.

LIGNIÈRE. That old vintner's cask

will roll through Phaedo very like a barrel.

What then?

RAGUENEAU. You didn't know there was a quarrel?

And that our friend in an excess of rage

forbade him for a month to tread the stage?

LIGNIÈRE. Well?
RAGUENEAU. He is acting.
LIGNIÈRE. C. can't stop him.
CUIGY, *joining the group.* No?
RAGUENEAU. You wait and see!
1ST MARQUIS. Who is this Cyrano?
CUIGY. No lad to play with in the fencing-yards!
1ST MARQUIS. Well-born?
CUIGY. A sub-lieutenant in the Guards. *Pointing to a man moving through the crowd in search of someone.*
His friend, Le Bret, will tell you more. *Calling.* Le Bret!
LE BRET *approaches.* Do you seek Cyrano?
LE BRET. I'm worried!
CUIGY. Say!
Isn't he a portent among men?
LE BRET. No less
than nature's final word in nobleness!
RAGUENEAU. A poet—
CUIGY. Fencer.
BRISSAILLE. Leech.
LE BRET. Hands to the lute.
LIGNIÈRE. And a face like an Arabesque to boot.
RAGUENEAU. Yes, I'll admit he'd never sit as model
to de Champaigne, that pompous mollycoddie.
But for poor Callot he'd have been the stuff—
divinely odd, extravagantly tough—
to serve him for the maddest of his maskers,
triple-plumed beaver, doublet fringed like whiskers,
sword at his coat-tail, cocked to heaven as sheer
as the pert panoply of Chanticleer.
He struts—of all the lads she ever grew—
Gascony—the old woman in the shoe—
proudest with his huge ruff—a roaring fellow,
his nose the very spit of Punchinello.
Did I say nose—it's not so much his feature
as a wit's outrage on the face of Nature!
Impossible—you'd cry—a nasal pose!
But Cyrano will never doff his nose.

ACT I] CYRANO DE BERGERAC 23

LE BRET, *with a significant nod.*
Put on for life—but death for its aggressors.

RAGUENEAU, *proudly.* His sword's the cutting half
of Clotho's scissors.

1ST MARQUIS, *shrugging.* He'll never come.

RAGUENEAU. I'll lay a capon roasted
as I know how.

1ST MARQUIS, *laughing.* Done with you.

Cries of admiration in the theatre. ROXANE *has entered her box. She sits in front, her duenna behind.* CHRISTIAN, *who is paying the barmaid, does not see her.*

2ND MARQUIS, *in ecstasy.* Heaven has hosted
in terrible loveliness!

1ST MARQUIS. She's beautiful
as a peach amused with strawberries.

2ND MARQUIS. So cool
that merely to see her is to enrheum the heart.

CHRISTIAN *raises his head, sees* ROXANE, *and grasps* LIGNIÈRE *eagerly by the arm.*

CHRISTIAN. 'Tis she!

LIGNIÈRE, *looking.* That she!

CHRISTIAN. Speak! lest my wits depart!

A distinguished figure, with a blue riband across his breast, enters the box and speaks to ROXANE.

LIGNIÈRE, *sipping his Rivesalte.*
Magdaleine Robin—Roxane to her set.
A wit!

CHRISTIAN. Alas!

LIGNIÈRE. An orphan, heartwhole yet,
cousin to Cyrano.

CHRISTIAN, *in a panic.* Who's that?

LIGNIÈRE. Well parried!
The Comte de Guiche. Mad for her. But married
to the niece of Richelieu. He means Roxane
for poor De Valvert—the sort of nobleman
who thinks girls will be girls. She bites the leash—
but he's a powerful creature—that De Guiche,
and might be cruel if a girl denied him.

But there's a poem of mine in which I've guyed him
with all his tricks. He's angry. There's a sting
in the tail. It runs like this.

CHRISTIAN. Good evening.

LIGNIÈRE. You're off?

CHRISTIAN. To find De Valvert.

LIGNIÈRE. And your end! *Indicating* ROXANE *with a glance.*
I'd stay, I think. She's watching you, my friend.

CHRISTIAN. 'Tis true. CHRISTIAN *remains rapt. The pickpocket's gang, seeing him moonstruck, begin to creep towards him.*

LIGNIÈRE. I'm off to save myself from parching.
Exit reeling.

LE BRET. No sign of Cyrano.

RAGUENEAU. I swear he's marching—

LE BRET. My hope is that he hasn't seen the bill.

THE PUBLIC. Time! Time!

A MARQUIS, *watching* DE GUICHE *leave the box surrounded by a group of sycophants, including* DE VALVERT.
De Guiche goes wooing with a will.

ANOTHER. A bloody Gascon!

THE FIRST. But with a supple mask on
of cold success. Come, let's salute this Gascon!
They go over to DE GUICHE.

2ND MARQUIS.
Enchanting ribands! What would you call the shade?
"The dappled faun" or "Kiss me, pretty maid!"

DE GUICHE. "Spaniard in Trouble."

1ST MARQUIS. A hit! a palable hit!
For, thanks to you, in Flanders it will fit
their army like a glove!

DE GUICHE. Gentlemen, I count
on a stage-seat. Come. *He goes, followed by lords and gentlemen to the theatre—he goes back and calls.* Valvert.

CHRISTIAN. That's the Viscount!
My gauntlet in his chops—*Plunges his hand in his pocket and finds the pickpocket's fingers there. He turns.* Well!
I'll be blessed!

PICKPOCKET. Oh!

ACT I] CYRANO DE BERGERAC 25

CHRISTIAN, *holding on*. Groping to find my glove.
PICKPOCKET, *with a pitiful smile*. —you found a fist.
Changing his note and whispering rapidly.
Release me. I've a secret—
CHRISTIAN, *holding on*. What?
PICKPOCKET. The stranger who has just left you—
CHRISTIAN, *still holding*. Well—
PICKPOCKET. His life's in danger.
His lampoon stung a nobleman whose one dread
is ridicule. A hundred wait.
CHRISTIAN. A hundred!
At whose behest?
PICKPOCKET. There's honour among thieves.
CHRISTIAN. Where are they posted?
PICKPOCKET. He'll find 'em when he leaves
by the Gate of Nesle. Warn him.
CHRISTIAN. I'm much beholden!
But where?
PICKPOCKET. Search all the taverns. Try "The Golden
Winepress," "The Pine Cone," and "The Bursting Belt."
"The Torches," "The Three Funnels."—"A rat is smelt."
Just leave that message and your job is done.
CHRISTIAN. I'll go. The swine! A hundred against one! *Looking at* ROXANE *with passion*. But leave her—*With fury at* VALVERT—and leave him. Lignière has called!
I fly!
He rushes out. DE GUICHE, THE VISCOUNT, *the* MARQUISES, *all the great world have disappeared behind the curtain to seats on the stage. The pit is full. Not an empty place in the gallery or boxes.*
THE PUBLIC. Begin.
CITIZEN, *whose wig disappears, caught by one of the* PAGES *from the gallery*. My wig.
Cries of satisfaction. The creature's bald!
Well done, you pages.
THE CITIZEN, *furiously shaking his fist.*
Offspring of the midden.
LAUGHTER, *beginning loudly and suddenly stilted.*
Ha! Ha! Ha! Ha! Ha! Ha!

LE BRET, *astonished.* What means this sudden silence. No, really!

SPECTATOR. Yes! the thing is certain!

MURMURS. Yes—he is here! No!—Yes, behind the curtain! The Cardinal himself—by God, that's news!

A PAGE. Children, we'll have to mind our Ps and Qs.

Knocking on the stage. Complete silence. Everybody waiting eagerly.

THE VOICE OF A MARQUIS, *behind the curtain.* Snuff me that candle.

ANOTHER MARQUIS, *sticking his head out of the curtain.* A chair here!

A chair is passed in from hand to hand over the heads of the crowd. The MARQUIS *takes it and disappears after having distributed kisses to the boxes.*

A SPECTATOR. Silence, all!

Three knocks. The curtain goes up. The MARQUISES *arrogantly grouped at the sides of the stage. The backcloth is a dim pastoral landscape. Four little cut-glass candelabra as lights. Soft music.*

LE BRET, *whispering to* RAGUENEAU. Is it Montfleury?

RAGUENEAU, *in the same tone.* Yes, he opens the ball!

LE BRET. Cyrano is not here.

RAGUENEAU. I've lost.

LE BRET. Don't worry! 'Tis better so!

Pipes. Enter MONTFLEURY, *gigantic, dressed as a shepherd, his rose-wreathed hat over his ear, and playing on a be-ribboned pipe.*

THE PIT, *cheering.* Montfleury! Hail, Montfleury!

MONTFLEURY *bows and begins the part of Phaedo.* Happy the man far from the Court who roves self-banished through these solitary groves, And who when Zephyrs whisper through the copses—

A VOICE. What! would you flout my orders, king of dropsies!

VOICES. What's up?

CUIGY. I'm damned.

LE BRET, *frightened.* Cyrano.

THE VOICE. Outside, scullion.

VOICES. Shut up—what is it?

THE VOICE. Would you try rebellion?

ACT I] CYRANO DE BERGERAC 27

VOICES. Stow it—play on—and send the swine to Hell!
MONTFLEURY, *in a shaky voice.*
Happy the man far from the Court who—
THE VOICE, *threatening.* Well!
It seems, my prince of zanies, that you lack
this sort of wood—to decorate your back.
A hand clutching a cane is raised above the heads of the audience.
MONTFLEURY, *with a voice growing steadily feebler.*
Happy the man—
THE VOICE. Tut!
THE PIT. Silence!
MONTFLEURY, *choking.* Happy the—
CYRANO *climbs on a chair in the pit, his arms crossed, his beaver cocked, his moustache bristling, and his nose crying ha-ha among the trumpets.*
CYRANO. Must I be angry?
Sensation.
MONTFLEURY, *to the* MARQUISES. Gentlemen, you see
this outrage.
A MARQUIS, *carelessly.* Act, my man.
CYRANO. You mountain of stuff, you.
Act—if you wish these hands of mine to cuff you.
THE MARQUIS. Have done!
CYRANO. Be seated, lest this cudgel bounces,
my pretty popinjays, among your flounces!
THE MARQUISES, *rising to their feet.*
You go too far! . . . Montfleury.
CYRANO. Unless he cuts
I'll slit his ears and paddle in his guts.
A VOICE. Hold!
CYRANO. Off!
ANOTHER VOICE. But——
CYRANO. Would the creature dare to bluff it?
Good! Then the stage shall serve me for a buffet,
whereat I'll slice him like his own Salami.
MONTFLEURY, *with assumed dignity.*
Striking at me you wound Thalia.
CYRANO. Dummy!

Don't claim to know a lady who never met you,
and who, were she so luckless, would, I'll bet you,
seeing you poke your swinish snout and tusk in
acquaint you with the toe-piece of her buskin.

THE PIT. We want Montfleury—get on with the acting.

CYRANO, *to the yelling mob round him*.

Gentlemen, I fear your clamour is distracting
the sword at peace as yet within my scabbard.

The crowd draws back.

MOB. Steady!

CYRANO, *to* MONTFLEURY. Outside.

MOB, *drawing near, threatening*. Shame! shame!

CYRANO, *turning sharply*. Who was it blubbered?

Crowd retreats again.

A VOICE, *from the back of the Pit*.

Cyrano de Bergerac
Wherefore bluster, why rant?
We will have the actors back,
Silly little tyrant.

THE AUDIENCE, *shouting*.

We want La Clorise. We want La Clorise.

CYRANO. Sing me that stuff again, and your doom slams on the lot of you!

A CITIZEN. Perhaps, sir, you are Samson.

CYRANO. Well, you'd provide the jawbone of an ass!

LADY, *in the boxes*. Shocking.

A GENTLEMAN. Disgraceful.

A CITIZEN. Here's a pretty pass!

A PAGE. What fun!

THE PIT. Shut up! Montfleury—Bergerac.

CYRANO. Silence, all.

THE PIT, *raging*. Cock-a-doodle-do. Quack, quack.

CYRANO. Beware—

A PAGE. Miaou—

CYRANO. Unless you shut that riot
I'll find a way to keep the whole pit quiet.
Inscribe your names. Roll up, my budding heroes.
Each shall be numbered upward from the zeros.

Come, lads of mettle, which of you's the jewel—
you sir, or you, or you, to start the duel.
With military honours, you understand.
Let those, who wish to earn them, raise their hand.
Silence.
This naked steel offends your maiden virtue.
No name? No hand? Your doctor, loth to hurt you—
Turns to the stage where MONTFLEURY *waits in an agony of doubt*—
nevertheless to end this painful history of local inflammation prescribes—*Sword in hand*—
the bistory.

MONTFLEURY. I——

CYRANO, *climbs down from the chair and sits down as at his own fireside in the middle of the circle about him.*
Bloated moon of fat, your course will run into eclipse
when I've clapped three.

THE PIT, *amused.* Ha!

CYRANO, *clapping.* One.

MONTFLEURY. I——

A VOICE, *from the boxes.* Stay.

THE PIT. He stays—he's going.

MONTFLEURY. It seems to me,
Gentlemen.

CYRANO. Two.

MONTFLEURY. 'Tis better, maybe——

CYRANO. Three!

MONTFLEURY *disappears as through a trap-door. Storm of laughter, hisses and booing.*

AUDIENCE. Poltroon! Come back!

CYRANO, *leaning back with his legs crossed, delighted.*
Yes, come—and get your dose.

A CITIZEN. Where is the company's orator?

BELLEROSE *appears and makes his bow.*

THE BOXES. Ah, Bellerose!

BELLEROSE, *elegantly.* My noble friends——

THE PIT. Where's Jodelet?

JODELET, *speaking through his nose.* Foul steers!

THE PIT. Good. Very good. Bravo.

JODELET. A truce to cheers!
Your favourite actor, bellied like a sack,
felt . . .

THE PIT. He's a coward.

JODELET. . . . Left.

THE PIT. Well! Send him back!

VOICES. No!

VOICES. Yes!

A YOUNG MAN, *to* CYRANO.
You hate the fellow, but can't refuse
to tell us why.

CYRANO. Child of the tribe of goose,
I have two reasons, either one enough.
First, he's a wretched mime who mouths his stuff,
and hauls up verse, that beauty should have quickened
into her flight, with a porter's "ho." And second
. . . but that's my secret.

AN OLD CITIZEN, *behind him.* Meanwhile you deprive us
of La Clorise.

CYRANO. Thersites redivivus,
d'you call that verse? I reckon it at zero,
and gladly interrupt it.

BLUE-STOCKINGS, *in the box.* What!—our Baro——
Insolence!

CYRANO, *turning to the boxes gallantly.*
Ladies, than the morning fairer,
'tis yours to blossom, shine and, dream's cupbearer,
to wet death's lips with the vintage of your laughter.
But don't inspire verse—and judge it after.

BELLEROSE. They'll want their money back.

CYRANO, *turning his chair to the stage.* My Bellerose
That's the first word of sense I've heard. God knows
I'd not have Thespis go in rags and tatters.
He rises and throws a purse on the stage.
Catch this—the only silencer that matters.

THE AUDIENCE. My God!

JODELET, *catching the purse neatly and weighing it.*

ACT I] CYRANO DE BERGERAC 31

For this on any night you please,
as far as I'm concerned, stop La Clorise!
  THE AUDIENCE. Shame, Jodelet!
  JODELET. And hoot your fill and bawl!
  BELLEROSE. We'd better clear the theatre.
  JODELET. Outside, all.
Exit begins, while CYRANO *gazes on satisfied. But the crowd almost immediately stops on hearing the following scene. The women in the boxes, standing with their cloaks on, first listen and then resume their seats.*
  LE BRET, *to* CYRANO. You're mad!
  A BORE, *approaching*. Montfleury! What a hornet's nest!
The man enjoys de Candal's interest.
Have you a patron?
  CYRANO. No!
  A BORE. D'you mean it?
  CYRANO. Yes.
  A BORE. No name of power to cloak your nakedness?
  CYRANO. I've said it twice, but why should that affect me?
No lord but—*his hand upon his sword*—this great lady to
protect me.
  THE BORE. You'll quit the city.
  CYRANO. If it suits.
  THE BORE. You're wrong.
De Candal's arm is long.
  CYRANO. But not so long
As this of mine—*showing his sword*—
when it prepares to thrust!
  THE BORE. You will not think of fighting!
  CYRANO. Won't I just!
  THE BORE. But——
  CYRANO. That's enough from you. Shove off!
  THE BORE. But!
  CYRANO. Fly!
Or does my nose amuse your worship?
  THE BORE. I——
  CYRANO, *advancing*. What's wrong with it?

THE BORE, *shrinking back*. Nothing, your grace.

CYRANO. You're drunk,
if you assert it dangles like a trunk!

THE BORE, *still retreating*. Far from it.

CYRANO. Or a beak an owl might sport?

THE BORE. I——

CYRANO. —perchance disfigured by a wart.

THE BORE. But——

CYRANO. —a fly promenades about the feature
or is it

THE BORE. Sir!

CYRANO. Clean contrary to nature?

THE BORE. I never looked; since there was naught to stare for!

CYRANO. You never looked! Explain the why and wherefore!

THE BORE. I swear.

CYRANO. The thing disgusts you.

THE BORE. Sir!

CYRANO. You mean
the colour's foul.

THE BORE. Dear sir!

CYRANO. The shape's obscene!

THE BORE. Certainly not!

CYRANO. Then why so critical?
Is it a trifle large, perhaps?

THE BORE. It's small.
Tiny; indeed, I'd call it microscopic!

CYRANO. What, would you vent your humour on this topic?
You dare to call it small.

THE BORE. God!

CYRANO. It's enormous.
You snub-nosed dolt, such vastness can't deform us!
'Tis my delight to face the world thus snouted,
for none but fools like you have ever doubted
that a great nose argues its owner lavish
gentle and brave, like me, and not a knavish
nincompoop such as you, whose featureless face,
which serves no purpose but its own disgrace

and some small entertainment for these fingers,
is as devoid—*boxes his ear*—

THE BORE. Stop it!

CYRANO. —of noble hungers
of lyric loveliness, of all that glows
with mere excess of being—in short, of Nose—
suiting the action to the word—
as this on which I exercise my boots.

THE BORE. Police! Help! Help!

CYRANO. I warn the world of brutes
who find my nose a joke and seek to crab it,
that, if the jester's noble, 'tis my habit
to touch him, ere he leaves me altogether,
in front, and higher up, with steel, not leather.

DE GUICHE, *coming down from stage*. He becomes tedious.

DE VALVERT, *shrugging his shoulders*.
He blows his trumpet.

DE GUICHE. Will none return his lead?

DE VALVERT. Watch me! I'll trump it!
You know my wit—its sudden thrust and parry.
He swaggers up to CYRANO *like a young turkey-cock.*
Your nose, sir, is—your nose—gigantic.

CYRANO. Very.

DE VALVERT, *laughing*. What?

CYRANO. Is that all?

DE VALVERT. But——

CYRANO. For a man of birth it almost seems immoral
to be so clumsy when he picks a quarrel.
Forgive me, therefore, if I adumbrate
merely in outline, I need hardly state,
certain suggestions, which you'll let me call
perhaps, "The Young Insulter's Manual."
First, then, I should have raised my beaver thus—
then, tapping my scabbard so, half courteous,
half wonderingly, I should have gazed awhile
upon the nose, then murmured with a smile
under my breath, "Impossible. My trouble

is that a drink or two makes me see double."
Then I'd have rubbed my eyes, straining my sight
and cried, "It's there. By God! I am not tight."
Then as my reason tottered and all went blacker
than midnight, I'd have moaned, "A Christmas cracker!
Of course he wears it," and I should have smiled
"because at heart he's simple as a child."
Then drawing near to nip the joke in the bud
I should have pinched, and found it flesh and blood.
Then shrinking back with a simulated start,
I should have muttered, a hand against my heart:
"Pardon the doubts, which, when the wits are gone, stir
the mind when first presented with a monster.
And if my curiosity is not imprudent
be good enough to tell an earnest student
of cookery (you'll tell me if I badger)
whether for food you use a bucket-dredger,
and when you drink, they fill you at the jump
with yards of piping from the village-pump!"
Then, "Though you're not the type of man to brag
what happens when you puff a ton of shag
and the heavens darken! As a sort of vengeance
do casual strangers summon the fire-engines?"
Then, "If a sneeze or two should make your girth quake
do the observatories record an earthquake?"
"And if it bleeds (remember Shakespeare's line)
do the green seas forthwith incarnadine?"
Then I'd have asked, "Tell me, do country cousins
when flocking to the Capital in dozens
inquire, as they give their eyes a cub-lick,
when is that open, Constable, to the public?"
Last in a parody of Marlowe—shout
summing it up, "Did that outrageous snout
launch all those ships with a blast and carry on
till it sneezed down the towers of Ilion?"
That is a sketch of what you might have said
had you been even moderately bred.
For any man, not stinking of the stable

ACT I] CYRANO DE BERGERAC 35

where you were born, had certainly been able
to decorate with breeding's natural empery,
in this great company, my rough extempore.
But had you done so, the fourth line, my lord,
would have been punctuated with my sword.
For though I mock myself with flawless verve,
my imitators get what they deserve.

DE GUICHE. Let be, my lord.

THE VISCOUNT. Intolerable vauntlets
of a lout, who doesn't even carry gauntlets,
no bows, no ruffles, naught that fashion fancies.

CYRANO. For my part mine are moral elegances.*

THE VISCOUNT. Damn you!

CYRANO. I have no gloves! Why should I care?
I have one only—of an ancient pair—
Which, as my calling card, at the earliest chance
I left upon some coward's countenance.

THE VISCOUNT. Cad, bounder, hairy-heeled performing hack!

CYRANO, *lifting his hat and returning the introduction.*
Let me in turn present de Bergerac!
Loud laughter.

THE VISCOUNT, *furious.* Revolting clown!

CYRANO, *groaning as though seized with cramp.* O God!

THE VISCOUNT, *who has gone upstage, turning back.*
What ails you, scum?

CYRANO, *feigning again.*
Massage is what it needs; it's all but numb.

---

* Humbert Wolfe omits a few lines here that Gertrude Hall translated thus: "My foppery is of the inner man. I do not trick myself out like a popinjay, but I am more fastidious if I am not so showy. I would not sally forth, by any chance, not quite washed clean of an affront; my conscience foggy about the eye, my honor crumpled, my nicety black-rimmed. I walk with all upon me furnished bright. I plume myself with independence and straightforwardness. It is not a handsome figure, it is my soul that I hold erect as in a brace. . . ." These lines render well the dignity of Cyrano's moral pose, which is remarked in the Commentary following the play. The reference to the soul is also of interest: Roxane subsequently expatiates on beauty of soul. She insists she loves Christian for his soul.

36   CYRANO DE BERGERAC   [ACT I

That's the result of idleness, my lord!
  THE VISCOUNT. What is it?
  CYRANO. Pins and needles in my sword.
  THE VISCOUNT, *drawing*. Have at you!
  CYRANO. O delicious gentle touch!
  THE VISCOUNT. You poetaster!
  CYRANO. No, a poet, and such
a poet that, as we fence, I'll dress your salad
with an impromptu effort.
  THE VISCOUNT. What?
  CYRANO. A ballade
gayest (you know it?) of extravaganzas.
  THE VISCOUNT. What's that?
  CYRANO. A composition of three stanzas
of eight lines each, the envoi having four.
  THE VISCOUNT. You mean——
  CYRANO. To fence while writing and to score
a hit at the last line!
  THE VISCOUNT. You will not.
  CYRANO. So!
Reciting. Ballade of the duel fought by Cyrano
with a rogue at the Burgundy.
  THE VISCOUNT. Your recital means what?
  CYRANO. It means that you have heard the title.
  THE AUDIENCE, *much excited*. Move on there! This is
fun!
*A circle in the pit of the gentry and officers mixed with citizens and
the proletariat; pages climbing on each other's shoulders to see better.
All the women standing in the boxes.* R., DE GUICHE *and his friend.*
L., LE BRET, RAGUENEAU, CYRANO.
  CYRANO, *closing his eyes for a second.*
Wait while I find my rhyme. . . . I'm with you, boys!

I doff my beaver with an air,
and then unfasten at my ease
the military cloak I wear!
Then out you best of snickersees!
Lo! neat as Alcibiades

and Scaramouche for agile wit
I give you warning, scum and lees,
you'll find the envoi scores a hit.

You should have minded your affair!
Where shall I stuff you, goose, with grease?
Here in the flank, the elbow there,
or give your ribands heart-disease?
Hark! the hilt-music on the breeze!
Look! here's a gnat: don't blink at it!
Is that your paunch? Dodge, as you please,
you'll find the envoi scores a hit.

Have you, perchance, a rhyme to spare?
Hold! when I see you, white as cheese,
I think the missing rhyme is "scare"!
Click! Thrust and bind? I parry these
thus, as you notice, with remise.
Now for a fleche—ah, clutch your spit
poor dastard. In extremities
you'll find the envoi scores a hit.

Prince, pray for pardon on your knees.
I thrust in carte! Ho there! admit
a feint in Prime. *He wounds the* VISCOUNT.
   St. Peter's keys!
you've found the envoi scores a hit.

Loud applause in the boxes. Flowers and handkerchiefs shower down. Officers surround and congratulate CYRANO. RAGUENEAU *dances with joy.* LE BRET *is beside himself with happiness. Friends of the* VISCOUNT *take him away.*

 THE CROWD, *shouting.* Oh!
 A TROOPER. It's superb!
 A WOMAN. Thrilling!
 RAGUENEAU. Divine!
 A MARQUIS. It's new!
 LE BRET. Madman.
Uproar around CYRANO.

THE CROWD. Bravo!—Cheers!—Too good to be true!

A WOMAN'S VOICE. A hero.

A MUSKETEER, *approaching* CYRANO *eagerly with outstretched hands.*
Sir, you do your country credit.
And if they ask you, tell them that I said it.
I stamped until my feet were almost gone. *Goes.*

CYRANO. Who was that musketeer?

CUIGY. One d'Artagnan.

LE BRET. Let's talk!

CYRANO. Let the crowd go first.
To BELLEROSE. Need I hurry?

BELLEROSE. Certainly not.
Cries without.

JODELET. They're hissing poor Montfleury.

BELLEROSE, *solemnly.* Sic transit—*with a changed note to the porter and the snuffer of the candles*—
Sweep! Shut down! But leave the light!
after our supper we return to-night
for a rehearsal—a new farce.
Exeunt JODELET *and* BELLEROSE, *with a deep bow to* CYRANO.

PORTER, *to* CYRANO. Say, boss!
What about dinner?

CYRANO. I'm staying.
Exit porter.

LE BRET, *to* CYRANO. Why?

CYRANO, *proudly.* Because—
on a changed note, seeing the porter is going—
I've got no money.

LE BRET, *imitating the act of throwing a purse.*
But your purse of gold?

CYRANO. 'Twas my allowance; 'tis a tale that's told!

LE BRET. How will you last the month?

CYRANO. On heaven's pasture!

LE BRET. Madness to fling the purse!

CYRANO. But what a gesture.

THE BARMAID, *coughing behind the counter.* Sir—
CYRANO *and* LE BRET *turn. She draws near timidly*—

ACT I] CYRANO DE BERGERAC 39

if you fast, you'll have my heartstrings rent.
Pointing to the bar.
Here's all you need. *Eagerly.* Take it!

CYRANO, *removing his beaver.* Dear Innocent!
Although my Gascon pride in face of plenty
forbids me to accept the smallest dainty,
lest I should hurt your gentle heart I'll take—
Goes to the bar—
not for my hunger, but for your charming sake,
this single grape.
She offers him the bunch, but he takes one only.
This glass of water—cool—
He stops her as she tries to pour out wine—
And half a macaroon. *He returns the other half.*

LE BRET. The man's a fool.

THE BARMAID. And nothing more?

CYRANO. Yes—this for all your trouble.
He kisses her hand, like that of a princess.

THE BARMAID. I thank you, sir.
Curtseying. Good night. *Exit.*

CYRANO, *to* LE BRET. Now let us babble!
He stands in front of the bar, and sets the macaroon in front of him.
Food.
—*the glass of water.* Wine.
—*the grape.* Dessert.
He sits. And so, my friend, to dinner.
I have a twist, Le Bret, a perfect stunner.
Eating. What were you saying?

LE BRET. Little good they'll do you
these fire-eating dolts whose cheers pursue you!
Ask men of sober common sense to lend us
their ears, and they will tell you——

CYRANO, *finishing his macaroon.* It's tremendous!

LE BRET. The Cardinal!

CYRANO, *enchanted.* You don't say he was present!

LE BRET. —No doubt esteemed it——

CYRANO. New—and, therefore, pleasant!

LE BRET. Still——

CYRANO. He's an author, hating the survival
of any play whatever, by a rival.

LE BRET. You make new foes, dear friend, at six a penny!

CYRANO. This evening, for example, say! How many?

LE BRET. Well! eight and forty—not counting women!

CYRANO. Where?

LE BRET. Montfleury, the townie, de Guiche, Valvert,
Baro, th'Academy!

CYRANO. They're what I'm needing.

LE BRET. Have you considered whither this life is leading?
Have you a plan?

CYRANO. I stumbled in a maze,
Confused between the parts the wanderer plays.
Now I have chosen——

LE BRET. What?

CYRANO. The simple plan
of being everything to every man.

LE BRET. So be it. But now tell me, as between us,
what has Montfleury done?

CYRANO. That old Silenus,
so fat his fingers cannot reach his navel,
with women thinks himself the very devil,
and makes sheep's eyes, while sputtering he flogs
his part, with eyes protruding like a frog's.
My hatred began when that pot-bellied thug
dared ogle her—as though a crawling slug
did at the heart of a lily blackly hover.

LE BRET, *astounded*. What! Is it possible?

CYRANO, *with a bitter smile*. That I'm a lover?
Changing his tone and speaking quietly.
Yes, I'm in love.

LE BRET. With whom? You never told.

CYRANO. My love! Perpend! I realized of old
this nose which runs before me like a flunkey
would scare a woman ugly as a monkey.
While she I love—but that's self-evident—
is what, when he planned loveliness, God meant.

LE BRET. So lovely.

CYRANO. Fair to thought's end—and beyond.
Most dazzling, rarest—*with increasing excitement*—
most superbly blonde.

LE BRET. Who is this woman?

CYRANO. A sweet unconscious danger,
walking with her own beauty as with a stranger.
The snare of nature, the musk-rose love has made
the stronghold of his scented ambuscade.
Her smile's all heaven in a little place,
and she does nothing with so supreme a grace
she traps all beauty in her negligent spell.
No Venus can as greatly ride her shell,
nor Dian as goddess skirt the woodland cherries
as in her chair she rides the streets of Paris.

LE BRET. 'Tis clear as daylight. I can guess——

CYRANO. You can.

LE BRET. It is your cousin Robin.

CYRANO. 'Tis Roxane.

LE BRET. That's right as rain. The brave deserve the fair.
She knows you brave. Tell her you love. You're there.

CYRANO. Look at me, damn you! and then shut your trap!
This nose that snuffles like a thunderclap
is made for love, you think! As God is my light!
Yes, sometimes I grow maudlin in the twilight.
Say, there's a garden. In the scented dusk
I wander there and with this nose, this tusk
I snuff all April. Under the moon's cold beam
I watch some girl with her lover and I dream
I too might loiter, changed by that silver charm,
sweetly with such another on my arm.
I tower, forget—until the wall discloses
suddenly the shadow of my damned proboscis.

LE BRET. Steady, old horse.

CYRANO. Steady yourself! But yes,
sometimes I grieve alone with ugliness.

LE BRET. Your eyes are wet!

CYRANO. You lie! I'm far too ugly

for tears along my nose to trickle smugly.
I'll not permit, while I am in control,
tears meant for beauty's cheeks in floods to roll
grossly, like tumblers in a circus. For tears
echo from far the music of the spheres,
and therefore not a tear, through me, shall thus
change the sublime for the ridiculous.

LE BRET. Pluck up your heart. In love you never know.

CYRANO. Fool! I love Juliet! Am I Romeo?
I am a moth that stumbles at a star.

LE BRET. Where is your courage wandered? At the bar
that little lass just now who bade you eat
looked well upon you—and did not retreat!

CYRANO. That's true.

LE BRET. Well, then! And Roxane, when you fought,
was pale with anguish!

CYRANO. Roxane was distraught?

LE BRET. Her heart and spirit unto wonder woke!
Courage, and speak!

CYRANO. And find my nose a joke!
'Tis the one thing in all the world I fear.

PORTER, *introducing someone to* CYRANO.
Sir, you are wanted!

CYRANO. Her duenna! here!

THE DUENNA. We ask her gallant cousin—meaning you—
if he'd accord us——

CYRANO. I?

THE DUENNA. A rendezvous.
Matters there are to mention!

CYRANO. Save me!

THE DUENNA. Matters!

CYRANO. God's wounds!

THE DUENNA. To-morrow when the dawnspring spatters
the world with rose, she goes to Mass.

CYRANO, *leaning on* LE BRET. St. Peter!

THE DUENNA. Is there perchance a place where you could
meet her?

CYRANO, *thunderstruck.* A place—I—but—my God.

ACT I]   CYRANO DE BERGERAC   43

   THE DUENNA. Be quick!
   CYRANO. I guess——
   THE DUENNA. Well——
   CYRANO. Ragueneau—the pastry-cook——
   THE DUENNA. Address?
   CYRANO. In the Street—of, O my God—St. Honoré.
   THE DUENNA. We'll come. Be there at seven!
   CYRANO. As you say!

Exit DUENNA.

   CYRANO, *falling into* LE BRET's *arms.* I—she—a rendezvous.
   LE BRET. Well! Duellist!
   CYRANO. Whatever it means, she knows that I exist!
   LE BRET. You will be calm!
   CYRANO. Now that my soul is tightening,
I will be wild and terrible as lightning!
An army will not sate my appetite,
who have ten hearts and twenty arms to-night.
Avaunt! you dwarves of valour.
He shouts. Forward! Titans!
For the last few minutes at the back of the stage the shadows of actors and actresses are visible in action; the rehearsals begin. The violins.
   A VOICE, *from the stage.*
Sir, our rehearsal this wild clamour frightens!
   CYRANO, *laughs.* We're going.
CUIGY, BRISSAILLE *and a number of officers holding up* LIGNIÈRE, *who is quite drunk, enter by the main door.*
   CUIGY. Cyrano!
   CYRANO. What now?
   CUIGY. A bird
We bring you.
   CYRANO, *recognizes him.* Lignière! Utterly absurd!
   CUIGY. He needs you.
   BRISSAILLE. Can't go home.
   CUIGY. But why?
   LIGNIÈRE, *pathetically showing a crumpled note.* This note
Warns me—a hundred at my single throat.
Because of a poem—there's danger—Gate de Nesle—
Ambush—and I must pass—you will not fail.

Lend me a bed—beneath your sacred dome!

CYRANO. A hundred men, you say? You'll sleep at home.

LIGNIÈRE, *terrified*. But——

CYRANO, *with a terrible voice, pointing to the porter's lantern, who is listening curiously*. Take this lantern!

LIGNIÈRE *seizes the lantern*. Yes, you have my oath
To-night I'll guard you against Behemoth!
To the officers. Follow behind, and be my witnesses!

CUIGY. A hundred men!

CYRANO. I would not fight with less!

Actors and actresses have come down from the stage in their costumes.

LE BRET. But why defend——

CYRANO. Le Bret would have me funk?

LE BRET. This useless sot——

CYRANO. Because the man is drunk!
This vat of muscat, this tun of vin rosé
like a great gentleman the other day,
when, after Mass, he saw his lady sip
the Holy Water of God's fellowship,
though terrified of aqua pura, quaffed
the total chalice at a single draught.

AN ACTRESS, *dressed as a soubrette*. A pretty deed!

CYRANO. Pretty of you to know it.

THE ACTRESS, *to the company*.
But why a hundred men against a poet?

CYRANO. Forward. *To the officers*. And, gentlemen,
when I'm attacked,
whatever danger threatens, I'll not be backed.

ANOTHER ACTRESS, *leaping from the stage*. I'm coming too.

CYRANO. You're welcome.

ANOTHER, *same action, to an old actor*. Come, Cassandre!

CYRANO. Come all, the Doctor, Isabelle, Leandre!
And see how your Italian farce will banish
the tragedy these ruffians think is Spanish,
and with the joy-bells of a tambourine
silence their fanfares, ringing in between!

THE WOMEN, *leaping with joy*. Bravo. My cloak. A hood.

JODELET. The play begins.

CYRANO, *to the fiddlers.* Play us a tune of action, violins!
The violins join the rout. They snatch and distribute the footlights. Then they become a torchlight procession.
Hurrah! Here captains, women here together,
and here in front, alone, crowned with the feather
that glory lends my helm, to point the way—so
I stride as proud as Scipio three times Naso.
—You understand? No help whate'er's in store?
All ready? One, two, three. Porter, the door.
The porter throws the doors wide. A picturesque corner of old Paris reveals itself.
See! Paris trembles in her midnight mist
her roofs moon-pencilled with dim amethyst.
The stage is set for wonder where the Seine
slips back her sliding scarves of cloud and rain—
a mirror night holds up to mystery.
Forward—and you shall see what you shall see!
    ALL. We for the Gate of Nesle.
    CYRANO, *on the threshold.* The Gate of Nesle.
Turning, as he goes out, to the soubrette.
You asked me why, if I remember well,
a hundred men attack a single poet?
He draws his sword and adds quietly.
The answer is, I love him—and they know it.

*Exit. The procession—*LIGNIÈRE *staggering in front, then the actresses arm-in-arm with the officers, then the actors dancing—marches through the night to the sound of violins in the faint light of the candles.*

Act II

THE POET'S TAVERN

RAGUENEAU'S *restaurant and confectioner's shop. A large kitchen at the corner of the Rue St. Honoré and the Rue de l'Arbre Sec seen in the background through the glass panels of the door, in the light of dawn.*

On the left in the foreground is a counter with a forged iron stand, from which hang geese, ducks, and white peacocks. There are tall vases with bunches of country flowers, chiefly yellow sunflowers. On the same side, in the background, there is an enormous fireplace in front of which the roasts are dripping into pans between huge firedogs, each of them supporting a little saucepan. On the right is the foreground with door. Further back a staircase giving access to a little attic room, of which the inside is visible through open shutters. The table is laid in this room, lighted by a small Flemish candelabra. It is a dining-room. A wooden gallery continuing the staircase appears to lead to other similar rooms.

In the middle of the shop there is an iron hoop, which can be pulled down with a cord, to which joints are fastened, which forms a sort of larder.

The ovens under the staircase glow in the semi-darkness. Copper pans shine, spits turn, food is displayed in heaps; there are hams suspended from the hoop. Morning bustle. Scurry of the personnel, fat cooks and tiny turnspits, their caps decorated with cocks' feathers or with a guinea-fowl's plumage. Piles of brioches and townships of petit fours are being brought in on metal and wicker trays.

The tables are covered with cakes and dishes; others are set with chairs for customers. A small one in a corner is hidden under papers. As the curtain rises, RAGUENEAU *is discovered at it writing.*

RAGUENEAU, PASTRYCOOKS. RAGUENEAU *writes at a little table, with an inspired air, though counting syllables on his fingers.*

1ST PASTRYCOOK, *trying an elaborate confection.*
Here's nougat.
    2ND PASTRYCOOK. Flan.
    3RD PASTRYCOOK, *with a decorated roast.* A peacock.
    4TH PASTRYCOOK, *with a tray of cakes.* Pastries.
    5TH PASTRYCOOK, *with a pie-dish.* Brawn.
    RAGUENEAU, *ceasing to write and raising his head.*
The copper pans are silvered by the dawn.
Shake off the Muse, that well-beloved sloven!
Later the lute, my man; now for the oven.
Rises. To Cook. Here, you; that's far too short. Extend it.

COOK. By?
RAGUENEAU. Three feet!
COOK. Mad!
1ST PASTRYCOOK. Here's a tart, sir.
2ND PASTRYCOOK. Here's a pie.
RAGUENEAU. Away, my Muse, lest, gazing on the spigots,
your eyes are reddened by these roaring faggots.
To a baker, pointing to the loaves.
Why don't you give these loaves their proper niches?
Caesuras must bisect the hemistiches.
To another, pointing to an unfinished pastry.
This palace needs a thatch; attend to it.
To a young apprentice, who is spitting fowls.
And you on your interminable spit
threading the modest fowl, the splendid turkey,
remember old Malherbe, how, when at work he
used longs and shorts alternately, and learn
like him your dithyrambic roasts to turn.

A 2ND APPRENTICE, *coming with a covered dish.*
Master, I thought of you when at the fire.
I moulded this especially.
RAGUENEAU, *delighted.* A lyre!
APPRENTICE. 'Tis a brioche!
RAGUENEAU. And stuffed with candied fruits.
APPRENTICE. With sugared strings most natural for lutes.
RAGUENEAU, *giving him money.* Drink to my health.
Seeing LISE *enter.* My wife! Off. Not a word!
and put the cash away.
Showing the lyre with a bashful air. Pretty?
LISE. Absurd!
She places a pile of paper-bags on the counter.
RAGUENEAU.
Paper-bags? Thank you. *He looks.*
What! the manuscript
of poems and my books obscenely ripped
to pouch an acid-drop or marzipan. 'Tis
Orpheus once more dismembered by Bacchantes.

LISE. And why not use the only thing that they meant
to leave behind as substitute for payment,
your wretched poetasters and their rant!

RAGUENEAU. Do not abuse divine cicadas—ant!

LISE. Nor ant, nor yet Bacchante I, until
you joined these porcine creatures at their swill.

RAGUENEAU. To use verse so!

LISE. Its only use, God knows!

RAGUENEAU. Madame, if so, what would you do
with prose?

TWO CHILDREN *enter the shop.*

RAGUENEAU. Well, children, what d'you lack?

FIRST CHILD. Three pies.

RAGUENEAU, *serving.* Well browned
and piping hot.

SECOND CHILD. Please will you wrap them round?

RAGUENEAU. One of my bags. *To the children.* Wrap up!
Well! Let me see.
He takes a bag, and before inserting the pies, reads.
"Ulysses when he left Penelope."
Not that one. *Takes another bag and reads.*
"Phoebus blonde" nor t'other one.

LISE, *impatiently.* Well! What's the trouble? Hurry up!

RAGUENEAU. 'Tis done! *Takes a third with resignation.*
Sonnet for Phyllis. May the Muse redeem us!

LISE. At last he's made his mind up!
Shrugs her shoulders. Nicodemus!
She climbs on a chair, and arranges plates on a dresser.

RAGUENEAU, *as she turns her back, recalls the children.*
Hush! Children! Give me back the wrapper, and see!
Here are six pastries in the place of three!
They give the bag back and rush out with the cakes.
"Phyllis"—a grease-spot on the sills of heaven.
Phyllis! CYRANO *strides in.*

CYRANO. What time is't?

RAGUENEAU, *greeting him warmly.* Six!

CYRANO, *with emotion.* An hour till seven.

RAGUENEAU, *following.* Bravo! I saw it—

CYRANO. What?
RAGUENEAU. Your duel.
CYRANO. Where?
RAGUENEAU. Fought at the Burgundy.
CYRANO. Oh—that affair!
RAGUENEAU, *admiringly*. The duel in verse.
LISE. He will remember it!
CYRANO. Bravo!
RAGUENEAU, *fencing with a spit*.
You'll find the envoi scores a hit.
The envoi scores a hit—how does it go?—
that envoi scores.
CYRANO. What time is't, Ragueneau?
RAGUENEAU, *stopping his antics before the clock*.
Five minutes past six. "That Death." O could I match
that ballade.
LISE, *to* CYRANO, *who has laid a hand carelessly on the counter*. You are wounded?
CYRANO. No! A scratch!
LISE. Were you in danger?
CYRANO. Danger? None whatever.
LISE, *shaking her finger*. You're fibbing, aren't you, sir?
CYRANO. Did my nose quiver?
It must have been no fiblet, but a giant.
Changing his voice. I expect someone. To oblige a client,
see that we aren't disturbed.
RAGUENEAU. My poets are coming.
LISE, *sarcastically*. For breakfast—when they start the day
with bumming!
CYRANO. Well, when I signal, see that they are gone!
What time?
RAGUENEAU. Six-ten.
CYRANO, *sitting down nervously and taking some paper*.
A pen?
RAGUENEAU, *taking the quill from behind his ear*.
Plucked from a swan!
Enter MUSKETEER *with magnificent moustaches and a stentorian voice*.
MUSKETEER. Good day!

CYRANO. Who's that?

RAGUENEAU. Friend of my wife. A sworder
by his account!

CYRANO *takes up the pen and waves* RAGUENEAU *away.*

CYRANO. Tut, write, then fold in order,
then give it her—and fly. A coward's crime!
Dropping the pen. To lack the courage to speak.
To RAGUENEAU. What is the time?

RAGUENEAU. Quarter-past six.

CYRANO. One word of all my store!
While if I write—*Resumes*—I'll write it down once more,
that letter which I've penned within my heart
a hundred times, so that no other art
is needed, but to set my soul beside it,
and write the spoken words my tongue denied it.
He writes. Behind the glass-panes of the door lean and hesitating figures appear. Enter the POETS *in black, with rumpled stockings all muddy.*

LISE, *entering, to* RAGUENEAU. Behold your rats!

1ST POET, *entering, to* RAGUENEAU. Hail, colleague.

2ND POET, *shaking hands.* Colleague, greeting.

3RD POET. Eagle of pastry-cooks—*Sniffs*—spiced wings are
beating!

4TH POET. Phoebus of Chefs!

5TH POET. Cook, rival of Apollo's.

RAGUENEAU, *surrounded, embraced, thumped.*
How soon one is at ease among these fellows.

1ST POET. We were delayed by a huge crowd assembled
at the Gate de Nesle.

2ND POET. Eight wounded wretches, tumbled
in a heap, were stretched out bleeding on the cobbles.

CYRANO, *raising his head.* Eight? There were only seven.

RAGUENEAU. What king of troubles
struck there?

CYRANO. I do not know.

RAGUENEAU, *to* MUSKETEER. And you?

MUSKETEER, *tugging at his moustache.* Perhaps.

CYRANO, *apart—he murmurs from time to time.*
"I love"——

ACT II] CYRANO DE BERGERAC 51

1ST POET. A single man, they tell me, chaps,
put the whole gang to flight!
2ND POET. The pavement lies
all strewn with pikes and broken cudgels.
CYRANO. Eyes——
3RD POET. Hats everywhere for miles.
1ST POET. A king of rips,
he seems, this fierce companion!
CYRANO. Your lips.
1ST POET. A dreadful ogre—the man who set about it.
CYRANO. I fear your beauty—and I die without it.
2ND POET, *gobbling a cake.*
Any new verses, Ragueneau?
CYRANO. Your lover—
No need to sign what I'll be handing over!
RAGUENEAU, *to 2nd poet.* A recipe in rhyme!
3RD POET, *with a plate of cream puffs.*
Silence for verse!
4TH POET, *looking at a brioche.*
This pastry's cap's too crooked to be hers!
He decapitates it at a bite.
1ST POET. This gingerbread would woo a maw of silica
with almond eyes 'neath lashes of angelica!
He swallows a slice of gingerbread.
2ND POET. We wait!
3RD POET, *crushing a cream puff.*
This puff dies with a creamy flourish!
2ND POET, *eating the pastry lyre.*
'Tis the first time I knew a lyre nourish!
RAGUENEAU, *preparing himself to recite.*
A recipe in verse.
2ND POET, *nudging 1st.* 'Tis breakfast.
1ST POET, *to 2nd.* Dinner!
RAGUENEAU. Recipe for almond tarts:
    Beat up eggs until they foam
        into chrome!
    When they're beaten soft as silk
      add some lemon-juice, and pour
        to be sure,

> almonds pounded into milk.
> Flank the sides with lemon-cheese,
> if you please,
> then with hands that lightly flutter,
> round the edges, I entreat,
> fold and pleat!
> Percolate the froth of batter
> on the little pastry-shelves;
> these themselves
> stack within the hottest parts
> of the oven; crisply toast
> for a host,
> piping hot, of almond tarts.

THE POETS, *mouths full.* Exquisite! Charming!

A POET, *choking.* Humph.

They go to the end of the room eating. CYRANO, *who has watched all this, goes over to* RAGUENEAU.

CYRANO. While you discourse,
did you see how they stuffed themselves?

RAGUENEAU, *low, and smiling.* Of course—
But I avert my eyes lest they be troubled,
and thus the joy my verse affords is doubled.
I read my poetry, and while I read
the hungry sheep on more than stanzas feed.

CYRANO, *clapping him on the shoulder.* I like you!

RAGUENEAU *goes off to his friends.* CYRANO *watches him and then calls* LISE. Listen, Lise!

LISE, *exchanging social nothings with the* MUSKETEER, *looks up startled, and comes to* CYRANO.

This Musketeer besieges you?

LISE, *offended.* That virtue has no fear
whose lofty gaze is proof against surprise.

CYRANO. Too oft the conquering are conquered eyes!

LISE. Sir——

CYRANO. I love Ragueneau. I warn you, therefore,
respect the dignity of him I care for.

LISE. Really!

CYRANO, *raising his voice so that the* MUSKETEER *can hear.*
Verb. sap.

ACT II] CYRANO DE BERGERAC 53

Salutes the MUSKETEER *and continues to watch the door, looking at the clock.*

LISE, *to the* MUSKETEER, *who has merely returned* CYRANO's *salute.*
Stand this and you are no man.
Mock me his nose!

THE MUSKETEER. His nose—his more than Roman!

Goes off quickly, followed by LISE.

CYRANO, *from the door signalling to* RAGUENEAU *to get rid of the poets.* Now!

RAGUENEAU, *pointing to the door, R.* For reading verse——

CYRANO, *impatient.* Hurry!

RAGUENEAU, *leading them off.* This is better.

1ST POET, *in despair, his mouth full.* What! leave the cakes?

2ND POET. Take them.

They follow RAGUENEAU *in procession, first piling up the cakes.*

CYRANO. I'll read the letter,
which I had written, on the instant when a
vestige of hope appears.

ROXANE, *masked, followed by the* DUENNA, *appears behind the pane.*

CYRANO *opens the door eagerly.* Enter!
Turning to the DUENNA. Duenna
a word!

DUENNA. Four!

CYRANO. Have you a sweet tooth?

DUENNA. I'd say I had!

CYRANO, *taking paper bags from the counter.*
Excellent! See! two sonnets by Benserade!

DUENNA. What?

CYRANO. Crammed with cream-buns in plenty.

DUENNA. Good enough!

CYRANO. What say you to a pastry called a puff?

DUENNA. Fill it with cream, it eats as sweet as salmon.

CYRANO. Take six wrapped in these verses by Saint-Amant.
And in this poem of Chapelain a slice
of ribbon-cake finished with almond-ice.
And new-baked scones?

DUENNA. Almost my favourite sweet!

CYRANO. Take the whole lot and eat them in the street!

DUENNA. But——

CYRANO. —and remain there till the last is swallowed!
He closes the door and returns to ROXANE, *uncovered, and at a respectful distance.*

CYRANO. Moment above all other moments hallowed,
wherein by you remembered it befell me
that you have stooped from heaven to say—to tell me——

ROXANE, *unmasking.*
Why, first to tell you that the oaf check-mated
by your bright sword had long been designated
by a great noble (for a purpose which
I dare not name) to be my lord.

CYRANO, *bowing.* De Guiche.
My sword—'tis my great fortune—did its duty
not for my blemishes, but for your beauty.

ROXANE. Then—I was minded—could speak it to no other
save you the nearest that I own of brother—
my playmate all those summers how far back—

CYRANO. Yes—every year you came to Bergerac!

ROXANE. Your swords were reeds plucked by the waterways!

CYRANO. And your dolls owed their flaxen locks to maize!

ROXANE. Playtime.

CYRANO. The time of brambles.

ROXANE. And the time
when disobedience to my whims was crime.

CYRANO. Roxane, with skirts to her knees, was Madeleine.

ROXANE. And was I beautiful?

CYRANO. You were not plain!

ROXANE. Often with hands from some cause or another
gashed you came running, when, an anxious mother,
I murmured with a voice that sought to grumble,
"What scratch is this caused by another tumble?"
She takes his hand. Good God! Incredible! A scratch!
CYRANO *seeks to withdraw his hand.* No! Show it!
At your age, too! What were you doing, poet?

CYRANO. Playing—as once I played when all was vernal!

ROXANE. Give me your hand. *Sitting by the table and dipping her handkerchief in water.*

CYRANO, *sitting by her side.* So tenderly maternal.

ROXANE. And tell me while I stanch the blood how many
you fought with?

CYRANO. A mere hundred, hardly any!

ROXANE. The tale!

CYRANO. O no! I pray, as you are fair,
speak what at first you dared not!

ROXANE. Now I dare,
because of that fragrance floating from the past,
to make avowal that I am held at last!

CYRANO. Ah!

ROXANE. But he does not know.

CYRANO. Knows not!

ROXANE. As yet.

CYRANO. Yes!

ROXANE. But he'll know before this sun is set!

CYRANO. He?

ROXANE. A poor lad, who hardly dared to move
his eyes to mine and never spoke——

CYRANO. his love!

ROXANE. But I—nay! leave your hand! 'tis in a fever—
saw on his lips his love unspoken hover.

CYRANO. His love!

ROXANE. And by the strangest accident
he serves, my cousin, in your regiment!

CYRANO. In mine!

ROXANE. A sub-Lieutenant of the Guard!

CYRANO. Yes.

ROXANE. By his brow with all that's noble starred
I know him proud, and young and noble, comely.

CYRANO, *rising, pale to the lips.* Comely!

ROXANE. What ails you?

CYRANO. Naught! This scratch—*showing his hand*—
scolds dumbly!

ROXANE. I love him—but I've only seen him, sir,
far off and lonely, at the theatre.

CYRANO. You have not spoken?

ROXANE. With our eyes—at times!

CYRANO. How do you know?

ROXANE. Gossip beneath the limes
about the playhouse whispered low—

CYRANO. That he—

ROXANE. Was sub-Lieutenant in your Company.

CYRANO. His name?

ROXANE. De Neuvillette.

CYRANO. There's no such man
in Ours!

ROXANE. He joined to-day—my Christian—
under your Captain Castel-Jaloux.

CYRANO. How wild,
how swift the heart is. But—belovéd child.

The DUENNA *appears.*

DUENNA. The cakes are done, Monsieur de Bergerac.

CYRANO. Well! go and read the verses on the back!

Exit DUENNA.

But you whom eloquence alone can ravage,
how will you suffer if the man's a savage!

ROXANE. His looks proclaim the hero of romance!

CYRANO. Bright hair, dull wits, would make you look askance!

ROXANE. His soul, I guess, soars upward like a bird's.

CYRANO. O yes, I know, fine feathers make fine words.
But if he proved a dolt?

ROXANE, *stamping her foot.* My heart would shatter.

CYRANO. And was it, madam, to ventilate this matter
you summoned me? I'm puzzled, I confess.

ROXANE. 'Twas yesterday they told me that your Mess
were Gascons all!

CYRANO. And that we tend to bully
those beardless lads who venture sorrowfully,
still milky from their mothers, with a mask on
that argues mongrel to a pure-bred Gascon?
'Twas this you heard?

ROXANE. 'Twas something of the sort!

CYRANO. Not without reason, madam.

ROXANE. And I thought

ACT II] CYRANO DE BERGERAC 57

you soldier of the world, when yesterday
you drubbed that wretch and held the mob at bay—
I thought if he, that all men fear, were ready——
  CYRANO. I will protect your little baron, lady!
  ROXANE. Cyrano, bless you! You'll be his defender?
My gentle friend—tender as I am tender.
  CYRANO. I swear.
  ROXANE. And be his friend.
  CYRANO. I'll fight for both.
  ROXANE. Even his duels?
  CYRANO. Roxane, you have my oath.
  ROXANE. I like you well. But the clock bids me go.
She resumes her mask eagerly, with lace on her forehead, and adds in an absent voice.
But tell me of your fight! Since Roncevaux
no knight has so prevailed on heathenness!
Tell him I'll write! *Blows him a kiss.* I love you!
  CYRANO. Yes, oh yes!
  ROXANE. A hundred against one—Farewell. My one dread
you've cured.
  CYRANO. Yes, yes.
  ROXANE. And bid him write!—a hundred!—
You'll tell me more! I fly! It makes me wince—
A hundred! Brave!
  CYRANO, *saluting her.* I have been braver since.
Exit. CYRANO *remains motionless, his eyes on the ground. Silence. The door opens;* RAGUENEAU *thrusts his head in.*
  RAGUENEAU. Can we return?
  CYRANO, *without moving.* Yes.
RAGUENEAU *signals and his friends enter. At the same moment* CARBON DE CASTEL-JALOUX, *in the uniform of a Captain in the Guards, appears, gesticulating wildly as he sees* CYRANO.
  C. DE C.-J. Cyrano.
  CYRANO, *raising his head.* You, Captain!
  C. DE C.-J., *loudly.* Brave lad! All's known! Come!
share the joy we're lapped in
with your admirers!
  CYRANO. But——

C. DE C.-J. They've stormed the bars
And now await you at the Cross of Stars.

CYRANO. I——

C. DE C.-J., *going to the door and shouting thunderously.*
He refuses. The Hero's got the hump!

A VOICE, *outside.* Mother of Jasus!

Tumult without, swords and bottles being brandished.

C. DE C.-J., *rubbing his hands.*
They're coming in a clump!

THE OFFICERS, *storming the inn.* Begob!
Bejabers! Saint Pather and Saint Paul!

RAGUENEAU, *retreating terrified.*
Are you all Gascons, gentlemen?

THE OFFICERS. Yes, all!

AN OFFICER, *to* CYRANO. Bravo!

CYRANO. Baron!

A 2ND, *shaking his hands.* Your health!

CYRANO. Baron!

A 3RD. Be kissed!—

CYRANO. Baron!

SEVERAL GASCONS. Embrace him.

CYRANO. Gentlemen, desist!

RAGUENEAU. Are you all Barons?

OFFICERS. All!

RAGUENEAU. No, really!

OFFICERS. Let's
build him a steeple with our coronets.

LE BRET, *enters and runs to* CYRANO.
A crowd of lunatics is out to find you
led by the mob who marched last night behind you.

CYRANO. You didn't tell them where I was?

LE BRET, *rubbing his hands.* I did.

A CITIZEN, *enters, followed by a group.*
Sir, the whole blooming town is on the skid.

Outside the street is packed. Sedan-chairs and carriages draw up.

LE BRET, *smiling, low to* CYRANO. What of Roxane?

CYRANO, *sharply.* Be silent!

THE CROWD, *without.* Cyrano!

ACT II] CYRANO DE BERGERAC

RAGUENEAU, *jumps on a table.*
Storm the shop! Sack it! Let the whole world go!
A CROWD, *about* CYRANO. My friend—my friend.
CYRANO. I had, of friends, the fewest
yesterday!
LE BRET. Thank success!
A YOUNG MARQUIS, *running with open arms.*
If thou but knewest!
CYRANO. If thou! When was't we herded swine together?
ANOTHER. Sir, certain ladies in my chaise ask whether
I will present you.
CYRANO, *coldly.* And who'll do the like
for you to me!
LE BRET, *bewildered.* What ails you?
CYRANO. Quiet, type!
A MAN OF LETTERS. A few details?
CYRANO. No.
LE BRET. This is Renaudot.
Invented the Gazette.
CYRANO. I tell you "No."
LE BRET. A sheet where all the news is printed. Some
think it will dominate the days to come.
POET, *advancing.* Sir.
CYRANO. Still they come!
POET. I'll write a pentacrostic
upon your name.
CYRANO. O Hell!
Commotion. DE GUICHE *enters with retinue of officers who accompanied* CYRANO *at the end of the last act.* CUIGY, BRISSAILLE. CUIGY *comes rapidly to* CYRANO.
CUIGY. De Guiche, old costic,
Murmurs. Everyone makes way.
Marshal de Gassion's envoy.
DE GUICHE, *saluting* CYRANO. And whose mission
is to express the Marshal's admiration
for this new feat, that caught us by the collar!
CROWD. Bravo!
CYRANO, *bows.* The Marshal is a judge of valour!

DE GUICHE. He had not credited a tale like this
had not these gentlemen——

CUIGY. Been witnesses!

LE BRET, *aside to* CYRANO, *who seems absent-minded.*
But——

CYRANO. Silence.

LE BRET. You're in pain.

CYRANO, *trembling, and pulling himself together.*
Before this crowd!
His moustache bristles! He puffs his chest out.
In pain! You watch me!

DE GUICHE, *to whom* CUIGY *is whispering.*
All your past speaks loud
with noble exploits, and you prove it thus
among these Gascons?

CYRANO. Yes.

AN OFFICER, *violently.* He's one of us!

DE GUICHE, *looking at the Gascons in a group behind* CYRANO. Well, well! And all these gentlemen so wrapped in their majesty are——

C. DE C.-J. Cyrano!

CYRANO. Yes, Captain!

C. DE C.-J. Since my whole company of savages
is mustered, make the presentations, please!

CYRANO. These are the Gascon Grenadiers.
Like soldiers into battle hurled,
so into life with reckless cheers,
thunder the Gascon Grenadiers.
They have all Paris by the ears,
their pedigrees like flags unfurled,
these high-born Gascon Grenadiers,
the noble riff-raff of the world.

They're eagles stooping to the kill,
though rusty as a moulting rook,
but rooks that tumble from a still
sky, eagles stooping to the kill.
They've never paid their tailor's bill
for all their carved ancestral look

of eagles stooping to the kill,
at whose descent the heavens shook.

The shop-assistants of the grave
who trade in death and peddle fame,
and on their tombstones for a name
scrawl, "Shop-assistants of the grave."
Too arrogant for breath they crave
to swap life's long domestic shame,
as shop-assistants of the grave,
for glory's swift and single flame.

They are all this—and one thing more—
[that every cuckold knows and fears]
the eternal lover waiting for
woman, the everlasting whore.
Sing loud, cuckoo! Old husband snore!
Your wives, long tortured by arrears,
moan, as they break the oaths they swore:
"These are the Gascon Grenadiers."

DE GUICHE, *sitting at ease in a chair that* RAGUENEAU *has quickly brought him.*
To-day your man of fashion must have his poet.
Will you be mine?
    CYRANO. Nobody's if I know it!
    DE GUICHE. Your feat amused my uncle. I might move
the Cardinal in your favour.
    LE BRET, *in raptures.* Heavens above!
    DE GUICHE. Some play perhaps the theatre has not seen?
    LE BRET, *whispers.*
You know you want to place your "Agrippine."
    DE GUICHE. Bring it!
    CYRANO, *tempted and attracted.* But, really——
    DE GUICHE. A great critic, who
will at the most correct a line or two!
    CYRANO, *instantly stiffening.*
Impossible. He'd set my poet's soul on
fire by altering one semi-colon.

DE GUICHE. But in revenge he planks down a king's ransom
for what he likes.

CYRANO. Handsome, but not as handsome
as my own bounty when, happy in my art,
I pay by learning my own verse by heart.

DE GUICHE. You're proud.

CYRANO. Perhaps I am. Do you complain?

AN OFFICER, *enters with a string of battered hats spitted on his sword.* Look, Cyrano. This morning by the Seine
we found these feathered trophies, left behind
by those you routed.

C. DE C.-J. Spoils of the noblest kind!

EVERYONE, *laughing.* Ha, ha!

CUIGY. The man who bade these feathers fly
must curse himself.

BRISSAILLE. Who was it?

DE GUICHE. It was I. *A sudden silence.*
I ordered them to thrash—since one can't plaster
one's hands with such—a drunken poetaster.
General embarrassment.

AN OFFICER, *aside to* CYRANO, *showing the feathers.*
They'd make a stew, or, better still, polonies.

CYRANO, *taking the sword on which they were spitted, and throwing them with a bow, at the feet of* DE GUICHE.
Perhaps, sir, you'd restore them to your cronies.

DE GUICHE, *rising sharply.*
My chair and chairmen instantly. *To* CYRANO *angrily.*
A word with you!

VOICE, *outside, shouting.* The chair of the most noble lord.

DE GUICHE, *controlling himself with a smile.*
D'you know "Don Quixote"?

CYRANO. Well—and I uncover
to the mad knight who turned the whole world over.

DE GUICHE. Study——

A PORTER, *appearing.* The chair!

DE GUICHE. —and find that it is apter
than you suppose, the windmills.

CYRANO, *bowing.* Thirteenth chapter.

DE GUICHE. For in that contest you may find——
CYRANO. I learn
I fight with those that every breeze can turn!
DE GUICHE. That one of the great sails may with its bars
shoot you in the mud——
CYRANO. or upward to the stars.

Exit DE GUICHE. *He enters the chair. His retinue follow, talking eagerly.* LE BRET *accompanies them to the door. Exit crowd. The officers drink and eat at tables R. and L.*

CYRANO, *bowing ironically to those who leave without greeting him.*
Your servant!
LE BRET, *in despair, with upraised arms.*
Here's a pretty kettle of fish.
CYRANO. What! Would you scold me?
LE BRET. Yes, because you wish,
it seems, to slaughter any hopes there are.
'Tis madness!
CYRANO. Very well. I go too far!
LE BRET. Then you admit it?
CYRANO. Principle and example,
if an excuse were needed, offer ample.
LE BRET. If you would leave your musketeering swagger,
Fortune would toss a ha'penny to a beggar!
CYRANO. To Hell with that and all the bloated tribe
of millionaires and marquises who bribe
each man, according to the lives we lead,
with reference to his especial need.
You'd have me write a book and dedicate it
to some illiterate bully, whom I hated,
some creature who could whisper to the Banks:
"Give the poor knave a little rope!" No thanks!
Or scribble pamphlets of the sort to curry
favour with politicians in a hurry,
proving that the very treason which they plot
proclaims the single-minded patriot.
Thank you for nothing. Or write gossip-notes
about some woman's lovers or petticoats,
and scrawl lampoons to order, safe from hurt

within the shelter of the creature's skirt.
No thanks! Become a literary sneak
who, by himself exceptionally meek,
joins with a pack of other curs, which tackles
lions from behind—as is the way with jackals.
I thank you, no! And lastly make it virtue
to hurt those only who can never hurt you,
side with the stronger always in your quarrels,
debauch the Muse, and therefore win the laurels
by living, like the lowest kind of varlet,
on the immoral earnings of a harlot.
I thank you, no, no, no and no again.
To be a poet is to be 'ware of pain,
and not to fear it, to follow to the end
the dream, to live with freedom as a friend,
to sing as though life trembled in his breath,
and look between the eyelashes of death.
Nor that's not all. For in a world of lies
he alone damns the devil's compromise,
and when he threatens, does not give a curse
and pinks him with a sword-thrust or a verse.
And what he writes, he writes because he must,
and scribbles with a finger in the dust:
"Let others boast. I, who was born a poet,
am brother to the dust and proudly owe it."
Thus glad of flowers, fruit, even of leaves
plucked in his garden under his own eaves
when others outclimb him by ladders not their own,
he laughs in their teeth because he climbs alone!

LE BRET. Alone, but not an outcast. Why the devil
need you be so confoundedly uncivil
and why insist on making enemies?

CYRANO. Because your easy popularities
stink in my nostrils. You may smirk and whimper
with your mouth like a puppy's pursed to simper.
I blast the swine to Hell, and, as they go,
shout to their backs, "Thank God! another foe."

LE BRET. An aberration!

CYRANO. Well! It is my foible!
To be detested always rings my joy-bell!
You little know, my friend, how a sharp volley
from hostile eyes disperses melancholy,
or how amusingly my suit's deflowered
by envy's gall or drivel from a coward!
The melting kindness with which you are surrounded
is an Italian collar, soft, unbounded,
in whose soft clasp your neck in woman's fashion
puts self-respect and manhood on a ration,
so that you bend this way and that, and wait, red
and cringing on the fleeting whims of time. But hatred
irons my spirit out with starch enough
to keep my neck unbending in my ruff,
and each new foe gophers another pleat
in the supreme denial of retreat.
For hatred, like the ruffles Spaniards roll,
grips like a vice, but makes an aureole.

LE BRET, *after a silence, taking* CYRANO'S *arm.*
Be proud and bitter. But underneath your breath
Whisper, "She loves me not—and that is death."

CYRANO, *sharply.* Silence!

CHRISTIAN *has just come in and joins the officers. They ignore him. Finally he sits down by himself at a table, where* LISE *waits on him.*

AN OFFICER, *at the table, glass in hand.*
Hi! Cyrano. The tale.

CYRANO. One minute.

Passes on LE BRET'S *arm. They speak in whispers.*

OFFICER. The story and the ring of glory in it
will teach our timid novice.

CYRANO. Novice! Who?

OFFICER. A Northerner and sickly!

CYRANO. Sickly too!

1ST OFFICER, *teasing.*
Monsieur de Neuvillette, pray understand—
there is one topic as absolutely banned,
as to breathe "halter" in a suicide's dwelling.

CHRISTIAN. And 'tis?

ANOTHER OFFICER, *loudly.* Observe.
He touches his nose thrice mysteriously.
You've guessed what I am telling?
 CHRISTIAN. Yes! 'Tis the——
 ANOTHER. Silence! That word is abhorred
Points to CYRANO *in conversation with* LE BRET.
Unless you seek acquaintance with his sword!
 ANOTHER, *who has noiselessly come up to the table.*
There were two fellows snuffled! Well! He slew them,
because he thought the topic must pursue them.
 ANOTHER, *sepulchrally, emerging from under the table, where he has crept on all fours.*
Unless you would die young, prithee abridge
the smallest reference to that cartilage!
 ANOTHER, *laying a hand on his shoulder.*
A word's enough! Nay more! One indiscreet
gesture may prove some blunderer's winding-sheet.
Silence. They surround him with crossed arms. He rises and crosses to CARBON DE C.-J., *who, in conversation with an officer, pretends to have noticed nothing.*
 CHRISTIAN. Captain.
 C. DE C.-J., *turning and eyeing him.* My friend?
 CHRISTIAN. When Southerners exhibit
their swagger, what do you advise?
 C. DE C.-J. Why! crab it
by proving that the North has courage! *Turns his back.*
 CHRISTIAN. Good!
 1ST OFFICER, *to* CYRANO. The tale.
 ALL. The tale!
 CYRANO. I'd drown it if I could.
All bring their stools and listen eagerly. CHRISTIAN *sits astride over a chair.*
Well! When I started out for this hotch-potch,
the moon shone round in heaven as a watch;
then of a sudden some horologist,
clearing the dial with a rag of mist,
muffled the argent circle of its light,
and the whole world was plunged in utmost night.

ACT II] CYRANO DE BERGERAC 67

There were no lamps in the streets, and I suppose
a man could see no further than
  CHRISTIAN. his nose.
Silence. Everybody rises slowly, watching CYRANO *in turn. He breaks
off astounded. A pause.*
  CYRANO. Who is this fellow?
  AN OFFICER. 'Tis a lad who came
only this morning.
  CYRANO, *advancing on* CHRISTIAN. This morning?
  CARBON, *under his breath*. And his name
Baron de Neuvill——
  CYRANO, *quickly, holding himself in*. What!
Goes pale and red, still moving towards CHRISTIAN.
I——*Then controlling himself, says in a low voice:*
Very well.
He continues. I was saying,—*with sudden fury*—God!
Continues naturally. the night was black as Hell!
And to protect this plate of warmed-up mince,
I thought, I shall offend some peer or prince,
Who'll pull
  CHRISTIAN. your nose——
Everyone rises. CHRISTIAN *remains seated.*
  CYRANO, *choking*. Who'll pull, I said, a tooth out.
A tooth, I said, and thought, to let the truth out,
I'll pinch——
  CHRISTIAN. Your nose——
  CYRANO. my finger in the crack
of the door, and when my noble answers back
he'll trap
  CHRISTIAN. Your nose.
  CYRANO, *mopping his brow*. my fingers in the jamb!
But then I thought: March, Gascon that I am!
On, Cyrano! and, though 'twas growing darker,
I held my way and met
  CHRISTIAN. some nosey Parker!
  CYRANO. I stand on guard and find me
  CHRISTIAN. —nose by nose,
  CYRANO, *leaping forward*. Thunder of God!

All the Gascons rush forward to see. CYRANO *on nearly reaching* CHRISTIAN *masters himself and continues—*
with drunken oafs in rows
who stank

CHRISTIAN. Your nose out——

CYRANO, *pale and smiling.* breathing beer at large!
I spring to action!

CHRISTIAN. Nose upwards.

CYRANO. and I charge!

Two disembowel, another I impale,
spit a fourth in riposte

CHRISTIAN. A likely tale!

CYRANO, *bursting.* Out, all of you.

1ST OFFICER. The tiger's roused. Beware!

CYRANO. Out! Leave us two alone!

2ND OFFICER. Death's in the air!
You'll find him chopped to mincemeat!

RAGUENEAU. Mincemeat!

ANOTHER OFFICER. Yes,
and dished up in your kitchen.

RAGUENEAU. I confess
I feel as limp and pale as any napkin!

CARBON. But——

ANOTHER. He'll not leave a crumb, no! not a scrapkin.

ANOTHER. I faint with terror of what is bound to happen.

ANOTHER, *closing door R.* Most horrible!

Exeunt all. CYRANO *and* CHRISTIAN *remain face to face, looking at one another.*

CYRANO. Hither, my arms are open.

CHRISTIAN. Sir!

CYRANO. It was brave!

CHRISTIAN. But——

CYRANO. Brave. Let's know each other!

CHRISTIAN. I do not understand.

CYRANO. Embrace her brother!

CHRISTIAN. Whose?

CYRANO. Hers.

ACT II] CYRANO DE BERGERAC 69

CHRISTIAN. Who's she?
CYRANO. Roxane!
CHRISTIAN, *running to him.* You Powers infernal!
her brother?
CYRANO. Almost! Say a cousin fraternal!
CHRISTIAN. She has
CYRANO. Told all.
CHRISTIAN. She loves me!
CYRANO. You've a faint chance.
CHRISTIAN. How proud and glad I am of your acquaintance.
CYRANO. You show your feelings suddenly—I swear!
CHRISTIAN. Forgive me——
CYRANO, *looking at him, with a hand on his shoulder.*
True, the wretch is passing fair!
CHRISTIAN. Sir, I admire you to the point of awe.
CYRANO. And these allusions to my——
CHRISTIAN. I withdraw!
CYRANO. Roxane expects a letter.
CHRISTIAN. Ah!
CYRANO. What now?
CHRISTIAN. I'm lost the moment that I utter!
CYRANO. How?
CHRISTIAN. I'm such a hopeless dolt I'd die of shame.
CYRANO. No man's a dolt who gives himself the name!
nor did you set about me like a dolt!
CHRISTIAN. O! Battle lends my lips a thunderbolt!
For action I'm sufficiently well-sprung,
but women simply make me hold my tongue.
Their eyes, perhaps, when I pass by are tender.
CYRANO.
And, when you pause, no doubt their hearts surrender?
CHRISTIAN. Never, for I am one—with shame 'tis said—
who cannot tell his love——
CYRANO. And I instead,
If God had cast me in a different mould,
had never failed to love—and always told.
CHRISTIAN. O, for the power to clothe my love with grace.

CYRANO. O, for that comely musketeering face!

CHRISTIAN. Roxane's a wit, and when I plead with her my chance is gone.

CYRANO. You've an interpreter
upon your brow would plead my suit in heaven!

CHRISTIAN. O, for the gift of tongues!

CYRANO. It shall be given!
while you in turn give me your conquering glance,
and lo! the perfect hero of romance!

CHRISTIAN. You mean?

CYRANO. Could you repeat at second-hand
gold words of mine?

CHRISTIAN. I do not understand!

CYRANO. Why should we let aught disappoint or harm her,
when we two spirits in one are leagued to charm her,
and with my soul, leaving this coat of leather
for yours of lace, we storm the stars together.

CHRISTIAN. Cyrano.

CYRANO. Christian.

CHRISTIAN. I'm all confusion.

CYRANO. But if you think you'd shatter her illusion,
why fear to tread the path that fortune blazes
when we collaborate—your lips, my phrases?

CHRISTIAN. How your eyes glitter!

CYRANO. Think what you'd be losing!

CHRISTIAN. 'Twould please you?

CYRANO, *shuddering*. Please!
Pulling himself together. At least 'twould be amusing!
It is the poet's perfect chance. Come! meet me!
I will complete you, you in turn complete me!
I darkling, you in light, will share the duty—
I'll be your soul, and you shall be my beauty.

CHRISTIAN. This note that she's expecting, were it better to venture on a scrawl——

CYRANO, *taking from his doublet the letter he had written.* Here is your letter!

CHRISTIAN. But——

CYRANO. Save the superscription, naught is lacking.
CHRISTIAN. I——
CYRANO. 'Tis well written! Fear not! Send it packing!
CHRISTIAN. 'Twas written!
CYRANO. See! how the poor heart can mock its
own emptiness. We've always in our pockets—
we that were never loved—to ease our troubles,
letters for Chloris, dreams, love's rainbow bubbles.
Take it and give this little ghost of passion
the substance my feigned raptures could not fashion,
and range the birds I loosed but to forsake them,
and in these burning words of mine—nay! take them,
find the less truth, the greater eloquence.
Take them—and end it all!
CHRISTIAN. But will the sense
unaltered serve, and will this feignéd love
so written, fit Roxane?
CYRANO. Like her own glove!
CHRISTIAN. But——
CYRANO. Love of self will never cease to warp us!
Roxane will think that it was writ on purpose.
CHRISTIAN. My dearest friend.
Throws himself into CYRANO'S *arms. They remain locked in an embrace.*
1ST CADET, *opening a door.* A silence you could touch!
I dare not look. *Peeps in.* What!
THE OFFICERS, *seeing* CYRANO *and* CHRISTIAN *embracing.*
'Swounds!
AN OFFICER. This is too much!
A MUSKETEER, *ironically.* Hallo!
C. DE C.-J. Our demon mild as Holy Brother
struck on one nostril simply turns the other.
THE MUSKETEER. Now is the time to quiz his nose, by God!
Calling LISE *with a conquering air.*
Come hither, Lise, and watch!
Sniffing the air. 'Tis very odd
the odour here.

Going up to CYRANO *and staring at his nose.*
Perhaps, sir, you would snuff it,
and tell me what it smells of?

CYRANO, *striking him.* Yes—of buffet!

Joy. The OFFICERS *have rediscovered their* CYRANO. *They dance wildly.*

Act III

THE KISS OF ROXANE

A small square in the old Marais. Old houses. A glimpse of small streets. Right, ROXANE's *house and the wall of her garden, which is covered with thick foliage. Above the door are a window and balcony. There is a seat in front.*

Ivy climbs up the wall, the balcony is wreathed with jasmine. It is quite easy to climb on to the balcony by the seat and the stones that jut out from the wall.

Opposite there is an old brick and stone house in the same style with a large door. The knocker of this door is bandaged like an injured thumb. As the curtain rises the DUENNA *is seated by the door. The window on* ROXANE's *balcony is open wide.* RAGUENEAU *is dressed in a sort of livery, standing close to the* DUENNA. *He is finishing a story, drying his tears.*

RAGUENEAU, *the* DUENNA, *to them* ROXANE, CYRANO, *and two* PAGES.

RAGUENEAU. And then she bolted with a musketeer.
Alone and ruined, I'd hanged myself, my dear,
when enter Cyrano! and ecce homo!—
saves, and appoints me Roxane's major-domo!

DUENNA. But how explain your ruin?

RAGUENEAU. Simply thus—
I loved the lute and Lise the blunderbuss!
Mars gobbled what was left him by Apollo—
and soon was nothing left for me to swallow!

DUENNA, *rising and calling to the open window.*
Roxane! come down. They're waiting!

ROXANE's *voice, through the window.* I'll just fit
this cloak and come!

ACT III] CYRANO DE BERGERAC 73

DUENNA, *to* RAGUENEAU, *showing him the door opposite.*
The party's opposite.
Clomire receives to-day in her apartment
to hear a lecture on what the lover's heart meant.
RAGUENEAU. The lover's heart?
DUENNA, *mincing.* Why, yes.
Calling up to the window. Roxane, dear, see. Come!
We mustn't miss the lover's Vade Mecum!
ROXANE. I come.
Sound of string instruments approaching.
CYRANO, *singing without.* La! La!
DUENNA, *surprised.* Music? Who's playing it?
CYRANO, *followed by* TWO PAGES *with triple lutes.*
A demi-semi-quaver, quarter-wit!
PAGES, *ironically.*
You have a close acquaintance with a quaver!
CYRANO. Gassendi taught me that, my little shaver,
and more.
PAGE, *playing and singing.* La! La!
CYRANO. I'll carry on the burden!
La! La! La! La!
ROXANE. 'Tis you.
CYRANO. To greet your garden—
the lily's bloom and what of scent the rose owes!
ROXANE, *leaving the balcony.* I will come down.
DUENNA, *pointing to the* PAGES. Who are these virtuosos?
CYRANO. A bet I won upon a point of grammar—
I, and D'Assoucy at it tongs and hammer—
when suddenly he shows me these tall felons
who scratch a nimble string with their long talons
and are his escort. "I will bet the cost,"
says he, "of a day's music"—and he lost!
Therefore till Phoebus shows his gilded foot
I am the master of their triple lute,
of all I do a soft harmonious witness,
whereof I now misdoubt its earlier fitness.
To the MUSICIANS.

Off—and with my regards play a Pavane
to old Montfleury.
The PAGES *leave by exit. To the* DUENNA.
I come to ask Roxane
as always—*To the* PAGES *as they go*—
discords which will make him shiver—
To the DUENNA—
if her soul's love is marvellous as ever.
  ROXANE, *coming out of the house.*
Comely as gifted, who'd not own his charm?
  CYRANO. So gifted?
  ROXANE. Even you must yield the palm.
  CYRANO. Gladly.
  ROXANE. There's none, I think, can turn like him
the airy nothings of the seraphim.
Sometimes he's absent, his Muse has closed her wings,
then suddenly one hears an angel's strings!
  CYRANO, *incredulously.* No?
  ROXANE. 'Tis too much. It seems he must act dumbly
(how like you men!) because the boy is comely!
  CYRANO. He tells his love with such imagination?
  ROXANE. 'Tis not his speech but love's own dissertation.
  CYRANO. He writes——
  ROXANE. Still better! Let me read to you:
"My heart grows with your thieving!"
Triumphant. Judge it!
  CYRANO. Pooh!
  ROXANE. And this: "Since pain only the heart endures,
and you have mine in keeping, send me yours."
  CYRANO. First too much heart, then not enough—the lad
can't find the happy mean.
  ROXANE. You drive me mad.
You're jealous.
  CYRANO, *trembling.* I?
  ROXANE. Yes, of a greater singer.
And here does love himself not sweetly linger:
"My heart, belovéd, is a single sigh,
and could but kisses, like my letter, fly,

you'd read it with your lips."
How soft that comes!
  CYRANO, *smiling in his own despite.*
The lines are well enough—but only crumbs.
  ROXANE. And this?
  CYRANO. But do you know them all by heart?
  ROXANE. All.
  CYRANO. 'Tis a noble tribute to his art.
  ROXANE. A master!
  CYRANO, *modestly.* What!
  ROXANE, *peremptorily.* Yes!
  CYRANO, *bowing.* Very well, a master.
  DUENNA, *coming to her quickly.* Monsieur de Guiche.
To CYRANO, *pushing him to the door.*
Go! It might spell disaster
if he should find you here.
  ROXANE, *to* CYRANO. Give him no clue
to my dear secret! Since he comes to woo,
and is most powerful, he must not guess
lest he destroy us out of wickedness!
  CYRANO, *entering the house.* O well!
Enter DE GUICHE.
  ROXANE, *curtseying.* I'm going!
  DE GUICHE. I come to say adieu!
  ROXANE. You're leaving?
  DE GUICHE. For the front.
  ROXANE. Ah!
  DE GUICHE. Now.
  ROXANE. Ah.
  DE GUICHE. New
orders. The siege of Arras.
  ROXANE. Is it so?
  DE GUICHE. My news would seem to leave you cold
as snow!
  ROXANE, *politely.* Oh!
  DE GUICHE. Parting will be long, too long for me!
You heard I was appointed G.O.C.?
  ROXANE, *bored.* Bravo.

DE GUICHE. And in the Guards.

ROXANE. The Guards are sent?

DE GUICHE. Your gasconading cousin's regiment.
I'll teach him manners there.

ROXANE. But God eternal!
The Guards!

DE GUICHE, *laughing.* But certainly, since I'm their Colonel!

ROXANE, *falling on the seat—aside.* Christian!

DE GUICHE. What ails you?

ROXANE. I am in despair!
War—and to know my dear acquaintance there.

DE GUICHE, *surprised and charmed.*
On your first word of kindness fate doth banish
your loving servant!

ROXANE, *changing her tone and fanning herself.*
And you seek to punish
my cousin?

DE GUICHE, *smiling.* Ah! you like him.

ROXANE. No, I swear!

DE GUICHE. You see him?

ROXANE. Seldom.

DE GUICHE. He goes everywhere
with a certain guardsman.
Tries to remember the name. Neuviller—or nearly.

ROXANE. Tall.

DE GUICHE. Blonde.

ROXANE. No, sandy!

DE GUICHE. Handsome.

ROXANE. Pooh!

DE GUICHE. Dull!

ROXANE. Really!
Her voice changes. Now as to Cyrano—our fire-eater
is for the front of the battle? but 'twere neater
and break his heart beside if——

DE GUICHE. You propose?

ROXANE. Leave him in Paris when the army goes
with all his fellow-rips for the duration
to cool his heels. 'Twould be the worst vexation

for such a man, to have to make a stranger
of his belovéd—the bright eyes of danger!

DE GUICHE. A woman, a woman against the universe
for subtlety!

ROXANE. He and his friends will curse
their luckless fate which keeps them out of action,
and there's your vengeance!

DE GUICHE. Does this prove affection?
She smiles. O let your dear espousal of this plan
bear that interpretation.

ROXANE. Sir, it can.

DE GUICHE, *showing a pile of folded papers.*
Here are the marching orders to be sent
forthwith to the entire regiment.
He detaches one.
This one I'll keep! And your proud heart will crack,
king of swashbucklers, my de Bergerac!
Laughing. And do you often trick your friends?

ROXANE. At times.

DE GUICHE.
You madden me! I ought when midnight chimes
to march—but since reveille love has sounded,
listen! near by's a House some monks have founded
in the Rue d'Orleans. Laymen are forbidden,
but I'll convert the angels of that Eden!
And there is room enough in the wide sleeves
the fathers wear to cloak love's gentle thieves!
They are the Cardinal's own Capuchins,
owing the nephew grace his uncle wins.
The world will think me gone. I'll enter masked!
Grant me this night, the first I ever asked.

ROXANE, *eagerly.* But were it known, your glory——

DE GUICHE. Glory!

ROXANE. Still
the siege.

DE GUICHE. What matter!

ROXANE. No.

DE GUICHE. You will, you will!

ROXANE, *tenderly.* For your sake, no!
DE GUICHE. My love!
ROXANE. March! *Aside.* Christian's saved.
Aloud. Come back a hero, Antoine!
DE GUICHE. I have craved
to hear you speak that name with love.
ROXANE. 'Tis spoken.
DE GUICHE, *transported with joy.* I go.
He kisses her hand. Are you content?
ROXANE. My hand's the token.
DUENNA, *making an ironical curtsey to his back.*
My hand's the token.
ROXANE, *to the* DUENNA. Silence, let us go!
I've robbed you of your war, poor Cyrano.
Calls to the House. Cousin. We're going to Clomire's. *Points to the door opposite.* Lysimon and Alcandre speak.
DUENNA, *putting her little finger in her ear.*
Yes, but this little demon
tells me we'll miss them.
CYRANO. Do not miss those apes!
They arrive at Clomire's door.
DUENNA, *delighted.*
O, look, the knocker muffled up with crapes!
To the knocker.
They've tied you up so that your metal boot
won't trample down their speeches—little brute!
She lifts the knocker with infinite care and raps softly.
ROXANE, *seeing the door open.* Enter!
From the doorstep to CYRANO.
If Christian comes, as I expect,
bid him to wait.
CYRANO, *eagerly as he enters.* Roxane! *She turns.*
What d'you select
to be your topic to-day?
ROXANE. I think——
CYRANO. She thinks!
ROXANE. You'll not betray me?

CYRANO. Secret as the Sphinx!

ROXANE. I'll say to him, "Go, gallop. Cast your bridle. Improvise—be magnificently tidal!"

CYRANO, *smiles*. Excellent!

ROXANE. Hush!

CYRANO. Hush!

ROXANE. Not a word! *Enters and closes the door.*

CYRANO. I can——

The door opens again, ROXANE'S *head protruding.*

ROXANE. He'll practise!

CYRANO. Never!

TOGETHER. Silence! *Door closes.*

CYRANO, *calling*. Christian!

Enter CHRISTIAN.

CYRANO. I know what's needed. Prepare to learn by rote
words that will take your triumph by the throat!
No time to lose. Don't glare upon me so!
Quick to your house and con your lesson.

CHRISTIAN. No!

CYRANO. What!

CHRISTIAN. I'll wait her here!

CYRANO. What vertigo
has seized you? Quick to lessons.

CHRISTIAN. I tell you—No!
I'm tired of alien letters, words dissembling,
of playing a part, and, while I play it, trembling!
It passed at first, but now her heart is plighted
I'll use no lamps save what my love has lighted!

CYRANO. God save us!

CHRISTIAN. And who'll swear that they will snuff!
I'm not so dull but they'll be well enough.
I'll speak, as you have taught me, passing well.
And if I fail, by all the devils in Hell,
I'll find a way, unless these arms deceive me!
Seeing ROXANE *leaving Clomire's house.*
'Tis she! Dear Cyrano, you will not leave me!

CYRANO, *bowing*.

Eat, since you chose it, your own sugar-candy!

ROXANE, *leaving Clomire's house with a company of highbrows of both sexes, whom she leaves; curtsies and greetings.* Ladies, good day!

DUENNA, *in despair.* We've missed the Ars Amandi!

ROXANE, *bowing again.* Farewell, dear ladies!

Greetings to ROXANE, *further interchange of greetings.*
All go by different ways. ROXANE *sees* CHRISTIAN.
Ah! 'tis you—*She goes to him*—and dusk!
Wait! Those far footsteps on the night all musk!
Let's sit—and speak. I listen while I dream.

CHRISTIAN. Love!

ROXANE. Speak of love!

CHRISTIAN. I love you!

ROXANE. That's the theme!
The variations!

CHRISTIAN. I——

ROXANE. Well?

CHRISTIAN. to distraction!

ROXANE. No doubt—and then——

CHRISTIAN. and then 'twere satisfaction
if you loved in exchange. You'll not be cruel!

ROXANE. I ask for pastries and you give me gruel.
Expound the nature of your love——

CHRISTIAN. Why—this!

ROXANE. Nay—sir, distil your passion!

CHRISTIAN. But one kiss
on that fair neck!

ROXANE. Sir!

CHRISTIAN. But I love.

ROXANE, *rising.* Once more!

CHRISTIAN, *holding her back.* No! for I love

ROXANE, *sitting again.* That's lucky.

CHRISTIAN. and adore.

ROXANE, *rising and leaving.* Really!

CHRISTIAN. But I grow dull.

ROXANE, *tartly.* Which gives me pain,
precisely as it would if you grew plain.

CHRISTIAN. But——

ACT III]   CYRANO DE BERGERAC   81

ROXANE. Find your vanished phrases on your way!
CHRISTIAN. I——
ROXANE. love. I know. Farewell to you! *Walks to house.*
CHRISTIAN. O stay!
For I would tell you——
ROXANE. You adore. I guess!
Pushing the door open. No! No! Begone!
CHRISTIAN. But I——*She closes the door in his face.*
CYRANO, *who has entered unseen.* A great success!
CHRISTIAN. Help! Help!
CYRANO. I cannot.
CHRISTIAN. If I'm not restored
to favour forthwith, I shall die.
CYRANO. Good Lord!
How can I teach you on the instant!
CHRISTIAN, *seizing his arm.* See!
The balcony window is lit.
CYRANO, *moves.* Her window!
CHRISTIAN, *softly.* I shall die.
CYRANO. Speak quietly!
CHRISTIAN, *in a whisper.* Death!
CYRANO. 'Tis pitch-black.
CHRISTIAN. Well!
CYRANO. Let me think! I suppose——
you don't deserve it, but——here on your toes
beside the balcony. I'll breathe your speech
in your ear.
CHRISTIAN. But——
CYRANO. Silence, I beseech!
THE PAGES, *reappearing, to* CYRANO. Hi!
CYRANO. Hush! *He signs to them to whisper.*
1ST PAGE, *whispering.* Montfleury's had his serenade!
CYRANO, *quick and low.*
Good! Now, go plant yourselves in ambuscade,
one at this corner, the other opposite,
and if a stranger passes, herald it
with a tune on the lute.
2ND PAGE. What tune, Sir Virtuoso?

CYRANO. Gay for a woman, for a man—why so-so.
Exeunt PAGES. *To* CHRISTIAN. Call her.

CHRISTIAN. Roxane!

CYRANO, *picking up pebbles and throwing them at the window.*
Wait! 'Twas a stone I threw!

ROXANE, *opening the window.* Who calls!

CHRISTIAN. 'Tis I.

ROXANE. Who's I?

CHRISTIAN. Christian.

ROXANE, *disdainfully.* You!

CHRISTIAN. I crave one word!

CYRANO, *under the balcony to* CHRISTIAN.
Don't let your accent harden!

ROXANE. No! You speak ill. Begone.

CHRISTIAN. I come for pardon!

ROXANE. You love no more!

CHRISTIAN. How you miscall my loving
by adding—"no" to "more."

ROXANE, *stops as she was closing the window.*
You are improving!

CHRISTIAN. This baby love grows cradled in my sorrow
so fast he'll use it as a pram to-morrow!

ROXANE, *walking on to the balcony.*
Better! But, if he is so cruel, what
kept you from strangling love within his cot?

CHRISTIAN. I tried, but all in vain . . . for, if you please,
this . . . new-born babe . . . is a young . . . Hercules.

ROXANE. Better!

CHRISTIAN. So that he crushed . . . as 'twere a reed,
two serpents . . . Pride . . . and Fear.

ROXANE, *leaning on the balustrade.* O good indeed!
But why d'you speak, and on a sudden stop?
Do you distil your fancy drop by drop?

CYRANO, *drawing* CHRISTIAN *under the balcony and taking his place.*
Shut up! Leave it to me!

ROXANE. Your words to-day
have lost their footing. Why?

CYRANO. They lose their way
by night, and grope through darkness to your ear.

ROXANE. My words have no such trouble.

CYRANO. Because they steer
straight for their goal and find it, where they start,
before you speak them, in my waiting heart!
And think how large that is, your ear so small!
Besides your words, breathed downward, swiftly fall,
while mine, as rising, need a longer time!

ROXANE. But latterly, it seems, they've learned to climb!

CYRANO. Practice makes perfect in this bright gymnastic!

ROXANE. It's true I speak from high!

CYRANO. Breathe one sarcastic,
one bitter word, and, tumbling from that height,
'twill slay me, shattering my heart outright.

ROXANE. I'll leave this height.

CYRANO, *quickly*. No!

ROXANE. There's a bench. Leap off it.

CYRANO, *shrinking back terrified*. No!

ROXANE. What means your "No"?

CYRANO. O madam! let us profit
by this dear moment, when the night between
unseen we murmur with muted voice!

ROXANE. Unseen?

CYRANO.
But yes! 'tis heaven in shadow like shade to glimmer,
I whiteness see and guess a robe of summer.
You faintly glimpse a cloak as black as night,
the shadow I by your consummate light.
You cannot guess what deeps these moments stir!
If I at times was eloquent——

ROXANE. You were.

CYRANO. it is because, until this moment, never
my heart spoke out——

ROXANE. And why?

CYRANO. I stumbled ever—entangled.

ROXANE. How entangled?

CYRANO. In your bright
misleading beauty. But my heart to-night
for the first time to its first love is speaking.

ROXANE. And with a different voice its love is seeking.

CYRANO. Aye, new and strange, for with the night as friend
I dare to be myself—Where will this end?
Forgive me—this—I know not what I do—
so sweet—and so intolerably new!

ROXANE. So new?

CYRANO. Yes, new—at last to be sincere!
To be a butt has been my lifelong fear.

ROXANE. A butt?

CYRANO. Of an unguarded moment. Hence
I always shroud my heart with common sense.
We go star-gathering, and lest laughter choke us,
my heart and I bring home a common crocus.

ROXANE. The flower's sweet.

CYRANO. But not to-night for us.

ROXANE. Never before have you entreated thus.

CYRANO. O, let us leave the fevered crowd and dare
return to nature and things fresh and fair!
Let's cease at some stale pool to sip and mumble
drops in the compass of a golden thimble,
and plunge into the flood, in whose great tide
we tipple freedom and are satisfied.

ROXANE. But wit?

CYRANO. A trick to hold your interest!
But in this perfumed hour of dream to jest
would be to emulate some mincing creature
who throws confetti in the face of nature.
Look at the stars, and let the heavens with this
strip all sophisticated artifice,
the cold fastidious alchemy of the head
which turns the gold of sentiment to lead.

ROXANE. And wit?

CYRANO. I hate it in love. It is a crime
to waste with fencing love's appointed time—
the inevitable instant when (I pity

all those who miss it) each elegant and witty
phrase, as we speak it, does to sadness move
hearts great with the nobility of love.

ROXANE. What, were this instant ours and you my lover,
words would you use?

CYRANO. All these! I toss them over——
wild flowers as I plucked them—blossoms tumbled
and crumpled leaf. I love you, I have trembled,
I love, I swoon; 'tis over and 'tis well.
Your name within my heart is like a bell
homeward to ring love's wandered flock and sound
with every stroke the heaven your name has found.
I'm but a chronicle remembering
all that you are. There was a day in spring
you dressed your hair anew, and all my sight
was so bedazzled by that dangerous light,
that, like a man who, gazing on the sun,
where'er he looks, beholds vermilion,
I turned away mine eyes bewitched, and fond,
and all the world was memorably blonde!

ROXANE. Aye! this is love indeed!

CYRANO. Before God, yes!
This that I feel, this lovely bitterness,
this pain, this terror, these are love—and yet
the more I love, the more I self forget!
All mine I'd give for your least happiness,
and though you never knew, and did not guess,
an echo of your laughter would suffice,
though heard in Hell, to crown my sacrifice.
Your lightest glance breeds virtue, binds me fast
with undreamed valour! O do you feel at last
what love ascends with what lost heart how beating
in the soul softly through the midnight fleeting?
It is too fair, this night; it is not true;
I do not speak, nor she who listens, you;
It cannot be! This loveliness outgraces
my wildest dream, and death alone outpaces
life as it leaps the dark. But God! she blanches!

O can it be my words among the branches
have made you tremble, leaf among fair leaves?
For you are trembling, and no night deceives
the little stir of your belovéd hand
that thrills along the jasmine strand by strand.
He kisses the jasmine in ecstasy.

ROXANE. I tremble, weep, surrender on the breath
of love upon your lips!

CYRANO. Then welcome death!
It is my words have brought her heart to this.
But one thing's left in the world to ask——

CHRISTIAN, *under the balcony.* —a kiss.

ROXANE, *withdrawing.* What?

CYRANO. Love!

ROXANE. You asked?

CYRANO. I asked! *To* CHRISTIAN. You go too fast.

CHRISTIAN. Since she's so moved, I'll have my turn at last!

CYRANO. O yes—I asked—but, you dark heavens above,
forgive the too great daring of my love!

ROXANE. Then you insist no further?

CYRANO. I insist that I refuse insistence. Be unkissed,
I pray you, and be kissed for ever so!

ROXANE. Why?

CYRANO. Silence, Christian!

ROXANE, *leaning forward.* What d'you whisper low?

CYRANO. For my great boldness, to myself I beckoned,
saying, "Poor Christian, hither."

The lutes play. Hush! a second! a stranger.

ROXANE *closes window.* CYRANO *listens to the lutes, one of which plays a comic, the other a tragic tune.*

Grave or gay? What do they mean?
A man? A woman? Hold! a Capuchin.

Enter CAPUCHIN, *going from house to house, a lantern in hand, scanning the doors.*

CYRANO, *to* CAPUCHIN. Who is this latter-day Diogenes?

CAPUCHIN. I seek the house of Madam——

CHRISTIAN. As you please?

CAPUCHIN. Robin?

ACT III]   CYRANO DE BERGERAC   87

CHRISTIAN. What does he say?
CYRANO. This alley leads
straight to her house on the right!
CAPUCHIN. I'll tell my beads
on your behalf to-night! *Exit.*
CYRANO. You midnight owl!
My blessings follow your retreating cowl!
CHRISTIAN. Win me that kiss!
CYRANO. No.
CHRISTIAN. Late or soon——
CYRANO. 'Tis true!
that moment of ecstasy must come to you,
when your two mouths must find each other, rose
lips underneath the blonde moustachios.
To himself. I'd rather be the cause——
The shutters open, CHRISTIAN *hides under balcony.*
ROXANE, *on the balcony.* 'Tis you again!
We spoke——
CYRANO. of kisses. Why should you refrain
from that sweet word, which, merely spoken, scorches
the lips, but acted, lights love home with torches?
Be not afraid. For you did lately glide
with scarcely a ripple on love's flowing tide
from gentle mockery to smiles, the near
neighbour of sighs, that yielded to a tear.
Glide on, glide out and learn the distance is
one heart-beat from a tear to the first kiss.
ROXANE. Be still!
CYRANO. What is a kiss that you should fear it?
It is the instant when the body and spirit
meet, and in some divine alembic stirred
merge their two virtues in a lovelier third.
It is the interchange of sun and rose,
whose gold in heaven to earth its fragrance owes;
time, as it darkly passes over, lit
with the brief radiance of the infinite.
It is God's shadow silencing the heart.
ROXANE. Be still!

CYRANO. A kiss has played so high a part
that one—the happiest of noblemen—
shared it with the Queen of France herself.
ROXANE. What then?
CYRANO. That I, like Buckingham, have wept unseen,
like Buckingham, in you adore a queen,
as sad as he and faithful——
ROXANE. Are you not
also as fair?
CYRANO, *aside, checked*. As fair. I had forgot.
ROXANE. Climb, then, and pluck the nonpareil of roses.
CYRANO, *pushing* CHRISTIAN *to the balcony*. Climb!
ROXANE. Taste to the heart——
CYRANO. Climb!
ROXANE. That the bee discloses.
CYRANO. Climb!
CHRISTIAN, *hesitating*.
But the moment has slipped by for action.
ROXANE. This summer of the south.
CYRANO, *pushing him*. Up with you, fiction!
CHRISTIAN *clambers up the columns and reaches the balustrade*.
CHRISTIAN. Roxane!
CYRANO. O strangest pain that, while it wrings
the heart, consoles it with immortal things.
A beggar in anguish, out of a single crumb
I build the turrets of love's kingdom come,
knowing that Roxane on his mouth must find,
and therefore kiss, the fragrance of my mind.
Lutes. Tune—grave and gay. The Capuchin.
He pretends to run as though arriving from a distance. Hallo!
ROXANE. What is it?
CYRANO. I was passing!
CHRISTIAN, *astonished*. Cyrano!
ROXANE. Good morning, cousin!
CYRANO. Cousin, good day to you.
ROXANE. I come. *Disappears. Enter* CAPUCHIN.
CHRISTIAN. O, once again! *Follows* ROXANE.

CAPUCHIN. 'Tis here—I knew—
Magdaleine Robin.
CYRANO. 'Twas Rolin, I swear!
CAPUCHIN. No. B.I.N.
ROXANE. What is't?
CAPUCHIN. A note.
CHRISTIAN. Who's there?
CAPUCHIN. A holy father on a holy mission,
sent by a worthy lord.
ROXANE, *to* CHRISTIAN. De Guiche!
CHRISTIAN. Damnation!
ROXANE. O, he'll not trouble us much longer, sweeting,
Unsealing the letter. I love you and—*She reads, in a low voice, by the light of* RAGUENEAU's *lantern*—
"Madame,
The drums are beating.
My soldiers gird their iron on. They march!
and think me gone, who leave them in the lurch.
I disobeyed and from this House I'll stir
only to bring you hither. My messenger,
my monkish postman, guiltless of all guile,
understands naught. Ensorceled by your smile
I cannot rest, till in a little while
one sweeter still, when we are close together,
pardons your most audacious servant——
To the CAPUCHIN. Father!
They all draw near. She reads.
This is the letter. Listen!
"As you treasure,
lady, your life, obey the Cardinal's pleasure,
whatever pain it brings. I, therefore, send
to its address this note, my lovely friend,
by the safe hands (at his express desire)
of this discreet, wise and most holy friar.
We wish that in your house this very night
the Capuchin—
Turns over the leaf—perform your marriage-rite!

You must wed Christian, whom I know you hate,
but you've no choice. Therefore accept your Fate,
and heaven your obedience will bless.
Believe me, madam, in all gentleness
your most obedient humble servant—and,
if you will have it so, your loving friend."
  CAPUCHIN, *radiant.* O worthy gentleman. I knew full well
what he devised for you was honourable.
  ROXANE, *whispers to* CHRISTIAN.
Don't I read letters admirably?
  CHRISTIAN. M'yes.
  ROXANE, *aloud, in despair.* Horrible!
  CAPUCHIN, *turning the lantern on* CYRANO. You?
  CHRISTIAN. No! I.
  CAPUCHIN, *turning his lantern and struck with doubt at the sight of his comeliness.* But——
  ROXANE. A P.S.
"Give six-score pistoles to the Fathers—signed——"
  CAPUCHIN. O noble lord.
To ROXANE. You're ready?
  ROXANE, *with resignation.* I'm resigned.
While RAGUENEAU *opens the door for the* CAPUCHIN, *whom* CHRISTIAN *beckons in, she whispers to* CYRANO.
Friend, keep De Guiche in play when he arrives.
He mustn't enter till——
  CYRANO. Good! *To* CAPUCHIN. To make wives
you take how long?
  CAPUCHIN. Say fifteen minutes.
  CYRANO, *pushing them to the house.* Hasten!
  ROXANE, *to* CHRISTIAN. Come. *They enter.*
  CYRANO. How shall I hold De Guiche and make him listen?
He jumps on the bench, and climbs up the wall towards the balcony.
Up! I've a plan!
The triple lutes play a melancholy air.
There's someone passing by!
A man this time!
He has reached the balcony. He crushes his beaver over his eyes, draws his sword, cloaks himself, then leans over.

'Tis high, but not too high.
He bestrides the balustrade, and gripping one of the long branches of the trees, hangs on to it, ready to drop.
I'll make a journey through the stratosphere.

DE GUICHE, *groping, masked.*
Where did that wretched father disappear?

CYRANO. He'll recognize my voice. I'll turn it back
into the Gascon brogue of Bergerac.

DE GUICHE, *looking at the house.* Ah! there's the house.
These velvet ribbons blind me!
He is entering when CYRANO *jumps from the balcony by the branch between* DE GUICHE *and the door. He pretends to fall heavily as if from a great height, and lies on the ground as though stunned.* DE GUICHE *leaps back.*

DE GUICHE. Good God!
He raises his eyes. The branch has swung back; he sees nothing but the sky, and is thunderstruck.
Whence come you?

CYRANO, *sitting up.* From the moon behind me!

DE GUICHE. The Moon!

CYRANO, *dreamily.* What is the time?

DE GUICHE. He's lost his reason!

CYRANO. The time, the day, the country and the season!

DE GUICHE. But, sir,

CYRANO. 'Tis mazed, I am.

DE GUICHE. Sir!

CYRANO. Like a shell
they shot me earthwards.

DE GUICHE, *impatiently.* Nonsense!

CYRANO, *loudly.* And I fell!

DE GUICHE, *recoiling.*
Yes! Yes! you fell from the moon. He's mad.

CYRANO. But really!
In sober fact, not metaphorically!

DE GUICHE. But——

CYRANO. Was it a hundred ages or a minute
that saffron monster with me bouncing in it
tumbled through heaven like an archangel?

DE GUICHE, *shrugging his shoulders.* Out of my way!

CYRANO. Throw off disguise and tell
where I have fallen in the roaring flight
across the heavens of an aerolite.

DE GUICHE. God's truth!

CYRANO. I fell so fast you couldn't blame me
for my bewilderment. So, therefore, name me
this moon or is it planet where I shot am
by the dead weight of my celestial bottom!

DE GUICHE. I tell you, sir!

CYRANO, *with a scream of terror, retreating.*
Preserve me! It appears
the man's a nigger!

DE GUICHE, *putting his hand to his face.* What!

CYRANO. Is it Algiers?
Or a Red Indian of the Shenandoah?
Feeling the mask. Why! 'tis a mask!
Then Venice or Genoa?

DE GUICHE. You keep a lady waiting!

CYRANO. Ah! 'tis Paris.

DE GUICHE, *laughing in spite of himself.*
That's rather funny!

CYRANO. You smile.

DE GUICHE. My mission tarries:
no time for jokes!

CYRANO, *cheerful.* Paris without a doubt
At his ease, laughs, dusts himself and bows.
whither I rode on the last waterspout!
I'm travel-stained with the ether. There is star-dust
still in my eyes, and on my spurs the far dust
from the shaggy gold of a planet, and I swear—
Picking something from his sleeve—
upon my doublet a strand of comet's hair!
He blows it away.

DE GUICHE, *beside himself.* Sir——

CYRANO, *as he passes, extends his leg, as though to show him something.* In my calf do you observe this high dent?
That's the Great Bear! And as to Neptune's Trident,

giving a miss to those three angry nails
I pitched head over heels into the Scales.
My weight's recorded in heaven by those light-bringers.
He holds back DE GUICHE, *who tries to pass, by his coat-button.*
If you should squeeze my nose between your fingers
'twould spurt with milk!

DE GUICHE. Milk!

CYRANO. From the Milky Way!

DE GUICHE. O, go to Hell!

CYRANO. To Heaven, you meant to say!

Crossing his arms.

I saw great Sirius, like some old suburban
grocer, at bedtime, muffled in his turban!

Confidentially.

The Little Bear was teething. I snapped a wire
by accident, in passing, in the Lyre!

Magnificently.

But all of this is for my travel-book!
And these gold stars that scorched my doublet. Look!
I pillaged at my peril. Their bright discs
will punctuate the page with asterisks!

DE GUICHE. Enough. I must—

CYRANO. I smoke you!

DE GUICHE. Have a care!

CYRANO. Is the moon made, you ask, of Camembert?
and are the folk—forgive my dithyrambic
raptures—that haunt its argentine alembic?

DE GUICHE, *shouting.* No! No! I wish

CYRANO. —to learn (what never men did
till I devised a means!) how I ascended!

DE GUICHE. He's mad!

CYRANO, *contemptuously.* No eagle did I top its ridge on,
like Regiomontanus, used no pigeon
like Archytas!

DE GUICHE. There's method in his ravings!

CYRANO. I do not borrow, sir, from other's savings!

DE GUICHE, *having got past, is on the way to* ROXANE'S *door.* CYRANO *follows him, prepared to knock him down.*

I know six ways to scale the sky and rape her!

DE GUICHE, *turning*. Six!

CYRANO. Stripping my body naked as a taper,
I'd furnish me with flasks where I'd refine all
the fallen tears of nature matutinal,
and when the sun did with his rays infuse
my frame, he'd suck it upward like the dews.

DE GUICHE, *surprised, and taking a step towards* CYRANO.
Yes, that's one way.

CYRANO. And then I could, of course,
to generate the wind's propelling force
rarify air, by using burning-glasses
arranged in twenty-sided cedar cases.

DE GUICHE, *taking another step*. Two!

CYRANO. Well! No more inventive than I'm skilful,
forge a steel-springed grasshopper I'd distil full
of raw saltpetre, which in successive blazes
would shoot me where the herd celestial grazes.

DE GUICHE, *follows him, unconsciously counting on his fingers*. Three!

CYRANO. Blow enough vapour into a balloon
(since it flies upward) to bear me to the moon.

DE GUICHE, *still following*. Four!

CYRANO. Since Phoebus at his Nadir sucks bull's marrow,
I'll use as ointment all that I can borrow!

DE GUICHE, *astounded*. Five!

CYRANO, *in speaking has drawn* DE GUICHE *to a bench across the square*. Last I'd essay the method of the drag-net.
On a steel tray seated I'd toss a magnet
into the air: the tray, of course, would shoot
after the flying magnet in pursuit.
Repeat continuously and despite hum
and ha of doubt, soar ad infinitum!

DE GUICHE. Here are six excellent ways of reaching heaven.
Which was your choice?

CYRANO. Sir, I chose number seven!

DE GUICHE. A seventh? Tell me!

CYRANO. I've a hundred more!

DE GUICHE. This is the comic I've been waiting for!
CYRANO, *with wide mysterious movements.* Roll on——
DE GUICHE. What's that?
CYRANO. You've guessed?
DE GUICHE. No!
CYRANO. Azure main!
When the high moon draws ocean home again
after a bathe, stretched on the sand, head-foremost
(for hair, which dries the slowest, tends to soar most)
under the moon's long pull I floated straight
as any angel to St. Peter's Gate!
Effortless, smooth, I rose and rose again
until I felt a shock, and then——
DE GUICHE, *drawn by curiosity, sits.* Yes?
CYRANO. Then——
Resuming his natural voice.
They've gone—the fifteen minutes. Did the gipsy
not say, "They will be married!"
DE GUICHE, *leaping up.* God! I'm tipsy.
That voice!
The door of the house opens. LACKEYS *appear carrying lighted candelabra.* CYRANO *removes his hat.*
That nose! 'Tis Cyrano.
CYRANO, *bowing.* It is!
—and they're exchanging gold acceptances!
DE GUICHE. What?
He turns. Tableau. Behind the LACKEYS, ROXANE *and* CHRISTIAN *hand in hand. The* CAPUCHIN *follows smiling.* RAGUENEAU *holds torch up. The* DUENNA *follows in the rear, all tousled from her bed.* God!
DE GUICHE, *to* ROXANE. You!
Recognizing CHRISTIAN *with amazement.* He?
Bowing to ROXANE *admiringly.*
Salute! thou subtlest eft!
To CYRANO. And you, inventor, almost as brightly deft!
Your story would have held a minor prophet
outside your Gate! Pray make a copy of it
for a book, "Peri outside Paradise."
CYRANO, *bowing.* Sir, I'll not fail to follow your advice.

CAPUCHIN, *pointing to the lovers and stroking his beard.*
A handsome pair, my son, your knot has tied.
DE GUICHE, *looking at them.* Yes.
To ROXANE.
Time for parting from your bridegroom, bride.
ROXANE. What do you mean?
DE GUICHE, *to* CHRISTIAN. Your regiment's about to march. Fall in, sir!
ROXANE. For the front?
DE GUICHE. No doubt!
ROXANE. But they're not going.
DE GUICHE. They will—now there's a war on.
Taking the orders from his pocket.
Pray be the bearer of this order, baron!
ROXANE, *throwing herself in* CHRISTIAN's *arms.* Christian!
DE GUICHE, *sneeringly, to* CYRANO.
The marriage-night must be postponed!
CYRANO, *aside.*
He little knows what respite I've been loaned!
CHRISTIAN, *to* ROXANE. Your lips again!
CYRANO. Enough! 'Tis time to go!
CHRISTIAN, *holding* ROXANE.
Parting is death. If you but knew——
CYRANO, *drawing his arm.* I know.
Drums off sound the march.
DE GUICHE, *from the back.* They're moving!
ROXANE, *to* CYRANO. Cyrano, a loving wife entrusts her dearest to you. Guard his life against all danger.
CYRANO. What I can, I will!
ROXANE. And see that he is prudent?
CYRANO. Prudent! Still I'll do my best.
ROXANE. And see that he keeps well throughout the siege!
CYRANO. I'll do what's possible.
ROXANE. And keep him faithful!
CYRANO. Faithful where the drum is!

ROXANE. And make him often write!

CYRANO, *pausing*. That I can promise.

Act IV

THE GASCON GRENADIERS

The position held by CARBON DE CASTEL-JALOUX'S *company at Arras. In the background an embankment fills the stage. Beyond that, view of a plain extending to the horizon, the countryside scarred with entrenchments. The walls of Arras, with its roof against the sky in the distance.*

Tents; arms littered about; drums, etc. Day breaks with a faint blonde light in the east. Sentinels at their posts. Watch-fires.

The Gascon Grenadiers are sleeping wrapped in their cloaks. CARBON DE CASTEL-JALOUX *and* LE BRET *are awake. They are very pale and thin.* CHRISTIAN *sleeps in the group, in his cape, his face lighted by a watch-fire. Silence.*

CHRISTIAN, CARBON DE CASTEL-JALOUX, LE BRET, *the Company, to them* CYRANO.

LE BRET. It's awful.

C. DE C.-J. Not a bite!

LE BRET. Hell!

C. DE C.-J. Hush! You'll scupper their dreams and wake them.

To OFFICERS. Sleep!

To LE BRET. Since sleep is supper!

LE BRET. When one can't sleep, it merely whets desire! I'm starving! *Distant firing.*

C. DE C.-J. Devil take them—and their fire! They'll wake my children.

To OFFICERS *raising their heads*. Sleep!

They lie down again. Further sounds of firing.

OFFICER, *moving*. What is it, Captain?

C. DE C.-J. Nothing except that Cyrano has tripped in!

SENTRY, *without*. Who goes there?

VOICE OF CYRANO. Bergerac!

SENTRY, *on the embankment.* I say: Who goes?
CYRANO, *appearing over the top.* Bergerac, idiot!
LE BRET. Heaven alone knows!
CYRANO, *making a sign for quiet.* Hush!
LE BRET. Wounded?
CYRANO. It's a habit they have got
of missing me at half-past seven.
LE BRET. Rot!
No letter's worth the daily risk you take
in posting it.
CYRANO, *stopping by* CHRISTIAN.
He sleeps. 'Tis for her sake.
I promised. And so pale. Did she but know
he dies of hunger. . . . But always comely!
LE BRET. So!
Your turn to sleep!
CYRANO. Don't scold, Le Bret, but wait!
I found a point at which to penetrate
the Spanish lines—where they are always drunk!
LE BRET. Then why not scrounge some victuals—
since we're sunk!
CYRANO. A man must travel light. But in their trench
I saw what makes me prophesy the French
will eat or die to-night.
LE BRET. What was it? Tell!
CYRANO. No! I'm not sure! You'll see.
C. DE C.-J. It's simply Hell,
to starve when we're besiegers.
LE BRET. 'Twould embarrass
old Hannibal himself, this siege of Arras.
We besiege Arras, good—and that obleeges us
to face the Crown Prince, who in turn besieges us.
CYRANO. Then someone should besiege the Prince—
to top it.
LE BRET. We're not amused.
CYRANO. Tut! Tut!
LE BRET. Why won't you stop it,

ACT IV] CYRANO DE BERGERAC 99

risking your life worth more than any other
for a letter.
Seeing him go. Off?
   CYRANO. I'm off to write another.
Lifts the flap and disappears.
Day is breaking. Rose shadows. The town of Arras glitters on the skyline. Cannon-shot followed by roll of drums in the far distance. Nearer drums beating. Interchange of gun-fire nearer and then moving R. Morning noises. OFFICERS' *voices off.*
   C. DE C.-J., *sighing.* Reveille.
His company move in their cloaks and stretch themselves.
Succulent sleep that know'st not blemish
Thou endest and they'll cry aloud.
   OFFICER, *sitting up.* —I famish.
   ANOTHER. I die.
   ALL. Oh.
   C. DE C.-J. Up with you!
   3RD OFFICER. Can't move!
   4TH OFFICER. Can't sneeze!
   1ST OFFICER, *looking at himself in his armour.*
My tongue's all yellow—I can't digest the breeze.
   ANOTHER. I'd give my title for a slice of Cheshire!
   ANOTHER. Unless they feed my belly what brews a measure
of necessary bile to cure the willies,
I'll keep my tent and sulk there like Achilles!
   ANOTHER. Bread?
   C. DE C.-J., *going to the tent where* CYRANO *is, in a low voice.*
Cyrano!
   OTHERS. We die!
   C. DE C.-J., *at the door of the tent.* A rescue hither!
Come, you whose humour pulls us all together,
and save us all.
   2ND OFFICER, *falling on the First.*
You're chewing something. Well met!
   1ST OFFICER. O! axle-grease well-basted in our helmet,
melted from cannon-waddings. Game don't harrass
with multitude the neighborhood of Arras.

ANOTHER, *entering.* I have been hunting.

ANOTHER. —fishing in the Scarpe.

ALL, *rising on them.*

Well, then? What luck?—a pheasant or a carp?
Quick! Show!

THE FISHERMAN. A gudgeon!

THE HUNTER. A sparrow!

God! I ask you!

ALL, *furious.* Let's chuck our hand in!

C. DE C.-J. Cyrano, a rescue!

CYRANO, *emerges from his tent calmly, pen behind his ear, book in hand.* Well?

To First Cadet.

Why d'you trail your legs as though they hurt you?

1ST OFFICER.

Because there's something has destroyed their virtue.

CYRANO. What?

1ST OFFICER. 'Tis my belly!

CYRANO. Haven't I a belly?

1ST OFFICER. And don't it snarl?

CYRANO. It sounds my soul's reveille.

2ND OFFICER. My teeth are long.

CYRANO. To bite on Kingdom Come!

3RD OFFICER. My maw rings hollow.

CYRANO. We'll beat it for a drum!

ANOTHER. I have strange noises in my ears.

CYRANO. You lie!

An empty maw has naught to listen by!

ANOTHER. O for a dish with oil on't!

CYRANO, *taking off his helmet and handing it over.*

Here, my lad!

ANOTHER. What can we feed on?

CYRANO, *throwing him the book.* Try the Iliad!

ANOTHER. Richelieu has his meals all fresh and hot.

CYRANO. He ought to send us partridges?

ANOTHER. Why not,
and wine!

CYRANO. A glass of Corton, if you please!

ANOTHER. Brought by a monk?
CYRANO. His Eminence of grease?
ANOTHER. I've got an ogre's twist!
CYRANO. To twist death's joints!
1ST OFFICER. I'm sick of repartee!
CYRANO. It has its points!
I'd choose to die under a setting sun,
outpunning glory with a final pun.
Aye! pierced with the noblest weapon of them all
to some great foe magnificently fall,
not in a bed but on the stricken field,
my heart with the sword, my lips with laughter steeled.
SHOUTS. We're starving!
CYRANO. Have a heart! Forget your maw!
Bertrandou, come. You were a shepherd. Draw
one of your fifes out of its leathern case,
and play me for these sots, with the old grace,
one of those country airs, whose sweet obsession
clings like a little sister, whose gentle fashion
echoes loved voices as in youth they spoke.
Those airs drift gentlier than the drifting smoke
over the village roof-trees of our birth.
They are not music, but are native earth.
And let the fife, conscripted for the wars,
remind us as the music dips and soars
in the swallow-dance that, ere with silver keyed
the varnish darkly glittered, she was a reed.
And let her be astonished with the dim rose
of rustic quiet returning with the primrose.
He begins to play the airs of Languedoc.
Listen, you Gascons! He pipes the neighbourhood
not of the camp, but of your native wood!
'Tis not the fife of battle, but the notes
the goatherd plays to fold his wandered goats.
Listen! It is the valley, the Landes, the very
tan of your youth beneath its crimson beret!
It is Dordogne all green on summer eves;
'Tis Gascony, you Gascons, and all its leaves!

C. DE C.-J. They weep!

CYRANO. O nobler the nostalgic quarrel
with fate than physical hunger. It is moral.—
For the wrung heart storms heaven with its avowals
unlike the earthbound anguish of the bowels!

C. DE C.-J. You'll sap their strength with tenderness!

CYRANO. Good Lud!
The heroic past they cherish in their blood
will wake on the instant.

He signals. The drum beats.

ALL, *tumbling into their armour.*
What is it? Where? And who?

CYRANO. At the first rumble of the first tattoo,
dreams, home, regret, and love itself are dumb
when the fife yields to the quick, alarming drum.

AN OFFICER, *looking in the distance.*
Look! here's De Guiche!

ALL. The swine!

CYRANO, *smiling.* Our noble charmer
annoys you?

1ST OFFICER. Pimp!

ANOTHER. He decorates his armour
with a great collar of lace!—the mumping siren!

ANOTHER. Who but a dolt would wear rosepoint on iron?

THE FIRST. It's well enough to cover a carbuncle!

SECOND. A courtier!

ANOTHER. The nephew of his uncle!

C. DE C.-J. But still a Gascon!

THE FIRST. Not a Gascon Lad!
No! to be a Gascon means you must be mad!
Nothing is worse than Gascony grown civil!

LE BRET. He's pale!

ANOTHER. Like any other starving devil!
But, since enamel all his harness flakes,
Phoebus-Apollo gilds his stomach-aches!

CYRANO, *quickly.*
Don't seem downhearted! Play a cheerful part!
Your pipes and dice

Games are spread out on the drums, stools, the ground and on their cloaks. They light their pipes.
and I will read Descartes.
He walks up and down and reads a booklet that he takes from his pocket. Tableau. Enter DE GUICHE. *Everybody interested and gay. He is very pale and goes up to* CARBON.

DE GUICHE. Good morning.
They look at each other with satisfaction. Is he sallow!
C. DE C.-J. Naught but eye!
DE GUICHE, *addressing the company.*
Salute! the rebels! They tell me you despise
De Guiche! It seems I am a laughing-stock
for every little dunghill mountain-cock,
Squireens of Bearn, Countlets of Perigord,
who make a washpot of their feudal lord,
call him intriguer, say that it disgraces
a soldier to bedizen mail with laces,
and think the fellow bound to be a scamp,
who, though a Gascon, does not look a tramp.
Silence. They smoke and play cards and dice.
How, Captain, will you curb my rebel minions?
C. DE C.-J. I'm free, my lord, and they are free companions!
DE GUICHE. Dear me!
C. DE C.-J. They're mine. I pay them. You can't trap me.
I only take strategic orders!
DE GUICHE. Slap me!
Enough! I am indifferent to your prattle
who give me answer in the field of battle!
It was Bapaume saw yesterday the valiance
with which, triumphant through Bucquoi's battalions,
I thundered like an avalanche to smash
thrice through their scattered ranks.
CYRANO. And your white sash?
DE GUICHE, *surprised and pleased.*
Ah, you heard that? Well! I was galloping
along the front to range my men, and fling
them in for the third time, when I was swirled
by a mob in panic-flight, and almost hurled

upon the Spanish lines. Capture and death
threatened. I took my cue, and, in a breath,
tore off the sash I wore, and let it fall,
and by that trick saved France her general.
I turned my horse, and from the danger-zone
of Spanish territory reached our own.
Whence I led forth my troops to nail their quarry!
The story likes you not?
The OFFICERS *pretend not to listen, but dice and cards are in fact suspended and they wait eagerly.*
    CYRANO. Our Gascon Harry
against a world in arms in peace or war
had never dipped the ensign of Navarre!
Silent manifestations of joy. The cards and dice fall. Pipes go out.
    DE GUICHE. The ruse succeeded.
The same anxious tension.
    CYRANO. Who would valour's star get
would think it honour to be made a target.
Extreme pleasure in the listening group.
We differ so upon the point of honour
that I'd have snatched and worn it like a banner,
and shown the enemy my battle-flag.
    DE GUICHE. Brag on, my Gascon fire-eater!
    CYRANO. Brag!
Lend it! This very night I'll wear the sash,
storming their battle-lines, as my panache!
    DE GUICHE. A very Gascon offer! Of course you know
it fell beside the Scarpe, a place the foe
with drum-fire makes as hot as Hell could make it.
No one could take it and live.
    CYRANO, *taking the sash from his pocket and handing it over.* Well, you can take it!
Silence. The OFFICERS *smother their laughter.* DE GUICHE *turns; they become serious at once, though one of them whistles the mountain-air played by the fife.*
    DE GUICHE, *taking the sash.*
Thank you. As you suggested I'll make this rag
perform the office of a signal-flag!

He mounts the trench and waves the flag repeatedly.

ALL. Hallo!

SENTINEL, *from above.* A man in flight on the horizon!

DE GUICHE. The man's a Spanish traitor—one who spies on
our army and who carries back the lies
which I invent to throw dust in their eyes,
and thus distort the plans our foes are laying.

CYRANO. A renegade!

DE GUICHE, *carelessly knotting his scarf.*
But useful. We were saying?
O yes! I meant to tell you. To replenish
our stores and finally defeat the Spanish,
the Marshal moved last night to Dourlens for
the Depot of the Army Service Corps.
He'll make the town, but to secure his flanks
he took so large a number of all ranks
that, if the enemy attacked, they'd find
that only half our force is left behind.

C. DE C.-J. That would be serious if the Spaniards knew.
But they don't know, of course?

DE GUICHE. Captain, they do!
they will attack!

C. DE C.-J. Ah!

DE GUICHE. 'Twas the traitor spy
who told me what they meditate and why.
He added: "Choose the spot along your line
that would best suit you. For the choice is mine!
I'll say it's weakest held, worst fortified.
The issue rests with you," and I replied,
"Good! Leave the camp at once and watch our front!
I'll signal at the point to bear the brunt."

C. DE C.-J., *to his men.* Gentlemen, action!

All leap to their feet and get ready.

DE GUICHE. In an hour.

1ST OFFICER. I'd worry!

All sit and resume their games.

DE GUICHE, *to* CARBON.
Until the Marshal comes, time mustn't hurry!

C. DE C.-J. And how arrest its march?

DE GUICHE. You, who despise all,
will be so good as to be killed.

CYRANO. Reprisal?

DE GUICHE. I'll not pretend that it was dear affection
that led me, Cyrano, to your selection,
but I'd not served, since you're the top of valour,
my King, had I not also served my choler.

CYRANO, *saluting*. We thank you for your courtesy, my lord.

DE GUICHE. You like, I know, a hundred for your sword.
Well! You shall have your chance.
Walks with CARBON.

CYRANO, *to the company*. Friends, to the rays on
the field of glory that is the Gascon blazon,
six chevrons, gold and azure, we will add—
a seventh gules—the blood of Galahad.

Upstage DE GUICHE *speaks to* CARBON DE CASTEL-JALOUX. *Orders are given. The company prepares for action.* CYRANO *goes across to* CHRISTIAN, *who is motionless with crossed arms.*

CYRANO, *with a hand on his shoulder*.
Christian, my friend!

CHRISTIAN, *shakes his head*. Roxane!

CYRANO. Alas!

CHRISTIAN. I must
utter my heart's last passion, ere 'tis dust!

CYRANO. Doom's for to-day. I knew: it was not guess!
Takes a letter from his doublet.
Here's your farewell.

CHRISTIAN. Show it.

CYRANO. You mean it?

CHRISTIAN. Yes!
Odd!

CYRANO. What is odd?

CHRISTIAN. Why, this!

CYRANO, *looking at the letter*. A smudge!

CHRISTIAN. A tear!

CYRANO. His fancied sorrow to the poet's so dear

that, when he writes farewell, to be in keeping,
he wakes from work to find that he is weeping.
  CHRISTIAN. Weeping?
  CYRANO. Death's nothing; but the long farewell
to love is double death, and death in Hell.
For I shall never—
CHRISTIAN *looks at him*—we—*Quickly*—you—
  CHRISTIAN. Have a care!
Give me the letter, man.
Noise without in the camp.
  SENTRY'S VOICE. Halt! Who goes there?
Sound of firing.
  C. DE C.-J. What is't?
  SENTRY, *on the parapet*. A carriage. *Runs to see.*
  CRIES. Crossing no-man's land
from the Spanish lines. Fire! No! hold your hand.
The coachman shouts while he is galloping.
What? "On the King's service."
Everybody cranes forward from the parapet.
  DE GUICHE. The service of the King.
They climb down and get into line.
  C. DE C.-J. Hats off.
  DE GUICHE. Fall in, vile scum, and let the coach
with such distinction, as befits the King, approach.
*The carriage drives in at a gallop. It is covered with mud and dust.
The blinds are drawn. Two* LACKEYS *ride behind. It draws up short.*
  C. DE C.-J., *shouting*. Present arms!
  DE GUICHE. Drop the bridge!
Two men rush forward. It is lowered.
  ROXANE, *opening coach door*. Is't to your liking?
The sound of a woman's voice brings the whole company to attention. General astonishment.
  DE GUICHE. In the King's service—you!
  ROXANE. Yes—Love, the High King!
  CYRANO. Great God!
  CHRISTIAN. You! Why?
  ROXANE. Your siege is a disgrace.

CHRISTIAN. Why?

ROXANE. I'll explain.

CYRANO, *who, at the sound of her voice, is struck to stone.*
I dare not see her face!

DE GUICHE. You cannot stay.

ROXANE, *gaily.* Will someone in the ranks
lend me a drum?
She sits on the drum. My most distinguished thanks!
She laughs.
They fired on my coach! Some Dick or Tomkin!
—It has the air of Cinderella's pumpkin
in the fairy-tale, with the footmen, you would say,
two rats.
Blowing a kiss to CHRISTIAN. Good morning, love—
Looking round. You don't look gay!
Arras lies far?
Observing CYRANO. Cousin, your greetings charm me!

CYRANO, *drawing near.* But how?

ROXANE. But how did I rejoin . . . the Army?
Nothing more simple. The only thing to do in
the case is follow in the tracks of ruin.
The sights I witnessed were so harrowing,
that if this be service of your King,
you'd better change for mine!

CYRANO. Madness, I swear.
How did you pass the lines, I ask, and——

ROXANE. Where? Across the Spaniards'.

AN OFFICER. Women take the biscuit!

DE GUICHE. The Spanish lines! How did you dare to
risk it?

LE BRET. Surely 'twas difficult.

ROXANE. Sir! it was not!
I simply drove straight forward at the trot!
When some Hidalgo showed his haughty brow,
I smiled upon him—as I'm smiling now.
And, as, save the French, they are the last
word in most gallant courtesy, I passed.

C. DE C.-J. Your smile's a passport, but it was their duty

to ask its mission even of such beauty.
Were you not often asked?

ROXANE. Over and over,
and I replied, "I go to seek my lover."
Whereat the fiercest Spaniard closed the door,
and, with the gesture of an emperor,
ordered his men with muskets at their shoulder,
to let me be. There could be nothing bolder,
and naught more tinged with melancholy graces,
than with his feather streaming out of laces,
his beaver held so that the plume might meet a
gay breath of air, he cried, "Pass, Senorita."

CHRISTIAN. Roxane——

ROXANE. I said, "my lover." Love, forgive me!
Had I said "husband," nobody, believe me,
had let me through.

CHRISTIAN. But——

ROXANE. Well?

DE GUICHE. You must go hence,
Madam, I fear.

ROXANE. I——

CYRANO. Speedily.

DE GUICHE. At once!

CHRISTIAN. Yes.

ROXANE. Tell me why!

CYRANO, *embarrassed*. Because

CHRISTIAN, *embarrassed*. —they will

DE GUICHE, *embarrassed*. or may—

C. DE C.-J., *embarrassed*. 'Twere well!

LE BRET, *embarrassed*. You could!

ROXANE. A battle! I shall stay.

ALL. No! No!

ROXANE, *throwing herself into* CHRISTIAN'S *arms*.
My husband—if you die, I die.

CHRISTIAN. How very strange you look!

ROXANE. I'll tell you why!

DE GUICHE, *in despair*. It is a danger post!

ROXANE, *to* DE GUICHE. Danger!

110   CYRANO DE BERGERAC   [ACT IV

CYRANO. Death's shadow!
De Guiche 'twas chose it.
   ROXANE, *to* DE GUICHE. To make Roxane a widow!
   DE GUICHE. I swear!
   ROXANE. No! I'll not go. I think I'm losing
my wits, and, anyhow, the thing's amusing.
   CYRANO. Would our blue-stocking play the heroine?
   ROXANE. Monsieur de Bergerac, I am your kin!
   AN OFFICER. We will protect you!
   ROXANE, *with mounting excitement.* I can swear to that!
   ANOTHER, *drunk with emotion.*
The camp is sweet with perfume.
   ROXANE. And my hat,
luckily, is the kind one wears for battles!
And if the Count, whom the situation rattles,
would leave us, we might start.
   DE GUICHE. A taunt I spurn.
I'm for the guns! There's time, ere I return
To change your mind.
   ROXANE. I—never.
Exit DE GUICHE.
   CHRISTIAN, *begging.* O, Roxane.
   ROXANE. No.
   1ST OFFICER, *to others.* She will stay!
   ALL, *rushing about.* A comb! Soap! Needle, man,
look at my coat! A bootlace! Looking-glass!
Cuffs! Got a razor? Curling-tongs, you ass!
   ROXANE, *to* CHRISTIAN, *who pleads with her.*
No! I'll not budge!
   C. DE C.-J., *after having tidied himself up like the rest,
approaches* ROXANE *with ceremony.*
Madam, if you permit
I will present these gentlemen. 'Tis fit
that you should meet your gladiators now,
qui morituri te salutant.
   ROXANE *curtsies and waits on* CHRISTIAN'S *arm.* CARBON *makes the
introductions.* Bow,
Baron de Colignac.

OFFICER, *saluting.* Your servant, Ma'am!

C. DE C.-J. Baron Casterac de Cahuzac. Vidame
De Malgouyre Estressac d'Escarabiot—,
Chevalier d'Antignoac-Juzet. Hillot
Baron de Blagnac Castel Crabioules.

ROXANE. You have long names?

BARON HILLOT. Like fishes, in a school!

C. DE C.-J., *to* ROXANE. Give me the handkerchief you hold!

ROXANE. But why?

C. DE C.-J. We have no ensign under which to die.
Now what you lend will give us pride of place.

ROXANE, *smiling.* It is a trifle small.

C. DE C.-J., *fixing it to his lance.* Little, but lace!

1ST OFFICER. She'd light death with the dawn-star, had I but
as much in all my stomach as a nut.

C. DE C.-J. Shame! To complain of food when loveliness——

ROXANE. But beauty's starving too, she must confess!
Pâté, chaud froids, good wine—my bill of fare!
Set that before me, pray!

AN OFFICER. All that!

ANOTHER. But where
In God's name, shall we find it?

ROXANE, *tranquilly.* In my coach.

ALL. What!

ROXANE. There's the carving, and the wine to broach.
Look at my coachman, sirs, with more attention,
and tell me if for sauces of invention
the world can show his equal!

OFFICERS, *rushing to the coach.* Holy Mary!
Ragueneau, is it you?

ROXANE, *watching them.* Poor boys!

CYRANO, *kissing her hand.* Good fairy!

RAGUENEAU, *standing up like a huckster.* Gentlemen!
Cheers.

OFFICERS. Good.

RAGUENEAU. The many charms that guard her
diverted those good Spaniards from the larder!
Applause.

CYRANO, *low to* **CHRISTIAN**. Christian.

RAGUENEAU, *holding up a dish*.
And as for galantine, they're too
gallant in love to see!
Applause. The dish is passed round.

CYRANO, *to* **CHRISTIAN**. A word with you!

RAGUENEAU. Venus misled them so that Artemis
displayed her calf unnoticed—
Flourishes a shoulder of veal—and here it is!
More cheers. The veal passes round.

CYRANO, *to* **CHRISTIAN**. Listen, my friend.

RAGUENEAU, *to* **OFFICERS** *returning loaded with food*.
Put it all down. *He sets the table on the grass, aided by the two imperturbable* **FOOTMEN**.
To **CHRISTIAN**. My lad
make yourself useful! A truffled peacock.

1ST OFFICER, *in ecstasy with a huge piece of ham*. Gad!
We shall not plunge into death's final hazard
unstuffed
Recovering himself as he sees **ROXANE**.
or rather, madam, unbalthazared.

RAGUENEAU, *throwing out the cushions*.
The cushions are stuffed with ortolans.

3RD OFFICER. The pope has——

RAGUENEAU, *throwing out bottles of red wine*.
no bottle as ruby—
white wine—or as purely topaz.

ROXANE, *throwing a folded napkin in* **CYRANO**'s *face*.
Unfold
that napkin—and jump to it.

RAGUENEAU, *flourishing a lamp*. 'Tis harder
to find than carriage-lamps a snugger larder!

CYRANO, *to* **CHRISTIAN**, *while they arrange the cloth*.
Before you speak to her, I have a message!

RAGUENEAU, *with mounting ecstasy*.
And my whip-handle's a Provençal sausage!

ROXANE. Since they have doomed us, let the ranks of Tuscany

ACT IV] CYRANO DE BERGERAC 113

starve and be damned! Roxane provisions Gascony!
And if De Guiche appears, no bite, no sup!
Going the rounds.
Slow! Plenty time!—No need to wolf it up!
Wine? You are weeping?

1ST OFFICER. Food goes to my head!

ROXANE. Tut! Red or white? What is it, Captain—bread?
A knife?—your plate!—a second helping?—Tart!
I'm coming—Wine?—a wing?

CYRANO, *following her, his arms laden.* Heart of my heart!

ROXANE, *to* CHRISTIAN. You?

CHRISTIAN. Nothing!

ROXANE. This biscuit dipped in muscat—taste it!

CHRISTIAN, *holding her back.* Why did you come?

ROXANE. Their hour—I must not waste it—
poor lads! I'll tell you later, sweet.

LE BRET, *who has gone to give the sentry on the parapet bread on the point of his lance.* De Guiche!

CYRANO. Flasks, dishes, pastries, hide them, I beseech!
Nothing has happened. Is it understood?

TO RAGUENEAU. Up with you! Is all hidden?

In a twinkling all the food is concealed. DE GUICHE *enters with rapid strides, and stops suddenly, sniffing the air. Silence.*

DE GUICHE. This smells good.

OFFICER, *humming, with an off-hand air.*
With a tol, lol, lay!

DE GUICHE, *stopping.* Why is your face so red?

OFFICER. My blood in battle rushes to my head!

ANOTHER. Tiddley-pom-pom!

DE GUICHE, *turning.* What's that?

ANOTHER. A song we had
that I was humming!

DE GUICHE. You're a cheerful lad!

OFFICER. 'Tis danger cheers me.

DE GUICHE, *calling the* CAPTAIN *to give his orders.*
Captain. *Stops on seeing him.* You've a grin on
like all the others.

C. DE C.-J., *red, hiding a bottle behind his back*. O!
DE GUICHE. I've brought one cannon—
pointing off—
and placed it in position there—d'you see?—
for use, if needed, by your company!
1ST OFFICER, *bowing*. A charming thought!
2ND OFFICER, *smiling graciously*. My lord, you are too kind!
DE GUICHE. They're mad as hatters!
Coldly. And look out behind
for its back action!
1ST OFFICER. Rot!
DE GUICHE. Sir!
1ST OFFICER. In attack,
the guns, worked by the Gascons, never back!
DE GUICHE, *taking him by the arm and shaking him*.
You're drunk, I ask myself on what!
OFFICER, *proudly*. On powder!
DE GUICHE, *shrugging his shoulders, crossing to* ROXANE.
Madame, have you decided? Death's voice calls louder!
ROXANE. I'm staying!
DE GUICHE. Fly!
ROXANE. Never!
DE GUICHE. Will one of you
lend me a musket?
C. DE C.-J. Why?
DE GUICHE. I'm staying too!
CYRANO. O, bravely said! Here's courage and here's grace!
OFFICER. Is there a Gascon under all that lace?
ROXANE. What?
DE GUICHE. I'll not leave a woman where there's danger!
2ND OFFICER, *to* 1ST.
Here! Give him something to appease his hunger!
All the food reappears as by enchantment.
DE GUICHE, *his eyes sparkling*. Victuals!
A THIRD. From every doublet a larder comes!
DE GUICHE, *mastering himself, haughtily*.
D'you think that I will batten on your crumbs?
CYRANO, *saluting*. Sir, you progress!

DE GUICHE, *proudly, with a faint Gascon accent.*
I'll fight still r-ravenous!
    1ST OFFICER, *cheering.* That "r's" pure Gascon.
    DE GUICHE, *laughing.* Well!
    OFFICER. He's one of us!
They break into a dance.
    C. DE C.-J., *who has disappeared behind the parapet, shows himself on the top.* The pikes are posted.
They'll only let death through them!
    DE GUICHE, *to* ROXANE, *bowing.*
Accept my escort, madam, while I review them.
She takes his hand. They walk to the parapet.
Everybody follows uncovered.
    CYRANO, *to* CHRISTIAN, *eagerly.* Quick!
As ROXANE *mounts the parapet the lances are sloped in salute. Shouting. She curtsies.*
    PIKEMEN, *off.* Hail! Roxane!
    CHRISTIAN. What is it?
    CYRANO. If she mentions
    CHRISTIAN. Yes, if she mentions
    CYRANO. letters!
    CHRISTIAN. Your inventions!
    CYRANO. Don't be surprised——
    CHRISTIAN. by what?——
    CYRANO. by reference—
'Tis naught—
    CHRISTIAN. Nay, tell me——
    CYRANO. Merely common sense.
Perfectly simple. Only I was bitten
by the thought to-day.
    CHRISTIAN. What thought?
    CYRANO. That you have written
more often than you knew!
    CHRISTIAN. More often?
    CYRANO. Yes,
I took it on myself, I must confess
to write without your knowledge!

CHRISTIAN. Man alive!
The Siege!

CYRANO. Quite simple!

CHRISTIAN. How did you contrive
to run the gauntlet?

CYRANO. Nobody was stirring
before dawn broke.

CHRISTIAN. How oft was it occurring—
this simple act—each week? What would you say?
Twice? Thrice?

CYRANO. No! More!

CHRISTIAN. More!

CYRANO. You wrote twice a day!

CHRISTIAN, *violently*.
And for vicarious love you could and can
outface insistent death!

CYRANO, *seeing* ROXANE *return*. Silence! Roxane.
He goes back quickly to his tent. In the background OFFICERS, CARBON
and DE GUICHE *are giving orders*.

ROXANE, *running to* CHRISTIAN. And now, my Christian!

CHRISTIAN, *taking her hands*. Now tell me why you came
by roads whose thousand terrors mock the name,
facing the brutal soldiery and the Ritters
to join me?

ROXANE. Dearest, you must blame your letters.

CHRISTIAN. What!

ROXANE. If I risk danger, all the fault is theirs;
they sweetly drugged me with divine despairs.
Think how you wrote, how many, how they grew
from beauty into beauty.

CHRISTIAN. For a few
brief letters of love!

ROXANE. Be still! You cannot guess
how I have loved, with what bright tenderness,
since underneath my window a voice unknown
revealed your spirit to its true stature grown.
For all this bitter month (my love, rejoice!)

far in your letters, but sweet, I heard that voice,
which since that evening clothes you like a cloak.
I heard. I came. Penelope, who broke
the web, had thrown the bobbins after it
if her Ulysses with your pen had writ,
and, wild as Helen, had the sails unfurled
to seek her absent lover through the world!

CHRISTIAN. But——

ROXANE. They were read, re-read, till love with grief
became a single chord of passion. Leaf
after leaf like petals from a flower,
whose heart is flame, bore witness to the power
and truth of love.

CHRISTIAN. Power and truth—they went together

ROXANE. Like that flower, and its scent.

CHRISTIAN. Therefore you came!

ROXANE. Therefore, my love, my lord,
I came. Your grace, I think, would not accord
my knees the right to stoop. Therefore, my sweet,
I lay my heart for ever at your feet.
And, love, forgive me ('tis the time and place
for pardon when death stares us in the face)
that I insulted love, when love began,
by loving the appearance, not the man.

CHRISTIAN. Roxane!

ROXANE. But later, as I grew more wise,
a bird that tests her wings before she flies,
charmed by your beauty, your spirit taught me how
to love the two together, sweet.

CHRISTIAN. And now?

ROXANE. Christian has triumphed over Christian.
I love the soul alone—which is the man.

CHRISTIAN. Roxane!

ROXANE. Be happy! When my heart confessed your
sway only in your beauty's fleeting vesture,
your nobler soul might meditate disgrace,

but when its greater beauty masked your face,
the lesser beauty, which held my heart in thrall,
seeing beyond it, I do not see at all.

CHRISTIAN. O——

ROXANE. Doubtful, victor, though my heart has said it,
of victory?

CHRISTIAN. Roxane!

ROXANE. You will not credit
such love!

CHRISTIAN. I do not wish such love. 'Tis more
and less that I would have you love me——

ROXANE. For
the beauty that did other women move?
This is, dear love, a better way of love!

CHRISTIAN. No!

ROXANE. Ah! my love, you vex your heart unduly!
How greater far my love now I love truly!
The real you, believe it, I adore,
and with less beauty—

CHRISTIAN. Hush!

ROXANE. I'd love still more!
Yes, if your beauty vanished, grain by grain!

CHRISTIAN. Hush!

ROXANE. It is true!

CHRISTIAN. If I were bitter plain?

ROXANE. I swear it.

CHRISTIAN. God!

ROXANE. Be glad and glory in it.

CHRISTIAN. Yes.

ROXANE. What?

CHRISTIAN, *gently putting her away*.
My love, have I your leave a minute?——

ROXANE. But——

CHRISTIAN, *pointing to a group of* OFFICERS.
Love has cheated those poor lads. I owe
their death the bounty of your smile. Sweet, go!

ROXANE, *melted*. Dear Christian!

She goes towards the GASCONS, *who crowd round her respectfully.*

CHRISTIAN, *outside* CYRANO's *tent*. Cyrano!
CYRANO, *appearing armed*. How strange you start!
CHRISTIAN. She does not love me!
CYRANO. What!
CHRISTIAN. You have her heart!
CYRANO. Nonsense!
CHRISTIAN. She only loves my soul!
CYRANO. No!
CHRISTIAN. Yes!
'Tis you she loves—and you who love no less!
CYRANO. I!
CHRISTIAN. Yes!
CYRANO. 'Tis true!
CHRISTIAN. And madly!
CYRANO. Desperately!
CHRISTIAN. Then tell her!
CYRANO. No!
CHRISTIAN. Why not?
CYRANO. Friend, look at me!
CHRISTIAN. She'd love me were I plain!
CYRANO. She said that!
CHRISTIAN. Aye!
CYRANO. Only an angel could so sweetly lie!
Go—and forget that dear insensate fib,
sweetest since Eve had commerce with a rib—
Be comely always as you were at first,
lest she be disillusioned and I accurst!
CHRISTIAN. We'll test it!
CYRANO. No!
CHRISTIAN. Yes, she shall judge between us!
You'll speak!
CYRANO. And suffer the thunderbolt of Venus!
CHRISTIAN. Because I'm comely must you fry in Hell?
I'll not abide it!
CYRANO. And you be miserable
because by accident my tongue is stealing
the lovelier rhapsodies that you are feeling!
CHRISTIAN. Tell all!

CYRANO. He tempts me! 'Tis intempestival!
CHRISTIAN. I'll brook myself no longer as a rival!
CYRANO. Christian!
CHRISTIAN. Our marriage—there is none to suborn.
It could be ended—if I live.
CYRANO. He's stubborn!
CHRISTIAN. I will be loved for myself—or not at all!
I'll leave you for the trenches. When you call
I'll know that she has chosen!
CYRANO. 'Twill be you!
CHRISTIAN. I do not know. God send it may be true.
He calls. Roxane! Belovéd!
ROXANE, *running up.* Yes?
CHRISTIAN. 'Tis Cyrano
wishes to speak.
She hastens to CYRANO. *Exit* CHRISTIAN.
ROXANE. To speak?
CYRANO, *in agony.* O, do not go!
To ROXANE.
He lends—you know—the sweet bewildered baby—
significance to naught!
ROXANE. He doubted maybe,
that what I said was spoken in good sooth!
CYRANO, *taking her hand.*
He doubted—that you uttered only truth?
ROXANE. Yes, yes, I'd love him even—
She hesitates.
CYRANO. Do not shun
the word!
ROXANE. But——
CYRANO. It is a familiar one!
You'd love him ugly!
ROXANE. Yes. Did the guns speak?
CYRANO, *with passion.* Hideous?
ROXANE. Yes!
CYRANO. Yes?
ROXANE. If he were nature's freak!
CYRANO. Grotesque?

ACT IV] CYRANO DE BERGERAC 121

ROXANE. He could not be grotesque to me!
CYRANO. The more he shocked——
ROXANE. The more belovéd he!
CYRANO, *aside, in wild exultation.*
Fate, can it be that you avert your rod?
To ROXANE. Roxane!
LE BRET, *coming in quickly, in a low voice.* Hey, Cyrano!
CYRANO, *turning.* Well?
LE BRET. Silence! *He whispers.*
CYRANO, *letting* ROXANE'S *hand fall with a groan.* God!
ROXANE. What ails you?
CYRANO, *aside.* 'Tis the end!
ROXANE, *going to look out.* The end—but how?
CYRANO. 'Tis ended! I can never tell her now.
ROXANE, *trying to leave.* What is it?
CYRANO, *holding her back.* Naught.

OFFICERS *enter carrying a hidden object. They group themselves so as to prevent* ROXANE'S *approach.*

ROXANE. What are these soldiers hiding?
CYRANO. Nothing!
ROXANE. What was it, then, you were confiding?
CYRANO. Confiding, I? Naught, Madam, naught. I swear it.
I swear the soul of Christian and his spirit
were——
Recovering himself with terror—are the noblest.
ROXANE, *with a great cry.* Were—oh!
She rushes through the crowd.
CYRANO. It is over!
ROXANE, *seeing* CHRISTIAN *wrapped in his cloak.* Christian!
LE BRET, *to* CYRANO. 'Twas the first volley killed her lover!
C. DE C.-J., *sword in hand.* They're here! Our muskets!
ROXANE. Christian!
C. DE C.-J. And despatch!
ROXANE. Christian!
C. DE C.-J. Form ranks!
ROXANE. Christian!
C. DE C.-J. Cut your match!

RAGUENEAU *has rushed up with water in a helmet.*

CHRISTIAN, *in a dying voice*. Roxane!

CYRANO, *quiet and low in* CHRISTIAN'S *ear, while* ROXANE *distractedly tears a piece of linen from her breast and dips in the water*. I told her all. You are her love.

CHRISTIAN *closes his eyes*.

ROXANE. Yes, love.

C. DE C.-J. Draw ramrods!

ROXANE, *to* CYRANO. Christ! he does not move!

C. DE C.-J. The charges out with teeth!

ROXANE. Cold, cold, already
his cheek against my cheek!

C. DE C.-J. All at the ready!

ROXANE. A letter—*opens*—and for me!

CYRANO, *aside*. My letter!

C. DE C.-J. Fire.

Firing. Shouts. Noise of battle.

CYRANO, *seeking to free his hand which* ROXANE *holds as she kneels*. Roxane, they're fighting!

ROXANE, *holding him*. Stay! The need is dire!
He's dead. You knew him. Stay! He was a man
such as in heaven the stars and nature plan
and lose the mould.

CYRANO, *standing bareheaded*. Most true!

ROXANE. The poet's guess
at beauty!

CYRANO. Yes.

ROXANE. A paragon.

CYRANO. Yes, yes, Roxane.

ROXANE. A heart beyond the limit that we can
reach to in dreams, and miss.

CYRANO, *firmly*. Yes, yes, Roxane.

ROXANE, *throwing herself on the body*. He's dead.

CYRANO. And in your turn, die, Cyrano!
whom in his death she mourns, and does not know!
Trumpets off.

DE GUICHE, *on the parapet, wounded and dishevelled, in a voice of thunder.*
It is the signal. The trumpets sound relief.

ACT IV]   CYRANO DE BERGERAC   123

The Marshal has returned. Friends, for a brief
moment hold on!

ROXANE. Look, where the blood did flow
and dyed the tears!

A VOICE, *off*. Surrender, Frenchmen!

VOICES OF OFFICERS. No!

RAGUENEAU, *who has jumped on the box, looking at the attack*.
Danger!

CYRANO, *to* DE GUICHE, *pointing to* ROXANE. I go! Save her!

ROXANE, *kissing the letter, faintly*. His blood, his tears.

RAGUENEAU, *leaping from the box and running to her*.
She's fainted!

DE GUICHE, *on the parapet, to the* OFFICER. Hold!

A VOICE. Surrender, musketeers!

OFFICERS. No!

CYRANO, *to* DE GUICHE.

You have proved your valour, sir! Away
and save her.

DE GUICHE, *running to* ROXANE, *and taking her in his arms*.
As you will. We've won the day
if you can hold them!

CYRANO. Good!

Calling to ROXANE, *whom* DE GUICHE, *helped by* RAGUENEAU, *carries off in a faint.* Farewell, Roxane!

Uproar, shouts, OFFICERS *reappear wounded and fall.* CYRANO, *rushing into battle, is stopped by* CARBON DE CASTEL-JALOUX, *covered with blood.*

C. DE C.-J. We break! I'm struck—I have done all I can.

CYRANO, *to the* GASCONS. On Gascons! Charge again!

To CARBON, *whom he holds in his arms*.

Captain, 'tis well!
I'll avenge Christian and my lost love in Hell!

They come down, CYRANO *brandishing the lance to which* ROXANE'S *handkerchief is tied.*

Fly, ensign of my love and of her life!

He plants it in the ground and cries to the company.

Fall on them! Smash them!

To the piper. Piper, play your fife!

The fife plays. The wounded rise. OFFICERS, *rushing down the parapet, group themselves round* CYRANO *and the little flag. The carriage is filled with men outside and in, and stiff with muskets, becomes a fortress.*

AN OFFICER, *appearing on the parapet, beaten back but fighting.*
They're on the parapet! *He falls dead.*
CYRANO. We'll bid them welcome!
The parapet is black with an enemy wave. The great imperial standards fill the air.
CYRANO. Fire!
VOICE, *in the enemy ranks.* Fire!
A deadly riposte. OFFICERS *fall on all sides.*
A SPANISH OFFICER, *uncovering.*
Who are these who bid their Hell come?
CYRANO, *reciting in the hail of shots.*
These are the Gascon Grenadiers,
Like soldiers into battle hurled.
He rushes in, followed by the survivors.
These, Spaniards, are the Grenadiers!
The rest is lost in battle.

Act V

CYRANO'S GAZETTE

Fifteen years after, in 1655. The Park at Paris of the Convent of the Sisters of the Cross.

Magnificent trees. The house is on the left. There are broad steps upon which other doors open. An immense tree in the middle of the stage which stands alone in a small oval space. Right, in the foreground, a semi-circular stone bench between tall bushes.

The whole background is traversed by an avenue of chestnut trees, leading to the door of the chapel, seen between the branches. Through the curtain of these trees lawns, avenues, clumps of trees, the further distances of the park and the sky are visible.

The chapel gives by a little side door on to a colonnade wreathed with reddening vine-leaves, and is lost to view behind boxwood on the right.

ACT V] CYRANO DE BERGERAC 125

It is autumn. All the foliage is changing over the green lawns. The box and the yew remain darkly green. There is a heap of yellow leaves under every tree. The leaves crackle underfoot and half cover the steps and the benches. Between the bench, right, and the door there is a large embroidery frame with a small chair in front of it. There are baskets full of skeins and balls of wool. The embroidery has been begun. When the curtain rises, Sisters are passing up and down in the park. A few of them are seated on the bench around an older Sister. Leaves are falling.

MOTHER MARGUERITE, SISTER MARTHE, SISTER CLAIRE, SISTERS.

S. MARTHE, *to* M. MARGUERITE.
Sister Claire looked again, and then again
at her wimple in the mirror.

M. MARGUERITE, *to* S. CLAIRE. 'Tis very plain.

S. CLAIRE. Well! Sister Marthe pilfered a second plum
out of the tart. I saw her.

M. MARGUERITE, *to* S. MARTHE. O, Marthe, come!

S. CLAIRE. Such a small look.

S. MARTHE. —And a plum even less.

M. MARGUERITE. Cyrano to-night shall hear your naughtiness.

S. CLAIRE, *shocked*. O no! He'll laugh.

S. MARTHE. The wearers of the hood
are flirts, he'll say—

S. CLAIRE. greedy—

M. MARGUERITE, *smiling*. but very good.

S. CLAIRE. Dear Mother in Jesus, 'tis ten years since he swore
to come here every Saturday.

M. MARGUERITE. 'Tis more!
Fourteen full years have passed since his fair cousin
mixed with our humble caps what veils bedizen
with lace great ladies' sorrow, and sang to rest—
an eagle homing in a pigeon's nest.

S. MARTHE. And only he has given her relief
housed in the cloisters, but alone with grief.

ALL THE SISTERS. He's such a wit.
The whole world laughs before him.

He teases.—He is charming.
—We adore him.
Therefore we bake him all our lightest pastries.

M. MARGUERITE.

He knows the cook-shop better than the vestries.

S. CLAIRE. We'll strive with him——

SISTERS. Yes! yes!

M. MARGUERITE. Children beware!
His soul, believe me, is not your affair!
He may not come so often! Leave him alone.

S. MARTHE. But God

M. MARGUERITE. —my children, God retrieves His own.

S. MARTHE. But every time on entering he'll say,
cheerfully, "Sister, I ate meat* yesterday."

M. MARGUERITE.
He tells you that? Well! last time, or some other,
two days had passed since he had eaten.

S. MARTHE. Mother!

M. MARGUERITE. He's poor.

S. MARTHE. Who told you?

M. MARGUERITE. Monsieur Le Bret.

S. MARTHE. Can no one help?

M. MARGUERITE. He drives all help away.
But let's go in. For with an escort mark!
where Madame Madeleine walks in the park.

ROXANE, *dressed in black in deep mourning, appears at the end of an alley.* DE GUICHE, *now the* DUKE DE GRAMMONT, *a magnificent old man, walks with her. They stroll gently.* MOTHER MARGUERITE *rises.*

S. MARTHE. It is De Grammont, the Duke-Marshal.

S. CLAIRE. Yes.

S. MARTHE. Months since he came to visit her.

SISTERS. The press
of business—the court—the camp.

S. CLAIRE. The world.

---

* The Wolfe version actually reads *fasted*, but the French *"j'ai fait gras"* means the opposite. The real Cyrano de Bergerac (1619–55) was a freethinker. In the last years of his life, his cousin Roxane joined others in a vain effort to convert him.

Exeunt. DE GUICHE *and* ROXANE *walk down in silence and stop by her embroidery. A pause.*

DUKE. And here, for ever, a loveliness unfurled
you mourn.

ROXANE. For ever.

DUKE. Faithful?

ROXANE. Until death.

DUKE, *after a pause.* Am I forgiven?

ROXANE, *simply looking at the Cross on the Convent.*
Pardon belongs to faith.

A silence.

DUKE. He was a man?

ROXANE. To know him was to kneel.

DUKE. Alas! I only know him in what you feel!
And his last words upon your heart you carry?

ROXANE. Hung here for ever, love's dear scapulary.

DUKE. He's dead, and yet you love him!

ROXANE. Almost he seems
'twixt death and life, the lover of my dreams,
whose love has power death itself to soften.

DUKE. And Cyrano still visits you?

ROXANE. Yes, often.
Friend of my youth, he comes, my gazetteer,
punctual to the hour. His chair is here
under that tree. The weather smiles. I bend
over my needle. Upon the stroke my friend
(I need not lift my head to hear his cane)
taps down the terrace, and settles to complain
against my everlasting needle's play.
Then to his weekly news.

LE BRET *appears on the terrace.*
Welcome, Le Bret.
How fares our friend?

LE BRET. But ill!

DUKE. What?

ROXANE, *to the* DUKE. Overstatement!

LE BRET. Grief and despair—I told you what his fate meant.
Always he makes new foes with letters that prod

nobles ignoble, hypocrites of God,
swashbuckler, plagiarist and all their horde!

ROXANE. They cringe before the terror of his sword.
He will outface them to the end.

DUKE, *nodding*. Who knows?

LE BRET. He has more perilous enemies than those—
loneliness dogs him, hunger, and December
with tired feet that pace a stricken chamber.
These and the bravoes will have him body and soul.
Each day his belt is tightened by a hole,
his nose is thin as ivory, and as yellow,
with one drab coat of serge to wear—poor fellow.

DUKE. Not a success maybe. Yet to the impartial
no subject for pity.

LE BRET. You are joking, Marshal.

DUKE. No subject for pity, whose life stands up and cries
"Free thought, free deeds. To hell with compromise."

LE BRET. I must protest——

DUKE, *coldly*. Enough. I understand:
but I would proudly shake him by the hand.
Farewell.

The DUKE *bows to* LE BRET *and walks with* ROXANE *towards the terrace.*

ROXANE. I'll show the way.

The DUKE, *waiting while she mounts the steps.*

DUKE. He makes me jealous.
When life goes all our way, or so they tell us,
one feels—with no great mischief to one's name—
a thousand small disgusts, a hidden shame—
hardly remorse, but maybe something worse;
For when His Grace the Duke, clad all in furs,
climbs the long steps of glory, his skirts jostle
illusions lost and vain regrets that rustle
about his steps, dry as on autumn eves,
about your widow's robes the fallen leaves.

ROXANE, *ironically*. You dream, I think, my lord.

DUKE. Perhaps.

At the moment of exit, suddenly. Le Bret!

To ROXANE. Have I your leave?

ACT V] CYRANO DE BERGERAC 129

To LE BRET. I have a word to say
privately in your ear! They dare not bait him
because of his sword, but there are many hate him.
'Twas yesterday at Court some creature bent
and lisped, "Suppose he had an accident."
  LE BRET. What!
  DUKE. Keep him at home and prudent!
  LE BRET. Prudence, Hell!
Nevertheless I'll warn him, Marshal.
ROXANE, *who has waited on the terrace, to a* SISTER *who walks towards her*. Well?
  THE SISTER. Ragueneau begs an audience.
To the DUKE *and* LE BRET.
  ROXANE. Let him spill
his evil tidings. From an author, sirs,
he has become the least of choristers.
  LE BRET. Bathkeeper
  ROXANE. Actor
  LE BRET. Beadle
  ROXANE. Barber
  LE BRET. Master
of the triple lute.
  ROXANE. But always a disaster!
  RAGUENEAU, *entering at top speed*. Ah, madam—
Seeing LE BRET. Sir, to you!
  ROXANE, *smiling*. Le Bret's all set
for horrors. I'll return.
  RAGUENEAU. But Madam!
ROXANE, *without listening, exits with* DUKE. RAGUENEAU *returns to join* LE BRET.
  RAGUENEAU. Yet!
Kinder to spare her for a moment! listen!
I go to visit your friend. I see him, hasten
to join him, but he turns the corner. Crash!
a flunkey from a window in a flash
drops a huge log—on purpose? it may be.
  LE BRET. O Cyrano! The cowards!
  RAGUENEAU. I run! I see!

LE BRET. O horrible!

RAGUENEAU. With a great wound in his head
I see our stricken friend, our poet.

LE BRET. Dead?

RAGUENEAU. No! but I bore him on these shoulders—I—
back to his room—did I say room?—a sty!

LE BRET. Is he in pain?

RAGUENEAU. Unconscious.

LE BRET. Who attends him?

RAGUENEAU. Some doctor of his kindliness befriends him.

LE BRET. My Cyrano! We'll keep the tidings back
from Roxane! But what says the leech?

RAGUENEAU. Alack!
babbles of fevers, membranes. God knows what,
and all the time he lies with that red spot
gaining upon the bandage. Come! None's by,
and if he moves, by God, he's like to die.

LE BRET *draws him away, R.*

LE BRET. This way. It's quicker. Through the Chapel. Come.

ROXANE. Monsieur Le Bret.

LE BRET *and* RAGUENEAU *rush off without answering.*
He does not answer. Some
new nonsense of that wretched Ragueneau!

ROXANE. How sweet the last days of September go!
My heart that April darkens, autumn beguiles
with her slow charm, and lo! my sorrow smiles.
She settles down to her embroidery. Two SISTERS *appear from the house and carry a large arm-chair which they place under the tree.*
Why, here's the chair sacred to Cyrano—
a classic—Sisters.

S. MARTHE. 'Tis the best we own.

ROXANE. Thank you. *Exeunt* SISTERS.
He's here. The clock begins to chime.
My skeins! But where is Cyrano? This time
will he be late and break his rule? I tremble!
But maybe the lay-Sister—where's my thimble?—
exhorts him to repent.
A further pause. 'Tis my belief

that she's about it now. Look, a dead leaf!
She shakes a dead leaf from her work with her fingers.
Besides, there's naught on earth could hold him back.
My scissors—ah!

A SISTER, *appearing on the terrace.* Monsieur de Bergerac!

ROXANE, *without looking up.* What was I saying?

She embroiders. CYRANO, *white to the teeth, with his hat crushed over his eyes, enters. He comes down the steps slowly, having to make an obvious effort to walk upright, leaning all the time on his cane.* ROXANE *is busy with her work.*
Look! how these dyes have perished.
They will not mix. For fourteen years I've cherished
your punctual step—and now to-day

CYRANO. I failed you!
It breaks my heart, but I was kept—

ROXANE. What ailed you?

CYRANO. A most untimely call.

ROXANE. Some stupid bore?

CYRANO. Yes, cousin, a most tedious visitor!

ROXANE. A woman? Well, you sent the wench away.

CYRANO. I said, "Forgive me, this is Saturday.
I have a tryst to which, did I play traitor,
all would be lost. Come back a little later."

ROXANE. Well, the good woman must wait upon your pleasure,
you shall stay here till nightfall at your leisure.

CYRANO. I may be earlier called to my own hearth.

CYRANO *closes his eyes and remains silent for an instant.* SISTER MARTHE *crosses the park from the Chapel on the way to the terrace.* ROXANE *sees her and nods.*

ROXANE, *to* CYRANO. Don't you see sister?

CYRANO, *gaily, opening his eyes.* Why, of course.
In a loud humorous voice. Dear Marthe.
Approach. *She glides towards him.*
But turn those veiléd eyes away.

S. MARTHE, *raising her eyes with a smile.* But—
She sees his face and falls back astonished. Oh.

CYRANO, *in a low voice, motioning towards* ROXANE.
'Tis naught. I ate meat* yesterday.

* See footnote on p. 126.

S. MARTHE, *speaking low and quickly.*
That's why you're pale. Swear me upon your troth
you'll come forthwith to sup a bowl of broth
in the refectory. You swear!

CYRANO. Yes, yes.

S. MARTHE. You show a most unwonted gentleness.

ROXANE, *who hears them whisper.*
She's trying to convert you.

S. MARTHE. Madame mocks.

CYRANO. No! she is right! My saintly chatterbox—
with comic fury—
have you no sermon for me? You astound me!
But I'll have my revenge, may heaven confound me!
Listen! You have my leave
He pretends to search for a joke and find it.
—the drollest thing—
to pray for me at Chapel this evening.

ROXANE. Heavens above!

CYRANO, *laughing.* She thinks her ears deceive!

S. MARTHE. My prayers have not been waiting on your leave!
Exit.

CYRANO, *returning to* ROXANE, *busy with her work.*
You sweetly cursed embroidery, I protest
you will outstitch me.

ROXANE. I waited on the jest!
At this moment a breath of wind shakes down the leaves.

CYRANO. The leaves.

ROXANE, *lifting her head and looking down the alleys.*
They have a blonde Venetian air.
Watch how they fall—over some divine affair!

CYRANO.
In that brief passage between the branch and the grass
how well they know with loveliness to pass,
and, though they fear the mould, they claim the right
to clothe their fall with the upward glory of flight.

ROXANE. So sad, dear friend?

CYRANO. Dear friend, not sad at all!

ROXANE. Enough of plane-trees, then, and leaves that fall . . .

Tell me instead what news has come your way,
My gazetteer.

CYRANO, *growing steadily paler and fighting against pain.*
The nineteenth, Saturday.
The king, although warned against it, thought he'd
chance it
and eat a surfeit of pears: a faithful lancet
passed judgment on the treasonable shiver,
and the pulse royal was straightway cured of fever.
On Sunday at the Queen's great ball—a scandal—
they burned about a ton of finest candle.
Our troops have beaten John of Austria.
Four sorcerers were hanged; the enema
on Madam Athis' lap-dog was a riot!

ROXANE. Monsieur de Bergerac, will you be quiet?

CYRANO. Naught—Monday—save a change of lovers.

ROXANE. Oh!

CYRANO. Tuesday the Court was held at Fontainebleau,
Wednesday, De Montglat told De Fresque—I mean
Thursday—Mancini, France's second Queen—
the twenty-fifth—Montglat grew well acquainted
with her—De Fresque. On Saturday——
He closes his eyes. His head falls. Silence.

ROXANE, *surprised to hear no more, turns to look, and rises in terror.* He's fainted.
She runs to him, calling. Cyrano!

CYRANO, *opening his eyes—with a trembling voice.*
Did you call me? Naught's amiss.
Pray be at ease.

ROXANE. But——

CYRANO. Yes, it hurts like this
at times, my Arras wound.

ROXANE. Poor Cyrano.

CYRANO. 'Tis nothing—watch my eyes—
he smiles painfully—and see it go!

ROXANE, *standing close by him.*
Each of us has a wound. I with the rest.
Aye, it is here—the wound within my breast—

She lays her hand on her breast—
under his letter whose yellow page nor tear
nor blood has blotted. Aye, the wound is here.
Dusk begins to fall.

CYRANO. His letter? Once you said (but do not heed it
if it should irk you—)

ROXANE. You would dare to read it?

CYRANO. Yes—I would dare—to-day.

ROXANE, *giving him the letter from her neck.* Then take it!

CYRANO. Why?

ROXANE. Open it and read it.

She returns to her work, folds and arranges her wools.

CYRANO. Farewell, Roxane. I die.

ROXANE, *stopping, astounded.* Louder.

CYRANO. "This very night, my love's dear token
with half that love in my deep heart unspoken,
I die, and never more that flock of birds
which are your gestures"—

ROXANE. How you read his words!

CYRANO. "shall brush mine eyelids with the butterfly kiss
of wings that hover, and snare the soul with this.
And most I see the small habitual wonder
of fingers on your brow, and, swooning under"

ROXANE. God, how you read!

The night gradually falls.

CYRANO. "that memory, I write
farewell."

ROXANE. You read—

CYRANO. "My heart, my soul's delight.
My life."

ROXANE. and while you read

CYRANO. "My love."

ROXANE. I know
the voice. It is the voice. Wait, Cyrano.

She draws near so gently that he does not notice, passes behind the chair, and leaning over silently, reads the letter. The darkness deepens.

CYRANO. "My heart has never wavered for a second.

I am and will be, now the dark has beckoned
he who has loved and loves you in death's despite."

ROXANE, *laying her hand on his shoulder.*
How can you read the letter? It is night.
He trembles, turns, sees her close to him, makes a movement of terror and bends his head. A long silence. Then, in the deep night, she says slowly with folded hands.
With all of heaven hidden in his heart
for fourteen years, how did he play his part?

CYRANO. Roxane.

ROXANE. 'Twas you.

CYRANO. No, no, Roxane.

ROXANE. For shame,
I should have guessed it when he spoke my name.

CYRANO. No! It was never I——

ROXANE. 'Twas you.

CYRANO. My oath!

ROXANE. At last I understand and know you—both.
The letter's you—

CYRANO. 'Tis false.

ROXANE. The sweet untrue
phrases were—

CYRANO. No!

ROXANE. and the voice on the midnight, you!

CYRANO. No. No!

ROXANE. You were his soul. You are the man!

CYRANO. I did not love——

ROXANE. You loved——

CYRANO. 'Twas Christian.

ROXANE. You loved me.

CYRANO, *with a faltering voice.* No.

ROXANE. Your failing tones disprove you.

CYRANO. No, no, my dear, dear love. I did not love you.

ROXANE. O what a world died then, what world has sprung
out of its grave. How could you hold your tongue
when on this letter, where he nothing is,
the very tears were yours.

CYRANO. The blood was his.

ROXANE, *releasing the letter.*
But why then choose to break your splendid vow
this day of all days?
 CYRANO. Why?
 LE BRET *and* RAGUENEAU *enter.*
 LE BRET. He's with her now.
What folly! But I guessed.
 CYRANO, *smiling as he recovers himself.* I kept my trust.
 LE BRET. He killed himself by coming here.
 ROXANE. O Christ!
Then a few instants ago—that sudden spell—
 CYRANO. 'Tis true. I did not end my chronicle—
Saturday the twenty-sixth, slain before dinner.
God rest the soul of Bergerac—a sinner.
He uncovers himself and displays his bandaged head.
 ROXANE. I cannot hear, I think. His head all bound!
What have they done? O why?
 CYRANO. "I'll take my wound
here in the heart upon a hero's blade."
Yes, I said that—but Fate's a fickle jade,
and lo! I die through a log dropped on my pate
from behind me by a lackey. Thank you, Fate.
You botched all else. 'Twas right to botch my end.
 RAGUENEAU. O Cyrano!
 CYRANO, *to* RAGUENEAU. Nay! do not weep, my friend.
He takes his hand.
But what will you do now, my dear confrère?
 RAGUENEAU. I snuff the candles for the great Molière.
 CYRANO. Molière!
 RAGUENEAU. But I shall sack myself to-morrow.
In his new play "Scapin" he dared to borrow
A scene from yours!
 LE BRET. The whole entire text!
 RAGUENEAU. Yes, sir, your famous, "What the devil next?"
 LE BRET, *furious.* Molière has stolen it!
 CYRANO, *to* RAGUENEAU. Tut, tut! Why worry?
If it went well, why should my friends be sorry?
 RAGUENEAU, *sobbing.* It fairly took the roof off.

CYRANO. It was written
that I should build for others, and be forgotten.
To ROXANE.
Do you remember when Christian wooed his wife
beneath your lattice at night? Well! there's my life!
I stand below in dark—'tis all my story—
while others climb to snatch the kiss of glory.
'Tis just, for, as I perish, I declare
Molière has genius, Christian was fair.
The convent-bell having rung, at the bottom of the avenue the Nuns are seen making their way to Service.
Pray, gentle sisters, now that your bells ring!

ROXANE, *rising to call for help.* Sister, oh, sister.

CYRANO, *holding her back.* No! Leave everything.
Go, and I'd not be here howe'er you hasten.
The Nuns have entered the chapel. The organ peals.
Who guessed that I needed a little music! Listen!

ROXANE. I love you; live!

CYRANO. No! in the fairy tale
when she has breathed "I love," the prince, all pale,
feels his own ugliness pour up in flame—
but I, belovéd, you see am still the same.

ROXANE. I broke your heart.

CYRANO. No! No!

ROXANE. I and no other.

CYRANO. You my one proof of women's grace. My mother
thought me ill-favoured. No sister whispered over
her brother, and I feared a cruel lover—
you the one woman in my loneliness,
who charmed it with the rustle of her dress.

LE BRET, *pointing to the moon shining through the branches.*
Behold your other friend.

CYRANO. Sweet moon, well met!

ROXANE. I loved but once and twice pay lost love's debt.

CYRANO. I'll plunge this night in the moon's sliding green
without the need to fashion a machine!

ROXANE. Dear friend, be calm!

CYRANO. Sweet, when a poet dies

the moon in heaven is his paradise:
and there I'll meet in exile, and at ease,
old Galileo and old Socrates.

LE BRET, *in revolt.* No! No! It cannot be. Hell's not so black
that the poet's heart of all the world shall crack
in a gutter.

CYRANO. There are no more Iliads,
Le Bret.

LE BRET. My friend.

CYRANO. These are the Gascon lads.
The primal element—the how and thus.

LE BRET. Still science—though he raves—

CYRANO. Copernicus
has said—

ROXANE. O God——

CYRANO. But what is he to us,
and what are we to old Copernicus?
—Philosopher, physician,
rhymer, brawler, and musician,
traveller abaft the skies,
wit who always answered back,
Lover—who found his love a foeman—
Hercule-Savinien here lies,
that Cyrano de Bergerac
who was all men, and therefore no man.
But I must go, forgive me. They are calling,
and for an escort see! the moonbeams falling!
To ROXANE.
I would not have you cease to mourn your lover
Christian, the good, the fair; but when all's over,
and the great cold has clapped me, body and sense,
do on your mourning with a difference,
and in his weeds give me at least a share.

ROXANE. I swear.

CYRANO, *shaken by a great agony, rises with a sudden.*
Not here! I say, not in this chair.
They run to him.
Off, all of you! I'll wait by this tree rooted. *Silence.*

Death comes. Already I'm with marble booted
and gloved with lead; but, as she comes, I'll stand
thus to attention with my sword in hand.
   LE BRET. Cyrano.
   ROXANE, *fainting.* Cyrano.
All draw back horror-stricken.
   CYRANO. Death's nose is snub,
therefore she quizzes mine. On guard, you drab!
Draws his sword.
What say you! It is useless! Well I know it.
It is the hope forlorn that seals the poet.
The desperate venture still rewards us most.
But what is this innumerable host?
I know them by the devil in their eyes.
Have at you, falsehood, that for compromise!
Prejudice, craven fear, you seek for terms?
Here is my sword! go ask them of the worms!
But now my victor overtops the rest.
Salute stupidity! Here is my breast!
He makes huge passes with his sword and stands gasping.
You have taken all—the laurel and the rose.
Take them. There is a secret my heart owes
in your despite, and when my feet have trod
to-night the azure ante-rooms of God,
what I bring home unstained with gold will splash
the basalt floors.
He lunges with the sword. It is
   ROXANE, *bending over him, kissing his forehead.* What?
   CYRANO, *opens his eyes, recognizes her and says wearily.*
My panache.

※

THE READER must already have some conception of melodrama which is sufficient for our purposes. A melodrama is a sort of adventure story for stage or screen. What we primarily expect from it is excitement. If the reader agrees that *Cyrano* is a cut above the average costume romance, he may be willing to ask why.

The simplest answer is that it is "much better written." But this is vague. *What* is better about the writing? The common reader today is certainly not predisposed in favor of *verse* plays. He probably thinks verse rather formidable. Yet undoubtedly the *rhymes* of Rostand (or of Humbert Wolfe) are the source of much of our amusement. Test this by translating Cyrano's tirade on noses into prose —or just consult one of the published prose versions of the speech. Among the qualities of the verse that no one would deny to it are *speed* and *lightness*. Granted a certain context, we enjoy such qualities in writing, just as we enjoy them in an athlete.

Pressed further to analyze his opinion of the play, the reader can quite properly muster the terms he learned at school: plot, character, theme, spectacle, and dialogue. The terms have an honorable history and can scarcely be dispensed with. If a reader is troubled because he "doesn't know what he's supposed to look for" in a play, he cannot do better than look for those standard things, jotting down in a notebook a summary of what is done, in a given play, with each. It is hard to be clear about any work of literature or other art until one has, as it were, itemized the ingredients in one's notebook. First of all come the matters of brute fact, which the memory is nonetheless adept at losing. *What* is the plot, *who* are the characters, *where* is the story set, etc.? These may seldom be questions to answer in public, but we can scarcely proceed to more subtle matters till we have answered them in our notebooks. By more subtle matters, I mean matters of value: here the pervading query is, how good is it? One cannot, as a beginner, press this question too much, since one's taste is undeveloped and, in any case, judgment is comparative: by "good" we mean better than X (if X is below par) and not so good as Y (if Y is outstanding). Nonetheless, one can make a beginning. One can begin with plot, which will tend, will it not? to be the core of melodrama, and which can also be regarded as the core of drama generally. Does the plot of *Cyrano* in any way commend itself to us? Is it exciting? Amusing? The reader can take the plot of *Cyrano* and say what he found most effective about it. Was any sequence of narrative more interesting than another? Can he tell why? Is the general layout of the story effective? Might one call Rostand's plot a good one? Can one compliment him on his handling of it? And, in all this, can one be specific?

What of the *characters*? Perhaps the only one who presents problems is Cyrano himself. "The comedy of a nose" does not seem a very promising subject. (Shakespeare had limited the idea to a very minor character [Bardolph]). If a playwright wants to make much of an idea like this he must, for one thing, *complicate* it, give it meaning—and a various meaning, at that. Did Rostand do this? It seems that he did. He made a great deal of fun out of the nose—and also a great deal of pathos. Where is the joke funniest? Where most pathetic? Is the pathos ever so soft and flabby that one can complain of sentimentality? Does the funniness of the joke have any relation to the pathos—i.e., does Rostand make these two "effects" interact in any way? An answer to this question can be approached by way of the last act of the play. Death is an event with solemn associations, and it would not be hard to recount the death of even a previously funny man in such a way as to arouse unmitigated sadness and even horror. Yet few spectators or readers think of the famous death scene as one of the really heartbreaking scenes in theater. Why not?

So much for Cyrano himself. What of the other characters in the play? They are not very realistically portrayed. Does this matter? Here the topic that arises for discussion is characterization in general. The opinion can be brought forward that dramatic characters need not be detailed psychological portraits; the criterion is whether they make a sufficient contribution to the total pattern of the play, provided that pattern is one we can accept. If we are impressed by the general nature of *Cyrano,* if we accept it as a witty melodrama, as a sad comedy, or even as an *x,* a something we cannot find a name for, the question to ask concerning the characters is, are they in place within the world (the *artificial* world, if you will) which is Rostand's creation? Roxane, for example. There are plays and novels where her presence would be an outrage—where the critics would have to write: "This play (or novel) has a fatal weakness: a wildly improbable heroine." But as the heroine of a play in rhymed verse, a play in romantic costume, a heroine of fairy tale and fancy, a heroine of *Cyrano de Bergerac?* Perhaps we can accept her. Perhaps (and this is the real point) we could not accept here a realistically portrayed heroine.

Has the play a *theme*? The leading idea of Cyrano, and of Rostand as far as this play goes, might be said to be that *life is a performance*. It has to be judged from the aesthetic point of view. Ragueneau, the cook who believes so profoundly that one lives to eat (i.e., for the aesthetics of eating) and that one does not eat merely to live, is a Cyrano on a lower plane. It will be noted that all Cyrano's protests against other people's behavior arise from the fact that they have broken the rules of a game—or rather the laws of an art. Much of the comedy of the play has its source in the application of an aesthetic criterion where we expect a practical one. Roxane's penetration of the battle lines is but one example.

Of course Rostand is not so interested in the statement and restatement of the idea as he is in such comic possibilities. The most serious and ludicrous of the jests is that our super-aesthete carries about with him so ugly a protuberance. Emphatically this is something one does not mention. But one sees the logic of Cyrano's career. He lives for beauty as an idea. As to the actual possession of it, he will realize that Christian has a prior claim. Yet he assigns to himself a rôle of more intelligence, talent, and heroism. And he plays it—plays it *as a rôle*—to the very end.

On the whole, then, what is true of characterization is true of theme: in this sort of entertainment a little goes a long way. If *Cyrano* has profundity of a kind, we shall find it rather by watching Rostand at work in the theater, by observing his artistic method, than by listing his opinions or, when we find that he is only advancing one opinion, counting how many times he states it. T. S. Eliot has some interesting comments on Cyrano as a man who watches himself act. He remarks that Rostand is not the first playwright to depict a character who sees himself in a dramatic light:

> The really fine rhetoric of Shakespeare occurs in situations where a character in the play *sees himself* in a dramatic light . . . But when a character in a play makes a direct appeal to us, we are either the victims of our own sentiment, or we are in the presence of a vicious rhetoric.

> These references [Mr. Eliot has cited Othello's last big speech and other passages in Shakespeare] ought to supply some evidence of the propriety of Cyrano and Noses. Is not Cyrano ex-

actly in this position of contemplating himself as a romantic, a dramatic figure? This dramatic sense on the part of the characters is rare in modern drama . . . Rostand had—whether he had anything else or not—this dramatic sense, and it is what gives life to Cyrano. It is a sense which is almost a sense of humour (for when anyone is conscious of himself as acting, something like a sense of humour is present.) It gives Rostand's characters —Cyrano at least—a gusto which is uncommon on the modern stage. No doubt Rostand's people play up to this too steadily. We recognize that in the love scene of Cyrano in the garden, for in *Romeo and Juliet* the profounder dramatist shows his lovers melting into unconsciousness of their isolated selves, shows the human soul in the process of forgetting itself. Rostand could not do that; but in the particular case of Cyrano on Noses, the character, the situation, the occasion were perfectly suited and combined. The tirade generated by this combination is not only genuinely and highly dramatic: it is possibly poetry also. . . . *Cyrano* satisfies, as far as scenes like this can satisfy, the requirements of poetic drama. It must take genuine and substantial human emotions, such emotions as observation can confirm, typical emotions, and give them artistic form; the degree of abstraction is a question for the method of each author. In Shakespeare the form is determined in the unity of the whole, as well as single scenes; it is something to attain this unity, as Rostand does, in scenes, if not in the whole play. Not only as a dramatist, but as a poet, he is superior to Maeterlinck [if the reader does not know Maeterlinck, he can *imagine* a writer of whom what Mr. Eliot here says is true] whose drama, in failing to be dramatic, fails also to be poetic. Maeterlinck has a literary perception of the dramatic and a literary conception of the poetic, and he joins the two; the two are not, as sometimes they are in the work of Rostand, fused. His characters take no conscious delight in their role—they are sentimental. With Rostand the center of gravity is in the expression of the emotion, not as with Maeterlinck in the emotion that cannot be expressed. . . .

This passage from Mr. Eliot is one to come back to, because it introduces the topic of poetic drama in general. For the present, however, its value is that it calls attention to the theatrical, rather than philosophical, character of Rostand's mind: only through this theatrical conception of a person's seeing himself as an actor can Rostand achieve any sort of profundity. The "sheer theatricality" of *Cyrano* is, therefore, not something to be lightly dismissed. *Spectacle,* that which is presented to the eye in the theater, is a basic dramatic category. Insofar as we can grasp the spectacular side of the play without seeing a performance, Rostand's stage directions and our own visual imagination will convince us that the play depends heavily on seen beauty and seen movement. A minute by minute examination of the visual element would be worth making. The reader might ask himself, how much of this play could be captured in a silent movie?

The theatricality of Rostand can be illustrated, not only from his method of *characterizing* Cyrano, and not only from his use of *spectacle,* but also from his *dialogue,* his style of writing. Verse and prose for theater have not only to be good by all the usual standards of good writing. They have in addition to have a certain projectile quality, something in their diction and rhetoric that lifts them off the page and projects them across the footlights to the ears of the audience. Poetry doesn't become dramatic by being spoken *in* the theater, as Jean Cocteau has put it; it is dramatic by being *of* the theater in its very nature. Actors acknowledge this fact when they talk of bad theatrical verse (which may be good verse otherwise) as being "unspeakable," good theatrical verse as being "speakable." Not that good theatrical verse is always easy on the performer; but at least it seems shaped to his lips, his vocal chords, even to his body, and at least it is so ordered as to enter the spectator's ear and give the right impression as something heard. The order in which words are presented to the ear decides the impression given. It gives to the words their special gesture. "Pluck thine eye out if it offend thee" is a perfectly logical and grammatical sentence. But the authors of the English Bible wrote, "If thine eye offend thee, pluck it out," which has a different rhetoric, a different *gesture:* the second half of the sentence conveys not only the idea but a shock. A writer for theater must be a master of gestures like this.

Obviously Rostand is a poet *of* the theater. And there is no need to define his talent in merely general terms. We can come down to brass tacks by considering one of the problems that faced Humbert

Wolfe when he made his English version. It was intended for use by the actor Charles Laughton. Wolfe and Laughton collaborated, in fact. Here is Wolfe's account of their approach to one passage in the play:

> Laughton was working on the ballade in Act I. He acted it first in French. Up went his left hand, out lunged his right, and as he shrugged his shoulders up I could hear the shiver of steel on steel. As he spoke he fenced, his eyes never leaving his opponent's face, and I became aware that, as Rostand had written it, not a line but might have been dictated by a *maître d'armes*. And when with the final stroke he cried with the ringing challenge of the Gallic cock, conjuring up the sun,
>
> > À la fin d'envoi je touche,
>
> if you had eyes in your head, you could see the little stain of red on the rapier's point.
>
> This finished, without a pause Laughton began, without comment, to act my original version with which I had been pleased when I wrote it. It seemed to me that not only had it taken the exact meaning of the French, but that in itself it was a good ballade, supple, and moving swiftly without jolt or hindrance. It read as follows:
>
> > I doff my beaver with a gesture
> > and then dismantle grave and slow
> > the laces of my outward vesture—
> > and give my blade its freedom—so.
> > Then, elegant as poor Pierrot
> > and dexterous as Harlequin,
> > I give you warning, child of woe,
> > with the last line, that Death comes in.
> >
> > You should have kept your distance, lest your
> > bones find a stuffing not of dough—
> > within the flank or if one pressed your
> > heart underneath its garter-bow!
> > Hark! How the iron musics go!
> > Watch my blade flutter round your skin

> —a stinging fly—which tends to show
> at the last line that Death comes in.
>
> And here's a rhyme, since you've confessed your
> terror, pale craven, that I owe
> to the white feather in your posture!
> See! now I turn what you bestow
> in my direction, blow for blow.
> Look, a parade in tierce! Begin
> to learn, my lily-livered foe,
> with the last line that Death comes in.
>
> Prince! Say your nunc dimittis, Lo!
> I shift my ground (God salve your sin!)
> I feint, I lunge—and now you know
> at the last line that Death came in.

As Laughton acted it, a doubt began to assail me. Why were the fencer's movements which in the French flowed with rhythmic ease hesitating and interrupted in the English? Was Laughton finding it difficult to remember? But no! he was word-perfect. Could it be that the very smoothness which I had imported was a mistake? Had Rostand introduced the breaks in the verse of set purpose, knowing the motions of the fence, and had I completely overlooked this essential point? I knew before Laughton had finished that this was so, and I knew also that the last line could not stand. Because Cyrano only scored a hit, a palpable hit on de Valvert. He did not kill him. It was therefore, an arrant mistranslation to write,

> at the last line that Death came in.

The French swordsman disappeared. Laughton stood before me smiling. "I see," he said, "that you agree. Your version may be a better ballade, but I can't fence it. Rostand knew what he was about." I tried four times, carefully watching Laughton act the French on each occasion, to get a version which would give the actor what he needed and still be a reasonable ballade. Finally, Laughton was satisfied that he could fight to the rendering which appears in the text [pp. 36-37 in this book]. For my part, though I recognize that it is less impracticable, I can't feel that it is a success. I have tried it a dozen times since, and failed as often. I leave it because Laughton could act to it.

Probably the best general appreciation of *Cyrano* is that (available only in French) of the critic Francisque Sarcey, reprinted in his *Quarante Ans de Théâtre*, Volume 8, "Cyrano de Bergerac." Sarcey gives instances not mentioned in the above commentary of Rostand's theatricality. He also helps us to imagine what the occasion of the première with Coquelin—December 28, 1897—was like.

2. THE IMPORTANCE OF BEING EARNEST · 1895

IF A MELODRAMA is a play which confines itself to being thrilling, and a farce is a play which confines itself to being funny, this play, which might be described as a superior farce, comes naturally enough after *Cyrano*, which is a superior melodrama. By "superior," in both instances, is meant that the playwright starts with the crude established form and, by deft manipulation, raises it above itself. In both cases the playwright has complicated his recipe by adding a little of the opposite: the farce has a serious flavoring, the melodrama is seasoned with wit.

We have, in effect, been considering the question, what raises *Cyrano* above ordinary melodrama and romance? The question to consider now is, what, if anything, raises *Earnest* above ordinary farce?

As with *Cyrano*, very little special knowledge is demanded of the reader. We are in upper-class England of the eighteen-nineties, and what we all think we know of this milieu or of similar milieus is as pertinent as what the informed historian of the period really knows.

THE IMPORTANCE OF BEING EARNEST

A Trivial Comedy for Serious People

by Oscar Wilde

*

The Importance of Being Earnest

Characters

JOHN WORTHING, J.P.
ALGERNON MONCRIEFF
REV. CANON CHASUBLE, D.D.
MERRIMAN, *butler*
LANE, *manservant*

LADY BRACKNELL
HON. GWENDOLEN FAIRFAX
CECILY CARDEW
MISS PRISM, *governess*

THE TIME: *The Present*

Act I

Morning room in ALGERNON'S *flat in Half-Moon Street. The room is luxuriously and artistically furnished. The sound of a piano is heard in the adjoining room.*

LANE *is arranging afternoon tea on the table, and after the music has ceased,* ALGERNON *enters.*

ALGERNON. Did you hear what I was playing, Lane?

LANE. I didn't think it polite to listen, sir.

ALGERNON. I'm sorry for that, for your sake. I don't play accurately—anyone can play accurately—but I play with wonderful expression. As far as the piano is concerned, sentiment is my forte. I keep science for Life.

LANE. Yes, sir.

ALGERNON. And, speaking of the science of Life, have you got the cucumber sandwiches cut for Lady Bracknell?

LANE. Yes, sir.   *Hands them on a salver.*

ALGERNON, *inspects them, takes two, and sits down on the sofa.* Oh! . . . by the way, Lane, I see from your book that on Thursday night, when Lord Shoreman and Mr. Worthing were dining with me, eight bottles of champagne are entered as having been consumed.

LANE. Yes, sir; eight bottles and a pint.

ALGERNON. Why is it that at a bachelor's establishment the servants invariably drink the champagne? I ask merely for information.

LANE. I attribute it to the superior quality of the wine, sir. I have often observed that in married households the champagne is rarely of a first-rate brand.

ALGERNON. Good heavens! Is marriage so demoralizing as that?

LANE. I believe it *is* a very pleasant state, sir. I have had very little experience of it myself up to the present. I have only been married once. That was in consequence of a misunderstanding between myself and a young person.

ALGERNON, *languidly*. I don't know that I am much interested in your family life, Lane.

LANE. No, sir; it is not a very interesting subject. I never think of it myself.

ALGERNON. Very natural, I am sure. That will do, Lane, thank you.

LANE. Thank you, sir. LANE *goes out*.

ALGERNON. Lane's views on marriage seem somewhat lax. Really, if the lower orders don't set us a good example, what on earth is the use of them? They seem, as a class, to have absolutely no sense of moral responsibility.

Enter LANE.

LANE. Mr. Ernest Worthing.

Enter JACK.

LANE *goes out*.

ALGERNON. How are you, my dear Ernest? What brings you up to town?

JACK. Oh, pleasure, pleasure! What else should bring one anywhere? Eating as usual, I see, Algy!

ALGERNON, *stiffly*. I believe it is customary in good society to take some slight refreshment at five o'clock. Where have you been since last Thursday?

JACK, *sitting down on the sofa*. In the country.

ALGERNON. What on earth do you do there?

JACK, *pulling off his gloves*. When one is in town one amuses oneself. When one is in the country one amuses other people. It is excessively boring.

ALGERNON. And who are the people you amuse?

JACK, *airily*. Oh, neighbors, neighbors.

ALGERNON. Got nice neighbors in your part of Shropshire?

JACK. Perfectly horrid! Never speak to one of them.

ALGERNON. How immensely you must amuse them! *Goes over and takes sandwich*. By the way, Shropshire is your county, is it not?

JACK. Eh? Shropshire? Yes, of course. Hallo! Why all these cups? Why cucumber sandwiches? Why such reckless extravagance in one so young? Who is coming to tea?

ALGERNON. Oh! merely Aunt Augusta and Gwendolen.

JACK. How perfectly delightful!

ALGERNON. Yes, that is all very well; but I am afraid Aunt Augusta won't quite approve of your being here.

JACK. May I ask why?

ALGERNON. My dear fellow, the way you flirt with Gwendolen is perfectly disgraceful. It is almost as bad as the way Gwendolen flirts with you.

JACK. I am in love with Gwendolen. I have come up to town expressly to propose to her.

ALGERNON. I thought you had come up for pleasure? . . . I call that business.

JACK. How utterly unromantic you are!

ALGERNON. I really don't see anything romantic in proposing. It is very romantic to be in love. But there is nothing romantic about a definite proposal. Why, one may be accepted. One usually is, I believe. Then the excitement is all over. The very essence of romance is uncertainty. If ever I get married, I'll certainly try to forget the fact.

JACK. I have no doubt about that, dear Algy. The Divorce Court was specially invented for people whose memories are so curiously constituted.

ALGERNON. Oh! there is no use speculating on that subject. Divorces are made in Heaven—— JACK *puts out his hand to take a sandwich*. ALGERNON *at once interferes*. Please don't touch the cucumber sandwiches. They are ordered specially for Aunt Augusta.

Takes one and eats it.

JACK. Well, you have been eating them all the time.

ALGERNON. That is quite a different matter. She is my aunt. *Takes plate from below.* Have some bread and butter. The bread and butter is for Gwendolen. Gwendolen is devoted to bread and butter.

JACK, *advancing to table and helping himself.* And very good bread and butter it is too.

ALGERNON. Well, my dear fellow, you need not eat as if you were going to eat it all. You behave as if you were married to her already. You are not married to her already, and I don't think you ever will be.

JACK. Why on earth do you say that?

ALGERNON. Well, in the first place girls never marry the men they flirt with. Girls don't think it right.

JACK. Oh, that is nonsense!

ALGERNON. It isn't. It is a great truth. It accounts for the extraordinary number of bachelors that one sees all over the place. In the second place, I don't give my consent.

JACK. Your consent!

ALGERNON. My dear fellow, Gwendolen is my first cousin. And before I allow you to marry her, you will have to clear up the whole question of Cecily. *Rings bell.*

JACK. Cecily! What on earth do you mean? What do you mean, Algy, by Cecily! I don't know anyone of the name of Cecily.

Enter LANE.

ALGERNON. Bring me that cigarette case Mr. Worthing left in the smoking room the last time he dined here.

LANE. Yes, sir. LANE *goes out.*

JACK. Do you mean to say you have had my cigarette case all this time? I wish to goodness you had let me know. I have been writing frantic letters to Scotland Yard about it. I was very nearly offering a large reward.

ALGERNON. Well, I wish you would offer one. I happen to be more than usually hard up.

JACK. There is no good offering a large reward now that the thing is found.

Enter LANE *with the cigarette case on a salver.* ALGERNON *takes it at once.* LANE *goes out.*

ALGERNON. I think that is rather mean of you, Ernest, I must say. *Opens case and examines it.* However, it makes no matter, for, now that I look at the inscription inside, I find that the thing isn't yours after all.

JACK. Of course it's mine. *Moving to him.* You have seen me with it a hundred times, and you have no right whatsoever to read what is written inside. It is a very ungentlemanly thing to read a private cigarette case.

ALGERNON. Oh! it is absurd to have a hard and fast rule about what one should read and what one shouldn't. More than half of modern culture depends on what one shouldn't read.

JACK. I am quite aware of the fact, and I don't propose to discuss modern culture. It isn't the sort of thing one should talk of in private. I simply want my cigarette case back.

ALGERNON. Yes; but this isn't your cigarette case. This cigarette case is a present from someone of the name of Cecily, and you said you didn't know anyone of that name.

JACK. Well, if you want to know, Cecily happens to be my aunt.

ALGERNON. Your aunt!

JACK. Yes. Charming old lady she is, too. Lives at Tunbridge Wells. Just give it back to me, Algy.

ALGERNON, *retreating to back of sofa.* But why does she call herself little Cecily if she is your aunt and lives at Tunbridge Wells? *Reading.* "From little Cecily with her fondest love."

JACK, *moving to sofa and kneeling upon it.* My dear fellow, what on earth is there in that? Some aunts are tall, some aunts are not tall. That is a matter that surely an aunt may be allowed to decide for herself. You seem to think that every aunt should be exactly like your aunt! That is absurd! For Heaven's sake give me back my cigarette case. *Follows* ALGERNON *round the room.*

ALGERNON. Yes. But why does your aunt call you her uncle? "From little Cecily, with her fondest love to her dear Uncle Jack." There is no objection, I admit, to an aunt being a small aunt, but why an aunt, no matter what her size may be, should call her own nephew her uncle, I can't quite make out. Besides, your name isn't Jack at all; it is Ernest.

JACK. It isn't Ernest; it's Jack.

ALGERNON. You have always told me it was Ernest. I have introduced you to everyone as Ernest. You answer to the name of Ernest. You look as if your name was Ernest. You are the most earnest-looking person I ever saw in my life. It is perfectly absurd your saying that your name isn't Ernest. It's on your cards. Here is one of them. *Taking it from case.* "Mr. Ernest Worthing, B. 4, The Albany." I'll keep this as a proof that your name is Ernest if ever you attempt to deny it to me, or to Gwendolen, or to anyone else.

Puts the card in his pocket.

JACK. Well, my name is Ernest in town and Jack in the country, and the cigarette case was given to me in the country.

ALGERNON. Yes, but that does not account for the fact that your small Aunt Cecily, who lives at Tunbridge Wells, calls you her dear uncle. Come, old boy, you had much better have the thing out at once.

JACK. My dear Algy, you talk exactly as if you were a dentist. It is very vulgar to talk like a dentist when one isn't a dentist. It produces a false impression.

ALGERNON. Well, that is exactly what dentists always do. Now, go on! Tell me the whole thing. I may mention that I have always suspected you of being a confirmed and secret Bunburyist; and I am quite sure of it now.

JACK. Bunburyist? What on earth do you mean by a Bunburyist?

ALGERNON. I'll reveal to you the meaning of that incomparable expression as soon as you are kind enough to inform me why you are Ernest in town and Jack in the country.

JACK. Well, produce my cigarette case first.

ALGERNON. Here it is. *Hands cigarette case.* Now produce your explanation, and pray make it improbable.   *Sits on sofa.*

JACK. My dear fellow, there is nothing improbable about my explanation at all. In fact it's perfectly ordinary. Old Mr. Thomas Cardew, who adopted me when I was a little boy, made me in his will guardian to his grand-daughter, Miss Cecily Cardew. Cecily, who addresses me as her uncle from motives of respect that you could not possibly appreciate, lives at my place in the country under the charge of her admirable governess, Miss Prism.

ALGERNON. Where is that place in the country, by the way?

JACK. That is nothing to you, dear boy. You are not going to be invited. . . . I may tell you candidly that the place is not in Shropshire.

ALGERNON. I suspected that, my dear fellow! I have Bunburyed all over Shropshire on two separate occasions. Now, go on. Why are you Ernest in town and Jack in the country?

JACK. My dear Algy, I don't know whether you will be able to understand my real motives. You are hardly serious enough. When one is placed in the position of guardian, one has to adopt a very high moral tone on all subjects. It's one's duty to do so. And as a high moral tone can hardly be said to conduce very much to either one's health or one's happiness, in order to get up to town I have always pretended to have a younger brother of the name of Ernest, who lives in the Albany, and gets into the most dreadful scrapes. That, my dear Algy, is the whole truth pure and simple.

ALGERNON. The truth is rarely pure and never simple. Modern life would be very tedious if it were either, and modern literature a complete impossibility!

JACK. That wouldn't be at all a bad thing.

ALGERNON. Literary criticism is not your forte, my dear fellow. Don't try it. You should leave that to people who haven't been at a University. They do it so well in the daily papers. What you really are is a Bunburyist. I was quite right in saying you were a Bunburyist. You are one of the most advanced Bunburyists I know.

JACK. What on earth do you mean?

ALGERNON. You have invented a very useful younger brother called Ernest, in order that you may be able to come up to town as often as you like. I have invented an invaluable permanent invalid called Bunbury, in order that I may be able to go down into the country whenever I choose. Bunbury is perfectly invaluable. If it wasn't for Bunbury's extraordinary bad health, for instance, I wouldn't be able to dine with you at Willis's to-night, for I have been really engaged to Aunt Augusta for more than a week.

JACK. I haven't asked you to dine with me anywhere to-night.

ALGERNON. I know. You are absurdly careless about sending out invitations. It is very foolish of you. Nothing annoys people so much as not receiving invitations.

JACK. You had much better dine with your Aunt Augusta.

ALGERNON. I haven't the smallest intention of doing anything of the kind. To begin with, I dined there on Monday, and once a week is quite enough to dine with one's own relations. In the second place, whenever I do dine there I am always treated as a member of the family, and sent down with either no woman at all, or two. In the third place, I know perfectly well whom she will place me next to, to-night. She will place me next Mary Farquhar, who always flirts with her own husband across the dinner table. That is not very pleasant. Indeed, it is not even decent . . . and that sort of thing is enormously on the increase. The amount of women in London who flirt with their own husbands is perfectly scandalous. It looks so bad. It is simply washing one's clean linen in public. Besides, now that I know you to be a confirmed Bunburyist, I naturally want to talk to you about Bunburying. I want to tell you the rules.

JACK. I'm not a Bunburyist at all. If Gwendolen accepts me, I am going to kill my brother, indeed I think I'll kill him in any case. Cecily is a little too much interested in him. It is rather a bore. So I am going to get rid of Ernest. And I strongly advise you to do the same with Mr. . . . with your invalid friend who has the absurd name.

ALGERNON. Nothing will induce me to part with Bunbury, and if you ever get married, which seems to me extremely problematic, you will be very glad to know Bunbury. A man who marries without knowing Bunbury has a very tedious time of it.

JACK. That is nonsense. If I marry a charming girl like Gwendolen, and she is the only girl I ever saw in my life that I would marry, I certainly won't want to know Bunbury.

ALGERNON. Then your wife will. You don't seem to realize, that in married life three is company and two is none.

JACK, *sententiously*. That, my dear young friend, is the theory that the corrupt French Drama has been propounding for the last fifty years.

ALGERNON. Yes; and that the happy English home has proved in half the time.

JACK. For Heaven's sake, don't try to be cynical. It's perfectly easy to be cynical.

ALGERNON. My dear fellow, it isn't easy to be anything nowadays. There's such a lot of beastly competition about. *The sound of an electric bell is heard.* Ah! that must be Aunt Augusta. Only relatives, or creditors, ever ring in that Wagnerian manner. Now, if I get her out of the way for ten minutes, so that you can have an opportunity for proposing to Gwendolen, may I dine with you to-night at Willis's?

JACK. I suppose so, if you want to.

ALGERNON. Yes, but you must be serious about it. I hate people who are not serious about meals. It is so shallow of them.

Enter LANE.

LANE. Lady Bracknell and Miss Fairfax. ALGERNON *goes forward to meet them.*

Enter LADY BRACKNELL *and* GWENDOLEN.

LADY BRACKNELL. Good afternoon, dear Algernon, I hope you are behaving very well.

ALGERNON. I'm feeling very well, Aunt Augusta.

LADY BRACKNELL. That's not quite the same thing. In fact the two things rarely go together.
Sees JACK *and bows to him with icy coldness.*

ALGERNON, *to* GWENDOLEN. Dear me, you are smart!

GWENDOLEN. I am always smart! Aren't I, Mr. Worthing?

JACK. You're quite perfect, Miss Fairfax.

GWENDOLEN. Oh! I hope I am not that. It would leave no room for developments, and I intend to develop in many directions.
GWENDOLEN *and* JACK *sit down together in the corner.*

LADY BRACKNELL. I'm sorry if we are a little late, Algernon, but I was obliged to call on dear Lady Harbury. I hadn't been there since her poor husband's death. I never saw a woman so altered; she looks quite twenty years younger. And now I'll have a cup of tea, and one of those nice cucumber sandwiches you promised me.

ALGERNON. Certainly, Aunt Augusta. *Goes over to tea table.*

LADY BRACKNELL. Won't you come and sit here, Gwendolen?

GWENDOLEN. Thanks, mamma, I'm quite comfortable where I am.

ALGERNON, *picking up empty plate in horror.* Good heavens! Lane! Why are there no cucumber sandwiches? I ordered them specially.

LANE, *gravely.* There were no cucumbers in the market this morning, sir. I went down twice.

ALGERNON. No cucumbers!

LANE. No, sir. Not even for ready money.

ALGERNON. That will do, Lane, thank you.

LANE. Thank you, sir. *Goes out.*

ALGERNON. I am greatly distressed, Aunt Augusta, about there being no cucumbers, not even for ready money.

LADY BRACKNELL. It really makes no matter, Algernon. I had some crumpets with Lady Harbury, who seems to me to be living entirely for pleasure now.

ALGERNON. I hear her hair has turned quite gold from grief.

LADY BRACKNELL. It certainly has changed its color. From what cause I, of course, cannot say. ALGERNON *crosses and hands tea.* Thank you. I've quite a treat for you to-night, Algernon. I am going to send you down with Mary Farquhar. She is such a nice woman, and so attentive to her husband. It's delightful to watch them.

ALGERNON. I am afraid, Aunt Augusta, I shall have to give up the pleasure of dining with you to-night after all.

LADY BRACKNELL, *frowning.* I hope not, Algernon. It would put my table completely out. Your uncle would have to dine upstairs. Fortunately he is accustomed to that.

ALGERNON. It is a great bore, and, I need hardly say, a terrible disappointment to me, but the fact is I have just had a telegram to say that my poor friend Bunbury is very ill again. *Exchanges glances with* JACK. They seem to think I should be with him.

LADY BRACKNELL. It is very strange. This Mr. Bunbury seems to suffer from curiously bad health.

ALGERNON. Yes; poor Bunbury is a dreadful invalid.

LADY BRACKNELL. Well, I must say, Algernon, that I think it is high time that Mr. Bunbury made up his mind whether he was going to live or to die. This shilly-shallying with the question is absurd. Nor do I in any way approve of the modern sympathy with invalids. I consider it morbid. Illness of any kind is hardly a thing to be encouraged in others. Health is the primary duty of life. I am always telling that to your poor uncle, but he never seems to take much notice . . . as far as any improvement in his ailments goes. I should be much obliged if you would ask Mr. Bunbury, from me, to be kind enough not to have a relapse on Saturday, for I rely on you to arrange my music for me. It is my last reception, and one wants something that will encourage conversation, particularly at the end of the season when every one has practically said whatever they had to say, which, in most cases, was probably not much.

ALGERNON. I'll speak to Bunbury, Aunt Augusta, if he is still conscious, and I think I can promise you he'll be all right by Saturday. Of course the music is a great difficulty. You see, if one plays good music, people don't listen, and if one plays bad music, people don't talk. But I'll run over the program I've drawn out, if you will kindly come into the next room for a moment.

LADY BRACKNELL. Thank you, Algernon. It is very thoughtful of you. *Rising, and following* ALGERNON. I'm sure the programme will be delightful, after a few expurgations. French songs I cannot possibly allow. People always seem to think that they are improper, and either look shocked, which is vulgar, or laugh, which is worse. But German sounds a thoroughly respectable language, and indeed, I believe is so. Gwendolen, you will accompany me.

GWENDOLEN. Certainly, mamma.

LADY BRACKNELL *and* ALGERNON *go into the music room,* GWENDOLEN *remains behind.*

JACK. Charming day it has been, Miss Fairfax.

GWENDOLEN. Pray don't talk to me about the weather, Mr. Worthing. Whenever people talk to me about the weather, I always feel quite certain that they mean something else. And that makes me so nervous.

JACK. I do mean something else.

GWENDOLEN. I thought so. In fact, I am never wrong.

JACK. And I would like to be allowed to take advantage of Lady Bracknell's temporary absence . . .

GWENDOLEN. I would certainly advise you to do so. Mamma has a way of coming back suddenly into a room that I have often had to speak to her about.

JACK, *nervously.* Miss Fairfax, ever since I met you I have admired you more than any girl . . . I have ever met since . . . I met you.

GWENDOLEN. Yes, I am quite aware of the fact. And I often wish that in public, at any rate, you had been more demonstrative. For me you have always had an irresistible fascination. Even before I met you I was far from indifferent to you. JACK *looks at her in amazement.* We live, as I hope you know, Mr. Worthing, in an age of ideals. The fact is constantly mentioned in the more expensive monthly magazines, and has reached the provincial pulpits I am told: and my ideal has always been to love some one of the name of Ernest. There is something in that name that inspires absolute confidence. The moment Algernon first mentioned to me that he had a friend called Ernest, I knew I was destined to love you.

JACK. You really love me, Gwendolen?

GWENDOLEN. Passionately!

JACK. Darling! You don't know how happy you've made me.

GWENDOLEN. My own Ernest!

JACK. But you don't really mean to say that you couldn't love me if my name wasn't Ernest?

GWENDOLEN. But your name is Ernest.

JACK. Yes, I know it is. But supposing it was something else? Do you mean to say you couldn't love me then?

GWENDOLEN, *glibly*. Ah! that is clearly a metaphysical speculation, and like most metaphysical speculations has very little reference at all to the actual facts of real life, as we know them.

JACK. Personally, darling, to speak quite candidly, I don't much care about the name of Ernest. . . . I don't think the name suits me at all.

GWENDOLEN. It suits you perfectly. It is a divine name. It has a music of its own. It produces vibrations.

JACK. Well, really, Gwendolen, I must say that I think there are lots of other much nicer names. I think Jack, for instance, a charming name.

GWENDOLEN. Jack? . . . No, there is very little music in the name Jack, if any at all, indeed. It does not thrill. It produces absolutely no vibrations. . . . I have known several Jacks, and they all, without exception, were more than usually plain. Besides, Jack is a notorious domesticity for John! And I pity any woman who is married to a man called John. She would probably never be allowed to know the entrancing pleasure of a single moment's solitude. The only really safe name is Ernest.

JACK. Gwendolen, I must get christened at once—I mean we must get married at once. There is no time to be lost.

GWENDOLEN. Married, Mr. Worthing?

JACK, *astounded*. Well . . . surely. You know that I love you, and

ACT I]   THE IMPORTANCE OF BEING EARNEST   163

you led me to believe, Miss Fairfax, that you were not absolutely indifferent to me.

GWENDOLEN. I adore you. But you haven't proposed to me yet. Nothing has been said at all about marriage. The subject has not even been touched on.

JACK. Well . . . may I propose to you now?

GWENDOLEN. I think it would be an admirable opportunity. And to spare you any possible disappointment, Mr. Worthing, I think it only fair to tell you quite frankly beforehand that I am fully determined to accept you.

JACK. Gwendolen!

GWENDOLEN. Yes, Mr. Worthing, what have you got to say to me?

JACK. You know what I have got to say to you.

GWENDOLEN. Yes, but you don't say it.

JACK. Gwendolen, will you marry me?   *Goes on his knees.*

GWENDOLEN. Of course I will, darling. How long you have been about it! I am afraid you have had very little experience in how to propose.

JACK. My own one, I have never loved anyone in the world but you.

GWENDOLEN. Yes, but men often propose for practice. I know my brother Gerald does. All my girl-friends tell me so. What wonderfully blue eyes you have, Ernest! They are quite, quite blue. I hope you will always look at me just like that, especially when there are other people present.

Enter LADY BRACKNELL.

LADY BRACKNELL. Mr. Worthing! Rise, sir, from this semi-recumbent posture. It is most indecorous.

GWENDOLEN. Mamma! *He tries to rise; she restrains him.* I must beg you to retire. This is no place for you. Besides, Mr. Worthing has not quite finished yet.

LADY BRACKNELL. Finished what, may I ask?

GWENDOLEN. I am engaged to Mr. Worthing, mamma.

They rise together.

LADY BRACKNELL. Pardon me, you are not engaged to anyone. When you do become engaged to someone, I, or your father, should his health permit him, will inform you of the fact. An engagement should come on a young girl as a surprise, pleasant or unpleasant, as the case may be. It is hardly a matter that she could be allowed to arrange for herself. . . . And now I have a few questions to put to you, Mr. Worthing. While I am making these inquiries, you, Gwendolen, will wait for me below in the carriage.

GWENDOLEN, *reproachfully.* Mamma!

LADY BRACKNELL. In the carriage, Gwendolen! GWENDOLEN *goes to the door. She and* JACK *blow kisses to each other behind* LADY BRACKNELL'S *back.* LADY BRACKNELL *looks vaguely about as if she could not understand what the noise was. Finally turns round.* Gwendolen, the carriage!

GWENDOLEN. Yes, mamma. *Goes out, looking back at* JACK.

LADY BRACKNELL, *sitting down.* You can take a seat, Mr. Worthing.
Looks in her pocket for notebook and pencil.

JACK. Thank you, Lady Bracknell, I prefer standing.

LADY BRACKNELL, *pencil and notebook in hand.* I feel bound to tell you that you are not down on my list of eligible young men, although I have the same list as the dear Duchess of Bolton has. We work together, in fact. However, I am quite ready to enter your name, should your answers be what a really affectionate mother requires. Do you smoke?

JACK. Well, yes, I must admit I smoke.

LADY BRACKNELL. I am glad to hear it. A man should always have an occupation of some kind. There are far too many idle men in London as it is. How old are you?

JACK. Twenty-nine.

LADY BRACKNELL. A very good age to be married at. I have always been of opinion that a man who desires to get married should know either everything or nothing. Which do you know?

JACK, *after some hesitation.* I know nothing, Lady Bracknell.

LADY BRACKNELL. I am pleased to hear it. I do not approve of anything that tampers with natural ignorance. Ignorance is like a delicate exotic fruit; touch it and the bloom is gone. The whole theory of modern education is radically unsound. Fortunately in England, at any rate, education produces no effect whatsoever. If it did, it would prove a serious danger to the upper classes, and probably lead to acts of violence in Grosvenor Square. What is your income?

ACT I] THE IMPORTANCE OF BEING EARNEST

JACK. Between seven and eight thousand a year.

LADY BRACKNELL. *Makes a note in her book.* In land, or in investments?

JACK. In investments, chiefly.

LADY BRACKNELL. That is satisfactory. What between the duties expected of one during one's lifetime, and the duties exacted from one after one's death, land has ceased to be either a profit or a pleasure. It gives one position, and prevents one from keeping it up. That's all that can be said about land.

JACK. I have a country house with some land, of course, attached to it, about fifteen hundred acres, I believe; but I don't depend on that for my real income. In fact, as far as I can make out, the poachers are the only people who make anything out of it.

LADY BRACKNELL. A country house! How many bedrooms? Well, that point can be cleared up afterwards. You have a town house, I hope? A girl with a simple, unspoiled nature, like Gwendolen, could hardly be expected to reside in the country.

JACK. Well, I own a house in Belgrave Square, but it is let by the year to Lady Bloxham. Of course, I can get it back whenever I like, at six months' notice.

LADY BRACKNELL. Lady Bloxham? I don't know her.

JACK. Oh, she goes about very little. She is a lady considerably advanced in years.

LADY BRACKNELL. Ah, nowadays that is no guarantee of respectability of character. What number in Belgrave Square?

JACK. 149.

LADY BRACKNELL, *shaking her head.* The unfashionable side. I thought there was something. However, that could easily be altered.

JACK. Do you mean the fashion, or the side?

LADY BRACKNELL, *sternly.* Both, if necessary, I presume. What are your politics?

JACK. Well, I am afraid I really have none. I am a Liberal Unionist.

LADY BRACKNELL. Oh, they count as Tories. They dine with us. Or come in the evening, at any rate. Now to minor matters. Are your parents living?

JACK. I have lost both my parents.

LADY BRACKNELL. Both? . . . That looks like carelessness. Who was your father? He was evidently a man of some wealth. Was he born in what the Radical papers call the purple of commerce, or did he rise from the ranks of the aristocracy?

JACK. I am afraid I really don't know. The fact is, Lady Bracknell, I said I had lost my parents. It would be nearer the truth to say that my parents seem to have lost me. . . . I don't actually know who I am by birth. I was . . . well, I was found.

LADY BRACKNELL. Found!

JACK. The late Mr. Thomas Cardew, an old gentleman of a very charitable and kindly disposition, found me, and gave me the name of Worthing, because he happened to have a first-class ticket for Worthing in his pocket at the time. Worthing is a place in Sussex. It is a seaside resort.

LADY BRACKNELL. Where did the charitable gentleman who had a first-class ticket for this seaside resort find you?

JACK, *gravely*. In a handbag.

LADY BRACKNELL. A handbag?

JACK, *very seriously*. Yes, Lady Bracknell. I was in a handbag—a somewhat large, black leather handbag, with handles to it—an ordinary handbag in fact.

LADY BRACKNELL. In what locality did this Mr. James, or Thomas, Cardew come across this ordinary handbag?

JACK. In the cloakroom at Victoria Station. It was given to him in mistake for his own.

LADY BRACKNELL. The cloakroom at Victoria Station?

JACK. Yes. The Brighton line.

LADY BRACKNELL. The line is immaterial. Mr. Worthing, I confess I feel somewhat bewildered by what you have just told me. To be born, or at any rate, bred in a handbag, whether it had handles or not, seems to me to display a contempt for the ordinary decencies of family life that reminds one of the worst excesses of the French Revolution. And I presume you know what that unfortunate movement led to? As for the particular locality in which the handbag was found, a cloakroom at a railway station might serve to conceal a social indiscretion—has probably, indeed, been used for that purpose before now—but it could hardly be regarded as an assured basis for a recognized position in good society.

JACK. May I ask you then what you would advise me to do? I need hardly say I would do anything in the world to ensure Gwendolen's happiness.

LADY BRACKNELL. I would strongly advise you, Mr. Worthing, to try and acquire some relations as soon as possible, and to make a definite effort to produce at any rate one parent, of either sex, before the season is quite over.

JACK. Well, I don't see how I could possibly manage to do that. I can produce the handbag at any moment. It is in my dressing room at home. I really think that should satisfy you, Lady Bracknell.

LADY BRACKNELL. Me, sir! What has it to do with me? You can hardly imagine that I and Lord Bracknell would dream of allowing our only daughter—a girl brought up with the utmost care—to marry into a cloakroom, and form an alliance with a parcel? Good morning, Mr. Worthing!

LADY BRACKNELL *sweeps out in majestic indignation.*
JACK. Good morning! ALGERNON, *from the other room, strikes up the Wedding March.* JACK *looks perfectly furious, and goes to the door.* For goodness' sake don't play that ghastly tune, Algy! How idiotic you are!

The music stops, and ALGERNON *enters cheerily.*

ALGERNON. Didn't it go off all right, old boy? You don't mean to say Gwendolen refused you? I know it is a way she has. She is always refusing people. I think it is most ill-natured of her.

JACK. Oh, Gwendolen is as right as a trivet. As far as she is concerned, we are engaged. Her mother is perfectly unbearable. Never met such a Gorgon. . . . I don't really know what a Gorgon is like, but I am quite sure that Lady Bracknell is one. In any case, she is a monster, without being a myth, which is rather unfair. . . . I beg your pardon, Algy, I suppose I shouldn't talk about your own aunt in that way before you.

ALGERNON. My dear boy, I love hearing my relations abused. It is the only thing that makes me put up with them at all. Relations are simply a tedious pack of people, who haven't got the remotest knowledge of how to live, nor the smallest instinct about when to die.

JACK. Oh, that is nonsense!
ALGERNON. It isn't!

JACK. Well, I won't argue about the matter. You always want to argue about things.

ALGERNON. That is exactly what things were originally made for.

JACK. Upon my word, if I thought that, I'd shoot myself. . . . *A pause.* You don't think there is any chance of Gwendolen becoming like her mother in about a hundred and fifty years, do you, Algy?

ALGERNON. All women become like their mothers. That is their tragedy. No man does. That's his.

JACK. Is that clever?

ALGERNON. It is perfectly phrased! and quite as true as any observation in civilized life should be.

JACK. I am sick to death of cleverness. Everybody is clever nowadays. You can't go anywhere without meeting clever people. The thing has become an absolute public nuisance. I wish to goodness we had a few fools left.

ALGERNON. We have.

JACK. I should extremely like to meet them. What do they talk about?

ALGERNON. The fools? Oh! about the clever people, of course.

JACK. What fools!

ALGERNON. By the way, did you tell Gwendolen the truth about your being Ernest in town, and Jack in the country?

JACK, *in a very patronizing manner.* My dear fellow, the truth isn't quite the sort of thing one tells to a nice, sweet, refined girl. What extraordinary ideas you have about the way to behave to a woman!

ALGERNON. The only way to behave to a woman is to make love to her, if she is pretty, and to someone else, if she is plain.

JACK. Oh, that is nonsense!

ALGERNON. What about your brother? What about the profligate Ernest?

JACK. Oh, before the end of the week I shall have got rid of him. I'll say he died in Paris of apoplexy. Lots of people die of apoplexy, quite suddenly, don't they?

ALGERNON. Yes, but it's hereditary, my dear fellow. It's a sort of thing that runs in families. You had much better say a severe chill.

JACK. You are sure a severe chill isn't hereditary, or anything of that kind?

ALGERNON. Of course it isn't!

JACK. Very well, then. My poor brother Ernest is carried off suddenly, in Paris, by a severe chill. That gets rid of him.

ALGERNON. But I thought you said that . . . Miss Cardew was a little too much interested in your poor brother Ernest? Won't she feel his loss a good deal?

JACK. Oh, that is all right. Cecily is not a silly romantic girl, I am glad to say. She has got a capital appetite, goes long walks, and pays no attention at all to her lessons.

ALGERNON. I would rather like to see Cecily.

JACK. I will take very good care you never do. She is excessively pretty, and she is only just eighteen.

ALGERNON. Have you told Gwendolen yet that you have an excessively pretty ward who is only just eighteen?

JACK. Oh! one doesn't blurt these things out to people. Cecily and Gwendolen are perfectly certain to be extremely great friends. I'll bet you anything you like that half an hour after they have met, they will be calling each other sister.

ALGERNON. Women only do that when they have called each other a lot of other things first. Now, my dear boy, if we want to get a good table at Willis's, we really must go and dress. Do you know it is nearly seven?

JACK, *irritably*. Oh! it always is nearly seven.

ALGERNON. Well, I'm hungry.

JACK. I never knew you when you weren't. . . .

ALGERNON. What shall we do after dinner? Go to a theater?

JACK. Oh, no! I loathe listening.

ALGERNON. Well, let us go to the club?

JACK. Oh, no! I hate talking.

ALGERNON. Well, we might trot round to the Empire at ten?

JACK. Oh, no! I can't bear looking at things. It is so silly.

ALGERNON. Well, what shall we do?

JACK. Nothing!

ALGERNON. It is awfully hard work doing nothing. However, I don't mind hard work where there is no definite object of any kind.

Enter LANE.

LANE. Miss Fairfax.

Enter GWENDOLEN. LANE *goes out.*

ALGERNON. Gwendolen, upon my word!

GWENDOLEN. Algy, kindly turn your back. I have something very particular to say to Mr. Worthing.

ALGERNON. Really, Gwendolen, I don't think I can allow this at all.

GWENDOLEN. Algy, you always adopt a strictly immoral attitude towards life. You are not quite old enough to do that.

ALGERNON *retires to the fireplace.*

JACK. My own darling!

GWENDOLEN. Ernest, we may never be married. From the expression on mamma's face I fear we never shall. Few parents nowadays pay any regard to what their children say to them. The old-fashioned respect for the young is fast dying out. Whatever influence I ever had over mamma, I lost at the age of three. But although she may prevent us from becoming man and wife, and I may marry someone else, and marry often, nothing that she can possibly do can alter my eternal devotion to you.

JACK. Dear Gwendolen!

GWENDOLEN. The story of your romantic origin, as related to me by mamma, with unpleasing comments, has naturally stirred the deeper fibers of my nature. Your Christian name has an irresistible fascination. The simplicity of your character makes you exquisitely incomprehensible to me. Your town address at the Albany I have. What is your address in the country?

JACK. The Manor House, Woolton, Hertfordshire.

ALGERNON, *who has been carefully listening, smiles to himself, and writes the address on his shirt cuff. Then picks up the Railway Guide.*

GWENDOLEN. There is a good postal service, I suppose? It may be necessary to do something desperate. That of course will require serious consideration. I will communicate with you daily.

JACK. My own one!

GWENDOLEN. How long do you remain in town?

JACK. Till Monday.

GWENDOLEN. Good! Algy, you may turn round now.

ALGERNON. Thanks, I've turned round already.

GWENDOLEN. You may also ring the bell.

JACK. You will let me see you to your carriage, my own darling?

GWENDOLEN. Certainly.

JACK, *to* LANE, *who now enters.* I will see Miss Fairfax out.

LANE. Yes, sir.   JACK *and* GWENDOLEN *go off.*

LANE *presents several letters on a salver to* ALGERNON. *It is to be surmised that they are bills, as* ALGERNON, *after looking at the envelopes, tears them up.*

ALGERNON. A glass of sherry, Lane.

LANE. Yes, sir.

ALGERNON. Tomorrow, Lane, I'm going Bunburying.

LANE. Yes, sir.

ALGERNON. I shall probably not be back till Monday. You can put up my dress clothes, my smoking jacket, and all the Bunbury suits . . .

LANE. Yes, sir.   *Handing sherry.*

ALGERNON. I hope tomorrow will be a fine day, Lane.

LANE. It never is, sir.

ALGERNON. Lane, you're a perfect pessimist.

LANE. I do my best to give satisfaction, sir.

Enter JACK. LANE *goes off.*

JACK. There's a sensible, intellectual girl! the only girl I ever cared for in my life. ALGERNON *is laughing immoderately.* What on earth are you so amused at?

ALGERNON. Oh, I'm a little anxious about poor Bunbury, that is all.

JACK. If you don't take care, your friend Bunbury will get you into a serious scrape some day.

ALGERNON. I love scrapes. They are the only things that are never serious.

JACK. Oh, that's nonsense, Algy. You never talk anything but nonsense.

ALGERNON. Nobody ever does.

JACK *looks indignantly at him, and leaves the room.* ALGERNON *lights a cigarette, reads his shirt cuff, and smiles.*

Act II

Garden at the Manor House. A flight of gray stone steps leads up to the house. The garden, an old-fashioned one, full of roses. Time of year, July. Basket chairs, and a table covered with books, are set under a large yew tree.

> MISS PRISM *discovered seated at the table.* CECILY
> *is at the back watering flowers.*

MISS PRISM, *calling.* Cecily, Cecily! Surely such a utilitarian occupation as the watering of flowers is rather Moulton's duty than yours? Especially at a moment when intellectual pleasures await you. Your German grammar is on the table. Pray open it at page fifteen. We will repeat yesterday's lesson.

CECILY, *coming over very slowly.* But I don't like German. It isn't at all a becoming language. I know perfectly well that I look quite plain after my German lesson.

MISS PRISM. Child, you know how anxious your guardian is that you should improve yourself in every way. He laid particular stress on your German, as he was leaving for town yesterday. Indeed, he always lays stress on your German when he is leaving for town.

CECILY. Dear Uncle Jack is so very serious! Sometimes he is so serious that I think he cannot be quite well.

MISS PRISM, *drawing herself up.* Your guardian enjoys the best of health, and his gravity of demeanor is especially to be commended in one so comparatively young as he is. I know no one who has a higher sense of duty and responsibility.

CECILY. I suppose that is why he often looks a little bored when we three are together.

MISS PRISM. Cecily! I am surprised at you. Mr. Worthing has many troubles in his life. Idle merriment and triviality would be out of place in his conversation. You must remember his constant anxiety about that unfortunate young man, his brother.

CECILY. I wish Uncle Jack would allow that unfortunate young man, his brother, to come down here sometimes. We might have a good influence over him, Miss Prism. I am sure you certainly would. You know German, and geology, and things of that kind influence a man very much.   CECILY *begins to write in her diary.*

MISS PRISM, *shaking her head.* I do not think that even I could produce any effect on a character that according to his own brother's admission is irretrievably weak and vacillating. Indeed I am not sure that I would desire to reclaim him. I am not in favor of this modern mania for turning bad people into good people at a moment's notice. As a man sows so let him reap. You must put away your diary, Cecily. I really don't see why you should keep a diary at all.

CECILY. I keep a diary in order to enter the wonderful secrets of my life. If I didn't write them down I should probably forget all about them.

MISS PRISM. Memory, my dear Cecily, is the diary that we all carry about with us.

CECILY. Yes, but it usually chronicles the things that have never happened, and couldn't possibly have happened. I believe that Memory is responsible for nearly all the three-volume novels that Mudie sends us.

MISSS PRISM. Do not speak slightingly of the three-volume novel, Cecily. I wrote one myself in earlier days.

CECILY. Did you really, Miss Prism? How wonderfully clever you are! I hope it did not end happily? I don't like novels that end happily. They depress me so much.

MISS PRISM. The good ended happily, and the bad unhappily. That is what Fiction means.

CECILY. I suppose so. But it seems very unfair. And was your novel ever published?

MISS PRISM. Alas! no. The manuscript unfortunately was abandoned. I use the word in the sense of lost or mislaid. To your work, child, these speculations are profitless.

CECILY, *smiling*. But I see dear Dr. Chasuble coming up through the garden.

MISS PRISM, *rising and advancing*. Dr. Chasuble! This is indeed a pleasure.

Enter CANON CHASUBLE.

CHASUBLE. And how are we this morning? Miss Prism, you are, I trust, well?

CECILY. Miss Prism has just been complaining of a slight headache. I think it would do her so much good to have a short stroll with you in the Park, Dr. Chasuble.

MISS PRISM. Cecily, I have not mentioned anything about a headache.

CECILY. No, dear Miss Prism, I know that, but I felt instinctively that you had a headache. Indeed I was thinking about that, and not about my German lesson, when the Rector came in.

CHASUBLE. I hope, Cecily, you are not inattentive.

CECILY. Oh, I am afraid I am.

CHASUBLE. That is strange. Were I fortunate enough to be Miss Prism's pupil, I would hang upon her lips. MISS PRISM *glares.* I spoke metaphorically.—My metaphor was drawn from bees. Ahem! Mr. Worthing, I suppose, has not returned from town yet?

MISS PRISM. We do not expect him till Monday afternoon.

CHASUBLE. Ah yes, he usually likes to spend his Sunday in London. He is not one of those whose sole aim is enjoyment, as, by all accounts, that unfortunate young man his brother seems to be. But I must not disturb Egeria and her pupil any longer.

MISS PRISM. Egeria? My name is Laetitia, Doctor.

CHASUBLE, *bowing.* A classical allusion merely, drawn from the Pagan authors. I shall see you both no doubt at Evensong?

MISS PRISM. I think, dear Doctor, I will have a stroll with you. I find I have a headache after all, and a walk might do it good.

CHASUBLE. With pleasure, Miss Prism, with pleasure. We might go as far as the schools and back.

MISS PRISM. That would be delightful. Cecily, you will read your Political Economy in my absence. The chapter on the Fall of the Rupee you may omit. It is somewhat too sensational. Even these metallic problems have their melodramatic side. *Goes down the garden with* DR. CHASUBLE.

CECILY, *picks up books and throws them back on table.* Horrid Political Economy! Horrid Geography! Horrid, horrid German!

Enter MERRIMAN *with a card on a salver.*

MERRIMAN. Mr. Ernest Worthing has just driven over from the station. He has brought his luggage with him.

CECILY. *Takes the card and reads it.* "Mr. Ernest Worthing, B. 4, The Albany, W." Uncle Jack's brother! Did you tell him Mr. Worthing was in town?

MERRIMAN. Yes, Miss. He seemed very much disappointed. I mentioned that you and Miss Prism were in the garden. He said he was anxious to speak to you privately for a moment.

CECILY. Ask Mr. Ernest Worthing to come here. I suppose you had better talk to the housekeeper about a room for him.

MERRIMAN. Yes, Miss. *MERRIMAN goes off.*

CECILY. I have never met any really wicked person before. I feel rather frightened. I am so afraid he will look just like everyone else. He does!

Enter ALGERNON, very gay and debonair.

ALGERNON, *raising his hat*. You are my little cousin Cecily, I'm sure.

CECILY. You are under some strange mistake. I am not little. In fact, I believe I am more than usually tall for my age. ALGERNON *is rather taken aback*. But I am your cousin Cecily. You, I see from your card, are Uncle Jack's brother, my cousin Ernest, my wicked cousin Ernest.

ALGERNON. Oh, I am not really wicked at all, cousin Cecily. You mustn't think that I am wicked.

CECILY. If you are not, then you have certainly been deceiving us all in a very inexcusable manner. I hope you have not been leading a double life, pretending to be wicked and being really good all the time. That would be hypocrisy.

ALGERNON. *Looks at her in amazement.* Oh! Of course I have been rather reckless.

CECILY. I am glad to hear it.

ALGERNON. In fact, now you mention the subject, I have been very bad in my own small way.

CECILY. I don't think you should be so proud of that, though I am sure it must have been very pleasant.

ALGERNON. It is much pleasanter being here with you.

CECILY. I can't understand how you are here at all. Uncle Jack won't be back till Monday afternoon.

ALGERNON. That is a great disappointment. I am obliged to go up by the first train on Monday morning. I have a business appointment that I am anxious . . . to miss.

CECILY. Couldn't you miss it anywhere but in London?

ALGERNON. No: the appointment is in London.

CECILY. Well, I know of course, how important it is not to keep a business engagement, if one wants to retain any sense of the beauty of life, but still I think you had better wait till Uncle Jack arrives. I know he wants to speak to you about your emigrating.

ALGERNON. About my what?

CECILY. Your emigrating. He has gone up to buy your outfit.

ALGERNON. I certainly wouldn't let Jack buy my outfit. He has no taste in neckties at all.

CECILY. I don't think you will require neckties. Uncle Jack is sending you to Australia.

ALGERNON. Australia! I'd sooner die.

CECILY. Well, he said at dinner on Wednesday night, that you would have to chose between this world, the next world, and Australia.

ALGERNON. Oh, well! The accounts I have received of Australia and the next world are not particularly encouraging. This world is good enough for me, cousin Cecily.

CECILY. Yes, but are you good enough for it?

ALGERNON. I'm afraid I'm not that. That is why I want you to reform me. You might make that your mission, if you don't mind, cousin Cecily.

CECILY. I'm afraid I've no time, this afternoon.

ALGERNON. Well, would you mind my reforming myself this afternoon?

CECILY. It is rather Quixotic of you. But I think you should try.

ALGERNON. I will. I feel better already.

CECILY. You are looking a little worse.

ALGERNON. That is because I am hungry.

CECILY. How thoughtless of me. I should have remembered that when one is going to lead an entirely new life, one requires regular and wholesome meals. Won't you come in?

ALGERNON. Thank you. Might I have a buttonhole first? I never have any appetite unless I have a buttonhole first.

CECILY. A Maréchal Niel? *Picks up scissors.*

ALGERNON. No, I'd sooner have a pink rose.

CECILY. Why? *Cuts a flower.*

ALGERNON. Because you are like a pink rose, cousin Cecily.

CECILY. I don't think it can be right for you to talk to me like that. Miss Prism never says such things to me.

ALGERNON. Then Miss Prism is a shortsighted old lady. CECILY *puts the rose in his buttonhole.* You are the prettiest girl I ever saw.

CECILY. Miss Prism says that all good looks are a snare.

ALGERNON. They are a snare that every sensible man would like to be caught in.

CECILY. Oh, I don't think I would care to catch a sensible man. I shouldn't know what to talk to him about.

They pass into the house. MISS PRISM *and* DR. CHASUBLE *return.*

MISS PRISM. You are too much alone, dear Dr. Chasuble. You should get married. A misanthrope I can understand—a womanthrope, never!

CHASUBLE, *with a scholar's shudder.* Believe me, I do not deserve so neologistic a phrase. The precept as well as the practice of the Primitive Church was distinctly against matrimony.

MISS PRISM, *sententiously.* That is obviously the reason why the Primitive Church has not lasted up to the present day. And you do not seem to realize, dear Doctor, that by persistently remaining single, a man converts himself into a permanent public temptation. Men should be more careful; this very celibacy leads weaker vessels astray.

CHASUBLE. But is a man not equally attractive when married?

MISS PRISM. No married man is ever attractive except to his wife.

CHASUBLE. And often, I've been told, not even to her.

MISS PRISM. That depends on the intellectual sympathies of the woman. Maturity can always be depended on. Ripeness can be trusted. Young women are green. DR. CHASUBLE *starts.* I spoke horticulturally. My metaphor was drawn from fruits. But where is Cecily?

CHASUBLE. Perhaps she followed us to the schools.

Enter JACK *slowly from the back of the garden. He is dressed in the deepest mourning, with crape hatband and black gloves.*

MISS PRISM. Mr. Worthing!

CHASUBLE. Mr. Worthing?

MISS PRISM. This is indeed a surprise. We did not look for you till Monday afternoon.

JACK. *Shakes* MISS PRISM'S *hand in a tragic manner.* I have returned sooner than I expected. Dr. Chasuble, I hope you are well?

CHASUBLE. Dear Mr. Worthing, I trust this garb of woe does not betoken some terrible calamity?

JACK. My brother.

MISS PRISM. More shameful debts and extravagance?

CHASUBLE. Still leading his life of pleasure?

JACK, *shaking his head.* Dead!

CHASUBLE. Your brother Ernest dead?

JACK. Quite dead.

MISS PRISM. What a lesson for him! I trust he will profit by it.

CHASUBLE. Mr. Worthing, I offer you my sincere condolence. You have at least the consolation of knowing that you were always the most generous and forgiving of brothers.

JACK. Poor Ernest! He had many faults, but it is a sad, sad blow.

CHASUBLE. Very sad indeed. Were you with him at the end?

JACK. No. He died abroad; in Paris, in fact. I had a telegram last night from the manager of the Grand Hotel.

CHASUBLE. Was the cause of death mentioned?

JACK. A severe chill, it seems.

MISS PRISM. As a man sows, so shall he reap.

CHASUBLE, *raising his hand.* Charity, dear Miss Prism, charity! None of us are perfect. I myself am peculiarly susceptible to draughts. Will the interment take place here?

JACK. No. He seemed to have expressed a desire to be buried in Paris.

CHASUBLE. In Paris! *Shakes his head.* I fear that hardly points to any very serious state of mind at the last. You would no doubt wish me to make some slight allusion to this tragic domestic affliction next Sunday. JACK *presses his hand convulsively.* My sermon on the meaning of the manna in the wilderness can be adapted to almost any occasion, joyful, or, as in the present case, distressing. *All sigh.* I have preached it at harvest celebrations, christenings, confirmations, on days of humiliation and festal days. The last time I delivered it was in the Cathedral, as a charity sermon on behalf of the Society for the Prevention of Discontent among the Upper Orders. The Bishop, who was present, was much struck by some of the analogies I drew.

JACK. Ah! that reminds me, you mentioned christenings, I think, Dr. Chasuble? I suppose you know how to christen all right? DR.

ACT II] THE IMPORTANCE OF BEING EARNEST 179

CHASUBLE *looks astounded.* I mean, of course, you are continually christening, aren't you?

MISS PRISM. It is, I regret to say, one of the Rector's most constant duties in this parish. I have often spoken to the poorer classes on the subject. But they don't seem to know what thrift is.

CHASUBLE. But is there any particular infant in whom you are interested, Mr. Worthing? Your brother was, I believe, unmarried, was he not?

JACK. Oh yes.

MISS PRISM, *bitterly.* People who live entirely for pleasure usually are.

JACK. But it is not for any child, dear Doctor. I am very fond of children. No! the fact is, I would like to be christened myself, this afternoon, if you have nothing better to do.

CHASUBLE. But surely, Mr. Worthing, you have been christened already?

JACK. I don't remember anything about it.

CHASUBLE. But have you any grave doubts on the subject?

JACK. I certainly intend to have. Of course I don't know if the thing would bother you in any way, or if you think I am a little too old now.

CHASUBLE. Not at all. The sprinkling, and, indeed, the immersion of adults is a perfectly canonical practice.

JACK. Immersion!

CHASUBLE. You need have no apprehensions. Sprinkling is all that is necessary, or indeed I think advisable. Our weather is so changeable. At what hour would you wish the ceremony performed?

JACK. Oh, I might trot round about five if that would suit you.

CHASUBLE. Perfectly, perfectly! In fact I have two similar ceremonies to perform at that time. A case of twins that occurred recently in one of the outlying cottages on your own estate. Poor Jenkins the carter, a most hard-working man.

JACK. Oh! I don't see much fun in being christened along with other babies. It would be childish. Would half-past five do?

CHASUBLE. Admirably! Admirably! *Takes out watch.* And now, dear Mr. Worthing, I will not intrude any longer into a house of sorrow. I would merely beg you not to be too much bowed down by grief. What seem to us bitter trials are often blessings in disguise.

MISS PRISM. This seems to me a blessing of an extremely obvious kind.

Enter CECILY *from the house.*

CECILY. Uncle Jack! Oh, I am pleased to see you back. But what horrid clothes you have got on! Do go and change them.

MISS PRISM. Cecily!

CHASUBLE. My child! my child!

CECILY *goes towards* JACK; *he kisses her brow in a melancholy manner.*

CECILY. What is the matter, Uncle Jack? Do look happy! You look as if you had toothache, and I have got such a surprise for you. Who do you think is in the dining room? Your brother!

JACK. Who?

CECILY. Your brother Ernest. He arrived about half an hour ago.

JACK. What nonsense! I haven't got a brother.

CECILY. Oh, don't say that. However badly he may have behaved to you in the past he is still your brother. You couldn't be so heartless as to disown him. I'll tell him to come out. And you will shake hands with him, won't you, Uncle Jack? *Runs back into the house.*

CHASUBLE. These are very joyful tidings.

MISS PRISM. After we had all been resigned to his loss, his sudden return seems to me peculiarly distressing.

JACK. My brother is in the dining room? I don't know what it all means. I think it is perfectly absurd.

Enter ALGERNON *and* CECILY *hand in hand. They come slowly up to* JACK.

JACK. Good heavens! *Motions* ALGERNON *away.*

ALGERNON. Brother John, I have come down from town to tell you that I am very sorry for all the trouble I have given you, and that I intend to lead a better life in the future.

JACK *glares at him and does not take his hand.*

CECILY. Uncle Jack, you are not going to refuse your own brother's hand?

JACK. Nothing will induce me to take his hand. I think his coming down here disgraceful. He knows perfectly well why.

CECILY. Uncle Jack, do be nice. There is some good in everyone.

Ernest has just been telling me about his poor invalid friend Mr. Bunbury whom he goes to visit so often. And surely there must be much good in one who is kind to an invalid, and leaves the pleasures of London to sit by a bed of pain.

JACK. Oh! he has been talking about Bunbury, has he?

CECILY. Yes, he has told me all about poor Mr. Bunbury, and his terrible state of health.

JACK. Bunbury! Well, I won't have him talk to you about Bunbury or about anything else. It is enough to drive one perfectly frantic.

ALGERNON. Of course I admit that the faults were all on my side. But I must say that I think that Brother John's coldness to me is peculiarly painful. I expected a more enthusiastic welcome, especially considering it is the first time I have come here.

CECILY. Uncle Jack, if you don't shake hands with Ernest I will never forgive you.

JACK. Never forgive me?

CECILY. Never, never, never!

JACK. Well, this is the last time I shall ever do it.

Shakes hands with ALGERNON *and glares.*

CHASUBLE. It's pleasant, is it not, to see so perfect a reconciliation? I think we might leave the two brothers together.

MISS PRISM. Cecily, you will come with us.

CECILY. Certainly, Miss Prism. My little task of reconciliation is over.

CHASUBLE. You have done a beautiful action today, dear child.

MISS PRISM. We must not be premature in our judgments.

CECILY. I feel very happy.

They all go off except JACK *and* ALGERNON.

JACK. You young scoundrel, Algy, you must get out of this place as soon as possible. I don't allow any Bunburying here.

Enter MERRIMAN.

MERRIMAN. I have put Mr. Ernest's things in the room next to yours, sir. I suppose that is all right?

JACK. What?

MERRIMAN. Mr. Ernest's luggage, sir. I have unpacked it and put it in the room next to your own.

JACK. His luggage?

MERRIMAN. Yes, sir. Three portmanteaus, a dressing case, two hat-boxes, and a large luncheon basket.

ALGERNON. I am afraid I can't stay more than a week this time.

JACK. Merriman, order the dogcart at once. Mr. Ernest has been suddenly called back to town.

MERRIMAN. Yes, sir. *Goes back into the house.*

ALGERNON. What a fearful liar you are, Jack! I have not been called back to town at all.

JACK. Yes, you have.

ALGERNON. I haven't heard anyone call me.

JACK. Your duty as a gentleman calls you back.

ALGERNON. My duty as a gentleman has never interfered with my pleasures in the smallest degree.

JACK. I can quite understand that.

ALGERNON. Well, Cecily is a darling.

JACK. You are not to talk of Miss Cardew like that. I don't like it.

ALGERNON. Well, I don't like your clothes. You look perfectly ridiculous in them. Why on earth don't you go up and change? It is perfectly childish to be in deep mourning for a man who is actually staying for a whole week with you in your house as a guest. I call it grotesque.

JACK. You are certainly not staying with me for a whole week as a guest or anything else. You have got to leave . . . by the four-five train.

ALGERNON. I certainly won't leave you so long as you are in mourning. It would be most unfriendly. If I were in mourning you would stay with me, I suppose. I should think it very unkind if you didn't.

JACK. Well, will you go if I change my clothes?

ALGERNON. Yes, if you are not too long. I never saw anybody take so long to dress, and with such little result.

JACK. Well, at any rate, that is better than being always overdressed as you are.

ALGERNON. If I am occasionally a little overdressed, I make up for it by being always immensely overeducated.

JACK. Your vanity is ridiculous, your conduct an outrage, and your presence in my garden utterly absurd. However, you have got to catch the four-five, and I hope you will have a pleasant journey back to

ACT II] THE IMPORTANCE OF BEING EARNEST 183

town. This Bunburying, as you call it, has not been a great success for you. *Goes into the house.*

ALGERNON. I think it has been a great success. I'm in love with Cecily, and that is everything.

Enter CECILY *at the back of the garden. She picks up the can and begins to water the flowers.*

But I must see her before I go, and make arrangements for another Bunbury. Ah, there she is.

CECILY. Oh, I merely came back to water the roses. I thought you were with Uncle Jack.

ALGERNON. He's gone to order the dogcart for me.

CECILY. Oh, is he going to take you for a nice drive?

ALGERNON. He's going to send me away.

CECILY. Then have we got to part?

ALGERNON. I am afraid so. It's a very painful parting.

CECILY. It is always painful to part from people whom one has known for a very brief space of time. The absence of old friends one can endure with equanimity. But even a momentary separation from anyone to whom one has just been introduced is almost unbearable.

ALGERNON. Thank you.

Enter MERRIMAN.

MERRIMAN. The dogcart is at the door, sir.

ALGERNON *looks appealingly at* CECILY.

CECILY. It can wait, Merriman . . . for . . . five minutes.

MERRIMAN. Yes, Miss. *Exit* MERRIMAN.

ALGERNON. I hope, Cecily, I shall not offend you if I state quite frankly and openly that you seem to me to be in every way the visible personification of absolute perfection.

CECILY. I think your frankness does you great credit, Ernest. If you will allow me I will copy your remarks into my diary.

Goes over to table and begins writing in diary.

ALGERNON. Do you really keep a diary? I'd give anything to look at it. May I?

CECILY. Oh, no! *Puts her hand over it.* You see, it is simply a very young girl's record of her own thoughts and impressions and consequently meant for publication. When it appears in volume form I hope you will order a copy. But pray, Ernest, don't stop. I delight in taking down from dictation. I have reached "absolute perfection." You can go on. I am quite ready for more.

ALGERNON, *somewhat taken aback*. Ahem! Ahem!

CECILY. Oh, don't cough, Ernest. When one is dictating one should speak fluently and not cough. Besides, I don't know how to spell a cough. *Writes as* ALGERNON *speaks*.

ALGERNON, *speaking very rapidly*. Cecily, ever since I first looked upon your wonderful and incomparable beauty, I have dared to love you wildly, passionately, devotedly, hopelessly.

CECILY. I don't think that you should tell me that you love me wildly, passionately, devotedly, hopelessly. Hopelessly doesn't seem to make much sense, does it?

ALGERNON. Cecily!

Enter MERRIMAN.

MERRIMAN. The dogcart is waiting, sir.

ALGERNON. Tell it to come round next week, at the same hour.

MERRIMAN. *Looks at* CECILY, *who makes no sign*. Yes, sir.

MERRIMAN *retires*.

CECILY. Uncle Jack would be very much annoyed if he knew you were staying on till next week, at the same hour.

ALGERNON. Oh, I don't care about Jack. I don't care for anybody in the whole world but you. I love you, Cecily. You will marry me, won't you?

CECILY. You silly boy! Of course! Why, we have been engaged for the last three months.

ALGERNON. For the last three months?

CECILY. Yes, it will be exactly three months on Thursday.

ALGERNON. But how did we become engaged?

CECILY. Well, ever since dear Uncle Jack first confessed to us that he had a younger brother who was very wicked and bad, you of course have formed the chief topic of conversation between myself and Miss Prism. And of course a man who is much talked about is always very attractive. One feels there must be something in him, after all. I daresay it was foolish of me, but I fell in love with you, Ernest.

ALGERNON. Darling! And when was the engagement actually settled?

CECILY. On the 14th of February last. Worn out by your entire ignorance of my existence, I determined to end the matter one way or the other, and after a long struggle with myself I accepted you under this dear old tree here. The next day I bought this little ring in your name, and this is the little bangle with the true lovers' knot I promised you always to wear.

ALGERNON. Did I give you this? It's very pretty, isn't it?

CECILY. Yes, you've wonderfully good taste, Ernest. It's the excuse I've always given for your leading such a bad life. And this is the box in which I keep all your dear letters.

Kneels at table, opens box, and produces letters tied up with blue ribbon.

ALGERNON. My letters! But my own sweet Cecily, I have never written you any letters.

CECILY. You need hardly remind me of that, Ernest. I remember only too well that I was forced to write your letters for you. I wrote always three times a week, and sometimes oftener.

ALGERNON. Oh, do let me read them, Cecily?

CECILY. Oh, I couldn't possibly. They would make you far too conceited. *Replaces box.* The three you wrote me after I had broken off the engagement are so beautiful, and so badly spelled, that even now I can hardly read them without crying a little.

ALGERNON. But was our engagement ever broken off?

CECILY. Of course it was. On the 22nd of last March. You can see the entry if you like. *Shows diary.* "To-day I broke off my engagement with Ernest. I feel it is better to do so. The weather still continues charming."

ALGERNON. But why on earth did you break it off? What had I done? I had done nothing at all. Cecily, I am very much hurt indeed to hear you broke it off. Particularly when the weather was so charming.

CECILY. It would hardly have been a really serious engagement if it hadn't been broken off at least once. But I forgave you before the week was out.

ALGERNON, *crossing to her, and kneeling.* What a perfect angel you are, Cecily!

CECILY. You dear romantic boy! *He kisses her, she puts her fingers through his hair.* I hope your hair curls naturally, does it?

ALGERNON. Yes, darling, with a little help from others.

CECILY. I am so glad.

ALGERNON. You'll never break off our engagement again, Cecily?

CECILY. I don't think I could break it off now that I have actually met you. Besides, of course, there is the question of your name.

ALGERNON. Yes, of course. *Nervously.*

CECILY. You must not laugh at me, darling, but it had always been a girlish dream of mine to love someone whose name was Ernest. ALGERNON *rises,* CECILY *also.* There is something in that name that seems to inspire absolute confidence. I pity any poor married woman whose husband is not called Ernest.

ALGERNON. But, my dear child, do you mean to say you could not love me if I had some other name?

CECILY. But what name?

ALGERNON. Oh, any name you like—Algernon—for instance . . .

CECILY. But I don't like the name of Algernon.

ALGERNON. Well, my own dear, sweet, loving little darling, I really can't see why you should object to the name of Algernon. It is not at all a bad name. In fact, it is rather an aristocratic name. Half of the chaps who get into the Bankruptcy Court are called Algernon. But seriously, Cecily . . . *Moving to her.* . . . . if my name was Algy, couldn't you love me?

CECILY, *rising.* I might respect you, Ernest, I might admire your character, but I fear that I should not be able to give you my undivided attention.

ALGERNON. Ahem! Cecily! *Picking up hat.* Your Rector here is, I suppose, thoroughly experienced in the practice of all the rites and ceremonials of the Church?

CECILY. Oh, yes. Dr. Chasuble is a most learned man. He has never written a single book, so you can imagine how much he knows.

ALGERNON. I must see him at once on a most important christening —I mean on most important business.

CECILY. Oh!

ALGERNON. I shan't be away more than half an hour.

CECILY. Considering that we have been engaged since February the 14th, and that I only met you today for the first time, I think it is rather hard that you should leave me for so long a period as half an hour. Couldn't you make it twenty minutes?

ALGERNON. I'll be back in no time.

Kisses her and rushes down the garden.

CECILY. What an impetuous boy he is! I like his hair so much. I must enter his proposal in my diary.

Enter MERRIMAN.

MERRIMAN. A Miss Fairfax has just called to see Mr. Worthing. On very important business Miss Fairfax states.

CECILY. Isn't Mr. Worthing in his library?

MERRIMAN. Mr. Worthing went over in the direction of the Rectory some time ago.

CECILY. Pray ask the lady to come out here; Mr. Worthing is sure to be back soon. And you can bring tea.

MERRIMAN. Yes, Miss. *Goes out.*

CECILY. Miss Fairfax! I suppose one of the many good elderly women who are associated with Uncle Jack in some of his philanthropic work in London. I don't quite like women who are interested in philanthropic work. I think it is so forward of them.

Enter MERRIMAN.

MERRIMAN. Miss Fairfax.

Enter GWENDOLEN.

Exit MERRIMAN.

CECILY, *advancing to meet her.* Pray let me introduce myself to you. My name is Cecily Cardew.

GWENDOLEN. Cecily Cardew? *Moving to her and shaking hands.* What a very sweet name! Something tells me that we are going to be great friends. I like you already more than I can say. My first impressions of people are never wrong.

CECILY. How nice of you to like me so much after we have known each other such a comparatively short time. Pray sit down.

GWENDOLEN, *still standing up.* I may call you Cecily, may I not?

CECILY. With pleasure!

GWENDOLEN. And you will always call me Gwendolen, won't you?

CECILY. If you wish.

GWENDOLEN. Then that is all quite settled, is it not?

CECILY. I hope so. *A pause. They both sit down together.*

GWENDOLEN. Perhaps this might be a favorable opportunity for my mentioning who I am. My father is Lord Bracknell. You have never heard of papa, I suppose?

CECILY. I don't think so.

GWENDOLEN. Outside of the family circle, papa, I am glad to say, is entirely unknown. I think that is quite as it should be. The home seems to me to be the proper sphere for the man. And certainly once a man begins to neglect his domestic duties he becomes painfully effeminate, does he not? And I don't like that. It makes men so very attractive. Cecily, mamma, whose views on education are remarkably strict, has brought me up to be extremely short-sighted; it is part of her system; so do you mind my looking at you through my glasses?

CECILY. Oh! not at all, Gwendolen. I am very fond of being looked at.

GWENDOLEN, *after examining* CECILY *carefully through a lorgnette.* You are here on a short visit I suppose.

CECILY. Oh no! I live here.

GWENDOLEN, *severely.* Really? Your mother, no doubt, or some female relative of advanced years, resides here also?

CECILY. Oh no! I have no mother, nor, in fact, any relations.

GWENDOLEN. Indeed?

CECILY. My dear guardian, with the assistance of Miss Prism, has the arduous task of looking after me.

GWENDOLEN. Your guardian?

CECILY. Yes, I am Mr. Worthing's ward.

GWENDOLEN. Oh! It is strange he never mentioned to me that he had a ward. How secretive of him! He grows more interesting hourly. I am not sure, however, that the news inspires me with feelings of unmixed delight. *Rising and going to her.* I am very fond of you, Cecily; I have liked you ever since I met you! But I am bound to state that now that I know that you are Mr. Worthing's ward, I cannot help expressing a wish you were—well just a little older than you seem to be—and not quite so very alluring in appearance. In fact, if I may speak candidly——

CECILY. Pray do! I think that whenever one has anything unpleasant to say, one should always be quite candid.

GWENDOLEN. Well, to speak with perfect candor, Cecily. I wish that you were fully forty-two, and more than usually plain for your age. Ernest has a strong upright nature. He is the very soul of truth and honor. Disloyalty would be as impossible to him as deception. But even men of the noblest possible moral character are extremely susceptible to the influence of the physical charms of others. Modern, no less than Ancient History, supplies us with many most painful examples of what I refer to. If it were not so, indeed, History would be quite unreadable.

CECILY. I beg your pardon, Gwendolen, did you say Ernest?

GWENDOLEN. Yes.

CECILY. Oh, but it is not Mr. Ernest Worthing who is my guardian. It is his brother—his elder brother.

GWENDOLEN, *sitting down again*. Ernest never mentioned to me that he had a brother.

CECILY. I am sorry to say they have not been on good terms for a long time.

GWENDOLEN. Ah! that accounts for it. And now that I think of it I have never heard any man mention his brother. The subject seems distasteful to most men. Cecily, you have lifted a load from my mind. I was growing almost anxious. It would have been terrible if any cloud had come across a friendship like ours, would it not? Of course you are quite, quite sure that it is not Mr. Ernest Worthing who is your guardian?

CECILY. Quite sure. *A pause*. In fact, I am going to be his.

GWENDOLEN, *inquiringly*. I beg your pardon?

CECILY, *rather shy and confidingly*. Dearest Gwendolen, there is no reason why I should make a secret of it to you. Our little county newspaper is sure to chronicle the fact next week. Mr. Ernest Worthing and I are engaged to be married.

GWENDOLEN, *quite politely, rising*. My darling Cecily, I think there must be some slight error. Mr. Ernest Worthing is engaged to me. The announcement will appear in the *Morning Post* on Saturday at the latest.

CECILY, *very politely, rising*. I am afraid you must be under some misconception. Ernest proposed to me exactly ten minutes ago.

Shows diary.

GWENDOLEN. *Examines diary through her lorgnette carefully*. It is certainly very curious, for he asked me to be his wife yesterday afternoon at 5.30. If you would care to verify the incident, pray do so. *Produces diary of her own*. I never travel without my diary. One should always have something sensational to read in the train. I am so sorry, dear Cecily, if it is any disappointment to you, but I am afraid *I* have the prior claim.

CECILY. It would distress me more than I can tell you, dear Gwendolen, if it caused you any mental or physical anguish, but I feel bound to point out that since Ernest proposed to you he clearly has changed his mind.

GWENDOLEN, *meditatively.* If the poor fellow has been entrapped into any foolish promise I shall consider it my duty to rescue him at once, and with a firm hand.

CECILY, *thoughtfully and sadly.* Whatever unfortunate entanglement my dear boy may have got into, I will never reproach him with it after we are married.

GWENDOLEN. Do you allude to me, Miss Cardew, as an entanglement? You are presumptuous. On an occasion of this kind it becomes more than a moral duty to speak one's mind. It becomes a pleasure.

CECILY. Do you suggest, Miss Fairfax, that I entrapped Ernest into an engagement? How dare you? This is no time for wearing the shallow mask of manners. When I see a spade I call it a spade.

GWENDOLEN, *satirically.* I am glad to say that I have never seen a spade. It is obvious that our social spheres have been widely different.

Enter MERRIMAN, *followed by the footman. He carries a salver, tablecloth, and plate stand.* CECILY *is about to retort. The presence of the servants exercises a restraining influence, under which both girls chafe.*

MERRIMAN. Shall I lay tea here as usual, Miss?

CECILY, *sternly, in a calm voice.* Yes, as usual.

MERRIMAN *begins to clear table and lay cloth. A long pause.* CECILY *and* GWENDOLEN *glare at each other.*

GWENDOLEN. Are there many interesting walks in the vicinity, Miss Cardew?

CECILY. Oh! yes! a great many. From the top of one of the hills quite close one can see five counties.

GWENDOLEN. Five counties! I don't think I should like that; I hate crowds.

CECILY, *sweetly*. I suppose that is why you live in town?

GWENDOLEN *bites her lip, and beats her foot nervously with her parasol.*

GWENDOLEN, *looking round*. Quite a well-kept garden this is, Miss Cardew.

CECILY. So glad you like it, Miss Fairfax.

GWENDOLEN. I had no idea there were any flowers in the country.

CECILY. Oh, flowers are as common here, Miss Fairfax, as people are in London.

GWENDOLEN. Personally I cannot understand how anybody manages to exist in the country, if anybody who is anybody does. The country always bores me to death.

CECILY. Ah! This is what the newspapers call agricultural depression, is it not? I believe the aristocracy are suffering very much from it just at present. It is almost an epidemic amongst them, I have been told. May I offer you some tea, Miss Fairfax?

GWENDOLEN, *with elaborate politeness*. Thank you. *Aside.* Detestable girl! But I require tea!

CECILY, *sweetly*. Sugar?

GWENDOLEN, *superciliously*. No, thank you. Sugar is not fashionable any more.

CECILY *looks angrily at her, takes up the tongs and puts four lumps of sugar into the cup.*

CECILY, *severely*. Cake or bread and butter?

GWENDOLEN, *in a bored manner*. Bread and butter, please. Cake is rarely seen at the best houses nowadays.

CECILY. *Cuts a very large slice of cake, and puts it on the tray.* Hand that to Miss Fairfax.

MERRIMAN *does so, and goes out with footman.* GWENDOLEN *drinks the tea and makes a grimace. Puts down cup at once, reaches out her hand to the bread and butter, looks at it, and finds it is cake. Rises in indignation.*

GWENDOLEN. You have filled my tea with lumps of sugar, and though I asked most distinctly for bread and butter, you have given me cake. I am known for the gentleness of my disposition, and the extraordinary sweetness of my nature, but I warn you, Miss Cardew, you may go too far.

CECILY, *rising*. To save my poor, innocent, trusting boy from the machinations of any other girl there are no lengths to which I would not go.

GWENDOLEN. From the moment I saw you I distrusted you. I felt that you were false and deceitful. I am never deceived in such matters. My first impressions of people are invariably right.

CECILY. It seems to me, Miss Fairfax, that I am trespassing on your valuable time. No doubt you have many other calls of a similar character to make in the neighborhood.

Enter JACK.

GWENDOLEN, *catching sight of him*. Ernest! My own Ernest!

JACK. Gwendolen! Darling! *Offers to kiss her.*

GWENDOLEN, *drawing back*. A moment! May I ask if you are engaged to be married to this young lady? *Points to* CECILY.

JACK, *laughing*. To dear little Cecily! Of course not! What could have put such an idea into your pretty little head?

GWENDOLEN. Thank you. You may! *Offers her cheek.*

CECILY, *very sweetly*. I knew there must be some misunderstanding, Miss Fairfax. The gentleman whose arm is at present round your waist is my dear guardian, Mr. John Worthing.

GWENDOLEN. I beg your pardon?

CECILY. This is Uncle Jack.

GWENDOLEN, *receding*. Jack! Oh!

Enter ALGERNON.

CECILY. Here is Ernest.

ALGERNON. *Goes straight over to* CECILY *without noticing anyone else*. My own love! *Offers to kiss her.*

CECILY, *drawing back*. A moment, Ernest! May I ask you—are you engaged to be married to this young lady?

ALGERNON, *looking round*. To what young lady? Good heavens! Gwendolen!

CECILY. Yes! to good heavens, Gwendolen, I mean to Gwendolen.

ALGERNON, *laughing*. Of course not! What could have put such an idea into your pretty little head?

CECILY. Thank you. *Presenting her cheek to be kissed*. You may.

ALGERNON *kisses her.*

GWENDOLEN. I felt there was some slight error, Miss Cardew. The gentleman who is now embracing you is my cousin, Mr. Algernon Moncrieff.

CECILY, *breaking away from* ALGERNON. Algernon Moncrieff! Oh!
The two girls move towards each other and put their arms round each other's waists as if for protection.

CECILY. Are you called Algernon?

ALGERNON. I cannot deny it.

CECILY. Oh!

GWENDOLEN. Is your name really John?

JACK, *standing rather proudly*. I could deny it if I liked. I could deny anything if I liked. But my name certainly is John. It has been John for years.

CECILY, *to* GWENDOLEN. A gross deception has been practised on both of us.

GWENDOLEN. My poor wounded Cecily!

CECILY. My sweet wronged Gwendolen!

GWENDOLEN, *slowly and seriously*. You will call me sister, will you not?

They embrace. JACK *and* ALGERNON *groan and walk up and down.*

CECILY, *rather brightly*. There is just one question I would like to be allowed to ask my guardian.

GWENDOLEN. An admirable idea! Mr. Worthing, there is just one question I would like to be permitted to put to you. Where is your brother Ernest? We are both engaged to be married to your brother Ernest, so it is a matter of some importance to us to know where your brother Ernest is at present.

JACK, *slowly and hesitatingly*. Gwendolen—Cecily—it is very painful for me to be forced to speak the truth. It is the first time in my life that I have ever been reduced to such a painful position, and I am really quite inexperienced in doing anything of the kind. However, I will tell you quite frankly that I have no brother Ernest. I have no brother at all. I never had a brother in my life, and I certainly have not the smallest intention of ever having one in the future.

CECILY, *surprised*. No brother at all?

JACK, *cheerily*. None!

GWENDOLEN, *severely*. Had you never a brother of any kind?

JACK, *pleasantly*. Never. Not even of any kind.

GWENDOLEN. I am afraid it is quite clear, Cecily, that neither of us is engaged to be married to anyone.

CECILY. It is not a very pleasant position for a young girl suddenly to find herself in. Is it?

GWENDOLEN. Let us go into the house. They will hardly venture to come after us there.

CECILY. No, men are so cowardly, aren't they?

They retire into the house with scornful looks.

JACK. This ghastly state of things is what you call Bunburying, I suppose?

ALGERNON. Yes, and a perfectly wonderful Bunbury it is. The most wonderful Bunbury I have ever had in my life.

JACK. Well, you've no right whatsoever to Bunbury here.

ALGERNON. That is absurd. One has a right to Bunbury anywhere one chooses. Every serious Bunburyist knows that.

JACK. Serious Bunburyist! Good heavens!

ALGERNON. Well, one must be serious about something, if one wants to have any amusement in life. I happen to be serious about Bunburying. What on earth you are serious about I haven't got the remotest idea. About everything, I should fancy. You have such an absolutely trivial nature.

JACK. Well, the only small satisfaction I have in the whole of this wretched business is that your friend Bunbury is quite exploded. You won't be able to run down to the country quite so often as you used to do, dear Algy. And a very good thing too.

ALGERNON. Your brother is a little off color, isn't he, dear Jack? You won't be able to disappear to London quite so frequently as your wicked custom was. And not a bad thing either.

JACK. As for your conduct towards Miss Cardew, I must say that your taking in a sweet, simple, innocent girl like that is quite inexcusable. To say nothing of the fact that she is my ward.

ALGERNON. I can see no possible defense at all for your deceiving a brilliant, clever, thoroughly experienced young lady like Miss Fairfax. To say nothing of the fact that she is my cousin.

JACK. I wanted to be engaged to Gwendolen, that is all. I love her.

ALGERNON. Well, I simply wanted to be engaged to Cecily. I adore her.

ACT II] THE IMPORTANCE OF BEING EARNEST 195

JACK. There is certainly no chance of your marrying Miss Cardew.

ALGERNON. I don't think there is much likelihood, Jack, of you and Miss Fairfax being united.

JACK. Well, that is no business of yours.

ALGERNON. If it was my business, I wouldn't talk about it. *Begins to eat muffins.* It is very vulgar to talk about one's business. Only people like stockbrokers do that, and then merely at dinner parties.

JACK. How you can sit there, calmly eating muffins when we are in this horrible trouble, I can't make out. You seem to me to be perfectly heartless.

ALGERNON. Well, I can't eat muffins in an agitated manner. The butter would probably get on my cuffs. One should always eat muffins quite calmly. It is the only way to eat them.

JACK. I say it's perfectly heartless your eating muffins at all, under the circumstances.

ALGERNON. When I am in trouble, eating is the only thing that consoles me. Indeed, when I am in really great trouble, as anyone who knows me intimately will tell you, I refuse everything except food and drink. At the present moment I am eating muffins because I am unhappy. Besides, I am particularly fond of muffins. *Rising.*

JACK, *rising.* Well, that is no reason why you should eat them all in that greedy way. *Takes muffins from* ALGERNON.

ALGERNON, *offering tea-cake.* I wish you would have tea-cake instead. I don't like tea-cake.

JACK. Good heavens! I suppose a man may eat his own muffins in his own garden.

ALGERNON. But you have just said it was perfectly heartless to eat muffins.

JACK. I said it was perfectly heartless of you, under the circumstances. That is a very different thing.

ALGERNON. That may be. But the muffins are the same.

He seizes the muffin dish from JACK.

JACK. Algy, I wish to goodness you would go.

ALGERNON. You can't possibly ask me to go without having some dinner. It's absurd. I never go without my dinner. No one ever does, except vegetarians and people like that. Besides I have just made arrangements with Dr. Chasuble to be christened at a quarter to six under the name of Ernest.

JACK. My dear fellow, the sooner you give up that nonsense the better. I made arrangements this morning with Dr. Chasuble to be christened myself at 5.30, and I naturally will take the name of Ernest. Gwendolen would wish it. We can't both be christened Ernest. It's absurd. Besides, I have a perfect right to be christened if I like. There is no evidence at all that I ever have been christened by anybody. I should think it extremely probable I never was, and so does Dr. Chasuble. It is entirely different in your case. You have been christened already.

ALGERNON. Yes, but I have not been christened for years.

JACK. Yes, but you have been christened. That is the important thing.

ALGERNON. Quite so. So I know my constitution can stand it. If you are not quite sure about your ever having been christened, I must say I think it rather dangerous your venturing on it now. It might make you very unwell. You can hardly have forgotten that someone very closely connected with you was very nearly carried off this week in Paris by a severe chill.

JACK. Yes, but you said yourself that a severe chill was not hereditary.

ALGERNON. It usen't to be, I know—but I dare to say it is now. Science is always making wonderful improvements in things.

JACK, *picking up the muffin dish*. Oh, that is nonsense; you are always talking nonsense.

ALGERNON. Jack, you are at the muffins again! I wish you wouldn't. There are only two left. *Takes them*. I told you I was particularly fond of muffins.

JACK. But I hate tea-cake.

ALGERNON. Why on earth then do you allow tea-cake to be served up for your guests? What ideas you have of hospitality!

JACK. Algernon! I have already told you to go. I don't want you here. Why don't you go!

ALGERNON. I haven't quite finished my tea yet! and there is still one muffin left.

JACK *groans, and sinks into a chair*. ALGERNON *still continues eating*.

Act III

Morning room at the Manor House.

GWENDOLEN *and* CECILY *are at the window, looking out into the garden.*

GWENDOLEN. The fact that they did not follow us at once into the house, as anyone else would have done, seems to me to show that they have some sense of shame left.

CECILY. They have been eating muffins. That looks like repentance.

GWENDOLEN, *after a pause.* They don't seem to notice us at all Couldn't you cough?

CECILY. But I haven't got a cough.

GWENDOLEN. They're looking at us. What effrontery!

CECILY. They're approaching. That's very forward of them.

GWENDOLEN. Let us preserve a dignified silence.

CECILY. Certainly. It's the only thing to do now.

Enter JACK *followed by* ALGERNON. *They whistle some dreadful popular air from a British Opera.*

GWENDOLEN. This dignified silence seems to produce an unpleasant effect.

CECILY. A most distasteful one.

GWENDOLEN. But we will not be the first to speak.

CECILY. Certainly not.

GWENDOLEN. Mr. Worthing, I have something very particular to ask you. Much depends on your reply.

CECILY. Gwendolen, your common sense is invaluable. Mr. Moncrieff, kindly answer me the following question. Why did you pretend to be my guardian's brother?

ALGERNON. In order that I might have an opportunity of meeting you.

CECILY, *to* GWENDOLEN. That certainly seems a satisfactory explanation, does it not?

GWENDOLEN. Yes, dear, if you can believe him.

CECILY. I don't. But that does not affect the wonderful beauty of his answer.

GWENDOLEN. True. In matters of grave importance, style, not sincerity is the vital thing. Mr. Worthing, what explanation can you offer to me for pretending to have a brother? Was it in order that you might have an opportunity of coming up to town to see me as often as possible?

JACK. Can you doubt it, Miss Fairfax?

GWENDOLEN. I have the gravest doubts upon the subject. But I intend to crush them. This is not the moment for German skepticism. *Moving to* CECILY. Their explanations appear to be quite satisfactory, especially Mr. Worthing's. That seems to me to have the stamp of truth upon it.

CECILY. I am more than content with what Mr. Moncrieff said. His voice alone inspires one with absolute credulity.

GWENDOLEN. Then you think we should forgive them?

CECILY. Yes. I mean no.

GWENDOLEN. True! I had forgotten. There are principles at stake that one cannot surrender. Which of us should tell them? The task is not a pleasant one.

CECILY. Could we not both speak at the same time?

GWENDOLEN. An excellent idea! I nearly always speak at the same time as other people. Will you take the time from me?

CECILY. Certainly. GWENDOLEN *beats time with uplifted finger.*

GWENDOLEN AND CECILY, *speaking together.* Your Christian names are still an insuperable barrier. That is all!

JACK AND ALGERNON, *speaking together.* Our Christian names! Is that all? But we are going to be christened this afternoon.

GWENDOLEN, *to* JACK. For my sake you are prepared to do this terrible thing?

JACK. I am.

CECILY, *to* ALGERNON. To please me you are ready to face this fearful ordeal?

ALGERNON. I am!

GWENDOLEN. How absurd to talk of the equality of the sexes! Where questions of self-sacrifice are concerned, men are infinitely beyond us.

JACK. We are. *Clasps hands with* ALGERNON.

CECILY. They have moments of physical courage of which we women know absolutely nothing.

GWENDOLEN, *to* JACK. Darling!
ALGERNON, *to* CECILY. Darling!   *They fall into each other's arms.*

Enter MERRIMAN. *When he enters he coughs loudly, seeing the situation.*

MERRIMAN. Ahem! Ahem! Lady Bracknell!
JACK. Good heavens!

Enter LADY BRACKNELL. *The couples separate in alarm.*

Exit MERRIMAN.

LADY BRACKNELL. Gwendolen! What does this mean?

GWENDOLEN. Merely that I am engaged to be married to Mr. Worthing, mamma.

LADY BRACKNELL. Come here. Sit down. Sit down immediately. Hesitation of any kind is a sign of mental decay in the young, of physical weakness in the old. *Turns to* JACK. Apprised, sir, of my daughter's sudden flight by her trusty maid, whose confidence I purchased by means of a small coin, I followed her at once by a luggage train. Her unhappy father is, I am glad to say, under the impression that she is attending a more than usually lengthy lecture by the University Extension Scheme on the Influence of a Permanent Income on Thought. I do not propose to undeceive him. Indeed I have never undeceived him on any question. I would consider it wrong. But of course, you will clearly understand that all communication between yourself and my daughter must cease immediately from this moment. On this point, as indeed on all points, I am firm.

JACK. I am engaged to be married to Gwendolen, Lady Bracknell!

LADY BRACKNELL. You are nothing of the kind, sir. And now as regards Algernon! . . . Algernon!

ALGERNON. Yes, Aunt Augusta.

LADY BRACKNELL. May I ask if it is in this house that your invalid friend Mr. Bunbury resides?

ALGERNON, *stammering*. Oh! No! Bunbury doesn't live here. Bunbury is somewhere else at present. In fact, Bunbury is dead.

LADY BRACKNELL. Dead! When did Mr. Bunbury die? His death must have been extremely sudden.

ALGERNON, *airily*. Oh! I killed Bunbury this afternoon. I mean poor Bunbury died this afternoon.

LADY BRACKNELL. What did he die of?

ALGERNON. Bunbury? Oh, he was quite exploded.

LADY BRACKNELL. Exploded! Was he the victim of a revolutionary outrage? I was not aware that Mr. Bunbury was interested in social legislation. If so, he is well punished for his morbidity.

ALGERNON. My dear Aunt Augusta, I mean he was found out! The doctors found out that Bunbury could not live, that is what I mean— so Bunbury died.

LADY BRACKNELL. He seems to have had great confidence in the opinion of his physicians. I am glad, however, that he made up his mind at the last to some definite course of action, and acted under the proper medical advice. And now that we have finally got rid of this Mr. Bunbury, may I ask, Mr. Worthing, who is that young person whose hand my nephew Algernon is now holding in what seems to me a peculiarly unnecessary manner?

JACK. That lady is Miss Cecily Cardew, my ward.

LADY BRACKNELL *bows coldly to* CECILY.

ALGERNON. I am engaged to be married to Cecily, Aunt Augusta.

LADY BRACKNELL. I beg your pardon?

CECILY. Mr. Moncrieff and I are engaged to be married, Lady Bracknell.

LADY BRACKNELL, *with a shiver, crossing to the sofa and sitting down*. I do not know whether there is anything peculiarly exciting in the air of this particular part of Hertfordshire, but the number of engagements that go on seems to me considerably above the proper average that statistics have laid down for our guidance. I think some preliminary inquiry on my part would not be out of place. Mr. Worthing, is Miss Cardew at all connected with any of the larger railway stations in London? I merely desire information. Until yesterday I had no idea that there were any families or persons whose origin was a Terminus.

JACK *looks perfectly furious, but restrains himself*.

JACK, *in a clear, cold voice*. Miss Cardew is the grand-daughter of the late Mr. Thomas Cardew of 149 Belgrave Square, S.W.; Gervase Park, Dorking, Surrey; and The Sporran, Fifeshire, N.B.

LADY BRACKNELL. That sounds not unsatisfactory. Three addresses always inspire confidence, even in tradesmen. But what proof have I of their authenticity?

JACK. I have carefully preserved the Court Guides of the period. They are open to your inspection, Lady Bracknell.

LADY BRACKNELL, *grimly*. I have known strange errors in that publication.

JACK. Miss Cardew's family solicitors are Messrs. Markby, Markby, and Markby.

LADY BRACKNELL. Markby, Markby, and Markby? A firm of the very highest position in their profession. Indeed I am told that one of the Mr. Markbys is occasionally to be seen at dinner parties. So far I am satisfied.

JACK, *very irritably*. How extremely kind of you, Lady Bracknell! I have also in my possession, you will be pleased to hear, certificates of Miss Cardew's birth, baptism, whooping cough, registration, vaccination, confirmation, and the measles; both the German and the English variety.

LADY BRACKNELL. Ah! A life crowded with incident, I see; though perhaps somewhat too exciting for a young girl. I am not myself in favor of premature experiences. *Rises, looks at her watch*. Gwendolen! the time approaches for our departure. We have not a moment to lose. As a matter of form, Mr. Worthing, I had better ask you if Miss Cardew has any little fortune?

JACK. Oh! about a hundred and thirty thousand pounds in the Funds. That is all. Goodby, Lady Bracknell. So pleased to have seen you.

LADY BRACKNELL, *sitting down again*. A moment, Mr. Worthing. A hundred and thirty thousand pounds! And in the Funds! Miss Cardew seems to me a most attractive young lady, now that I look at her. Few girls of the present day have any really solid qualities, any of the qualities that last, and improve with time. We live, I regret to say, in an age of surfaces. *To* CECILY. Come over here, dear. CECILY *goes across*. Pretty child! your dress is sadly simple, and your hair seems almost as Nature might have left it. But we can soon alter all that. A thoroughly experienced French maid produces a really marvelous result in a very brief space of time. I remember recommending one to young Lady Lancing, and after three months her own husband did not know her.

JACK, *aside*. And after six months nobody knew her.

LADY BRACKNELL. *Glares at* JACK *for a few moments. Then bends, with a practised smile, to* CECILY. Kindly turn round, sweet child. CECILY *turns completely round*. No, the side view is what I want. CECILY *presents her profile*. Yes, quite as I expected. There are distinct social possibilities in your profile. The two weak points in our age are its want of principle and its want of profile. The chin a little higher, dear. Style largely depends on the way the chin is worn. They are worn very high, just at present. Algernon!

ALGERNON. Yes, Aunt Augusta!

LADY BRACKNELL. There are distinct social possibilities in Miss Cardew's profile.

ALGERNON. Cecily is the sweetest, dearest, prettiest girl in the whole world. And I don't care twopence about social possibilities.

LADY BRACKNELL. Never speak disrespectfully of Society, Algernon. Only people who can't get into it do that. *To* CECILY. Dear child, of course you know that Algernon has nothing but his debts to depend upon. But I do not approve of mercenary marriages. When I married Lord Bracknell I had no fortune of any kind. But I never dreamed for a moment of allowing that to stand in my way. Well, I suppose I must give my consent.

ALGERNON. Thank you, Aunt Augusta.

LADY BRACKNELL. Cecily, you may kiss me!

CECILY. *Kisses her*. Thank you, Lady Bracknell.

LADY BRACKNELL. You may also address me as Aunt Augusta for the future.

CECILY. Thank you, Aunt Augusta.

LADY BRACKNELL. The marriage, I think, had better take place quite soon.

ALGERNON. Thank you, Aunt Augusta.

CECILY. Thank you, Aunt Augusta.

LADY BRACKNELL. To speak frankly, I am not in favor of long engagements. They give people the opportunity of finding out each other's character before marriage, which I think is never advisable.

JACK. I beg your pardon for interrupting you, Lady Bracknell, but this engagement is quite out of the question. I am Miss Cardew's guardian, and she cannot marry without my consent until she comes of age. That consent I absolutely decline to give.

LADY BRACKNELL. Upon what grounds may I ask? Algernon is an extremely, I may almost say an ostentatiously, eligible young man. He has nothing, but he looks everything. What more can one desire?

JACK. It pains me very much to have to speak frankly to you, Lady Bracknell, about your nephew, but the fact is that I do not approve at all of his moral character. I suspect him of being untruthful.

ALGERNON *and* CECILY *look at him in indignant amazement.*

LADY BRACKNELL. Untruthful! My nephew Algernon? Impossible! He is an Oxonian.

JACK. I fear there can be no possible doubt about the matter. This afternoon, during my temporary absence in London on an important question of romance, he obtained admission to my house by means of the false pretense of being my brother. Under an assumed name he drank, I've just been informed by my butler, an entire pint bottle of my Perrier-Jouet, Brut, '89; a wine I was specially reserving for myself. Continuing his disgraceful deception, he succeeded in the course of the afternoon in alienating the affections of my only ward. He subsequently stayed to tea, and devoured every single muffin. And what makes his conduct all the more heartless is, that he was perfectly well aware from the first that I have no brother, that I never had a brother, and that I don't intend to have a brother, not even of any kind. I distinctly told him so myself yesterday afternoon.

LADY BRACKNELL. Ahem! Mr. Worthing, after careful consideration I have decided entirely to overlook my nephew's conduct to you.

JACK. That is very generous of you, Lady Bracknell. My own decision, however, is unalterable. I decline to give my consent.

LADY BRACKNELL, *to* CECILY. Come here, sweet child. CECILY *goes over.* How old are you, dear?

CECILY. Well, I am really only eighteen, but I always admit to twenty when I go to evening parties.

LADY BRACKNELL. You are perfectly right in making some slight alteration. Indeed, no woman should ever be quite accurate about her age. It looks so calculating. . . . *In a meditative manner.* Eighteen, but admitting to twenty at evening parties. Well, it will not be very long before you are of age and free from the restraints of tutelage. So I don't think your guardian's consent is, after all, a matter of any importance.

JACK. Pray excuse me, Lady Bracknell, for interrupting you again, but it is only fair to tell you that according to the terms of her grandfather's will Miss Cardew does not come legally of age till she is thirty-five.

LADY BRACKNELL. That does not seem to me to be a grave objection. Thirty-five is a very attractive age. London society is full of women of the very highest birth who have, of their own free choice, remained thirty-five for years. Lady Dumbleton is an instance in point. To my own knowledge she has been thirty-five ever since she arrived at the age of forty, which was many years ago now. I see no reason why our dear Cecily should not be even still more attractive at the age you mention than she is at present. There will be a large accumulation of property.

CECILY. Algy, could you wait for me till I was thirty-five?

ALGERNON. Of course I could, Cecily. You know I could.

CECILY. Yes, I felt it instinctively, but I couldn't wait all that time. I hate waiting even five minutes for anybody. It always makes me rather cross. I am not punctual myself, I know, but I do like punctuality in others, and waiting, even to be married, is quite out of the question.

ALGERNON. Then what is to be done, Cecily?

CECILY. I don't know, Mr. Moncrieff.

LADY BRACKNELL. My dear Mr. Worthing, as Miss Cardew states positively that she cannot wait till she is thirty-five—a remark which I am bound to say seems to me to show a somewhat impatient nature —I would beg of you to reconsider your decision.

JACK. But my dear Lady Bracknell, the matter is entirely in your own hands. The moment you consent to my marriage with Gwendolen, I will most gladly allow your nephew to form an alliance with my ward.

LADY BRACKNELL, *rising and drawing herself up.* You must be quite aware that what you propose is out of the question.

JACK. Then a passionate celibacy is all that any of us can look forward to.

LADY BRACKNELL. That is not the destiny I propose for Gwendolen. Algernon, of course, can choose for himself. *Pulls out her watch.* Come, dear—GWENDOLEN *rises*—we have already missed five, if not six, trains. To miss any more might expose us to comment on the platform.

ACT III] THE IMPORTANCE OF BEING EARNEST   205

Enter DR. CHASUBLE.

CHASUBLE. Everything is quite ready for the christenings.

LADY BRACKNELL. The christenings, sir! Is not that somewhat premature?

CHASUBLE, *looking rather puzzled, and pointing to* JACK *and* ALGERNON. Both these gentlemen have expressed a desire for immediate baptism.

LADY BRACKNELL. At their age? The idea is grotesque and irreligious! Algernon, I forbid you to be baptized. I will not hear of such excesses. Lord Bracknell would be highly displeased if he learned that that was the way in which you wasted your time and money.

CHASUBLE. Am I to understand then that there are to be no christenings at all this afternoon?

JACK. I don't think that, as things are now, it would be of much practical value to either of us, Dr. Chasuble.

CHASUBLE. I am grieved to hear such sentiments from you, Mr. Worthing. They savor of the heretical views of the Anabaptists, views that I have completely refuted in four of my unpublished sermons. However, as your present mood seems to be one peculiarly secular, I will return to the church at once. Indeed, I have just been informed by the pew-opener that for the last hour and a half Miss Prism has been waiting for me in the vestry.

LADY BRACKNELL, *starting*. Miss Prism! Did I hear you mention a Miss Prism?

CHASUBLE. Yes, Lady Bracknell. I am on my way to join her.

LADY BRACKNELL. Pray allow me to detain you for a moment. This matter may prove to be one of vital importance to Lord Bracknell and myself. Is this Miss Prism a female of repellent aspect, remotely connected with education?

CHASUBLE, *somewhat indignantly*. She is the most cultivated of ladies, and the very picture of respectability.

LADY BRACKNELL. It is obviously the same person. May I ask what position she holds in your household?

CHASUBLE, *severely*. I am a celibate, madam.

JACK, *interposing*. Miss Prism, Lady Bracknell, has been for the last three years Miss Cardew's esteemed governess and valued companion.

LADY BRACKNELL. In spite of what I hear of her, I must see her at once. Let her be sent for.

CHASUBLE, *looking off.* She approaches; she is nigh.

Enter MISS PRISM *hurriedly.*

MISS PRISM. I was told you expected me in the vestry, dear Canon. I have been waiting for you there for an hour and three quarters. *Catches sight of* LADY BRACKNELL *who has fixed her with a stony glare.* MISS PRISM *grows pale and quails. She looks anxiously round as if desirous to escape.*

LADY BRACKNELL. *In a severe, judicial voice.* Prism! MISS PRISM *bows her head in shame.* Come here, Prism! MISS PRISM *approaches in a humble manner.* Prism! Where is that baby? *General consternation. The* CANON *starts back in horror.* ALGERNON *and* JACK *pretend to be anxious to shield* CECILY *and* GWENDOLEN *from hearing the details of a terrible public scandal.* Twenty-eight years ago, Prism, you left Lord Bracknell's house, Number 104, Upper Grosvenor Street, in charge of a perambulator that contained a baby, of the male sex. You never returned. A few weeks later, through the elaborate investigations of the Metropolitan police, the perambulator was discovered at midnight, standing by itself in a remote corner of Bayswater. It contained the manuscript of a three-volume novel of more than usually revolting sentimentality. MISS PRISM *starts in involuntary indignation.* But the baby was not there! *Everyone looks at* MISS PRISM. Prism! Where is that baby? *A pause.*

MISS PRISM. Lady Bracknell, I admit with shame that I do not know. I only wish I did. The plain facts of the case are these. On the morning of the day you mention, a day that is for ever branded on my memory, I prepared as usual to take the baby out in its perambulator. I had also with me a somewhat old, but capacious handbag in which I had intended to place the manuscript of a work of fiction that I had written during my few unoccupied hours. In a moment of mental abstraction, for which I never can forgive myself, I deposited the manuscript in the basinette, and placed the baby in the handbag.

JACK, *who has been listening attentively.* But where did you deposit the handbag?

MISS PRISM. Do not ask me, Mr. Worthing.

JACK. Miss Prism, this is a matter of no small importance to me. I

ACT III] THE IMPORTANCE OF BEING EARNEST 207

insist on knowing where you deposited the handbag that contained that infant.

MISS PRISM. I left it in the cloakroom of one of the larger railway stations in London.

JACK. What railway station?

MISS PRISM, *quite crushed*. Victoria. The Brighton line.

Sinks into a chair.

JACK. I must retire to my room for a moment. Gwendolen, wait here for me.

GWENDOLEN. If you are not too long, I will wait here for you all my life. *Exit* JACK *in great excitement.*

CHASUBLE. What do you think this means, Lady Bracknell?

LADY BRACKNELL. I dare not even suspect, Dr. Chasuble. I need hardly tell you that in families of high position strange coincidences are not supposed to occur. They are hardly considered the thing.

Noises heard overhead as if someone was throwing trunks about. Everyone looks up.

CECILY. Uncle Jack seems strangely agitated.

CHASUBLE. Your guardian has a very emotional nature.

LADY BRACKNELL. This noise is extremely unpleasant. It sounds as if he was having an argument. I dislike arguments of any kind. They are always vulgar, and often convincing.

CHASUBLE, *looking up*. It has stopped now.

The noise is redoubled.

LADY BRACKNELL. I wish he would arrive at some conclusion.

GWENDOLEN. This suspense is terrible. I hope it will last.

Enter JACK *with a handbag of black leather in his hand.*

JACK, *rushing over to* MISS PRISM. Is this the handbag, Miss Prism? Examine it carefully before you speak. The happiness of more than one life depends on your answer.

MISS PRISM, *calmly*. It seems to be mine. Yes, here is the injury it received through the upsetting of a Gower Street omnibus in younger and happier days. Here is the stain on the lining caused by the explosion of a temperance beverage, an incident that occurred at Leamington. And here, on the lock, are my initials. I had forgotten that in an extravagant mood I had had them placed there. The bag is undoubtedly mine. I am delighted to have it so unexpectedly restored to me. It has been a great inconvenience being without it all these years.

JACK, *in a pathetic voice*. Miss Prism, more is restored to you than this handbag. I was the baby you placed in it.

MISS PRISM, *amazed*. You?

JACK, *embracing her*. Yes . . . mother!

MISS PRISM, *recoiling in indignant astonishment*. Mr. Worthing! I am unmarried!

JACK. Unmarried! I do not deny that is a serious blow. But after all, who has the right to cast a stone against one who has suffered? Cannot repentance wipe out an act of folly? Why should there be one law for men, and another for women? Mother, I forgive you.

Tries to embrace her again.

MISS PRISM, *still more indignant*. Mr. Worthing, there is some error. *Pointing to* LADY BRACKNELL. There is the lady who can tell you who you really are.

JACK, *after a pause*. Lady Bracknell, I hate to seem inquisitive, but would you kindly inform me who I am?

LADY BRACKNELL. I am afraid that the news I have to give you will not altogether please you. You are the son of my poor sister, Mrs. Moncrieff, and consequently Algernon's elder brother.

JACK. Algy's elder brother! Then I have a brother after all. I knew I had a brother! I always said I had a brother! Cecily—how could you have ever doubted that I had a brother? *Seizes hold of* ALGERNON. Dr. Chasuble, my unfortunate brother. Miss Prism, my unfortunate brother. Gwendolen, my unfortunate brother. Algy, you young scoundrel, you will have to treat me with more respect in the future. You have never behaved to me like a brother in all your life.

ALGERNON. Well, not till today, old boy, I admit. I did my best, however, though I was out of practice. *Shakes hands*.

GWENDOLEN, *to* JACK. My own! But what own are you? What is your Christian name, now that you have become someone else?

JACK. Good heavens! . . . I had quite forgotten that point. Your decision on the subject of my name is irrevocable, I suppose?

GWENDOLEN. I never change, except in my affections.

CECILY. What a noble nature you have, Gwendolen!

JACK. Then the question had better be cleared up at once. Aunt

Augusta, a moment. At the time when Miss Prism left me in the handbag, had I been christened already?

LADY BRACKNELL. Every luxury that money could buy, including christening, had been lavished on you by your fond and doting parents.

JACK. Then I was christened! That is settled. Now, what name was I given? Let me know the worst.

LADY BRACKNELL. Being the eldest son you were naturally christened after your father.

JACK, *irritably*. Yes, but what was my father's Christian name?

LADY BRACKNELL, *meditatively*. I cannot at the present moment recall what the General's Christian name was. But I have no doubt he had one. He was eccentric, I admit. But only in later years. And that was the result of the Indian climate, and marriage, and indigestion, and other things of that kind.

JACK. Algy! Can't you recollect what our father's Christian name was?

ALGERNON. My dear boy, we were never even on speaking terms. He died before I was a year old.

JACK. His name would appear in the Army Lists of the period, I suppose, Aunt Augusta?

LADY BRACKNELL. The General was essentially a man of peace, except in his domestic life. But I have no doubt his name would appear in any military directory.

JACK. The Army Lists of the last forty years are here. These delightful records should have been my constant study. *Rushes to bookcase and tears the books out.* M. Generals . . . Mallam, Maxbohm, Magley, what ghastly names they have—Markby, Migsby, Mobbs, Moncrieff! Lieutenant 1840, Captain, Lieutenant-Colonel, Colonel, General 1869, Christian names, Ernest John. *Puts book very quietly down and speaks quite calmly.* I always told you, Gwendolen, my name was Ernest, didn't I? Well, it is Ernest after all. I mean it naturally is Ernest.

LADY BRACKNELL. Yes, I remember now that the General was called Ernest. I knew I had some particular reason for disliking the name.

GWENDOLEN. Ernest! My own Ernest! I felt from the first that you could have no other name!

JACK. Gwendolen, it is a terrible thing for a man to find out suddenly that all his life he has been speaking nothing but the truth. Can you forgive me?

GWENDOLEN. I can. For I feel that you are sure to change.

JACK. My own one!

CHASUBLE, *to* MISS PRISM. Laetitia! *Embraces her.*

MISS PRISM, *enthusiastically*. Frederick! At last!

ALGERNON. Cecily! *Embraces her.* At last!

JACK. Gwendolen! *Embraces her.* At last!

LADY BRACKNELL. My nephew, you seem to be displaying signs of triviality.

JACK. On the contrary, Aunt Augusta, I've now realized for the first time in my life the vital Importance of Being Earnest.

*

THE MOST thorough way of investigating the dramatic art of Oscar Wilde would be to read many of the farces that were popular in his day and to compare his plays with them. A slightly less laborious task would be to compare Wilde with whatever farces one happens to know already. For, as has already been intimated, *Earnest* is a variant of farce. Consequently nothing is easier than to handle the play without noticing what it contains. The tone, characterization, and plot are so consistently farcical that very few readers or even producers care to root out any more serious content. A common conclusion has been that Wilde simply decorated a silly play with a flippant wit. Those who compare it with the comic classics will probably dismiss it as *slight*.

One must retort that insensitivity to slight and delicate things is insensitivity pure and simple. Wilde himself said that the man who despises superficiality is himself superficial. The idea is not unconnected with *Earnest*. The play is confessedly about *earnestness,* that is, Victorian solemnity—a kind of false seriousness involving priggishness, hypocrisy, lack of irony. Wilde proclaims that earnestness is less praiseworthy than the ironical attitude to life, which the serious denounce as superficial. His own art and the comic spirit generally were thereby vindicated. Wilde calls *Earnest* "a trivial comedy for serious people," meaning, in the first place, a comedy which the earnest will think negligible, and in the second, a *comedy of surface* for the non-earnest. The latter will perceive that Wilde is, after all, very much of a moralist, but that, instead of presenting the problems of modern society directly, he flits around them, teasing them, declining to grapple with them. His wit is no "searchlight into the darkness of modern life." It is a flickering, a coruscation, intermittently revealing the upper class of England in a harsh, bizarre light. This upper class has been able to feel about Bernard Shaw that at least he takes them seriously. But the outrageous Oscar refused to see the importance of—being earnest.

One does not find Wilde's satire embedded in plot and character as we shall find Molière's. It is a running accompaniment to the play, and this fact is the making of a unique sort of comedy. The plot is one of those absurdities of lost infants and recovered brothers which can only be thought of to be laughed at. Yet the dialogue which sustains the plot, or is sustained by it, is an unbroken stream of comment on all the themes of life which the plot is so far from broaching. Perhaps *comment* is too flat and downright a conception. Wildean "comment" is a pseudo-irresponsible jabbing at all the great problems, and we should be justified in removing the adjective "pseudo" if the Wildean satire, for all its naughtiness, had not a cumulative and paradoxical effect. Flippancies repeated, developed, and, so to say, elaborated into a system amount to something in the end—and thereby cease to be flippant. What begins as a prank ends as a criticism of life. What begins as intellectual high-kicking ends as intellectual sharpshooting.

The margins of an annotated copy of *Earnest* would show such headings as: death, money and marriage, the nature of style, ideology and economics, beauty and truth, the psychology of philanthropy, the decline of aristocracy, nineteenth-century morals, the class system of society. The possibility of such notations means little in itself, but if we bear in mind that Wilde is skimming steadily over more and more topics all through the play, we should turn to a particular page to see precisely how this works. Look back at the first page of the play (p. 151 above).

To choose the opening page is not to load the dice in a playwright's favor, since that page is usually either heavy-going exposition or mere patter which allows late-comers to get seated. On *his* opening page, Wilde attaches to every remark a serious and satirical allusion. The butler's "I didn't think it polite to listen, sir" is a prelude to the jokes against class society which run through the play. Algernon's first little speech touches on the foolish opposition of life and sentiment, science and art. Talk of science and life leads by Wildean transition back to the action and the cucumber sandwiches. Champagne takes the action to speculation on servants and masters, and thence to marriage and morals. A little dialectical climax is reached with the answer to the question: "Is marriage so demoralizing as that?" when Lane coolly replies: "I believe it *is* a very pleasant state, sir" and adds, by way of an explanation not less disconcerting, especially by Victorian standards, "I have had very little experience of it myself up to the present. I have only been married once." Which is followed by an explanation of this explanation: "That was in consequence of a misunderstanding. . . ." It cannot be said that, in this passage, marriage receives the "staggering blows" which some modern writers are said to have given to it. But it does not receive poisoned pinpricks that are just as effective? Are not the inversions and double inversions of standards handled with dexterous delicacy? "No, sir, it is not a very interesting subject." A delicious turn in the argument! And then Algernon's little moralistic summing-up: "Lane's views on marriage seem somewhat lax. Really, if the lower orders don't set us a good example. . . ." And so it ripples on.

Most of us have seen plays or films in which a serious plot or theme is enlivened—"dramatized," as we say—by comic incident and witticism. Such plays and films are at best sweetened pills. "Entertainment value" is added as an afterthought, reminding one of the man who, having watched for weeks the construction of a modern Gothic building, cried one day: "Oh look, they're putting the architecture on now!" Oscar Wilde's procedure is the opposite of all this. He has no serious plot, no credible characters. His witticisms are not comic relief: they are serious relief. They function in ironic counterpoint with the absurdities of the action. This counterpoint is Wilde's method. It is what gives him his peculiar voice and his peculiar triumph. It is what makes him hard to catch: the fish's tail flicks, flashes, and disappears. Perhaps *Earnest* should be defined as "almost a satire." As the conversations in *Alice in Wonderland* hover on the frontier of sense without ever quite crossing it, so the dialogue in *Earnest* is forever on the frontier of satire, forever on the point of breaking into bitter criticism. It never breaks. The ridiculous action constantly steps in to prevent the break. That is its function. Before the enemy can denounce Wilde, the agile outburst is over, and we are back among the cucumber sandwiches.

If in drama we always look for contrasts, the crucial one in this play—the one that establishes the principal interactions—is that between the elegant *savoir-faire* of these people and the absurdity of what they do. It is a contrast between, on the one hand, character, spectacle, and dialogue and, on the other, plot. The plot has thus to counterbalance the three other components. Silly as a story considered separately, it is highly important in the structure of a play which has its serious side, which ends, indeed, in being a criticism of life. Beware of calling Wilde's comedy unreal! The contrast between smooth, assured appearances and inner emptiness is nothing more nor less than a fact, a fact of sociology and history. Wilde knew his England and, after his fashion, painted her portrait.

> If Sarcey tells us about the "first night" of *Cyrano,* we learn of the first night of *Earnest* from Bernard Shaw—see his *Dramatic Opinions,* Volume I, "An Old New Play and a New Old One"—who is also one of Wilde's acutest critics. There is a notable appreciation of Wilde as playwright in St. John Hankin's *Dramatic Works,* Volume III, *The Collected Plays of Oscar Wilde.*

3. THE MISER · 1668

IF ROSTAND AND WILDE may be said to be at one remove from the average modern play, and thus from the average modern person's experience, the older theatrical classics are at three removes: the time that separates their age from ours constitutes the second, and the greatness that renders their work rich and complex constitutes the third remove. If, then, the reader felt that *Cyrano* and *Earnest* made some demands on his intellect and on his sympathy, he will find Molière and Shakespeare making much greater ones. If he still wishes to extend his experience and understanding of drama, he must now summon all his strength and take a leap.

For here the matter of historical background becomes a problem. The reader needs some knowledge of Molière's life and times, but how much? (See Letter to the Reader, pp. 4-5.) A possible reply to this all but impossible question is: "You must have some sense of Molière as a bourgeois (middle-class) poet in an aristocratic (upper-class) age, in an age when a king, served by certain notable members of the bourgeoisie, established his ascendancy over an initially rebellious nobility. You must understand that Molière was both a court poet who on occasion arranged lavish entertainments for the king and a touring actor-manager who performed in improvised conditions before popular audiences. In short, anything you know about France in the age of Louis XIV, anything that is not a mere fact lying fallow in your mind, isolated or as an item in a catalogue. What you need is a *vivid impression* of the age of Louis XIV, and that is to be obtained less from history textbooks than from imaginative histories and biographies—and from pictorial material, especially, for our purposes, pictures in the standard histories of the theater, such as *A History of the Theatre*, by Freedley and Reeves.

'For historical background means not only the political and general background but also that specific background of drama which is—theater. You must know, for example, what kind of comedy lay to hand when Molière began to look about him, namely, the *commedia dell'arte* (Italian for "comedy of art") a kind of comedy in which the dialogue follows certain set forms and the actors always play the same roles: Mr. A always plays the imbecile old man, Mr. B always the boastful soldier, Mr. C the romantic lover, Mr. D the clown, and so on."

One is tempted to add: "You must know French." For no translation quite gives us the spirit of Molière, his special tone and temper. One could also add: "You must know France." Even someone ignorant of French might learn more about Molière in a Paris theater today than from all the books on the seventeenth century. He would, at least partially, sense what the spirit of Molière, his tone and temper, are. He would feel the rhythm of the plays and would see how it is communicated to an audience.

But it is assumed that many readers of this book have neither studied French nor visited French theaters. Such readers must simply try hard. They must use whatever they possess of historical and theatrical imagination. Molière's greatness may not be immediately apparent to them. They must have the will to understand what his enormous reputation rests on. In many modern persons there interferes at this point a certain philistinism or "muckerism," that is, an evil spirit that whispers: "If you don't see it at once, it probably isn't there. You are clever; other people are snobs. Therefore the reputation that other people have created for an author is probably bogus, your own first impression a pointer to the truth. In any event, one should never be over-impressed. Be bluff and blunt, and someday they'll make you a professional theater critic." Certainly, patient truth-seeking makes less noise in the world than brash self-assurance. It all depends what you want. It is assumed here that you want to understand Molière.

THE MISER

by Molière

TRANSLATED BY LLOYD PARKS

✷

Used by permission of Lloyd Parks. All rights whatsoever in this translation are strictly reserved, and applications for performances, etc., should be made to Mr. Parks, Uhrichsville, Ohio.

The Miser

Characters

HARPAGON, *father of Cleanth and Elise, and in love with Marianne*
CLEANTH, *Harpagon's son, and in love with Marianne*
ELISE, *Harpagon's daughter, and in love with Valère*
VALÈRE, *Anselm's son, and in love with Elise*
MARIANNE, *Anselm's daughter, and in love with Cleanth*
ANSELM, *father of Valère and Marianne*
FROSINE, *a woman of intrigue*
MASTER SIMON, *a broker*
MASTER JACQUES, *Harpagon's coachman and cook*
LA FLÈCHE, *Cleanth's valet*
DAME CLAUDE, *Harpagon's maid*
BRINDAVOINE, *Harpagon's lackey*
LA MERLUCHE, *Harpagon's lackey*

A Commissary and his clerk

THE PLACE: *Paris. Harpagon's house.*

Act I

Enter VALÈRE *and* ELISE.

VALÈRE. What is it, charming Elise? Are you melancholy? After all the obliging assurances you so kindly gave of faith in me? Alas! I see you sighing in the midst of my joy! Tell me, do you regret our engagement—to which my ardour has perhaps constrained you?

ELISE. No, Valère, I could not regret what I have done for you. I feel myself drawn by powers far too sweet, and I lack strength to wish that things were not as they are. But to tell the truth, I fear to think of the consequences. I am much afraid that I love you a little more than I ought.

VALÈRE. Ah! Elise, what can you have to fear from the kindness you have shown me?

ELISE. Alas! a hundred things: my father's wrath, reproaches from my family, the censure of the world—but most of all, Valère, a change in your heart and that criminal coldness with which those of your sex most often repay the over-ardent testimonies of innocent love.

VALÈRE. Oh! do not do me the wrong of judging me by others. Suspect me of anything, Elise, but not that I should fail in my duty to you. I love you too much for that, and I will love you as long as I live.

ELISE. Ah! that is the way you all talk. All men are alike in their speech; their actions alone reveal their differences.

VALÈRE. If our actions alone reveal what we are, then at least wait and judge my heart by mine; and do not invent crimes for me simply because unhappy apprehension has bred unjust fear. I beg you, do not kill me with mortal blows of outrageous suspicion. Give me time to convince you, by a thousand and one proofs, that my intentions are honorable.

ELISE. Alas! how easily we are persuaded by those we love! Yes, Valère, I think you have no room in your heart for deceit. I am convinced that you love me truly, and will always be faithful to me. I have no wish to doubt you; I am sad only because I fear I may be blamed by others.

VALÈRE. What is it that worries you?

ELISE. I would have nothing to fear if everyone saw you as I do. For in your very person I see enough to justify what I have done. My heart has all your merit for its defense, reinforced by that gratitude which Heaven has bade me owe you. Not an hour passes but I picture to myself the terrible catastrophe which brought us into one another's sight; your amazing generosity, which made you risk your life to preserve mine from the fury of the waves; the great pains you took, how tenderly you cared for me after lifting me from the water; and the assiduous homage of your ardent love, which neither time nor difficulty has discouraged; which causes you to neglect both family and fatherland; which detains you in this place, and makes you hide your rank for my sake; and which has reduced you to wearing my father's livery. All of this has certainly made a wonderful impression on me, and in my eyes is justification enough for the engagement I have consented to. But perhaps that is not enough to justify it to the world, nor am I sure that every one feels as I do.

VALÈRE. For all that you have said, it is only through my love that I pretend to merit your esteem, and as for your scruples, a father like yours is justification enough for anything you might do. His excessive avarice and the austere manner in which he lives with his children might well authorize far stranger things than this. Pardon me, charming Elise, for talking this way in front of you, but you know there is no good to be said on that score. But, if, as I hope, I can finally find my parents again, it will not be hard to win him over. I am waiting impatiently for news of them, and I will go and inquire if it is much longer in coming.

ELISE. Oh! Valère, do not go away, I beg you. Think only of winning my father's confidence.

VALÈRE. You have seen how I go about it; you saw how artfully compliant I was obliged to be in order to introduce myself into his service—under what mask of sympathy and agreement I disguise my feelings to please him—what role I play to gain his affection. And I am making admirable progress. I have discovered that, to win men over, there is no better way than to trick yourself out in their inclinations, fall in with their maxims, burn incense to their faults, and applaud everything they do. One need have no fear of overdoing complaisance. No matter how obviously you play on their feelings, the shrewdest men are always the greatest dupes when it comes to flattery. There is nothing so impertinent or so ridiculous that you can't make them swallow it—if you season it well with praise. Sincerity, of course, suffers a little by this trade. But if you need certain men, you must adapt yourself to them. And, since there is no other way of winning them over, it is not the flatterers who are at fault, but those who wish to be flattered.

ELISE. Why don't you try to gain my brother's support too—in the event my maid should decide to tell our secret?

VALÈRE. I cannot manage both of them at the same time. The father's temperament and the son's are so opposed, it would be hard to accommodate the confidings of both at once. But you, for your part, could approach your brother, and avail yourself of his friendship to get him to act on our behalf. There he comes now. I'll withdraw. Use the occasion to sound him out, but don't disclose our affair unless you think the time is ripe. *Exit.*

ELISE. I don't know if I will have the courage to confide in him.

Enter CLEANTH.

CLEANTH. I am very happy to find you alone, Elise. I have been burning to unburden a secret to you.

ELISE. Here I am, ready to listen, Cleanth. What do you wish to tell me?

CLEANTH. A thousand things, Elise—all bound up in three words: I'm in love.

ELISE. You are in love?

CLEANTH. I am in love. But before I say more, I know I am dependent on my father; that the name of son subjects me to his wishes; that we should not commit ourselves without the consent of those who brought us into the world; that Heaven has made them the masters of our truth; that we are enjoined not to pledge it except by their direction; that having never been affected by foolish passions, they are in a condition to be deceived much less often than we are, and can see more clearly what is best for us. I know that we ought to trust the light of their prudence rather than the blindness of our passion and that the extravagance of youth most often lures us toward the precipice of sorrow. I am telling all this to you, Elise, so that you won't take the trouble to tell it to *me*. For, to tell the truth, my love will not listen. So, please do not make objections.

ELISE. Are you engaged, Cleanth, to her whom you love?

CLEANTH. No, but I am resolved to be. And again I beg you not to offer any reasons to dissuade me.

ELISE. Am I such a stranger, Cleanth?

CLEANTH. No, Elise; but you are not in love. You do not know the violence that tender love does to our hearts. I mistrust your prudence.

ELISE. Alas! Cleanth, let us not talk of my prudence. There is no one who is not deficient in that at least once in a lifetime; and if I opened my heart to you, perhaps in your eyes I should seem far less prudent than you are.

CLEANTH. Ah! I wish to Heaven, that your heart, like mine. . . .

ELISE. First of all, let us finish with your affair. Tell me, who is she. . . .

CLEANTH. A young lady who has lived but a short time in this neighborhood, and who seems to have been made to inspire love in all who see her. Nature never shaped anything more lovable. I felt transported the moment I saw her. Her name is Marianne and she lives under the protection of her mother—a good woman who is almost always ill, and whom her daughter holds in such loving regard, it is unbelievable. She waits on her, takes pity on her, and consoles her so tenderly that it touches your heart. She has the most charming way in the world of going about her business. A thousand graces shine through her every action. Such alluring sweetness, such engaging goodness, such adorable civility! such. . . . Oh! Elise, if you could only see her!

ELISE. I see a great deal of her, Cleanth, through what you have told me. And to understand her, it is enough for me that you love her.

CLEANTH. I have discovered, in a roundabout way, that they are not very well provided for, and that even with frugal management, they can hardly stretch their income far enough to cover all their needs. Imagine, Elise, what a pleasure it would be to be able to raise the fortunes of the person one loves, adroitly to supply a little help for the modest needs of a virtuous family. And think how unpleasant it must be for me to be powerless to taste that pleasure because of my father's stinginess, to be powerless to surprise this beautiful girl with some proof of my love for her.

ELISE. Oh! Cleanth, I can easily conceive how exasperated you must feel.

CLEANTH. Ah! Elise, much more so than you can imagine. Really, have you ever seen anything more cruel than the rigorous economy he imposes on us, than this queer stinginess under which we languish? What good will wealth do us, if it comes only when we are past the age when we can most enjoy it, if even to maintain myself I am now obliged to go into debt on every side, and if I am reduced with you to seeking help from tradesmen to find the means to wear decent clothes? I really wanted to ask you to help me find out father's attitude toward my present feelings. If I find him contrary, I am resolved to go away, in the company of that wonderful creature, to enjoy whatever fortune Providence may offer us. I am having somebody look everywhere for money to borrow for this purpose;

and, if your affairs are in the same state as mine, if father insists on opposing our desires, we will both leave him, and free ourselves of this tyranny, to which his insupportable avarice has so long subjected us.

ELISE. It is only too true that he gives us more reason every day to regret our mother's death, and that. . . .

CLEANTH. I can hear his voice. Let us go somewhere else to conclude our confidences. Later we will join forces and assault his hard heart together. *Exeunt.*

Enter HARPAGON *and* LA FLÈCHE.

HARPAGON. Get out of here at once, and don't answer back! Go on, leave my house! You master-mind of crime! You born gallow's bait!

FLÈCHE, *aside*. I have never seen anything so wicked as this cursèd old man, and I believe, begging your pardon, he has a devil in his flesh.

HARPAGON. Are you muttering between your teeth?

FLÈCHE. Why chase me out of the house?

HARPAGON. As though you didn't know why! Scoundrel! Go quickly before I beat you!

FLÈCHE. What have I done?

HARPAGON. You have done enough to make me want you to leave.

FLÈCHE. My master your son gave me orders to wait for him.

HARPAGON. Go and wait for him in the street, not here in my house, standing there as stiff and straight as a post to watch what goes on and profit from everything. . . . I will not have someone continually spying on my business, a traitor whose cursèd eyes besiege all my actions, devour all I possess, and ferret about in every corner for something to steal.

FLÈCHE. How the deuce do you expect anyone to steal from you? Can you rob a man when he keeps everything under lock and key, and stands guard day and night?

HARPAGON. I will lock up whatever I think should be locked up, and I will stand guard as I please. *To audience.* There, isn't that the talk of a spy who watches everything you do? I tremble lest he suspects something about my money. *To* LA FLÈCHE. Are you the kind of man who would go about spreading the story that I have money hidden away?

FLÈCHE. *Do* you have money hidden away?

HARPAGON. No, you rascal, I didn't say that. *Aside.* I'm losing my temper. *To* LA FLÈCHE. I mean, would you go around spreading the story that I do have some—out of malice?

FLÈCHE. Hoho! what difference does it make to us, if you have or have not? Things are always the same for us anyway.

HARPAGON. Ha! you play the reasoner! I'll teach you how to reason with your ears. *Lifting his hand to give* LA FLÈCHE *a box on the ear.* One last time—get out of here!

FLÈCHE. All right, I'm going.

HARPAGON. Wait. You're not taking anything of mine with you?

FLÈCHE. What could I take of yours?

HARPAGON. Come here, so I can see. Show me your hands.

FLÈCHE. There they are.

HARPAGON, *sarcastically*. Your other hands.

FLÈCHE. My other hands?

HARPAGON. Yes.

FLÈCHE, *good-humoredly*. There they are.

HARPAGON, *pointing to* LA FLÈCHE'S *breeches*. Have you put anything inside there?

FLÈCHE. See for yourself.

HARPAGON, *feeling the knees of* LA FLÈCHE'S *breeches*. These breeches are just right for hiding stolen goods, and I wish somebody had been hanged for it. . . .

FLÈCHE. Ah! how well a man like that deserves what he fears, and what pleasure it would give me to steal from him.

HARPAGON. Eh?

FLÈCHE. What?

HARPAGON. What did you say about stealing?

FLÈCHE. I said that you are poking everywhere to see if I have stolen anything from you.

HARPAGON. That's what I intend to do.

FLÈCHE, *aside*. A pox on avarice and the avaricious!

HARPAGON. How's that? What did you say?

FLÈCHE. What did I say?

HARPAGON. Yes. What did you say about avarice and the avaricious?

FLÈCHE. I said, a pox on avarice and the avaricious.

HARPAGON. Who are you talking about?

FLÈCHE. About avaricious men.

HARPAGON. And who are they, these avaricious men?

FLÈCHE. They are misers and villains.

HARPAGON. But who do you mean by that?

FLÈCHE. What are you so upset about?

HARPAGON. I am upset about what I ought to be upset about.

FLÈCHE. Do you think I mean you?

HARPAGON. I think what I think. But I want you to tell me who you were speaking to when you said that.

FLÈCHE. I . . . . I was speaking to my beret.

HARPAGON. And I might well knock it off.

FLÈCHE. Would you stop me from cursing avaricious men?

HARPAGON. No, but I'll stop you from chattering and being insolent. Keep quiet.

FLÈCHE. I haven't named anybody.

HARPAGON. I'll thrash you if you talk.

FLÈCHE. If your nose feels snotty, blow it.

HARPAGON. Will you be quiet?

FLÈCHE. Yes, in spite of myself.

HARPAGON. Ah! ah!

FLÈCHE, *showing him one of his waist-coat pockets.* Look, here's another pocket. Are you satisfied?

HARPAGON. Come now, give it back to me without any more searching.

FLÈCHE. What?

HARPAGON. What you took from me.

FLÈCHE. I took nothing from you.

HARPAGON. Are you sure?

FLÈCHE. Positive.

HARPAGON. Goodbye! Go to the devil!

FLÈCHE. Well, I must say, I have been very handsomely dismissed!

HARPAGON. At least I have laid something to your conscience.

Exit LA FLÈCHE.

HARPAGON. That rascal of a valet makes me uneasy, and I don't care to see the limping cur around here. *Alone.* It's certainly no small worry having a large sum of money in this house, and it's a lucky

ACT I] THE MISER 227

man who has his fortune well invested, and can carry what he needs for expenses on his own person. It's no little problem to find, in an entire house, a safe hiding place for it. Because, to my way of thinking, your strong-boxes are suspect; I'd never trust my money to one. In my opinion they are nothing but bait for thieves, they are what a thief always goes after first. *Enter* CLEANTH *and* ELISE *unnoticed*. Still, I don't know if it was wise to bury the ten thousand écus I was paid yesterday in the garden. Ten thousand gold écus is a rather large sum to have about the house. Oh! Heavens! I must have given myself away! I must have been carried away by anxiety—and I think I spoke out loud while I was reasoning with myself all alone here. . . . . *Noticing* CLEANTH *and* ELISE. What's the matter?

CLEANTH. Nothing, father.

HARPAGON. Have you been there very long?

ELISE. We have just come.

HARPAGON. You heard. . . .

CLEANTH. What, father?

HARPAGON. There. . . .

ELISE. What?

HARPAGON. What I just said.

CLEANTH. No.

HARPAGON. Yes, you did, you did.

ELISE. I beg your pardon, but we didn't.

HARPAGON. I can plainly see you heard something. I was talking to myself about how hard it is to find money these days, and I said that anyone who happens to have ten thousand écus about the house is a very lucky man.

CLEANTH. We held back for fear of interrupting you.

HARPAGON. I am only too glad to let you know what I said. So you won't get it all wrong and think it is I who have the ten thousand écus.

CLEANTH. We don't concern ourselves with your affairs.

HARPAGON. Would to God I had that much money, ten thousand écus!

CLEANTH. I don't believe it.

HARPAGON. It would be a fine thing for me.

ELISE. These are matters. . . .

HARPAGON. I could certainly use it.

CLEANTH. I think that. . . .

HARPAGON. It would set me up very comfortably.

ELISE. You are. . . .

HARPAGON. I wouldn't complain then, as I do now, about how hard the times are!

CLEANTH. My God, father, you have no room to complain: everyone knows you are well-off.

HARPAGON. What! I am well-off? Those who say so are liars. Nothing could be more untrue. And those who go around spreading such a story are all villains.

ELISE. Don't be angry.

HARPAGON. It is very strange that my own children should betray me and become my enemies.

CLEANTH. Am I your enemy because I say you are well-off?

HARPAGON. Yes. That kind of talk and your extravagant spending will one day cause somebody to come here and to cut my throat, under the impression that my clothes are lined with money.

CLEANTH. What extravagant spending have I done?

HARPAGON. What? Is there anything more scandalous than the sumptuous clothes that you parade all over the city? Yesterday I was criticizing your sister, but this is far worse. This cries out to Heaven for vengeance; and, taking you from head to foot, there is enough on you to buy a good piece of property. I have told you twenty times, son, that your ways displease me very much. You are breaking your neck to look like a marquis, and in order to go about dressed as you are, I am sure you must be stealing from me.

CLEANTH. Ha! how could I steal from you?

HARPAGON. How should I know? Then were do you get the means to keep up your fashionable appearance?

CLEANTH. I, father? Why, I gamble, and, since I am very lucky, I put all the money I win on my back.

HARPAGON. That is very ill-advised. If you are lucky at cards you ought to profit by it, and invest your money at an honest interest, so that one day you will find it has. . . . I should like very much to know, not to mention the rest, what good are all those ribbons you are garnished with from head to foot, as if half a dozen laces would not be enough to hold up your breeches? Is it really necessary to spend your money on wigs, when you can wear the hair that grows

ACT I]   THE MISER   229

on your head, which doesn't cost a sou? I'll wager your wigs and ribbons alone are worth at least twenty pistoles. And twenty pistoles bring in eight francs, six sols, and eight deniers a year, even at eight per cent interest.

CLEANTH. You are quite right.

HARPAGON. Enough of that; let us talk about something else. Eh? *Aside, seeing* CLEANTH *and* ELISE *making signs to one another.* I think they are signalling one another to pick my pockets. *To* CLEANTH *and* ELISE. What do those signs mean?

ELISE. We were bargaining as to who should speak first, my brother or myself. Both of us have something to tell you.

HARPAGON. And I, too, have something to tell both of you.

CLEANTH. It is about marriage, father, that we wish to speak with you.

HARPAGON. And it is marriage also that I want to discuss with you.

ELISE. Oh! father!

HARPAGON. Why "Oh! father!"? Is it the word, daughter, or the thing that frightens you?

CLEANTH. Marriage could be frightening in both respects, depending on how you mean it. And we are afraid that our inclinations might not agree with your choice.

HARPAGON. Have a little patience. Don't get alarmed. I know what is best for you both, and neither one of you will have reason to complain of anything I intend to do. Now, to begin at the beginning, tell me, have you ever seen a girl named Marianne, who lives not far from here?

CLEANTH. Yes, father.

HARPAGON, *to* ELISE. And you?

ELISE. I have heard of her.

HARPAGON. What do you think of this girl, Cleanth?

CLEANTH. An extremely charming person.

HARPAGON. Her physiognomy?

CLEANTH. Very honest and intelligent.

HARPAGON. Her air and manner?

CLEANTH. Exquisite, to be sure.

HARPAGON. Don't you think a girl like that is worth some consideration?

CLEANTH. Yes, father.

HARPAGON. That she might be a very desirable match?

CLEANTH. Very desirable.

HARPAGON. That she looks very much as though she would make a good housewife?

CLEANTH. No doubt.

HARPAGON. And that a husband would be completely satisfied with her?

CLEANTH. Surely.

HARPAGON. There is one slight obstacle. I am afraid she may not have as much money as one might reasonably expect.

CLEANTH. Ah! father, money is no consideration when it is a question of marrying an honest woman.

HARPAGON. Pardon me, if I disagree! But there is always this to be said: if a fortune does not measure up to one's expectations, one can always try to make it up some other way.

CLEANTH. Of course.

HARPAGON. Well—I am happy to find that you agree with me, because her maidenly conduct and sweet disposition have won my heart, and I am resolved to marry her. Provided she has some kind of property.

CLEANTH. Eh?

HARPAGON. What?

CLEANTH. You say you have resolved. . . .

HARPAGON. To marry Marianne.

CLEANTH. Who? you, you?

HARPAGON. Yes. I, I, I! What do you mean by that?

CLEANTH. I feel dizzy all of a sudden. I think I'll go.   *Exit* CLEANTH.

HARPAGON. It will pass. Quick, go into the kitchen and drink a large glass of plain water. *To* ELISE. There's one of your lily-livered dandies—no more constitution than a chicken! Well, daughter, that's what I have decided for myself. As for your brother, I have a certain widow in mind that someone spoke to me about this very morning. And as for you, I am going to give you to Signor Anselm.

ELISE. To Signor Anselm?

HARPAGON. Yes. A man who is mature, prudent and wise, who is not over fifty, and who is famous for his great wealth.

ELISE. I would rather not get married at all, father, if you please.

HARPAGON. And I, my little girl, my pet, would rather you did get married, if you please.

ELISE. I beg your pardon, father.

HARPAGON. I beg your pardon, daughter.

ELISE. I am Signor Anselm's most humble servant, but, with your permission, I will not marry him.

HARPAGON. I am your very humble valet, but, with your permission, you shall marry him—this very evening.

ELISE. This very evening?

HARPAGON. This very evening.

ELISE. That shall never be, father.

HARPAGON. That shall be, daughter.

ELISE. No.

HARPAGON. Yes.

ELISE. I tell you, no.

HARPAGON. I tell you, yes.

ELISE. You shall never force me to do such a thing.

HARPAGON. I shall force you to do such a thing.

ELISE. I would kill myself sooner than marry such a husband.

HARPAGON. You will not kill yourself, and you shall marry him. Such audacity! Did you ever hear of a daughter talking to her father that way?

ELISE. Did you ever hear of a father marrying off his daughter that way?

HARPAGON. It is a match which will admit of no objection. And I will wager that everyone will approve my choice.

ELISE. And I will wager that no reasonable person could possibly approve it.

HARPAGON. Here is Valère. Would you be willing to let him be the judge of this matter for both of us?

ELISE. I'll consent to that.

HARPAGON. Will you abide by his decision?

ELISE. Yes. I will stand by whatever he says.

HARPAGON. It's settled then.

Enter VALÈRE.

HARPAGON. Here, Valère. We have elected you to decide who is in the right, my daughter or myself.

VALÈRE. You sir, there's no contradicting that.

HARPAGON. You know, of course, what we are talking about.

VALÈRE. No, but you couldn't be wrong; you are reason itself.

HARPAGON. Tonight I want to give her a husband who is as rich as he is wise, and the hussy tells me to my face she will have no part of him. What do you say to that?

VALÈRE. What do I say to that?

HARPAGON. Yes.

VALÈRE. Hoho!

HARPAGON. What?

VALÈRE. I say that fundamentally I am of your opinion; and that you couldn't possibly be wrong; but on the other hand, she is not absolutely in the wrong either, and. . . .

HARPAGON. How so! Signor Anselm is a considerable match. He is a gentleman: noble, cultured, poised, intelligent and very rich; and he has no children left from his first marriage. Could she do better?

VALÈRE. True, but she might tell you that you are hurrying things somewhat, and that she ought to have a little time at least to find out whether she can adapt her temperament to. . . .

HARPAGON. This is an opportunity that must be grasped by the forelock. This match offers me an advantage which I would find in no other. He has agreed to take her without a dowry and. . . .

VALÈRE. Without a dowry?

HARPAGON. Yes.

VALÈRE. Ah! I have nothing more to say. You see, here is a reason that is entirely convincing; one can only defer to it. . . . .

HARPAGON. To me it represents a considerable saving.

VALÈRE. Certainly. There's no denying it. It's true your daughter may suggest to you that marriage is a more important step than you are inclined to think; that it is a question of being happy or unhappy for the rest of one's life; and that a partnership which will last till death should never be entered on without great precaution.

HARPAGON. Without a dowry!

VALÈRE. You are right. That decides everything, naturally. Though there are those who might tell you that in such matters you certainly ought to have some regard for your daughter's inclinations, and that the great difference in age, in temperament, and in sensibility would render such a marriage liable to very unhappy accidents.

HARPAGON. Without a dowry!

VALÈRE. Oh! there's no gainsaying that, as everyone knows. Who the deuce would argue the point? Not that there aren't many fathers who are more interested in their daughter's happiness than in the money they give with them; who would never sacrifice them to their own interest; and who seek, above all else, to insure that sweet conformity in marriage which is a continuous source of honor, tranquillity and joy, and which. . . .

HARPAGON. Without a dowry!

VALÈRE. Very true. That closes every mouth. Without a dowry! An irrefutable argument!

HARPAGON. Wait! I think I hear a dog barking. *Aside.* Is someone trying to get at my money? *To* VALÈRE. Don't move; I'll be back in a minute. *Exit* HARPAGON.

ELISE. Are you joking, Valère, talking to him this way?

VALÈRE. I don't want to sour him. This way I can better accomplish my own ends. Opposing his ideas to his face is a sure way to spoil everything. There are certain minds you have to take by the bias. Some temperaments are inimical to any kind of resistance: they stiffen themselves against the truth, and always balk when they confront the straight road of reason. You can guide them where you want to take them only by leading them in a roundabout way. Pretend that you consent to what he wants; you will be more certain to get your way in the end. . . . .

ELISE. But this marriage, Valère?

VALÈRE. We'll break it on the bias.

ELISE. What can we contrive if it is to be concluded tonight?

VALÈRE. You must ask them to delay it. Feign a sickness.

ELISE. But they will discover the pretense—if they call in the doctor.

VALÈRE. Are you joking? Do doctors know anything about sickness? Come now, with doctors you can have any sickness you please, and they will find reasons for your having it, and tell you where it comes from.

Enter HARPAGON.

HARPAGON, *aside*. It was nothing, thank God!

VALÈRE. As a last resort we could run away and leave all this behind. And if your love, Elise, is capable of firmness. . . . *Seeing* HARPAGON. Yes, a daughter should obey her father. She should have no concern for what her husband is like; and, when such a powerful argument as *without a dowry* intervenes, she should be ready to accept whatever is given her.

HARPAGON. Good! That was well said, that!

VALÈRE. Sir, I beg pardon if I have been too forward, and for having made so bold as to talk to her this way.

HARPAGON. What do you mean? I am delighted. And I want to give you absolute power over her. *To* ELISE. There's no good running away. ELISE *moves to the end of the stage.* I give him the same authority over you that God gave me, and I expect you to do everything he tells you.

VALÈRE, *to* ELISE. After that how can you resist my remonstrances! Sir, I will follow her and continue the lessons I have been giving her.

HARPAGON. Yes, you will oblige me. Truly. . . .

VALÈRE. I think it is good to pull in the reins with her.

HARPAGON. That's right, you should. . . . .

VALÈRE. Don't worry about a thing; I am sure I can manage this.

HARPAGON. Do, do as you like. I am going to take a little walk through the city. I'll be back shortly.

VALÈRE. Yes, money is the most precious thing in the world, and you ought to thank God for the honest father He has given you. He knows what it takes to live. When someone offers to take a girl without a dowry, she ought not to look any further. Everything is included in *without a dowry;* it takes the place of beauty, youth, birth, honor, intelligence and probity. *Exeunt* VALÈRE *and* ELISE.

HARPAGON. Ah! bravo, bravo! Spoken like an oracle. Lucky the man with such a servant!

Act II

CLEANTH *is on stage. Enter* LA FLÈCHE.

CLEANTH. Ah! you traitor! What new mischief have you been getting into? Didn't I give you orders? . . . . .

FLÈCHE. Yes sir! I came here with every intention of waiting for you, but your father, the most ungracious man in the world, chased me out of the house, in spite of myself, and I came close to getting a beating.

CLEANTH. How goes our business? Things are more pressing now than ever. Since I last saw you, I have discovered that my own father is my rival.

FLÈCHE. Your father is in love?

CLEANTH. Yes; and I had all the trouble in the world to keep him from seeing how much this news distressed me.

FLÈCHE. Him, dabbling in love? What the devil can he be thinking of? Does public opinion mean nothing to him? Was love made for men built like that?

CLEANTH. It must be for my sins that he has got this idea into his head.

FLÈCHE. For what reason do you keep your love a secret from him?

CLEANTH. So that he will be less suspicious. So that he won't suspect my actions should it become necessary to try and prevent his marriage. What answer did they give you?

FLÈCHE. By Heaven, sir, those that have to borrow are in a very bad way! A man has to put up with strange things when he is reduced, as you are, to putting himself into the hands of sharks.

CLEANTH. You couldn't get the money?

FLÈCHE. Not exactly. Our Master Simon, the broker, who was recommended to us as an energetic, determined man, assures me he has left no stone unturned to serve you—and that your face alone has won his heart.

CLEANTH. Will I get the fifteen thousand francs I asked for?

FLÈCHE. Yes, but there are some trifling conditions attached—which you must accept, if you expect anything to be done.

CLEANTH. Did he let you speak to the man who is supposed to lend the money?

FLÈCHE. Oh, really, it is not so simple as all that. He took more pains to hide himself than you do yourself; it is all much more mysterious than you might think. They will by no means tell his name, and they are going to bring you together today in a private house, so that he can learn from your own lips who your family is and what your expectations are. But I don't have the slightest doubt that your father's name alone will make things easy for you.

CLEANTH. And especially the fact that our mother is dead, whose property no one can take from me.

FLÈCHE. Here are a few articles which he himself dictated to our go-between, to be shown to you before any action will be taken.

"Supposing that the lender is satisfied with the collateral offered, and that the borrower has reached his majority and is from a family whose estate is large, solid, assured and free from all encumbrance, a valid and precise contract will be drawn up in the presence of a notary, the most honest man available, who, for that reason, must be chosen by the lender, to whom it is of the utmost importance that the contract be properly drawn up."

CLEANTH. I have no objection to that.

FLÈCHE. "The lender, in order not to burden his conscience with any scruples, intends to charge no more than six per cent interest."

CLEANTH. Six per cent interest? By Jove, an honest fellow indeed! There is no reason to complain about that.

FLÈCHE. Indeed not!

"But, since the said lender does not have the sum required in his own house, and because, in order to oblige the borrower, he is forced to borrow himself at the rate of twenty per cent, it is only fair that the said, first borrower should pay this interest without prejudice to the other, considering that it is only to oblige him that the said lender will borrow the sum requested."

CLEANTH. What the devil! What Jew, what Arab am I dealing with? That's more than twenty five per cent interest!

FLÈCHE. That's right. That's what I told him. You had better look into it yourself.

CLEANTH. What is there to look into? I need money. I will have to agree to anything.

FLÈCHE. That's what I told him.

CLEANTH. Is there something else?

FLÈCHE. Only a small item.

"Of the fifteen thousand francs that are requested, the lender can count on only twelve thousand francs in cash. As for the remaining thousand écus, the borrower must take them in furniture, clothing, and jewelry, a list of which follows this note, and which the said lender has, in all good faith, priced as moderately as he possibly can."

CLEANTH. What does he mean by that?

FLÈCHE. Listen to the list.

"First: one four-poster bed, with Hungarian point lace handsomely sewn on olive-coloured cloth, with six chairs, and a counterpane of the same material; all in good condition and lined with changeable red and blue taffeta.

"In addition: one bedstead canopy of good, dry rose-coloured serge, with silk fringes."

CLEANTH. What does he expect me to do with that?

FLÈCHE. Hold on.

"In addition: a set of tapestries; the subject of which is *The Amours of Gombaut and Macaea*.

"In addition: one large walnut table, with twelve columns, or turned pillars, pulling out at either end, and fitted with half-a-dozen joint stools under it."

CLEANTH. My God! What good will that do me!

FLÈCHE. Be patient.

"In addition: three large muskets inlaid with mother-of-pearl, with three matching tripods.

"In addition: one brick furnace with two retorts and three recipients, very useful for anyone interested in distilling.

"In addition: a Bologna lute with all its strings, or few lacking.

"In addition: a troll-madam table and a chess board, with a goose game restored from the Greeks; all very fine to pass away the time when one has nothing to do.

"In addition: a lizard skin, three feet long, and half-filled with straw—a very agreeable curiosity to hang from a bedroom ceiling.

"The total mentioned above, easily worth more than four thousand, five hundred francs, is reduced in price to one thousand écus by the moderation of the lender."

CLEANTH. May the plague choke him and his moderation, the traitor! Cut-throat that he is! Have you ever heard of such usury? Can't he be satisfied with the furious interest he demands, without making me take all the junk he has heaped up, for three thousand francs? I won't get more than two hundred écus for the lot! And yet I must resign myself and consent to whatever he wants. He is in a position to make me accept anything. The dog has me by the throat.

FLÈCHE. Sir, I see you taking the very same road, no offense intended, that Panurge followed to his ruin: taking money in advance, buying dear and selling cheap, and eating your wheat in the blade.*

CLEANTH. What would you have me do? You see what young men are reduced to by the cursèd avarice of their fathers! Is it any wonder, after this, that the sons should wish their fathers' death?

FLÈCHE. I must confess, the stinginess of your's would infuriate the calmest man in the world. I am not strongly inclined toward the gallows, thank God, and when I am with my colleagues, seeing them taking big chances for small gains, I always know when to pull my iron out of the fire, and when it is prudent to drop out of any adventure that smells ever so little of the gallows. But, to tell the truth, the way your father acts tempts me very much to steal from him. And I think, if I did rob him, I would be doing a good deed.

CLEANTH. Give me the note; I want to look it over again.

Enter MASTER SIMON *and* HARPAGON.

SIMON. Yes sir, he is a young man in need of money. The state of his affairs obliges him to find some, and he will agree to anything you prescribe.

HARPAGON. But are you convinced, Master Simon, that I will run no risk? Are you acquainted with the name, the fortune and the family of the party for whom you are speaking?

SIMON. No, I cannot give you any definite information about him; and it was only by chance that he was directed to me; but he himself will enlighten you about everything. And his man assures me that you will be satisfied when you meet him. All I can tell you is that his family is very rich, that his mother is already dead, and that he will guarantee, if you wish it, that his father will die before eight months are out.

---

* Rabelais, *Gargantua and Pantagruel*, Book 3, Chapter 2.

HARPAGON. That is something, indeed. Charity, Master Simon, obliges us to make others happy when it is in our power to do so.

SIMON. To be sure.

FLÈCHE, *low to* CLEANTH. What does this mean? Our Master Simon talking to your father!

CLEANTH, *low to* LA FLÈCHE. Could they have told him who I am? or have you betrayed me?

SIMON, *noticing* CLEANTH *and* LA FLÈCHE. Aha! you are in a hurry! Who told you this was the house? *To* HARPAGON. In any event, sir, it was not I who revealed your name and lodgings. But, in my opinion, no great harm has been done: they are discreet fellows, and now you can discuss your business together.

HARPAGON. What?

SIMON. This is the gentleman who wants to borrow the fifteen thousand francs, the one I was telling you about.

HARPAGON. What! you rascal! It is you who abandons yourself to such culpable extremities!

CLEANTH. What! father, it is you who carries on this shameful business! *Exit* MASTER SIMON *and* LA FLÈCHE.

HARPAGON. It is you who wants to ruin yourself by such deplorable borrowing!

CLEANTH. It is you who seek to enrich yourself by this criminal usury!

HARPAGON. Do you dare, after that, to show your face to me?

CLEANTH. Do you dare, after that, to show your face to the world?

HARPAGON. Tell me, aren't you ashamed to descend to such debauchery, to hurl yourself into horrible expenditure, and shamefully to squander the wealth that your ancestors have amassed for you by the sweat of their brows?

CLEANTH. How can you help but blush for disgracing your class this way with this trade you practise, sacrificing your honor and reputation to your insatiable desire to pile écu on écu and outdoing, in point of interest, the most infamous subtleties ever invented by the most notorious usurers?

HARPAGON. Get out of my sight, scoundrel, get out of my sight!

CLEANTH. Who is the greater criminal in your opinion: the man who buys money because he needs it, or the man who steals money but has no use for it?

HARPAGON. Leave the room I tell you, and stop chafing my ears.

Exit CLEANTH.

I am not a bit sorry that this has happened; it is a warning to me to watch everything he does more closely than ever.

Enter FROSINE.

FROSINE. Sir. . . .

HARPAGON. Wait a moment. I'll be back to talk with you. *Aside.* It's about time I take a peek at my money. *Exit.*

Enter LA FLÈCHE.

FLÈCHE. The whole thing is very amusing. He must surely have a large store of supplies somewhere in the house, because we couldn't find a thing that's listed in the inventory he gave us.

FROSINE. Ah! it's you, my poor La Flèche! To what do we owe this meeting?

FLÈCHE. Aha! it's you Frosine! What are *you* doing here?

FROSINE. What I do everywhere else: play the go-between in negotiations, make myself useful to others, and profit as much as I possibly can by whatever slight talent I may have. You know that in this world one is obliged to live by one's wits. And for women like myself Heaven has provided no other source of income than intrigue and persistency.

FLÈCHE. Do you have some business with the master of the house?

FROSINE. Yes, I am transacting some small business for him—for which I hope to be compensated.

FLÈCHE. By him? Ah! in faith, you'll have to be pretty sharp to get anything out of *him;* I warn you, money costs very dearly in this house.

FROSINE. There are certain services that are wonderfully effective.

FLÈCHE. I am your humble servant. But you don't know Signor Harpagon, yet. Signor Harpagon is of all humans the least human, the hardest and tightest mortal of all mortals. No service can push his gratitude far enough to make him unclench his fists. Of praise, esteem, benevolent words and friendship as much as you like, but money?—nothing doing. There is nothing more dry and withered than his favors and caresses, and "give" is a word for which he has such an aversion that he never says "I give," but "I lend, you good-day."

FROSINE. Mercy me! I know the art of milking a man. I have the secret for bringing out his tenderness, for tickling his heart, for finding his soft spot.

FLÈCHE. Useless here! If money is involved, I defy you to touch the man in question. On that score he is a Turk; and his turkery is the despair of all who know him; you could be dying, and he wouldn't turn a hair. In a word, he loves money more than reputation, honor or virtue, and the sight of anyone who expects to be paid throws him into convulsions. It wounds him mortally. It pierces his heart. It tears out his entrails. And if. . . . He's coming back; I must be going.

Enter HARPAGON.

HARPAGON, *aside*. All is as it should be. *To* FROSINE. How now! What is it, Frosine?

FROSINE. Ah! Mercy me, how well you are looking! You are the very picture of health!

HARPAGON. Who? I?

FROSINE. Never have I seen your color so fresh and jovial.

HARPAGON. Really?

FROSINE. Never in your life were you as young as you are now; I see men of twenty-five who are older than you.

HARPAGON. Nevertheless, Frosine, I'm a good sixty years old.

FROSINE. Well, what is that, sixty years old? A worry indeed! It's the bloom of life, that is. And now you are entering on a man's prime season.

HARPAGON. That's true. However, twenty years less wouldn't do me any harm, as I see it.

FROSINE. Are you joking? You have no need of them. You bid fair to live to be a hundred.

HARPAGON. Do you think so?

FROSINE. Of course. You show every indication. Hold still a bit. Oh, there it is! There it is! Between your two eyes!—a sign of long life!

HARPAGON. Do you know something about these things?

FROSINE. Certainly. Show me your hand. Ah! Mercy me, what a life line!

HARPAGON. How's that?

FROSINE. Don't you see how far that line goes?

HARPAGON. Well, yes. What does it mean?

FROSINE. By my faith, I said a hundred years, but you will pass the one hundred and twenty mark.

HARPAGON. Is it possible?

FROSINE. You deserve a beating. I tell you, you will bury your children and your children's children.

HARPAGON. So much the better! How goes our little transaction?

FROSINE. Need you ask? Did anyone ever see me start anything I couldn't finish? I have an especially wonderful talent for marriages. There aren't two people in the world that I couldn't find a way to couple in no time at all. If I had the notion, I believe I could marry the Grand Turk to the Republic of Venice. But, to be sure, there wasn't any such great difficulty involved in this affair. Since I have business at their house, I have already discussed you at length with both of them; and I told the mother what plans you had conceived for Marianne, on seeing her pass through the street and take the air at her window.

HARPAGON. She answered. . . .

FROSINE. She received the proposition with joy! And when I informed her that you are very desirous her daughter should be present tonight at the signing of the marriage contract which is to take place here she readily consented. And she has entrusted her daughter to me for the evening.

HARPAGON. I am obliged, Frosine, to give a supper for Signor Anselm, and I would like her to attend this feast.

FROSINE. A good idea. After dinner, she is to pay your daughter a visit; from here she plans to go and see the fair; and afterwards she can come back for supper.

HARPAGON. Fine! They can go together in my carriage. Which I will lend them.

FROSINE. That will suit her perfectly.

HARPAGON. But, Frosine, have you talked to the mother about the money she can give her daughter? Did you tell her she ought to help a little, herself? That she should make some special effort? That she should bleed herself for an occasion like this? For, I tell you again, no one marries a girl unless she brings something in.

FROSINE. What! This is a girl who will bring you twelve thousand francs a year.

HARPAGON. Twelve thousand francs a year?

FROSINE. Yes. First of all: those who raised and nurtured her were very sparing on food. She is a girl used to living on salad, milk, cheese, and apples, and consequently doesn't require a richly set table, or fancy jellies or barley syrup all the time, or all the other delicacies that most women must have. And this is no trifling matter. It will make a difference of at least three thousand francs a year. Besides, she feels that true elegance lies in simplicity, and she doesn't care for magnificent clothes, or rich jewelry, or sumptuous furniture —things which young ladies are usually so passionately addicted to. And that little item is worth more than four thousand francs a year. What's more, she has a tremendous aversion to cards—a thing not common in women nowadays. I know of one in our neighbourhood who, at thirties and forties mind you, lost twenty thousand francs this year! But suppose we take only a quarter of that. Five thousand francs a year for cards, and four thousand francs for clothes and jewelry, make nine thousand francs. And we will figure one thousand écus for food. Isn't that your twelve thousand francs a year —every sou of it?

HARPAGON. Yes, not bad: but this account has nothing real in it.

FROSINE. I beg your pardon. Is the great sobriety that she will bring to your marriage nothing real? Or her inheritance of a great love for simplicity in dress? Or the acquisition of a great fund of hatred for cards?

HARPAGON. It is a mockery to try and make up a dowry out of the expenses that she won't put me to. I won't give a receipt for something I don't receive. I must be able to touch something.

FROSINE. Mercy me! you will touch enough. They spoke to me about a certain country where they have some property. You shall be the master of it.

HARPAGON. That remains to be seen. But Frosine, there is something else that bothers me. The girl is young, as you can see, and young people usually like only their own kind, and seek only their company. I am afraid that a man of my age might not be to her taste, and that this might cause some little disorder in my house, which would not suit me at all!

FROSINE. Ah! how little you know her! This is another thing about her that I was going to mention. She has a frightful aversion to all young men, and feels no love except for the old.

HARPAGON. Her?

FROSINE. Yes, her. I wish you could hear her on that subject. She can't so much as stand the sight of a young fellow; but she is in ecstasy, she tells me, when she can look at a handsome old man with a majestic beard. For her, the oldest are the most charming. And I warn you not to go and make yourself look younger than you are. She likes a man to be sixty at the very least. It wasn't four months ago, that, all set to be married, she broke off the marriage on the spot because her lover let it be known he was only fifty-six years old—and didn't use spectacles to sign the contract.

HARPAGON. Just for that?

FROSINE. Yes. She says she simply couldn't be satisfied with a man of fifty-six, and above all, she is for the nose that wears spectacles.

HARPAGON. Really, this is something altogether new!

FROSINE. It goes much deeper than most people know. Like most young girls she has a few paintings and a few prints in her room, but what do you think the subjects are? Adonises? Cephaluses? Parises? or Apollos? No. They are handsome portraits of Saturn, of King Priam, of old Nestor, and good father Anchises on his son's shoulders!

HARPAGON. That is admirable! I should never have suspected it. And I am very happy to learn she has that kind of disposition. In fact, had *I* been a woman, I wouldn't have liked young men at all.

FROSINE. I can well believe you. What are they but fancy drugs? And to love them, ha! They are nothing but handsome idiots, good-looking fops that make you envy their complexions. I'd really like to know what there is to them!

HARPAGON. As for me, I can't understand it. I don't know why some women are so fond of them.

FROSINE. They must be stark mad. To find youth amiable! Is there any common sense in it? Are they men, these young dandies? Can you become attached to one of those animals?

HARPAGON. That's what I have always said—with their effeminate, milk-fed voices, and their three little wisps of beard turned up like cat's whiskers, with their mouse-colored wigs, and their sloppy breeches, and their puffed-out stomachs!

FROSINE. They are well-built, indeed, compared with a person like you! *To the audience.* There's a man for you! There is someone who is a pleasure to look at! This is how a man should be made and dressed to inspire love.

HARPAGON. You like the way I look?

FROSINE. I should say! You are ravishing, you ought to have your portrait painted. Turn round a bit, if you please. You couldn't be better. Let me see you walk. *To the audience.* Here is a body that is trim, supple and tall as it ought to be. And not marked by any infirmity.

HARPAGON. None to speak of, thank God! *Coughs.*—Except my catarrh that bothers me from time to time.

FROSINE. That is nothing. Your catarrh is not unbecoming to you. You cough gracefully.

HARPAGON. But tell me, hasn't Marianne seen me yet? Hasn't she noticed me at all, passing by her house?

FROSINE. No. But we have talked about you a great deal. I sketched a portrait of your person for her. And I did not fail to boast of your merits and the advantage it would be for her to have a husband like you.

HARPAGON. You have done well. And I thank you.

FROSINE. I would like, sir, to ask a small favour of you. I have a lawsuit that I am on the point of losing for want of a little money; and you could easily assure my winning this suit if you would show me some little kindness. HARPAGON *frowns*. Ah! how well you will please her! What a marvellous impression your old-fashioned ruff will make! But she will be especially charmed by your breeches, attached to your doublet with laces; they'll make her go wild over you. A laced-up lover will seem to her a wonderful treat.

HARPAGON. Really, it delights me to hear you say it.

FROSINE. To tell the truth, sir, this suit is of the utmost importance to me. I am ruined if I lose it, and the least bit of help would set everything right for me. HARPAGON *frowns*. I wish you could have seen the rapture in her face when she heard me speak of you. Her eyes sparkled with joy as I recited your qualities. In short, I left her in a state of extreme impatience to see this marriage entirely concluded.

HARPAGON. You have given me great pleasure, Frosine. And I must confess, I am under all the obligation in the world to you.

FROSINE. I beg you, sir, to give me the slight help I need. It will put me on my feet again. And I will be eternally indebted to you.

HARPAGON. Goodbye! I must get my mail ready.

FROSINE. I assure you, sir, you couldn't relieve me in a greater need.

HARPAGON. I will leave orders, so my coach will be ready to take you to the fair.

FROSINE. I would not importune you, were I not forced to do so—out of necessity.

HARPAGON. And I'll see to it that supper is ready early so that you won't get sick.

FROSINE. Do not refuse me this favor, I beg of you.

HARPAGON. I am going. There, someone is calling me. I'll see you by and by. *Exit* HARPAGON.

FROSINE. May the fever rack you! Cur! Villain! The devil take you! The miser was deaf to all my attacks. Nevertheless I must not drop his suit: for in any case, there is the other party. I am sure of a good reward from them!

Act III

On stage. HARPAGON, CLEANTH, ELISE, VALÈRE, DAME CLAUDE, MASTER JACQUES, BRINDAVOINE *and* LA MERLUCHE.

HARPAGON. Here, all of you come here. I want to give you orders for this evening, and assign everyone a job. Step forward Dame Claude. Let's begin with you. Good, I see you are already armed. I consign to you the task of cleaning up the house; but be especially careful not to rub the furniture too hard, or you'll wear it out. Furthermore, I assign you to see to the bottles during supper. And if any of them are carried off, or if anything is broken, you will be responsible, and I'll deduct it from your wages.

JACQUES, *aside*. A convenient punishment.

HARPAGON, *to* DAME CLAUDE. Go. . . . *Exit* DAME CLAUDE. You Brindavoine, and you La Merluche, are appointed to rinse the glasses, and to serve the wine—but only when someone is thirsty. And don't follow the example of those impudent lackies who go and *incite* people to drink and put the notion in their heads when they aren't even thinking about it. Wait until they have asked you more than once, and remember always to bring a lot of water.

JACQUES, *aside*. Yes, pure wine goes to the head.

MERLUCHE. Shall we take our canvas smocks off, sir?

HARPAGON. Yes, when you see the guests coming, and be careful not to spoil your clothes.

BRINDAVOINE. You know very well, sir, that one side of my doublet is covered with a big spot of lamp-oil.

MERLUCHE. And I, sir, have a big hole in the back of my breeches, and I can be seen, begging your pardon. . . . .

HARPAGON. Peace! Keep that side discreetly turned toward the wall, and always show your front side to the world. And you, always hold your hat like this—*holds his hat over his chest*—when you serve. *Exeunt* LA MERLUCHE *and* BRINDAVOINE. And as for you, my daughter, keep an eye open when they clear away the table, and see to it that nothing goes to waste. That's a proper job for a young girl. But meanwhile, prepare yourself to receive my fiancée, who is coming to pay you a visit, and take you to the fair with her. Did you hear what I said?

ELISE. Yes, father.

HARPAGON. And you, my son, the dandy whose latest escapade I was so good as to forgive, don't you go getting any ideas either and make sour faces at her.

CLEANTH. I, father? Sour faces? And for what reason?

HARPAGON. By God, we know the drift of children whose fathers remarry, and how they feel toward what is called a stepmother. But, if you would like me to forget your last prank, I especially recommend that you treat this person to some of your most cheerful looks and give her the best reception you possibly can.

CLEANTH. To tell you the truth, father, I cannot promise you to be very glad she is to become my stepmother. I should be lying if I told you I would. But as for receiving her well and showing her a pleasant face, I promise to obey you punctually on that score.

HARPAGON. At least take care you do.

CLEANTH. You will see you will have no reason to complain.

HARPAGON. You will do wisely. *Exeunt* CLEANTH *and* ELISE. Valère, help me with this. Oh, there you are, Master Jacques! come here. I have saved you for the last.

JACQUES. Is it to your coachman, sir, or is it to your cook you wish to speak? For I am one and the other.

HARPAGON. To the two of you.

JACQUES. But to which of us first?

HARPAGON. To the cook.

JACQUES. One moment then if you please. *Takes off his coachman's coat and appears dressed as a cook.*

HARPAGON. What the deuce kind of ceremony is this?

JACQUES. You have only to speak.

HARPAGON. I have committed myself, Master Jacques, to give a supper tonight.

JACQUES, *aside*. This is miraculous!

HARPAGON. Tell me now, will you give us a fine feast?

JACQUES. Yes, if you give me a good deal of money.

HARPAGON. What the devil! always money! It seems they have nothing else to say: money, money, money! That's the sword they keep by their bed, money!

VALÈRE. I have never heard a more impertinent answer. How miraculous it is to be able to set out a fine feast when you have a lot of money! It is the easiest thing in the world to do, and there is no man so poor in wit that he couldn't do as much. But it is a clever man who can talk about providing a fine feast for little money!

JACQUES. A fine feast for little money?

VALÈRE. Yes.

JACQUES. By my faith, Mr. Steward, you would oblige us if you would let us in on your secret—and if you will take my place as cook! You meddle so much in this house already, you might as well be the factotum.

HARPAGON. Be quiet. What will we need?

JACQUES. There is your steward who will provide a fine feast at small cost.

HARPAGON. Ha! I want you to answer me.

JACQUES. How many will you be at table?

HARPAGON. We will be eight or ten. When there is enough for eight, there is plenty for ten.

ACT III] THE MISER 249

VALÈRE. Naturally.

JACQUES. Very well, we will need four kinds of soup and five other dishes. Soups, entrées. . . .

HARPAGON. What the devil! That's enough to feed a whole city.

JACQUES. Roast. . . .

HARPAGON, *putting his hand over* MASTER JACQUES' *mouth*. Ah! traitor, you are eating up all my money!

JACQUES. Side dishes. . . .

HARPAGON, *putting his hand over* MASTER JACQUES' *mouth again*. More?

VALÈRE. Do you want to make everybody split open? Do you think our master invites people in order to *murder* them with food? Go and read the rules of health a while—and ask the doctors if there is anything more prejudicial to man than excessive eating.

HARPAGON. He is right.

VALÈRE. Learn, Master Jacques, you and the like of you, that a table overloaded with food is a cut-throat; that if you want to prove yourself a friend to those you invite, frugality should reign at the meals you serve; and that, according to the saying of the ancients, we should eat to live, and not live to eat.

HARPAGON. Oh! but that was well said! Come here, I want to embrace you for that saying. It is the most beautiful sentence I have ever heard in my life. We should live to eat, and not eat to li. . . . No, that isn't it. How was it you said it?

VALÈRE. We should eat to live, and not live to eat.

HARPAGON. Yes, do you hear that? Who was the great man who said it?

VALÈRE. At the moment I can't recall his name.

HARPAGON. Remember to write it down for me. I want to have it carved in gold letters above the mantlepiece in my dining room.

VALÈRE. I won't forget. And as for your supper, you have only to leave it to me. I will order things to be done as they should be.

HARPAGON. Take care of it then.

JACQUES. So much the better; it will mean less trouble for me.

HARPAGON. We should have those things that people don't eat much of, that satisfy the appetite quickly: a nice mutton stew, rather fat, with some kind of a meat-pie well garnished and chestnuts to go with it. Yes, that! And let there be a lot of it.

VALÈRE. Leave everything to me.

HARPAGON. Now, Master Jacques, my coach must be cleaned up.

JACQUES. One moment. That was addressed to the coachman. *Exit, and reappears in his coachman's coat.* You said. . . . ?

HARPAGON. That you should clean up my coach, and have my horses ready to drive to the fair.

JACQUES. Your horses, sir? Faith, they are in no condition to walk. I won't say they are down on their litters. The poor beasts don't have any, so I'd be speaking very improperly. But you make them observe such strict fasts that they are now no more than ideas or ghosts or appearances of horses.

HARPAGON. No wonder they are sick; they do nothing.

JACQUES. And because they do nothing, sir, must they eat nothing? It would be much better for them, poor animals, to work a lot, and to eat accordingly. It breaks my heart to see them so weak, because, to tell the truth, I have so much affection for my horses, that when I see them suffer, it's just as though it were myself. Everyday I take food out of my own mouth to feed them; it is a very hard nature, sir, that feels no pity for the next one.

HARPAGON. It won't be much work for them to go as far as the fair.

JACQUES. No, sir, I haven't the courage to drive them, and it would lie on my conscience if I hit them with the whip, in the condition they're in. How do you expect them to pull a carriage; they can't even pull themselves.

VALÈRE. Sir, I will ask our neighbour Picard if he will be good enough to drive them. Besides, we shall need him here to help prepare the supper.

JACQUES. Very well! I'd still rather they died under someone else's hands and not mine.

VALÈRE. Master Jacques is intent on cavilling.

JACQUES. Mister Steward is intent on seeming indispensable.

HARPAGON. Peace!

JACQUES. Sir, I can't stand flatterers, and I can see what he is doing. He continually restricts the bread, the wine, the wood, the salt, and the candles just to scratch your ear, to win your favor. It makes me angry. And it grieves me to hear what people say about you every day. Because I feel a real affection for you, in spite of myself; and after my horses, you are the person I like most.

HARPAGON. Could I learn from you, Master Jacques, what people say about me?

JACQUES. Yes, sir, if I could be sure it wouldn't make you angry.

HARPAGON. No, not in the least.

JACQUES. Pardon me, but I know very well you'd fly into a rage.

HARPAGON. Not at all. On the contrary, it will give me great pleasure to learn what is said about me.

JACQUES. Sir, since it is your wish, I tell you frankly: people everywhere are laughing at you. They taunt us with a thousand jokes about you on all sides, and they are never so happy as when tearing you to ribbons or making up countless stories about your stinginess. One says that you have special almanacs printed, in which you have doubled the quarter-days and vigils, so you can take advantage of the fasts you impose on your household. Another says you always have a quarrel ready to pick with your valets when it is time for holiday gifts, or when they are leaving, so you'll have a reason for not giving them anything. This one tells the story that you once tried to bring your neighbor's cat to court for eating up the remainder of a leg of mutton. Somebody else says that you yourself were caught coming to steal your horses' oats, and that in the dark your coachman, the one before me, gave you I don't know how many blows with his stick, which you didn't care to say anything about. Shall I go on? We can't go anywhere without hearing people pull you apart. You are the talk of the town, the laughing-stock of the world. And they never refer to you except by the name of miser, cut-throat, villain, or shark.

HARPAGON. You are a fool, a scoundrel, a rascal, an insolent knave!
Beats him.

JACQUES. There! Didn't I say it would be that way? You wouldn't believe me. I warned you that you would get angry if I told you the truth.

HARPAGON. Then learn how to talk. *Exit* HARPAGON.

Enter VALÈRE.

VALÈRE. As far as I can see, Master Jacques, you are poorly paid for your frankness.

JACQUES. By God! Mister Upstart, playing the man of importance, it is none of your business. Save your laughs for your own beating when you get it, and don't come laughing at mine.

VALÈRE. Ah! good Master Jacques, please don't be angry.

JACQUES, *aside*. He's backing down. I'll pretend to be tough, and if he is fool enough to be afraid of me, I'll give him a little thrashing. Did you know, Mister Comedian, that I myself never laugh?—and that if you get my temper up you are likely to be laughing out of the other side of your mouth?

VALÈRE. Gently now!

JACQUES. Why gently? What if I don't feel like being gentle?

VALÈRE. Please!

JACQUES. You are an impertinent fellow.

VALÈRE. Good Master Jacques!

JACQUES. There is no such person as good Master Jacques. If I get a stick, I'll beat the importance out of you.

VALÈRE, *picking up the stick on the table*. What did you say? a stick?

JACQUES. Oh! I wasn't talking about that one.

VALÈRE. Did you know, Mister Fool, that I am man enough to thrash you?

JACQUES. I don't doubt it.

VALÈRE. That you are, by any standard, nothing but a miserable cook?

JACQUES. I know very well.

VALÈRE. And that you don't know me yet?

JACQUES. I beg your pardon.

VALÈRE. You'll beat me, you say?

JACQUES. I was joking.

VALÈRE. And your joking is not to my taste. This will teach you that you're a scurvy joker. *Beats him.* *Exit* VALÈRE.

JACQUES. A pox on sincerity! It's a wretched practice. Here and now I renounce it, and I will never tell the truth again. As for my master, I'll let that go—he has some right to beat me. But, as for this steward, I'll take my revenge if I can.

Enter FROSINE *and* MARIANNE.

FROSINE. Do you know, Master Jacques, if your master is at home?

JACQUES. Yes, he certainly is. I know it all too well!

FROSINE. Tell him, pray, that we are here. *Exit* MASTER JACQUES.

MARIANNE. Ah! Frosine, I am in such a strange state! If I must tell what I feel: I am very much afraid of this interview.

FROSINE. But why? What is it that worries you?

MARIANNE. Alas! Need you ask? Can't you imagine the alarm of a person just about to see the rack she is to be tortured on?

FROSINE. I can plainly see that Harpagon is not the rack you would choose to embrace if you're thinking of an agreeable death. And I know by your expression that the dandy you were telling me about is somewhere in your thoughts.

MARIANNE. Yes, Frosine. That I do not wish to deny. The respectful visits he paid at our house have had, I must confess, some effect on my heart.

FROSINE. But have you learned *who* he is?

MARIANNE. No, I don't in the least know *who* he is, but I do know he is fashioned in a way that inspires love and that, if the choice were left at my disposal, I would take him sooner than any other, and that he contributes not a little to make me find the husband you would give me a horrible torment.

FROSINE. Mercy me! all those dandies are agreeable enough, and they play their parts very well, but most of them are poor as church-mice. You would do much better to take an old husband who will leave you a lot of money. I will admit that the senses will not find full measure on the side which I am speaking for, and there are some slightly distasteful details to be endured with such a husband—but it won't be for long. His death, believe me, will soon put you in a position to pick a more attractive one, who will make up for everything.

MARIANNE. Bless me, Frosine, it seems a very strange business when, to be happy, one must hope or wait for the demise of someone. And death does not always lend itself to the plans we make.

FROSINE. Are you joking? You are marrying him only on the understanding that he will soon leave you a widow. That ought to be one of the articles in the contract. It would be very impertinent in him not to die before three months are out.   *Enter* HARPAGON. Speak of the devil. . . .

MARIANNE. Ah! Frosine, what a face!

HARPAGON. Do not be offended, my beauty, if I come to you wearing spectacles. I know that your charms are striking enough—are visible enough by themselves—that there is no need of glasses to perceive them. But after all, it is through glasses we observe the stars, and I maintain and guarantee that you are a star. And what a star! The most beautiful star in the realm of stars. Frosine, she doesn't say a word, and she doesn't show, so it seems to me, that she is at all pleased to see me.

FROSINE. That is because she is still all surprise. And then, the girls nowadays are always shy about showing straightway what is in their hearts.
Enter ELISE.

HARPAGON. You are right. *To* MARIANNE. Here, darling beauty, is my daughter, who has come to greet you.

MARIANNE. I acquit myself, madam, much too tardily of this visit.

ELISE. You have done that, madam, which I ought to have done. It was my place to anticipate you.

HARPAGON. You see how tall she is; but weeds grow fast.

MARIANNE, *aside to* FROSINE. Oh, what an unpleasant man!

HARPAGON. What does the beauty say?

FROSINE. That she thinks you are wonderful.

HARPAGON. You do me too much honor, adorable darling.

MARIANNE, *aside to* FROSINE. Such an animal!

HARPAGON. I am obliged for your sentiments.

MARIANNE, *aside to* FROSINE. I can't stand any more of this.

Enter CLEANTH.

HARPAGON. Here is my son, who also comes to pay you his respects.

MARIANNE, *aside to* FROSINE. Ah! Frosine, what a coincidence! This is the very person I spoke to you about.

FROSINE. The adventure is fantastic.

HARPAGON. I see you are astonished to find that I have such big children; but I shall soon be rid of them both.

CLEANTH. Madam, to tell the truth, this is an encounter which I by no means expected; and my father surprised me not a little when he told me a while ago of his intentions.

MARIANNE. I can say the same for myself. This is an unforeseen meeting, which has surprised me as much as it has you. I too was not at all prepared for such an encounter.

CLEANTH. It is true that my father, madam, could not make a handsomer choice, and the honor of seeing you is a real joy for me; but for all that, I will not assure you that I rejoice over the design you may have to become my mother-in-law. That compliment, I confess, is too much for me; it is a title, if you please, that I do not want for you. This speech may seem brutal in the eyes of some, but I am sure you are a person who will take it in the right sense. You can easily imagine, madam, that this is a marriage which is bound to be somewhat repugnant to me; for you know what kind of a man I am and how much it clashes with my interests. In short, you will not be offended if I tell you, with my father's permission, that if things depended on me, these nuptials would never take place.

HARPAGON. Your compliment is very impertinent! What a nice confession to make to her!

MARIANNE. And I, in answer to you, have this to say: our feelings are quite mutual. If it is true that you would find it repugnant to have me for a mother-in-law, it would be no less so for me, I assure you, to have you for a son-in-law. Do not think, pray, that it is I who seek to be the source of your uneasiness. I should be very sorry to cause you any displeasure; and if I did not see myself forced to it by an absolute power, I give you my word, I would never consent to a marriage that pains you.

HARPAGON. She is right. A stupid compliment like that deserves a stupid answer. I beg pardon, my beauty, for my son's impertinence. He is a young ass who doesn't yet know the weight of his own words.

MARIANNE. I assure you that what he said has not offended me in the least. On the contrary, it has been a pleasure to hear him express his true sentiments. I like that kind of confession from him. If he had spoken in any other way, I would have far less esteem for him.

HARPAGON. It is very kind of you to forgive his faults this way. Time will make him wiser, and you will see that he will have a change of heart.

CLEANTH. No, father, it is not capable of change; and I earnestly entreat madam to believe that.

HARPAGON. Just see how extravagant he is! He goes on more rashly than ever.

CLEANTH. Would you have me belie my heart?

HARPAGON. Again! Would you mind changing the subject?

CLEANTH. Very well, since you wish me to speak in a different manner. . . . . Permit me, madam, to put myself in my father's place, to confess that I have never seen anything in the world as lovely as you; that I can conceive nothing to equal the happiness of pleasing you; and that the title of your husband is a glory, a felicity, that I would prefer to the destiny of the greatest prince on earth. Yes, madam, the happiness of possessing you, is in my estimation, the fairest of all fortunes; it is the goal of my whole ambition. I would do anything to make such a conquest; and the most powerful obstacles. . . .

HARPAGON. Moderation, son, if you please.

CLEANTH. This is a compliment I am paying the lady, for you.

HARPAGON. By God! I have a tongue to express myself, and I have no need of a proxy the likes of you. Here, bring chairs.

FROSINE. No. It will be better for us to go directly to the fair. Then we'll be back early and have the whole time afterward to talk with you.

HARPAGON. Then tell them to hitch up the horses to the carriage. I beg you to excuse me, my beauty, for not having thought to give you a little refreshment before you start out.

CLEANTH. I have provided for that, father. I had them bring a few plates of Chinese oranges, some lemons, and some preserves; which I sent for in your name.

HARPAGON, *aside to* VALÈRE. Valère!

VALÈRE. He's out of his head.

CLEANTH. Do you think, father, that it isn't enough? Madam will please have the kindness to excuse it.

MARIANNE. It was not at all necessary.

CLEANTH. Have you ever, madam, seen more fire in a diamond than in this one you see on my father's finger?

Takes ring off HARPAGON'S *finger.*

MARIANNE. It is true that it shines quite brightly.

CLEANTH. You must see it from close up.

Puts ring on MARIANNE'S *hand.*

MARIANNE. It is very handsome, I must say, and it sparkles a great deal. *Begins to take ring off her finger.*

CLEANTH. No, no, madam; it is on hands much too lovely. My father makes you a present of it.

HARPAGON. I?

CLEANTH. Isn't it true, father, that you want the lady to keep it for love of you?

HARPAGON, *aside to* CLEANTH. What is this?

CLEANTH. Foolish question. He makes a sign to me that I should make you accept it.

MARIANNE. I don't at all want. . . .

CLEANTH. Are you joking? He has no intention of taking it back.

HARPAGON, *aside*. I'm losing my temper.

MARIANNE. It would be. . . .

CLEANTH. No, I tell you, you will offend him.

MARIANNE. Please. . . .

CLEANTH. Out of the question.

HARPAGON, *aside*. A pox. . . .

CLEANTH. Your refusal is making him angry.

HARPAGON, *aside to* CLEANTH. Ah! you traitor!

CLEANTH. You see he's getting desperate.

HARPAGON, *aside to* CLEANTH. You murderer, you!

CLEANTH. Father, it's not my fault. I am doing what I can to oblige her to keep it, but she is determined.

HARPAGON, *aside to* CLEANTH. Scoundrel!

CLEANTH. You are the cause, madam, of my father's quarreling with me.

HARPAGON, *aside to* CLEANTH. Knave!

CLEANTH. You will make him ill. Please, madam, do not resist any longer.

FROSINE. Mercy me! what a fuss! Keep the ring if the gentleman wants you to have it.

MARIANNE. So that you won't fly into a rage, I will keep it for the time being; and I will find another opportunity to return it.

Enter BRINDAVOINE.

BRINDAVOINE. Sir, there's a man here who wants to talk to you.

HARPAGON. Tell him I am busy, and to come back some other time.

BRINDAVOINE. He says he has money for you.

HARPAGON, *to* MARIANNE. Please excuse me. I'll be back presently.

Enter LA MERLUCHE.

MERLUCHE, *comes running and knocks* HARPAGON *down*. Sir. . . .

HARPAGON. Ah! I am dying!

CLEANTH. What is it, father, are you hurt?

HARPAGON. The traitor must surely have been paid by my debtors to make me break my neck.

VALÈRE, *to* HARPAGON. There's no harm done.

MERLUCHE. I beg your pardon, sir, I thought I did right to come running.

HARPAGON. What are you here for, murderer?

MERLUCHE. To tell you that neither of your horses has any shoes.

HARPAGON. Take them to the blacksmith, right away.

CLEANTH. While waiting for the horses to be shod, father, I will do the honors of the house for you, and conduct madam into the garden where I shall have the refreshments served.

Exeunt FROSINE, ELISE, MARIANNE *and* CLEANTH.

HARPAGON. Valère, keep an eye on all that; and take care, pray, to save me as much as you can, so that we can send it back to the dealer.

VALÈRE. Rest assured. *Exit* VALÈRE.

HARPAGON. Oh, impertinent son! You are trying to ruin me!

Act IV

Enter CLEANTH, MARIANNE, ELISE *and* FROSINE.

CLEANTH. Let us go in again; we shall be much better off in here. There is no longer anyone suspect around, and we can speak freely.

ELISE. Yes, madam, my brother has confided to me the love he bears you. I know what pain and frustration such obstacles can cause; and it is a most kindly sympathy, I assure you, that provokes my interest in your adventure.

MARIANNE. It is a sweet consolation to see a person like you interested in oneself, and I implore you, madam, always to cherish your generous friendship for me—so capable of softening the cruel blows of misfortune.

FROSINE. By my faith, you are unlucky people, both of you, for not having told me about your affair before all this happened. I could, no doubt, have warded off these troubles. I wouldn't have brought matters to such a pass as this.

CLEANTH. What can you expect? It is my evil destiny has willed it so. But, dear Marianne, what have you resolved to do?

MARIANNE. Alas! am I in a position to resolve anything? Dependent as I am, can I do more than hope?

CLEANTH. Is there nothing in your heart to encourage me but barren hope? No benevolent pity? No helpful kindness? No lively affection at all?

MARIANNE. What can I tell you? Put yourself in my place, and see what I can do. Advise me. Order me. I put myself in your hands. And I believe you are too reasonable to demand more of me than is allowed by honor and decorum.

CLEANTH. Alas! to what am I reduced if you limit me to the pallid sentiments that rigorous honor and scrupulous decorum will allow?

MARIANNE. But what would you have me do? Even though I could ignore many of the niceties which our sex is obliged to observe, I have too much consideration for my mother. She has reared me with extreme tenderness. I could never resolve to do anything that would cause her displeasure. Go and speak to her. Do everything in your power to win her over. You may do and say whatever you please; I give you my permission. And if it is only a question of declaring in your favor, I readily consent to make a confession to her of all that I feel for you.

CLEANTH. Frosine, my poor Frosine, would you help us?

FROSINE. By my faith, is there any need to ask? I will with all my heart. You know that by nature I am human enough. Heaven didn't give me a heart of bronze, and I am only too eager to do little services for people when I see they love one another sincerely and honorably. What can we do about this?

CLEANTH. Think a little; I beg you.

MARIANNE. Show us a way.

ELISE. Invent something that will undo what you have done.

FROSINE. That is rather difficult. *To* MARIANNE. As to your mother, she is not altogether unreasonable: perhaps you could win her over, and make her decide to transfer the gift she intends for the father to the son. *To* CLEANTH. But the worst part of this is that your father is—your father.

CLEANTH. That's understood.

FROSINE. I mean he will bear a grudge if she refuses him openly, and he will be in no humour afterward to give his consent to your marriage. It will be necessary, to do it well, that the refusal come from himself. We must try by some means to make her distasteful to him.

CLEANTH. You are right.

FROSINE. Yes, I am right. I know it very well. That is what has to be done. But the deuce of it is to find a way. Wait; if we had a woman, getting on in years, with my talent, and who could act well enough to counterfeit a lady of quality, with the help of a train made up in a hurry and some bizarre name of marchioness or viscountess, who we could pretend comes from Brittany, I could be clever enough to convince him that she was a rich person who, besides her houses, had a hundred thousand écus in solid silver, that she was hopelessly in love with him, and wanted to be his wife so badly that she would sign over all her property to him in a marriage contract. I don't in the least doubt that he would lend an ear to the proposition. For, in short, although he loves you very much, he loves money a little more. And, once blinded by this illusion, once he has consented to what concerns you most, it will matter little afterward if he is undeceived when he looks more closely into the estate of our marchioness.

CLEANTH. This is all very well thought out.

FROSINE. Leave it to me. I just thought of a friend of mine who is the very woman we want.

CLEANTH. Rest assured, Frosine, of my gratitude if you succeed in this. But dear Marianne, let us begin by persuading your mother; there is still much to be done to break off this marriage. For your part, I beseech you, make every effort you possibly can. Use all the power that her love for you gives you over her. Unfold your eloquent graces without reserve—those all-powerful charms that Heaven has located in your eyes and lips. And forget none, please, of those tender expressions, or those soft entreaties, or those touching caresses to which, I am persuaded, no one could refuse anything.

Enter HARPAGON.

MARIANNE. I will do all in my power, and I won't forget a thing.

HARPAGON, *aside*. Hey! what's this? My son kisses the hand of his future stepmother; and his future stepmother does not offer much resistance. Could there be more to this than meets the eye?

ELISE. Here is my father.

HARPAGON. The carriage is ready. You can leave when you please.

CLEANTH. Since you are not going, father, I will drive them myself.

HARPAGON. No, stay. They can go just as well by themselves. I need you here.   *Exeunt* FROSINE, ELISE *and* MARIANNE.

HARPAGON. Oh! by the way, apart from the question of her becoming your stepmother, what do you think of this person?

CLEANTH. What do I think of her?

HARPAGON. Yes—of her manner, her figure, her beauty, and her wit?

CLEANTH. So so.

HARPAGON. What do you mean?

CLEANTH. To tell you frankly, I did not find her what I thought her to be. She has the manner of an out-and-out coquette, her figure is rather awkward, her beauty is mediocre, and she has a very common kind of wit. But don't think, father, that I am trying to set you against her. Because, stepmother for stepmother, I like this one as much as I would any other.

HARPAGON. Nevertheless you were telling her a while ago. . . .

CLEANTH. I did say a few nice things to her in your name—but that was to please you.

HARPAGON. So then, you don't feel the slightest inclination for her?

CLEANTH. I? None at all.

HARPAGON. That's too bad, for it puts an end to an idea that came into my head. Seeing her here made me reflect on my age, and I thought to myself that people might find fault with me for marrying such a young girl. This consideration made me abandon my plans; but, since I have already asked her to marry and am bound by my word, I would have given her to you—if you had not shown such an aversion.

CLEANTH. To me?

HARPAGON. To you.

CLEANTH. In marriage?

HARPAGON. In marriage.

CLEANTH. Listen. It is true she is not much to my taste. But to make you happy, father, I will resign myself to marrying her—since it is your wish.

HARPAGON. Mine? I am more reasonable than you think. I would not force your inclination.

CLEANTH. Pardon me, I will do myself this violence out of love for you.

HARPAGON. No, no. A marriage can never be happy where there is no affection.

CLEANTH. Affection is something, father, that will come afterwards, perhaps. They say that love is often the fruit of marriage.

HARPAGON. No, the venture ought not to be risked on the man's side. There may be painful consequences to which I would not care to expose myself. If you had felt some inclination for her earlier, I would have had you marry her in my place. But since that is not the case, I will carry out my first plan, and marry her myself.

CLEANTH. Very well, father, since this is the way things are, I am obliged to bare my heart to you: I must reveal our secret. The truth is that I have loved her since the first time I saw her out walking, that my intention up to a while ago was to ask you if I could have her for my wife, and that nothing has held me back but your declaration of your own sentiments and fear of displeasing you.

HARPAGON. Have you visited her?

CLEANTH. Yes father.

HARPAGON. Very often?

CLEANTH. Often enough—for the time I had.

HARPAGON. Were you well received?

CLEANTH. Very well. But they did not know who I was. That is why Marianne was so surprised a while ago.

HARPAGON. Did you declare your passion to her, and your intention of marrying her?

CLEANTH. Certainly, and I have even broached the subject a little to her mother.

HARPAGON. Did she give your proposal a hearing?

CLEANTH. Yes, a very civil one.

HARPAGON. And does her daughter return your love appreciably?

CLEANTH. If appearances are to be trusted, I am persuaded, father, that she feels some affection for me.

HARPAGON. I am happy to learn such a secret. It is exactly what I wanted to know. And now, son, do you know what you will have to do? You will have to think, if you please, about getting over your love, about giving up your pursuit of this person whom I intend for myself, and about marrying, in a short time, the woman I have chosen for you!

CLEANTH. So, father, you have tricked me! Very well! Since things have come to this pass, I declare to you that I will never cease loving Marianne, that I will go to any limit to dispute the conquest with you, and though you have the mother's consent on your side, I will perhaps find others who will fight for me.

HARPAGON. What? You scoundrel! You have the audacity to stalk my game?

CLEANTH. It is you who are stalking mine: I knew her first.

HARPAGON. Am I not your father? Don't you owe me your respect?

CLEANTH. These are not matters in which the children are obliged to defer to their fathers. Love knows no master.

HARPAGON. I'll teach you to know me—by the mastery of a good stick.

CLEANTH. All your threats will do no good.

HARPAGON. Will you renounce Marianne?

CLEANTH. On no account.

HARPAGON. Bring me a stick, quickly.

Enter MASTER JACQUES.

JACQUES. Now, now, now! gentlemen, what is this? What can you be thinking of?

CLEANTH. I laugh at it all.

JACQUES. Ah! gently, sir.

HARPAGON. To talk with such impudence!

JACQUES. Oh! sir, please.

CLEANTH. I won't yield an inch.

JACQUES. Eh, what? to your father?

HARPAGON. Leave him to me.   *Menaces* CLEANTH *with his stick.*

JACQUES. Eh, what? to your son? Once more, leave off, for my sake.

HARPAGON. I want to make *you*, Master Jacques, judge of this affair—to prove I am right.

JACQUES. I am willing. *To* CLEANTH. Go a little farther off.

HARPAGON. I am in love with a girl I want to marry, and that scoundrel has the impudence to be in love with the same girl at the same time, and intends, despite my orders, to marry her.

JACQUES. Ah! he is in the wrong.

HARPAGON. Isn't it a shocking thing for a son to enter into competition with his father? Shouldn't he, out of respect, refrain from meddling where my affections are involved?

JACQUES. You are right. Let me talk to him. Stay here.

CLEANTH. Yes, of course, since he has chosen you for judge, I'll not back out. It isn't important to me who it is, and I too am willing to refer myself to you, Master Jacques, in this matter of our difference.

JACQUES. You do me great honor.

CLEANTH. I am very much taken with a young lady who returns all my interest, and who has tenderly received the offer of my heart; and my father has taken it into his head to trouble our love by making her an offer of marriage.

JACQUES. He is in the wrong, surely.

CLEANTH. Isn't he ashamed, at his age, to dream of marrying? Is it becoming in him to be amorous? Wouldn't he do better to leave that business to young fellows?

JACQUES. You are right; he is making a fool of himself. Let me say a few words to him. *He returns to* HARPAGON. Well, your son is not so strange as you make him out to be; he has submitted to reason. He says he knows that he owes you respect, that he was carried away by the heat of the argument, and that he will not refuse to submit to anything that pleases you, provided you intend to treat him better than you have done, and that you give him someone in marriage with whom he will have reason to be satisfied.

HARPAGON. Ah, tell him, Master Jacques, that with this provision, he may expect anything he *wants* from me; and that, Marianne excepted, he is at liberty to choose any girl he pleases.

JACQUES. Leave it to me. *To* CLEANTH. Well, your father is not as unreasonable as you make him out to be, and he admitted to me that it was only your rage that roused his temper, that he is angry only about the way you conducted yourself, and that he will be very much disposed to grant all your wishes provided you will go about it gently, and show him the deference, respect, and submission that a son owes his father.

CLEANTH. Ah! Master Jacques, you can assure him that if he grants me Marianne, he will see that I will always be the most submissive

ACT IV] THE MISER 265

man in the world, and that I will never do anything except by his wish.

JACQUES, *going to* HARPAGON. It's done. He consents to what you ask.

HARPAGON. It's the happiest conclusion in the world.

JACQUES, *going to* CLEANTH. It's all decided. He is satisfied with your promises.

CLEANTH. Heaven be praised!

JACQUES, *in the middle of the stage*. Gentlemen, you have only to talk together. Here you are in agreement now, and you were about to fall out because of a misunderstanding!

CLEANTH. My poor Master Jacques, I will be obliged to you for life.

JACQUES. It was nothing, sir.

HARPAGON. You have made me happy, Master Jacques, and you deserve a reward. MASTER JACQUES *puts out his hand*. Go—I shall remember it, I assure you.

JACQUES. I kiss your hand. *Exit* MASTER JACQUES.

CLEANTH. I beg your pardon, father, for showing my temper in that way.

HARPAGON. It was nothing.

CLEANTH. I assure you, it gives me all the concern in the world.

HARPAGON. As for myself, it gives me all the joy in the world to see you reasonable.

CLEANTH. How good of you to forget my fault so quickly!

HARPAGON. One easily forgets his child's faults when one sees him return to the path of duty.

CLEANTH. What! you harbour no resentment for all my extravagance?

HARPAGON. You oblige me not to by the submission and respect you show.

CLEANTH. And I, I promise you, father, will bear the memory of your kindness to the grave.

HARPAGON. And I, I promise you that there is nothing you shall not have from me.

CLEANTH. Ah! father, I have nothing more to ask: you gave me all when you gave me Marianne.

HARPAGON. What?

CLEANTH. I say, father, that you have made me too happy. You gave me all when you agreed to give me Marianne.

HARPAGON. Who said anything about giving you Marianne?

CLEANTH. You, father.

HARPAGON. I?

CLEANTH. Certainly.

HARPAGON. What! You are the one who promised to renounce her.

CLEANTH. I renounce her?

HARPAGON. Yes.

CLEANTH. Not in the least.

HARPAGON. You haven't abandoned your pretensions to her?

CLEANTH. On the contrary, I am more determined than ever.

HARPAGON. What! you rascal, again?

CLEANTH. Nothing can change my mind.

HARPAGON. Let me at you, traitor!

CLEANTH. Do whatever you please.

HARPAGON. I forbid you ever to see me again.

CLEANTH. It's all the same to me.

HARPAGON. I abandon you.

CLEANTH. Abandon me.

HARPAGON. I disown you as my son.

CLEANTH. So be it.

HARPAGON. I disinherit you.

CLEANTH. Anything you like.

HARPAGON. And I give you my curse.

CLEANTH. I have no need of your gifts. *Exit* HARPAGON.

Enter LA FLÈCHE.

FLÈCHE. Ah! sir! I have found you just in time! Follow me quickly.

CLEANTH. What's the matter?

FLÈCHE. Follow me, I tell you—our troubles are over.

CLEANTH. What?

FLÈCHE, *shows him the chest.* Here's your way out.

CLEANTH. How?

FLÈCHE. Your father's treasure. I dug it up!

CLEANTH. Where was it?

FLÈCHE. You shall know everything. Run. I hear him screaming.

Exeunt LA FLÈCHE *and* CLEANTH.

Enter HARPAGON.

HARPAGON. Stop thief! Stop thief! Stop assassin! Stop murderer! Justice, Divine Justice! I am ruined! I've been murdered! He cut my throat, he stole my money! Who can it be? What's become of him? Where is he? Where is he hiding? What shall I do to find him? Where shall I run? Where shan't I run? Isn't that he there? Isn't this he here? Who's this? *Sees his own shadow and grabs his own arm.* Stop! Give me back my money, you rogue. . . . Ah! it is myself. My mind is unhinged, and I don't know where I am, who I am, or what I am doing. *Falls to his knees.* Alas! my poor money, my poor money, my dear friend, they have taken you from me. And since they carried you off, I've lost my support, my consolation, my joy. Everything is at an end for me; I have no more to do in this world! I cannot live without you! It's finished. I can no more. *Lies down.* I am dying. I am dead. I am buried! Isn't there anybody who would like to bring me back to life by returning my dear money or by telling me who took it? *Rising to his knees.* What did you say? It was nobody. *Stands.* Whoever did the job must have watched very closely for his chance; for he chose exactly the time when I was talking to my treacherous son. *Takes his hat and cane.* I'll go out. I'll go and demand justice. I'll order them to torture everyone in my house for a confession: the maids, the valets, my son, my daughter—and myself too! What a crowd of people! Everybody I cast my eyes on arouses my suspicion, and everything seems to be my thief. Eh! what are you talking about there? About the man that robbed me? Why are you making that noise up there? Is my thief there? *Kneels and addresses the audience.* Please, if anyone has any information about my thief, I beg you to tell me. Are you sure he isn't hidden there among you? They all look at me and laugh. *Rises.* You will probably see that they all had a part in this robbery. Here, quick, commissaries, archers, provosts, judges, tortures, scaffolds, and executioners! I want to have everybody hanged. And if I don't recover my money, I'll hang myself afterward!

Exit.

Act V

On stage: HARPAGON, *the* COMMISSARY, *and his clerk.*

COMMISSARY. Leave me alone. I know my business, thank God! I didn't start investigating robberies yesterday. I wish I had a sack of francs for every man I've sent to the gallows!

HARPAGON. All the magistrates are interested in taking this case in hand. What's more, if no one sees to it that I recover my money, I shall demand justice from Justice herself!

COMMISSARY. We must follow the prescribed procedure. How much was it you said was in this money box?

HARPAGON. Ten thousand écus, to the sou.

COMMISSARY. Ten thousand écus?

HARPAGON. Ten thousand écus.

COMMISSARY. It was a considerable theft.

HARPAGON. No penalty would be too great for the enormity of the crime. If it goes unpunished, nothing is too sacred to be safe.

COMMISSARY. In what coin was the sum?

HARPAGON. In good gold louis and solid pistoles.

COMMISSARY. Whom do you suspect of this theft?

HARPAGON. Everybody! I want you to arrest the whole city and the suburbs!

COMMISSARY. We mustn't frighten anyone, take my word for it. We must try and obtain some evidence quietly. Then afterward we can proceed more rigorously in recovering the deniers that were taken from you.

Enter MASTER JACQUES *from the kitchen.*

JACQUES. I'll be back in a little while. First I want you to cut his throat. Then I want you to singe his feet. Then I want you to put him in boiling water. Then I want you to hang him from the ceiling.

HARPAGON. Who? The man who robbed me?

JACQUES. I was talking about the suckling pig your steward just sent me. I want to dress him for you according to my fancy.

HARPAGON. That is not the question. You must talk to this gentleman about something else.

COMMISSARY. Don't be frightened. I am not a man who would cause you scandal. Everything will be done quietly.

JACQUES. Is the gentleman one of your supper guests?

COMMISSARY. Now, my dear friend, you must hide nothing from your master.

JACQUES. Faith, sir, I will show you all I know: I will treat you the best I possibly can.

HARPAGON. We aren't talking about that.

JACQUES. If I can't give you as fine a feast as I want to, it's the fault of a certain gentleman, a certain steward, who has clipped my wings with the scissors of his economy.

HARPAGON. Traitor! We are investigating something more important than supper. I want you to give me information about the money that was stolen from me.

JACQUES. Did someone steal your money?

HARPAGON. Yes, you rascal! And I'll have you hanged if you don't give it back.

COMMISSARY. For Heaven's sake, don't bully him! I can see by his face he's an honest man. Without making us send him to jail, he will tell you everything you want to know. Yes, my friend, if you tell us what you know, no harm will come to you. You will be rewarded by your master, as you deserve to be. Just this morning someone took his money. Is it possible you don't have some information about this matter?

JACQUES, *aside*. Exactly what I need to get my revenge on our steward! Ever since he came into this house he has been the favorite —only *his* advice is listened to. Then, too, the beating he gave me sticks in my craw.

HARPAGON. What are you mumbling about?

COMMISSARY. Leave him alone. He is preparing to give you satisfaction. I told you he is an honest man.

JACQUES. Sir, since you want me to tell you something about this business, I think it was a certain gentleman, a certain steward, who did the job.

HARPAGON. Valère?

JACQUES. Yes.

HARPAGON. He? Who seemed to be so trustworthy?

JACQUES. Himself. I think he is the one who robbed you.

HARPAGON. On what grounds do you think so?

JACQUES. On what grounds?

HARPAGON. Yes.

JACQUES. I think so. . . . on the grounds that. . . . I think so.

COMMISSARY. But it is necessary that you tell us what proof you have.

HARPAGON. Did you see him sneaking around the place where I kept my money?

JACQUES. Yes, certainly. Where did you keep your money?

HARPAGON. In the garden.

JACQUES. Exactly. I saw him sneaking through the garden. What was this money in?

HARPAGON. A moneybox.

JACQUES. That's it. I saw him with a moneybox.

HARPAGON. This moneybox. . . . What did it look like? I'll soon see if it was mine.

JACQUES. What did it look like?

HARPAGON. Yes.

JACQUES. It looked like. . . . it looked like a moneybox.

COMMISSARY. Of course. But describe it a little, so we can see. . . .

JACQUES. It was a large moneybox.

HARPAGON. The one that was stolen from me was small.

JACQUES. Oh, yes—it was small if you want to look at it that way. I call it large on account of what it contained.

COMMISSARY. What color was it?

JACQUES. What color?

COMMISSARY. Yes.

JACQUES. It was the color of. . . . yes, the color of it was. . . . Can't you help me out a bit?

HARPAGON. Eh!

JACQUES. Wasn't it red?

HARPAGON. No, gray.

JACQUES. Oh! yes, grayish-red. That's what I meant to say.

HARPAGON. There isn't the slightest doubt. That is definitely it. Write, sir, write down his testimony. Heavens! who's to be trusted nowadays? You can't put your faith in anything! After this, I fear I am a man who might rob himself.

ACT V] THE MISER

JACQUES. Sir, he is coming back. At least don't go and tell him it was I who told you this.

Enter VALÈRE.

HARPAGON. Advance. Come. Confess the darkest deed, the most horrible atrocity ever committed.

VALÈRE. What do you mean, sir?

HARPAGON. What! traitor, you do not even blush for your crime?

VALÈRE. What crime can you be talking of?

HARPAGON. What crime am I talking of? Infamous! As though you didn't know what I mean! It is useless for you to try and cover up. The deed has been discovered. Someone has just told me all. Really! How could you abuse my kindness that way—insinuate yourself into my house to betray me—to play a trick of that kind on me!

VALÈRE. Sir, since someone has told you all, I shall not try to find a way out. I deny nothing.

JACQUES, *aside*. Hoho! Could I have guessed right without thinking?

VALÈRE. It was my intention to speak to you about it, and I wanted to wait for more favorable conditions to do so. But since things are the way they are, I beg you not to be angry. Be good enough to hear my reasons.

HARPAGON. And what wonderful reasons can you give me, infamous thief?

VALÈRE. Ah! sir, I have not deserved those names. It is true I am guilty of an offense against you. But, after all, my fault is pardonable.

HARPAGON. How, pardonable? A premeditated crime? An assassination of this sort?

VALÈRE. Please don't lose your temper. When you have heard me, you will see that the evil done is not so great as you make it out.

HARPAGON. The evil is not so great as I make it out! What? My blood! My entrails!—You scoundrel!

VALÈRE. Your blood, sir, has not fallen into evil hands. I belong to a class which is not beneath it, and there is nothing in all this for which I cannot make full reparation.

HARPAGON. That is my intention precisely—that you shall make full restitution of what you have ravished from me.

VALÈRE. Your honor, sir, shall be fully satisfied.

HARPAGON. It has nothing to do with honor. But, tell me, what ever possessed you to do it?

VALÈRE. Alas! You are asking me?

HARPAGON. Yes I really am.

VALÈRE. A god who is his own excuse for everything he does: Love.

HARPAGON. Love?

VALÈRE. Yes.

HARPAGON. A beautiful love, a beautiful love indeed! Love of my gold louis.

VALÈRE. No, sir, it was not in the least your wealth that tempted me. That wasn't what dazzled me. And I swear I will make no claims whatsoever on your property, provided you let me keep what I have.

HARPAGON. I will do no such thing, by God! See how insolent he is! He wants to keep the proceeds of his theft.

VALÈRE. Do you call it a theft?

HARPAGON. Do I call it a theft! A treasure like that!

VALÈRE. A treasure indeed! The most precious you have, without a doubt! But your giving me such a treasure would be no real loss to you. I ask you on bended knee to give me this enchanting treasure. If you want to do right you will grant my request.

HARPAGON. I will do nothing of the kind. What is he saying?

VALÈRE. We have promised to be faithful to one another. We have vowed never to separate.

HARPAGON. Your vow is admirable. Your promise is amusing.

VALÈRE. We are engaged to an eternal union.

HARPAGON. I shall forbid the banns, I assure you.

VALÈRE. Naught but death can part us.

HARPAGON. You are certainly bewitched by my money.

VALÈRE. I have told you, sir, it was not selfish interest that drove me to do what I have done. My heart was not impelled by the motives you suspect. A nobler idea was my inspiration.

HARPAGON. You'll see: it is out of Christian charity he wants to keep my money! But I'll set all to rights. The law, you brazen scoundrel, will make me amends for everything!

VALÈRE. You may proceed as you like in the matter. I am ready to suffer any violence that will please you. But at least believe, I beg, that if any harm is done, I am the only one to accuse. Your daughter is in no way to blame for any of this.

HARPAGON. Certainly I believe that. It would be very strange, indeed, if my daughter had a part in this crime. But I want to get my treasure back. I want you to confess where you have carried it off to!

VALÈRE. I? Your treasure has not been carried off at all, but is here —at home.

HARPAGON, *aside*. Oh, my dear moneybox! *To* VALÈRE. My treasure has not left the house?

VALÈRE. No, sir.

HARPAGON. Well. Tell me now, haven't you even. . . . tampered a bit?

VALÈRE. I, tamper? Ah! you do us both a great wrong. The love that consumes me is wholly pure and respectful.

HARPAGON, *aside*. He's consumed with love for my moneybox?

VALÈRE. I would have died rather than reveal to your treasure a single offensive thought. It would have been an insult to so much honor and virtue.

HARPAGON, *aside*. My moneybox honorable and virtuous?

VALÈRE. I limited my desires to the pleasure of merely seeing. No criminal act has profaned the passion that is inspired by those lovely eyes.

HARPAGON, *aside*. My moneyboxes lovely eyes? He talks like a lover discussing his mistress.

VALÈRE. Dame Claude, sir, knows the truth of this adventure. She can bear witness. . . .

HARPAGON. What! my maid is an accomplice in this business?

VALÈRE. Yes, sir, she stood as a witness at our engagement. But it was not until she had learned how honorable were my intentions that she helped me to persuade your daughter to pledge her fidelity to me and accept my pledge in return.

HARPAGON, *aside*. Ha? Is his fear of the law making his mind wander? *To* VALÈRE. Why confuse us by bringing my daughter into this?

VALÈRE. I tell you, sir, I had all the trouble in the world to persuade modesty to grant what love desired.

HARPAGON. Whose modesty?

VALÈRE. Your daughter's. And it wasn't until yesterday that she was able to make up her mind and sign a mutual promise of marriage with me.

HARPAGON. My daughter signed a promise of marriage with you?

VALÈRE. Just as I, on my part, signed one with her.

HARPAGON. O Heavens! Another disgrace!

JACQUES, *to the* COMMISSARY. Write, sir, write.

HARPAGON. Aggravation of misfortune! Excess of despair! Come, sir, do the duty of your office. Draw me up an indictment against him as a thief and an instigator.

VALÈRE. Those are names which do not belong to me. When it is known who I am. . . .

Enter ELISE, MARIANNE, *and* FROSINE.

HARPAGON. Ah! profligate daughter! Unworthy of a father like me! This is how you put into practice the lessons I gave you! You let yourself beome infatuated with an infamous thief! You promise him your hand without my consent! But you will be undone, both of you. *To* ELISE. Four good, strong walls will answer for your conduct. *To* VALÈRE. A good, tall gallows will give me satisfaction for your audacity.

VALÈRE. It is not your passion that will judge the matter. I will at least be heard before I am condemned.

HARPAGON. I was mistaken to say the gallows. You will be broken alive on the wheel.

ELISE. Ah! father, be a little more human in your sentiments, I beseech you. Do not push things to the violent extreme of paternal power. Do not let yourself be carried away by the first impulse of passion. Give yourself time. Consider what you wish to do. Take pains. Look more closely at the person who has roused your wrath. He is not what your eyes have judged him to be. You will find it far less strange that I should have given myself to him when you learn that, were it not for him, you would have lost me long ago, and forever. Yes, father, he is the man who saved me from the great peril, the peril you know I was so close to in the water—the man to whom you owe the life of the same daughter who—

HARPAGON. All that is nothing. It would have been better for me had he let you drown and not do what he has done.

ELISE. Father, out of paternal love for me. . . .

ACT V]   THE MISER   275

HARPAGON. No, no! I won't hear another word. The law must do its duty.

JACQUES, *aside*. You'll pay for the beating you gave me.

FROSINE, *aside*. This is a queer mix-up.

Enter ANSELM.

ANSELM. What is it, Signor Harpagon? I see you are very much disturbed.

HARPAGON. Ah! Signor Anselm, you now behold the most unfortunate of men. Here is I don't know how much trouble and disorder to complicate the contract you came to sign! My money has been attacked! My honor has been attacked! And there stands a traitor, a profligate who has violated all that is most sacred to man—who has insinuated himself into my house under the name of servant in order to steal my money and seduce my daughter!

VALÈRE. Who cares about this money that you make so much noise about?

HARPAGON. Yes, they have made each other a promise of marriage. This outrage is your concern, Signor Anselm. You are the man who ought to take action against him. Have him prosecuted by the law! Revenge yourself for his insolence!

ANSELM. I have no intention of forcing myself on anybody or of making any claims to a heart that has already given itself to another. But of course I am ready to fight for your interests. As if the cause were my own.

HARPAGON. This gentleman here is an honest commissary, who assures me that he will neglect no part of his official duty. *To the* COMMISSARY. Indict him, sir, in due form! And make everything sound very criminal!

VALÈRE. I don't see what sort of crime you can make out of my passion for your daughter or what punishment you think I can be condemned to for our engagement. When it is known who I am. . . .

HARPAGON. I don't give a damn for all those tales. Nowadays the world is only too full of thieves of nobility, of impostors who take advantage of their insignificance and impudently bedeck themselves with the first illustrious name they take a fancy to.

VALÈRE. I'll have you know I am too honest to adorn myself with aught that is not mine. All Naples can testify to my birth.

ANSELM. Careful. Watch what you say. You run a greater risk here than you think. You have before you a man to whom all Naples is known and who can easily see through a trumped-up story.

VALÈRE. I am a man with nothing to fear. If you know Naples, you know who Don Thomas d'Alburcy was.

ANSELM. Of course I know who he was. Few people were better acquainted with him than I.

HARPAGON. I don't give a damn for Don Thomas or Don Smith.

ANSELM. Please, let him talk. We will see what he has to say about him.

VALÈRE. I have this to say: it was he who brought me into the world.

ANSELM. He?

VALÈRE. Yes.

ANSELM. Come now. You deceive yourself. Try some other story that might be more successful. Don't expect to save yourself by this imposture.

VALÈRE. Watch what you say. This is no imposture. I advance no claim that I cannot easily justify.

ANSELM. What! You dare to call yourself the son of Thomas d'Alburcy?

VALÈRE. I dare. And I am ready to defend that truth against no matter whom.

ANSELM. Fantastic audacity! Learn to your confusion that it was sixteen years ago, at the very least, that the man you speak of perished at sea with his wife and children while trying to save their lives from the cruel persecutions that accompanied the disorder at Naples and which precipitated the exile of more than one noble family.

VALÈRE. Yes, but learn to your own confusion, that his seven-year-old son, with a single servant, was saved from the shipwreck by a Spanish vessel—and that the son then saved now speaks to you. Learn that the captain of that vessel, touched by my misfortune, took a liking to me and brought me up as his own son—that arms have been my occupation since the time I was able to hold them—that I learned a short time ago that my father is not dead, as I had always thought—that while passing through this city in search of him an adventure planned by Heaven gave me a glimpse of charming Elise—that the sight of her made me a slave to her beauty—and that the violence of my love and her father's severity made me resolve to enter into his house and send another in search of my parents.

ANSELM. What proof do you have beyond your bare word that this is not a fable you have constructed on a foundation of truth?

VALÈRE. The Spanish captain, a ruby signet that belonged to my father, an agate bracelet that my mother placed upon my arm, and old Pedro, the servant who with me was saved from the shipwreck.

MARIANNE. Alas! I myself can answer for what you have said. You are not deceiving us. Your account has made clear to me that you are my brother!

VALÈRE. You, my sister?

MARIANNE. Yes. My heart was moved the moment you opened your mouth. Our mother, whom you will see again, has diverted me a thousand times with the misfortunes of our family. Heaven did not suffer us either to perish in that unhappy shipwreck—but our lives were saved only at the expense of our liberty. They were pirates who took us, my mother and me, off the wreckage of our vessel. After ten years of slavery, we regained our liberty through a happy accident, and returned to Naples. There we found that all our property had been sold and were not able to uncover any news of my father. We sailed for Genoa, where my mother went to gather up the sad remains of our dissipated family fortune. From there, fleeing the barbarous injustice of her kinsmen, she came to these parts, where she has lived scarcely more than a languishing life.

ANSELM. O Heaven—such are the signs of Thy power! How clearly Thou hast shown us that Thou alone canst work miracles! Embrace me, children both! Mingle your joy with that of your father!

VALÈRE. You are our father?

MARIANNE. Is it for you my mother has shed so many tears?

ANSELM. Yes, my daughter, yes, my son, I am Don Thomas d'Alburcy, whom Heaven saved from the waves with all the money he had with him—and who, believing for more than sixteen years you all were dead, was preparing, after long voyages, to seek the consolation of a new family through marriage with a good and gentle young lady. When I saw how much my life would be in danger should I return to Naples, I abandoned the idea forever. Having found a way to sell what I had there, I established my residence here. Under the name of Anselm I sought to leave behind the sorrows of the name which has caused me so many reverses.

HARPAGON. Is that your son?

ANSELM. Yes.

HARPAGON. I hold you responsible for the ten thousand écus he stole from me.

ANSELM. He? He stole from you?

HARPAGON. He himself.

VALÈRE. Who told you?

HARPAGON. Master Jacques.

VALÈRE. It is you that says so?

JACQUES. Look, I'm not saying a thing.

HARPAGON. Yes. This gentleman is the commissary who took down his testimony.

VALÈRE. Can you believe me capable of such a villainous deed?

HARPAGON. Capable or not capable, I want my money back.

Enter CLEANTH *and* LA FLÈCHE.

CLEANTH. Torment yourself no longer, father. Accuse no one. I have uncovered some information about your affair, and I have come to tell you that, if you will resign yourself to letting me marry Marianne, your money will be returned to you.

HARPAGON. Where is it?

CLEANTH. Don't worry. It's in a place that I will answer for. Everything depends on me. It only remains for you to tell me your decision. You can choose whether to give me Marianne or lose your moneybox.

HARPAGON. Nothing has been removed from it?

CLEANTH. Nothing. Let us see if it is your intention to subscribe to this marriage and join your consent to that of her mother—who has given her the liberty to choose between us two.

MARIANNE. But you do not realize that his consent is not enough, or that Heaven, along with my brother, whom you now behold—*points to* VALÈRE—has restored my father to me. You must win me from *him*.

ANSELM. Heaven, my children, did not restore me to you in order that I should oppose your desires. Signor Harpagon, you very well know that the choice of a young lady falls to the son and not to the father. Come now, don't make people say what is too obvious to need expression. Give your consent to this double ceremony as I have.

HARPAGON. Before I can make up my mind, I must see my moneybox.

CLEANTH. You shall see it safe and sound.

HARPAGON. I have no money to give my children for their marriages.

ANSELM. Oh well, I have some for both of them. Don't let that bother you.

HARPAGON. You will commit yourself to stand the cost of both these marriages?

ANSELM. Yes, I will commit myself. Are you satisfied?

HARPAGON. Yes, provided that you have me a suit made for the wedding.

ANSELM. Agreed. Come, let us indulge the happiness which this joyous day bestows upon us.

COMMISSARY. Hold, gentlemen! Hold on, one moment, if you please! Who is going to pay for all the writing I've done?

HARPAGON. We have no need of your writing.

COMMISSARY. No? But I, on the other hand, can't pretend to have done it for nothing.

HARPAGON, *points to* MASTER JACQUES. As payment I give you this man. Take him and hang him.

JACQUES. Alas! what is a man supposed to do? They beat me before for telling the truth. Now they want to hang me for lying.

ANSELM. Signor Harpagon, you ought to pardon him his trickery.

HARPAGON. You'll pay the commissary then.

ANSELM. So be it. Let us go at once and share our joy with your mother.

HARPAGON. And I, to see my dear, dear moneybox.

✷

IT WOULD BE an unusual reader who found this version of *The Miser* more amusing at first acquaintance than Wilde's *Earnest*. The technique is alien to us, and we miss the witticisms of the Anglo-Saxon tradition. However, even at a first reading, if we survive the rather formidable opening scene, we may have a foothold in certain recognizable and half-familiar devices. In the scene between Harpagon and La Flèche (beginning above, p. 224), where, we may feel, the play really gets going, we recognize, for example, *the patter of comedians*. And this is an important clue, for the present-day comedian is the point of contact between us and the older comedy, of which Molière is the great exponent.

Many modern persons protest against artifice in dramatic art, yet the patter of comedians abounds in artifice that everyone accepts because it makes for good fun. The justification of all artifice in art is similar: it is acceptable when it makes for good fun, for good work, for good art. At this point, the best thing is to read Bergson's essay *Laughter* and E. E. Stoll's pieces on "Comedy" and "Comic Method" in *Art and Artifice in Shakespeare* and *Shakespeare Studies,* respectively. Bergson and Stoll make one aware that, like the radio, stage, or screen comedian, the classic writer of comedy has a bag of tricks. Deception, disguise, misrepresentation, misunderstanding, mistaken identity, the calumniator credited, hoax, coincidence, repetition, inversion, reversal, discovery, recognition—these terms are not limited to the criticism of comedy, and in any case they overlap each other, but they inevitably enter into analyses of comedies. And the beginner who is stumped, as beginners are, for something to say about a work of art can approach any comedy by asking which of these devices or processes are to be found in it and how are they employed.

In *The Miser,* for example, *comic repetition* is the very basis of the dialogue. "A pox on avarice and the avaricious!" "How's that? What did you say?" "What did I say?" "Yes. What did you say about avarice and the avaricious?" "I said, a pox on avarice and the avaricious" (p. 225 above). And so forth. *Comic coincidence* lies at the center of Molière's story (as of Wilde's in *Earnest*). "You are our father?" "Is it for you my mother has shed so many tears?" "Yes, my daughter, yes, my son, I am Don Thomas d'Alburcy. . . ." (p. 277 above). And so forth. The reader will do well to list all the comic devices he can find in the play if he wants to know what Molière's technical resources are.

He will realize, however, that such a list does not tell us whether a play is a good one or not. An equally long and impressive list might be compiled from the works of minor authors. The question to ask here is, of what use were the various artifices to Molière? The modern reader often resents the artificial as such; he prefers the "life-like." If Molière were confronted with modern naturalism, he might, however, complain that it *limits* the playwright too much. Take the matter of coincidences. In modern colleges, students of playwriting are often told to avoid the use of startling coincidences. If a character suddenly enters, we must know that there is good reason for his doing so. (In technical language: entrances and exits should be motivated.) In Molière, on the other hand, coincidence is not occasional but constant. Molière uses it, you might also say, on principle. He takes no pains to provide motives for entrances and exits. He is *free*—free to manipulate, free to exploit artifice to the top of its bent. For what purpose? Just to increase the immediate effectiveness of farce and melodrama? Such are perhaps the loaded questions of those who defend realism at all costs. In actual practice, Molière used his freedom *to bring his subject into high relief*. Having no need to keep up appearances, he is free to arrange his devices in whatever combination most brilliantly makes his points.

The examples of repetition given above are trivial. Something of the sort can be heard every evening on the radio. The repetition of the phrase "without a dowry" in Act I (pp. 232-33 above) is of a different order. It is not just a trick of language but also an attempt to define a trick of mind. It points to Harpagon's obsession (money) and to its consequence: that he doesn't hear what he doesn't wish to hear. Here we have a human trait that at its mildest we might describe as absentmindedness but, at its extreme, as in Harpagon, is *narrow*-mindedness, even insanity.

Perhaps a more special device than the repetition of a phrase is Talking at Cross Purposes (one of the varieties of comic misunderstanding). A simple instance is to be found in Act I (p. 230 above). Harpagon seems to be offering Marianne to Cleanth. The speeches pass quickly back and forth like a fencing match. Then suddenly: ". . . and I am resolved to marry her. . ." "Eh?" "What?" "You say you have resolved . . ." "To marry Marianne." The news will not go into Cleanth's head. "Who, you, you?" "Yes. I, I, I!" Such a misunderstanding is quite simply funny and could be paralleled in a hundred little comedies with no pretensions to greatness. Much more meaningful is the misunderstanding in Act V (pp. 271-73 above). The tables are now being turned. This time it is Harpagon who is being deceived. He thinks Valère is talking about his casket when actually he is talking about Elise. The confusion is deeply psychological. Harpagon is driven into it by his obsession. And Molière is able to make the point that Harpagon loves his casket as a human being. The comedy ends with the lovers coming together—Valère and Elise, Cleanth and Marianne, *Harpagon and the casket.*

Molière, then, *makes points* and he *notes psychological traits.* These are hard things to do in a play, and the student of dramatic art would do well to list the "points" made in a given scene and the traits that are noted, just as he has listed the comic devices. When he has done all this he will have before him an impressive list of fine details. Can he stop here—with the sound conclusion that a "masterpiece is full of fine details and the critic (or student) takes note of them"? No, he has to ask if the parts have been organized into a whole. Probably he has thought of this when considering the characters and has asked himself, are the individual traits organized into the wholeness of portraiture? This is to ask whether Molière has created satisfactory characters; and some critics are content as soon as they have assured themselves that he has. It cannot, however, be taken as axiomatic that a portrait or a series of portraits amounts to a play, let alone to an integrated play. The simple reader may here be a safer guide than the sophisticated critic in his feeling that plot or action is the ground-plan of such a play and that all the rest—individual devices, satiric points, and even character—have to be subordinated to it. These other things are coaches drawn along by a swift locomotive, which is comic plot.

Look back at the last scenes of Act IV. The action shuttles to and fro. Harpagon and Cleanth quarrel, are reconciled by Master Jacques, quarrel again. The sequence, and with it the whole play, reaches a climax in Harpagon's long and famous soliloquy (p. 267). However *unrealistic* we may have considered Molière's story to be, we have here to acknowledge how brilliantly it permits him to handle *reality*. For it is precisely the artifice of the to and fro movement that gives form and body to Harpagon's state of mind. Character is dependent on plot. How close the "unrealism" may come to reality is nowhere more apparent than in Harpagon's seizing the thief's arm and finding it to be his own. It is a comedian's stunt, and requires for its execution on the stage a comedian's special dexterity; but it is also a perfect vehicle for the idea of mania, the disintegration of a man.

The man is not depicted alone or simply *alongside* others: he is seen *in relation to* others. His relations with others give Molière his chance to introduce *plot*—which involves his whole bag of comic tricks. In the end, then, we see a number of people whose relationships to each other amount to Molière's subject. The word *subject* here is used in the sense in which a painter might use it. He doesn't mean his theme or idea or message. He means that particular grouping of houses, trees, people, or whatever that struck him as something for his canvas. The painter's subject is, of course, static; the playwright's is not seen entire at any one moment, it is in motion. It is given a beginning, middle, and end. It is given shape, form, definition—by plot.

Plot material seems at first bewilderingly various. Millions of stories have been written, and millions more will be. Yet there seem to be only a few basic narrative patterns. A French critic has written a book to show, for example, that there are only thirty-six dramatic situations, and even some of these are not clearly distinct. Viewed as a machine for the definition of subject, plot can indeed be reduced to our principle of like and unlike. (See p. 9 above.) In *The Miser* we have noted the parallelism and contrast of three couples: Valère and Elise, Cleanth and Marianne, Harpagon and the casket. The horrible meaning of Harpagon's love of the casket is defined by contrast with the healthy, human love of the young people for each other.

This is a convenient point at which to mention Molière's *theme*. He is dealing with love and money—fundamental topics of drama as of life. The two are, for many purposes, antithetic. Hence the pure romantic lover has no interest in money, while the pure villain has no interest in love. In life, there is little "purity." Consequently in serious art (which, by definition, is at grips with life) impurity or disorder is always involved. In *The Miser* the disorder is complete in that Harpagon has turned morality upside down by making money the object of love. Returning to the end of Act IV, we find that one of the things that makes it great is the highly imaginative identification of love and money. Highly imaginative: that is, very completely dramatized, very clearly seen, very exactly reproduced down to the last desired detail of tone. "And since they carried you off, I've lost my support, my consolation, my joy. Everything is at an end for me. . ." It is the way a tragic hero might talk of the loss of his lady.

Such a precise realization of a theme, a character, a situation in a particular way—this is what the reader who is in search of dramatic art should study, this and its inclusion within the larger unit, ultimately within the play as a whole.

4. TWELFTH NIGHT · 1602

WHETHER the foregoing comments cut any ice the reader himself will judge. Much depends on whether he has already found Molière amusing before reading them. Unless one starts by being amused—unless one's attention is pleasurably engaged—one does not end by being impressed. As has already been intimated (p. 12), pleasure may not, in art, be the only end in view, but it is an absolute prerequisite (p. 3), because, as Dr. Johnson said, "that book is good in vain which the reader throws away."

A distinguished dramatic critic wrote to the present editor: "If you can interest the Anglo-Saxon reader in Molière you're a better man than I." Presumably Shakespeare is less of a bugbear. There is no translation problem. Here is an author who can even be seen on the stage, where he still amuses and excites popular audiences. Any reader of this book who finds the very notion of Shakespeare unpleasant can probably overcome his dread by seeing the poet in stage or screen performance. (It is at once the merit and the limitation of the Shakespeare films that they are addressed to a public that is assumed to be prejudiced against Shakespeare. A book by the makers of the *Hamlet* film—*The Film Hamlet,* Auvergne Publishers, New York, 1949—is full of evidence on the point.)

A competent production proves this at least to the sceptical and the hardboiled: that Shakespeare is an entertainer. Scenes where the dialogue is rather too laboriously funny (i.e., rather too *unfunny*) as one reads them often prove to be really amusing, or otherwise convincing, as one watches them acted out. Since the low comedy scenes in *Twelfth Night* are instances, the reader who has not seen the play must make every effort to visualize the stage action for these episodes.

A tip as to Elizabethan stage technique may be in order. *Ignore the scene divisions.* At any rate don't take them to mean an intermission and change of scenery. As one group of characters leaves the stage another comes on. Like the film, but unlike most modern plays, the Elizabethan play consists of a busy succession of short scenes.

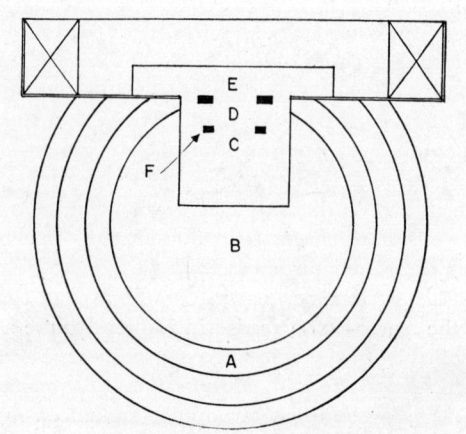

Piero D'Orazio, after Gervais, Propos sur la Mise en Scène.

SHAKESPEARE'S THEATER—GROUND PLAN

A. Galleries for seated spectators.
B. Open space—originally an inn-yard—for mass of standees.
C. The *apron* of the stage (spectators on three sides).
D. Here a roof defines another playing area.
E. Inner stage. Two stories. Below, can be revealed or cut off by a curtain —hence is useful for bedroom scenes as in *Othello*. Above is a balcony, used famously in *Romeo*.
F. The letter F points to one of the four pillars that sustain roof D.

A remark on the language of Shakespeare may be added. As more and more time separates us from the Elizabethans, their language becomes more and more foreign; it will before long differ as much from modern English as, say, Swedish does from Norwegian. Hence it is absurd to present a Shakespeare text to the general reader without notes. But who is the general reader? No two people need exactly the same notes. Each reader is bound to think the editor provides either too many or too few. Too many clutter up the text and waste the reader's time. Too few prevent him knowing what he is reading or force him to get up and hunt for the encyclopedia. The present editor has assumed that the reader knows a few Elizabethanisms (such as "Zounds!" and "Marry!"). But, with a few such exceptions, he has assumed that the reader will not know words that are no longer in use or archaic senses of words which *are* in use. He has also assumed that the general reader does not wish to be distracted from his reading by a whole paragraph of editorial matter about each difficult point. It is true that the full sense can sometimes not be unraveled without such extensive

THE EXTERIOR OF THE GLOBE PLAYHOUSE

From a Model by Dr. J. C. Adams

THE STAGE OF THE GLOBE PLAYHOUSE

investigation; but the reader who is after this "full sense" will simply have to go to a big scholarly edition of Shakespeare. One should not imagine that even Shakespeare scholars ever feel that they have mastered the "full sense" of every word; it is something to master the approximate sense.

Sometimes the editor had no idea whether most of his readers would know a word or not. The word *cuckold*, for instance. A few usages proved so common and/or important in the two texts that they should perhaps be given here once and for all. They are *still* in the sense of *always*, *fancy* in the sense of *love*, *abuse* (the verb) in the sense of *deceive*, *ancient* in the sense of *ensign*, *for that* in the sense of *because*. Some words that *are* annotated in the text might also be carried in mind from the outset. They include *practice* in the sense of *plotting*, *owe* in the sense of *possess*, *free* in the sense of *generous*, and *honest* in the sense of (1) *honorable* and (2) *chaste*.

TWELFTH NIGHT

OR, WHAT YOU WILL

by William Shakespeare

✶

Twelfth Night

Characters

ORSINO, *Duke of Illyria*
SEBASTIAN, *brother to Viola*
ANTONIO, *a sea captain, friend to Sebastian*
A SEA CAPTAIN, *friend to Viola*
VALENTINE } *gentlemen attending*
CURIO } *on the Duke*
SIR TOBY BELCH, *uncle to Olivia*
SIR ANDREW AGUECHEEK
MALVOLIO, *steward to Olivia*
FABIAN } *servants*
FESTE, *a clown* } *to Olivia*
OLIVIA
VIOLA
MARIA, *Olivia's woman*

Lords, Priests, Sailors, Officers, Musicians, and other Attendants

THE PLACE: *A city in Illyria, and the sea-coast near it.*

Act I

SCENE 1. *The* DUKE'S *palace.*

Enter DUKE, CURIO, *and other* LORDS; MUSICIANS *attending.*

DUKE. If music be the food of love, play on;
Give me excess of it, that, surfeiting,
The appetite may sicken, and so die.
That strain again! it had a dying fall;
O, it came o'er my ear like the sweet sound
That breathes upon a bank of violets,
Stealing and giving odour! Enough; no more:
'T is not so sweet now as it was before.
O spirit of love, how quick and fresh art thou,
That, notwithstanding thy capacity   10
Receiveth as the sea, nought enters there,
Of what validity and pitch soe'er,

ACT I, SC. 1: 4. *fall:* cadence. 5. *sound:* i.e., of the wind. 9. *quick:* alive.
12. *validity and pitch:* value and excellence.

But falls into abatement and low price,
Even in a minute! so full of shapes is fancy
That it alone is high fantastical.
  CURIO. Will you go hunt, my lord?
  DUKE.   What, Curio?
  CURIO. The hart.
  DUKE. Why, so I do, the noblest that I have;
O, when mine eyes did see Olivia first,
Methought she purg'd the air of pestilence!
That instant was I turn'd into a hart;
And my desires, like fell and cruel hounds,
E'er since pursue me.—

Enter VALENTINE.

                           How now! what news from her?
  VALENTINE. So please my lord, I might not be admitted,
But from her handmaid do return this answer:
The element itself, till seven years' heat,
Shall not behold her face at ample view;
But, like a cloistress, she will veiled walk
And water once a day her chamber round
With eye-offending brine; all this to season
A brother's dead love, which she would keep fresh
And lasting in her sad remembrance.
  DUKE. O, she that hath a heart of that fine frame
To pay this debt of love but to a brother,
How will she love when the rich golden shaft
Hath kill'd the flock of all affections else
That live in her; when liver, brain, and heart,
These sovereign thrones, are all supplied and fill'd—
Her sweet perfections—with one self king!
Away before me to sweet beds of flowers!
Love-thoughts lie rich when canopied with bowers.   *Exeunt.*

---

15. *fantastical:* imaginative. 17-18. *hart:* pun—heart/hart. 22. i.e., like the dogs that pursued Actaeon in the old story. 26. *element:* sky. *heat:* course. 28. *cloistress:* nun. 30. *season:* preserve. 35. *shaft:* i.e., Cupid's arrow. 37-38. *liver, brain, heart* are thrones of love, thought, feeling.

SCENE 2. *The sea-coast.*

Enter VIOLA, *a* CAPTAIN, *and* SAILORS.

VIOLA. What country, friends, is this?
CAPTAIN. This is Illyria, lady.
VIOLA. And what should I do in Illyria?
My brother he is in Elysium.
Perchance he is not drown'd; what think you, sailors?
  CAPTAIN. It is perchance that you yourself were sav'd.
  VIOLA. O my poor brother! and so perchance may he be.
  CAPTAIN. True, madam: and, to comfort you with chance,
Assure yourself, after our ship did split,
When you and those poor number saved with you   10
Hung on our driving boat, I saw your brother,
Most provident in peril, bind himself,
Courage and hope both teaching him the practice,
To a strong mast that liv'd upon the sea;
Where, like Arion on the dolphin's back,
I saw him hold acquaintance with the waves
So long as I could see.
  VIOLA. For saying so, there's gold;
Mine own escape unfoldeth to my hope,
Whereto thy speech serves for authority,   20
The like of him. Know'st thou this country?
  CAPTAIN. Ay, madam, well; for I was bred and born
Not three hours' travel from this very place.
  VIOLA. Who governs here?
  CAPTAIN. A noble duke, in nature as in name.
  VIOLA. What is his name?
  CAPTAIN. Orsino.
  VIOLA. Orsino! I have heard my father name him;
He was a bachelor then.
  CAPTAIN. And so is now, or was so very late;   30
For but a month ago I went from hence,

---

sc. 2: 8. *you:* yourself. 10. *poor number:* few. 13. *practice:* i.e., how to do it. 14. *liv'd:* floated. 15. i.e., like a famous singer whose life was so saved. 19-21. i.e., unfoldeth a like escape for him.

And then 't was fresh in murmur—as, you know,
What great ones do the less will prattle of—
That he did seek the love of fair Olivia.

VIOLA. What's she?

CAPTAIN. A virtuous maid, the daughter of a count
That died some twelvemonth since, then leaving her
In the protection of his son, her brother,
Who shortly also died; for whose dear love,
They say, she hath abjur'd the company   40
And sight of men.

VIOLA.   O that I serv'd that lady,
And might not be deliver'd to the world,
Till I had made mine own occasion mellow,
What my estate is!

CAPTAIN.   That were hard to compass;
Because she will admit no kind of suit,
No, not the duke's.

VIOLA. There is a fair behaviour in thee, captain;
And though that nature with a beauteous wall
Doth oft close in pollution, yet of thee
I will believe thou hast a mind that suits   50
With this thy fair and outward character.
I prithee,—and I'll pay thee bounteously,—
Conceal me what I am, and be my aid
For such disguise as haply shall become
The form of my intent. I'll serve this duke;
Thou shalt present me as an eunuch to him:
It may be worth thy pains; for I can sing
And speak to him in many sorts of music
That will allow me very worth his service.
What else may hap to time I will commit;   60
Only shape thou thy silence to my wit.

CAPTAIN. Be you his eunuch, and your mute I'll be;
When my tongue blabs, then let mine eyes not see.

VIOLA. I thank thee; lead me on.   *Exeunt.*

---

42. *deliver'd:* revealed. 43. *made . . . mellow:* made . . . ready. 44. i.e., "as to what my condition is." *compass:* manage. 49. *close in:* enclose, conceal. 55. *form:* character. 62. *mute:* dumb attendant.

SCENE 3. OLIVIA'S *house*.

Enter SIR TOBY BELCH *and* MARIA.

SIR TOBY. What a plague means my niece, to take the death of her brother thus? I am sure care's an enemy to life.

MARIA. By my troth, Sir Toby, you must come in earlier o' nights; your cousin, my lady, takes great exceptions to your ill hours.

SIR TOBY. Why, let her except before excepted.

MARIA. Ay, but you must confine yourself within the modest limits of order.

SIR TOBY. Confine! I'll confine myself no finer than I am: these clothes are good enough to drink in; and so be these boots too; an they be not, let them hang themselves in their own straps. 10

MARIA. That quaffing and drinking will undo you: I heard my lady talk of it yesterday; and of a foolish knight that you brought in one night here to be her wooer.

SIR TOBY. Who, Sir Andrew Aguecheek?

MARIA. Ay, he.

SIR TOBY. He's as tall a man as any's in Illyria.

MARIA. What's that to the purpose?

SIR TOBY. Why, he has three thousand ducats a year.

MARIA. Ay, but he'll have but a year in all these ducats; he's a very fool and a prodigal. 20

SIR TOBY. Fie, that you'll say so! he plays o' the viol-de-gamboys, and speaks three or four languages word for word without book, and hath all the good gifts of nature.

MARIA. He hath indeed, almost natural: for besides that he's a fool, he's a great quarreller; and but that he hath the gift of a coward to allay the gust he hath in quarrelling, 't is thought among the prudent he would quickly have the gift of a grave.

SIR TOBY. By this hand, they are scoundrels and substractors that say so of him. Who are they?

MARIA. They that add, moreover, he's drunk nightly in your [30 company.

---

sc. 3: 4. *cousin:* relative. 5. "Let her object to what she has objected to before" (word play as in *confine, fine,* ll. 7-9 below). 16. *tall:* able. 19. i.e., he'll run through them in a year. 24. *natural:* fool. 28. *substractors:* detractors.

298   TWELFTH NIGHT   [ACT I

SIR TOBY. With drinking healths to my niece; I'll drink to her as long as there is a passage in my throat and drink in Illyria: he's a coward and a coystril that will not drink to my niece till his brains turn o' the toe like a parish-top. What, wench!—Castiliano vulgo! for here comes Sir Andrew Agueface.

Enter SIR ANDREW AGUECHEEK.

SIR ANDREW. Sir Toby Belch! how now, Sir Toby Belch!
SIR TOBY. Sweet Sir Andrew!
SIR ANDREW. Bless you, fair shrew!
MARIA. And you too, sir.   40
SIR TOBY. Accost, Sir Andrew, accost.
SIR ANDREW. What's that?
SIR TOBY. My niece's chambermaid.
SIR ANDREW. Good Mistress Accost, I desire better acquaintance.
MARIA. My name is Mary, sir.
SIR ANDREW. Good Mistress Mary Accost,—
SIR TOBY. You mistake, knight; accost is front her, board her, woo her, assail her.
SIR ANDREW. By my troth, I would not undertake her in this company. Is that the meaning of accost?   50
MARIA. Fare you well, gentlemen.
SIR TOBY. An thou let part so, Sir Andrew, would thou mightst never draw sword again!
SIR ANDREW. An you part so, mistress, I would I might never draw sword again! Fair lady, do you think you have fools in hand?
MARIA. Sir, I have not you by the hand.
SIR ANDREW. Marry, but you shall have; and here's my hand.
MARIA. Now, sir, thought is free; I pray you, bring your hand to the buttery-bar and let it drink.
SIR ANDREW. Wherefore, sweet-heart? what's your metaphor?   60
MARIA. It's dry, sir.
SIR ANDREW. Why, I think so; I am not such an ass but I can keep my hand dry. But what's your jest?
MARIA. A dry jest, sir.

---

34. *a coystril:* a nobody. 35. *castiliano*—nonsense. 58-9. Perhaps Maria places Andrew's hand on her bosom.

SCENE 3]   TWELFTH NIGHT   299

SIR ANDREW. Are you full of them?

MARIA. Ay, sir, I have them at my fingers' ends; marry, now I let go your hand, I am barren. *Exit.*

SIR TOBY. O knight, thou lackest a cup of canary! when did I see thee so put down?

SIR ANDREW. Never in your life, I think; unless you see [70 canary put me down. Methinks sometimes I have no more wit than a Christian or an ordinary man has; but I am a great eater of beef, and I believe that does harm to my wit.

SIR TOBY. No question.

SIR ANDREW. An I thought that, I'd forswear it. I'll ride home to-morrow, Sir Toby.

SIR TOBY. Pourquoi, my dear knight?

SIR ANDREW. What is pourquoi? do or not do? I would I had bestowed that time in the tongues that I have in fencing, dancing, and bear-baiting! O, had I but followed the arts! 80

SIR TOBY. Then hadst thou had an excellent head of hair.

SIR ANDREW. Why, would that have mended my hair?

SIR TOBY. Past question; for thou seest it will not curl by nature.

SIR ANDREW. But it becomes me well enough, does't not?

SIR TOBY. Excellent: it hangs like flax on a distaff; and I hope to see a housewife take thee and spin it off.

SIR ANDREW. Faith, I'll home to-morrow, Sir Toby. Your niece will not be seen; or if she be, it's four to one she'll none of me: the count himself here hard by wooes her.

SIR TOBY. She'll none o' the count. She'll not match above [90 her degree, neither in estate, years, nor wit; I have heard her swear 't. Tut, there's life in 't, man.

SIR ANDREW. I'll stay a month longer. I am a fellow o' the strangest mind i' the world; I delight in masques and revels sometimes altogether.

SIR TOBY. Art thou good at these kickshawses, knight?

SIR ANDREW. As any man in Illyria, whatsoever he be, under the degree of my betters; and yet I will not compare with an old man.

---

80. i.e., the sport of baiting bears with dogs. 80-3. Pun on *tongues*. Hair is curled with *tongs*. 90. *count*: i.e., duke. 96. *kickshawses*: trifles. 98. *degree*: social rank.

SIR TOBY. What is thy excellence in a galliard, knight?
SIR ANDREW. Faith, I can cut a caper. 100
SIR TOBY. And I can cut the mutton to 't.
SIR ANDREW. And I think I have the back-trick simply as strong as any man in Illyria.
SIR TOBY. Wherefore are these things hid? wherefore have these gifts a curtain before 'em? are they like to take dust, like Mistress Mall's picture? why dost thou not go to church in a galliard and come home in a coranto? My very walk should be a jig. What dost thou mean? Is it a world to hide virtues in? I did think, by the excellent constitution of thy leg, it was formed under the star of a galliard.
SIR ANDREW. Ay, 't is strong, and it does indifferent well in [110 a flame-coloured stock. Shall we set about some revels?
SIR TOBY. What shall we do else? were we not born under Taurus?
SIR ANDREW. Taurus! That's sides and heart.
SIR TOBY. No, sir; it is legs and thighs. Let me see thee caper. Ha! higher! ha, ha! excellent! *Exeunt.*

SCENE 4. *The* DUKE'S *palace.*

Enter VALENTINE, *and* VIOLA *in man's attire.*

VALENTINE. If the duke continue these favours towards you, Cesario, you are like to be much advanced; he hath known you but three days, and already you are no stranger.

VIOLA. You either fear his humour or my negligence, that you call in question the continuance of his love. Is he inconstant, sir, in his favours?

VALENTINE. No, believe me.

VIOLA. I thank you. Here comes the count.

Enter DUKE, CURIO, *and* ATTENDANTS.

DUKE. Who saw Cesario, ho?
VIOLA. On your attendance, my lord; here. 10
DUKE. Stand you awhile aloof.—Cesario,

---

99. *galliard:* a kind of gay and lively dance. 100. *caper:* (1) leap; (2) a sauce. 102. *back-trick:* caper backwards. 105-6. *Mall:* Moll Cutpurse—or anyone. 107. *coranto:* another dance. 109 ff. *star . . . Taurus:* parts of the body were believed affected by the stars.

Thou know'st no less but all; I have unclasp'd
To thee the book even of my secret soul:
Therefore, good youth, address thy gait unto her;
Be not denied access, stand at her doors,
And tell them, there thy fixed foot shall grow
Till thou have audience.

VIOLA.   Sure, my noble lord,
If she be so abandon'd to her sorrow
As it is spoke, she never will admit me.

DUKE. Be clamorous and leap all civil bounds   20
Rather than make unprofited return.

VIOLA. Say I do speak with her, my lord, what then?

DUKE. O, then unfold the passion of my love,
Surprise her with discourse of my dear faith.
It shall become thee well to act my woes;
She will attend it better in thy youth
Than in a nuncio of more grave aspect.

VIOLA. I think not so, my lord.

DUKE.   Dear lad, believe it;
For they shall yet belie thy happy years,
That say thou art a man: Diana's lip   30
Is not more smooth and rubious; thy small pipe
Is as the maiden's organ, shrill and sound,
And all is semblative a woman's part.
I know thy constellation is right apt
For this affair.—Some four or five attend him;
All, if you will; for I myself am best
When least in company.—Prosper well in this,
And thou shalt live as freely as thy lord,
To call his fortunes thine.

VIOLA.   I'll do my best
To woo your lady.—*Aside.* Yet, a barful strife!   40
Whoe'er I woo, myself would be his wife.   *Exeunt.*

---

sc. 4: 14. *address . . .* : go. 16. *fixed foot . . . grow:* i.e., there you'll stay. 19. *As . . .* : as people say. 27. *nuncio:* envoy. 30. *Diana:* virgin goddess. 31. *rubions:* ruby-red. 34. influence of stars again. 40. *barful:* full of barriers.

SCENE 5. OLIVIA'S *house*.

Enter MARIA *and* CLOWN.

MARIA. Nay, either tell me where thou hast been, or I will not open my lips so wide as a bristle may enter in way of thy excuse. My lady will hang thee for thy absence.

CLOWN. Let her hang me; he that is well hanged in this world needs to fear no colours.

MARIA. Make that good.

CLOWN. He shall see none to fear.

MARIA. A good lenten answer. I can tell thee where that saying was born, of 'I fear no colours.'

CLOWN. Where, good Mistress Mary?

MARIA. In the wars; and that may you be bold to say in your foolery.

CLOWN. Well, God give them wisdom that have it; and those that are fools, let them use their talents.

MARIA. Yet you will be hanged for being so long absent; or, to be turned away, is not that as good as a hanging to you?

CLOWN. Many a good hanging prevents a bad marriage; and, for turning away, let summer bear it out.

MARIA. You are resolute, then?

CLOWN. Not so, neither; but I am resolved on two points.

MARIA. That if one break, the other will hold; or, if both break, your gaskins fall.

CLOWN. Apt, in good faith; very apt. Well, go thy way; if Sir Toby would leave drinking, thou wert as witty a piece of Eve's flesh as any in Illyria.

MARIA. Peace, you rogue, no more o' that. Here comes my lady; make your excuse wisely, you were best. *Exit.*

CLOWN. Wit, an 't be thy will, put me into good fooling! Those wits, that think they have thee, do very oft prove fools; and I, that am sure I lack thee, may pass for a wise man: for what says Quinapalus? 'Better a witty fool than a foolish wit.'—

---

sc. 5: 2-3. *in way of thy excuse:* to make excuses for you. 5. *colours:* flags. 8. *lenten:* meager. 12. *"that have it":* the proverb reads "that have none." 17. i.e., it would be bearable in summer (not in winter). 19. *points:* suspenders. 21. *gaskins:* breeches. 29. *Quinapalus:* here and later the Fool invents his sages.

Enter LADY OLIVIA *with* MALVOLIO.

God bless thee, lady!

OLIVIA. Take the fool away.

CLOWN. Do you not hear, fellows? Take away the lady.

OLIVIA. Go to, you're a dry fool; I'll no more of you: besides, you grow dishonest.

CLOWN. Two faults, madonna, that drink and good counsel will amend: for give the dry fool drink, then is the fool not dry: bid the dishonest man mend himself, if he mend, he is no longer dishonest; if he cannot, let the botcher mend him. Any thing that's mended is but patched; virtue that transgresses is but patched with [40 sin; and sin that amends is but patched with virtue. If that this simple syllogism will serve, so; if it will not, what remedy? As there is no true cockold but calamity, so beauty's a flower. The lady bade take away the fool; therefore, I say again, take her away.

OLIVIA. Sir, I bade them take away you.

CLOWN. Misprision in the highest degree! Lady, cucullus non facit monachum; that's as much to say as I wear not motley in my brain. Good madonna, give me leave to prove you a fool.

OLIVIA. Can you do it?

CLOWN. Dexteriously, good madonna. 50

OLIVIA. Make your proof.

CLOWN. I must catechise you for it, madonna; good my mouse of virtue, answer me.

OLIVIA. Well, sir, for want of other idleness, I'll bide your proof.

CLOWN. Good madonna, why mournest thou?

OLIVIA. Good fool, for my brother's death.

CLOWN. I think his soul is in hell, madonna.

OLIVIA. I know his soul is in heaven, fool.

CLOWN. The more fool, madonna, to mourn for your brother's soul being in heaven.—Take away the fool, gentlemen. 60

OLIVIA. What think you of this fool, Malvolio? doth he not mend?

MALVOLIO. Yes, and shall do till the pangs of death shake him; infirmity, that decays the wise, doth ever make the better fool.

CLOWN. God send you, sir, a speedy infirmity, for the better in-

---

39. *botcher:* mender of old clothes. 42. *so:* very good. 46. *misprision:* a mistake. 46-7. *cucullus . . . :* "the cowl does not make the monk."

creasing your folly! Sir Toby will be sworn that I am no fox; but he will not pass his word for twopence that you are no fool.

OLIVIA. How say you to that, Malvolio?

MALVOLIO. I marvel your ladyship takes delight in such a barren rascal; I saw him put down the other day with an ordinary fool that has no more brain than a stone. Look you now, he's out of his [70 guard already; unless you laugh and minister occasion to him, he is gagged. I protest, I take these wise men, that crow so at these set kind of fools, no better than the fools' zanies.

OLIVIA. O, you are sick of self-love, Malvolio, and taste with a distempered appetite. To be generous, guiltless, and of free disposition, is to take those things for bird-bolts that you deem cannon-bullets. There is no slander in an allowed fool, though he do nothing but rail; nor no railing in a known discreet man, though he do nothing but reprove.

CLOWN. Now Mercury endue thee with leasing, for thou [80 speakest well of fools!

Re-enter MARIA.

MARIA. Madam, there is at the gate a young gentleman much desires to speak with you.

OLIVIA. From the Count Orsino, is it?

MARIA. I know not, madam; 't is a fair young man, and well attended.

OLIVIA. Who of my people hold him in delay?

MARIA. Sir Toby, madam, your kinsman.

OLIVIA. Fetch him off, I pray you; he speaks nothing but madman: fie on him!—*Exit* MARIA. Go you, Malvolio: if it be a suit from the count, I am sick, or not at home; what you will, to dismiss it. [90 —*Exit* MALVOLIO. Now you see, sir, how your fooling grows old, and people dislike it.

CLOWN. Thou hast spoke for us, madonna, as if thy eldest son should be a fool; whose skull Jove cram with brains! for—here he comes—one of thy kin has a most weak pia mater.

Enter SIR TOBY.

---

73. *zanies:* underlings. 76. *bird-bolts:* short arrows. 80. *Mercury endue thee with leasing:* may the goddess of wisdom teach you to lie. 95. *pia mater:* brain.

SCENE 5] TWELFTH NIGHT 305

OLIVIA. By mine honour, half drunk.—What is he at the gate, cousin?
SIR TOBY. A gentleman.
OLIVIA. A gentleman! what gentleman?
SIR TOBY. 'T is a gentleman here—a plague o' these pickle-herring! —How now, sot! 100
CLOWN. Good Sir Toby!
OLIVIA. Cousin, cousin, how have you come so early by this lethargy?
SIR TOBY. Lechery! I defy lechery. There's one at the gate.
OLIVIA. Ay, marry, what is he?
SIR TOBY. Let him be the devil, an he will, I care not; give me faith, say I. Well, it's all one. *Exit.*
OLIVIA. What's a drunken man like, fool?
CLOWN. Like a drowned man, a fool, and a madman: one draught above heat makes him a fool; the second mads him; and a third drowns him. 110
OLIVIA. Go thou and seek the crowner, and let him sit o' my coz; for he's in the third degree of drink, he's drowned: go, look after him.
CLOWN. He is but mad yet, madonna; and the fool shall look to the madman. *Exit.*

Re-enter MALVOLIO.

MALVOLIO. Madam, yond young fellow swears he will speak with you. I told him you were sick; he takes on him to understand so much, and therefore comes to speak with you. I told him you were asleep; he seems to have a foreknowledge of that too, and therefore comes to speak with you. What is to be said to him, lady? he's fortified against any denial. 120
OLIVIA. Tell him he shall not speak with me.
MALVOLIO. He has been told so; and he says, he'll stand at your door like a sheriff's post, and be the supporter to a bench, but he'll speak with you.
OLIVIA. What kind o' man is he?
MALVOLIO. Why, of mankind.
OLIVIA. What manner of man?
MALVOLIO. Of very ill manner; he'll speak with you, will you or no.

---

111. *crowner:* coroner. 123. *sheriff's post:* fixed posts for proclamations. *supporter* . . . : i.e., as stationary as the legs of a bench.

OLIVIA. Of what personage and years is he?

MALVOLIO. Not yet old enough for a man, nor young [130 enough for a boy; as a squash is before 't is a peascod, or a codling when 't is almost an apple: 't is with him in standing water, between boy and man. He is very well-favoured and he speaks very shrewishly; one would think his mother's milk were scarce out of him.

OLIVIA. Let him approach: call in my gentlewoman.

MALVOLIO. Gentlewoman, my lady calls. *Exit.*

Re-enter MARIA.

OLIVIA. Give me my veil; come, throw it o'er my face. We'll once more hear Orsino's embassy.

Enter VIOLA, *and* ATTENDANTS.

VIOLA. The honourable lady of the house, which is she?

OLIVIA. Speak to me; I shall answer for her. Your will? 140

VIOLA. Most radiant, exquisite, and unmatchable beauty,—I pray you, tell me if this be the lady of the house, for I never saw her: I would be loath to cast away my speech, for besides that it is excellently well penned, I have taken great pains to con it. Good beauties, let me sustain no scorn; I am very comptible, even to the least sinister usage.

OLIVIA. Whence came you, sir?

VIOLA. I can say little more than I have studied, and that question's out of my part. Good gentle one, give me modest assurance if you be the lady of the house, that I may proceed in my speech.

OLIVIA. Are you a comedian? 150

VIOLA. No, my profound heart; and yet, by the very fangs of malice I swear, I am not that I play. Are you the lady of the house?

OLIVIA. If I do not usurp myself, I am.

VIOLA. Most certain, if you are she, you do usurp yourself; for what is yours to bestow is not yours to reserve. But this is from my commission; I will on with my speech in your praise, and then show you the heart of my message.

---

131. *squash:* unripe peascod (peapod). *codling:* unripe apple. 132. *standing water:* between ebb and flow. 144. *con:* learn by heart. 145. *comptible:* sensitive. *sinister:* unfriendly. 150. *comedian:* actor. 153-4. *usurp oneself:* claim more than one's rights. 155. *from:* beyond.

SCENE 5]   TWELFTH NIGHT   307

OLIVIA. Come to what is important in 't; I forgive you the praise.

VIOLA. Alas, I took great pains to study it, and 't is poetical.

OLIVIA. It is the more like to be feigned; I pray you, keep [160 it in. I heard you were saucy at my gates, and allowed your approach rather to wonder at you than to hear you. If you be not mad, be gone; if you have reason, be brief: 't is not that time of moon with me to make one in so skipping a dialogue.

MARIA. Will you hoist sail, sir? here lies your way.

VIOLA. No, good swabber; I am to hull here a little longer.—Some mollification for your giant, sweet lady. Tell me your mind: I am a messenger.

OLIVIA. Sure, you have some hideous matter to deliver, when the courtesy of it is so fearful. Speak your office. 170

VIOLA. It alone concerns your ear. I bring no overture of war, no taxation of homage: I hold the olive in my hand; my words are as full of peace as matter.

OLIVIA. Yet you began rudely. What are you? what would you?

VIOLA. The rudeness that hath appeared in me have I learned from my entertainment. What I am, and what I would, are as secret as maidenhead: to your ears, divinity; to any other's, profanation.

OLIVIA. Give us the place alone; we will hear this divinity.—*Exeunt* MARIA *and* ATTENDANTS. Now, sir, what is your text?

VIOLA. Most sweet lady,— 180

OLIVIA. A comfortable doctrine, and much may be said of it. Where lies your text?

VIOLA. In Orsino's bosom.

OLIVIA. In his bosom! In what chapter of his bosom?

VIOLA. To answer by the method, in the first of his heart.

OLIVIA. O, I have read it; it is heresy. Have you no more to say?

VIOLA. Good madam, let me see your face.

OLIVIA. Have you any commission from your lord to negotiate with my face? You are now out of your text; but we will draw the curtain and show you the picture. Look you, sir, such a one I was [190

---

164. *make one:* take part. 165-6. Nautical figures. *hull:* beat about. 166-7. *Some mollification:* please pacify. 170. *office:* commission. 172. *taxation:* demand. 176. *entertainment:* the way I was treated. 185. *the method:* i.e., your method.

308 TWEFLTH NIGHT [ACT I

this present; is 't not well done? *Unveiling.*

VIOLA. Excellently done, if God did all.

OLIVIA. 'T is in grain, sir; 't will endure wind and weather.

VIOLA. 'T is beauty truly blent, whose red and white
Nature's own sweet and cunning hand laid on:
Lady, you are the cruell'st she alive,
If you will lead these graces to the grave
And leave the world no copy.

OLIVIA. O, sir, I will not be so hard-hearted; I will give out divers schedules of my beauty. It shall be inventoried, and every [200 particle and utensil labelled to my will; as, item, two lips, indifferent red; item, two grey eyes, with lids to them; item, one neck, one chin, and so forth. Were you sent hither to praise me?

VIOLA. I see you what you are, you are too proud;
But, if you were the devil, you are fair.
My lord and master loves you; O, such love
Could be but recompens'd, though you were crown'd
The nonpareil of beauty!

OLIVIA. How does he love me?

VIOLA. With adorations, with fertile tears,
With groans that thunder love, with sighs of fire.   210

OLIVIA. Your lord does know my mind; I cannot love him:
Yet I suppose him virtuous, know him noble,
Of great estate, of fresh and stainless youth;
In voices well divulg'd, free, learn'd, and valiant;
And in dimension and the shape of nature
A gracious person: but yet I cannot love him;
He might have took his answer long ago.

VIOLA. If I did love you in my master's flame,
With such a suffering, such a deadly life,
In your denial I would find no sense;   220
I would not understand it.

OLIVIA. Why, what would you?

VIOLA. Make me a willow cabin at your gate,

---

191. *this present:* for this moment. 194. *blent:* blended. 196. *she:* woman. 206-8. i.e., could only be paid for if your beauty were unequalled. 214. *in voices well divulg'd:* well spoken of. 215. *of nature:* conferred by nature. 218. *in:* with. 221. *Why, what would you* do? I would . . .

SCENE 5]   TWELFTH NIGHT   309

And call upon my soul within the house;
Write loyal cantons of contemned love,
And sing them loud even in the dead of night;
Halloo your name to the reverberate hills,
And make the babbling gossip of the air
Cry out Olivia! O, you should not rest
Between the elements of air and earth,
But you should pity me!
    OLIVIA.   You might do much.   230
What is your parentage?
    VIOLA. Above my fortunes, yet my state is well;
I am a gentleman.
    OLIVIA.   Get you to your lord;
I cannot love him: let him send no more;
Unless, perchance, you come to me again,
To tell me how he takes it. Fare you well:
I thank you for your pains; spend this for me.
    VIOLA. I am no fee'd post, lady; keep your purse:
My master, not myself, lacks recompense.
Love make his heart of flint that you shall love;   240
And let your fervour, like my master's, be
Plac'd in contempt! Farewell, fair cruelty.   *Exit.*
    OLIVIA. What is your parentage?
'Above my fortunes, yet my state is well;
I am a gentleman.' I'll be sworn thou art;
Thy tongue, thy face, thy limbs, actions, and spirit,
Do give thee five-fold blazon.—Not too fast! soft, soft!
Unless the master were the man.—How now!
Even so quickly may one catch the plague?
Methinks I feel this youth's perfections   250
With an invisible and subtle stealth
To creep in at mine eyes. Well, let it be.—
What ho, Malvolio!

                Re-enter MALVOLIO.

---

224. *cantons:* cantos, verses. 227. i.e., echo. 232. *fortunes:* i.e., my present position. *state:* condition. 238. *post:* messenger. 247. *blazon:* coat of arms.

MALVOLIO.   Here, madam, at your service.

OLIVIA. Run after that same peevish messenger,
The county's man: he left this ring behind him,
Would I or not; tell him I'll none of it.
Desire him not to flatter with his lord,
Nor hold him up with hopes; I am not for him.
If that the youth will come this way to-morrow,
I'll give him reasons for 't. Hie thee, Malvolio.   260

MALVOLIO. Madam, I will.   *Exit.*

OLIVIA. I do I know not what, and fear to find
Mine eye too great a flatterer for my mind.
Fate, show thy force: ourselves we do not owe;
What is decreed must be, and be this so!   *Exit.*

Act II

SCENE I. *The sea-coast.*

Enter ANTONIO *and* SEBASTIAN.

ANTONIO. Will you stay no longer? nor will you not that I go with you?

SEBASTIAN. By your patience, no. My stars shine darkly over me: the malignancy of my fate might perhaps distemper yours; therefore I shall crave of you your leave that I may bear my evils alone: it were a bad recompense for your love, to lay any of them on you.

ANTONIO. Let me yet know of you whither you are bound.

SEBASTIAN. No, sooth, sir; my determinate voyage is mere extravagancy. But I perceive in you so excellent a touch of modesty, that you will not extort from me what I am willing to keep in; there-   [10
fore it charges me in manners the rather to express myself. You must know of me then, Antonio, my name is Sebastian, which I called Roderigo. My father was that Sebastian of Messaline, whom I know you have heard of. He left behind him myself and a sister, both born in an hour. If the heavens had been pleased, would we had so ended!

---

254. *peevish:* wilful. 255. *county:* count, duke. 264. *owe:* own.

ACT II, SC. I: 4. *distemper:* damage. 8-9. "My purposed travel is just wandering about."

SCENE 2] TWELFTH NIGHT 311

but you, sir, altered that; for some hour before you took me from the breach of the sea was my sister drowned.

ANTONIO. Alas the day!

SEBASTIAN. A lady, sir, though it was said she much resembled me, was yet of many accounted beautiful; but, though I could not [20 with such estimable wonder overfar believe that, yet thus far I will boldly publish her: she bore a mind that envy could not but call fair. She is drowned already, sir, with salt water, though I seem to drown her remembrance again with more.

ANTONIO. Pardon me, sir, your bad entertainment.

SEBASTIAN. O good Antonio, forgive me your trouble.

ANTONIO. If you will not murther me for my love, let me be your servant.

SEBASTIAN. If you will not undo what you have done, that is, kill him whom you have recovered, desire it not. Fare ye well at [30 once; my bosom is full of kindness, and I am yet so near the manners of my mother, that upon the least occasion more mine eyes will tell tales of me. I am bound to the Count Orsino's court; farewell. *Exit.*

ANTONIO. The gentleness of all the gods go with thee!
I have many enemies in Orsino's court,
Else would I very shortly see thee there.
But, come what may, I do adore thee so,
That danger shall seem sport, and I will go. *Exit.*

SCENE 2. *A street.*

Enter VIOLA, MALVOLIO *following.*

MALVOLIO. Were not you even now with the Countess Olivia?

VIOLA. Even now, sir; on a moderate pace I have since arrived but hither.

MALVOLIO. She returns this ring to you, sir; you might have saved me my pains, to have taken it away yourself. She adds, moreover, that you should put your lord into a desperate assurance she will none of him; and one thing more, that you be never so hardy to come

---

17. *breach:* breaking (of waves). 21. *estimable:* estimating. 31. *manners:* behavior.

SC. 2: 2. *on a moderate pace:* walking moderately fast.

312   TWELFTH NIGHT   [ACT II

again in his affairs, unless it be to report your lord's taking of this.
Receive it so.

 VIOLA. She took the ring of me; I'll none of it. 10

 MALVOLIO. Come, sir, you peevishly threw it to her; and her will is,
it should be so returned. If it be worth stooping for, there it lies
in your eye; if not, be it his that finds it. *Exit.*

 VIOLA. I left no ring with her; what means this lady?
Fortune forbid my outside have not charm'd her!
She made good view of me; indeed, so much,
That sure methought her eyes had lost her tongue,
For she did speak in starts distractedly.
She loves me, sure; the cunning of her passion
Invites me in this churlish messenger. 20
None of my lord's ring! why, he sent her none.
I am the man; if it be so, as 't is,
Poor lady, she were better love a dream.
Disguise, I see, thou art a wickedness,
Wherein the pregnant enemy does much.
How easy is it for the proper-false
In women's waxen hearts to set their forms!
Alas, our frailty is the cause, not we!
For such as we are made of, such we be.
How will this fadge? my master loves her dearly; 30
And I, poor monster, fond as much on him;
And she, mistaken, seems to dote on me.
What will become of this? As I am man,
My state is desperate for my master's love;
As I am woman,—now alas the day!—
What thriftless sighs shall poor Olivia breathe!
O time! thou must untangle this, not I;
It is too hard a knot for me to untie! *Exit.*

SCENE 3. OLIVIA'S *house.*

Enter SIR TOBY *and* SIR ANDREW.

 SIR TOBY. Approach, Sir Andrew: not to be a-bed after midnight is

---

13. *in your eye:* where you can see it. 25. *pregnant:* inventive, tricky. 26. *proper-false:* handsome and deceitful (cf. III, iv, 322: beauteous-evil). 30. *fadge:* turn out. 31. *fond:* dote.

SCENE 3] TWELFTH NIGHT 313

to be up betimes; and 'diluculo surgere,' thou know'st,—

SIR ANDREW. Nay, by my troth, I know not; but I know, to be up late is to be up late.

SIR TOBY. A false conclusion; I hate it as an unfilled can. To be up after midnight and to go to bed then, is early; so that to go to bed after midnight is to go to bed betimes. Does not our life consist of the four elements?

SIR ANDREW. Faith, so they say; but I think it rather consists of eating and drinking. 10

SIR TOBY. Thou 'rt a scholar; let us therefore eat and drink.—Marian, I say! a stoup of wine!

Enter CLOWN.

SIR ANDREW. Here comes the fool, i' faith.

CLOWN. How now, my hearts! did you never see the picture of we three?

SIR TOBY. Welcome, ass. Now let's have a catch.

SIR ANDREW. By my troth, the fool has an excellent breast. I had rather than forty shillings I had such a leg, and so sweet a breath to sing, as the fool has.—In sooth, thou wast in very gracious fooling last night, when thou spokest of Pigrogromitus, of the Vapians [20 passing the equinoctial of Queubus; 't was very good, i' faith. I sent thee sixpence for thy leman; hadst it?

CLOWN. I did impeticos thy gratillity; for Malvolio's nose is no whipstock: my lady has a white hand, and the Myrmidons are no bottle-ale houses.

SIR ANDREW. Excellent! why, this is the best fooling, when all is done. Now, a song.

SIR TOBY. Come on; there is sixpence for you: let's have a song.

SIR ANDREW. There's a testril of me too: if one knight give a—

CLOWN. Would you have a love-song, or a song of good [30 life?

SIR TOBY. A love-song, a love-song.

SC. 3: 2. *betimes:* early. "*diluculo surgere* saluberrimum est": "to rise at dawn is most healthy." 8. *four elements* of medieval physics: fire, air, earth, water. 12. *stoup:* vessel. 14-15. Refers to an ale-house sign. 16. *catch:* part song. 17. *breast:* voice. 20-21. Made-up names. 22. *leman:* girl friend. 23-5. Nonsense suggesting "I put your gratuity in my petticoat . . ." 29. *testril:* a coin.

SIR ANDREW. Ay, ay; I care not for good life.
CLOWN, *sings.*

    'O mistress mine, where are you roaming?
     O, stay and hear; your true love's coming,
       That can sing both high and low:
      Trip no further, pretty sweeting;
      Journeys end in lovers meeting,
       Every wise man's son doth know.'

SIR ANDREW. Excellent good, i' faith. 40
SIR TOBY. Good, good.
CLOWN, *sings.*

    'What is love? 't is not hereafter;
    Present mirth hath present laughter;
     What's to come is still unsure:
    In delay there lies no plenty;
    Then come kiss me, sweet and twenty;
     Youth's a stuff will not endure.'

SIR ANDREW. A mellifluous voice, as I am true knight.
SIR TOBY. A contagious breath.
SIR ANDREW. Very sweet and contagious, i' faith. 50
SIR TOBY. To hear by the nose, it is dulcet in contagion. But shall we make the welkin dance indeed? shall we rouse the night-owl in a catch that will draw three souls out of one weaver? shall we do that?
SIR ANDREW. An you love me, let's do 't: I am dog at a catch.
CLOWN. By 'r lady, sir, and some dogs will catch well.
SIR ANDREW. Most certain. Let our catch be, 'Thou knave.'
CLOWN. 'Hold thy peace, thou knave,' knight? I shall be constrained in 't to call thee knave, knight.
SIR ANDREW. 'T is not the first time I have constrained one to call me knave. Begin, fool: it begins 'Hold thy peace.' 60
CLOWN. I shall never begin if I hold my peace.
SIR ANDREW. Good, i' faith. Come, begin. *Catch sung.*

Enter MARIA.

MARIA. What a caterwauling do you keep here! If my lady have not called up her steward Malvolio and bid him turn you out of

---

51. *dulcet:* sweet (not foul as *breath* often is). 52. *welkin:* sky. 53. Weavers liked singing. 63. *caterwauling:* a cat's noise.

SCENE 3]   TWELFTH NIGHT   315

doors, never trust me.

SIR TOBY. My lady's a Cataian, we are politicians, Malvolio's a Peg-a-Ramsey, and 'Three merry men be we.' Am not I consanguineous? am I not of her blood? Tillyvally, lady! *Sings.* 'There dwelt a man in Babylon, lady, lady!'

CLOWN. Beshrew me, the knight's in admirable fooling.   70

SIR ANDREW. Ay, he does well enough if he be disposed, and so do I too; he does it with a better grace, but I do it more natural.

SIR TOBY, *sings.* 'O, the twelfth day of December.'—

MARIA. For the love of God, peace!

Enter MALVOLIO.

MALVOLIO. My masters, are you mad? or what are you? Have you no wit, manners, nor honesty, but to gabble like tinkers at this time of night? Do ye make an alehouse of my lady's house, that ye squeak out your coziers' catches without any mitigation or remorse of voice? Is there no respect of place, persons, nor time in you?

SIR TOBY. We did keep time, sir, in our catches. Sneck up!   80

MALVOLIO. Sir Toby, I must be round with you. My lady bade me tell you, that, though she harbours you as her kinsman, she's nothing allied to your disorders. If you can separate yourself and your misdemeanours, you are welcome to the house; if not, an it would please you to take leave of her, she is very willing to bid you farewell.

SIR TOBY. 'Farewell, dear heart, since I must needs be gone.'

MARIA. Nay, good Sir Toby.

CLOWN. 'His eyes do show his days are almost done.'

MALVOLIO. Is 't even so?

SIR TOBY. 'But I will never die.'   90

CLOWN. Sir Toby, there you lie.

MALVOLIO. This is much credit to you.

SIR TOBY. 'Shall I bid him go?'

CLOWN. 'What an if you do?'

SIR TOBY. 'Shall I bid him go, and spare not?'

CLOWN. 'O, no, no, no, no, you dare not.'

---

66. *Cataian* may mean *Chinese:* Sir Toby is drunk. 78. *cozier:* artisan. *remorse:* restraint. 80. *sneck up:* go to hell. 81. *round:* plainspoken.

SIR TOBY. Out o' time, sir? ye lie.—Art any more than a steward? Dost thou think, because thou art virtuous, there shall be no more cakes and ale?

CLOWN. Yes, by Saint Anne, and ginger shall be hot i' the mouth too. [100

SIR TOBY. Thou 'rt i' the right.—Go, sir, rub your chain with crumbs.—A stoup of wine, Maria!

MALVOLIO. Mistress Mary, if you prized my lady's favour at any thing more than contempt, you would not give means for this uncivil rule; she shall know of it, by this hand. *Exit.*

MARIA. Go shake your ears.

SIR ANDREW. 'T were as good a deed as to drink when a man's a-hungry, to challenge him the field, and then to break promise with him and make a fool of him. 110

SIR TOBY. Do 't, knight! I'll write thee a challenge; or I'll deliver thy indignation to him by word of mouth.

MARIA. Sweet Sir Toby, be patient for to-night; since the youth of the count's was to-day with my lady, she is much out of quiet. For Monsieur Malvolio, let me alone with him; if I do not gull him into a nayword, and make him a common recreation, do not think I have wit enough to lie straight in my bed: I know I can do it.

SIR TOBY. Possess us, possess us, tell us something of him.

MARIA. Marry, sir, sometimes he is a kind of puritan.

SIR ANDREW. O, if I thought that, I'd beat him like a dog! 120

SIR TOBY. What, for being a puritan? thy exquisite reason, dear knight?

SIR ANDREW. I have no exquisite reason for 't, but I have reason good enough.

MARIA. The devil a puritan that he is, or any thing constantly, but a time-pleaser; an affectioned ass, that cons state without book and utters it by great swarths; the best persuaded of himself, so crammed, as he thinks, with excellencies, that it is his ground of faith that all that look on him love him: and on that vice in him will my revenge find notable cause to work. 130

---

106. *rule:* conduct. 109. *the field* i.e., to a duel. *promise:* faith. 115. *gull:* hoax, trick. 115-16. *into a nayword:* till he's a byword. 116. *common recreation:* general joke. 118. *possess:* tell. 121. *exquisite:* subtle. 126. *time-pleaser:* a yes-man (following the current vogue of puritanism). *state:* deportment.

SCENE 3]   TWELFTH NIGHT   317

SIR TOBY. What wilt thou do?

MARIA. I will drop in his way some obscure epistles of love; wherein, by the colour of his beard, the shape of his leg, the manner of his gait, the expressure of his eye, forehead, and complexion, he shall find himself most feelingly personated. I can write very like my lady your niece; on a forgotten matter we can hardly make distinction of our hands.

SIR TOBY. Excellent! I smell a device.

SIR ANDREW. I have 't in my nose too.

SIR TOBY. He shall think, by the letters that thou wilt drop, [140 that they come from my niece, and that she's in love with him.

MARIA. My purpose is, indeed, a horse of that colour.

SIR ANDREW. And your horse now would make him an ass.

MARIA. Ass, I doubt not.

SIR ANDREW. O, 't will be admirable!

MARIA. Sport royal, I warrant you; I know my physic will work with him. I will plant you two, and let the fool make a third, where he shall find the letter; observe his construction of it. For this night, to bed, and dream on the event. Farewell.   *Exit.*

SIR TOBY. Good night, Penthesilea.   150

SIR ANDREW. Before me, she's a good wench.

SIR TOBY. She's a beagle, true-bred, and one that adores me. What o' that?

SIR ANDREW. I was adored once too.

SIR TOBY. Let's to bed, knight.—Thou hadst need send for more money.

SIR ANDREW. If I cannot recover your niece, I am a foul way out.

SIR TOBY. Send for money, knight; if thou hast her not i' the end, call me cut.

SIR ANDREW. If I do not, never trust me, take it how you [160 will.

SIR TOBY. Come, come, I'll go burn some sack; 't is too late to go to bed now. Come, knight; come, knight.   *Exeunt.*

---

135. *personated:* indicated. 136-7. "when we've forgotten the document in question we can hardly distinguish our handwritings." 138. *device:* trick. 147. *let the fool make a third:* oddly enough Shakespeare has *Fabian* make a third. See II, 5. 150. *Penthesilea:* queen of the Amazons. 152. *beagle:* hound. 157. *recover:* win. *out:* i.e., of pocket. 159. *cut:* gelded (like a horse). 162. *burn . . . sack:* warm . . . wine.

318   TWELFTH NIGHT   [ACT II

scene 4. *The* duke's *palace.*

Enter duke, viola, curio, *and others.*

duke. Give me some music.—Now, good morrow, friends.—
Now, good Cesario, but that piece of song,
That old and antique song we heard last night;
Methought it did relieve my passion much,
More than light airs and recollected terms
Of these most brisk and giddy-paced times.
Come, but one verse.
   curio. He is not here, so please your lordship, that should sing it.
   duke. Who was it?
   curio. Feste, the jester, my lord; a fool that the lady Olivia's   [10
father took much delight in. He is about the house.
   duke. Seek him out, and play the tune the while.—

Exit curio. *Music plays.*

Come hither, boy. If ever thou shalt love,
In the sweet pangs of it remember me;
For such as I am all true lovers are,
Unstaid and skittish in all motions else,
Save in the constant image of the creature
That is belov'd. How dost thou like this tune?
   viola. It gives a very echo to the seat
Where love is thron'd.
   duke.   Thou dost speak masterly: 20
My life upon 't, young though thou art, thine eye
Hath stay'd upon some favour that it loves;
Hath it not, boy?
   viola.   A little, by your favour.
   duke. What kind of woman is 't?
   viola.   Of your complexion.
   duke. She is not worth thee, then. What years, i' faith?
   viola. About your years, my lord.
   duke. Too old, by heaven! Let still the woman take
An elder than herself; so wears she to him,

---

sc. 4: 5. *recollected:* cliché. 19. *the seat,* i.e., the heart. 22. *favour:* (1) personal appearance; (2) kindness. 27. *still:* always.

SCENE 4] TWELFTH NIGHT 319

So sways she level in her husband's heart:
For, boy, however we do praise ourselves,
Our fancies are more giddy and unfirm,
More longing, wavering, sooner lost and worn,
Than women's are.
 VIOLA. I think it well, my lord.
 DUKE. Then let thy love be younger than thyself,
Or thy affection cannot hold the bent;
For women are as roses, whose fair flower,
Being once display'd, doth fall that very hour.
 VIOLA. And so they are: alas, that they are so;
To die, even when they to perfection grow!

Re-enter CURIO *and* CLOWN.

 DUKE. O, fellow, come, the song we had last night.— 40
Mark it, Cesario, it is old and plain;
The spinsters and the knitters in the sun
And the free maids that weave their thread with bones
Do use to chant it: it is silly sooth,
And dallies with the innocence of love,
Like the old age.
 CLOWN. Are you ready, sir?
 DUKE. Ay; prithee, sing. *Music.*

Song

 CLOWN. 'Come away, come away, death,
  And in sad cypress let me be laid; 50
 Fly away, fly away, breath;
  I am slain by a fair cruel maid.
 My shroud of white, stuck all with yew,
  O, prepare it
 My part of death, no one so true
  Did share it.'

---

33. "I am sure of it." 34. *love:* lover (feminine). 42. *spinsters:* spinners. 43. *free:* carefree. *bones:* (lace-makers used bone bobbins). 44. *silly sooth:* simple truth. 46. "As was usual in olden times." 49. *Come away:* come here. (This song of a lover slain by his mistress's indifference is worth contrasting with the song Feste sings for the revelers in II, 3.)

'Not a flower, not a flower sweet,
　　On my black coffin let there be strown;
Not a friend, not a friend greet
　　My poor corpse, where my bones shall be thrown:　60
A thousand sighs to save,
　　Lay me, O, where
Sad true lover never find my grave,
　　To weep there!'

DUKE. There's for thy pains.

CLOWN. No pains, sir; I take pleasure in singing, sir.

DUKE. I'll pay thy pleasure then.

CLOWN. Truly, sir, and pleasure will be paid, one time or another.

DUKE. Give me now leave to leave thee.

CLOWN. Now the melancholy god protect thee; and the [70 tailor make thy doublet of changeable taffeta, for thy mind is a very opal!—I would have men of such constancy put to sea, that their business might be every thing and their intent every where; for that's it that always makes a good voyage of nothing.—Farewell. *Exit.*

DUKE. Let all the rest give place.—　CURIO *and* ATTENDANTS *retire.*
　　　　　　　　　　　Once more, Cesario,
Get thee to yond same sovereign cruelty:
Tell her, my love, more noble than the world,
Prizes not quantity of dirty lands;
The parts that fortune hath bestow'd upon her,
Tell her, I hold as giddily as fortune;　　　　　　　　　　80
But 't is that miracle and queen of gems
That nature pranks her in attracts my soul.

VIOLA. But if she cannot love you, sir?

DUKE. I cannot be so answer'd.

VIOLA.　　　　　　　　　　Sooth, but you must.
Say that some lady, as perhaps there is,
Hath for your love as great a pang of heart
As you have for Olivia: you cannot love her;

---

68. *will be paid:* has to be paid for. 71. *changeable taffeta:* shot silk (resembling opal). 72. *constancy:* i.e., inconsistency. 73. *that's it:* viz., constant change, etc. 76. *sovereign cruelty:* woman unrivalled for cruelty. 79. *parts:* gifts. 80. *hold as giddily as fortune:* prize as little as I do fortune. 81. *queen of gems:* i.e., beauty. 82. *pranks:* decks out.

SCENE 4] TWELFTH NIGHT 321

You tell her so; must she not then be answer'd?
 DUKE. There is no woman's sides
Can bide the beating of so strong a passion 90
As love doth give my heart; no woman's heart
So big to hold so much; they lack retention.
Alas, their love may be call'd appetite,—
No motion of the liver, but the palate,—
That suffer surfeit, cloyment, and revolt;
But mine is all as hungry as the sea,
And can digest as much.
      Make no compare
Between that love a woman can bear me
And that I owe Olivia.
 VIOLA.   Ay, but I know—
 DUKE. What dost thou know? 100
 VIOLA. Too well what love women to men may owe;
In faith, they are as true of heart as we.
My father had a daughter lov'd a man,
As it might be, perhaps, were I a woman,
I should your lordship.
 DUKE.   And what's her history?
 VIOLA. A blank, my lord. She never told her love,
But let concealment, like a worm i' the bud,
Feed on her damask cheek; she pin'd in thought,
And with a green and yellow melancholy
She sat like Patience on a monument, 110
Smiling at grief. Was not this love indeed?
We men may say more, swear more, but indeed
Our shows are more than will; for still we prove
Much in our vows, but little in our love.
 DUKE. But died thy sister of her love, my boy?
 VIOLA. I am all the daughters of my father's house,
And all the brothers too;—and yet I know not.
Sir, shall I to this lady?

---

94. *liver,* again the seat of love. (Appetite can be satisfied, love is insatiable.) 99. *owe:* feel for. 108. *damask:* pale red. 110-11. "sat smiling at grief, like a figure of Patience on a monument." 113. *shows:* display. *will:* our purposiveness.

322   TWELFTH NIGHT   [ACT II

DUKE.   Ay, that's the theme.
To her in haste; give her this jewel; say,
My love can give no place, bide no denay.   *Exeunt.*   120

SCENE 5. OLIVIA's *Garden.*

Enter SIR TOBY, SIR ANDREW, *and* FABIAN.

SIR TOBY. Come thy ways, Signior Fabian.

FABIAN. Nay, I'll come; if I lose a scruple of this sport, let me be boiled to death with melancholy.

SIR TOBY. Wouldst thou not be glad to have the niggardly rascally sheep-biter come by some notable shame?

FABIAN. I would exult, man; you know, he brought me out o' favour with my lady about a bear-baiting here.

SIR TOBY. To anger him we'll have the bear again; and we will fool him black and blue:—shall we not, Sir Andrew?

SIR ANDREW. An we do not, it is pity of our lives.   10

SIR TOBY. Here comes the little villain.—

Enter MARIA.

How now, my metal of India!

MARIA. Get ye all three into the box-tree; Malvolio's coming down this walk. He has been yonder i' the sun practising behaviour to his own shadow this half hour: observe him, for the love of mockery; for I know this letter will make a contemplative idiot of him. Close, in the name of jesting!—Lie thou there—*throws down a letter*—for here comes the trout that must be caught with tickling.   *Exit.*

Enter MALVOLIO.

MALVOLIO. 'T is but fortune; all is fortune. Maria once told me she did affect me; and I have heard herself come thus near,   [20 that, should she fancy, it should be one of my complexion. Besides, she uses me with a more exalted respect than any one else that follows her. What should I think on 't?

---

sc. 5: 1. *thy ways:* with me. 2. *scruple:* small portion. 5. *sheep-biter:* thief. 12. *metal of India:* gold, ∴ "my precious." 16. *close:* keep close. 21. *complexion:* character. 22. *uses:* treats.

SCENE 5] TWELFTH NIGHT 323

SIR TOBY. Here's an overweening rogue!

FABIAN. O, peace! Contemplation makes a rare turkey-cock of him! how he jets under his advanced plumes!

SIR ANDREW. 'Slight, I could so beat the rogue!

SIR TOBY. Peace, I say.

MALVOLIO. To be Count Malvolio!

SIR TOBY. Ah, rogue? 30

SIR ANDREW. Pistol him, pistol him.

SIR TOBY. Peace, peace!

MALVOLIO. There is example for 't; the lady of the Strachy married the yeoman of the wardrobe.

SIR ANDREW. Fie on him, Jezebel!

FABIAN. O, peace! now he's deeply in; look how imagination blows him.

MALVOLIO. Having been three months married to her, sitting in my state,—

SIR TOBY. O for a stone-bow, to hit him in the eye! 40

MALVOLIO. Calling my officers about me, in my branched velvet gown; having come from a day-bed, where I have left Olivia sleeping,—

SIR TOBY. Fire and brimstone!

FABIAN. O, peace, peace!

MALVOLIO. And then to have the humour of state; and after a demure travel of regard, telling them I know my place as I would they should do theirs, to ask for my kinsman Toby,—

SIR TOBY. Bolts and shackles!

FABIAN. O, peace, peace, peace! now, now. 50

MALVOLIO. Seven of my people, with an obedient start, make out for him: I frown the while; and perchance wind up my watch, or play with my—some rich jewel. Toby approaches; courtesies there to me,—

SIR TOBY. Shall this fellow live?

FABIAN. Though our silence be drawn from us with cars, yet peace.

MALVOLIO. I extend my hand to him thus, quenching my familiar

---

26. *advanced:* outspread. 33-4. No doubt a once well-known instance of lady marrying servant. 35. Andrew finds the wrong Biblical name. 39. *state:* a canopied chair. 40. *stone-bow:* crossbow. 41. *branched:* figured. 46. *humour of state:* attitude of a "big shot." 47. *travel of regard:* looking them over. 53. *courtesies:* bows. 56. *cars:* carts (i.e., violence).

smile with an austere regard of control,—

SIR TOBY. And does not Toby take you a blow o' the lips then?

MALVOLIO. Saying, 'Cousin Toby, my fortunes having cast me on your niece give me this prerogative of speech,'—

SIR TOBY. What, what?

MALVOLIO. 'You must amend your drunkenness.'

SIR TOBY. Out, scab!

FABIAN. Nay, patience, or we break the sinews of our plot.

MALVOLIO. 'Besides, you waste the treasure of your time with a foolish knight,'—

SIR ANDREW. That's me, I warrant you.

MALVOLIO. 'One Sir Andrew,'—

SIR ANDREW. I knew 't was I; for many do call me fool.

MALVOLIO. What employment have we here?

Taking up the letter.

FABIAN. Now is the woodcock near the gin.

SIR TOBY. O, peace! and the spirit of humours intimate reading aloud to him!

MALVOLIO. By my life, this is my lady's hand: these be her very C's, her U's, and her T's; and thus makes she her great P's. It is, in contempt of question, her hand.

SIR ANDREW. Her C's, her U's, and her T's; why that?

MALVOLIO, *reads*. 'To the unknown beloved, this, and my good wishes.'—Her very phrases!—By your leave, wax.—Soft! and the impressure her Lucrece, with which she uses to seal; 't is my lady. To whom should this be?

FABIAN. This wins him, liver and all.

MALVOLIO, *reads*. 'Jove knows I love:
    But who?
  Lips, do not move;
  No man must know.'

'*No man must know.*'—What follows? the numbers altered?—'*No man must know.*'—If this should be thee, Malvolio?

SIR TOBY. Marry, hang thee, brock!

MALVOLIO, *reads*.

---

72. *woodcock:* (1) bird; (2) fool. *gin:* trap. 73. *humours:* mischief. 75-6. *C-U-*-T:* a "four-letter word." 76. "*to make P's*": to p*** (urinate). 81. *impressure:* impression. *Lucrece:* a seal. 88. *numbers:* metre. 90. *brock:* badger.

SCENE 5]   TWELFTH NIGHT   325

'I may command where I adore;
   But silence, like a Lucrece knife,
With bloodless stroke my heart doth gore:
   M, O, A, I, doth sway my life.'

FABIAN. A fustian riddle!

SIR TOBY. Excellent wench, say I.

MALVOLIO. 'M, O, A, I, doth sway my life.'—Nay, but first, let me see, let me see, let me see.

FABIAN. What dish o' poison has she dressed him!

SIR TOBY. And with what wing the staniel checks at it!   100

MALVOLIO. 'I may command where I adore.'—Why, she may command me; I serve her, she is my lady. Why, this is evident to any formal capacity; there is no obstruction in this: and the end,— what should that alphabetical position portend? If I could make that resemble something in me,—Softly! *M, O, A, I,—*

SIR TOBY. O, ay, make up that!—he is now at a cold scent.

FABIAN. Sowter will cry upon 't for all this, though it be as rank as a fox.

MALVOLIO. *M,*—Malvolio; *M,*—why, that begins my name.

FABIAN. Did not I say he would work it out? the cur is excellent at faults.   [110

MALVOLIO. *M,*—but then there is no consonancy in the sequel; that suffers under probation: *A* should follow, but *O* does.

FABIAN. And *O* shall end, I hope.

SIR TOBY. Ay, or I'll cudgel him, and make him cry O!

MALVOLIO. And then *I* comes behind.

FABIAN. Ay, an you had any eye behind you, you might see more detraction at your heels than fortunes before you.

MALVOLIO. *M, O, A, I;* this simulation is not as the former: and yet, to crush this a little, it would bow to me, for every one of   [120 these letters are in my name. Soft! here follows prose.

Reads. 'If this fall into thy hand, revolve. In my stars I am above thee; but be not afraid of greatness: some are born great,

---

95. *fustian:* absurd. 100. *staniel:* hawk. *checks:* pounces. 103. *formal capacity:* well-regulated understanding. *obstruction:* obscurity. 107. *Sowter will cry:* the dog will bark. *rank:* strong (of scent). 112. *consonancy:* coherence. 113. *under probation:* when tested. 113-17. Puns on O (oh) and I (ay). 119 *simulation:* disguise. 122. *stars:* social position.

some achieve greatness, and some have greatness thrust upon 'em. Thy Fates open their hands; let thy blood and spirit embrace them; and, to inure thyself to what thou art like to be, cast thy humble slough and appear fresh. Be opposite with a kinsman, surly with servants; let thy tongue tang arguments of state; put thyself into the trick of singularity: she thus advises thee that sighs for thee. Remember who commended thy yellow stockings, and wished to see [130] thee ever cross-gartered; I say, remember. Go to, thou art made, if thou desirest to be so; if not, let me see thee a steward still, the fellow of servants, and not worthy to touch Fortune's fingers. Farewell. She that would alter services with thee,

THE FORTUNATE-UNHAPPY.'

Daylight and champaign discovers not more; this is open. I will be proud, I will read politic authors, I will baffle Sir Toby, I will wash off gross acquaintance, I will be point-devise the very man. I do not now fool myself, to let imagination jade me; for every reason excites to this, that my lady loves me. She did commend my yellow [140] stockings of late, she did praise my leg being cross-gartered; and in this she manifests herself to my love, and with a kind of injunction drives me to these habits of her liking. I thank my stars I am happy. I will be strange, stout, in yellow stockings, and cross-gartered, even with the swiftness of putting on. Jove and my stars be praised! Here is yet a postscript.

Reads. 'Thou canst not choose but know who I am. If thou entertainest my love, let it appear in thy smiling; thy smiles become thee well; therefore in my presence still smile, dear my sweet, I prithee.'

Jove, I thank thee!—I will smile; I will do everything that [150] thou wilt have me. *Exit.*

FABIAN. I will not give my part of this sport for a pension of thousands to be paid from the Sophy.

SIR TOBY. I could marry this wench for this device.

SIR ANDREW. So could I too.

SIR TOBY. And ask no other dowry with her but such another jest.

---

125. *blood:* courage. 127. *opposite:* hostile. 128. *of state:* of politics. 135. *champaign:* open country. 136. *politic:* on politics. 137. *gross:* lowborn. *point-devise:* to the minutest point (the very man she wants). 138. *jade:* deceive. 143. *happy:* fortunate. 145. "As swiftly as I can put them on." 149. *still:* always. 153. *Sophy:* Shah (of Persia).

SIR ANDREW. Nor I neither.
FABIAN. Here comes my noble gull-catcher.

Re-enter MARIA.

SIR TOBY. Wilt thou set thy foot o' my neck?
SIR ANDREW. Or o' mine either?
SIR TOBY. Shall I play my freedom at tray-trip, and become thy bond-slave?
SIR ANDREW. I' faith, or I either?
SIR TOBY. Why, thou hast put him in such a dream, that when the image of it leaves him he must run mad.
MARIA. Nay, but say true; does it work upon him?
SIR TOBY. Like aqua-vitæ with a midwife.
MARIA. If you will then see the fruits of the sport, mark his first approach before my lady: he will come to her in yellow stockings,— and 't is a colour she abhors; and cross-gartered,—a fashion she detests; and he will smile upon her, which will now be so unsuitable to her disposition, being addicted to a melancholy as she is, that it cannot but turn him into a notable contempt. If you will see it, follow me.
SIR TOBY. To the gates of Tartar, thou most excellent devil of wit!
SIR ANDREW. I'll make one too. *Exeunt.*

Act III

SCENE 1. OLIVIA'S *garden*.

Enter VIOLA *and* CLOWN *with a tabor*.

VIOLA. Save thee, friend, and thy music! Dost thou live by thy tabor?
CLOWN. No, sir, I live by the church.
VIOLA. Art thou a churchman?
CLOWN. No such matter, sir: I do live by the church; for I do live

---

161. *play:* stake. *tray-trip:* a dice game. 175. *Tartar:* Tartarus, hell. 176. *make one:* be of the party.

ACT III, SC. 1: 1. *Save thee:* God save thee. 2. *tabor:* drum.

at my house, and my house doth stand by the church.

VIOLA. So thou mayest say, the king lies by a beggar, if a beggar dwell near him; or, the church stands by thy tabor, if thy tabor stand by the church.

CLOWN. You have said, sir.—To see this age!—A sentence is but a cheveril glove to a good wit; how quickly the wrong side may be turned outward!

VIOLA. Nay, that's certain; they that dally nicely with words may quickly make them wanton.

CLOWN. I would, therefore, my sister had had no name, sir.

VIOLA. Why, man?

CLOWN. Why, sir, her name's a word; and to dally with that word might make my sister wanton. But indeed words are very rascals since bonds disgraced them.

VIOLA. Thy reason, man?

CLOWN. Troth, sir, I can yield you none without words; and words are grown so false, I am loath to prove reason with them.

VIOLA. I warrant thou art a merry fellow and carest for nothing.

CLOWN. Not so, sir, I do care for something; but in my conscience, sir, I do not care for you: if that be to care for nothing, sir, I would it would make you invisible.

VIOLA. Art not thou the Lady Olivia's fool?

CLOWN. No, indeed, sir; the Lady Olivia has no folly: she will keep no fool, sir, till she be married; and fools are as like husbands as pilchards are to herrings, the husband's the bigger. I am indeed not her fool, but her corrupter of words.

VIOLA. I saw thee late at the Count Orsino's.

CLOWN. Foolery, sir, does walk about the orb like the sun, it shines every where. I would be sorry, sir, but the fool should be as oft with your master as with my mistress. I think I saw your wisdom there.

VIOLA. Nay, an thou pass upon me, I'll no more with thee. Hold, there's expenses for thee.

CLOWN. Now Jove, in his next commodity of hair, send thee a beard!

---

11. *cheveril:* kid. 13. *dally:* fool around. 15-18. A bastard has no name. 19. *bonds:* a reference to money bonds. 26. *make you invisible:* make you go away. 30. *pilchard:* a small fish. 33. *orb:* globe. 34. *but the fool should be:* if the fool were not. 35. Sc. "Which should be counteracted by my fooling." 36. *pass upon:* make jokes about.

SCENE 1] TWELFTH NIGHT 329

VIOLA. By my troth, I'll tell thee, I am almost sick for one— [40
aside—though I would not have it grown on my chin. Is thy lady within?

CLOWN. Would not a pair of these have bred, sir?

VIOLA. Yes, being kept together and put to use.

CLOWN. I would play Lord Pandarus of Phrygia, sir, to bring a Cressida to this Troilus.

VIOLA. I understand you, sir; 't is well begged.

CLOWN. The matter, I hope, is not great, sir, begging but a beggar; Cressida was a beggar. My lady is within, sir. I will construe to them whence you come; who you are and what you would are out of [50 my welkin,—I might say element, but the word is over-worn. *Exit.*

VIOLA. This fellow is wise enough to play the fool;
And to do that well craves a kind of wit:
He must observe their mood on whom he jests,
The quality of persons, and the time,
Not, like the haggard, check at every feather
That comes before his eye. This is a practice
As full of labour as a wise man's art:
For folly that he wisely shows is fit;
But wise men's folly shown quite taints their wit.   60

Enter SIR TOBY *and* SIR ANDREW.

SIR TOBY. Save you, gentleman.

VIOLA. And you, sir.

SIR ANDREW. Dieu vous garde, monsieur.

VIOLA. Et vous aussi; votre serviteur.

SIR ANDREW. I hope, sir, you are; and I am yours.

SIR TOBY. Will you encounter the house? my niece is desirous you should enter, if your trade be to her.

VIOLA. I am bound to your niece, sir; I mean, she is the list of my voyage.

SIR TOBY. Taste your legs, sir; put them to motion.   70

---

43. "these" i.e., coins. 45. "I would be a pander to bring together two coins . . ." 49. *construe:* explain. 51. *welkin:* sky. 56. *haggard:* wild hawk, *check:* pounce. 63-4. "God protect you, sir." "And you too; your servant." 66 ff. Deliberately fancy language. 68. *list:* goal.

330   TWELFTH NIGHT   [ACT III

VIOLA. My legs do better understand me, sir, than I understand what you mean by bidding me taste my legs.

SIR TOBY. I mean, to go, sir, to enter.

VIOLA. I will answer you with gait and entrance. But we are prevented.—

Enter OLIVIA *and* MARIA.

Most excellent accomplished lady, the heavens rain odours on you!

SIR ANDREW. That youth's a rare courtier. 'Rain odours!' well!

VIOLA. My matter hath no voice, lady, but to your own most pregnant and vouchsafed ear.

SIR ANDREW. 'Odours,' 'pregnant,' and 'vouchsafed:' I'll get [80 'em all three all ready.

OLIVIA. Let the garden door be shut, and leave me to my hearing. —*Exeunt* SIR TOBY, SIR ANDREW, *and* MARIA. Give me your hand, sir.

VIOLA. My duty, madam, and most humble service.

OLIVIA. What is your name?

VIOLA. Cesario is your servant's name, fair princess.

OLIVIA. My servant, sir! 't was never merry world
Since lowly feigning was call'd compliment;
You're servant to the Count Orsino, youth.

VIOLA. And he is yours, and his must needs be yours;   90
Your servant's servant is your servant, madam.

OLIVIA. For him, I think not on him; for his thoughts,
Would they were blanks, rather than fill'd with me!

VIOLA. Madam, I come to whet your gentle thoughts
On his behalf.

OLIVIA.   O, by your leave, I pray you,
I bade you never speak again of him;
But, would you undertake another suit,
I had rather hear you to solicit that
Than music from the spheres.

VIOLA.   Dear lady,—

---

74. *with gait:* by going. 78-9. *pregnant:* attentive. 80. *vouchsafed:* vouchsafing. 81. *ready:* i.e., for use. 88. *lowly feigning:* a pretence of humility. 99. The allusion is to the Ptolemaic spheres, which spin around the globe emitting music.

SCENE 1] TWELFTH NIGHT 331

OLIVIA. Give me leave, beseech you. I did send, 100
After the last enchantment you did here,
A ring in chase of you; so did I abuse
Myself, my servant, and, I fear me, you.
Under your hard construction must I sit,
To force that on you, in a shameful cunning,
Which you knew none of yours; what might you think?
Have you not set mine honour at the stake,
And baited it with all the unmuzzled thoughts
That tyrannous heart can think? To one of your receiving
Enough is shown; a cypress, not a bosom, 110
Hideth my heart. So, let me hear you speak.

VIOLA. I pity you.

OLIVIA. That's a degree to love.

VIOLA. No, not a grise; for 't is a vulgar proof,
That very oft we pity enemies.

OLIVIA. Why, then, methinks 't is time to smile again.
O world, how apt the poor are to be proud!
If one should be a prey, how much the better
To fall before the lion than the wolf! *Clock strikes.*
The clock upbraids me with the waste of time.—
Be not afraid, good youth, I will not have you; 120
And yet, when wit and youth is come to harvest,
Your wife is like to reap a proper man.—
There lies your way, due west.

VIOLA. Then westward-ho!
Grace and good disposition attend your ladyship!
You'll nothing, madam, to my lord by me?

OLIVIA. Stay!
I prithee, tell me what thou think'st of me.

VIOLA. That you do think you are not what you are.

OLIVIA. If I think so, I think the same of you.

VIOLA. Then think you right; I am not what I am. 130

OLIVIA. I would you were as I would have you be!

107-09. In bear-baiting the bear is "set at the stake." 109. *receiving:* understanding. 110. *a cypress, not a bosom:* i.e., only a thin fabric tantamount to nothing. 113. *grise:* step. *vulgar proof:* thing often proved. 118. The lion is generous, the wolf is not.

VIOLA. Would it be better, madam, than I am?
I wish it might, for now I am your fool.

OLIVIA. O, what a deal of scorn looks beautiful
In the contempt and anger of his lip!
A murtherous guilt shows not itself more soon
Than love that would seem hid; love's night is noon.—
Cesario, by the roses of the spring,
By maidhood, honour, truth, and every thing,
I love thee so, that, maugre all thy pride, 140
Nor wit nor reason can my passion hide.
Do not extort thy reasons from this clause,
For that I woo, thou therefore hast no cause;
But rather reason thus with reason fetter,—
Love sought is good, but given unsought is better.

VIOLA. By innocence I swear, and by my youth,
I have one heart, one bosom, and one truth,
And that no woman has; nor never none
Shall mistress be of it, save I alone.
And so adieu, good madam; never more 150
Will I my master's tears to you deplore.

OLIVIA. Yet come again; for thou perhaps mayst move
That heart, which now abhors, to like his love. *Exeunt.*

SCENE 2. OLIVIA'S *house.*

Enter SIR TOBY, SIR ANDREW, *and* FABIAN.

SIR ANDREW. No, faith, I'll not stay a jot longer.

SIR TOBY. Thy reason, dear venom, give thy reason.

FABIAN. You must needs yield your reason, Sir Andrew.

SIR ANDREW. Marry, I saw your niece do more favours to the count's serving-man than ever she bestowed upon me: I saw 't i' the orchard.

SIR TOBY. Did she see thee the while, old boy? tell me that.

SIR ANDREW. As plain as I see you now.

FABIAN. This was a great argument of love in her toward you.

SIR ANDREW. 'Slight! will you make an ass o' me?

---

137. *night is noon:* secrecy is clear as daylight. 140. *maugre:* despite. 147-8. "given to one person and not a woman at that."

sc. 2: 2. *venom:* angry fellow. 8. *argument:* proof.

FABIAN. I will prove it legitimate, sir, upon the oaths of [10
judgment and reason.

SIR TOBY. And they have been grand-jurymen since before Noah was a sailor.

FABIAN. She did show favour to the youth in your sight only to exasperate you, to awake your *dormouse valour,* to put fire in your heart, and brimstone in your liver. You should then have accosted her; and with some excellent jests, fire-new from the mint, you should have banged the youth into dumbness. This was looked for at your hand, and this was balked: the double gilt of this opportunity you let time wash off, and you are now sailed into the north of my [20 lady's opinion; where you will hang like an icicle on a Dutchman's beard, unless you do redeem it by some laudable attempt either of valour or policy.

SIR ANDREW. An 't be any way, it must be with valour; for policy I hate: I had as lief be a Brownist as a politician.

SIR TOBY. Why, then, build me thy fortunes upon the basis of valour. Challenge me the count's youth to fight with him; hurt him in eleven places: my niece shall take note of it; and assure thyself, there is no love-broker in the world can more prevail in man's commendation with woman than report of valour. 30

FABIAN. There is no way but this, Sir Andrew.

SIR ANDREW. Will either of you bear me a challenge to him?

SIR TOBY. Go, write it in a martial hand; be curst and brief; it is no matter how witty, so it be eloquent and full of invention; taunt him with the license of ink; if thou thou'st him some thrice, it shall not be amiss; and as many lies as will lie in thy sheet of paper, although the sheet were big enough for the bed of Ware in England, set 'em down: go, about it. Let there be gall enough in thy ink, though thou write with a goose-pen, no matter: about it.

SIR ANDREW. Where shall I find you? 40

SIR TOBY. We'll call thee at the cubiculo; go.   *Exit* SIR ANDREW.

FABIAN. This is a dear manikin to you, Sir Toby.

---

10. *legitimate:* logical. 19. *balked:* withheld. 25. *Brownist:* rebel from Church of England. *politician:* intriguer, man of "policy." 33. *curst:* surly. 35. *license of ink:* the freedom ink permits. *thou'st:* call him *thou* (to strangers, an insult). 37. *bed of Ware:* famous for its size. 41. *cubiculo:* apartment.

SIR TOBY. I have been dear to him, lad, some two thousand strong, or so.

FABIAN. We shall have a rare letter from him; but you'll not deliver 't?

SIR TOBY. Never trust me, then; and by all means stir on the youth to an answer. I think oxen and wainropes cannot hale them together. For Andrew, if he were opened, and you find so much blood in his liver as will clog the foot of a flea, I'll eat the rest of the anatomy. [50

FABIAN. And his opposite, the youth, bears in his visage no great presage of cruelty.

Enter MARIA.

SIR TOBY. Look, where the youngest wren of nine comes.

MARIA. If you desire the spleen, and will laugh yourselves into stitches, follow me. Yond gull Malvolio is turned heathen, a very renegado; for there is no Christian, that means to be saved by believing rightly, can ever believe such impossible passages of grossness. He's in yellow stockings.

SIR TOBY. And cross-gartered? 60

MARIA. Most villanously; like a pedant that keeps a school i' the church. I have dogged him like his murtherer. He does obey every point of the letter that I dropped to betray him; he does smile his face into more lines than is in the new map with the augmentation of the Indies: you have not seen such a thing as 't is. I can hardly forbear hurling things at him. I know my lady will strike him; if she do, he'll smile and take 't for a great favour.

SIR TOBY. Come, bring us, bring us where he is. *Exeunt.*

SCENE 3. *A street.*

Enter SEBASTIAN *and* ANTONIO.

SEBASTIAN. I would not by my will have troubled you

---

43. *dear:* expensive. *two thousand* pounds—or an Italian currency? 48. *wain-:* waggon-. 54. *youngest wren:* smallest of a small species. 58. *passages of grossness:* passages, in scripture, of such gross absurdity. 64. *new map . . . :* with the West Indies newly added because recently discovered.

SCENE 3] TWELFTH NIGHT 335

But, since you make your pleasure of your pains,
I will no further chide you.

ANTONIO. I could not stay behind you: my desire,
More sharp than filed steel, did spur me forth;
And not all love to see you, though so much
As might have drawn one to a longer voyage,
But jealousy what might befall your travel,
Being skilless in these parts; which to a stranger,
Unguided and unfriended, often prove
Rough and unhospitable. My willing love,
The rather by these arguments of fear,
Set forth in your pursuit.

SEBASTIAN.   My kind Antonio,
I can no other answer make but thanks,
And thanks, and ever thanks; and oft good turns
Are shuffled off with such uncurrent pay:
But, were my worth as is my conscience firm,
You should find better dealing. What's to do?
Shall we go see the reliques of this town?

ANTONIO. To-morrow, sir; best first go see your lodging.

SEBASTIAN. I am not weary, and 't is long to night;
I pray you, let us satisfy our eyes
With the memorials and the things of fame
That do renown this city.

ANTONIO.   Would you 'd pardon me!
I do not without danger walk these streets:
Once, in a sea-fight, 'gainst the count his galleys
I did some service; of such note indeed,
That were I ta'en here it would scarce be answer'd.

SEBASTIAN. Belike you slew great number of his people.

ANTONIO. The offence is not of such a bloody nature;
Albeit the quality of the time and quarrel
Might well have given us bloody argument.
It might have since been answer'd in repaying

---

sc. 3: 6. *not all love:* not merely love. 9. *skilless:* a stranger. 19. *reliques:* ancient things "of fame." 26. *count his galleys:* count's galleys. 28. *ta'en:* taken prisoner. *answer'd:* counteracted, countervailed.

What we took from them; which, for traffic's sake,
Most of our city did: only myself stood out;
For which, if I be lapsed in this place,
I shall pay dear.

SEBASTIAN.   Do not then walk too open.

ANTONIO. It doth not fit me. Hold, sir, here's my purse.
In the south suburbs, at the Elephant,
Is best to lodge; I will bespeak our diet,   40
Whiles you beguile the time and feed your knowledge
With viewing of the town: there shall you have me.

SEBASTIAN. Why I your purse?

ANTONIO. Haply your eye shall light upon some toy
You have desire to purchase; and your store,
I think, is not for idle markets, sir.

SEBASTIAN. I'll be your purse-bearer and leave you
For an hour.

ANTONIO. To the Elephant.

SEBASTIAN.   I do remember.   *Exeunt.*

SCENE 4. OLIVIA'S *garden.*

Enter OLIVIA *and* MARIA.

OLIVIA. I have sent after him; he says he'll come.
How shall I feast him? what bestow of him?
For youth is bought more oft than begg'd or borrow'd.
I speak too loud.—
Where is Malvolio?—he is sad and civil,
And suits well for a servant with my fortunes;—
Where is Malvolio?

MARIA. He's coming, madam; but in very strange manner. He is, sure, possessed, madam.

OLIVIA. Why, what's the matter? does he rave?   10

MARIA. No, madam, he does nothing but smile: your ladyship were best to have some guard about you, if he come; for, sure, the man is tainted in 's wits.

---

34. *traffic:* trade. 36. *lapsed:* taken unawares. 45. *store:* supply of money. 46. *idle:* filled with valuable luxuries.

SC. 4: 2. *of:* on.

OLIVIA. Go call him hither.—*Exit* MARIA. I am as mad as he,
If sad and merry madness equal be.—

Re-enter MARIA, *with* MALVOLIO.

How now, Malvolio!

MALVOLIO. Sweet lady, ho, ho.

OLIVIA. Smilest thou?
I sent for thee upon a sad occasion.

MALVOLIO. Sad, lady! I could be sad: this does make some [20]
obstruction in the blood, this cross-gartering; but what of that? if it
please the eye of one, it is with me as the very true sonnet is, 'Please
one, and please all.'

OLIVIA. Why, how dost thou, man? what is the matter with thee?

MALVOLIO. Not black in my mind, though yellow in my legs.—It
did come to his hands, and commands shall be executed; I think we
do know the sweet Roman hand.

OLIVIA. Wilt thou go to bed, Malvolio?

MALVOLIO. To bed! ay, sweet-heart, and I'll come to thee.

OLIVIA. God comfort thee! Why dost thou smile so and kiss [30]
thy hand so oft?

MARIA. How do you, Malvolio?

MALVOLIO. At your request! yes; nightingales answer daws.

MARIA. Why appear you with this ridiculous boldness before my
lady?

MALVOLIO. 'Be not afraid of greatness;'—'t was well writ.

OLIVIA. What meanest thou by that, Malvolio?

MALVOLIO. 'Some are born great,'—

OLIVIA. Ha!

MALVOLIO. 'Some achieve greatness,'—

OLIVIA. What sayest thou?

MALVOLIO. 'And some have greatness thrust upon them.'

OLIVIA. Heaven restore thee!

MALVOLIO. 'Remember who commended thy yellow stockings,'—

OLIVIA. Thy yellow stockings!

MALVOLIO. 'And wished to see thee cross-gartered.'

22-3. "Please one . . .": refrain of a ballad. 27. Italian handwriting. 33. "nightingales . . .": i.e., high people may condescend to speak to low.

OLIVIA. Cross-gartered!

MALVOLIO. 'Go to, thou art made, if thou desirest to be so;'—

OLIVIA. Am I made?

MALVOLIO. 'If not, let me see thee a servant still.' 50

OLIVIA. Why, this is very midsummer madness.

Enter SERVANT.

SERVANT. Madam, the young gentleman of the Count Orsino's is returned; I could hardly entreat him back: he attends your ladyship's pleasure.

OLIVIA. I'll come to him.—*Exit* SERVANT. Good Maria, let this fellow be looked to. Where's my cousin Toby? Let some of my people have a special care of him; I would not have him miscarry for the half of my dowry. *Exeunt* OLIVIA *and* MARIA.

MALVOLIO. O, ho! do you come near me now? no worse man than Sir Toby to look to me! This concurs directly with the letter: [60 she sends him on purpose, that I may appear stubborn to him; for she incites me to that in the letter. 'Cast thy humble slough,' says she; 'be opposite with a kinsman, surly with servants; let thy tongue tang with arguments of state; put thyself into the trick of singularity;' and consequently sets down the manner how: as, a sad face, a reverend carriage, a slow tongue, in the habit of some sir of note, and so forth. I have limed her; but it is Jove's doing, and Jove make me thankful! And when she went away now, 'Let this fellow be looked to;' fellow! not Malvolio, nor after my degree, but fellow. Why, every thing adheres together, that no dram of a scruple, no scruple of a scru- [70 ple, no obstacle, no incredulous or unsafe circumstance,—what can be said? Nothing that can be can come between me and the full prospect of my hopes. Well, Jove, not I, is the doer of this, and he is to be thanked.

Re-enter MARIA, *with* SIR TOBY *and* FABIAN.

SIR TOBY. Which way is he, in the name of sanctity? If all the devils of hell be drawn in little, and Legion himself possessed him, yet I'll

---

57-8. "I'd rather lose half my dowry than have something happen to him."
66. *habit:* manner. *sir:* gentleman. 67. *limed:* caught. 71. *incredulous:* incredible. 76. *Legion:* the unclean spirit in the Bible: "My name is Legion, for we are many."

speak to him.

FABIAN. Here he is, here he is.—How is 't with you, sir? how is 't with you, man?

MALVOLIO. Go off; I discard you: let me enjoy my private; [80 go off.

MARIA. Lo, how hollow the fiend speaks within him! did not I tell you?—Sir Toby, my lady prays to have a care of him.

MALVOLIO. Ah, ha! does she so?

SIR TOBY. Go to, go to; peace, peace; we must deal gently with him: let me alone.—How do you, Malvolio? how is 't with you? What, man! defy the devil; consider, he's an enemy to mankind.

MALVOLIO. Do you know what you say?

MARIA. La you, an you speak ill of the devil, how he takes it at heart! Pray God, he be not bewitched! 90

FABIAN. Carry his water to the wise woman.

MARIA. Marry, and it shall be done to-morrow morning, if I live. My lady would not lose him for more than I'll say.

MALVOLIO. How now, mistress!

MARIA. O Lord!

SIR TOBY. Prithee, hold thy peace; this is not the way; do you not see you move him? let me alone with him.

FABIAN. No way but gentleness; gently, gently: the fiend is rough, and will not be roughly used.

SIR TOBY. Why, how now, my bawcock! how dost thou, chuck? 100

MALVOLIO. Sir!

SIR TOBY. Ay, Biddy, come with me. What, man! 't is not for gravity to play at cherry-pit with Satan. Hang him, foul collier!

MARIA. Get him to say his prayers, good Sir Toby, get him to pray.

MALVOLIO. My prayers, minx!

MARIA. No, I warrant you, he will not hear of godliness.

MALVOLIO. Go, hang yourselves all! you are idle shallow things. I am not of your element; you shall know more hereafter. *Exit.*

SIR TOBY. Is 't possible?

FABIAN. If this were played upon a stage now, I could con- [110 demn it as an improbable fiction.

---

80. *private:* privacy. 100. *bawcock:* from French beau coq, fine fellow. *chuck:* chicken, darling. 102. *Biddy:* hen. 103. *cherry-pit:* a game. *collier*—because black.

340 TWELFTH NIGHT [ACT III

SIR TOBY. His very genius hath taken the infection of the device, man.

MARIA. Nay, pursue him now, lest the device take air and taint.

FABIAN. Why, we shall make him mad indeed.

MARIA. The house will be the quieter.

SIR TOBY. Come, we'll have him in a dark room and bound. My niece is already in the belief that he's mad: we may carry it thus, for our pleasure and his penance, till our very pastime, tired out of breath, prompt us to have mercy on him; at which time we [120 will bring the device to the bar, and crown thee for a finder of madmen. But see, but see.

Enter SIR ANDREW.

FABIAN. More matter for a May morning.

SIR ANDREW. Here's the challenge, read it; I warrant there's vinegar and pepper in 't.

FABIAN. Is 't so saucy?

SIR ANDREW. Ay, is 't, I warrant him; do but read.

SIR TOBY. Give me. *Reads.* 'Youth, whatsoever thou art, thou art but a scurvy fellow.'

FABIAN. Good, and valiant. 130

SIR TOBY, *reads.* 'Wonder not, nor admire not in thy mind, why I do call thee so, for I will show thee no reason for 't.'

FABIAN. A good note; that keeps you from the blow of the law.

SIR TOBY, *reads.* 'Thou comest to the Lady Olivia, and in my sight she uses thee kindly: but thou liest in thy throat; that is not the matter I challenge thee for.'

FABIAN. Very brief, and to exceeding good sense—less.

SIR TOBY, *reads.* 'I will waylay thee going home; where if it be thy chance to kill me,'—

FABIAN. Good. 140

SIR TOBY, *reads.* 'Thou killest me like a rogue and a villain.'

FABIAN. Still you keep o' the windy side of the law: good.

SIR TOBY, *reads.* 'Fare thee well; and God have mercy upon one of our souls! He may have mercy upon mine; but my hope is better, and

---

112. *genius:* nature. 121. *bar*—of justice. 123. *May:* on May 1st, as on Twelfth Night, topsy-turvydom is in order. 131. *admire:* marvel.

SCENE 4] TWELFTH NIGHT 341

so look to thyself. Thy friend, as thou usest him, and thy sworn
enemy, ANDREW AGUECHEEK.'
If this letter move him not, his legs cannot; I'll give 't him.

MARIA. You may have very fit occasion for 't; he is now in some
commerce with my lady, and will by and by depart.

SIR TOBY. Go, Sir Andrew; scout me for him at the corner [150
of the orchard like a bum-baily. So soon as ever thou seest him, draw;
and, as thou drawest, swear horrible; for it comes to pass oft that a
terrible oath, with a swaggering accent sharply twanged off, gives
manhood more approbation than ever proof itself would have earned
him. Away!

SIR ANDREW. Nay, let me alone for swearing. *Exit.*

SIR TOBY. Now will not I deliver his letter; for the behaviour of the
young gentleman gives him out to be of good capacity and breeding;
his employment between his lord and my niece confirms no less:
therefore this letter, being so excellently ignorant, will breed [160
no terror in the youth; he will find it comes from a clodpole. But,
sir, I will deliver his challenge by word of mouth; set upon Aguecheek
a notable report of valour; and drive the gentleman, as I know his
youth will aptly receive it, into a most hideous opinion of his rage,
skill, fury, and impetuosity. This will so fright them both that they
will kill one another by the look, like cockatrices.

Re-enter OLIVIA, *with* VIOLA.

FABIAN. Here he comes with your niece; give them way till he take
leave, and presently after him.

SIR TOBY. I will meditate the while upon some horrid message for
a challenge. *Exeunt* SIR TOBY, FABIAN, *and* MARIA. 170

OLIVIA. I have said too much unto a heart of stone,
And laid mine honour too unchary on 't:
There's something in me that reproves my fault;
But such a headstrong potent fault it is,
That it but mocks reproof.

VIOLA. With the same haviour that your passion bears

---

151. *bum-baily:* bailiff. *draw*—your sword. 153-4. *gives manhood more approbation:* imparts more faith in a man's courage. 162. *set upon:* give to. 163. *report:* reputation. 166. *cockatrice:* mythical animal. 176. *haviour:* behavior.

342   TWELFTH NIGHT   [ACT III

Goes on my master's grief.

OLIVIA. Here, wear this jewel for me, 't is my picture:
Refuse it not, it hath no tongue to vex you;
And I beseech you come again to-morrow.   180
What shall you ask of me that I'll deny,
That honour sav'd may upon asking give?

VIOLA. Nothing but this,—your true love for my master.

OLIVIA. How with mine honour may I give him that
Which I have given to you?

VIOLA.   I will acquit you.

OLIVIA. Well, come again to-morrow: fare thee well;
A fiend like thee might bear my soul to hell.   *Exit.*

Re-enter SIR TOBY *and* FABIAN.

SIR TOBY. Gentleman, God save thee.

VIOLA. And you, sir.

SIR TOBY. That defence thou hast, betake thee to 't: of what [190
nature the wrongs are thou hast done him, I know not; but thy intercepter, full of despite, bloody as the hunter, attends thee at the orchard-end: dismount thy tuck, be yare in thy preparation, for thy assailant is quick, skilful, and deadly.

VIOLA. You mistake, sir; I am sure no man hath any quarrel to me: my remembrance is very free and clear from any image of offence done to any man.

SIR TOBY. You'll find it otherwise, I assure you: therefore, if you hold your life at any price, betake you to your guard; for your opposite hath in him what youth, strength, skill, and wrath can [200
furnish man withal.

VIOLA. I pray you, sir, what is he?

SIR TOBY. He is knight, dubbed with unhatched rapier and on carpet consideration; but he is a devil in private brawl: souls and bodies hath he divorced three; and his incensement at this moment is so implacable, that satisfaction can be none but by pangs of death and sepulchre. Hob, nob, is his word; give 't or take 't.

---

182. "That honor, when asked, may give—without giving itself." 190. *That:* whatever. 191-2. *intercepter:* viz., Sir Andrew. 193. *tuck:* rapier. *yare:* brisk. 199-200. *opposite:* opponent. 201. *withal:* with. 203. *dubbed with unhatched:* knighted with unstained. 203-04. *carpet:* a carpet knight, in fact.

SCENE 4] TWELFTH NIGHT 343

VIOLA. I will return again into the house and desire some conduct of the lady. I am no fighter. I have heard of some kind of men that put quarrels purposely on others, to taste their valour; belike [210 this is a man of that quirk.

SIR TOBY. Sir, no; his indignation derives itself out of a very competent injury: therefore, get you on and give him his desire. Back you shall not to the house, unless you undertake that with me which with as much safety you might answer him: therefore, on, or strip your sword stark naked; for meddle you must, that's certain, or forswear to wear iron about you.

VIOLA. This is as uncivil as strange. I beseech you, do me this courteous office, as to know of the knight what my offence to him is; it is something of my negligence, nothing of my purpose. 220

SIR TOBY. I will do so.—Signior Fabian, stay you by this gentleman till my return. *Exit.*

VIOLA. Pray you, sir, do you know of this matter?

FABIAN. I know the knight is incensed against you, even to a mortal arbitrement; but nothing of the circumstance more.

VIOLA. I beseech you, what manner of man is he?

FABIAN. Nothing of that wonderful promise, to read him by his form, as you are like to find him in the proof of his valour. He is, indeed, sir, the most skilful, bloody, and fatal opposite that you could possibly have found in any part of Illyria. Will you walk to- [230 wards him? I will make your peace with him if I can.

VIOLA. I shall be much bound to you for 't: I am one that had rather go with sir priest than sir knight; I care not who knows so much of my mettle. *Exeunt.*

Re-enter SIR TOBY, *with* SIR ANDREW.

SIR TOBY. Why, man, he's a very devil; I have not seen such a firago. I had a pass with him, rapier, scabbard, and all, and he gives me the stuck in with such a mortal motion, that it is inevitable; and on the answer, he pays you as surely as your feet hit the ground they step on. They say he has been fencer to the Sophy.

SIR ANDREW. Pox on 't, I'll not meddle with him. 240

224-5. *mortal arbitrement:* life and death decision. 228. *form:* body. 234. *mettle:* character. 235. *firago:* virago, fierce woman. 239. *Sophy:* Shah.

SIR TOBY. Ay, but he will not now be pacified; Fabian can scarce hold him yonder.

SIR ANDREW. Plague on 't, an I thought he had been valiant and so cunning in fence, I'd have seen him damned ere I'd have challenged him. Let him let the matter slip, and I'll give him my horse, grey Capilet.

SIR TOBY. I'll make the motion. Stand here, make a good show on 't; this shall end without the perdition of souls. *Aside.* Marry, I'll ride your horse as well as I ride you.—

Re-enter FABIAN *and* VIOLA.

To FABIAN. I have his horse to take up the quarrel; I have [250 persuaded him the youth's a devil.

FABIAN. He is as horribly conceited of him; and pants and looks pale, as if a bear were at his heels.

SIR TOBY, *to* VIOLA. There's no remedy, sir; he will fight with you for 's oath sake. Marry, he hath better bethought him of his quarrel, and he finds that now scarce to be worth talking of: therefore draw, for the supportance of his vow; he protests he will not hurt you.

VIOLA, *aside.* Pray God defend me! A little thing would make me tell them how much I lack of a man.

FABIAN. Give ground, if you see him furious. 260

SIR TOBY. Come, Sir Andrew, there's no remedy; the gentleman will, for his honour's sake, have one bout with you; he cannot by the duello avoid it; but he has promised me, as he is a gentleman and a soldier, he will not hurt you. Come on; to 't.

SIR ANDREW. Pray God, he keep his oath!

VIOLA. I do assure you, 't is against my will. *They draw.*

Enter ANTONIO.

ANTONIO. Put up your sword. If this young gentleman
Have done offence, I take the fault on me;
If you offend him, I for him defy you.

SIR TOBY. You, sir! why, what are you? 270

ANTONIO. One, sir, that for his love dares yet do more

---

249. Toby will keep the horse for himself. 252. *is . . . conceited:* imagines. 263. *duello:* laws of duelling.

SCENE 4] TWELFTH NIGHT 345

Than you have heard him brag to you he will.

SIR TOBY. Nay, if you be an undertaker, I am for you. *They draw.*

Enter OFFICERS.

FABIAN. O good Sir Toby, hold! here come the officers.

SIR TOBY. I'll be with you anon.

VIOLA. Pray, sir, put your sword up, if you please.

SIR ANDREW. Marry, will I, sir; and, for that I promised you, I'll be as good as my word; he will bear you easily and reins well.

1 OFFICER. This is the man; do thy office.

2 OFFICER. Antonio, I arrest thee at the suit of Count Orsino.   280

ANTONIO. You do mistake me, sir.

1 OFFICER. No, sir, no jot; I know your favour well,
Though now you have no sea-cap on your head.—
Take him away; he knows I know him well.

ANTONIO. I must obey.—*To* VIOLA. This comes with seeking you:
But there's no remedy; I shall answer it.
What will you do, now my necessity
Makes me to ask you for my purse? It grieves me
Much more for what I cannot do for you
Than what befalls myself. You stand amaz'd;   290
But be of comfort.

2 OFFICER. Come, sir, away.

ANTONIO. I must entreat of you some of that money.

VIOLA. What money, sir?
For the fair kindness you have show'd me here,
And, part, being prompted by your present trouble,
Out of my lean and low ability
I'll lend you something. My having is not much;
I'll make division of my present with you:
Hold, there's half my coffer.

ANTONIO.   Will you deny me now?   300
Is 't possible that my deserts to you
Can lack persuasion? Do not tempt my misery,
Lest that it make me so unsound a man

---

273. *undertaker:* one who takes on others' quarrels. 277. i.e., the horse. 282. *favour:* appearance. 298. *my present:* present resources. 300. *coffer:* possessions.

As to upbraid you with those kindnesses
That I have done for you.
　　VIOLA.　　　　　　　　I know of none;
Nor know I you by voice or any feature:
I hate ingratitude more in a man
Than lying, vainness, babbling, drunkenness,
Or any taint of vice whose strong corruption
Inhabits our frail blood.
　　ANTONIO.　　　　　O heavens themselves!　　　　　310
　　2 OFFICER. Come, sir, I pray you, go.
　　ANTONIO. Let me speak a little. This youth that you see here
I snatch'd one half out of the jaws of death,
Reliev'd him with such sanctity of love,
And to his image, which methought did promise
Most venerable worth, did I devotion.
　　1 OFFICER. What's that to us? The time goes by: away!
　　ANTONIO. But, O, how vile an idol proves this god!—
Thou hast, Sebastian, done good feature shame.—
In nature there's no blemish but the mind;　　　　　320
None can be call'd deform'd but the unkind.
Virtue is beauty, but the beauteous evil
Are empty trunks o'erflourish'd by the devil.
　　1 OFFICER. The man grows mad; away with him!—Come, come, sir.
　　ANTONIO. Lead me on.　　　　　　　*Exit with* OFFICERS.
　　VIOLA. Methinks his words do from such passion fly,
That he believes himself; so do not I.
Prove true, imagination, O, prove true,
That I, dear brother, be now ta'en for you!
　　SIR TOBY. Come hither, knight; come hither, Fabian: we'll　[330
whisper o'er a couplet or two of most sage saws.
　　VIOLA. He nam'd Sebastian: I my brother know
Yet living in my glass; even such and so
In favour was my brother, and he went
Still in this fashion, colour, ornament,
For him I imitate. O, if it prove,

---

315. *image:* person. 319. *done good feature shame:* cast a slur on good looks. 323. *o'erflourish'd:* finely painted on the outside. 331. *saws:* adages. 332-3. "I can tell what my brother looks like by consulting a mirror." 336. *O, if it prove* to be so.

ACT IV, SCENE 1]   TWELFTH NIGHT   347

Tempests are kind, and salt waves fresh in love!   *Exit.*

SIR TOBY. A very dishonest, paltry boy, and more a coward than a hare: his dishonesty appears in leaving his friend here in necessity and denying him; and for his cowardship, ask Fabian.   340

FABIAN. A coward, a most devout coward, religious in it.

SIR ANDREW. 'Slid, I'll after him again and beat him.

SIR TOBY. Do; cuff him soundly, but never draw thy sword.

SIR ANDREW. An I do not,—   *Exit.*

FABIAN. Come, let's see the event.

SIR TOBY. I dare lay any money 't will be nothing yet.   *Exeunt.*

Act IV

SCENE 1. *Before* OLIVIA'S *house.*

Enter SEBASTIAN *and* CLOWN.

CLOWN. Will you make me believe that I am not sent for you?

SEBASTIAN. Go to, go to, thou art a foolish fellow;
Let me be clear of thee.

CLOWN. Well held out, i' faith! No, I do not know you; nor I am not sent to you by my lady, to bid you come speak with her; nor your name is not Master Cesario; nor this is not my nose neither. Nothing that is so is so.

SEBASTIAN. I prithee, vent thy folly somewhere else;
Thou know'st not me.

CLOWN. Vent my folly! he has heard that word of some great [10 man, and now applies it to a fool. Vent my folly! I am afraid this great lubber, the world, will prove a cockney.—I prithee now, ungird thy strangeness, and tell me what I shall vent to my lady; shall I vent to her that thou art coming?

SEBASTIAN. I prithee, foolish Greek, depart from me:
There's money for thee; if you tarry longer,
I shall give worse payment.

CLOWN. By my troth, thou hast an open hand.—These wise men

ACT IV, SC. 1: 12. *lubber:* lout. *cockney:* fop. 15. *Greek:* jester. 17. *worse payment:* i.e., a beating. 18. *open:* generous.

that give fools money get themselves a good report—after fourteen
years' purchase.   20

Enter SIR ANDREW, SIR TOBY, *and* FABIAN.

SIR ANDREW. Now, sir, have I met you again? there's for you.
SEBASTIAN. Why, there's for thee, and there, and there, and there.
Are all the people mad?
SIR TOBY. Hold, sir, or I'll throw your dagger o'er the house.
CLOWN. This will I tell my lady straight; I would not be in some of
your coats for two pence.   *Exit.*
SIR TOBY. Come on, sir; hold.
SIR ANDREW. Nay, let him alone: I'll go another way to work with
him; I'll have an action of battery against him, if there be any law in
Illyria: though I struck him first, yet it's no matter for that.   30
SEBASTIAN. Let go thy hand.
SIR TOBY. Come, sir, I will not let you go. Come, my young soldier,
put up your iron: you are well fleshed; come on.
SEBASTIAN. I will be free from thee. What wouldst thou now?
If thou dar'st tempt me further, draw thy sword.
SIR TOBY. What, what? Nay, then I must have an ounce or two of
this malapert blood from you.

Enter OLIVIA.

OLIVIA. Hold, Toby; on thy life I charge thee, hold!
SIR TOBY. Madam!
OLIVIA. Will it be ever thus? Ungracious wretch,   40
Fit for the mountains and the barbarous caves,
Where manners ne'er were preach'd! out of my sight!—
Be not offended, dear Cesario.—
Rudesby, be gone!—   *Exeunt* SIR TOBY, SIR ANDREW, *and* FABIAN.
    I prithee, gentle friend,
Let thy fair wisdom, not thy passion, sway
In this uncivil and unjust extent

---

19. *report:* reputation. 19-20. *fourteen years' purchase:* a long time. 21.
there's for you: said when striking a blow. 25. *straight:* at once. 29. *action
of battery:* lawsuit for assault. 33. *are well fleshed:* have tasted blood. *come
on:* come away. 37. *malapert:* saucy. 44. *Rudesby:* clumsy fellow. 46. *extent:*
behavior.

SCENE 2]   TWELFTH NIGHT   349

Against thy peace. Go with me to my house,
And hear thou there how many fruitless pranks
This ruffian hath botch'd up, that thou thereby
Mayst smile at this: thou shalt not choose but go;   50
Do not deny. Beshrew his soul for me,
He started one poor heart of mine in thee.

SEBASTIAN. What relish is in this? how runs the stream?
Or I am mad, or else this is a dream:
Let fancy still my sense in Lethe steep;
If it be thus to dream, still let me sleep!

OLIVIA. Nay, come, I prithee; would thou 'dst be rul'd by me!

SEBASTIAN. Madam, I will.

OLIVIA.   O, say so, and so be!   *Exeunt.*

SCENE 2. OLIVIA'S *house.*

Enter MARIA *and* CLOWN.

MARIA. Nay, I prithee, put on this gown and this beard, make him believe thou art Sir Topas the curate: do it quickly; I'll call Sir Toby the whilst.   *Exit.*

CLOWN. Well, I'll put it on, and I will dissemble myself in 't; and I would I were the first that ever dissembled in such a gown. I am not tall enough to become the function well, nor lean enough to be thought a good student; but to be said an honest man and a good housekeeper goes as fairly as to say a careful man and a great scholar. The competitors enter.

Enter SIR TOBY *and* MARIA.

SIR TOBY. Jove bless thee, master Parson.   10

CLOWN. Bonos dies, Sir Toby: for, as the old hermit of Prague, that never saw pen and ink, very wittily said to a niece of King Gorboduc, 'That that is;' so I, being master Parson, am master Parson; for, what is that but that, and is but is?

SIR TOBY. To him, Sir Topas.

CLOWN. What, ho, I say! peace in this prison!

---

51. *Beshrew his soul:* may he be damned. 52. Pun—"started one poor *hart.*" 54. *Or I am:* Either I am.

sc. 2: 2. *Sir*—here a priest's title. 9. *competitors:* confederates. 11. *bonos dies:* happy days.

SIR TOBY. The knave counterfeits well; a good knave.

MALVOLIO, *within*. Who calls there?

CLOWN. Sir Topas the curate, who comes to visit Malvolio the lunatic.

MALVOLIO. Sir Topas, Sir Topas, good Sir Topas, go to my lady.

CLOWN. Out, hyperbolical fiend! how vexest thou this man! talkest thou nothing but of ladies?

SIR TOBY. Well said, master Parson.

MALVOLIO. Sir Topas, never was man thus wronged; good Sir Topas, do not think I am mad: they have laid me here in hideous darkness.

CLOWN. Fie, thou dishonest Satan! I call thee by the most modest terms; for I am one of those gentle ones that will use the devil himself with courtesy: sayest thou that house is dark?

MALVOLIO. As hell, Sir Topas.

CLOWN. Why, it hath bay-windows transparent as barricadoes, and the clear-stores towards the south-north are as lustrous as ebony; and yet complainest thou of obstruction?

MALVOLIO. I am not mad, Sir Topas; I say to you, this house is dark.

CLOWN. Madman, thou errest: I say, there is no darkness but ignorance; in which thou art more puzzled than the Egyptians in their fog.

MALVOLIO. I say, this house is as dark as ignorance, though ignorance were as dark as hell; and I say, there was never man thus abused. I am no more mad than you are; make the trial of it in any constant question.

CLOWN. What is the opinion of Pythagoras concerning wild fowl?

MALVOLIO. That the soul of our grandam might happily inhabit a bird.

CLOWN. What thinkest thou of his opinion?

MALVOLIO. I think nobly of the soul, and no way approve his opinion.

CLOWN. Fare thee well. Remain thou still in darkness; thou shalt hold the opinion of Pythagoras ere I will allow of thy wits, and fear to kill a woodcock lest thou dispossess the soul of thy grandam. Fare thee well.

MALVOLIO. Sir Topas, Sir Topas!

---

22. *out:* fie. *hyperbolical:* exaggerating. 32. *clear-stores:* windows. 36. *fog:* i.e., the darkness God sent: Exodus X, 21, 2. 40. *constant:* logical. 41-50. Pythagoras believed in transmigration of souls.

SCENE 2] TWELFTH NIGHT 351

SIR TOBY. My most exquisite Sir Topas!

CLOWN. Nay, I am for all waters.

MARIA. Thou mightst have done this without thy beard and gown; he sees thee not.

SIR TOBY. To him in thine own voice, and bring me word how thou findest him; I would we were well rid of this knavery. If he may be conveniently delivered, I would he were, for I am now so far in offence with my niece that I cannot pursue with any safety this sport to the upshot. Come by and by to my chamber. 60

Exeunt SIR TOBY *and* MARIA.

CLOWN, *singing*. 'Hey, Robin, jolly Robin,
  Tell me how thy lady does.'

MALVOLIO. Fool!

CLOWN. 'My lady is unkind, perdy.'

MALVOLIO. Fool!

CLOWN. 'Alas, why is she so?'

MALVOLIO. Fool, I say!

CLOWN. 'She loves another'—Who calls, ha?

MALVOLIO. Good fool, as ever thou wilt deserve well at my hand, help me to a candle, and pen, ink, and paper; as I am a gentle- [70 man, I will live to be thankful to thee for 't.

CLOWN. Master Malvolio?

MALVOLIO. Ay, good fool.

CLOWN. Alas, sir, how fell you besides your five wits?

MALVOLIO. Fool, there was never man so notoriously abused; I am as well in my wits, fool, as thou art.

CLOWN. But as well? then you are mad indeed, if you be no better in your wits than a fool.

MALVOLIO. They have here propertied me; keep me in darkness, send ministers to me, asses, and do all they can to face me out [80 of my wits.

CLOWN. Advise you what you say; the minister is here.—Malvolio, Malvolio, thy wits the heavens restore! endeavour thyself to sleep, and leave thy vain bibble babble.

---

53. *am for all waters:* am versatile. 60. *by and by:* soon (this line shows how intimate Toby already is with Maria). 61-8. As ever, the clown's singing bears on the action. 79. *propertied:* used as property. 80-1. "make me seem out of my senses." 82 ff. The clown now enacts a dialogue between himself and Sir Topas.

MALVOLIO. Sir Topas!

CLOWN. Maintain no words with him, good fellow.—Who, I, sir? not I, sir. God be wi' you, good Sir Topas.—Marry, amen.—I will, sir, I will.

MALVOLIO. Fool, fool, fool, I say!

CLOWN. Alas, sir, be patient. What say you, sir? I am shent [90 for speaking to you.

MALVOLIO. Good fool, help me to some light and some paper; I tell thee, I am as well in my wits as any man in Illyria.

CLOWN. Well-a-day that you were, sir!

MALVOLIO. By this hand, I am. Good fool, some ink, paper, and light; and convey what I will set down to my lady: it shall advantage thee more than ever the bearing of letter did.

CLOWN. I will help you to 't. But tell me true, are you not mad indeed? or do you but counterfeit?

MALVOLIO. Believe me I am not; I tell thee true. 100

CLOWN. Nay, I'll ne'er believe a madman till I see his brains. I will fetch you light and paper and ink.

MALVOLIO. Fool, I'll requite it in the highest degree; I prithee, be gone.

CLOWN, *singing.* 'I am gone, sir,
  And anon, sir,
   I'll be with you again
  In a trice,
  Like to the old Vice,
   Your need to sustain;' 110

'Who, with dagger of lath,
In his rage and his wrath,
 Cries, ah, ha! to the devil:
Like a mad lad,
Pare thy nails, dad;
 Adieu, goodman devil.' *Exit.*

---

90. *shent:* scolded. 109. *Vice:* a character in the morality plays.

SCENE 3. OLIVIA'S *garden*.

Enter SEBASTIAN.

SEBASTIAN. This is the air; that is the glorious sun;
This pearl she gave me, I do feel 't and see 't;
And though 't is wonder that enwraps me thus,
Yet 't is not madness. Where's Antonio, then?
I could not find him at the Elephant:
Yet there he was; and there I found this credit,
That he did range the town to seek me out.
His counsel now might do me golden service;
For though my soul disputes well with my sense,
That this may be some error, but no madness, 10
Yet doth this accident and flood of fortune
So far exceed all instance, all discourse,
That I am ready to distrust mine eyes
And wrangle with my reason that persuades me
To any other trust but that I am mad
Or else the lady's mad; yet, if 't were so,
She could not sway her house, command her followers,
Take and give back affairs and their dispatch
With such a smooth, discreet, and stable bearing
As I perceive she does. There's something in 't 20
That is deceivable.—But here the lady comes.

Enter OLIVIA *and* PRIEST.

OLIVIA. Blame not this haste of mine. If you mean well,
Now go with me and with this holy man
Into the chantry by: there, before him,
And underneath that consecrated roof,
Plight me the full assurance of your faith;
That my most jealous and too doubtful soul
May live at peace. He shall conceal it
Whiles you are willing it shall come to note,

SC. 3: 6. *credit:* belief. 9. *sense:* evidence of my senses. 12. *discourse:* reason. 15. *trust:* belief. 21. *deceivable:* delusive. 24. *chantry:* chapel. 26. *assurance:* i.e., betrothal not marriage. 29. *Whiles:* till. *to note:* to be known.

354 TWELFTH NIGHT [ACT V

What time we will our celebration keep 30
According to my birth.—What do you say?
  SEBASTIAN. I'll follow this good man, and go with you;
And, having sworn truth, ever will be true.
  OLIVIA. Then lead the way, good father; and heavens so shine,
That they may fairly note this act of mine! *Exeunt.*

Act V

SCENE 1. *Before* OLIVIA'S *house.*

Enter CLOWN *and* FABIAN.

FABIAN. Now, as thou lovest me, let me see his letter.
CLOWN. Good Master Fabian, grant me another request.
FABIAN. Any thing.
CLOWN. Do not desire to see this letter.
FABIAN. This is, to give a dog, and in recompense desire my dog again.

Enter DUKE, VIOLA, CURIO, *and* LORDS.

DUKE. Belong you to the Lady Olivia, friends?
CLOWN. Ay, sir; we are some of her trappings.
DUKE. I know thee well; how dost thou, my good fellow?
CLOWN. Truly, sir, the better for my foes and the worse for [10
my friends.
DUKE. Just the contrary; the better for thy friends.
CLOWN. No, sir, the worse.
DUKE. How can that be?
CLOWN. Marry, sir, they praise me and make an ass of me; now my foes tell me plainly I am an ass: so that by my foes, sir, I profit in the knowledge of myself, and by my friends I am abused: so that, conclusions to be as kisses, if your four negatives make your two affirmatives, why then, the worse for my friends and the better for my foes. 20
DUKE. Why, this is excellent.

---

30. *What time:* at which time. *celebration:* marriage. 31. *according:* suitably.
  ACT V, SC. 1: 18. It takes two people to make one kiss.

SCENE 1] TWELFTH NIGHT 355

CLOWN. By my troth, sir, no; though it please you to be one of my friends.

DUKE. Thou shalt not be the worse for me; there's gold.

CLOWN. But that it would be double-dealing, sir, I would you could make it another.

DUKE. O, you give me ill counsel.

CLOWN. Put your grace in your pocket, sir, for this once, and let your flesh and blood obey it.

DUKE. Well, I will be so much a sinner to be a double-dealer; [30 there's another.

CLOWN. Primo, secundo, tertio, is a good play; and the old saying is, the third pays for all: the triplex, sir, is a good tripping measure; or the bells of Saint Bennet, sir, may put you in mind; one, two, three.

DUKE. You can fool no more money out of me at this throw; if you will let your lady know I am here to speak with her, and bring her along with you, it may awake my bounty further.

CLOWN. Marry, sir, lullaby to your bounty till I come again. I go, sir; but I would not have you to think that my desire of having is the sin of covetousness: but, as you say, sir, let your bounty take [40 a nap, I will awake it anon.   *Exit.*

VIOLA. Here comes the man, sir, that did rescue me.

Enter ANTONIO *and* OFFICERS.

DUKE. That face of his I do remember well;
Yet, when I saw it last, it was besmear'd
As black as Vulcan in the smoke of war.
A bawbling vessel was he captain of,
For shallow draught and bulk unprizable;
With which such scathful grapple did he make
With the most noble bottom of our fleet,
That very envy and the tongue of loss   50
Cried fame and honour on him.—What's the matter?

1 OFFICER. Orsino, this is that Antonio

---

28. *grace:* virtue. 32. *Primo, secundo, tertio:* first, second, third. 33. *triplex:* triple time (in music). 34. He mimics the chime. 45. *Vulcan:* blacksmith-god. 46. *bawbling:* paltry. 47. *unprizable:* of little worth. 48. *scathful:* damaging. 49. *bottom:* vessel. 50. "that those who envied him and declared what losses he had inflicted on them . . ."

That took the Phœnix and her fraught from Candy;
And this is he that did the Tiger board,
When your young nephew Titus lost his leg.
Here in the streets, desperate of shame and state,
In private brabble did we apprehend him.

VIOLA. He did me kindness, sir, drew on my side;
But in conclusion put strange speech upon me:
I know not what 't was but distraction.

DUKE. Notable pirate! thou salt-water thief!
What foolish boldness brought thee to their mercies,
Whom thou, in terms so bloody and so dear,
Hast made thine enemies?

ANTONIO. Orsino, noble sir,
Be pleas'd that I shake off these names you give me;
Antonio never yet was thief or pirate,
Though I confess, on base and ground enough,
Orsino's enemy. A witchcraft drew me hither:
That most ingrateful boy there by your side,
From the rude sea's enrag'd and foamy mouth
Did I redeem; a wrack past hope he was:
His life I gave him, and did thereto add
My love, without retention or restraint,
All his in dedication; for his sake
Did I expose myself, pure for his love,
Into the danger of this adverse town;
Drew to defend him when he was beset:
Where being apprehended, his false cunning,
Not meaning to partake with me in danger,
Taught him to face me out of his acquaintance,
And grew a twenty-years-removed thing
While one would wink; denied me mine own purse,
Which I had recommended to his use
Not half an hour before.

VIOLA. How can this be?
DUKE. When came he to this town?

---

57. *brabble:* squabble. 60. *distraction:* madness. 71. "There was no hope for him." 74. *in dedication:* dedicated. 75. *pure:* purely. 76. *adverse:* hostile. 78. *being apprehended:* when I was arrested. 83. *recommended:* entrusted.

ANTONIO. To-day, my lord; and for three months before,
No interim, not a minute's vacancy,
Both day and night did we keep company.

Enter OLIVIA *and* ATTENDANTS.

DUKE. Here comes the countess; now heaven walks on earth.—
But for thee, fellow—fellow, thy words are madness: 90
Three months this youth hath tended upon me;
But more of that anon.—Take him aside.
 OLIVIA. What would my lord, but that he may not have,
Wherein Olivia may seem serviceable?—
Cesario, you do not keep promise with me.
 VIOLA. Madam!
 DUKE. Gracious Olivia,—
 OLIVIA. What do you say, Cesario?—Good my lord,—
 VIOLA. My lord would speak, my duty hushes me.
 OLIVIA. If it be aught to the old tune, my lord 100
It is as fat and fulsome to mine ear
As howling after music.
 DUKE.   Still so cruel?
 OLIVIA. Still so constant, lord.
 DUKE. What, to perverseness? you uncivil lady,
To whose ingrate and unauspicious altars
My soul the faithfull'st offerings hath breath'd out
That e'er devotion tender'd! What shall I do?
 OLIVIA. Even what it please my lord, that shall become him.
 DUKE. Why should I not, had I the heart to do it,
Like to the Egyptian thief at point of death, 110
Kill what I love?—a savage jealousy
That sometime savours nobly. But hear me this:
Since you to non-regardance cast my faith,
And that I partly know the instrument
That screws me from my true place in your favour,
Live you the marble-breasted tyrant still;
But this your minion, whom I know you love,

---

87. *vacancy:* duration. 110. The story is told of a certain Thyamis: he tried to kill his sweetheart so that no one else should have her. 117. *minion:* "boy friend."

358   TWELFTH NIGHT   [ACT V

And whom, by heaven I swear, I tender dearly,
Him will I tear out of that cruel eye,
Where he sits crowned in his master's spite.—   120
Come, boy, with me; my thoughts are ripe in mischief:
I'll sacrifice the lamb that I do love,
To spite a raven's heart within a dove.
   VIOLA. And I, most jocund, apt, and willingly,
To do you rest, a thousand deaths would die.
   OLIVIA. Where goes Cesario?
   VIOLA.   After him I love
More than I love these eyes, more than my life,
More, by all mores, than e'er I shall love wife.—
If I do feign, you witnesses above
Punish my life for tainting of my love!   130
   OLIVIA. Ay me, detested! how am I beguil'd!
   VIOLA. Who does beguile you? who does do you wrong?
   OLIVIA. Hast thou forgot thyself! is it so long?
Call forth the holy father.
   DUKE.   Come, away!
   OLIVIA. Whither, my lord?—Cesario, husband, stay.
   DUKE. Husband!
   OLIVIA.   Ay, husband; can he that deny?
   DUKE. Her husband, sirrah!
   VIOLA.   No, my lord, not I.
   OLIVIA. Alas, it is the baseness of thy fear
That makes thee strangle thy propriety!
Fear not, Cesario; take thy fortunes up: 140
Be that thou know'st thou art, and then thou art
As great as that thou fear'st.—

Enter PRIEST.

                    O, welcome, father!
Father, I charge thee, by thy reverence,
Here to unfold, though lately we intended
To keep in darkness what occasion now

---

119. *cruel eye:* i.e., the eye of Olivia. 120. *in his master's spite:* in order to cast spite on his master. 122 ff. This "artificial" climax is appropriately in rhymed couplets.

SCENE 1] TWELFTH NIGHT 359

Reveals before 't is ripe, what thou dost know
Hath newly pass'd between this youth and me.
  PRIEST. A contract of eternal bond of love,
Confirm'd by mutual joinder of your hands,
Attested by the holy close of lips, 150
Strengthen'd by interchangement of your rings,
And all the ceremony of this compact
Seal'd in my function, by my testimony;
Since when, my watch hath told me, toward my grave
I have travell'd but two hours.
  DUKE. O thou dissembling cub! what wilt thou be
When time hath sow'd a grizzle on thy case?
Or will not else thy craft so quickly grow,
That thine own trip shall be thine overthrow?
Farewell, and take her; but direct thy feet 160
Where thou and I henceforth may never meet.
  VIOLA. My lord, I do protest—
  OLIVIA.   O, do not swear!
Hold little faith, though thou hast too much fear.

Enter SIR ANDREW.

  SIR ANDREW. For the love of God, a surgeon! Send one presently to Sir Toby.
  OLIVIA. What's the matter?
  SIR ANDREW. He has broke my head across and has given Sir Toby a bloody coxcomb too; for the love of God, your help! I had rather than forty pound I were at home.
  OLIVIA. Who has done this, Sir Andrew? 170
  SIR ANDREW. The count's gentleman, one Cesario; we took him for a coward, but he's the very devil incardinate.
  DUKE. My gentleman, Cesario?
  SIR ANDREW. 'Od's lifelings, here he is!—You broke my head for nothing; and that that I did, I was set on to do 't by Sir Toby.
  VIOLA. Why do you speak to me? I never hurt you:
You drew your sword upon me without cause;

---

149. *joinder:* joining. 157. *case:* body. 159. *thine own trip:* thy tripping-up of others. 163. *hold little faith:* have at least a little faith. 168. *coxcomb:* head. 172. *incardinate:* an Aguecheekism for *incarnate.*

But I bespake you fair, and hurt you not.

SIR ANDREW. If a bloody coxcomb be a hurt, you have hurt me; I think you set nothing by a bloody coxcomb. 180

Enter SIR TOBY *and* CLOWN.

Here comes Sir Toby halting; you shall hear more: but if he had not been in drink, he would have tickled you othergates than he did.

DUKE. How now, gentleman! how is 't with you?

SIR TOBY. That's all one; he has hurt me, and there's the end on 't. —Sot, didst see Dick surgeon, sot?

CLOWN. O, he's drunk, Sir Toby, an hour agone; his eyes were set at eight i' the morning.

SIR TOBY. Then he's a rogue, and a passy-measures pavin I hate a drunken rogue.

OLIVIA. Away with him!—Who hath made this havoc with them? [190

SIR ANDREW. I'll help you, Sir Toby, because we'll be dressed together.

SIR TOBY. Will you help? an ass-head and a coxcomb and a knave, a thin-faced knave, a gull!

OLIVIA. Get him to bed, and let his hurt be look'd to.

Exeunt CLOWN, FABIAN, SIR TOBY, *and* SIR ANDREW.

Enter SEBASTIAN.

SEBASTIAN. I am sorry, madam, I have hurt your kinsman.
But, had it been the brother of my blood,
I must have done no less with wit and safety.
You throw a strange regard upon me, and by that 200
I do perceive it hath offended you;
Pardon me, sweet one, even for the vows
We made each other but so late ago.

DUKE. One face, one voice, one habit, and two persons.
A natural perspective, that is and is not!

SEBASTIAN. Antonio, O my dear Antonio!

---

178. *bespake you fair:* spoke courteously to you. 182. *othergates:* otherwise. 186. *set:* fixed (he is drunk). 188. *passy-measures pavin:* a dance. Nonsense? 192. *be dressed:* have our wounds dressed. 194-5. For the moment, at any rate, Sir Toby is willing to let Andrew—and his money—go.

How have the hours rack'd and tortur'd me
Since I have lost thee!

ANTONIO. Sebastian are you?

SEBASTIAN. Fear'st thou that, Antonio?

ANTONIO. How have you made division of yourself?— 210
An apple, cleft in two, is not more twin
Than these two creatures. Which is Sebastian?

OLIVIA. Most wonderful!

SEBASTIAN. Do I stand there? I never had a brother;
Nor can there be that deity in my nature,
Of here and everywhere. I had a sister,
Whom the blind waves and surges have devour'd.—
Of charity, what kin are you to me?
What countryman? what name? what parentage?

VIOLA. Of Messaline: Sebastian was my father; 220
Such a Sebastian was my brother too,
So went he suited to his watery tomb.
If spirits can assume both form and suit,
You come to fright us.

SEBASTIAN. A spirit I am indeed;
But am in that dimension grossly clad
Which from the womb I did participate.
Were you a woman, as the rest goes even,
I should my tears let fall upon your cheek,
And say, Thrice-welcome, drowned Viola!

VIOLA. My father had a mole upon his brow. 230

SEBASTIAN. And so had mine.

VIOLA. And died that day when Viola from her birth
Had number'd thirteen years.

SEBASTIAN. O, that record is lively in my soul!
He finished indeed his mortal act
That day that made my sister thirteen years.

VIOLA. If nothing lets to make us happy both
But this my masculine usurp'd attire,

215-16. "the divine ability to be in two places at once." 222. *suited:* dressed.
223. *suit:* dress. 224. *A spirit I am:* i.e., I have a soul. 225. *dimension:* shape.
226. *participate:* acquire. 227. *as the rest goes even:* since all else fits in.
235. *act:* i.e., an act in a play. 237. *lets:* hinders.

362 TWELFTH NIGHT [ACT V

Do not embrace me till each circumstance
Of place, time, fortune, do cohere and jump 240
That I am Viola: which to confirm,
I'll bring you to a captain in this town,
Where lie my maiden weeds; by whose gentle help
I was preserv'd to serve this noble count.
All the occurrence of my fortune since
Hath been between this lady and this lord.
    SEBASTIAN, *to* OLIVIA. So comes it, lady, you have been mistook;
But nature to her bias drew in that.
You would have been contracted to a maid;
Nor are you therein, by my life, deceiv'd,
You are betroth'd both to a maid and man. 250
    DUKE. Be not amaz'd; right noble is his blood.—
If this be so, as yet the glass seems true,
I shall have share in this most happy wrack.—
To VIOLA. Boy, thou hast said to me a thousand times
Thou never shouldst love woman like to me.
    VIOLA. And all those sayings will I over-swear;
And all those swearings keep as true in soul
As doth that orbed continent the fire
That severs day from night.
    DUKE.   Give me thy hand; 260
And let me see thee in thy woman's weeds.
    VIOLA. The captain that did bring me first on shore
Hath my maid's garments; he upon some action
Is now in durance, at Malvolio's suit,
A gentleman, and follower of my lady's.
    OLIVIA. He shall enlarge him.—Fetch Malvolio hither;—
And yet, alas, now I remember me,
They say, poor gentleman, he's much distract.

    Re-enter CLOWN *with a letter, and* FABIAN.

---

240. *Jump:* tally. 243. *weeds:* clothes. 248. *to her bias drew:* went her own way. 253. The *perspective* of l. 205 above is probably a *glass* that produces an optical illusion of two instead of one. 259-60. Possibly, "as the firmament, an orbed continent, keeps the fire that severs day from night, this fire being the sun." 264. *durance:* prison. 266. *enlarge:* set free. 268. *distract:* mad.

A most extracting frenzy of mine own
From my remembrance clearly banish'd his.—   270
How does he, sirrah?

CLOWN. Truly, madam, he holds Belzebub at the stave's end as well as a man in his case may do: he has here writ a letter to you; I should have given 't you to-day morning, but as a madman's epistles are no gospels, so it skills not much when they are delivered.

OLIVIA. Open 't, and read it.

CLOWN. Look then to be well edified when the fool delivers the madman. *Reads.* 'By the Lord, madam,'—

OLIVIA. How now! art thou mad?

CLOWN. No, madam, I do but read madness: an your lady- [280 ship will have it as it ought to be, you must allow vox.

OLIVIA. Prithee, read i' thy right wits.

CLOWN. So I do, madonna; but to read his right wits is to read thus: therefore perpend, my princess, and give ear.

OLIVIA, *to* FABIAN. Read it you, sirrah.

FABIAN, *reads.* 'By the Lord, madam, you wrong me, and the world shall know it; though you have put me into darkness and given your drunken cousin rule over me, yet have I the benefit of my senses as well as your ladyship. I have your own letter that induced me to the semblance I put on; with the which I doubt not but to   [290 do myself much right, or you much shame. Think of me as you please. I leave my duty a little unthought of, and speak out of my injury.

                                    THE MADLY-USED MALVOLIO.'

OLIVIA. Did he write this?

CLOWN. Ay, madam.

DUKE. This savours not much of distraction.

OLIVIA. See him deliver'd, Fabian; bring him hither.—

                                                Exit FABIAN.

My lord, so please you, these things further thought on,
To think me as well a sister as a wife,
One day shall crown the alliance on 't, so please you,   300
Here at my house and at my proper cost.

DUKE. Madam, I am most apt to embrace your offer.—

---

269. *extracting:* distracting. 272. *Belzebub:* the devil. 275. *skills:* matters. 281. *vox:* voice. 284. *perpend:* ponder.

To VIOLA. Your master quits you; and for your service done him,
So much against the mettle of your sex,
So far beneath your soft and tender breeding,
And since you call'd me master for so long,
Here is my hand; you shall from this time be
Your master's mistress.

OLIVIA.   A sister! you are she.

Re-enter FABIAN, *with* MALVOLIO.

DUKE. Is this the madman?

OLIVIA.   Ay, my lord, this same.—
How now, Malvolio!

MALVOLIO.   Madam, you have done me wrong,   310
Notorious wrong.

OLIVIA.   Have I, Malvolio? no.

MALVOLIO. Lady, you have. Pray you, peruse that letter.
You must not now deny it is your hand:
Write from it, if you can, in hand or phrase;
Or say 't is not your seal, not your invention.
You can say none of this: well, grant it then,
And tell me, in the modesty of honour,
Why you have given me such clear lights of favour,
Bade me come smiling and cross-garter'd to you,
To put on yellow stockings and to frown   320
Upon Sir Toby and the lighter people;
And, acting this in an obedient hope,
Why have you suffer'd me to be imprison'd,
Kept in a dark house, visited by the priest,
And made the most notorious geck and gull
That e'er invention play'd on? tell me why.

OLIVIA. Alas, Malvolio, this is not my writing,
Though, I confess, much like the character
But out of question 't is Maria's hand.
And now I do bethink me, it was she   330
First told me thou wast mad; then cam'st in smiling,

---

304. *mettle:* nature. 314. *from:* different from. 318. *lights:* indications. 325. *geck:* dupe.

SCENE 1]   TWELFTH NIGHT   365

And in such forms which here were presuppos'd
Upon thee in the letter. Prithee, be content:
This practice hath most shrewdly pass'd upon thee;
But when we know the grounds and authors of it,
Thou shalt be both the plaintiff and the judge
Of thine own cause.

FABIAN.   Good madam, hear me speak,
And let no quarrel nor no brawl to come
Taint the condition of this present hour,
Which I have wonder'd at. In hope it shall not,   340
Most freely I confess, myself and Toby
Set this device against Malvolio here,
Upon some stubborn and uncourteous parts
We had conceiv'd against him. Maria writ
The letter at Sir Toby's great importance;
In recompense whereof he hath married her.
How with a sportful malice it was follow'd,
May rather pluck on laughter than revenge;
If that the injuries be justly weigh'd
That have on both sides pass'd.   350

OLIVIA. Alas, poor fool, how have they baffled thee!

CLOWN. Why, 'some are born great, some achieve greatness, and some have greatness thrown upon them.' I was one, sir, in this interlude; one Sir Topas, sir; but that's all one.—'By the Lord, fool, I am not mad.'—But do you remember? 'Madam, why laugh you at such a barren rascal? an you smile not, he's gagged.' And thus the whirligig of time brings in his revenges.

MALVOLIO. I'll be reveng'd on the whole pack of you.   *Exit.*

OLIVIA. He hath been most notoriously abus'd.

DUKE. Pursue him and entreat him to a peace.   360
He hath not told us of the captain yet;
When that is known and golden time convents,
A solemn combination shall be made
Of our dear souls.—Meantime, sweet sister,
We will not part from hence.—Cesario, come;

---

339. *condition:* viz., happiness. 343. *Upon:* because of. 344. "which we believed he showed us." 345. *importance:* importunity. 354. *interlude:* drama. 362. *golden time convents:* happy moment is convenient.

366 TWELFTH NIGHT

For so you shall be, while you are a man;
But when in other habits you are seen,
Orsino's mistress and his fancy's queen. *Exeunt all, except* CLOWN.
 CLOWN, *sings.*

    'When that I was and a little tiny boy,
     With hey, ho, the wind and the rain,   370
    A foolish thing was but a toy,
     For the rain it raineth every day.'

    'But when I came to man's estate,
     With hey, ho, the wind and the rain,
    'Gainst knaves and thieves men shut their gate
     For the rain it raineth every day.'

    'But when I came, alas! to wive,
     With hey, ho, the wind and the rain,
    By swaggering could I never thrive,
     For the rain it raineth every day.'   380

    'But when I came unto my beds,
     With hey, ho, the wind and the rain,
    With toss-pots still had drunken heads,
     For the rain it raineth every day.'

    'A great while ago the world begun,
     With hey, ho, the wind and the rain,
    But that's all one, our play is done,
     And we'll strive to please you every day.'   *Exit.*

*

TAKING THE TIP given in the last editorial comment, the reader may ask: to what effect does Shakespeare use his "cinematic" structure? The basic pattern seems to be the alternation of scenes. There are two types of material in *Twelfth Night:* the romance of Viola and Sebastian, and the low comedy of Sir Toby and Sir Andrew. Shakespeare alternates them.

---

367. *habits:* clothes. 369. *and*—a superfluous word. 371. *a toy:* triviality.

Asked why Shakespeare does this, the reader might suggest that he is aiming at variety or (putting the same thought negatively) at preventing the audience from going to sleep. This is to regard Shakespeare as simply an entertainer and as an entertainer in our modern world where boredom is taken to be the state of mind into which we all descend unless redeemed from it by special stimulus. A less cynical reader might suggest that dramatic art consists of this sort of entertainment *plus an instructive element:* it is common nowadays to speak separately of what a work of art teaches (its "message") and of the pleasure it imparts (its "entertainment value"). But is this the best account of dramatic art? The present editor suggests that a playwright is a man who makes statements about life—more precisely, who defines a subject—by theatrical means. If we like the way he does it, we are *ipso facto* entertained. Thus the question whether a work is entertaining does not arise as a separate problem. We need only ask whether it is good.

This is a very general question until we apply it. Let us push further the investigation of the alternation of scenes in *Twelfth Night*. It might be regarded as Shakespeare's way of defining his theme. What *is* his theme? Another big, hard question. Shakespearean drama is about as far removed as possible from crude propaganda, Drama with a Message. It is true that books on Shakespeare used to be full of talk about his wisdom, supported by quotation of edifying passages; we have all seen such quotations adorning the houses of our elderly relatives. However, we can only regard these fine sentiments as the themes of Shakespeare's plays if we commit the Number 1 Error in dramatic criticism, which is to assume that what a character says the author would endorse. Even if there *is* a character who speaks the author's views he is not necessarily announcing also the theme of the play! Just as the word *plot* implies a unification of the action, the word *theme* implies a unification of the meaning. Is there any idea that runs through the whole of *Twelfth Night*? Which is therefore present in both strands of the plot? Short of finding a formula to sum up the play, one might suggest that *the idea of love* is deeply embedded in it. If we follow the idea of love through the play we shall, perhaps, uncover most of Shakespeare's thematic material. (In approaching other Shakespeare plays later this procedure may be found useful: to find *an* idea, *a* theme, and, without assuming that it is *the* idea, *the* theme, to find what is done with it from one end of the play to the other. If such a theme does not itself embrace the whole meaning of the play, the hope is that it may lead us to it.)

Twelfth Night presents love on different levels, not merely to the end of amusing us with life's variety, but of distinguishing between (*a*) higher and lower and (*b*) truer and falser. The romance shows love on the higher plane, the comedy of Sir Toby love on a lower plane. On either plane love may be true or false, genuine or spurious. Sir Andrew's love for Olivia is spurious. It is not a spontaneous or maturely human feeling. It is something he considers to be expected of him. It is ridiculous because mechanical. Sir Toby's love for Maria, on the other hand, is, for all its limitations, genuine enough, a natural and straightforward attachment. On the higher plane, three kinds of false love are defined: Orsino's, Olivia's, and Malvolio's. All are founded on vanity. All three of these people speak in a vein of neurotic intensity. Orsino is the most obvious case. "Give me excess of it" seems to be his motto. He is in love with love. It is appropriate that he sound the theme of love in the opening and closing lines of the play: "If music be the food of love, play on," and "Orsino's mistress and his fancy's [love's] queen." But Orsino's own love seems close to a death-wish, and the Clown knows what he is about when he sings "Come away, death" to him ("away" meaning "here"). Olivia's love, when we first meet her, is for her brother, but, since he is dead, her giving undivided attention to him seems strained and unnatural. She too is in love, not with a person, but with one of her own attitudes—grief. That she is courted by Orsino is an ironical fact. Parallelism and contrast. In such juxtapositions and confrontations Shakespeare renders his idea.

Take Malvolio. As a solemn humbug he is a fit companion for Olivia's "false" love. When he is made to smile, Olivia sees the falseness of the merry mood but realizes that her own sadness is just as false. "I am as mad as he/If sad and merry madness equal be." Shakespeare has used a piece of comic business to bring something home to one of his characters. Olivia grants that her sadness is "mad" —that is, beyond the bounds of commonsense and humanity.

Twelfth Night describes the "education" of Olivia and (perhaps) Orsino at the hands of fate and—Viola. Audiences and critics have always found Viola a charming heroine; it is only necessary to add that the charm has a dramatic and thematic function. Viola is the still point in all the bustle of the action, in all the critical analysis of love. Her love is as natural as Sir Toby's and on as high a plane of imagination as Orsino's. In order to appreciate the beauty and theme might be described as the contrast of the natural and the arti-subtlety of the portrayal, as well as its point, one should look back at her early scenes with Orsino and Olivia respectively. Here the ficial—of Viola's natural feelings with the self-dramatizations of her two lovers.

Viola occupies so crucial a place in Shakespeare's scheme that he involves her in both plots, the romance and the low comedy. There is another character who passes easily from one plot to the other: Feste the Jester or Clown. What—to Shakespeare—is a clown? Not what he is to the modern circus or rodeo audience, nothing so broad and acrobatic. He wears cap and bells but a fairly natural make-up. He is a court entertainer, and his specialty is a sort of word-play that today we do not find very funny. Luckily, Shakespeare was not content to give us the conventional clown. Just as in *The Merchant of Venice* he interests himself in the man's heart that beats beneath the conventional gabardine of the stage Jew, so in *Twelfth Night* he gives his clown a realistic twist. When we learn that Feste is past his best and that Malvolio would like to have him dismissed, our attention is called from arid word-play to a sad human situation.

An actor playing Feste can easily exaggerate the sadness. There have been productions in which his melancholy has overwhelmed the play and in which he has been added to the list of Olivia's wooers! What is delicate and marvelous in Shakespeare's creation, surely, is the way the balance is held between the fun and the sadness. Pushed a little further, *Twelfth Night* might, like *The Miser,* have become a pathetic drama, if not a tragedy. The way Shakespeare refuses to "push" can best be illustrated by the final song, where so fine a balance between the trivial and the significant is struck. "A long time ago the world begun. . . ." It is as though Feste were about to utter grave cosmic reflections, were about to interpret the whole of history. "But that's all one: our play is done." The thing is a joke —a celebration for the twelfth night after Christmas, when life was turned topsy-turvy under the patronage of a Lord of Misrule. Feste himself is the Lord of Misrule in this revel in which appearances, traditionally, contradict realities. "Nothing that is so is so," he declares (IV. 1. 6-7). Watch his seemingly casual entrances and exits, and you will find he is brought up against all the major characters, that he exchanges words with all of them, and always—in a deeper sense —comes off best. (Only Viola shares his knowledge of life's contradictions. It is she who uses the terms *fair-cruelty*, I. 5. 242; *proper-false*, II. 2. 26; *beauteous evil*, III. 4. 322.)

If *Twelfth Night* is *about* the things just discussed, we can return to our original question as to structure and form: the alternation of scenes is an apt—indeed obvious—way of rendering high and low life and contrasting them. In this way Shakespeare gives us his impression of the mixed character of life.

But this is not all. Supposing we had the romance alone, and no Sir Toby or Sir Andrew. It isn't comic relief that would be missing. It is—reality. Even with Viola in it, the romance can scarcely be said to have any anchor in common life. It is the comic subplot that provides this—and constantly, by the continuous reminder of the alternate scenes. Probably no modern reader would even *want* the romance alone. On the contrary, some might gladly take Sir Toby and Sir Andrew and throw the romance overboard. If one has never read a story like that of these twins before, or if one associates such stories only with bad literature, one may at first reject the romance as silly. Even so, one may come to accept (say) the marriage of Olivia and Sebastian if one lives for a short time within the world of romance and myth as Shakespeare has created it—if one reads and re-reads or if one takes part in a production. After this one would find the comic subplot *in itself* rather dull. Only in alternation with the romance is it either significant or amusing. If the romance is all love (of one kind and another), the low comedy balances it with the power-motif: it is a matter of social status (Malvolio) and money (Sir Andrew is only present at all because Sir Toby wants his money). At this point it becomes necessary to enlarge our conception of *realism*. If it is the unrealistic elements of their technique that first strike us in Molière and Shakespeare, we are later impressed by the tough, seamy realism of their social and economic analyses.

In their realism the two great playwrights join hands. They also have in common a narrative pattern: both *Twelfth Night* and *The*

Miser tell a story of shipwreck and long-lost relatives, of parting and reunion, disguise and unmasking. If we wish to know what is different in Shakespeare, we shall find it partly (if we have time to look) in the different technique of Elizabethan theater and partly (if we have the critical gift to find it) in his special genius as a dramatic poet. Here one of the leading topics for investigation is Shakespeare's language. One way of entering upon the topic is by tracing through a play certain key-words or ideas, such as (in *Twelfth Night*) *time, fortune, madness*. If one follows the *music* of its first line and the *storm* of its second scene through the final *song* about *rain,* one discovers the "recurring imagery" of the play, a "recurring image" being comparable to a recurring theme in music. Stretch this point a little, and we can say that Shakespeare uses symbolism. Storms and music are a symbolic contrast, the former (obviously) standing for disorder, the latter for order. . . . It is for each reader to decide how far to continue such analyses and speculations. Here our concern is to show how full a field for investigation a Shakespeare play is. Not least a comedy. T. S. Eliot has called the pattern of *Twelfth Night* (and *A Midsummer Night's Dream*) "more complex and elaborate than any constructed by a dramatist before or since."

5. OTHELLO · 1604

Twelfth Night is called a comedy, *Othello* a tragedy. We shall not be concerned here with the definition of these terms, beyond observing that whereas Shakespeare (as already noted) seems deliberately to prevent the sad situations in his comedies from developing beyond a certain stage, the tragedies are the plays in which he lets them develop to the limit. If this observation is correct, the tragedies and comedies differ, so to say, only in degree. As to plot, character, theme and so forth, they have much in common.

A convenient starting-point for the study of *Othello* is the idea of a contradiction between appearances and reality. It is an idea that pervades *Twelfth Night*. "Nothing that is so is so." The whole story of the twins enforces the idea: "I am ready to distrust mine eyes / And wrangle with my reason. . . . There's something in't / That is deceivable" (IV, 3, 13 ff.). In *Othello* Iago seems honest and isn't. Othello does not seem jealous but is. Desdemona is given a double twist. She seems chaste and is; but Othello doesn't think so; his opinion is that, though she seems chaste, she isn't; his discovery is that, though in Iago's accounts she seemed unchaste, she is actually chaste. "Men should be what they seem" (III. 3. 130).

Dramatic irony, then, the irony of things not being as they seem, is equally pervasive in *Twelfth Night* and *Othello*. But, whereas in the comedy the irony of a happy ending is added to it, in the tragedy it is allowed to work itself out to what is aptly termed the bitter (i.e., unironical) end. In the last act of *Twelfth Night* the ironies are straightened out by a time-honored comic device, the dénouement or untying of the knots. At the beginning Viola says: "O time! Thou must untie this knot, not I," and at the end the clown pronounces: "And thus the whirligig of time brings in his revenges." The disorder of person, events, and time is dissolved. In *Othello* Shakespeare drives his hero to the very threshold of death—and beyond.

The reader is invited to read *Othello* with the idea of appearance and reality in mind. It is not to be assumed that the idea is "the theme" of the play. The idea has utility of the kind suggested above (pp. 367-68): it will lead deep into the play. It is something to focus the attention, for, in confronting a work of art, one can never begin by looking with equal attention at all its parts.

If Shakespearean comedy and tragedy are similar, it follows that anything learned from the reading of *Twelfth Night* can be applied to the reading of *Othello*. In both plays, Shakespeare's scenes are assembled like music, in that deliberate changes of tempo and tone are of their very substance. This does *not* mean that we are to fall into that habit of "just listening to the poetry" which in practice means "not listening to the sense." A Shakespeare play is not a series of arias or recitations. It is not a bundle of Famous Passages. Total ignorance of all Shakespeare's lines is a better starting-point for the understanding of Shakespeare than is a knowledge of tags, famous soliloquies, purple passages. Like the Bible, Shakespeare has been ruined by the quoters and reciters. Someone starts to intone, and we give to what we hear a special and inferior sort of attention: the words wash over us, we know them almost by heart, but we limit our attention to their "music," and are indifferent to their context, their vitality, their meaning. Shakespearean actors who chant their lines resemble preachers who use the narcotic Bible Voice.

As much as Molière, Shakespeare presents a plot, and usually a pretty complicated one. It is obvious that the Elizabethans loved complications of plot, expected masses of narrative. Unless we can share this passionate interest of theirs, we shall not understand them. Perhaps we need to forget what we have learned about Shakespeare and remember what we know about the detective story. *What Happens in Hamlet* is the title of a modern book, but it is a topic seldom considered by modern readers, spectators, directors, or actors. Modern productions are so heavily and unwisely cut that it is often impossible to follow the plot; but nobody complains, because it is assumed either that Shakespeare's plots are "unfollowable" in the first place or that plot is unimportant. Such assumptions must not be made.

OTHELLO

by William Shakespeare

*

Othello

Characters

DUKE OF VENICE
BRABANTIO, *a senator*
OTHER SENATORS
GRATIANO, *brother to Brabantio*
LODOVICO, *kinsman to Brabantio*
OTHELLO, *a noble Moor in the service of the Venetian state*
CASSIO, *his lieutenant*
IAGO, *his ancient*
RODERIGO, *a Venetian gentleman*
MONTANO, *Othello's predecessor in the government of Cyprus*
CLOWN, *servant to Othello*
DESDEMONA, *daughter to Brabantio and wife to Othello*
EMILIA, *wife to Iago*
BIANCA, *mistress to Cassio*

Sailor, Messenger, Herald, Officers, Gentlemen, Musicians, and Attendants.

THE PLACE: *Venice and a seaport on the island of Cyprus.*

Act I

SCENE 1. *Venice. A street.*

Enter RODERIGO *and* IAGO.

RODERIGO. Tush, never tell me; I take it much unkindly
That thou, Iago, who hast had my purse
As if the strings were thine, shouldst know of this.
    IAGO. 'Sblood, but you will not hear me:
If ever I did dream of such a matter,
Abhor me.

378   OTHELLO   [ACT I

RODERIGO. Thou told'st me thou didst hold him in thy hate.

IAGO. Despise me, if I do not. Three great ones of the city,
In personal suit to make me his lieutenant,
Off-capp'd to him: and, by the faith of man,   10
I know my price, I am worth no worse a place:
But he, as loving his own pride and purposes,
Evades them, with a bombast circumstance
Horribly stuff'd with epithets of war;
And, in conclusion,
Nonsuits my mediators; for, 'Certes,' says he,
'I have already chose my officer.'
And what was he?
Forsooth, a great arithmetician,
One Michael Cassio, a Florentine,   20
A fellow almost damn'd in a fair wife;
That never set a squadron in the field,
Nor the division of a battle knows
More than a spinster; unless the bookish theoric,
Wherein the togèd consuls can propose
As masterly as he: mere prattle without practice
Is all his soldiership. But he, sir, had the election
And I, of whom his eyes had seen the proof
At Rhodes, at Cyprus, and on other grounds
Christian and heathen, must be be-lee'd and calm'd   30
By debitor and creditor: this counter-caster,
He, in good time, must his lieutenant be,
And I—God bless the mark!—his Moorship's ancient.

RODERIGO. By heaven, I rather would have been his hangman.

IAGO. Why, there's no remedy; 'tis the curse of service,

ACT I, SC. 1: 11. *price:* value. 13. *circumstance:* harangue. *bombast:* bombastic. 14. *epithets:* technical terms. 16. *nonsuits:* dismisses. 19. *arithmetician:* mathematician. 21. *wife:* woman (i.e., with a fatal weakness for women) (?) 23. *division:* how any army is divided into squadrons, etc. 24. *unless:* except. *theoric:* theory. 25. *togèd:* clad in togas, robes. *consuls:* counsellors, senators. *propose:* talk. 27. *had the election:* was selected. 30. *be-lee'd:* have the wind taken out of my sails. 31. *debitor and creditor:* a mere "arithmetician." *counter-caster:* one who counts by means of tokens, counters. 33. *ancient:* ensign. 35. *service:* military service.

Preferment goes by letter and affection,
And not by old gradation, where each second
Stood heir to the first. Now, sir, be judge yourself
Whether I in any just term am affined
To love the Moor.
  RODERIGO.   I would not follow him then.   40
  IAGO. O, sir, content you;
I follow him to serve my turn upon him:
We cannot all be masters, nor all masters
Cannot be truly follow'd. You shall mark
Many a duteous and knee-crooking knave,
That doting on his own obsequious bondage
Wears out his time, much like his master's ass,
For nought but provender, and when he's old, cashier'd:
Whip me such honest knaves. Others there are
Who, trimm'd in forms and visages of duty,   50
Keep yet their hearts attending on themselves,
And throwing but shows of service on their lords
Do well thrive by them, and when they have lined their coats
Do themselves homage: these fellows have some soul,
And such a one do I profess myself.
For, sir,
It is as sure as you are Roderigo,
Were I the Moor, I would not be Iago:
In following him, I follow but myself;
Heaven is my judge, not I for love and duty,   60
But seeming so, for my peculiar end:
For when my outward action doth demonstrate
The native act and figure of my heart
In compliment extern, 'tis not long after

---

36. *preferment:* promotion. *letter:* i.e., of recommendation. *affection:* love, favoritism. 37. *gradation:* proceeding regularly from one rank to the next. 39. *affined:* related in such a way as. 40. *follow:* serve. 47. *time:* lifetime. 48. *cashier'd:* turned away. 49. *honest knaves:* honorable fellows. (*Honest* is a key-word in the play: it can also mean *chaste.*) 50. *trimm'd:* dressed. 52. *throwing:* giving. 54. "*Do . . .*": i.e., serve only themselves. 58. Inference: "But being Iago, I am not the Moor." 60. *not I:* I do not do so. 63. *figure:* purpose. 64. *compliment extern:* external appearance.

380   OTHELLO   [ACT I

But I will wear my heart upon my sleeve
For daws to peck at: I am not what I am.
  RODERIGO. What a full fortune does the thick-lips owe,
If he can carry 't thus!
  IAGO.   Call up her father,
Rouse him: make after him, poison his delight,
Proclaim him in the streets; incense her kinsmen,   70
And, though he in a fertile climate dwell,
Plague him with flies: though that his joy be joy,
Yet throw such changes of vexation on 't
As it may lose some colour.
  RODERIGO. Here is her father's house; I'll call aloud.
  IAGO. Do; with like timorous accent and dire yell
As when, by night and negligence, the fire
Is spied in populous cities.
  RODERIGO. What, ho, Brabantio! Signior Brabantio, ho!
  IAGO. Awake! what, ho, Brabantio! thieves! thieves! thieves!   80
Look to your house, your daughter and your bags!
Thieves! thieves!

             BRABANTIO *appears above, at a window.*

  BRABANTIO. What is the reason of this terrible summons?
What is the matter there?
  RODERIGO. Signior, is all your family within?
  IAGO. Are your doors lock'd?
  BRABANTIO.   Why, wherefore ask you this?
  IAGO. 'Zounds, sir, you're robb'd; for shame, put on your gown;
Your heart is burst, you have lost half your soul;
Even now, now, very now, an old black ram
Is tupping your white ewe. Arise, arise;   90
Awake the snorting citizens with the bell,
Or else the devil will make a grandsire of you:
Arise, I say.
  BRABANTIO. What, have you lost your wits?
  RODERIGO. Most reverend signior, do you know my voice?

---

66. *daws:* jackdaws (stupid birds). 67. *a full fortune:* good luck. *owe:* have.
71. *fertile climate:* fortunate circumstances. 90. *tupping:* lying on top of.
91. *snorting:* snoring.

SCENE 1]   OTHELLO   381

 BRABANTIO. Not I: what are you?
 RODERIGO. My name is Roderigo.
 BRABANTIO.   The worser welcome:
I have charged thee not to haunt about my doors:
In honest plainness thou hast heard me say
My daughter is not for thee; and now, in madness,
Being full of supper and distempering draughts,   100
Upon malicious bravery, dost thou come
To start my quiet.
 RODERIGO. Sir, sir, sir,—
 BRABANTIO.   But thou must needs be sure.
My spirit and my place have in them power
To make this bitter to thee.
 RODERIGO.   Patience, good sir.
 BRABANTIO. What tell'st thou me of robbing? this is Venice;
My house is not a grange.
 RODERIGO.   Most grave Brabantio,
In simple and pure soul I come to you.
 IAGO. 'Zounds, sir, you are one of those that will not serve God, if
the devil bid you. Because we come to do you service and [110
you think we are ruffians, you'll have your daughter covered with a
Barbary horse; you'll have your nephews neigh to you; you'll have
coursers for cousins, and gennets for germans.
 BRABANTIO. What profane wretch art thou?
 IAGO. I am one, sir, that comes to tell you your daughter and the
Moor are now making the beast with two backs.
 BRABANTIO. Thou art a villain.
 IAGO.   You are—a senator.
 BRABANTIO. This thou shalt answer; I know thee, Roderigo.
 RODERIGO. Sir, I will answer any thing. But, I beseech you, 120
If 't be your pleasure and most wise consent,
As partly I find it is, that your fair daughter,
At this odd-even and dull watch o' the night,

---

100. *distempering:* disturbing. 101. *Upon malicious bravery:* from a malicious wish to brave me. 102. *start:* startle. 107. *grange:* farmhouse. 111. *covered:* "tupped." 112. *Barbary:* North Africa. 113. *cousins, germans:* relatives. *gennets:* Barbary horses. 116. *beast with two backs:* visual image of copulation. 119. *answer* for. 123. *odd-even:* vague hour. *dull watch:* sleepy time.

Transported with no worse nor better guard
But with a knave of common hire, a gondolier,
To the gross clasps of a lascivious Moor,—
If this be known to you, and your allowance,
We then have done you bold and saucy wrongs;
But if you know not this, my manners tell me
We have your wrong rebuke. Do not believe 130
That, from the sense of all civility,
I thus would play and trifle with your reverence:
Your daughter, if you have not given her leave,
I say again, hath made a gross revolt,
Tying her duty, beauty, wit and fortunes,
In an extravagant and wheeling stranger
Of here and every where. Straight satisfy yourself:
If she be in her chamber or your house,
Let loose on me the justice of the state
For thus deluding you.
   BRABANTIO.   Strike on the tinder, ho! 140
Give me a taper! call up all my people!
This accident is not unlike my dream:
Belief of it oppresses me already.
Light, I say! light!   *Exit above.*
   IAGO.   Farewell; for I must leave you:
It seems not meet, nor wholesome to my place,
To be produced—as, if I stay, I shall—
Against the Moor: for I do know, the state,
However this may gall him with some check,
Cannot with safety cast him; for he's embark'd
With such loud reason to the Cyprus wars, 150
Which even now stand in act, that, for their souls,
Another of his fathom they have none
To lead their business: in which regard,
Though I do hate him as I do hell pains,

---

126. *gross clasps:* coarse embraces. 127. *your allowance:* allowed by you. 129. *manners:* knowledge of conduct. 131. *from:* contrary to. 132. *your reverence:* respect due you. 136. *extravagant, wheeling:* wandering, changing residence. 137. *straight:* at once. 142. *my dream:* a dream I was just having. 145. *meet:* suitable. *place:* job. 146. *produced*—as a witness. 148. *gall:* irritate. 149. *cast him* off. 150. *loud:* imperious. 152. *fathom:* ability.

SCENE 1] OTHELLO 383

Yet for necessity of present life,
I must show out a flag and sign of love,
Which is indeed but sign. That you shall surely find him,
Lead to the Sagittary the raised search;
And there will I be with him. So farewell. *Exit.*

Enter, below, BRABANTIO, *in his night-gown, and* SERVANTS
with torches.

BRABANTIO. It is too true an evil: gone she is; 160
And what's to come of my despised time
Is nought but bitterness. Now, Roderigo,
Where didst thou see her? O unhappy girl!
With the Moor, say'st thou? Who would be a father!
How didst thou know 'twas she? O, she deceives me
Past thought! What said she to you? Get more tapers.
Raise all my kindred. Are they married, think you?

RODERIGO. Truly, I think they are.

BRABANTIO. O heaven! How got she out? O treason of the blood!
Fathers, from hence trust not your daughters' minds 170
By what you see them act. Is there not charms
By which the property of youth and maidhood
May be abused? Have you not read, Roderigo,
Of some such thing?

RODERIGO. Yes, sir, I have indeed.

BRABANTIO. Call up my brother. O, would *you* had had her!
Some one way, some another. Do you know
Where we may apprehend her and the Moor?

RODERIGO. I think I can discover him, if you please
To get good guard and go along with me.

BRABANTIO. Pray you, lead on. At every house I'll call; 180
I may command at most. Get weapons, ho!
And raise some special officers of night.
On, good Roderigo; I'll deserve your pains. *Exeunt.*

---

155. *life:* livelihood. 158. *Sagittary:* name of an inn (like Elephant in *Twelfth Night*). 161. *time:* lifetime. 169. Fornication would be treason against the aristocratic family ideal. 171. *charms:* love potions, etc. 172. *property:* nature. *maidhood:* virginity. 173. *abused:* deceived. 175-7. Brabantio wishes Roderigo, rather than Othello, had "had" Desdemona. He is talking to different people in different directions. 177. *apprehend:* arrest. 181. *most* of them. 182. *of night:* on night duty.

384 OTHELLO [ACT I

SCENE 2. *Another street.*

Enter OTHELLO, IAGO, *and* ATTENDANTS *with torches.*

IAGO. Though in the trade of war I have slain men,
Yet do I hold it very stuff o' the conscience
To do no contrived murder: I lack iniquity
Sometimes to do me service: nine or ten times
I had thought to have yerk'd him here under the ribs.
  OTHELLO. 'Tis better as it is.
  IAGO.   Nay, but he prated
And spoke such scurvy and provoking terms
Against your honour,
That, with the little godliness I have,
I did full hard forbear him. But I pray you, sir,   10
Are you fast married? Be assured of this,
That the magnifico is much beloved,
And hath in his effect a voice potential
As double as the duke's: he will divorce you,
Or put upon you what restraint and grievance
The law, with all his might to enforce it on,
Will give him cable.
  OTHELLO.   Let him do his spite:
My services, which I have done the signiory,
Shall out-tongue his complaints. 'Tis yet to know—
Which, when I know that boasting is an honour,   20
I shall promulgate—I fetch my life and being
From men of royal siege, and my demerits
May speak unbonneted to as proud a fortune
As this that I have reach'd: for know, Iago,
But that I love the gentle Desdemona,
I would not my unhoused free condition

SC. 2: 3. *contrived:* deliberate. 5. *yerk'd:* struck. 12. *magnifico:* grandee (i.e., Brabantio). 13. *in his effect a voice potential:* a voice powerful in its effect. 14. *double:* counting as two votes. 15. *what:* whatever. *grievance:* annoyance. 17. *cable* to do. *spite:* worst. 18. *signiory:* government. 22. *siege:* seat (i.e., who sat on thrones). *demerits:* merits, deserts. 24. *this:* viz., alliance with Brabantio's family.

SCENE 2] OTHELLO 385

Put into circumscription and confine
For the sea's worth. But, look! what lights come yond?
  IAGO. Those are the raised father and his friends:
You were best go in.
  OTHELLO.   Not I; I must be found:
My parts, my title and my perfect soul,
Shall manifest me rightly. Is it they?
  IAGO. By Janus, I think no.

Enter CASSIO, *and certain* OFFICERS *with torches.*

  OTHELLO. The servants of the duke, and my lieutenant.
The goodness of the night upon you, friends!
What is the news?
  CASSIO.   The duke does greet you, general,
And he requires your haste-post-haste appearance,
Even on the instant.
  OTHELLO.   What is the matter, think you?
  CASSIO. Something from Cyprus, as I may divine:
It is a business of some heat: the galleys
Have sent a dozen sequent messengers
This very night at one another's heels;
And many of the consuls, raised and met,
Are at the duke's already: you have been hotly call'd for;
When, being not at your lodging to be found,
The senate hath sent about three several quests
To search you out.
  OTHELLO.   'Tis well I am found by you.
I will but spend a word here in the house,
And go with you.   *Exit.*
  CASSIO.   Ancient, what makes he here?
  IAGO. Faith, he to-night hath boarded a land carack:
If it proved lawful prize, he's made for ever.
  CASSIO. I do not understand.
  IAGO.   He's married.
  CASSIO.   To who?

---

31. i.e., "My deeds, my rank, and my unstained conscience." 38. *matter:*
business. 41. *sequent:* following one another. 43. *consuls:* senators. 50.
carack: merchant vessel. 51. *made:* his fortune's made (cf. Malvolio: "Am I
made?")

Re-enter OTHELLO.

IAGO. Marry, to—Come, captain, will you go?
OTHELLO. Have with you.
CASSIO. Here comes another troop to seek for you.
IAGO. It is Brabantio: general, be advised;
He comes to bad intent.

Enter BRABANTIO, RODERIGO, *and* OFFICERS
with torches and weapons.

OTHELLO. Holla! stand there!
RODERIGO. Signior, it is the Moor.
BRABANTIO. Down with him, thief!
They draw on both sides.
IAGO. You, Roderigo! come, sir, I am for you.
OTHELLO. Keep up your bright swords, for the dew will rust them.
Good signior, you shall more command with years 60
Than with your weapons.
BRABANTIO. O thou foul thief, where hast thou stow'd my daughter?
Damn'd as thou art, thou hast enchanted her;
For I'll refer me to all things of sense,
If she in chains of magic were not bound,
Whether a maid so tender, fair and happy,
So opposite to marriage that she shunn'd
The wealthy curled darlings of our nation,
Would ever have, to incur a general mock,
Run from her guardage to the sooty bosom 70
Of such a thing as thou, to fear, not to delight.
Judge me the world, if 'tis not gross in sense
That thou hast practised on her with foul charms,
Abused her delicate youth with drugs or minerals
That weaken motion: I'll have 't disputed on;
'Tis probable, and palpable to thinking.
I therefore apprehend and do attach thee
For an abuser of the world, a practiser

---

53. *Have with you:* I'm coming. 59. *up:* in the scabbard (cf. Sir Toby's "put up your swords"). 64. "For I'll appeal to all men in their senses." 72. *gross in sense:* obvious to the senses. 73. *practised on:* plotted against.

Of arts inhibited and out of warrant.
Lay hold upon him: if he do resist, 80
Subdue him at his peril.

OTHELLO.   Hold your hands,
Both you of my inclining and the rest:
Were it my cue to fight, I should have known it
Without a prompter. Where will you that I go
To answer this your charge?

BRABANTIO.   To prison, till fit time
Of law and course of direct session
Call thee to answer.

OTHELLO.   What if I do obey?
How may the duke be therewith satisfied,
Whose messengers are here about my side,
Upon some present business of the state 90
To bring me to him?

1 OFFICER.   'Tis true, most worthy signior;
The duke's in council, and your noble self,
I am sure, is sent for.

BRABANTIO.   How! the duke in council!
In this time of the night! Bring him away:
Mine's not an idle cause: the duke himself,
Or any of my brothers of the state,
Cannot but feel this wrong as 'twere their own;
For if such actions may have passage free,
Bond-slaves and pagans shall our statesmen be.   *Exeunt.*

SCENE 3. *A council-chamber.*

The DUKE *and* SENATORS *sitting at a table;* OFFICERS *attending.*

DUKE. There is no composition in these news
That gives them credit.

1 SENATOR.   Indeed they are disproportion'd;

---

79. *inhibited:* prohibited. *out of warrant:* unwarranted, illegal. 82. *of my inclining:* on my side. 86. *direct:* regular. 99. "Slaves and pagans shall marry into our families and take over."

sc. 3: 1. *composition:* consistency. 2. *gives them credit:* makes them believed. *disproportion'd:* disagree as to numbers.

388 OTHELLO [ACT I

My letters say a hundred and seven galleys.
  DUKE. And mine, a hundred and forty.
  2 SENATOR.   And mine, two hundred:
But though they jump not on a just account,—
As in these cases, where the aim reports,
'Tis oft with difference,—yet do they all confirm
A Turkish fleet, and bearing up to Cyprus.
  DUKE. Nay, it is possible enough to judgement:
I do not so secure me in the error,   10
But the main article I do approve
In fearful sense.
  SAILOR, *within*. What, ho! what, ho! what, ho!
  1 OFFICER. A messenger from the galleys.

                    Enter SAILOR.

  DUKE.   Now, what's the business?
  SAILOR. The Turkish preparation makes for Rhodes;
So was I bid report here to the state
By Signior Angelo.
  DUKE. How say you by this change?
  1 SENATOR.   This cannot be,
By no assay of reason: 'tis a pageant
To keep us in false gaze. When we consider
The importancy of Cyprus to the Turk,   20
And let ourselves again but understand
That as it more concerns the Turk than Rhodes,
So may he with more facile question bear it,
For that it stands not in such warlike brace,
But altogether lacks the abilities
That Rhodes is dress'd in: if we make thought of this,
We must not think the Turk is so unskilful
To leave that latest which concerns him first,
Neglecting an attempt of ease and gain,

---

5. *jump:* tally. 10. *secure me in:* lull myself with. 11. *article:* point. *approve:* believe. 12. *in fearful sense:* so as to be alarmed. 14. *for Rhodes:* i.e., *not* for Cyprus. 18. *assay:* test. *pageant:* show. 19. *false gaze:* looking the wrong way. 23. "So he can capture it with less trouble." 24. *brace:* posture. 25. *abilities:* resources.

SCENE 3]   OTHELLO   389

To wake and wage a danger profitless.   30
    DUKE. Nay, in all confidence, he's not for Rhodes.
    1 OFFICER. Here is more news.

Enter a MESSENGER.

    MESSENGER. The Ottomites, reverend and gracious,
Steering with due course toward the isle of Rhodes,
Have there injointed them with an after fleet.
    1 SENATOR. Ay, so I thought. How many, as you guess?
    MESSENGER. Of thirty sail: and now they do re-stem
Their backward course, bearing with frank appearance
Their purposes toward Cyprus. Signior Montano,
Your trusty and most valiant servitor,   40
With his free duty recommends you thus,
And prays you to believe him.
    DUKE. 'Tis certain then for Cyprus.
Marcus Luccicos, is not he in town?
    1 SENATOR. He's now in Florence.
    DUKE. Write from us to him; post-post-haste dispatch.
    1 SENATOR. Here comes Brabantio and the valiant Moor.

Enter BRABANTIO, OTHELLO, IAGO, RODERIGO, *and* OFFICERS.

    DUKE. Valiant Othello, we must straight employ you
Against the general enemy Ottoman.
To BRABANTIO. I did not see you; welcome, gentle signior;   50
We lack'd your counsel and your help to-night.
    BRABANTIO. So did I yours. Good your grace, pardon me;
Neither my place nor aught I heard of business
Hath raised me from my bed, nor doth the general care
Take hold on me; for my particular grief
Is of so flood-gate and o'erbearing nature
That it engluts and swallows other sorrows,
And it is still itself.
    DUKE.   Why, what's the matter?

---

35. *injointed them:* joined themselves. *after:* second. 37-8. *re-stem their backward . . . :* steer back.

BRABANTIO. My daughter! O, my daughter!
ALL.   Dead?
BRABANTIO.   Ay, to me;
She is abused, stol'n from me and corrupted
By spells and medicines bought of mountebanks;
For nature so preposterously to err,
Being not deficient, blind, or lame of sense,
Sans witchcraft could not.
   DUKE. Whoe'er he be that in this foul proceeding
Hath thus beguiled your daughter of herself
And you of her, the bloody book of law
You shall yourself read in the bitter letter
After your own sense, yea, though our proper son
Stood in your action.
   BRABANTIO.   Humbly I thank your grace.
Here is the man, this Moor; whom now, it seems,
Your special mandate for the state-affairs
Hath hither brought.
   ALL.   We are very sorry for 't.
   DUKE, *to* OTHELLO. What in your own part can you say to this?
   BRABANTIO. Nothing, but this is so.
   OTHELLO. Most potent, grave, and reverend signiors,
My very noble and approved good masters,
That I have ta'en away this old man's daughter,
It is most true; true, I have married her:
The very head and front of my offending
Hath this extent, no more. Rude am I in my speech,
And little blest with the soft phrase of peace;
For since these arms of mine had seven years' pith,
Till now some nine moons wasted, they have used
Their dearest action in the tented field;
And little of this great world can I speak,
More than pertains to feats of broil and battle;
And therefore little shall I grace my cause

---

61. *mountebanks:* quacks. 63. *lame of sense:* lacking in intelligence. 64. *sans:* without. *could not* happen. 69. *sense:* interpretation. 70. *stood in:* was exposed to. 81. *rude:* crude. 84. i.e., till some ninth months ago. 84-5. *used their dearest action:* been most intensely active.

SCENE 3] OTHELLO 391

In speaking for myself. Yet, by your gracious patience,
I will a round unvarnish'd tale deliver 90
Of my whole course of love; what drugs, what charms,
What conjuration and what mighty magic—
For such proceeding I am charged withal—
I won his daughter.
    BRABANTIO.   A maiden never bold;
Of spirit so still and quiet that her motion
Blush'd at herself; and she—in spite of nature,
Of years, of country, credit, every thing—
To fall in love with what she fear'd to look on!
It is a judgement maim'd and most imperfect,
That will confess perfection so could err 100
Against all rules of nature; and must be driven
To find out practices of cunning hell,
Why this should be. I therefore vouch again,
That with some mixtures powerful o'er the blood,
Or with some dram conjured to this effect,
He wrought upon her.
    DUKE.   To vouch this, is no proof,
Without more certain and more overt test
Than these thin habits and poor likelihoods
Of modern seeming do prefer against him.
    1 SENATOR. But, Othello, speak: 110
Did you by indirect and forced courses
Subdue and poison this young maid's affections?
Or came it by request, and such fair question
As soul to soul affordeth?
    OTHELLO.   I do beseech you,
Send for the lady to the Sagittary,
And let her speak of me before her father:
If you do find me foul in her report,
The trust, the office I do hold of you,

---

90. *round:* blunt. 93. *withal:* with. 95-6. *her motion blushed:* strong emotion made her blush. 101. *must be driven:* one is forced. 104. *blood:* passions. 105. *conjured:* made efficacious. 103, 106. *vouch:* assent. 108. *habits:* clothes. 109. *modern seeming:* mere appearances. 111. *courses:* means. 114. the lovers' heart to heart. 117. *foul:* guilty.

Not only take away, but let your sentence
Even fall upon my life.

DUKE. Fetch Desdemona hither,

OTHELLO. Ancient, conduct them; you best know the place.

Exeunt IAGO *and* ATTENDANTS.

And till she come, as truly as to heaven
I do confess the vices of my blood,
So justly to your grave ears I'll present
How I did thrive in this fair lady's love
And she in mine.

DUKE. Say it, Othello.

OTHELLO. Her father loved me, oft invited me,
Still questioned me the story of my life
From year to year, the battles, sieges, fortunes,
That I have pass'd.
I ran it through, even from my boyish days
To the very moment that he bade me tell it:
Wherein I spake of most disastrous chances,
Of moving accidents by flood and field,
Of hair-breath 'scapes i' the imminent deadly breach,
Of being taken by the insolent foe,
And sold to slavery, of my redemption thence,
And portance in my travels' history:
Wherein of antres vast and deserts idle,
Rough quarries, rocks, and hills whose heads touch heaven,
It was my hint to speak,—such was the process;
And of the Cannibals that each other eat,
The Anthropophagi, and men whose heads
Do grow beneath their shoulders. This to hear
Would Desdemona seriously incline:
But still the house-affairs would draw her thence;
Which ever as she could with haste dispatch,
She 'ld come again, and with a greedy ear
Devour up my discourse: which I observing,

---

135. *accidents:* events. 136. *imminent deadly:* threatening imminent death.
139. *portance:* conduct. 140. *antres:* caves. *idle:* empty. 142. *hint:* opportunity (as in l. 166 below). *process:* story. 144. *Anthropophagi:* cannibals.

SCENE 3]   OTHELLO   393

Took once a pliant hour, and found good means
To draw from her a prayer of earnest heart
That I would all my pilgrimage dilate,
Whereof by parcels she had something heard,
But not intentively: I did consent,
And often did beguile her of her tears
When I did speak of some distressful stroke
That my youth suffer'd. My story being done,
She gave me for my pains a world of sighs:
She swore, in faith, 'twas strange, 'twas passing strange;   160
'Twas pitiful, 'twas wondrous pitiful:
She wish'd she had not heard it, yet she wish'd
That heaven had made her such a man: she thank'd me,
And bade me, if I had a friend that loved her,
I should but teach him how to tell my story,
And that would woo her. Upon this hint I spake:
She loved me for the dangers I had pass'd,
And I loved her that she did pity them.
This only is the witchcraft I have used.
Here comes the lady; let her witness it.   170

Enter DESDEMONA, IAGO, *and* ATTENDANTS.

DUKE. I think this tale would win my daughter too.
Good Brabantio,
Take up this mangled matter at the best:
Men do their broken weapons rather use
Than their bare hands.
  BRABANTIO.   I pray you, hear her speak:
If she confess that she was half the wooer,
Destruction on my head, if my bad blame
Light on the man! Come hither, gentle mistress:
Do you perceive in all this noble company
Where most you owe obedience?
  DESDEMONA.   My noble father,   180
I do perceive here a divided duty:

---

151. *pliant:* favorable. 154. *by parcels:* piecemeal. 155. *intentively:* with full attention. 173. "Make the best of a bad job."

To you I am bound for life and education;
My life and education both do learn me
How to respect you; you are the lord of duty,
I am hitherto your daughter: but here's my husband,
And so much duty as my mother show'd
To you, preferring you before her father,
So much I challenge that I may profess
Due to the Moor my lord.
  BRABANTIO.   God be with you! I have done.
Please it your grace, on to the state-affairs: 190
I had rather to adopt a child than get it.
Come hither, Moor:
I here do give thee that with all my heart,
Which, but thou hast already, with all my heart
I would keep from thee. For your sake, jewel,
I am glad at soul I have no other child;
For thy escape would teach me tyranny,
To hang clogs on them. I have done, my lord.
  DUKE. Let me speak like yourself, and lay a sentence
Which, as a grise or step, may help these lovers   200
Into your favour.
When remedies are past, the griefs are ended
By seeing the worst, which late on hopes depended.
To mourn a mischief that is past and gone
Is the next way to draw new mischief on.
What cannot be preserved when fortune takes,
Patience her injury a mockery makes.
The robb'd that smiles steals something from the thief;
He robs himself that spends a bootless grief.
  BRABANTIO. So let the Turk of Cyprus us beguile;   210
We lose it not so long as we can smile.
He bears the sentence well, that nothing bears

---

184. *How to respect you:* in what light to regard you. 188. *challenge that I may profess:* claim the right to declare. 191. *get:* beget. 194. *but thou hast:* but for the fact that thou hast it. 197. *escape:* escapade. 198. *clogs:* encumbrances. 199. *lay a sentence:* pronounce a principle. 200. *grise:* step. 203. *hopes:* expectations. 204. *mischief:* misfortune. 205. *next:* nearest. 207. Patience makes light of Fortune's injury. 209. *spends:* indulges. *bootless:* pointless.

But the free comfort which from thence he hears;
But he bears both the sentence and the sorrow,
That, to pay grief, must of poor patience borrow.
These sentences, to sugar or to gall,
Being strong on both sides, are equivocal:
But words are words; I never yet did hear
That the bruised heart was pieced through the ear.
I humbly beseech you, proceed to the affairs of state. 220

DUKE. The Turk with a most mighty preparation makes for Cyprus. Othello, the fortitude of the place is best known to you; and though we have there a substitute of most allowed sufficiency, yet opinion, a sovereign mistress of effects, throws a more safer voice on you: you must therefore be content to slubber the gloss of your new fortunes with this more stubborn and boisterous expedition.

OTHELLO. The tyrant custom, most grave senators,
Hath made the flinty and steel couch of war
My thrice-driven bed of down: I do agnize
A natural and prompt alacrity 230
I find in hardness; and do undertake
These present wars against the Ottomites.
Most humbly therefore bending to your state,
I crave fit disposition for my wife,
Due reference of place and exhibition,
With such accommodation and besort
As levels with her breeding.

DUKE.   If you please,
Be 't at her father's.

BRABANTIO.   I'll not have it so.

OTHELLO. Nor I.

DESDEMONA. Nor I, I would not there reside, 240
To put my father in impatient thoughts
By being in his eye. Most gracious duke,

---

213. *free:* i.e., from care. 219. *piecèd:* repaired. 222. *fortitude:* strength. 223. *substitute:* second-in-command (viz., Montano). *sufficiency:* ability. 224. *mistress of effects:* determinant of results. 225. *slubber:* smear. 229. *thrice-driven:* thrice sorted out (for softest feathers). *agnize:* recognize. 230. *alacrity:* stimulus. 233. *state:* authority. 234. *disposition:* provision. 235. *reference:* assignment. *exhibition:* money allowance. 236. *besort:* fitness.

To my unfolding lend your prosperous ear,
And let me find a charter in your voice
To assist my simpleness.
  DUKE. What would you, Desdemona?
  DESDEMONA. That I did love the Moor to live with him,
My downright violence and storm of fortunes
May trumpet to the world: my heart's subdued
Even to the very quality of my lord: 250
I saw Othello's visage in his mind,
And to his honours and his valiant parts
Did I my soul and fortunes consecrate.
So that, dear lords, if I be left behind,
A moth of peace, and he go to the war,
The rights for which I love him are bereft me,
And I a heavy interim shall support
By his dear absence. Let me go with him.
  OTHELLO. Let her have your voices.
Vouch with me, heaven, I therefore beg it not, 260
To please the palate of my appetite;
Nor to comply with heat—the young affects
In me defunct—and proper satisfaction;
But to be free and bounteous to her mind:
And heaven defend your good souls, that you think
I will your serious and great business scant
For she is with me. No, when light-wing'd toys
Of feather'd Cupid seel with wanton dullness
My speculative and officed instruments,
That my disports corrupt and taint my business, 270
Let housewives make a skillet of my helm,
And all indign and base adversities
Make head against my estimation!
  DUKE. Be it as you shall privately determine,

---

243. *unfolding:* disclosing. *prosperous:* friendly. 244. *charter:* authority. 248. "my violent action." 250. *quality:* profession. 256. i.e., rights to share his life. 259. *voices:* votes. 262. *heat:* sexual desire. *young affects:* feelings of youth. 263. *and proper satisfaction:* and I am satisfied. 265. *defend:* forbid. 267. *for:* because. *toys:* frivolities. 268. *seel:* close. 269. *speculative:* seeing. *officed:* having duties. 270. *disports:* pastimes. 271. *helm:* helmet. 272. *indign:* base. 273. *make head:* muster an army. *estimation:* reputation.

SCENE 3] OTHELLO 397

Either for her stay or going: the affair cries haste,
And speed must answer 't; you must hence to-night.

DESDEMONA. To-night, my lord?

DUKE.   This night.

OTHELLO.   With all my heart.

DUKE. At nine i' the morning here we'll meet again.
Othello, leave some officer behind,
And he shall our commission bring to you;   280
With such things else of quality and respect
As doth import you.

OTHELLO.   So please your grace, my ancient;
A man he is of honesty and trust:
To his conveyance I assign my wife,
With what else needful your good grace shall think
To be sent after me.

DUKE.   Let it be so.
Good night to every one. *To* BRABANTIO. And, noble signior,
If virtue no delighted beauty lack,
Your son-in-law is far more fair than black.

1 SENATOR. Adieu, brave Moor; use Desdemona well.   290

BRABANTIO. Look to her, Moor, if thou hast eyes to see:
She has deceived her father, and may thee.

                    Exeunt DUKE, SENATORS, OFFICERS, *&c.*

OTHELLO. My life upon her faith! Honest Iago,
My Desdemona must I leave to thee:
I prithee, let thy wife attend on her;
And bring them after in the best advantage.
Come, Desdemona; I have but an hour
Of love, of worldly matters and direction,
To spend with thee: we must obey the time.

                    Exeunt OTHELLO *and* DESDEMONA.

RODERIGO. Iago!   300

IAGO. What say'st thou, noble heart?

RODERIGO. What will I do, thinkest thou?

IAGO. Why, go to bed and sleep.

---

281. *quality and respect:* rank and honor. 282. *doth import:* are important to. 288. *delighted:* delighting. 296. *in the best advantage:* at the most favorable time. 298. The second *of* means *out of, stolen from.* 299. *the time:* i.e., the exigencies of the time.

RODERIGO. I will incontinently drown myself.

IAGO. If thou dost, I shall never love thee after. Why, thou silly gentleman!

RODERIGO. It is silliness to live when to live is torment; and then have we a prescription to die when death is our physician.

IAGO. O villanous! I have looked upon the world for four times seven years; and since I could distinguish betwixt a benefit and an injury, I never found man that knew how to love himself. Ere I would say I would drown myself for the love of a guinea-hen, I would change my humanity with a baboon.

RODERIGO. What should I do? I confess it is my shame to be so fond; but it is not in my virtue to amend it.

IAGO. Virtue! a fig! 'tis in ourselves that we are thus or thus. Our bodies are gardens; to the which our wills are gardeners: so that if we will plant nettles or sow lettuce, set hyssop and weed up thyme, supply it with one gender of herbs or distract it with many, either to have it sterile with idleness or manured with industry, why, the power and corrigible authority of this lies in our wills. If the balance of our lives had not one scale of reason to poise another of sensuality, the blood and baseness of our natures would conduct us to most preposterous conclusions: but we have reason to cool our raging motions, our carnal stings, our unbitted lusts; whereof I take this, that you call love, to be a sect or scion.

RODERIGO. It cannot be.

IAGO. It is merely a lust of the blood and a permission of the will. Come, be a man: drown thyself! drown cats and blind puppies. I have professed me thy friend, and I confess me knit to thy deserving with cables of perdurable toughness: I could never better stead thee than now. Put money in thy purse; follow thou the wars; defeat thy favour with an usurped beard; I say, put money in thy purse. It cannot be that Desdemona should long continue her love

---

304. *incontinently:* at once. 309-10. Thus we learn Iago's age. 312. *guinea-hen:* i.e., a woman. 313. *change:* exchange. 315. *fond:* foolish. *virtue:* character (strength of). 319. *gender:* species. *distract it with:* divide it among. 321. *corrigible:* correcting. 323. *blood:* passion. 325. *motions:* emotions. *unbitted:* without bit. 326. *sect:* cutting. 331. *perdurable:* enduring. 332. *stead:* stand in good stead. 333. *defeat thy favour:* spoil your looks. *usurped:* to which the face has no right.

SCENE 3]　　　　　　　　　　　　　OTHELLO　　　　　　　399

to the Moor—put money in thy purse—nor he his to her: it was a violent commencement, and thou shalt see an answerable sequestration; put but money in thy purse. These Moors are changeable in their wills:—fill thy purse with money. The food that to him now is as luscious as locusts, shall be to him shortly as bitter as colo- [339 quintida. She must change for youth: when she is sated with his body, she will find the error of her choice: she must have change, she must: therefore put money in thy purse. If thou wilt needs damn thyself, do it a more delicate way than drowning. Make all the money thou canst: if sanctimony and a frail vow betwixt an erring barbarian and a supersubtle Venetian be not too hard for my wits and all the tribe of hell, thou shalt enjoy her; therefore make money. A pox of drowning thyself! it is clean out of the way: seek thou rather to be hanged in compassing thy joy than to be drowned and go without her.　　　　　　　　　　　　　　　　　　　　　　　　　　　　　349

RODERIGO. Wilt thou be fast to my hopes, if I depend on the issue?

IAGO. Thou art sure of me: go, make money: I have told thee often, and I re-tell thee again and again, I hate the Moor: my cause is hearted; thine hath no less reason. Let us be conjunctive in our revenge against him: if thou canst cuckold him, thou dost thyself a pleasure, me a sport. There are many events in the womb of time, which will be delivered. Traverse; go, provide thy money. We will have more of this to-morrow. Adieu.

RODERIGO. Where shall we meet i' the morning?

IAGO. At my lodging.

RODERIGO. I'll be with thee betimes.　　　　　　　　　　　　　　　360

IAGO. Go to; farewell. Do you hear, Roderigo?

RODERIGO. What say you?

IAGO. No more of drowning, do you hear?

RODERIGO. I am changed: I'll go sell all my land.　　　　　　*Exit.*

IAGO. Thus do I ever make my fool my purse;
For I mine own gain'd knowledge should profane,

336-7. *sequestration:* estrangement. 339-40. *coloquintida:* a bitter medicine. 340. *change for youth:* change lovers in favour of a younger. 343. *Make:* assemble. 344. *sanctimony:* religion. *erring:* wandering. 348. *compassing:* achieving. 350. *fast:* loyal. 353. *hearted:* heartfelt. *conjunctive:* in partnership. 356. *Traverse:* go ahead. 364. *I am:* i.e., my mind is. 365. Exactly Sir Toby's attitude to Sir Andrew.

400 OTHELLO   [ACT II

If I would time expend with such a snipe
But for my sport and profit. I hate the Moor;
And it is thought abroad that 'twixt my sheets
He has done my office: I know not if 't be true;   370
But I for mere suspicion in that kind
Will do as if for surety. He holds me well;
The better shall my purpose work on him.
Cassio's a proper man: let me see now;
To get his place, and to plume up my will
In double knavery—How, how?—Let's see:—
After some time, to abuse Othello's ear
That he is too familiar with his wife.
He hath a person and a smooth dispose
To be suspected; framed to make women false.   380
The Moor is of a free and open nature,
That thinks men honest that but seem to be so;
And will as tenderly be led by the nose
As asses are.
I have 't. It is engender'd. Hell and night
Must bring this monstrous birth to the world's light.   *Exit.*

Act II

SCENE 1. *A sea-port in Cyprus. An open place near the quay.*

Enter MONTANO *and two* GENTLEMEN.

MONTANO. What from the cape can you discern at sea?
1 GENTLEMAN. Nothing at all: it is a high-wrought flood;
I cannot, 'twixt the heaven and the main,
Descry a sail.
MONTANO. Methinks the wind hath spoke aloud at land;
A fuller blast ne'er shook our battlements:
If it hath ruffian'd so upon the sea,

---

367. *snipe:* fool. 369. *'twixt my sheets:* in bed with my wife. 370. *office:* function. 371. *kind:* regard. 372. *for surety:* it were sure. *well:* in high regard. 374. *proper:* good-looking. 375. *place:* job. 377. *abuse:* deceive. 379. *dispose:* disposition. 381. *free:* frank. 383. *tenderly:* tamely.

SCENE 1]   OTHELLO   401

What ribs of oak, when mountains melt on them,
Can hold the mortise? What shall we hear of this?
  2 GENTLEMAN. A segregation of the Turkish fleet: 10
For do but stand upon the foaming shore,
The chidden billow seems to pelt the clouds;
The wind-shaked surge, with high and monstrous mane,
Seems to cast water on the burning bear,
And quench the guards of the ever-fixed pole:
I never did like molestation view
On the enchafed flood.
  MONTANO.   If that the Turkish fleet
Be not enshelter'd and embay'd, they are drown'd;
It is impossible to bear it out.

                Enter a third GENTLEMAN.

  3 GENTLEMAN. News, lads! our wars are done.   20
The desperate tempest hath so bang'd the Turks,
That their designment halts: a noble ship of Venice
Hath seen a grievous wreck and sufferance
On most part of their fleet.
  MONTANO. How! is this true?
  3 GENTLEMAN.   The ship is here put in,
A Veronesa; Michael Cassio,
Lieutenant to the warlike Moor Othello,
Is come on shore: the Moor himself at sea,
And is in full commission here for Cyprus.
  MONTANO. I am glad on 't; 'tis a worthy governor.   30
  3 GENTLEMAN. But this same Cassio, though he speak of comfort
Touching the Turkish loss, yet he looks sadly
And prays the Moor be safe; for they were parted
With foul and violent tempest.
  MONTANO.   Pray heavens he be;

ACT II, SC. 1: 8-9. Can the tenon stay in the mortise? 10. *segregation:* dispersal. 12. *chidden:* i.e., scolded by the wind. 14. *bear:* i.e., the Great Bear. 15. *guards:* i.e., two stars of the Little Bear. *pole:* pole star. 16. *molestation:* disorder. 17. *enchafed:* enraged. 19. *it:* the storm. *bear out:* survive. 22. *designment:* plan. 23. *sufferance:* disaster. 26. *a Veronesa:* a ship from Verona.

For I have served him, and the man commands
Like a full soldier. Let's to the seaside, ho!
As well to see the vessel that's come in
As to throw out our eyes for brave Othello,
Even till we make the main and the aerial blue
An indistinct regard.

3 GENTLEMAN.   Come, let's do so;
For every minute is expectancy
Of more arrivance.

Enter CASSIO.

CASSIO. Thanks, you the valiant of this warlike isle,
That so approve the Moor! O, let the heavens
Give him defence against the elements,
For I have lost him on a dangerous sea.

MONTANO. Is he well shipp'd?

CASSIO. His bark is stoutly timber'd, and his pilot
Of very expert and approved allowance;
Therefore my hopes, not surfeited to death,
Stand in bold cure.   *A cry within:* 'A sail, a sail, a sail!'

Enter a fourth GENTLEMAN.

CASSIO. What noise?

4 GENTLEMAN. The town is empty; on the brow o' the sea
Stand ranks of people, and they cry 'A sail!'

CASSIO. My hopes do shape him for the governor.   *Guns heard.*

2 GENTLEMAN. They do discharge their shot of courtesy:
Our friends at least.

CASSIO.   I pray you, sir, go forth,
And give us truth who 'tis that is arrived.

2 GENTLEMAN. I shall.   *Exit.*

MONTANO. But, good lieutenant, is your general wived?

CASSIO. Most fortunately: he hath achieved a maid

---

39. *main:* sea. *blue* air. 40. *an indistinct regard:* not distinct to the eye. 42. *arrivance:* arrivals. 44. *approve:* praise. 49. i.e., of allowed and approved expertness. 51. *Stand in bold cure:* are likely to be cured. 56. *shot of courtesy:* salute.

SCENE 1] OTHELLO 403

That paragons description and wild fame;
One that excels the quirks of blazoning pens,
And in the essential vesture of creation
Does tire the ingener.

Re-enter second GENTLEMAN.

               How now! who has put in?
  2 GENTLEMAN. 'Tis one Iago, ancient to the general.
  CASSIO. He has had most favourable and happy speed:
Tempests themselves, high seas, and howling winds,
The gutter'd rocks, and congregated sands,
Traitors ensteep'd to clog the guiltless keel,   70
As having sense of beauty, do omit
Their mortal natures, letting go safely by
The divine Desdemona.
  MONTANO.   What is she?
  CASSIO. She that I spake of, our great captain's captain,
Left in the conduct of the bold Iago;
Whose footing here anticipates our thoughts
A se'nnight's speed. Great Jove, Othello guard,
And swell his sail with thine own powerful breath,
That he may bless this bay with his tall ship,
Make love's quick pants in Desdemona's arms,   80
Give renew'd fire to our extincted spirits,
And bring all Cyprus comfort.

Enter DESDEMONA, EMILIA, IAGO, RODERIGO, *and* ATTENDANTS.

               O, behold,
The riches of the ship is come on shore!
Ye men of Cyprus, let her have your knees.
Hail to thee, lady! and the grace of heaven,
Before, behind thee, and on every hand,
Enwheel thee round!
  DESDEMONA.   I thank you, valiant Cassio.

---

62. *paragons:* outdoes. *fame:* rumor. 63. *quirks:* flourishes. *blazoning:* descriptive. 65. *ingener:* the inventive mind. 70. *ensteep'd:* sunk. 71. *omit:* forego. 72. *mortal:* lethal. 75. *conduct:* escort. 76. *footing:* landing. 77. *se'nnight:* week. 81. *extincted:* depressed.

What tidings can you tell me of my lord?

CASSIO. He is not yet arrived: nor know I aught
But that he's well and will be shortly here.   90

DESDEMONA. O, but I fear—How lost you company?

CASSIO. The great contention of the sea and skies
Parted our fellowship—But, hark! a sail.

A cry within: 'A sail, a sail!' *Guns heard.*

2 GENTLEMAN. They give their greeting to the citadel:
This likewise is a friend.

CASSIO.   See for the news.   *Exit* GENTLEMAN.
Good ancient, your are welcome. *To* EMILIA. Welcome, mistress:
Let it not gall your patience, good Iago,
That I extend my manners; 'tis my breeding
That gives me this bold show of courtesy.   *Kissing her.*

IAGO. Sir, would she give you so much of her lips   100
As of her tongue she oft bestows on me,
You 'ld have enough.

DESDEMONA.   Alas, she has no speech.

IAGO. In faith, too much;
I find it still when I have list to sleep:
Marry, before your ladyship, I grant,
She puts her tongue a little in her heart
And chides with thinking.

EMILIA. You have little cause to say so.

IAGO. Come on, come on; you are pictures out of doors,
Bells in your parlours, wild-cats in your kitchens,   110
Saints in your injuries, devils being offended,
Players in your housewifery, and housewives in your beds.

DESDEMONA. O, fie upon thee, slanderer!

IAGO. Nay, it is true, or else I am a Turk:
You rise to play, and go to bed to work.

EMILIA. You shall not write my praise.

IAGO.   No, let me not.

DESDEMONA. What wouldst thou write of me, if thou shouldst

---

98. *extend:* make show of. 104. *list:* inclination. 109. "you are [as pretty as] pictures." 111. "Saints when you injure people." 112. *Players:* triflers. *housewives:* hussies. 115. This ribald remark is apparently not thought out of keeping.

praise me?

IAGO. O gentle lady, do not put me to 't;
For I am nothing if not critical.

DESDEMONA. Come on, assay—There's one gone to the [120
harbour?

IAGO. Ay, madam.

DESDEMONA. I am not merry; but I do beguile
The thing I am by seeming otherwise.
Come, how wouldst thou praise me?

IAGO. I am about it; but indeed my invention
Comes from my pate as birdlime does from frize;
It plucks out brains and all: but my Muse labours,
And thus she is deliver'd.
If she be fair and wise, fairness and wit,
The one's for use, the other useth it.   130

DESDEMONA. Well praised! How if she be black and witty?

IAGO. If she be black, and thereto have a wit,
She'll find a white that shall her blackness fit.

DESDEMONA. Worse and worse.

EMILIA. How if fair and foolish?

IAGO. She never yet was foolish that was fair;
For even her folly help'd her to an heir.

DESDEMONA. These are old fond paradoxes to make fools laugh i' the alehouse. What miserable praise hast thou for her that's foul and foolish?   140

IAGO. There's none so foul, and foolish thereunto,
But does foul pranks which fair and wise ones do.

DESDEMONA. O heavy ignorance! thou praisest the worst best. But what praise couldst thou bestow on a deserving woman indeed, one that in the authority of her merit did justly put on the vouch of very malice itself?

IAGO. She that was ever fair and never proud,
Had tongue at will and yet was never loud,
Never lack'd gold and yet went never gay,

---

119. *critical:* fault-finding. 120. *assay:* try. 123. *The thing I am:* viz., sad. 126. *birdlime:* a sticky substance. *frize:* a cloth. 131. *black:* dark, brunette, (considered ugly). 133. *white:* blond (considered beautiful). 138. *fond:* foolish. 139. *foul:* ugly. 143. *heavy:* stupid. 145. *put on the vouch:* win the approval. 149. *gay:* lavishly dressed.

Fled from her wish and yet said 'Now I may;'   150
She that, being anger'd, her revenge being nigh,
Bade her wrong stay and her displeasure fly;
She that in wisdom never was so frail
To change the cod's head for the salmon's tail;
She that could think and ne'er disclose her mind,
See suitors following and not look behind;
She was a wight, if ever such wight were,—

DESDEMONA. To do what?

IAGO. To suckle fools and chronicle small beer.

DESDEMONA. O most lame and impotent conclusion! Do not [160 learn of him, Emilia, though he be thy husband. How say you, Cassio? is he not a most profane and liberal counsellor?

CASSIO. He speaks home, madam: you may relish him more in the soldier than in the scholar.

IAGO, *aside.* He takes her by the palm: ay, well said, whisper: with as little a web as this will I ensnare as great a fly as Cassio. Ay, smile upon her, do; I will gyve thee in thine own courtship. You say true; 'tis so, indeed: if such tricks as these strip you out of your lieutenantry, it had been better you had not kissed your three fingers so oft, which now again you are most apt to play the sir [170 in. Very good; well kissed! an excellent courtesy! 'tis so, indeed. Yet again your fingers to your lips? would they were clyster-pipes for your sake!—   *Trumpet within.*
The Moor! I know his trumpet.

CASSIO. 'Tis truly so.

DESDEMONA. Let's meet him and receive him.

CASSIO. Lo, where he comes!

Enter OTHELLO *and* ATTENDANTS.

OTHELLO. O my fair warrior!

DESDEMONA.   My dear Othello!

---

154. i.e., to exchange the best part of a simple thing for the worst part of something with more prestige. 157. *wight:* person. 159. *chronicle:* write down (household accounts). 162. *liberal:* licentious. 165. *well said:* well done. 167. *gyve:* shackle. 170. *apt to play the sir:* ready to act the gentleman. 172. *clyster-pipes:* medical syringes (used for purging).

SCENE 1] OTHELLO 407

OTHELLO. It gives me wonder great as my content
To see you here before me. O my soul's joy! 180
If after every tempest come such calms,
May the winds blow till they have waken'd death!
And let the labouring bark climb hills of seas
Olympus-high, and duck again as low
As hell's from heaven! If it were now to die,
'Twere now to be most happy; for I fear,
My soul hath her content so absolute
That not another comfort like to this
Succeeds in unknown fate.
DESDEMONA.   The heavens forbid
But that our loves and comforts should increase, 190
Even as our days do grow!
OTHELLO.   Amen to that, sweet powers!
I cannot speak enough of this content;
It stops me here; it is too much of joy:
And this, and this, the greatest discords be   *Kissing her.*
That e'er our hearts shall make!
IAGO, *aside.*   O, you are well tuned now!
But I'll set down the pegs that make this music,
As honest as I am.
OTHELLO.   Come, let us to the castle.
News, friends; our wars are done, the Turks are drown'd.
How does my old acquaintance of this isle?
Honey, you shall be well desired in Cyprus; 200
I have found great love amongst them. O my sweet,
I prattle out of fashion, and I dote
In mine own comforts. I prithee, good Iago,
Go to the bay, and disembark my coffers:
Bring thou the master to the citadel;
He is a good one, and his worthiness
Does challenge much respect. Come, Desdemona,
Once more well met at Cyprus.   *Exeunt all but* IAGO *and* RODERIGO.
IAGO. Do thou meet me presently at the harbour. Come hither. If

---

179. *content:* contentment (also 187 and 192). 196. *the pegs:* of a string instrument. 203. *In mine own comforts:* because of my own joys. 205. *master:* ship's captain. 207. *challenge:* claim.

thou be'st valiant—as, they say, base men being in love [210 have then a nobility in their natures more than is native to them —list me. The lieutenant to-night watches on the court of guard. First, I must tell thee this: Desdemona is directly in love with him.

RODERIGO. With him! why, 'tis not possible.

IAGO. Lay thy finger thus, and let thy soul be instructed. Mark me with what violence she first loved the Moor, but for bragging and telling her fantastical lies: and will she love him still for prating? let not thy discreet heart think it. Her eye must be fed; and what delight shall she have to look on the devil? When the blood is made [220 dull with the act of sport, there should be, again to inflame it and to give satiety a fresh appetite, loveliness in favour, sympathy in years, manners and beauties; all which the Moor is defective in: now, for want of these required conveniences, her delicate tenderness will find itself abused, begin to heave the gorge, disrelish and abhor the Moor; very nature will instruct her in it and compel her to some second choice. Now, sir, this granted—as it is a most pregnant and unforced position—who stands so eminently in the degree of this fortune as Cassio does? a knave very voluble; no further conscionable than in putting on the mere form of civil and humane seeming, for [230 the better compassing of his salt and most hidden loose affection? why, none; why, none: a slipper and subtle knave; a finder out of occasions; that has an eye can stamp and counterfeit advantages, though true advantage never present itself: a devilish knave! Besides, the knave is handsome, young, and hath all those requisites in him that folly and green minds look after: a pestilent complete knave; and the woman hath found him already.

RODERIGO. I cannot believe that in her; she's full of most blest condition.

IAGO. Blest fig's-end! the wine she drinks is made of grapes: [240 if she had been blest, she would never have loved the Moor: blest

---

212. *list:* listen to. *watches:* keeps watch. *the court of:* the headquarters of the. 220. *blood:* passions. 221. *act of sport:* sexual intercourse. 222. *favour:* looks. 224. *tenderness:* fastidiousness. 227. *pregnant:* obvious. 228. *degree:* ladder. 229. *conscionable:* conscientious. 230. *civil, humane:* polite. 231. *compassing:* achieving. *salt, loose:* lecherous. 232. *slipper:* slippery. 233. *advantages:* opportunities. 236. *green:* naive. *pestilent:* 'damned.' 238-9. *blest condition:* heavenly qualities.

SCENE 1]   OTHELLO   409

pudding! Didst thou not see her paddle with the palm of his hand? didst not mark that?

RODERIGO. Yes, that I did; but that was but courtesy.

IAGO. Lechery, by this hand; an index and obscure prologue to the history of lust and foul thoughts. They met so near with their lips that their breaths embraced together. Villanous thoughts, Roderigo! when these mutualities so marshal the way, hard at hand comes the master and main exercise, the incorporate conclusion: pish! But, sir, be you ruled by me: I have brought you from Venice. Watch [250 you to-night; for the command, I'll lay 't upon you: Cassio knows you not: I'll not be far from you: do you find some occasion to anger Cassio, either by speaking too loud, or tainting his discipline, or from what other course you please, which the time shall more favourably minister.

RODERIGO. Well.

IAGO. Sir, he is rash and very sudden in choler, and haply may strike at you: provoke him, that he may; for even out of that will I cause these of Cyprus to mutiny; whose qualification shall come into no true taste again but by the displanting of Cassio. So shall [260 you have a shorter journey to your desires by the means I shall then have to prefer them, and the impediment most profitably removed, without the which there were no expectation of our prosperity.

RODERIGO. I will do this, if I can bring it to any opportunity.

IAGO. I warrant thee. Meet me by and by at the citadel: I must fetch his necessaries ashore. Farewell.

RODERIGO. Adieu.   *Exit.*

IAGO. That Cassio loves her, I do well believe it;
That she loves him, 'tis apt and of great credit:
The Moor, howbeit that I endure him not,   270
Is of a constant, loving, noble nature;
And I dare think he'll prove to Desdemona
A most dear husband. Now, I do love her too,

---

242. *paddle:* play (erotically). 245. *index:* forerunner. 248. *mutualities:* reciprocity. *marshal:* lead. 249. *master:* main. *incorporate:* (?) corporate, carnal. 250. *Watch:* be on guard duty. 251. *for:* as for. 253. *tainting:* throwing doubt on. 257. *choler:* anger. 259. *whose qualification:* the pacifying of whom. 259-60. *come into no true taste:* not resume its flavor. 262. *prefer:* promote. *removed:* shall be removed. 263. *prosperity:* success. 269. *apt:* likely. *of great credit:* very credible.

410   OTHELLO   [ACT II

Not out of absolute lust, though peradventure
I stand accountant for as great a sin,
But partly led to diet my revenge,
For that I do suspect the lusty Moor
Hath leap'd into my seat: the thought whereof
Doth like a poisonous mineral gnaw my inwards;
And nothing can or shall content my soul   280
Till I am even'd with him, wife for wife;
Or failing so, yet that I put the Moor
At least into a jealousy so strong
That judgement cannot cure. Which thing to do,
If this poor trash of Venice, whom I trash
For his quick hunting, stand the putting on,
I'll have our Michael Cassio on the hip,
Abuse him to the Moor in the rank garb;
For I fear Cassio with my night-cap too;
Make the Moor thank me, love me and reward me,   290
For making him egregiously an ass
And practising upon his peace and quiet
Even to madness. 'Tis here, but yet confused:
Knavery's plain face is never seen till used.   *Exit.*

SCENE 2. *A street.*

Enter a HERALD *with a proclamation; People following.*

HERALD. It is Othello's pleasure, our noble and valiant general, that upon certain tidings now arrived, importing the mere perdition of the Turkish fleet, every man put himself into triumph; some to dance, some to make bonfires, each man to what sport and revels his addiction leads him: for, besides these beneficial news, it is the celebration of his nuptial. So much was his pleasure should be pro-

---

275. *accountant:* accountable. 276. *diet:* feed. 278. *leap'd into my seat:* slept with my wife. 285. *whom I trash for:* whom I restrain from. 286. *stand:* go through with. 287. *on the hip:* in my power. 288. *rank garb:* coarse way. 289. He fears that Cassio too has slept with Emilia. 292. *practising:* plotting. 293. *Even to madness:* even if it drives him insane. *here:* i.e., in Iago's head. *but yet:* as yet.

sc. 2: 2. *mere perdition:* total loss. 3. *triumph:* celebrating. 6. *nuptial:* marriage.

claimed. All offices are open, and there is full liberty of feasting from this present hour of five till the bell have told eleven. Heaven bless the isle of Cyprus and our noble general Othello!   *Exeunt.*

SCENE 3. *A hall in the castle.*

Enter OTHELLO, DESDEMONA, CASSIO, *and* ATTENDANTS.

OTHELLO. Good Michael, look you to the guard to-night:
Let's teach ourselves that honourable stop,
Not to outsport discretion.
   CASSIO. Iago hath direction what to do;
But notwithstanding with my personal eye
Will I look to 't.
   OTHELLO.   Iago is most honest.
Michael, good night: to-morrow with your earliest
Let me have speech with you. Come, my dear love,
The purchase made, the fruits are to ensue;
That profit's yet to come 'tween me and you.   10
Good night.   *Exeunt* OTHELLO, DESDEMONA, *and* ATTENDANTS.

Enter IAGO.

CASSIO. Welcome, Iago; we must to the watch.
   IAGO. Not this hour, lieutenant; 'tis not yet ten o' the clock. Our general cast us thus early for the love of his Desdemona; who let us not therefore blame: he hath not yet made wanton the night with her, and she is sport for Jove.
   CASSIO. She's a most exquisite lady.
   IAGO. And, I'll warrant her, full of game.
   CASSIO. Indeed she's a most fresh and delicate creature.
   IAGO. What an eye she has! methinks it sounds a parley to [20 provocation.
   CASSIO. An inviting eye; and yet methinks right modest.
   IAGO. And when she speaks, is it not an alarum to love?
   CASSIO. She is indeed perfection.

---

7. *offices:* kitchen, etc. 8. *told:* numbered.
   sc. 3: 9-10. He refers to the consummation of their marriage. 14. *cast us:* cast us off. 15-22. Iago speaks in metaphors of sport and army life.

IAGO. Well, happiness to their sheets! Come, lieutenant, I have a stoup of wine; and here without are a brace of Cyprus gallants that would fain have a measure to the health of black Othello.

CASSIO. Not to-night, good Iago: I have very poor and unhappy brains for drinking: I could well wish courtesy would invent some other custom of entertainment.

IAGO. O, they are our friends; but one cup: I'll drink for you.

CASSIO. I have drunk but one cup to-night, and that was craftily qualified too, and behold what innovation it makes here: I am unfortunate in the infirmity, and dare not task my weakness with any more.

IAGO. What, man! 'tis a night of revels: the gallants desire it.

CASSIO. Where are they?

IAGO. Here at the door; I pray you, call them in.

CASSIO. I'll do 't; but it dislikes me.   *Exit.*

IAGO. If I can fasten but one cup upon him,
With that which he hath drunk to-night already,
He'll be as full of quarrel and offence
As my young mistress' dog. Now my sick fool Roderigo,
Whom love hath turn'd almost the wrong side out,
To Desdemona hath to-night caroused
Potations pottle-deep; and he's to watch:
Three lads of Cyprus, noble swelling spirits,
That hold their honours in a wary distance,
The very elements of this warlike isle,
Have I to-night fluster'd with flowing cups,
And they watch too. Now, 'mongst this flock of drunkards,
Am I to put our Cassio in some action
That may offend the isle. But here they come:
If consequence do but approve my dream,
My boat sails freely, both with wind and stream.

Re-enter CASSIO; *with him* MONTANO *and* GENTLEMEN;
SERVANTS *following with wine.*

---

26. *stoup:* flagon. 27. *measure:* draught. 32. *craftily:* on the sly. 33. *qualified:* diluted. *innovation:* change. 39. i.e., *I* dislike *it*. 46. *potations:* drinks. *pottle:* goblet. 48. *in a wary distance:* i.e., very gingerly. 49. i.e., they are typical of warlike Cyprus. 54. *consequence:* what follows. *approve:* confirm. *my dream:* what I have dreamt.

SCENE 3]   OTHELLO   413

CASSIO. 'Fore God, they have given me a rouse already.

MONTANO. Good faith, a little one; not past a pint, as I am a soldier.

IAGO. Some wine, ho!

Sings.   'And let me the canakin clink, clink   60
                And let me the canakin clink:
                    A soldier's a man;
                    A life's but a span;
                Why then let a soldier drink.'

Some wine, boys!

CASSIO. 'Fore God, an excellent song.

IAGO. I learned it in England, where indeed they are most potent in potting: your Dane, your German, and your swag-bellied Hollander,—Drink, ho!—are nothing to your English.

CASSIO. Is your Englishman so expert in his drinking?   70

IAGO. Why, he drinks you with facility your Dane dead drunk; he sweats not to overthrow your Almain; he gives your Hollander a vomit ere the next pottle can be filled.

CASSIO. To the health of our general!

MONTANO. I am for it, lieutenant, and I'll do you justice.

IAGO. O sweet England!

Sings.   'King Stephen was a worthy peer,
                His breeches cost him but a crown;
                He held them sixpence all too dear,
                With that he call'd the tailor lown.'   80

                'He was a wight of high renown,
                And thou art but of low degree:
                'Tis pride that pulls the country down;
                Then take thine auld cloak about thee.'

Some wine, ho!

CASSIO. Why, this is a more exquisite song than the other.

IAGO. Will you hear 't again?

---

56. *rouse:* a drink. 68. *potting:* drinking. 72. *Almain:* German. 75. *do you justice:* drink as much as you. 80. *lown:* villain. 81. *wight:* man. 83. *pride:* i.e., dressing too lavishly.

CASSIO. No; for I hold him to be unworthy of his place that does those things. Well: God's above all; and there be souls must be saved, and there be souls must not be saved. 90

IAGO. It's true, good lieutenant.

CASSIO. For mine own part—no offence to the general, nor any man of quality—I hope to be saved.

IAGO. And so do I too, lieutenant.

CASSIO. Ay, but, by your leave, not before me; the lieutenant is to be saved before the ancient. Let's have no more of this; let's to our affairs. God forgive us our sins! Gentlemen, let's look to our business. Do not think, gentlemen, I am drunk: this is my ancient: this is my right hand, and this is my left. I am not drunk now; I can stand well enough, and speak well enough. 100

ALL. Excellent well.

CASSIO. Why, very well then; you must not think then that I am drunk. *Exit.*

MONTANO. To the platform, masters; come, let's set the watch.

IAGO. You see this fellow that is gone before;
He is a soldier fit to stand by Cæsar
And give direction: and do but see his vice;
'Tis to his virtue a just equinox,
The one as long as the other: 'tis pity of him.
I fear the trust Othello puts him in 110
On some odd time of his infirmity
Will shake this island.

MONTANO. But is he often thus?

IAGO. 'Tis evermore the prologue to his sleep:
He'll watch the horologe a double set,
If drink rock not his cradle.

MONTANO. It were well
The general were put in mind of it.
Perhaps he sees it not, or his good nature
Prizes the virtue that appears in Cassio
And looks not on his evils: is not this true?

Enter RODERIGO.

---

104. *platform:* courtyard. 108. *equinox:* equivalent. 111. i.e., when he's drunk. 114. *horologe:* clock. *double set:* 24 hours.

SCENE 3] OTHELLO 415

IAGO, *aside to him.* How now, Roderigo! 120
I pray you, after the lieutenant; go. *Exit* RODERIGO.
  MONTANO. And 'tis great pity that the noble Moor
Should hazard such a place as his own second
With one of an ingraft infirmity:
It were an honest action to say
So to the Moor.
  IAGO.   Not I, for this fair island:
I do love Cassio well, and would do much
To cure him of this evil:—But, hark! what noise?
                    A cry within: 'Help! help!'

  Re-enter CASSIO, *driving in* RODERIGO.

  CASSIO. 'Zounds! you rogue! you rascal!
  MONTANO. What's the matter, lieutenant? 130
  CASSIO. A knave teach me my duty! But I'll beat the knave into a wicker bottle.
  RODERIGO. Beat me!
  CASSIO. Dost thou prate, rogue? *Striking* RODERIGO.
  MONTANO. Nay, good lieutenant; I pray you, sir, hold your hand.
  CASSIO. Let me go, sir, or I'll knock you o'er the mazzard.
  MONTANO. Come, come, you're drunk.
  CASSIO. Drunk! *They fight.*
  IAGO, *aside to* RODERIGO. Away, I say; go out, and cry a mutiny.
                    Exit RODERIGO.
Nay, good lieutenant! God's will, gentlemen! 140
Help, ho!—Lieutenant,—sir,—Montano,—sir;—
Help, masters!—Here's a goodly watch indeed! *A bell rings.*
Who's that that rings the bell?—Diablo, ho!
The town will rise: God's will, lieutenant, hold;
You will be shamed for ever.

  Re-enter OTHELLO *and* ATTENDANTS.

  OTHELLO.   What is the matter here?
  MONTANO. 'Zounds, I bleed still; I am hurt to the death. *Faints.*

---

124. *ingraft:* grafted on. 136. *mazzard:* head. 142. Roderigo has cried mutiny, and the alarm is ringing. 143. *Diablo:* the devil.

OTHELLO. Hold, for your lives!
IAGO. Hold, ho! Lieutenant,—sir,—Montano,—gentlemen,—
Have you forgot all sense of place and duty?
Hold! the general speaks to you; hold, hold, for shame! 150
OTHELLO. Why, how now, ho! from whence ariseth this?
Are we turn'd Turks, and to ourselves do that
Which heaven hath forbid the Ottomites?
For Christian shame, put by this barbarous brawl:
He that stirs next to carve for his own rage
Holds his soul light; he dies upon his motion.
Silence that dreadful bell: it frights the isle
From her propriety. What is the matter, masters?
Honest Iago, that look'st dead with grieving,
Speak, who began this? on thy love, I charge thee. 160
IAGO. I do not know: friends all but now, even now,
In quarter, and in terms like bride and groom
Devesting them for bed; and then, but now,
As if some planet had unwitted men,
Swords out, and tilting one at other's breast,
In opposition bloody. I cannot speak
Any beginning to this peevish odds;
And would in action glorious I had lost
Those legs that brought me to a part of it!
OTHELLO. How comes it, Michael, you are thus forgot? 170
CASSIO. I pray you, pardon me; I cannot speak.
OTHELLO. Worthy Montano, you were wont be civil;
The gravity and stillness of your youth
The world hath noted, and your name is great
In mouths of wisest censure: what's the matter,
That you unlace your reputation thus,
And spend your rich opinion for the name
Of a night-brawler? give me answer to it.
MONTANO. Worthy Othello, I am hurt to danger:
Your officer, Iago, can inform you— 180

---

155. *carve for:* indulge. 158. *propriety:* identity. 162. *quarter:* amity. 164. *unwitted:* driven mad. 167 *odds:* quarrel. 175. *censure:* judgment. 177. *opinion:* reputation. 179. *to danger:* dangerously.

While I spare speech, which something now offends me—
Of all that I do know: nor know I aught
By me that's said or done amiss this night;
Unless self-charity be sometimes a vice,
And to defend ourselves it be a sin
When violence assails us.

OTHELLO.   Now, by heaven,
My blood begins my safer guides to rule,
And passion, having my best judgement collied,
Assays to lead the way: if I once stir,
Or do but lift this arm, the best of you   190
Shall sink in my rebuke. Give me to know
How this foul rout began, who set it on,
And he that is approved in this offence,
Though he had twinn'd with me, both at a birth,
Shall lose me. What! in a town of war,
Yet wild, the people's hearts brimful of fear,
To manage private and domestic quarrel,
In night, and on the court and guard of safety!
'Tis monstrous. Iago, who began 't?

MONTANO. If partially affined, or leagued in office,   200
Thou dost deliver more or less than truth,
Thou art no soldier.

IAGO.   Touch me not so near:
I had rather have this tongue cut from my mouth
Than it should do offence to Michael Cassio;
Yet, I persuade myself, to speak the truth
Shall nothing wrong him. Thus it is, general.
Montano and myself being in speech,
There comes a fellow crying out for help,
And Cassio following him with determined sword,
To execute upon him. Sir, this gentleman   210
Steps in to Cassio and entreats his pause:

---

181. *something offends:* somewhat hurts. 187. *blood:* passion, temper. *safer guides:* e.g., reason. 188. *collied:* darkened. 192. *rout:* brawl. 193. i.e., proved the offender. 194. i.e., were my twin brother. 198. *court:* headquarters. 200. *partially:* not impartially. *affined:* related. 202. "You needn't go so far." 210. *execute:* act.

Myself the crying fellow did pursue,
Lest by his clamour—as it so fell out—
The town might fall in fright: he, swift of foot,
Outran my purpose; and I return'd the rather
For that I heard the clink and fall of swords,
And Cassio high in oath; which till to-night
I ne'er might say before. When I came back—
For this was brief—I found them close together,
At blow and thrust; even as again they were   220
When you yourself did part them.
More of this matter cannot I report:
But men are men; the best sometimes forget:
Though Cassio did some little wrong to him,
As men in rage strike those that wish them best,
Yet surely Cassio, I believe, received
From him that fled some strange indignity,
Which patience could not pass.
    OTHELLO.   I know, Iago,
Thy honesty and love doth mince this matter,
Making it light to Cassio. Cassio, I love thee;   230
But never more be officer of mine.

Re-enter DESDEMONA, *attended.*

Look, if my gentle love be not raised up!
I'll make thee an example.
    DESDEMONA.   What's the matter?
    OTHELLO. All's well now, sweeting; come away to bed.
Sir, for your hurts, myself will be your surgeon:
                        To MONTANO, *who is led off.*
Lead him off.
Iago, look with care about the town,
And silence those whom this vile brawl distracted.
Come, Desdemona: 'tis the soldiers' life
To have their balmy slumbers waked with strife.   240
                     Exeunt all but IAGO *and* CASSIO.
    IAGO. What, are you hurt, lieutenant?

---

215. *rather:* sooner. 224. *him:* i.e., Montano.

CASSIO. Ay, past all surgery.

IAGO. Marry, heaven forbid!

CASSIO. Reputation, reputation, reputation! O, I have lost my reputation! I have lost the immortal part of myself, and what remains is bestial. My reputation, Iago, my reputation!

IAGO. As I am an honest man, I thought you had received some bodily wound; there is more sense in that than in reputation. Reputation is an idle and most false imposition; oft got without merit and lost without deserving: you have lost no reputation at [250 all, unless you repute yourself such a loser. What, man! there are ways to recover the general again: you are but now cast in his mood, a punishment more in policy than in malice; even so as one would beat his offenceless dog to affright an imperious lion: sue to him again, and he's yours.

CASSIO. I will rather sue to be despised than to deceive so good a commander with so slight, so drunken, and so indiscreet an officer. Drunk? and speak parrot? and squabble? swagger? swear? and discourse fustian with one's own shadow? O thou invisible spirit of wine, if thou hast no name to be known by, let us call thee [260 devil!

IAGO. What was he that you followed with your sword? What had he done to you?

CASSIO. I know not.

IAGO. Is 't possible?

CASSIO. I remember a mass of things, but nothing distinctly; a quarrel, but nothing wherefore. O God, that men should put an enemy in their mouths to steal away their brains! that we should, with joy, pleasance, revel and applause, transform ourselves into beasts! 270

IAGO. Why, but you are now well enough: how came you thus recovered?

CASSIO. It hath pleased the devil drunkenness to give place to the devil wrath: one unperfectness shows me another, to make me frankly despise myself.

---

248. *sense:* feeling. 252. *recover:* win back. *cast:* cast off. *in his mood:* when he was angry. 257. *slight:* worthless. 258. *parrot:* i.e., not knowing what one says. 259. *fustian:* nonsense.

420   OTHELLO   [ACT II

IAGO. Come, you are too severe a moraler: as the time, the place, and the condition of this country stands, I could heartily wish this had not befallen; but since it is as it is, mend it for your own good.

CASSIO. I will ask him for my place again; he shall tell me I am a drunkard! Had I as many mouths as Hydra, such an answer [280 would stop them all. To be now a sensible man, by and by a fool, and presently a beast! O strange! Every inordinate cup is unblest, and the ingredient is a devil.

IAGO. Come, come, good wine is a good familiar creature, if it be well used: exclaim no more against it. And, good lieutenant, I think you think I love you.

CASSIO. I have well approved it, sir. I drunk!

IAGO. You or any man living may be drunk at some time, man. I'll tell you what you shall do. Our general's wife is now the general. I may say so in this respect, for that he hath devoted and [290 given up himself to the contemplation, mark and denotement of her parts and graces: confess yourself freely to her; importune her help to put you in your place again: she is of so free, so kind, so apt, so blessed a disposition, she holds it a vice in her goodness not to do more than she is requested: this broken joint between you and her husband entreat her to splinter; and, my fortunes against any lay worth naming, this crack of your love shall grow stronger than it was before.

CASSIO. You advise me well.

IAGO. I protest, in the sincerity of love and honest kindness.   300

CASSIO. I think it freely; and betimes in the morning I will beseech the virtuous Desdemona to undertake for me: I am desperate of my fortunes if they check me here.

IAGO. You are in the right. Good night, lieutenant;
I must to the watch.

CASSIO. Good night, honest Iago.   *Exit.*

IAGO. And what's he then that says I play the villain?
When this advice is free I give and honest,

---

276. *moraler:* moralist. 280. *Hydra:* many-headed monster. 282. *inordinate:* beyond the limit. 284. *familiar:* useful. 287. *approved:* proved. 291. *mark, denotement:* contemplation. 292. *parts:* good qualities. 293. *free:* generous. 296. *lay:* stake. 297. *crack:* broken bone. 302. *undertake:* undertake this task. *am desperate:* lose hope. 303. *check:* fail. 308. *free:* i.e., from malice.

SCENE 3] OTHELLO 421

Probal to thinking, and indeed the course
To win the Moor again? For 'tis most easy   310
The inclining Desdemona to subdue
In any honest suit. She's framed as fruitful
As the free elements. And then for her
To win the Moor, were 't to renounce his baptism,
All seals and symbols of redeemed sin,
His soul is so enfetter'd to her love,
That she may make, unmake, do what she list,
Even as her appetite shall play the god
With his weak function. How am I then a villain
To counsel Cassio to this parallel course,   320
Directly to his good? Divinity of hell!
When devils will the blackest sins put on,
They do suggest at first with heavenly shows,
As I do now: for whiles this honest fool
Plies Desdemona to repair his fortunes,
And she for him pleads strongly to the Moor,
I'll pour this pestilence into his ear,
That she repeals him for her body's lust;
And by how much she strives to do him good,
She shall undo her credit with the Moor.   330
So will I turn her virtue into pitch;
And out of her own goodness make the net
That shall enmesh them all.

Enter RODERIGO.

How now, Roderigo!

RODERIGO. I do follow here in the chase, not like a hound that hunts, but one that fills up the cry. My money is almost spent; I have been to-night exceedingly well cudgelled; and I think the issue will be, I shall have so much experience for my pains; and so, with no money at all and a little more wit, return again to Venice.

IAGO. How poor are they that have not patience!
What wound did ever heal but by degrees?   340

---

309. *probal to:* to be approved by. 312-13. *fruitful, free:* bounteous. 314. *win:* persuade. 320. "parallel to his good"? 323. *suggest:* tempt. 328. *repeals:* recalls. 335. *cry:* pack. 338. *wit:* intelligent planning (also ll. 341-2).

Thou know'st we work by wit and not by witchcraft,
And wit depends on dilatory time.
Does 't not go well? Cassio hath beaten thee,
And thou by that small hurt hast cashier'd Cassio:
Though other things grow fair against the sun,
Yet fruits that blossom first will first be ripe:
Content thyself awhile. By the mass, 'tis morning;
Pleasure and action make the hours seem short.
Retire thee; go where thou art billeted:
Away, I say; thou shalt know more hereafter: 350
Nay, get thee gone. *Exit* RODERIGO. Two things are to be done:
My wife must move for Cassio to her mistress;
I'll set her on;
Myself the while to draw the Moor apart,
And bring him jump when he may Cassio find
Soliciting his wife: ay, that's the way;
Dull not device by coldness and delay. *Exit.*

Act III

SCENE 1. *Before the castle.*

Enter CASSIO *and some* MUSICIANS.

CASSIO. Masters, play here; I will content your pains;
Something that's brief; and bid 'Good morrow, general.' *Music.*

Enter CLOWN.

CLOWN. Why, masters, have your instruments been in Naples, that they speak i' the nose thus?

1 MUSICIAN. How, sir, how?

CLOWN. Are these, I pray you, wind-instruments?

---

352. *move for:* make a move in favor of. 355. *jump:* exactly. 357. *coldness:* sluggishness.

ACT III, SC. 1: 1. *content your pains:* reward your trouble. 2. So to greet a married couple with music was customary. 3. The clown is just a comical servant. 4. Naples was associated with syphilis. 5-10. The joke is about farting.

SCENE 1]   OTHELLO   423

1 MUSICIAN. Ay, marry, are they, sir.
CLOWN. O, thereby hangs a tail.
1 MUSICIAN. Whereby hangs a tale, sir?
CLOWN. Marry, sir, by many a wind-instrument that I know. [10 But, masters, here's money for you: and the general so likes your music, that he desires you, for love's sake, to make no more noise with it.
1 MUSICIAN. Well, sir, we will not.
CLOWN. If you have any music that may not be heard, to 't again: but, as they say, to hear music the general does not greatly care.
1 MUSICIAN. We have none such, sir.
CLOWN. Then put up your pipes in your bag, for I'll away: go; vanish into air; away!   *Exeunt* MUSICIANS.
CASSIO. Dost thou hear, my honest friend?   20
CLOWN. No, I hear not your honest friend; I hear you.
CASSIO. Prithee, keep up thy quillets. There's a poor piece of gold for thee: if the gentlewoman that attends the general's wife be stirring, tell her there's one Cassio entreats her a little favour of speech: wilt thou do this?
CLOWN. She is stirring, sir: if she will stir hither, I shall seem to notify unto her.
CASSIO. Do, good my friend.   *Exit* CLOWN.

Enter IAGO.

                In happy time, Iago.
IAGO. You have not been a-bed, then?
CASSIO. Why, no; the day had broke   30
Before we parted. I have made bold, Iago,
To send in to your wife: my suit to her
Is, that she will to virtuous Desdemona
Procure me some access.
  IAGO.   I'll send her to you presently;
And I'll devise a mean to draw the Moor
Out of the way, that your converse and business
May be more free.

---

22. *keep up:* i.e., to yourself. *quillets:* quips. 34. *presently:* at once. 36. *converse:* conversation.

CASSIO. I humbly thank you for 't. *Exit* IAGO. I never knew
A Florentine more kind and honest.

Enter EMILIA.

EMILIA. Good morrow, good lieutenant: I am sorry 40
For your displeasure; but all will sure be well.
The general and his wife are talking of it,
And she speaks for you stoutly: the Moor replies,
That he you hurt is of great fame in Cyprus
And great affinity, and that in wholesome wisdom
He might not but refuse you; but he protests he loves you,
And needs no other suitor but his likings
To take the safest occasion by the front
To bring you in again.
  CASSIO.   Yet, I beseech you,
If you think fit, or that it may be done, 50
Give me advantage of some brief discourse
With Desdemona alone.
  EMILIA.   Pray you, come in:
I will bestow you where you shall have time
To speak your bosom freely.
  CASSIO.   I am much bound to you.   *Exeunt.*

SCENE 2. *A room in the castle.*

Enter OTHELLO, IAGO, *and* GENTLEMEN.

OTHELLO. These letters give, Iago, to the pilot;
And by him do my duties to the senate:
That done, I will be walking on the works;
Repair there to me.
  IAGO.   Well, my good lord, I'll do 't.
OTHELLO. This fortification, gentlemen, shall we see 't?
GENTLEMEN. We'll wait upon your lordship.   *Exeunt.*

---

44. *fame:* reputation. 45. *affinity:* family. 46. *might:* could. 48. *front:* forelock. 53. *time:* opportunity. 54. *bosom:* inmost thoughts.
SC. 2: 3. *works:* fortifications.

SCENE 3. *The garden of the castle.*

Enter DESDEMONA, CASSIO, *and* EMILIA.

DESDEMONA. Be thou assured, good Cassio, I will do
All my abilities in thy behalf.
　EMILIA. Good madam, do: I warrant it grieves my husband
As if the case were his.
　DESDEMONA. O, that's an honest fellow. Do not doubt, Cassio,
But I will have my lord and you again
As friendly as you were.
　CASSIO.　　　　　　Bounteous madam,
Whatever shall become of Michael Cassio,
He's never any thing but your true servant.
　DESDEMONA. I know 't: I thank you. You do love my lord:　　10
You have known him long; and be you well assured
He shall in strangeness stand no farther off
Than in a politic distance.
　CASSIO.　　　　　　Ay, but, lady,
That policy may either last so long,
Or feed upon such nice and waterish diet,
Or breed itself so out of circumstance,
That, I being absent and my place supplied,
My general will forget my love and service.
　DESDEMONA. Do not doubt that; before Emilia here
I give thee warrant of thy place: assure thee,　　20
If I do vow a friendship, I'll perform it
To the last article: my lord shall never rest;
I'll watch him tame and talk him out of patience;
His bed shall seem a school, his board a shrift;
I'll intermingle every thing he does
With Cassio's suit: therefore be merry, Cassio;
For thy solicitor shall rather die
Than give thy cause away.

Enter OTHELLO *and* IAGO, *at a distance.*

---

sc. 3: 12. *strangeness:* estrangement. 16. *out of circumstance:* by finding circumstances. 19. *doubt:* fear. 23. *watch him tame:* keep him awake till he's tamed. 24. *shrift:* confessional.

EMILIA. Madam, here comes my lord.
CASSIO. Madam, I'll take my leave.
DESDEMONA. Nay, stay and hear me speak.
CASSIO. Madam, not now: I am very ill at ease,
Unfit for mine own purposes.
DESDEMONA. Well, do your discretion. *Exit* CASSIO.
IAGO. Ha! I like not that.
OTHELLO. What dost thou say?
IAGO. Nothing, my lord: or if—I know not what.
OTHELLO. Was not that Cassio parted from my wife?
IAGO. Cassio, my lord! No, sure, I cannot think it,
That he would steal away so guilty-like,
Seeing you coming.
OTHELLO. I do believe 'twas he.
DESDEMONA. How now, my lord!
I have been talking with a suitor here.
A man that languishes in your displeasure.
OTHELLO. Who is 't you mean?
DESDEMONA. Why, your lieutenant, Cassio. Good my lord,
If I have any grace or power to move you,
His present reconciliation take;
For if he be not one that truly loves you,
That errs in ignorance and not in cunning,
I have no judgement in an honest face:
I prithee, call him back.
OTHELLO. Went he hence now?
DESDEMONA. Ay, sooth; so humbled,
That he hath left part of his grief with me,
To suffer with him. Good love, call him back.
OTHELLO. Not now, sweet Desdemona; some other time.
DESDEMONA. But shall 't be shortly?
OTHELLO. The sooner, sweet, for you.
DESDEMONA. Shall 't be to-night at supper?
OTHELLO. No, not to-night.
DESDEMONA. To-morrow dinner then?
OTHELLO. I shall not dine at home;
I meet the captains at the citadel.

---

47. *grace:* favour. *move:* influence. 50. *in cunning:* knowingly.

SCENE 3] OTHELLO 427

DESDEMONA. Why then to-morrow night; or Tuesday morn;
On Tuesday noon, or night; on Wednesday morn:
I prithee, name the time; but let it not
Exceed three days: in faith, he's penitent;
And yet his trespass, in our common reason—
Save that, they say, the wars must make examples
Out of their best—is not almost a fault
To incur a private check. When shall he come?
Tell me, Othello: I wonder in my soul,
What you would ask me, that I should deny, 70
Or stand so mammering on. What! Michael Cassio,
That came a-wooing with you, and so many a time
When I have spoke of you dispraisingly
Hath ta'en your part; to have so much to do
To bring him in! Trust me, I could do much—

OTHELLO. Prithee, no more: let him come when he will;
I will deny thee nothing.

DESDEMONA.   Why, this is not a boon;
'Tis as I should entreat you wear your gloves,
Or feed on nourishing dishes, or keep you warm,
Or sue to you to do a peculiar profit 80
To your own person: nay, when I have a suit
Wherein I mean to touch your love indeed,
It shall be full of poise and difficult weight,
And fearful to be granted.

OTHELLO.   I will deny thee nothing:
Whereon, I do beseech thee, grant me this,
To leave me but a little to myself.

DESDEMONA. Shall I deny you? no: farewell, my lord.

OTHELLO. Farewell, my Desdemona: I'll come to thee straight.

DESDEMONA. Emilia, come. Be as your fancies teach you;
Whate'er you be, I am obedient. 90

Exeunt DESDEMONA *and* EMILIA.

OTHELLO. Excellent wretch! Perdition catch my soul,

---

65. *in our common reason:* as we commonly judge. 67. *not almost:* hardly.
68. *a private check:* even a private rebuke. 71. *mammering:* hesitating. 80.
peculiar: personal. 82. *touch:* test. 83. *poise:* weight. 91. *wretch:* **term of
endearment.**

But I do love thee! and when I love thee not,
Chaos is come again.
  IAGO. My noble lord,—
  OTHELLO.   What dost thou say, Iago?
  IAGO. Did Michael Cassio, when you woo'd my lady,
Know of your love?
  OTHELLO. He did, from first to last: why dost thou ask?
  IAGO. But for a satisfaction of my thought;
No further harm.
  OTHELLO.   Why of thy thought, Iago?
  IAGO. I did not think he had been acquainted with her.   100
  OTHELLO. O, yes, and went between us very oft.
  IAGO. Indeed!
  OTHELLO. Indeed! ay, indeed: discern'st thou aught in that?
Is he not honest?
  IAGO. Honest, my lord!
  OTHELLO. Honest! ay, honest.
  IAGO. My lord, for aught I know.
  OTHELLO. What dost thou think?
  IAGO. Think, my lord!
  OTHELLO. Think, my lord! By heaven, he echoes me,   110
As if there were some monster in his thought
Too hideous to be shown. Thou dost mean something:
I heard thee say even now, thou likedst not that,
When Cassio left my wife: what didst not like?
And when I told thee he was of my counsel
In my whole course of wooing, thou criedst 'Indeed!'
And didst contract and purse thy brow together,
As if thou then hadst shut up in thy brain
Some horrible conceit: if thou dost love me,
Show me thy thought.   120
  IAGO. My lord, you know I love you.
  OTHELLO.   I think thou dost;
And for I know thou 'rt full of love and honesty
And weigh'st thy words before thou givest them breath,
Therefore these stops of thine fright me the more:

---

93. *chaos:* the disorder that preceded the creation of the world. 115. *of my counsel:* in my confidence. 119. *conceit:* idea.

SCENE 3] OTHELLO 429

For such things in a false disloyal knave
Are tricks of custom; but in a man that's just
They 're close delations, working from the heart,
That passion cannot rule.
   IAGO.   For Michael Cassio,
I dare be sworn I think that he is honest.
   OTHELLO. I think so too.
   IAGO.   Men should be what they seem;   130
Or those that be not, would they might seem none!
   OTHELLO. Certain, men should be what they seem.
   IAGO. Why then I think Cassio's an honest man.
   OTHELLO. Nay, yet there's more in this:
I prithee, speak to me as to thy thinkings,
As thou dost ruminate, and give thy worst of thoughts
The worst of words.
   IAGO.   Good my lord, pardon me:
Though I am bound to every act of duty,
I am not bound to that all slaves are free to.
Utter my thoughts? Why, say they are vile and false;   140
As where's that palace whereinto foul things
Sometimes intrude not? who has a breast so pure,
But some uncleanly apprehensions
Keep leets and law-days, and in session sit
With meditations lawful?
   OTHELLO. Thou dost conspire against thy friend, Iago,
If thou but think'st him wrong'd and makest his ear
A stranger to thy thoughts.
   IAGO.   I do beseech you—
Though I perchance am vicious in my guess,
As, I confess, it is my nature's plague   150
To spy into abuses, and oft my jealousy
Shapes faults that are not—that your wisdom yet,
From one that so imperfectly conceits,
Would take no notice, nor build yourself a trouble

---

126. *of custom:* customary. 127. *close delations:* secret emotions. 131. *none:* not men. 139. i.e., which even slaves are *not* bound to. 143. *apprehensions:* ideas. 144. *leets:* sessions. 149. *vicious:* mistaken. 151. *jealousy:* suspicion. 153. *conceits:* thinks.

Out of his scattering and unsure observance.
It were not for your quiet nor your good,
Nor for my manhood, honesty, or wisdom,
To let you know my thoughts.

OTHELLO. What dost thou mean?

IAGO. Good name in man and woman, dear my lord,
Is the immediate jewel of their souls:
Who steals my purse steals trash; 'tis something, nothing;
'Twas mine, 'tis his, and has been slave to thousands;
But he that filches from me my good name
Robs me of that which not enriches him
And makes me poor indeed.

OTHELLO. By heaven, I'll know thy thoughts.

IAGO. You cannot, if my heart were in your hand;
Nor shall not, whilst 'tis in my custody.

OTHELLO. Ha!

IAGO. O, beware, my lord, of jealousy;
It is the green-eyed monster, which doth mock
The meat it feeds on: that cuckold lives in bliss
Who, certain of his fate, loves not his wronger;
But, O, what damned minutes tells he o'er
Who dotes, yet doubts, suspects, yet strongly loves!

OTHELLO. O misery!

IAGO. Poor and content is rich, and rich enough;
But riches fineless is as poor as winter
To him that ever fears he shall be poor:
Good heaven, the souls of all my tribe defend
From jealousy!

OTHELLO. Why, why is this!
Think'st thou I 'ld make a life of jealousy,
To follow still the changes of the moon
With fresh suspicions? No; to be once in doubt
Is once to be resolved: exchange me for a goat,
When I shall turn the business of my soul
To such exsufflicate and blown surmises,

---

167. *if:* even if. 170. *mock:* i.e., playing cat and mouse. 172. *wronger:* i.e., his unfaithful wife. 173. *tells:* counts. 177. *fineless:* boundless. 184. *resolved:* to have the doubt settled. 186. *exsufflicate, blown:* fly-blown, spit out.

Matching thy inference. 'Tis not to make me jealous
To say my wife is fair, feeds well, loves company,
Is free of speech, sings, plays and dances well;
Where virtue is, these are more virtuous:
Nor from mine own weak merits will I draw
The smallest fear or doubt of her revolt;
For she had eyes, and chose me. No, Iago;
I'll see before I doubt; when I doubt, prove;
And on the proof, there is no more but this,
Away at once with love or jealousy!

IAGO. I am glad of it; for now I shall have reason
To show the love and duty that I bear you
With franker spirit: therefore, as I am bound,
Receive it from me. I speak not yet of proof.
Look to your wife: observe her well with Cassio;
Wear your eye thus, not jealous nor secure:
I would not have your free and noble nature
Out of self-bounty be abused; look to 't:
I know our country disposition well;
In Venice they do let heaven see the pranks
They dare not show their husbands; their best conscience
Is not to leave 't undone, but keep 't unknown.

OTHELLO. Dost thou say so?

IAGO. She did deceive her father, marrying you;
And when she seem'd to shake and fear your looks,
She loved them most.

OTHELLO.   And so she did.

IAGO.   Why, go to then;
She that so young could give out such a seeming,
To seel her father's eyes up close as oak—
He thought 'twas witchcraft—but I am much to blame;
I humbly do beseech you of your pardon
For too much loving you.

OTHELLO.   I am bound to thee for ever.

---

187. *matching:* in accordance with. 191. *merits:* physical attributes. 194. *prove:* put to test. 203. *free:* generous. 204. *self-bounty:* inborn goodness. *abused:* deceived. 205. i.e., our country's disposition. 214. *seel:* close.

IAGO. I see this hath a little dash'd your spirits.

OTHELLO. Not a jot, not a jot.

IAGO. I' faith, I fear it has.
I hope you will consider what is spoke 220
Comes from my love; but I do see you're moved:
I am to pray you not to strain my speech
To grosser issues nor to larger reach
Than to suspicion.

OTHELLO. I will not.

IAGO. Should you do so, my lord,
My speech should fall into such vile success
As my thoughts aim not at. Cassio's my worthy friend—
My lord, I see you're moved.

OTHELLO. No, not much moved:
I do not think but Desdemona's honest.

IAGO. Long live she so! and long live you to think so! 230

OTHELLO. And yet, how nature erring from itself—

IAGO. Ay, there's the point: as—to be bold with you—
Not to affect many proposed matches
Of her own clime, complexion and degree,
Whereto we see in all things nature tends—
Foh! one may smell in such a will most rank,
Foul disproportion, thoughts unnatural.
But pardon me: I do not in position
Distinctly speak of her; though I may fear
Her will, recoiling to her better judgement, 240
May fall to match you with her country forms,
And happily repent.

OTHELLO. Farewell, farewell:
If more thou dost perceive, let me know more;
Set on thy wife to observe: leave me, Iago.

IAGO, *going*. My lord, I take my leave.

OTHELLO. Why did I marry? This honest creature doubtless
Sees and knows more, much more, than he unfolds.

---

223. *grosser:* larger. *issues:* results. *reach:* scope. 233. *affect:* like. 234. *complexion:* temperament. 236. *will:* sexual desire (also l. 240). 238. *in position:* as a proposition. 240. *recoiling:* reverting. 241. "May chance to compare you with her country's forms." 242. *happily:* haply, maybe.

SCENE 3] OTHELLO 433

   IAGO, *returning*. My lord, I would I might entreat your honour
To scan this thing no further; leave it to time:
Though it be fit that Cassio have his place, 250
For sure he fills it up with great ability,
Yet, if you please to hold him off awhile,
You shall by that perceive him and his means:
Note if your lady strain his entertainment
With any strong or vehement importunity;
Much will be seen in that. In the mean time,
Let me be thought too busy in my fears—
As worthy cause I have to fear I am—
And hold her free, I do beseech your honour.
   OTHELLO. Fear not my government. 260
   IAGO. I once more take my leave. *Exit*.
   OTHELLO. This fellow's of exceeding honesty,
And knows all qualities, with a learned spirit,
Of human dealings. If I do prove her haggard,
Though that her jesses were my dear heart-strings,
I 'ld whistle her off and let her down the wind
To prey at fortune. Haply, for I am black
And have not those soft parts of conversation
That chamberers have, or for I am declined
Into the vale of years,—yet that's not much— 270
She's gone; I am abused, and my relief
Must be to loathe her. O curse of marriage,
That we can call these delicate creatures ours,
And not their appetites! I had rather be a toad,
And live upon the vapour of a dungeon,
Than keep a corner in the thing I love
For others' uses. Yet, 'tis the plague of great ones;
Prerogatived are they less than the base;
'Tis destiny unshunnable, like death:

---

253. *means*: methods. 254. *strain*: press for. *entertainment*: reinstatement. 259. *free*: innocent. 260. *government*: self control. 263. *qualities*: natures. 263-4. i.e., learned as to human dealings. 264. *haggard*: unfaithful. 264-7. i.e., though the hawk's (haggard's) thongs (jesses—by which the hawk was tied) were my heart-strings, I'd whistle to her to go. 268. *parts*: qualities. 269. *chamberers*: bedroom gallants. 277-8. i.e., adultery is more prevalent in the best families.

Even then this forked plague is fated to us 280
When we do quicken. Desdemona comes:

Re-enter DESDEMONA *and* EMILIA.

If she be false, O, then heaven mocks itself!
I'll not believe 't.
   DESDEMONA.   How now, my dear Othello!
Your dinner, and the generous islanders
By you invited, do attend your presence.
   OTHELLO. I am to blame.
   DESDEMONA.   Why do you speak so faintly?
Are you not well?
   OTHELLO. I have a pain upon my forehead here.
   DESDEMONA. Faith, that's with watching; 'twill away again:
Let me but bind it hard, within this hour 290
It will be well.
   OTHELLO.   Your napkin is too little;
      He puts the handkerchief from him; and she drops it.
Let it alone. Come, I'll go in with you.
   DESDEMONA. I am very sorry that you are not well.
                    Exeunt OTHELLO *and* DESDEMONA.
   EMILIA. I am glad I have found this napkin:
This was her first remembrance from the Moor:
My wayward husband hath a hundred times
Woo'd me to steal it; but she so loves the token,
For he conjured her she should ever keep it,
That she reserves it evermore about her
To kiss and talk to. I'll have the work ta'en out, 300
And give 't Iago: what he will do with it
Heaven knows, not I;
I nothing but to please his fantasy.

Re-enter IAGO.

   IAGO. How now! what do you here alone?

---

280. *forked plague:* horns are supposed to grow on a cuckold's head. (See also l. 288.) 281. *quicken:* are born. 285. *attend:* await. 289. *watching:* not sleeping. 291, 294. *napkin:* handkerchief. 295. *remembrance:* keepsake. 300. *work ta'en out:* embroidery pattern copied. 303. *fantasy:* whim.

SCENE 3] OTHELLO 435

EMILIA. Do not you chide; I have a thing for you.
IAGO. A thing for me? it is a common thing—
EMILIA. Ha!
IAGO. To have a foolish wife.
EMILIA. O, is that all? What will you give me now
For that same handkerchief?
IAGO.   What handkerchief?   310
EMILIA. What handkerchief!
Why, that the Moor first gave to Desdemona;
That which so often you did bid me steal.
IAGO. Hast stol'n it from her?
EMILIA. No, faith; she let it drop by negligence,
And, to the advantage, I being here took 't up.
Look, here it is.
IAGO.   A good wench; give it me.
EMILIA. What will you do with 't, that you have been so earnest
To have me filch it?
IAGO, *snatching it.* Why, what's that to you?   320
EMILIA. If 't be not for some purpose of import,
Give 't me again: poor lady, she'll run mad
When she shall lack it.
IAGO. Be not acknown on 't; I have use for it.
Go, leave me.   *Exit* EMILIA.
I will in Cassio's lodging lose this napkin,
And let him find it. Trifles light as air
Are to the jealous confirmations strong
As proofs of holy writ: this may do something.
The Moor already changes with my poison: 330
Dangerous conceits are in their natures poisons,
Which at the first are scarce found to distaste,
But with a little act upon the blood
Burn like the mines of sulphur. I did say so:
Look, where he comes!

Re-enter OTHELLO.

---

316. *to the advantage:* opportunely. 321. *import:* i.e., importance. 324. *acknown:* don't let on you know. 331. *conceits:* ideas. 333. *act:* action.

436   OTHELLO   [ACT III

                    Not poppy, nor mandragora,
Nor all the drowsy syrups of the world,
Shall ever medicine thee to that sweet sleep
Which thou owedst yesterday.
  OTHELLO.   Ha! ha! false to me?
  IAGO. Why, how now, general! no more of that.
  OTHELLO. Avaunt! be gone! thou hast set me on the rack: 340
I swear 'tis better to be much abused
Than but to know 't a little.
  IAGO.   How now, my lord!
  OTHELLO. What sense had I of her stol'n hours of lust?
I saw 't not, thought it not, it harm'd not me:
I slept the next night well, was free and merry;
I found not Cassio's kisses on her lips:
He that is robb'd, not wanting what is stol'n,
Let him not know 't and he's not robb'd at all.
  IAGO. I am sorry to hear this.
  OTHELLO. I had been happy, if the general camp,   350
Pioners and all, had tasted her sweet body,
So I had nothing known. O, now for ever
Farewell the tranquil mind! farewell content!
Farewell the plumed troop and the big wars
That make ambition virtue! O, farewell,
Farewell the neighing steed and the shrill trump,
The spirit-stirring drum, the ear-piercing fife,
The royal banner and all quality,
Pride, pomp and circumstance of glorious war!
And, O you mortal engines, whose rude throats   360
The immortal Jove's dread clamours counterfeit,
Farewell! Othello's occupation's gone!
  IAGO. Is 't possible, my lord?
  OTHELLO. Villain, be sure thou prove my love a whore;
Be sure of it; give me the ocular proof;
Or, by the worth of man's eternal soul,

---

335. *mandragora:* like poppy, a narcotic. 338. *owedst:* possessed. 340. *rack:* instrument to stretch limbs out of joint. 341. *abused:* deceived (sexually). 345. *free:* care-free. 347. *wanting:* missing. 351. *pioners:* lowest artisans. 356. *trump:* trumpet. 358. *quality:* nature. 359. *circumstance:* pageantry. 360. *engines:* machines, i.e., cannon. 361. *counterfeit:* imitate.

SCENE 3] OTHELLO 437

Thou hadst been better have been born a dog
Than answer my waked wrath!
  IAGO.   Is 't come to this?
  OTHELLO. Make me to see 't; or at the least so prove it,
That the probation bear no hinge nor loop   370
To hang a doubt on; or woe upon thy life!
  IAGO. My noble lord,—
  OTHELLO. If thou dost slander her and torture me,
Never pray more; abandon all remorse;
On horror's head horrors accumulate;
Do deeds to make heaven weep, all earth amazed;
For nothing canst thou to damnation add
Greater than that.
  IAGO.   O grace! O heaven defend me!
Are you a man? have you a soul or sense?
God be wi' you; take mine office. O wretched fool,   380
That livest to make thine honesty a vice!
O monstrous world! Take note, take note, O world,
To be direct and honest is not safe.
I thank you for this profit, and from hence
I'll love no friend sith love breeds such offence.
  OTHELLO. Nay, stay: thou shouldst be honest.
  IAGO. I should be wise; for honesty's a fool,
And loses that it works for.
  OTHELLO.   By the world,
I think my wife be honest, and think she is not;
I think that thou art just, and think thou art not: 390
I'll have some proof. Her name, that was as fresh
As Dian's visage, is now begrimed and black
As mine own face. If there be cords, or knives,
Poison, or fire, or suffocating streams,
I'll not endure it. Would I were satisfied!
  IAGO. I see, sir, you are eaten up with passion:
I do repent me that I put it to you.

---

370. *probation:* proof. 374. *remorse:* pity. 379. *sense:* feeling. 380. *office:* job (he pretends to resign). 381. *vice:* fault. 384. *profit:* lesson. 385. *sith:* since (also l. 416 below). 392. Diana was a virgin. 395. *satisfied:* I knew the truth (also l. 399).

You would be satisfied?
>OTHELLO.   Would! nay, I will.
>IAGO. And may: but, how? how satisfied, my lord?
Would you, the supervisor, grossly gape on?
Behold her topp'd?
>OTHELLO.   Death and damnation! O!
>IAGO. It were a tedious difficulty, I think,
To bring them to that prospect: damn them then,
If ever mortal eyes do see them bolster
More than their own! What then? how then?
What shall I say? Where's satisfaction?
It is impossible you should see this,
Were they as prime as goats, as hot as monkeys,
As salt as wolves in pride, and fools as gross
As ignorance made drunk. But yet, I say,
If imputation and strong circumstances,
Which lead directly to the door of truth,
Will give you satisfaction, you may have 't.
>OTHELLO. Give me a living reason she's disloyal.
>IAGO. I do not like the office:
But sith I am enter'd in this cause so far,
Prick'd to 't by foolish honesty and love,
I will go on. I lay with Cassio lately,
And being troubled with a raging tooth,
I could not sleep.
There are a kind of men so loose of soul,
That in their sleeps will mutter their affairs:
One of this kind is Cassio:
In sleep I heard him say 'Sweet Desdemona,
Let us be wary, let us hide our loves;'
And then, sir, would he gripe and wring my hand,
Cry 'O sweet creature!' and then kiss me hard,
As if he pluck'd up kisses by the roots,
That grew upon my lips: then laid his leg

---

400. *supervisor:* eyewitness. 401. *topp'd:* same as *tupp'd* above. 403. *prospect:* (?) to be seen. 404. *bolster:* copulate. 404-5. Any eyes more than (in addition to) their own. 408. *prime:* hot (sexually). 409. *salt:* lecherous. 415. *office:* job. 418. *lay:* shared a bed.

SCENE 3] OTHELLO 439

Over my thigh, and sigh'd and kiss'd, and then 430
Cried 'Cursed fate that gave thee to the Moor!'
  OTHELLO. O monstrous! monstrous!
  IAGO.   Nay, this was but his dream.
  OTHELLO. But this denoted a foregone conclusion:
'Tis a shrewd doubt, though it be but a dream.
  IAGO. And this may help to thicken other proofs
That do demonstrate thinly.
  OTHELLO.   I'll tear her all to pieces.
  IAGO. Nay, but be wise: yet we see nothing done;
She may be honest yet. Tell me but this;
Have you not sometimes seen a handkerchief
Spotted with strawberries in your wife's hand? 440
  OTHELLO. I gave her such a one; 'twas my first gift.
  IAGO. I know not that: but such a handkerchief—
I am sure it was your wife's—did I to-day
See Cassio wipe his beard with.
  OTHELLO.   If it be that,—
  IAGO. If it be that, or any that was hers,
It speaks against her with the other proofs.
  OTHELLO. O, that the slave had forty thousand lives!
One is too poor, too weak for my revenge.
Now do I see 'tis true. Look here, Iago;
All my fond love thus do I blow to heaven: 450
'Tis gone.
Arise, black vengeance, from thy hollow cell!
Yield up, O love, thy crown and hearted throne
To tyrannous hate! Swell, bosom, with thy fraught,
For 'tis of aspics' tongues!
  IAGO.   Yet be content.
  OTHELLO. O, blood, blood, blood!
  IAGO. Patience, I say; your mind perhaps may change.
  OTHELLO. Never, Iago. Like to the Pontic sea,
Whose icy current and compulsive course

---

433. *foregone conclusion:* something that had already happened. 434. *shrewd doubt:* very suspicious thing. 450. *thus*—with a gesture. 453. *hearted:* in my heart. 454. *fraught:* freight. 455. *aspics':* asps'. 458. *Pontic:* Black Sea. 459. *compulsive:* compelling.

Ne'er feels retiring ebb, but keeps due on 460
To the Propontic and the Hellespont;
Even so my bloody thoughts, with violent pace,
Shall ne'er look back, ne'er ebb to humble love,
Till that a capable and wide revenge
Swallow them up. Now, by yond marble heaven,
In the due reverence of a sacred vow *Kneels.*
I here engage my words.

IAGO. Do not rise yet. *Kneels.*
Witness, you ever-burning lights above,
You elements that clip us round about,
Witness that here Iago doth give up 470
The execution of his wit, hands, heart,
To wrong'd Othello's service! Let him command,
And to obey shall be in me remorse,
What bloody business ever. *They rise.*

OTHELLO. I greet thy love,
Not with vain thanks, but with acceptance bounteous,
And will upon the instant put thee to 't:
Within these three days let me hear thee say
That Cassio's not alive.

IAGO. My friend is dead; 'tis done at your request:
But let her live.

OTHELLO. Damn her, lewd minx! O, damn her! 480
Come, go with me apart; I will withdraw,
To furnish me with some swift means of death
For the fair devil. Now art thou my lieutenant.

IAGO. I am your own for ever. *Exeunt.*

SCENE 4. *Before the castle.*

Enter DESDEMONA, EMILIA, *and* CLOWN.

DESDEMONA. Do you know, sirrah, where Lieutenant Cassio lies?
CLOWN. I dare not say he lies any where.

---

461. *Propontic:* Sea of Marmora. *Hellespont:* Bosporus. 464. *capable:* capacious. 468. *lights:* stars. 469. *clip:* embrace. 471. *execution of his wit:* action of his intellect. 473. *remorse:* compassion. 476. i.e., "put thee to work on it."
SC. 4: 1. *lies:* lodges.

SCENE 4] OTHELLO 441

DESDEMONA. Why, man?

CLOWN. He's a soldier; and for one to say a soldier lies, is stabbing.

DESDEMONA. Go to: where lodges he?

CLOWN. To tell you where he lodges, is to tell you where I lie.

DESDEMONA. Can any thing be made of this?

CLOWN. I know not where he lodges; and for me to devise a lodging, and say he lies here or he lies there, were to lie in mine own throat. 10

DESDEMONA. Can you inquire him out and be edified by report?

CLOWN. I will catechize the world for him; that is, make questions and by them answer.

DESDEMONA. Seek him, bid him come hither: tell him I have moved my lord on his behalf and hope all will be well.

CLOWN. To do this is within the compass of man's wit, and therefore I will attempt the doing it. *Exit.*

DESDEMONA. Where should I lose that handkerchief, Emilia?

EMILIA. I know not, madam.

DESDEMONA. Believe me, I had rather have lost my purse 20
Full of crusadoes: and, but my noble Moor
Is true of mind and made of no such baseness
As jealous creatures are, it were enough
To put him to ill thinking.

EMILIA. Is he not jealous?

DESDEMONA. Who, he? I think the sun where he was born
Drew all such humours from him.

EMILIA. Look, where he comes.

DESDEMONA. I will not leave him now till Cassio
Be call'd to him.

Enter OTHELLO.

How is 't with you, my lord?

OTHELLO. Well, my good lady. *Aside.* O, hardness to dissemble!
How do you, Desdemona?

DESDEMONA. Well, my good lord. 30

OTHELLO. Give me your hand: this hand is moist, my lady.

---

11. *edified:* instructed. 21. *crusadoes:* gold coins. 26. *humours:* attitudes.
31. A moist hand indicates sensuality; a dry hand (remember Maria's joke in *Twelfth Night*, p. 298) the opposite.

DESDEMONA. It yet has felt no age nor known no sorrow.

OTHELLO. This argues fruitfulness and liberal heart:
Hot, hot, and moist: this hand of yours requires
A sequester from liberty, fasting and prayer,
Much castigation, exercise devout;
For here's a young and sweating devil here,
That commonly rebels. 'Tis a good hand,
A frank one.

DESDEMONA. You may, indeed, say so;
For 'twas that hand that gave away my heart.   40

OTHELLO. A liberal hand: the hearts of old gave hands;
But our new heraldry is hands, not hearts.

DESDEMONA. I cannot speak of this. Come now, your promise.

OTHELLO. What promise, chuck?

DESDEMONA. I have sent to bid Cassio come speak with you.

OTHELLO. I have a salt and sorry rheum offends me;
Lend me thy handkerchief.

DESDEMONA. Here, my lord.

OTHELLO. That which I gave you.

DESDEMONA. I have it not about me.   50

OTHELLO. Not?

DESDEMONA. No, indeed, my lord.

OTHELLO. That's a fault. That handkerchief
Did an Egyptian to my mother give;
She was a charmer, and could almost read
The thoughts of people: she told her, while she kept it
'Twould make her amiable and subdue my father
Entirely to her love, but if she lost it
Or made a gift of it, my father's eye
Should hold her loathed and his spirits should hunt   60
After new fancies: she dying gave it me,
And bid me, when my fate would have me wife,
To give it her. I did so: and take heed on 't;
Make it a darling like your precious eye;

---

33. *fruitfulness:* bearing of children. *liberal:* sensual (also l. 41). 35. *sequester:* retirement. 36. *castigation:* self-discipline. 42. *heraldry:* symbolism. 44. *chuck:* chick, darling. 46. *rheum:* a cold. 54. *Egyptian:* i.e., a gypsy. 55. *charmer:* magician. 61. *fancies:* loves.

To lose 't or give 't away were such perdition
As nothing else could match.
DESDEMONA. Is 't possible?
OTHELLO. 'Tis true: there's magic in a web of it:
A sibyl, that had number'd in the world
The sun to course two hundred compasses,
In her prophetic fury sew'd the work; 70
The worms were hallow'd that did breed the silk;
And it was dyed in mummy which the skilful
Conserved of maidens' hearts.
DESDEMONA. Indeed! is 't true?
OTHELLO. Most veritable; therefore look to 't well.
DESDEMONA. Then would to God that I had never seen 't!
OTHELLO. Ha! wherefore?
DESDEMONA. Why do you speak so startingly and rash?
OTHELLO. Is 't lost? is 't gone? speak, is it out o' the way?
DESDEMONA. Heaven bless us!
OTHELLO. Say you? 80
DESDEMONA. It is not lost; but what an if it were?
OTHELLO. How!
DESDEMONA. I say, it is not lost.
OTHELLO. Fetch 't, let me see it.
DESDEMONA. Why, so I can, sir, but I will not now.
This is a trick to put me from my suit:
Pray you, let Cassio be received again.
OTHELLO. Fetch me the handkerchief: my mind misgives.
DESDEMONA. Come, come;
You'll never get a more sufficient man. 90
OTHELLO. The handkerchief!
DESDEMONA. I pray, talk me of Cassio.
OTHELLO. The handkerchief!
DESDEMONA. A man that all his time
Hath founded his good fortunes on your love,
Shared dangers with you,—
OTHELLO. The handkerchief!
DESDEMONA. In sooth, you are to blame.

---

65. *perdition:* loss. 68. *sibyl:* prophetess. 69. *compasses:* annual circuits. 72. *mummy:* corpse. 73. *conserved:* prepared. *of:* from. 90. *sufficient:* able.

OTHELLO. Away! *Exit.*
EMILIA. Is not this man jealous?
DESDEMONA. I ne'er saw this before.
Sure there's some wonder in this handkerchief: 100
I am most unhappy in the loss of it.
EMILIA. 'Tis not a year or two shows us a man:
They are all but stomachs and we all but food;
They eat us hungerly, and when they are full
They belch us. Look you, Cassio and my husband.

Enter CASSIO *and* IAGO.

IAGO. There is no other way; 'tis she must do 't:
And, lo, the happiness! go and importune her.
DESDEMONA. How now, good Cassio! what's the news with you?
CASSIO. Madam, my former suit: I do beseech you
That by your virtuous means I may again 110
Exist, and be a member of his love
Whom I with all the office of my heart
Entirely honour: I would not be delay'd.
If my offence be of such mortal kind,
That nor my service past nor present sorrows
Nor purposed merit in futurity
Can ransom me into his love again,
But to know so must be my benefit;
So shall I clothe me in a forced content
And shut myself up in some other course 120
To fortune's alms.
DESDEMONA. Alas, thrice-gentle Cassio!
My advocation is not now in tune;
My lord is not my lord, nor should I know him
Were he in favour as in humour alter'd.
So help me every spirit sanctified,
As I have spoken for you all my best
And stood within the blank of his displeasure
For my free speech! you must awhile be patient:

---

111. *be a member of:* have a share in. 112. *office:* devotion. 120-21. i.e., "limiting myself to fortune's smallest gifts." 124. *favour:* looks. 127. *blank:* direct line of fire.

SCENE 4] OTHELLO 445

What I can do I will; and more I will
Than for myself I dare: let that suffice you. 130
 IAGO. Is my lord angry?
 EMILIA. He went hence but now,
And certainly in strange unquietness.
 IAGO. Can he be angry? I have seen the cannon,
When it hath blown his ranks into the air,
And, like the devil, from his very arm
Puff'd his own brother; and can he be angry?
Something of moment then: I will go meet him:
There's matter in 't indeed if he be angry.
 DESDEMONA. I prithee, do so. *Exit* IAGO.
 Something sure of state,
Either from Venice some unhatch'd practice 140
Made demonstrable here in Cyprus to him,
Hath puddled his clear spirit; and in such cases
Men's natures wrangle with inferior things,
Though great ones are their object. 'Tis even so;
For let our finger ache, and it indues
Our other healthful members even to that sense
Of pain: nay, we must think men are not gods,
Nor of them look for such observancy
As fits the bridal. Beshrew me much, Emilia,
I was, unhandsome warrior as I am, 150
Arraigning his unkindness with my soul;
But now I find I had suborn'd the witness,
And he's indicted falsely.
 EMILIA. Pray heaven it be state-matters, as you think,
And no conception nor no jealous toy
Concerning you.
 DESDEMONA. Alas the day, I never gave him cause!
 EMILIA. But jealous souls will not be answer'd so;
They are not ever jealous for the cause,
But jealous for they are jealous: 'tis a monster 160
Begot upon itself, born on itself.

---

140. *unhatch'd practice:* plot not yet matured. 146. *sense:* feeling. 148. *of:* from. *observancy:* attention. 149. *Beshrew me:* oh dear. 150. *unhandsome:* unfair. 155. *toy:* whim.

DESDEMONA. Heaven keep that monster from Othello's mind!
EMILIA. Lady, amen.
DESDEMONA. I will go seek him. Cassio, walk hereabout:
If I do find him fit, I'll move your suit,
And seek to effect it to my uttermost.
    CASSIO. I humbly thank your ladyship.

Exeunt DESDEMONA *and* EMILIA.

Enter BIANCA.

BIANCA. Save you, friend Cassio!
    CASSIO.   What make you from home?
How is it with you, my most fair Bianca?
I' faith, sweet love, I was coming to your house.   170
    BIANCA. And I was going to your lodging, Cassio.
What, keep a week away? seven days and nights?
Eight score eight hours? and lovers' absent hours,
More tedious than the dial eight score times?
O weary reckoning!
    CASSIO.   Pardon me, Bianca:
I have this while with leaden thoughts been press'd;
But I shall in a more continuate time
Strike off this score of absence. Sweet Bianca,

            Giving her DESDEMONA'S *handkerchief.*

Take me this work out.
    BIANCA.   O Cassio, whence came this?
This is some token from a newer friend: 180
To the felt absence now I feel a cause:
Is 't come to this? Well, well.
    CASSIO.   Go to, woman!
Throw your vile guesses in the devil's teeth,
From whence you have them. You are jealous now
That this is from some mistress, some remembrance:
No, by my faith, Bianca.
    BIANCA.   Why, whose is it?
    CASSIO. I know not, sweet: I found it in my chamber.
I like the work well: ere it be demanded—

---

174. *the dial:* the "round" of the clock. 177. *more continuate:* less interrupted. 185. *remembrance:* keepsake.

ACT IV, SCENE 1]   OTHELLO   447

As like enough it will—I 'ld have copied:
Take it, and do 't; and leave me for this time.
  BIANCA. Leave you! wherefore?
  CASSIO. I do attend here on the general;
And think it no addition, nor my wish,
To have him see me woman'd.
  BIANCA.   Why, I pray you?
  CASSIO. Not that I love you not.
  BIANCA.   But that you do not love me.
I pray you, bring me on the way a little;
And say if I shall see you soon at night.
  CASSIO. 'Tis but a little way that I can bring you;
For I attend here: but I'll see you soon.
  BIANCA. 'Tis very good; I must be circumstanced. *Exeunt.*   [200

Act IV

SCENE 1. *Cyprus. Before the castle.*

Enter OTHELLO *and* IAGO.

  IAGO. Will you think so?
  OTHELLO.   Think so, Iago!
  IAGO.   What,
To kiss in private?
  OTHELLO.   An unauthorized kiss.
  IAGO. Or to be naked with her friend in bed
An hour or more, not meaning any harm?
  OTHELLO. Naked in bed, Iago, and not mean harm!
It is hypocrisy against the devil:
They that mean virtuously and yet do so,
The devil their virtue tempts and they tempt heaven.
  IAGO. So they *do* nothing, 'tis a venial slip:
But if I give my wife a handkerchief—   10

---

193. *addition:* credit to me. 199. *attend:* wait. 200. "I yield to circumstances."

ACT IV, SC. 1: 2. *unauthorized:* unwarrantable. 6. i.e., with appearance of evil but meaning well. 9. *so:* provided that.

OTHELLO. What then?

IAGO. Why, then, 'tis hers, my lord; and being hers,
She may, I think, bestow 't on any man.

OTHELLO. She is protectress of her honour too:
May she give that?

IAGO. Her honour is an essence that's not seen;
They have it very oft that have it not:
But for the handkerchief—

OTHELLO. By heaven, I would most gladly have forgot it:
Thou said'st—O, it comes o'er my memory,
As doth the raven o'er the infected house,
Boding to all—he had my handkerchief.

IAGO. Ay, what of that?

OTHELLO. That's not so good now.

IAGO. What,
If I had said I had seen him do you wrong?
Or heard him say—as knaves be such abroad,
Who having, by their own importunate suit,
Or voluntary dotage of some mistress,
Convinced or supplied them, cannot choose
But they must blab—

OTHELLO. Hath he *said* anything?

IAGO. He hath, my lord; but be you well assured,
No more than he'll unswear.

OTHELLO. What hath he said?

IAGO. Faith, that he did—I know not what he did.

OTHELLO. What, what?

IAGO. Lie—

OTHELLO. With her?

IAGO. With her, on her; what you will.

OTHELLO. Lie with her! lie on her!—We say lie on her, when they belie her.—Lie with her! 'Zounds, that's fulsome! Handkerchief—confessions—handkerchief!—"To confess, and be hanged for his labour;" first, to be hanged, and then to confess. I tremble at it. Nature would not invest herself in such shadowing passion without some instruction. It is not words that shakes me thus. Pish! [40

---

17. "They [claim to] have it . . ." 21. *infected:* with the plague in it. 22. *Boding:* ominous. 28. *convinced:* overcome. *supplied:* slept with. 39. *My* nature. 40. *instruction:* correct information.

Noses, ears and lips. Is 't possible?—Confess?—Handkerchief?—O
devil! *Falls in a trance.*

IAGO. Work on,
My medicine, work! Thus credulous fools are caught:
And many worthy and chaste dames even thus,
All guiltless, meet reproach. What, ho! my lord!
My lord, I say! Othello!

Enter CASSIO.

How now, Cassio!
CASSIO. What's the matter?
IAGO. My lord is fall'n into an epilepsy:
This is his second fit; he had one yesterday. 50
CASSIO. Rub him about the temples.
IAGO. No, forbear;
The lethargy must have his quiet course:
If not, he foams at mouth, and by and by
Breaks out to savage madness. Look, he stirs:
Do you withdraw yourself a little while,
He will recover straight: when he is gone,
I would on great occasion speak with you. *Exit* CASSIO.
How is it, general? have you not hurt your head?
OTHELLO. Dost thou mock me?
IAGO. I mock you! no, by heaven.
Would you would bear your fortune like a man! 60
OTHELLO. A horned man's a monster and a beast.
IAGO. There's many a beast then in a populous city,
And many a civil monster.
OTHELLO. Did he confess it?
IAGO. Good sir, be a man;
Think every bearded fellow that's but yoked
May draw with you: there's millions now alive
That nightly lie in those unproper beds
Which they dare swear peculiar: your case is better.
O, 'tis the spite of hell, the fiend's arch-mock,
To lip a wanton in a secure couch, 70

58-61. The cuckold's horns again. 63. *civil:* civilized. 65. *yoked:* married. 66. *draw:* (?) be the same. 67. *unproper:* not peculiar to them. 70. *lip a wanton:* kiss a wild wench. *secure:* carefree.

And to suppose her chaste! No, let me know;
And knowing what I am, I know what she shall be.

OTHELLO. O, thou art wise; 'tis certain.

IAGO.   Stand you awhile apart;
Confine yourself but in a patient list.
Whilst you were here o'erwhelmed with your grief—
A passion most unsuiting such a man—
Cassio came hither: I shifted him away,
And laid good 'scuse upon your ecstasy;
Bade him anon return and here speak with me;
The which he promised. Do but encave yourself,   80
And mark the fleers, the gibes and notable scorns,
That dwell in every region of his face;
For I will make him tell the tale anew,
Where, how, how oft, how long ago and when
He hath and is again to cope your wife:
I say, but mark his gesture. Marry, patience;
Or I shall say you are all in all in spleen,
And nothing of a man.

OTHELLO.   Dost thou hear, Iago?
I will be found most cunning in my patience;
But—dost thou hear?—most bloody.

IAGO.   That's not amiss;   90
But yet keep time in all. Will you withdraw? OTHELLO *retires*.
Now will I question Cassio of Bianca,
A huswife that by selling her desires
Buys herself bread and clothes: it is a creature
That dotes on Cassio; as 'tis the strumpet's plague
To beguile many and be beguiled by one.
He, when he hears of her, cannot refrain
From the excess of laughter. Here he comes.

Re-enter CASSIO.

As he shall smile, Othello shall go mad;

---

74. *in a patient list:* within the bounds of patience. 78. *ecstasy:* fainting fit. 80. *encave:* conceal. 81. *fleers, scorns:* gibes. 85. *cope:* cope with. 87. *all in all in spleen:* governed by your impulses. 91. *keep time:* don't loose your grip. 93. *huswife:* hussy. 95. *strumpet:* whore.

SCENE 1]   OTHELLO   451

And his unbookish jealousy must construe   100
Poor Cassio's smiles, gestures and light behaviour,
Quite in the wrong. How do you now, lieutenant?

CASSIO. The worser that you give me the addition
Whose want even kills me.

IAGO. Ply Desdemona well, and you are sure on 't.
Now, if this suit lay in Bianca's power,
How quickly should you speed!

CASSIO.   Alas, poor caitiff!

OTHELLO. Look, how he laughs already!

IAGO. I never knew a woman love man so.

CASSIO. Alas, poor rogue! I think, i' faith, she loves me.   110

OTHELLO. Now he denies it faintly and laughs it out.

IAGO. Do you hear, Cassio?

OTHELLO.   Now he importunes him
To tell it o'er: go to; well said, well said.

IAGO. She gives it out that you shall marry her:
Do you intend it?

CASSIO. Ha, ha, ha!

OTHELLO. Do you triumph, Roman? do you triumph?

CASSIO. I marry her! what, a customer! I prithee, bear some charity
to my wit; do not think it so unwholesome. Ha, ha, ha!

OTHELLO. So, so, so, so: they laugh that win.   120

IAGO. Faith, the cry goes that you shall marry her.

CASSIO. Prithee, say true.

IAGO. I am a very villain else.

OTHELLO. Have you scored me? Well.

CASSIO. This is the monkey's own giving out: she is persuaded I will
marry her, out of her own love and flattery, not out of my promise.

OTHELLO. Iago beckons me; now he begins the story.

CASSIO. She was here even now: she haunts me in every place. I
was the other day talking on the sea-bank with certain Venetians;
and thither comes the bauble, and, by this hand, she falls me   [130
thus about my neck—

OTHELLO. Crying 'O dear Cassio!' as it were: his gesture imports it.

105-07. Othello hears 105 but not 106-07, etc. 107. *speed:* succeed. *caitiff:* wretch. 117. *Roman:* proud man. 118. *customer:* whore. 124. (?) "you know what my score is?" 130. *bauble:* plaything.

CASSIO. So hangs and lolls and weeps upon me; so hales and pulls me: ha, ha, ha!

OTHELLO. Now he tells how she plucked him to my chamber. O, I see that nose of yours, but not that dog I shall throw it to.

CASSIO. Well, I must leave her company.

IAGO. Before me! look, where she comes.

CASSIO. 'Tis such another fitchew! marry, a perfumed one.

Enter BIANCA.

What do you mean by this haunting of me?   140

BIANCA. Let the devil and his dam haunt you! What did you mean by that same handkerchief you gave me even now! I was a fine fool to take it. I must take out the work? A likely piece of work, that you should find it in your chamber, and not know who left it there! This is some minx's token, and I must take out the work? There; give it your hobby-horse: wheresoever you had it, I'll take out no work on 't.

CASSIO. How now, my sweet Bianca! how now! how now!

OTHELLO. By heaven, that should be my handkerchief!

BIANCA. An you'll come to supper to-night, you may; an you will not, come when you are next prepared for.   *Exit.*   150

IAGO. After her, after her.

CASSIO. Faith, I must; she'll rail i' the street else.

IAGO. Will you sup there?

CASSIO. Faith, I intend so.

IAGO. Well, I may chance to see you; for I would very fain speak with you.

CASSIO. Prithee, come; will you?

IAGO. Go to; say no more.   *Exit* CASSIO.

OTHELLO, *advancing*. How shall I murder him, Iago?

IAGO. Did you perceive how he laughed at his vice?   160

OTHELLO. O Iago!

IAGO. And did you see the handkerchief?

OTHELLO. Was that mine?

IAGO. Yours, by this hand: and to see how he prizes the foolish woman your wife! she gave it him, and he hath given it his whore.

---

139. *such another:* such. *fitchew:* polecat (known for sensuality). 145 ff. *work:* pattern (as above).

OTHELLO. I would have him nine years a-killing. A fine woman! a fair woman! a sweet woman!

IAGO. Nay, you must forget that.

OTHELLO. Ay, let her rot, and perish, and be damned to-night; for she shall not live: no, my heart is turned to stone; I strike it, [170 and it hurts my hand. O, the world hath not a sweeter creature: she might lie by an emperor's side, and command him tasks.

IAGO. Nay, that's not your way.

OTHELLO. Hang her! I do but say what she is: so delicate with her needle: an admirable musician: O, she will sing the savageness out of a bear: of so high and plenteous wit and invention:—

IAGO. She's the worse for all this.

OTHELLO. O, a thousand thousand times: and then, of so gentle a condition!

IAGO. Ay, too gentle. 180

OTHELLO. Nay, that's certain: but yet the pity of it, Iago! O Iago, the pity of it, Iago!

IAGO. If you are so fond over her iniquity, give her patent to offend; for, if it touch not you, it comes near nobody.

OTHELLO. I will chop her into messes: cuckold me!

IAGO. O, 'tis foul in her.

OTHELLO. With mine officer!

IAGO. That's fouler.

OTHELLO. Get me some poison, Iago; this night. I'll not expostulate with her, lest her body and beauty unprovide my mind [190 again: this night, Iago.

IAGO. Do it not with poison, strangle her in her bed, even the bed she hath contaminated.

OTHELLO. Good, good: the justice of it pleases: very good.

IAGO. And for Cassio, let me be his undertaker: you shall hear more by midnight.

OTHELLO. Excellent good. *A trumpet within.* What trumpet is that same?

IAGO. Something from Venice, sure. 'Tis Lodovico
Come from the duke: and, see, your wife is with him. 200

---

176. *wit:* intellect. *invention:* originality. 179. *condition:* disposition. 183. *fond:* foolishly in love. *patent:* charter. 189-90. *expostulate:* reason. 190. *unprovide:* disarm. 195. *undertaker:* the one who "takes him on."

Enter LODOVICO, DESDEMONA, *and* ATTENDANTS.

LODOVICO. God save the worthy general!
OTHELLO. With all my heart, sir.
LODOVICO. The duke and senators of Venice greet you.
Gives him a letter.
OTHELLO. I kiss the instrument of their pleasures.
Opens the letter, and reads.
DESDEMONA. And what's the news, good cousin Lodovico?
IAGO. I am very glad to see you, signior;
Welcome to Cyprus.
LODOVICO. I thank you. How does Lieutenant Cassio?
IAGO. Lives, sir.
DESDEMONA. Cousin, there's fall'n between him and my lord
An unkind breach: but you shall make all well. 210
OTHELLO. Are you sure of that?
DESDEMONA. My lord?
OTHELLO, *reads.* 'This fail you not to do, as you will—'
LODOVICO. He did not call; he's busy in the paper.
Is there division 'twixt my lord and Cassio?
DESDEMONA. A most unhappy one: I would do much
To atone them, for the love I bear to Cassio.
OTHELLO. Fire and brimstone!
DESDEMONA. My lord?
OTHELLO. Are you wise?
DESDEMONA. What, is he angry?
LODOVICO. May be the letter moved him;
For, as I think, they do command him home, 220
Deputing Cassio in his government.
DESDEMONA. By my troth, I am glad on 't.
OTHELLO. Indeed!
DESDEMONA. My lord?
OTHELLO. I am glad to see you mad.
DESDEMONA. Why, sweet Othello?
OTHELLO. Devil! *Striking her.*
DESDEMONA. I have not deserved this.
LODOVICO. My lord, this would not be believed in Venice,

---

216. *atone:* put them at one. 221. *government:* position.

SCENE 1] OTHELLO 455

Though I should swear I saw 't: 'tis very much:
Make her amends; she weeps.
    OTHELLO.   O devil, devil!
If that the earth could teem with woman's tears,
Each drop she falls would prove a crocodile.
Out of my sight!   230
    DESDEMONA.   I will not stay to offend you.   *Going.*
    LODOVICO. Truly, an obedient lady:
I do beseech your lordship, call her back.
    OTHELLO. Mistress!
    DESDEMONA. My lord?
    OTHELLO. What would you with her, sir?
    LODOVICO.   Who, I, my lord?
    OTHELLO. Ay; you did wish that I would make her turn:
Sir, she can turn and turn, and yet go on,
And turn again; and she can weep, sir, weep;
And she's obedient, as you say, obedient,   240
Very obedient. Proceed you in your tears.
Concerning this, sir,—O well-painted passion!—
I am commanded home. Get you away;
I'll send for you anon. Sir, I obey the mandate,
And will return to Venice. Hence, avaunt!   *Exit* DESDEMONA.
Cassio shall have my place. And, sir, to-night,
I do entreat that we may sup together:
You are welcome, sir, to Cyprus. Goats and monkeys!   *Exit.*
    LODOVICO. Is this the noble Moor whom our full senate
Call all in all sufficient? This the nature   250
Whom passion could not shake? whose solid virtue
The shot of accident nor dart of chance
Could neither graze nor pierce?
    IAGO.   He is much changed.
    LODOVICO. Are his wits safe? is he not light of brain?
    IAGO. He's that he is: I may not breathe my censure
What he might be: if what he might he is not,
I would to heaven he were!
    LODOVICO.   What, strike his wife.

---

228. *teem:* be fruitful. 237. i.e., she is devious. 248. *goats, monkeys*—sensual beasts. 250. *sufficient:* able.

IAGO. Faith, that was not so well; yet would I knew
That stroke would prove the worst!

LODOVICO.   Is it his use?
Or did the letters work upon his blood,   260
And new create this fault?

IAGO.   Alas, alas!
It is not honesty in me to speak
What I have seen and known. You shall observe him,
And his own courses will denote him so
That I may save my speech: do but go after,
And mark how he continues.

LODOVICO. I am sorry that I am deceived in him.   *Exeunt.*

SCENE 2. *A room in the castle.*

Enter OTHELLO *and* EMILIA.

OTHELLO. You have seen nothing, then?
EMILIA. Nor ever heard, nor ever did suspect.
OTHELLO. Yes, you have seen Cassio and she together.
EMILIA. But then I saw no harm, and then I heard
Each syllable that breath made up between them.
OTHELLO. What, did they never whisper?
EMILIA.   Never, my lord.
OTHELLO. Nor send you out o' the way?
EMILIA. Never.
OTHELLO. To fetch her fan, her gloves, her mask, nor nothing?
EMILIA. Never, my lord.   10
OTHELLO. That's strange.
EMILIA. I durst, my lord, to wager she is honest,
Lay down my soul at stake: if you think other,
Remove your thought; it doth abuse your bosom.
If any wretch have put this in your head,
Let heaven requite it with the serpent's curse!
For if she be not honest, chaste and true,
There's no man happy; the purest of their wives

---

259. *use:* habit.

   sc. 2: 14. *abuse your bosom:* deceive your heart. 16. *serpent:* the devil
(? the curse of Genesis III, 14).

SCENE 2] OTHELLO 457

Is foul as slander.
  OTHELLO.   Bid her come hither: go.   *Exit* EMILIA.
She says enough: yet she's a simple bawd 20
That cannot say as much. This is a subtle whore,
A closet lock and key of villanous secrets:
And yet she'll kneel and pray; I have seen her do 't.

Enter DESDEMONA *with* EMILIA.

  DESDEMONA. My lord, what is your will?
  OTHELLO.   Pray, chuck, come hither.
  DESDEMONA. What is your pleasure?
  OTHELLO.   Let me see your eyes;
Look in my face.
  DESDEMONA.   What horrible fancy's this?
  OTHELLO, *to* EMILIA. Some of your function, mistress,
Leave procreants alone and shut the door;
Cough, or cry hem, if any body come:
Your mystery, your mystery: nay, dispatch.   *Exit* EMILIA. 30
  DESDEMONA. Upon my knees, what doth your speech import?
I understand a fury in your words,
But not the words.
  OTHELLO. Why, what art thou?
  DESDEMONA. Your wife, my lord; your true and loyal wife.
  OTHELLO. Come, swear it, damn thyself;
Lest, being like one of heaven, the devils themselves
Should fear to seize thee: therefore be double-damn'd;
Swear thou art honest.
  DESDEMONA.   Heaven doth truly know it.
  OTHELLO. Heaven truly knows that thou art false as hell. 40
  DESDEMONA. To whom, my lord? with whom? how am I false?
  OTHELLO. O Desdemona! Away! away! away!
  DESDEMONA. Alas the heavy day! Why do you weep?
Am I the motive of these tears, my lord?
If haply you my father do suspect
An instrument of this your calling back,
Lay not your blame on me: if you have lost him,

---

20. *bawd:* go-between, pimp. 27. *some of your function:* i.e., some bawds.
28. *procreants:* copulators. 30. *mystery:* job.

Why, I have lost him too.
  OTHELLO.   Had it pleased heaven
To try me with affliction; had they rain'd
All kinds of sores and shames on my bare head,   50
Steep'd me in poverty to the very lips,
Given to captivity me and my utmost hopes,
I should have found in some place of my soul
A drop of patience: but, alas, to make me
A fixed figure for the time of scorn
To point his slow unmoving finger at!
Yet could I bear that too; well, very well:
But there, where I have garner'd up my heart,
Where either I must live or bear no life,
The fountain from the which my current runs,   60
Or else dries up; to be discarded thence!
Or keep it as a cistern for foul toads
To knot and gender in! Turn thy complexion *there,*
Patience, thou young and rose-lipp'd cherubin,
Ay, *there,* look grim as hell!
  DESDEMONA. I hope my noble lord esteems me honest.
  OTHELLO. O, ay; as summer flies are in the shambles,
That quicken even with blowing. O thou weed,
Who art so lovely fair and smell'st so sweet
That the sense aches at thee, would thou hadst ne'er been born!   70
  DESDEMONA. Alas, what ignorant sin have I committed?
  OTHELLO. Was this fair paper, this most goodly book,
Made to write 'whore' upon? What committed!
Committed! O thou public commoner!
I should make very forges of my cheeks,
That would to cinders burn up modesty,
Did I but speak thy deeds. What committed!
Heaven stops the nose at it, and the moon winks;
The bawdy wind, that kisses all it meets,
Is hush'd within the hollow mine of earth,   80
And will not hear it. What committed!

---

55. *of scorn:* scornful. 62. *cistern:* cesspool. 63. *knot:* copulate. *gender:* engender. 68. *quicken:* come to life (image of maggots in flyblown meat). 71. *ignorant:* in ignorance. 74. *commoner:* whore. 78. *winks:* shuts her eyes.

SCENE 2] OTHELLO 459

Impudent strumpet!
  DESDEMONA.   By heaven, you do me wrong.
  OTHELLO. Are not you a strumpet?
  DESDEMONA.   No, as I am a Christian:
If to preserve this vessel for my lord
From any other foul unlawful touch
Be not to be a strumpet, I am none.
  OTHELLO. What, not a whore?
  DESDEMONA.   No, as I shall be saved.
  OTHELLO. Is 't possible?
  DESDEMONA. O, heaven forgive us!
  OTHELLO.   I cry you mercy then:
I took you for that cunning whore of Venice   90
That married with Othello. *Raising his voice.* You, mistress,
That have the office opposite to Saint Peter,
And keep the gate of hell!

Re-enter EMILIA.

                You, you, ay, you!
We have done our course; there's money for your pains:
I pray you, turn the key, and keep our counsel.   *Exit.*
  EMILIA. Alas, what does this gentleman conceive?
How do you, madam? how do you, my good lady?
  DESDEMONA. Faith, half asleep.
  EMILIA. Good madam, what's the matter with my lord?
  DESDEMONA. With who?   100
  EMILIA. Why, with my lord, madam.
  DESDEMONA. Who is thy lord?
  EMILIA.   He that is yours, sweet lady.
  DESDEMONA. I have none: do not talk to me, Emilia;
I cannot weep, nor answer have I none
But what should go by water. Prithee, to-night
Lay on my bed my wedding sheets: remember;
And call thy husband hither.

---

84. *this vessel:* i.e., her body. 92. *office:* position. 94-5. Othello keeps up the pretence that he is the customer, Desdemona the whore, Emilia the "madam." 95. *keep our counsel:* don't tell anyone. 105. *go by water:* come out in tears.

460   OTHELLO   [ACT IV

EMILIA.   Here's a change indeed!   *Exit.*
DESDEMONA. 'Tis meet I should be used so, very meet.
How have I been behaved, that he might stick
The small'st opinion on my least misuse?   110

Re-enter EMILIA, *with* IAGO.

IAGO. What is your pleasure, madam? How is 't with you?
DESDEMONA. I cannot tell. Those that do teach young babes
Do it with gentle means and easy tasks:
He might have chid me so; for, in good faith,
I am a child to chiding.
IAGO.   What's the matter, lady?
EMILIA. Alas, Iago, my lord hath so bewhored her,
Thrown such despite and heavy terms upon her,
As true hearts cannot bear.
DESDEMONA. Am I that name, Iago?
IAGO.   What name, fair lady?
DESDEMONA. Such as she says my lord did say I was.   120
EMILIA. He call'd her whore: a beggar in his drink
Could not have laid such terms upon his callet.
IAGO. Why did he so?
DESDEMONA. I do not know: I am sure I am none such.
IAGO. Do not weep, do not weep. Alas the day!
EMILIA. Hath she forsook so many noble matches,
Her father and her country and her friends,
To be call'd whore? would it not make one weep?
DESDEMONA. It is my wretched fortune.
IAGO.   Beshrew him for 't!
How comes this trick upon him?
DESDEMONA.   Nay, heaven doth know.   130
EMILIA. I will be hang'd, if some eternal villain,
Some busy and insinuating rogue,
Some cogging, cozening slave, to get some office,
Have not devised this slander; I'll be hang'd else.
IAGO. Fie, there is no such man; it is impossible.

---

108. *used:* treated. 110. *misuse:* misconduct. 116. *bewhored:* called a whore.
122. *callet:* mate, whore. 129. *Beshrew:* curse. 130. *trick:* freak. 133. *cogging:* tricky. *cozening:* deceiving. *office:* position.

SCENE 2] OTHELLO 461

DESDEMONA. If any such there be, heaven pardon him!
EMELIA. A halter pardon him! and hell gnaw his bones!
Why should he call her whore? who keeps her company?
What place? what time? what form? what likelihood?
The Moor's abused by some most villanous knave, 140
Some base notorious knave, some scurvy fellow.
O heaven, that such companions thou 'ldst unfold,
And put in every honest hand a whip
To lash the rascals naked through the world
Even from the east to the west!
IAGO.   Speak within door.
EMILIA. O, fie upon them! Some such squire he was
That turn'd your wit the seamy side without,
And made you to suspect me with the Moor.
IAGO. You are a fool; go to.
DESDEMONA.   O good Iago,
What shall I do to win my lord again? 150
Good friend, go to him; for, by this light of heaven,
I know not how I lost him. Here I kneel:
If e'er my will did trespass 'gainst his love
Either in discourse of thought or actual deed,
Or that mine eyes, mine ears, or any sense,
Delighted them in any other form,
Or that I do not yet, and ever did,
And ever will, though he do shake me off
To beggarly divorcement, love him dearly,
Comfort forswear me! Unkindness may do much; 160
And *his* unkindness may defeat my life,
But never taint my love. I cannot say 'whore':
It doth abhor me now I speak the word;
To do the act that might the addition earn
Not the world's mass of vanity could make me.
IAGO. I pray you, be content; 'tis but his humour:
The business of the state does him offence,
And he does chide with you.
DESDEMONA. If 'twere no other,—

---

137. *halter:* noose. 148. *suspect me* [of having slept]. 161. *defeat:* destroy. 164. *addition:* title.

IAGO.   'Tis but so, I warrant.

Trumpets within.

Hark, how these instruments summon to supper!   170
The messengers of Venice stay the meat:
Go in, and weep not; all things shall be well.

Exeunt DESDEMONA *and* EMILIA.

Enter RODERIGO.

How now, Roderigo!

RODERIGO. I do not find that thou dealest justly with me.

IAGO. What in the contrary?

RODERIGO. Every day thou daffest me with some device, Iago; and rather, as it seems to me now, keepest from me all conveniency than suppliest me with the least advantage of hope. I will indeed no longer endure it; nor am I yet persuaded to put up in peace what already I have foolishly suffered.   180

IAGO. Will you hear me, Roderigo?

RODERIGO. Faith, I have heard too much; for your words and performances are no kin together.

IAGO. You charge me most unjustly.

RODERIGO. With nought but truth. I have wasted myself out of my means. The jewels you have had from me to deliver to Desdemona would half have corrupted a votarist: you have told me she hath received them and returned me expectations and comforts of sudden respect and acquaintance; but I find none.

IAGO. Well; go to; very well.   190

RODERIGO. Very well! go to! I cannot go to, man; nor 'tis not very well: by this hand, I say 'tis very scurvy, and begin to find myself fopped in it.

IAGO. Very well.

RODERIGO. I tell you 'tis not very well. I will make myself known to Desdemona: if she will return me my jewels, I will give over my suit and repent my unlawful solicitation; if not, assure yourself I will seek satisfaction of you.

IAGO. You have said now.

---

171. *stay the meat:* stay for supper. 176. *daffest:* put off. 177. *conveniency:* opportunity. 187. *votarist:* a nun. 188. *comforts:* reports. *sudden:* immediate. 193. *fopped:* made a fool of.

RODERIGO. Ay, and said nothing but what I protest intend- [200
ment of doing.

IAGO. Why, now I see there's mettle in thee; and even from this instant do build on thee a better opinion than ever before. Give me thy hand, Roderigo: thou hast taken against me a most just exception; but yet, I protest, I have dealt most directly in thy affair.

RODERIGO. It hath not appeared.

IAGO. I grant indeed it hath not appeared, and your suspicion is not without wit and judgement. But, Roderigo, if thou hast that in thee indeed, which I have greater reason to believe now than ever, I mean purpose, courage and valour, this night show it: if thou [210 the next night following enjoy not Desdemona, take me from this world with treachery and devise engines for my life.

RODERIGO. Well, what is it? is it within reason and compass?

IAGO. Sir, there is especial commission come from Venice to depute Cassio in Othello's place.

RODERIGO. Is that true? why then Othello and Desdemona return again to Venice.

IAGO. O, no; he goes into Mauritania, and takes away with him the fair Desdemona, unless his abode be lingered here by some accident: wherein none can be so determinate as the removing of [220 Cassio.

RODERIGO. How do you mean, removing of him?

IAGO. Why, by making him uncapable of Othello's place; knocking out his brains.

RODERIGO. And that you would have me to do?

IAGO. Ay, if you dare do yourself a profit and a right. He sups to-night with a harlotry, and thither will I go to him: he knows not yet of his honourable fortune. If you will watch his going thence, which I will fashion to fall out between twelve and one, you may take him at your pleasure: I will be near to second your attempt, and [230 he shall fall between us. Come, stand not amazed at it, but go along with me; I will show you such a necessity in his death that you shall think yourself bound to put it on him. It is now high supper-time, and the night grows to waste: about it.

---

202. *mettle:* courage. 212. *engines for:* plots against. 227. *harlotry:* harlot. 234. *grows to waste:* is passing.

RODERIGO. I will hear further reason for this.
IAGO. And you shall be satisfied. *Exeunt.*

SCENE 3. *Another room in the castle.*

Enter OTHELLO, LODOVICO, DESDEMONA, EMILIA, *and* ATTENDANTS.

LODOVICO. I do beseech you, sir, trouble yourself no further.
OTHELLO. O, pardon me; 'twill do me good to walk.
LODOVICO. Madam, good night; I humbly thank your ladyship.
DESDEMONA. Your honour is most welcome.
OTHELLO. Will you walk, sir?
O,—Desdemona,—
DESDEMONA. My lord?
OTHELLO. Get you to bed on the instant; I will be returned forthwith: dismiss your attendant there:
look it be done.
DESDEMONA. I will, my lord. 10
Exeunt OTHELLO, LODOVICO, *and* ATTENDANTS.
EMILIA. How goes it now? he looks gentler than he did.
DESDEMONA. He says he will return incontinent:
He hath commanded me to go to bed,
And bade me to dismiss you.
EMILIA. Dismiss me!
DESDEMONA. It was his bidding; therefore, good Emilia,
Give me my nightly wearing, and adieu:
We must not now displease him.
EMILIA. I would you had never seen him!
DESDEMONA. So would not I: my love doth so approve him,
That even his stubbornness, his checks, his frowns,— 20
Prithee, unpin me,—have grace and favour in them.
EMILIA. I have laid those sheets you bade me on the bed.
DESDEMONA. All's one. Good faith, how foolish are our minds!
If I do die before thee, prithee, shroud me
In one of those same sheets.
EMILIA. Come, come, you talk.
DESDEMONA. My mother had a maid call'd Barbara:

---

sc. 3: 12. *incontinent:* at once. 20. *stubbornness:* roughness. *checks:* rebukes.

SCENE 3] OTHELLO 465

She was in love; and he she loved proved mad
And did forsake her: she had a song of 'willow;'
An old thing 'twas, but it express'd her fortune,
And she died singing it: that song to-night 30
Will not go from my mind; I have much to do
But to go hang my head all at one side
And sing it like poor Barbara. Prithee, dispatch.
 EMILIA. Shall I go fetch your night-gown?
 DESDEMONA. No, unpin me here.
This Lodovico is a proper man.
 EMILIA. A very handsome man.
 DESDEMONA. He speaks well.
 EMILIA. I know a lady in Venice would have walked barefoot to
Palestine for a touch of his nether lip.

 DESDEMONA, *singing*. 'The poor soul sat sighing by a syca- [40
 more tree,
 Sing all a green willow;
Her hand on her bosom, her head on her knee,
 Sing willow, willow, willow:
The fresh streams ran by her, and murmur'd her moans;
 Sing willow, willow, willow;
Her salt tears fell from her, and soften'd the stones;—'

Lay by these:—

Singing. 'Sing willow, willow, willow;'
Prithee, hie thee; he'll come anon:—
Singing. 'Sing all a green willow must be my garland. 50
 Let nobody blame him; his scorn I approve,—'

Nay, that's not next. Hark! who is 't that knocks?
 EMILIA. It's the wind.

 DESDEMONA, *singing*. 'I call'd my love false love; but what said he
 then?
 Sing willow, willow, willow:
If I court moe women, you'll couch with moe men.'

---

35. *proper:* handsome. 56. *moe:* more. *couch:* sleep.

So get thee gone; good night. Mine eyes do itch;
Doth that bode weeping?

EMILIA. 'Tis neither here nor there.

DESDEMONA. I have heard it said so. O, these men, these men!
Dost thou in conscience think,—tell me, Emilia,— 60
That there be women do abuse their husbands
In such gross kind?

EMILIA. There be some such, no question.

DESDEMONA. Wouldst thou do such a deed for all the world?

EMILIA. Why, would not you?

DESDEMONA. No, by this heavenly light!

EMILIA. Nor I neither by this heavenly light; I might do 't as well i' the dark.

DESDEMONA. Wouldst thou do such a deed for all the world?

EMILIA. The world's a huge thing: it is a great price
For a small vice.

DESDEMONA. In troth, I think thou wouldst not.

EMILIA. In troth, I think I should; and undo 't when I had [70
done. Marry, I would not do such a thing for a joint-ring, nor for measures of lawn, nor for gowns, petticoats, nor caps, nor any petty exhibition; but, for the whole world,—why, who would not make her husband a cuckold to make him a monarch? I should venture purgatory for 't.

DESDEMONA. Beshrew me, if I would do such a wrong
For the whole world.

EMILIA. Why, the wrong is but a wrong i' the world; and having the world for your labour, 'tis a wrong in your own world, and you might quickly make it right. 80

DESDEMONA. I do not think there is *any* such woman.

EMILIA. Yes, a dozen; and as many to the vantage as would store the world they played for.
But I do think it is their husbands' faults
If wives do fall: say that they slack their duties
And pour our treasures into foreign laps,

---

58. *'Tis neither* . . . : it bodes nothing. 62. *kind:* way. 71. *joint-ring:* double ring. 72. *lawn:* linen. 82. *to the vantage:* more. *store:* populate. 86. *our treasures:* what should be ours. *foreign laps:* the laps of others.

ACT V, SCENE 1] OTHELLO 467

Or else break out in peevish jealousies,
Throwing restraint upon us, or say they strike us,
Or scant our former having in despite,
Why, we have galls, and though we have some grace, 90
Yet have we some revenge. Let husbands know
Their wives have sense like them: they see and smell
And have their palates both for sweet and sour,
As husbands have. What is it that they do
When they change us for others? Is it sport?
I think it is: and doth affection breed it?
I think it doth: is 't frailty that thus errs?
It is so too: and have not we affections,
Desires for sport, and frailty, as men have?
Then let them use us well: else let them know, 100
The ills we do, their ills instruct us so.

DESDEMONA. Good night, good night: heaven me such uses send,
Not to pick bad from bad, but by bad mend! *Exeunt.*

Act V

SCENE 1. *Cyprus. A street.*

Enter IAGO *and* RODERIGO.

IAGO. Here, stand behind this bulk; straight will he come;
Wear thy good rapier bare, and put it home:
Quick, quick; fear nothing; I'll be at thy elbow:
It makes us, or it mars us; think on that,
And fix most firm thy resolution.

RODERIGO. Be near at hand; I may miscarry in 't.

IAGO. Here, at thy hand: be bold, and take thy stand. *Retires.*

RODERIGO. I have no great devotion to the deed;
And yet he hath given me satisfying reasons:
'Tis but a man gone. Forth, my sword: he dies. 10

IAGO. I have rubb'd this young quat almost to the sense,

---

89. *having:* money allowance. 90. *galls:* capacities for resentment. *grace:* virtue. 92. *sense:* feeling. 102. *uses:* ways. 103. *pick:* learn.

ACT V, SC. 1: 1. *bulk:* of a building. 2. *put:* drive. 11. *quat:* pimple.

And he grows angry. Now, whether he kill Cassio,
Or Cassio him, or each do kill the other,
Every way makes my gain: live Roderigo,
He calls me to a restitution large
Of gold and jewels that I bobb'd from him,
As gifts to Desdemona:
It must not be: if Cassio do remain,
He hath a daily beauty in his life
That makes me ugly; and besides, the Moor 20
May unfold me to him; there stand I in much peril:
No, he must die. Be 't so. I hear him coming.

Enter CASSIO.

RODERIGO. I know his gait; 'tis he. Villain, thou diest!
Makes a pass at CASSIO.
CASSIO. That thrust had been mine enemy indeed,
But that my coat is better than thou know'st:
I will make proof of thine.   *Draws, and wounds* RODERIGO.
RODERIGO.   O, I am slain!
IAGO *from behind wounds* CASSIO *in the leg, and exit.*
CASSIO. I am maim'd for ever. Help, ho! murder! murder!   *Falls.*

Enter OTHELLO.

OTHELLO. The voice of Cassio: Iago keeps his word.
RODERIGO. O, villain that I am!
OTHELLO.   It is even so.
CASSIO. O, help, ho! light! a surgeon! 30
OTHELLO. 'Tis he. O brave Iago, honest and just,
That hast such noble sense of thy friend's wrong!
Thou teachest *me*. Minion, your dear lies dead,
And your unblest fate hies: strumpet, I come!
Forth of my heart those charms, thine eyes, are blotted:
Thy bed lust-stain'd shall with lust's blood be spotted.   *Exit.*

Enter LODOVICO *and* GRATIANO.

---

16. *bobb'd:* got by cheating. 21. *unfold:* reveal. 33. *minion:* "boy friend."
35. *Forth of:* out of.

CASSIO. What, ho! no watch? no passage? murder! murder!
GRATIANO. 'Tis some mischance; the cry is very direful.
CASSIO. O, help!
LODOVICO. Hark!
RODERIGO. O wretched villain.
LODOVICO. Two or three groan: it is a heavy night:
These may be counterfeits: let's think 't unsafe
To come into the cry without more help.
RODERIGO. Nobody come? then shall I bleed to death.
LODOVICO. Hark!

Re-enter IAGO, *with a light.*

GRATIANO. Here's one comes in his shirt, with light and weapons.
IAGO. Who's there? whose noise is this that cries on murder?
LODOVICO. We do not know.
IAGO.   Did not you hear a cry?
CASSIO. Here, here! for heaven's sake, help me!
IAGO.   What's the matter?
GRATIANO. This is Othello's ancient, as I take it.
LODOVICO. The same indeed; a very valiant fellow.
IAGO. What are you here that cry so grievously?
CASSIO. Iago? O, I am spoil'd, undone by villains!
Give me some help.
IAGO. O me, lieutenant! what villains have done this?
CASSIO. I think that one of them is hereabout,
And cannot make away.
IAGO.   O treacherous villains!
What are you there? come in and give some help.

                                     To LODOVICO *and* GRATIANO.

RODERIGO. O, help me here!
CASSIO. That's one of them.
IAGO.   O murderous slave! O villain!

                                          Stabs RODERIGO.

RODERIGO. O damn'd Iago! O inhuman dog!
IAGO. Kill men i' the dark! Where be these bloody thieves?
How silent is this town! Ho! murder! murder!

---

37. *passage:* passers-by. 44. *into:* near.

470   OTHELLO   [ACT V

What may you be? are you of good or evil?
  LODOVICO. As you shall prove us, praise us.
  IAGO. Signior Lodovico?
  LODOVICO. He, sir.
  IAGO. I cry you mercy. Here's Cassio hurt by villains.
  GRATIANO. Cassio!   70
  IAGO. How is 't, brother?
  CASSIO. My leg is cut in two.
  IAGO.   Marry, heaven forbid!
Light, gentlemen: I'll bind it with my shirt.

Enter BIANCA.

  BIANCA. What is the matter, ho? who is 't that cried?
  IAGO. Who is 't that cried!
  BIANCA. O my dear Cassio! my sweet Cassio! O
Cassio, Cassio, Cassio!
  IAGO. O notable strumpet! Cassio, may you suspect
Who they should be that have thus mangled you?
  CASSIO. No.   80
  GRATIANO. I am sorry to find you thus: I have been to seek you.
  IAGO. Lend me a garter. So. O, for a chair,
To bear him easily hence!
  BIANCA. Alas, he faints! O Cassio, Cassio, Cassio!
  IAGO. Gentlemen all, I do suspect this trash
To be a party in this injury.
Patience awhile, good Cassio. Come, come;
Lend me a light. Know we this face or no?
Alas, my friend and my dear countryman
Roderigo? no:—yes, sure: O heaven! Roderigo.   90
  GRATIANO. What, of Venice?
  IAGO. Even he, sir: did you know him?
  GRATIANO.   Know him! ay.
  IAGO. Signior Gratiano? I cry you gentle pardon;
These bloody accidents must excuse my manners,
That so neglected you.
  GRATIANO.   I am glad to see you.

---

85. *trash:* i.e., Bianca.

SCENE 1]   OTHELLO   471

 IAGO. How do you, Cassio? O, a chair, a chair!
 GRATIANO. Roderigo!
 IAGO. He, he, 'tis he. *A chair brought in.* O, that's well said; the chair;
Some good man bear him carefully from hence;
I'll fetch the general's surgeon. *To* BIANCA. For you, mistress, 100
Save you your labour. He that lies slain here, Cassio,
Was my dear friend: what malice was between you?
 CASSIO. None in the world; nor do I know the man.
 IAGO, *to* BIANCA. What, look you pale? O, bear him out o' the air.
          CASSIO *and* RODERIGO *are borne off.*
Stay you, good gentlemen. Look you pale, mistress?
Do you perceive the gastness of her eye?
Nay, if you stare, we shall hear more anon.
Behold her well; I pray you, look upon her:
Do you see, gentlemen? nay, guiltiness will speak,
Though tongues were out of use. 110

      Enter EMILIA.

 EMILIA. 'Las, what's the matter? what's the matter, husband?
 IAGO. Cassio hath here been set on in the dark
By Roderigo, and fellows that are 'scaped:
He's almost slain, and Roderigo dead.
 EMILIA. Alas, good gentleman! alas, good Cassio!
 IAGO. This is the fruit of whoring. Prithee, Emilia,
Go know of Cassio where he supp'd to-night.
What, do you shake at that?
 BIANCA. He supp'd at my house; but I therefore shake not.
 IAGO. O, did he so? I charge you, go with me. 120
 EMILIA. Fie, fie upon thee, strumpet!
 BIANCA. I am no strumpet; but of life as honest
As you that thus abuse me.
 EMILIA.   As I! foh! fie upon thee!

---

102. *malice:* enmity. 106. *gastness:* terror. 123. At the end of IV, 3, Shakespeare indicates the difference in level of Emilia and Desdemona. We here see how much higher than Bianca Emilia considers herself, however. A Shakespearean "subject" involves many levels, many viewpoints.

472   OTHELLO   [ACT V

IAGO. Kind gentlemen, let's go see poor Cassio dress'd.
Come, mistress, you must tell 's another tale.
Emilia, run you to the citadel,
And tell my lord and lady what hath happ'd!
Will you go on? I pray. *Aside.* This is the night
That either makes me or fordoes me quite.   *Exeunt.*

SCENE 2. *A bedchamber in the castle:* DESDEMONA *in bed asleep;
a light burning.*

Enter OTHELLO.

OTHELLO. It is the cause, it is the cause, my soul:
Let me not name it to you, you chaste stars!
It is the cause. Yet I'll not shed her blood,
Nor scar that whiter skin of hers than snow
And smooth as monumental alabaster.
Yet she must die, else she'll betray more men.
Put out the light, and then put out the light:
If I quench thee, thou flaming minister,
I can again thy former light restore,
Should I repent me: but once put out thy light,   10
Thou cunning'st pattern of excelling nature,
I know not where is that Promethean heat
That can thy light relume. When I have pluck'd the rose,
I cannot give it vital growth again,
It must needs wither: I'll smell it on the tree.   *Kissing her.*
Ah, balmy breath, that dost almost persuade
Justice to break her sword! One more, one more:
Be thus when thou art dead, and I will kill thee,
And love thee after: one more, and this the last:
So sweet was ne'er so fatal. I must weep,   20
But they are cruel tears: this sorrow's heavenly;

---

124. *dress'd:* i.e., the wound. 129. *fordoes:* ruins.
  SC. 2: 1. i.e., It is the just cause for murder, not personal resentment, that he is trying to convince himself of. 7. "and then put out *her* light." 8. *thee:* i.e., the light in the room. 10. *thy:* i.e., Desdemona's. 12. Prometheus brought us fire. 21. *heavenly*—like that of God punishing whom he loves.

SCENE 2]   OTHELLO   473

It strikes where it doth love. She wakes.
  DESDEMONA. Who's there? Othello?
  OTHELLO.   Ay, Desdemona.
  DESDEMONA. Will you come to bed, my lord?
  OTHELLO. Have you pray'd to-night, Desdemona?
  DESDEMONA. Ay, my lord.
  OTHELLO. If you bethink yourself of any crime
Unreconciled as yet to heaven and grace,
Solicit for it straight.
  DESDEMONA. Alas, my lord, what may you mean by that?   30
  OTHELLO. Well, do it, and be brief; I will walk by:
I would not kill thy unprepared spirit;
No; heaven forfend! I would not kill thy soul.
  DESDEMONA. Talk you of killing?
  OTHELLO. Ay, I do.
  DESDEMONA. Then heaven have mercy on me!
  OTHELLO. Amen, with all my heart!
  DESDEMONA. If you say so, I hope you will not kill me.
  OTHELLO. Hum!
  DESDEMONA. And yet I fear you; for you are fatal then   40
When your eyes roll so: why I should fear I know not,
Since guiltiness I know not; but yet I feel I fear.
  OTHELLO. Think on thy sins.
  DESDEMONA.   They are loves I bear to you.
  OTHELLO. Ay, and for that thou diest.
  DESDEMONA. That death's unnatural that kills for loving.
Alas, why gnaw you so your nether lip?
Some bloody passion shakes your very frame:
These are portents; but yet I hope, I hope,
They do not point on me.
  OTHELLO.   Peace, and be still!
  DESDEMONA. I will so. What's the matter?   50
  OTHELLO. That handkerchief which I so loved and gave thee
Thou gavest to Cassio.
  DESDEMONA.   No, by my life and soul!
Send for the man, and ask him.
  OTHELLO.   Sweet soul, take heed,

---

31. *walk by:* step aside. 44. *that:* i.e., love. 48. *portents:* ominous signs.

474   OTHELLO   [ACT V

Take heed of perjury; thou art on thy death-bed.
  DESDEMONA. Ay, but not yet to die.
  OTHELLO.   Yes, presently:
Therefore confess thee freely of thy sin;
For to deny each article with oath
Cannot remove nor choke the strong conception
That I do groan withal. Thou art to die.
  DESDEMONA. Then Lord have mercy on me!
  OTHELLO.   I say, amen.   60
  DESDEMONA. And have you mercy too! I never did
Offend you in my life; never loved Cassio
But with such general warranty of heaven
As I might love: I never gave him token.
  OTHELLO. By heaven, I saw my handkerchief in 's hand.
O perjured woman! thou dost stone my heart,
And makest me call what I intend to do
A murder, which I thought a sacrifice:
I saw the handkerchief.
  DESDEMONA.   He found it then;
I never gave it him: send for him hither;   70
Let him confess a truth.
  OTHELLO.   He hath confess'd.
  DESDEMONA. What, my lord?
  OTHELLO. That he hath used thee.
  DESDEMONA.   How? unlawfully?
  OTHELLO. Ay.
  DESDEMONA. He will not say so.
  OTHELLO.   No, his mouth is stopp'd;
Honest Iago hath ta'en order for 't.
  DESDEMONA. O, my fear interprets! what, is he dead?
  OTHELLO. Had all his hairs been lives, my great revenge
Had stomach for them all.
  DESDEMONA. Alas, he is betray'd, and I undone!   80
  OTHELLO. Out, strumpet! weep'st thou for him to my face?
  DESDEMONA. O, banish me, my lord, but kill me not!

---

58. *conception:* idea. 59. *withal:* with. 62. *offend:* sin against. 63. "As warranted by religious law."

SCENE 2] OTHELLO 475

OTHELLO. Down, strumpet!
DESDEMONA. Kill me to-morrow; let me live to-night!
OTHELLO. Nay, if you strive,—
DESDEMONA. But half an hour!
OTHELLO.   Being done, there is no pause.
DESDEMONA. But while I say one prayer!
OTHELLO.   It is too late.

He stifles her.

EMILIA, *within*. My lord, my lord! what, ho! my lord, my lord!
OTHELLO. What noise is this? Not dead? not yet quite dead?
I that am cruel am yet merciful;   90
I would not have thee linger in thy pain:
So, so.
 EMILIA, *within*. What, ho! my lord, my lord!
OTHELLO.   Who's there?
EMILIA, *within*. O, good my lord, I would speak a word with you!
OTHELLO. Yes: 'tis Emilia. By and by. She's dead.
'Tis like she comes to speak of Cassio's death.
The noise was here. Ha! no more moving?
Still as the grave. Shall she come in? were 't good?
I think she stirs again. No. What's best to do?
If she come in, she'll sure speak to my wife: 100
My wife! my wife! what wife? I have no wife.
O, insupportable! O heavy hour!
Methinks it should be now a huge eclipse
Of sun and moon, and that the affrighted globe
Should yawn at alteration.
 EMILIA, *within*.   I do beseech you
That I may speak with you, O, good my lord!
OTHELLO. I had forgot thee: O, come in, Emilia.
Soft; by and by. Let me the curtains draw.
Where art thou?   *Unlocks the door.*

Enter EMILIA.

What's the matter with thee now?

---

86. *being done:* since it's over now. *pause:* delay. 96. *like:* likely. 105. *yawn:* split open in earthquake. *alteration:* the change (indicated by the eclipse). 108. *Soft:* wait.

EMILIA. O, my good lord, yonder's foul murders done! 110
OTHELLO. What, now?
EMILIA. But now, my lord.
OTHELLO. It is the very error of the moon;
She comes more nearer earth than she was wont
And makes men mad.
EMILIA. Cassio, my lord, hath kill'd a young Venetian
Call'd Roderigo.
OTHELLO.   Roderigo kill'd!
And Cassio kill'd!
EMILIA.   No, Cassio is not kill'd.
OTHELLO. Not Cassio kill'd! then murder's out of tune,
And sweet revenge grows harsh. 120
DESDEMONA. O, falsely, falsely murder'd!
EMILIA.   Alas, what cry is that?
OTHELLO. That! what?
EMILIA. Out, and alas! that was my lady's voice.
Help! help, ho! help! O lady, speak again!
Sweet Desdemona! O sweet mistress, speak!
DESDEMONA. A guiltless death I die.
EMILIA. O, who hath done this deed?
DESDEMONA. Nobody; I myself. Farewell:
Commend me to my kind lord: O, farewell! *Dies.*
OTHELLO. Why, how should she be murder'd?
EMILIA.   Alas, who knows? 130
OTHELLO. You heard her say herself, It was not I.
EMILIA. She said so: I must needs report the truth.
OTHELLO. She's like a liar gone to burning hell:
'Twas I that kill'd her.
EMILIA.   O, the more angel she,
And you the blacker devil!
OTHELLO. She turn'd to folly, and she was a whore.
EMILIA. Thou dost belie her, and thou art a devil.
OTHELLO. She was false as water.
EMILIA.   Thou art rash as fire, to say
That she was false: O, she was heavenly true!
OTHELLO. Cassio did top her; ask thy husband else. 140

---

113. *error:* wandering.   140. *top:* sleep with.

O, I were damn'd beneath all depth in hell,
But that I did proceed upon just grounds
To this extremity. Thy husband knew it all.
  EMILIA. My husband!
  OTHELLO. Thy husband.
  EMILIA. That she was false to wedlock?
  OTHELLO. Ay, with Cassio. Nay, had she been true,
If heaven would make me such another world
Of one entire and perfect chrysolite,
I 'ld not have sold her for it.   150
  EMILIA. My husband!
  OTHELLO.   Ay, 'twas he that told me first:
An honest man he is, and hates the slime
That sticks on filthy deeds.
  EMILIA.   My husband!
  OTHELLO. What needs this iteration, woman? I say thy husband.
  EMILIA. O mistress, villany hath made mocks with love!
My husband say that she was false!
  OTHELLO.   He, woman;
I say thy husband: dost understand the word?
My friend, thy husband, honest, honest Iago.
  EMILIA. If he say so, may his pernicious soul
Rot half a grain a day! he lies to the heart: 160
She was too fond of her most filthy bargain.
  OTHELLO. Ha!
  EMILIA. Do thy worst:
This deed of thine is no more worthy heaven
Than thou wast worthy her.
  OTHELLO.   Peace, you were best.
  EMILIA. Thou hast not half that power to do me harm
As I have to be hurt. O gull! O dolt!
As ignorant as dirt! thou hast done a deed—
I care not for thy sword; I'll make thee known,
Though I lost twenty lives. Help! help, ho! help!   170
The Moor hath kill'd my mistress! Murder! murder!

---

149. *chrysolite:* a precious stone.   155. *made mocks with:* mocked, made mockery of.

Enter MONTANO, GRATIANO, IAGO, *and others.*

MONTANO. What is the matter? How now, general!

EMILIA. O, are you come, Iago? you have done well,
That men must lay their murders on your neck.

GRATIANO. What is the matter?

EMILIA. Disprove this villain, if thou be'st a man:
He says thou told'st him that his wife was false:
I know thou didst not, thou 'rt not such a villain.
Speak, for my heart is full.

IAGO. I told him what I thought, and told no more   180
Than what he found himself was apt and true.

EMILIA. But did you ever tell him she was false?

IAGO. I did.

EMILIA. You told a lie, an odious, damned lie;
Upon my soul, a lie, a wicked lie!
She false with Cassio! Did you say with Cassio?

IAGO. With Cassio, mistress. Go to, charm your tongue.

EMILIA. I will not charm my tongue; I am bound to speak:
My mistress here lies murder'd in her bed,—

ALL. O heavens forfend!   190

EMILIA. And your reports have set the murder on.

OTHELLO. Nay, stare not, masters: it is true indeed.

GRATIANO. 'Tis a strange truth.

MONTANO. O monstrous act!

EMILIA.   Villany, villany, villany!
I think upon 't: I think: I smell 't: O villany!
I thought so then: I'll kill myself for grief:
O villany, villany!

IAGO. What, are you mad? I charge you, get you home.

EMILIA. Good gentlemen, let me have leave to speak:
'Tis proper I obey him, but not now.   200
Perchance, Iago, I will ne'er go home.

OTHELLO. O! O! O!   *Falling on the bed.*

EMILIA.   Nay, lay thee down and roar;
For thou hast kill'd the sweetest innocent

---

187. *charm:* put under a spell. 202-04. It is worth noting what effect Emilia's speeches have on the tone of the play here (as in IV, 3).

That e'er did lift up eye.

OTHELLO, *rising*.   O, she was foul!
I scarce did know you, uncle: there lies your niece,
Whose breath indeed these hands have newly stopp'd:
I know this act shows horrible and grim.

GRATIANO. Poor Desdemona! I am glad thy father's dead:
Thy match was mortal to him, and pure grief
Shore his old thread in twain: did he live now, 210
This sight would make him do a desperate turn,
Yea, curse his better angel from his side,
And fall to reprobation.

OTHELLO.   'Tis pitiful; but yet Iago knows
That she with Cassio hath the act of shame
A thousand times committed; Cassio confess'd it:
And she did gratify his amorous works
With that recognizance and pledge of love
Which I first gave her; I saw it in his hand:
It was a handkerchief, an antique token 220
My father gave my mother.

EMILIA. O heaven! O heavenly powers!

IAGO. 'Zounds! hold your peace.

EMILIA.   'Twill out, 'twill out. I peace!
No, I will speak as liberal as the north:
Let heaven and men and devils, let them all,
All, all, cry shame against me, yet I'll speak.

IAGO. Be wise, and get you home.

EMILIA.   I will not.

IAGO offers to stab EMILIA.

GRATIANO.   Fie!
Your sword upon a woman!

EMILIA. O thou dull Moor! that handkerchief thou speak'st of
I found by fortune and did give my husband; 230
For often with a solemn earnestness,
More than indeed belong'd to such a trifle,
He begg'd of me to steal it.

IAGO.   Villanous whore!

---

210. Here we learn what happened to Brabantio. 213. *reprobation:* being a reprobate. 217. *works:* deeds. 224. *liberal:* freely. 229. *dull:* stupid.

EMILIA. She give it Cassio! no, alas, I found it,
And I did give 't my husband.

IAGO. Filth, thou liest!

EMILIA. By heaven, I do not, I do not, gentlemen.
O murderous coxcomb! what should such a fool
Do with so good a wife?

OTHELLO. Are there no stones in heaven
But what serve for the thunder? Precious villain!

He runs at IAGO: IAGO, *from behind, stabs* EMILIA, *and exit*.

GRATIANO. The woman falls; sure, he hath kill'd his wife.   240

EMILIA. Ay, ay: O, lay me by my mistress' side.

GRATIANO. He's gone, but his wife's kill'd.

MONTANO. 'Tis a notorious villain. Take you this weapon,
Which I have here recover'd from the Moor:
Come, guard the door without; let him not pass,
But kill him rather. I'll after that same villain,
For 'tis a damned slave.   *Exeunt all but* OTHELLO *and* EMILIA.

OTHELLO. I am not valiant neither,
But every puny whipster gets my sword.
But why should honour outlive honesty?
Let it go all.

EMILIA. What did thy song bode, lady?   250
Hark, canst thou hear me? I will play the swan,
And die in music. *Singing*. Willow, willow, willow.
Moor, she was chaste; she loved thee, cruel Moor;
So come my soul to bliss, as I speak true;
So speaking as I think, I die, I die.   *Dies*.

OTHELLO. I have another weapon in this chamber;
It is a sword of Spain, the ice-brook's temper.—
O, here it is. Uncle, I must come forth.

GRATIANO, *within*. If thou attempt it, it will cost thee dear:
Thou hast no weapon, and perforce must suffer.   260

OTHELLO. Look in upon me then, and speak with me,
Or, naked as I am, I will assault thee.

Re-enter GRATIANO.

---

243. *notorious:* notable. 248. *whipster:* whippersnapper. 257. "Tempered in the icy brook." 262. *naked:* unarmed.

SCENE 2]   OTHELLO   481

GRATIANO. What is the matter?
OTHELLO.   Behold, I have a weapon;
A better never did itself sustain
Upon a soldier's thigh: I have seen the day
That with this little arm and this good sword
I have made my way through more impediments
Than twenty times your stop: but, O vain boast!
Who can control his fate? 'tis not so now.
Be not afraid, though you do see me weapon'd; 270
Here is my journey's end, here is my butt
And very sea-mark of my utmost sail.
Do you go back dismay'd? 'tis a lost fear:
Man but a rush against Othello's breast,
And he retires. Where should Othello go?
Now, how dost thou look now? O ill-starr'd wench!
Pale as thy smock! when we shall meet at compt,
This look of thine will hurl my soul from heaven,
And fiends will snatch at it. Cold, cold, my girl!
Even like thy chastity. O cursed slave! 280
Whip me, ye devils,
From the possession of this heavenly sight!
Blow me about in winds! roast me in sulphur!
Wash me in steep-down gulfs of liquid fire!
O Desdemona! Desdemona! dead!
Oh! Oh! Oh!

Enter LODOVICO, MONTANO, CASSIO *carried in a chair, and* OFFICERS *with* IAGO, *prisoner.*

LODOVICO. Where is this rash and most unfortunate man?
OTHELLO. That's he that was Othello: here I am.
LODOVICO. Where is that viper? bring the villain forth.
OTHELLO. I look down towards his feet; but that's a fable. 290
If that thou be'st a devil, I cannot kill thee.   *Wounds* IAGO.
LODOVICO. Wrench his sword from him.
IAGO.   I bleed, sir, but not kill'd.

---

268. *stop:* barrier. 271. *butt:* limit of arrow's flight. 272. *sea-mark:* beacon. 273. *lost:* wasted. 277. *compt:* judgment day. 290. i.e., to see whether, like the devil's, they are cloven.

OTHELLO. I am not sorry neither: I 'ld have thee live;
For, in my sense, 'tis happiness to die.

LODOVICO. O thou Othello, that wert once so good,
Fall'n in the practice of a damned slave,
What shall be said to thee?

OTHELLO. Why, any thing:
An honourable murderer, if you will;
For nought did I in hate, but all in honour.

LODOVICO. This wretch hath part confess'd his villany: 300
Did you and he consent in Cassio's death?

OTHELLO. Ay.

CASSIO. Dear general, I never gave you cause.

OTHELLO. I do believe it, and I ask your pardon.
Will you, I pray, demand that demi-devil
Why he hath thus ensnared my soul and body?

IAGO. Demand me nothing; what you know, you know:
From this time forth I never will speak word.

LODOVICO. What, not to pray?

GRATIANO. Torments will ope your lips.

OTHELLO. Well, thou dost best. 310

LODOVICO. Sir, you shall understand what hath befall'n,
Which, as I think, you know not. Here is a letter
Found in the pocket of the slain Roderigo,
And here another: the one of them imports
The death of Cassio to be undertook
By Roderigo.

OTHELLO. O villain!

CASSIO. Most heathenish and most gross!

LODOVICO. Now here's another discontented paper,
Found in his pocket too; and this, it seems,
Roderigo meant to have sent this damned villain; 320
But that, belike, Iago in the interim
Came in and satisfied him.

OTHELLO. O the pernicious caitiff!
How came you, Cassio, by that handkerchief
That was my wife's?

---

294. *sense:* opinion. 296. *practice:* plotting. 314. *imports:* tells us.

SCENE 2] OTHELLO 483

CASSIO.   I found it in my chamber:
And he himself confess'd but even now
That there he dropp'd it for a special purpose
Which wrought to his desire.
   OTHELLO.   O fool! fool! fool!
   CASSIO. There is besides in Roderigo's letter,
How he upbraids Iago, that he made him
Brave me upon the watch; whereon it came   330
That I was cast: and even but now he spake
After long seeming dead, Iago hurt him,
Iago set him on.
   LODOVICO. You must forsake this room, and go with us:
Your power and your command is taken off,
And Cassio rules in Cyprus. For this slave,
If there be any cunning cruelty
That can torment him much and hold him long,
It shall be his. You shall close prisoner rest,
Till that the nature of your fault be known   340
To the Venetian state. Come, bring away.
   OTHELLO. Soft you; a word or two before you go.
I have done the state some service, and they know 't.
No more of that. I pray you, in your letters,
When you shall these unlucky deeds relate,
Speak of me as I am; nothing extenuate,
Nor set down aught in malice: then must you speak
Of one that loved not wisely but too well;
Of one not easily jealous, but, being wrought,
Perplex'd in the extreme; of one whose hand,   350
Like the base Indian, threw a pearl away
Richer than all his tribe; of one whose subdued eyes,
Albeit unused to the melting mood,
Drop tears as fast as the Arabian trees
Their medicinal gum. Set you down this;
And say besides, that in Aleppo once,
Where a malignant and a turban'd Turk

---

327. *wrought:* worked out. *to:* in accordance with. 331. *cast:* cast off. 351. *Like the base Indian:* as a base Indian might.

Beat a Venetian and traduced the state,
I took by the throat the circumcised dog
And smote him, thus. *Stabs himself.* 360
  LODOVICO. O bloody period!
  GRATIANO.   All that's spoke is marr'd.
  OTHELLO. I kiss'd thee ere I kill'd thee: no way but this,
Killing myself, to die upon a kiss. *Falls on the bed, and dies.*
  CASSIO. This did I fear, but thought he had no weapon;
For he was great of heart.
  LODOVICO. *To* IAGO. O Spartan dog,
More fell than anguish, hunger, or the sea!
Look on the tragic loading of this bed;
This is thy work: the object poisons sight;
Let it be hid. Gratiano, keep the house,
And seize upon the fortunes of the Moor, 370
For they succeed on you. To you, lord governor,
Remains the censure of this hellish villain,
The time, the place, the torture: O, enforce it!
Myself will straight abroad, and to the state
This heavy act with heavy heart relate. *Exeunt.*

✳

IN APPROACHING older works of art, one has always to ask: in what way, if any, am I likely to misread them because my views and attitudes are different from those of the playwright and his original audience? Such misreadings can be *wholly* eliminated, if at all, only by a very considerable historical knowledge—and, equally important, historical imagination. But they can be reduced in number and scope by a few commonsense considerations.

In *Othello* the most obvious stumbling-block is the story or, more precisely, Shakespeare's handling of it. The present-day reader may

---

361. *period:* conclusion. 365. Spartan dogs were fierce. 366. *fell:* fierce. *anguish:* physical hurt. 368. *object:* i.e., the "loading." 372. *censure:* judging. 375. *heavy:* sad.

consider the treatment of love, marriage, family, and adultery old-fashioned or even wrong. Two rejoinders are possible. One is that we must regard moral standards as historical phenomena. This is what men *did* believe; it is therefore important. The other is that the play is, after all, not *about* views of love, marriage, etc., and is thus not dependent for its effect upon the truth or untruth of the views expressed. Like *Twelfth Night,* it is about the corruption of the human, which can take place within this or any other ideological scheme. The play has a moral-psychological substance that is independent of the particular mores of the characters. (See Letter to the Reader, pp. 6-7.)

Even so, the reader may find the handling of the story questionable. If the theme is so serious, why is the action so melodramatic? Here much depends on how far the reader has been convinced by *Twelfth Night*. If he allowed Shakespeare a liberal use of convention *there*, if he allowed him the comic devices of mistaken identity, far-fetched coincidence, etc., yet admitted that the theme was "love: false and true" and that this theme was pushed to "the brink of tragedy," he may allow Shakespeare to pass that brink without an essential change in procedure. Thus, Iago's eavesdropping can be accepted as a theatrical device. In the story of the handkerchief, verisimilitude is sacrificed, but the *subject* is brought into high relief. Again, we have reality, if not realistic procedures. The reader has already conceded the idea in principle by allowing Shakespeare's characters to speak soliloquies—or even to speak blank verse—or even to speak before an audience! In other words, artifice is in the nature of theater and of art generally. All Shakespeare asks is a greater degree of it (or a different kind of it?) from what we are used to nowadays.

The detective story writer shares Shakespeare's interest in plot; but with a different emphasis. He asks us to look hard for improbability in a narrative sequence and to pounce on him—the author—if we find it. Detective-readers of *Othello* have discovered that Shakespeare builds everything on a possible adultery but actually does not leave Desdemona time to commit it. Judged by detective story standards, Shakespeare has bungled the job. Judged by the standards of a poetic theater (which is more akin to conjuring and acrobatics) he is to be congratulated on skillful sleight of hand. Because so little time has passed we have an impression of great speed, tremendous fatality. Because our eyes are so often distracted from the clock, we do not notice that Cassio couldn't have managed it.

There are readers who grant all this but boggle at the characters. "Your plot may not be real," they say, "but your characters must be. Who ever met an Iago? A Desdemona? They're not human beings: they're just types." Now what is a "real" human being? And how do you place him on the stage? Are not all the great characters "typical"? Hamlet is considered "highly individualized," but would we be interested in him if we didn't find something of him in ourselves? Comedy, at least, has always welcomed types. *Earnest, The Miser,* and *Twelfth Night* are full of them. We judge them according to their relevance in context and the degree of their vitality. Unrealistic conventions of character have the same justification as other unrealistic conventions.

We no longer expect Shakespeare to proceed differently in his tragedies. Iago is not a realistic portrait out of a modern novel. He is an embodiment of evil. (Modern realism, in making a character more plausible, finds it hard to express and project the evil. In art, when something is gained, something else is lost. One method, on the aggregate, scarcely seems better than another.) Our attention is to be directed less to the attribution of motives for Iago's deeds (though one or two are suggested) than to the defining of the deeds themselves. And to the defining also of the evil that envelops the deeds. So too with Desdemona. Twentieth-century persons, if prepared to foist their own viewpoint on Shakespeare, can dismiss her as naïve, ignorant, incredible. Others (not so unbending) can feel that she is a symbol—of purity or what not—as in an allegory: but is this more friendly interpretation more correct than the other? Shakespeare's plays are not abstract allegories. If Shakespeare does not build up a painstaking psychological study, he expertly suggests the livingness of his characters, the *feel* of them. Of course a good character may always be said to symbolize goodness, but what catches the attention in the portrayal of Desdemona is the amount of concrete detail provided in part by the action (the disrobing scene, for example) and in even larger part by the language she speaks.*

---

* "A living character is not necessarily 'true to life.' It is a person whom we can see and hear, whether he be true or false to human nature as we

OTHELLO 487

Othello himself is a supreme example of a character rendered by the method, not of the modern novel, but of a poetic theater. The visual image of a Moor in Renaissance Venice is a theatrical demonstration of Shakespeare's whole subject. (A Moor may not properly be defined as a Negro, is at any rate brown rather than black. But did Shakespeare know this? Or care? He seems to envisage his hero as black, and though the meaning of this for his audience is not what it would be for a Southern reactionary in America, it does indicate the exotic and, in the popular sense of the word, the primitive—the man whose passions when roused are more violent than those of the civilized.) Othello is a noble savage: "an erring [i.e., wandering] barbarian" whom Iago asks us to contrast with the "supersubtle Venetian." His character is defined by his color, physique, rank, and costume—and above all by the especially melodious and majestic verse which he is given to speak.

The melody and majesty raise questions. What do they tell us about Othello? The naïvest answer is: they tell us that he is a great poet. By the criterion thus implied *every* character in a good poetic play would have to be considered a good poet. Yet the naïve comment (which was not invented by the present editor) springs from a true response to something that is really there: Shakespeare uses his highest poetry to suggest that Othello dramatizes himself. This is, perhaps, the central and inner tragedy of the character and the play. On this view, the temptation of Othello by Iago would be a subordinate and external matter; for the worst deception is self-deception—Othello can describe himself as "not easily jealous" after showing himself very easily jealous indeed.

What are we to make of Othello's final burst of eloquence? It has usually been taken as Othello's pulling himself together and achieving dignity in death. Another view is that it is his supreme piece of

---

know it. What the creator of character needs is not so much knowledge of motives as keen sensibility; the dramatist need not understand people; but he must be exceptionally aware of them." —From T. S. Eliot's *Selected Essays*.

"The Shakespearian delineation of character owes all its magic to the turn of the line, which lets you into the secret of its utterer's mood and temperament, not by its commonplace meaning, but by some subtle exaltation, or stultification, or shyness, or delicacy, or hesitancy, or what not, in the sound of it." —From Bernard Shaw's *Dramatic Opinions*.

self-dramatization, self-deception. How do we decide which view to take? It is largely a matter of tone: if, after reading the passage many times in and out of context, the reader judges the tone to be firmly heroic, he will take the first view. If he concludes that Shakespeare is writing with deliberate over-emphasis, with inflated rhetoric, he will take the second.

>The first of the two views just mentioned has been championed at length by A. C. Bradley in his *Shakespearean Tragedy*, the second by F. R. Leavis in an essay, "Diabolic Intellect and the Noble Hero," to be found in the magazine *Scrutiny*, Volume VI, Number 3. Indeed, Bradley goes much further than this first view: he does not acknowledge the existence of the "inner tragedy" at all, for he does not consider Othello easily jealous. Leavis takes the opposite tack, and finds confirmation in T. S. Eliot's essays—e.g., in the passage mentioned above, page 142.
>
>Bernard Shaw's *Dramatic Opinions* contain an attack upon *Othello*: refusing to accept Shakespeare's conventions, Shaw finds his play disastrously melodramatic. E. E. Stoll, on the other hand, has made the defence of Shakespeare's "unrealistic" characterization his special subject—for example, in essays on *Othello* in *Art and Artifice in Shakespeare* and *Shakespeare and Other Masters*.
>
>Probably the most eloquent account of the tenor and force of the play as a whole is that given by G. Wilson Knight in *The Wheel of Fire*.

6. ANTIGONE · 441 B.C.

IF IT REQUIRES an effort of historical imagination to understand a playwright of around 1600 who wrote in English, how shall we hope to understand playwrights of the fifth century before Christ who wrote in Greek? We have seen that the interpretation of a key passage in *Othello* depends on our feeling for the tone. Only if we know English extremely well, only if we have some training in the reading of English verse, have we any right to expect that our opinion will be correct. Now, even if we were to take up Greek, could we ever know it well enough to form a correct opinion of such passages? It seems doubtful. Yet, reading such passages translated into another tongue in another place at another time, reading *Othello*, let us say in Russian in Moscow today, what could one say then about the tone of the final great speech? It has become something different according to the gifts and opinions and attitudes of the translator. If the translator says he has been very faithful, "changing the form but preserving the content," one recalls that in art, form and content are fused. To change one is to change the other. The wonder is that, in a translation, anything of note is kept at all.

And yet it is. One can read a translation of a Greek drama and be impressed—by something; and it is hard to believe that this something is wholly the translator's original contribution. Much of the plot, the theme, and the characterization seems to survive in any reasonably well-written translation. What kind of translation gives us most? Some would say: a literal prose version. Yet many sentences of the *Antigone*, rendered in unmetrical, unfastidious English words, communicate nothing. A generation ago Gilbert Murray saw this and tried to recreate the spirit of the original by writing highly poetic versions. But to reproduce great poetry *in* great poetry one has to be a great poet; and Murray wasn't. Today his versions are harder to read than any of the literal versions.

It is conceivable that a great English poet might give to Greek plays with which he happened to be in harmony a form that would become permanent in our own tradition. But so far it has not happened. The next best thing is that each generation should translate the Greeks into its own idiom without excessive literalness, without "poetic" flights. Thus each generation can read the Greeks in a language which sets up a minimum of interference.

Among several modern versions, the present editor has chosen one that was conceived by the French poet and playwright Jean Cocteau.

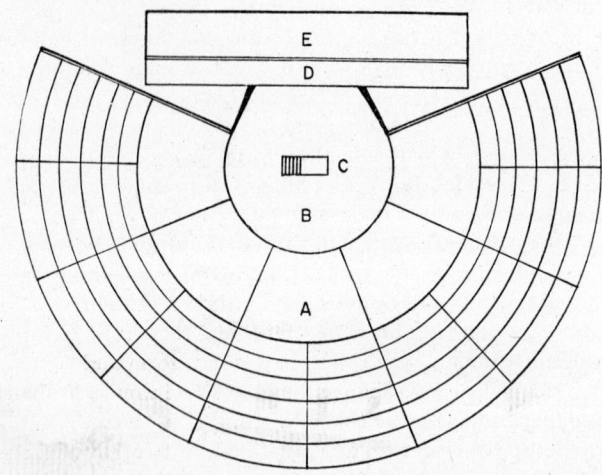

Piero D'Orazio, after Gervais, Propos sur la Mise en Scène.

THE THEATER OF SOPHOCLES

A. The auditorium. Out-of-doors on a hillside. Rises in steps like a modern stadium.
B. The fore-stage where the chorus danced and sang.
C. The altar of the god Dionysos round which the chorus revolved.
D. The stage proper. Unlike the *fore-stage,* it is raised above ground level.
E. The back-stage area. A two-story building containing dressing-rooms, etc.

It is what would be called in the commercial theater a streamlined version, that is, a sort of synopsis, rather than a line-by-line rendering of the original. Such a version would be uncalled for in the case of plays that *could* be plausibly rendered line by line. Cocteau's procedure is defensible on the grounds that much of Sophocles is lost anyway. *Words which add little or nothing should be deleted:* if this principle were applied to older English versions of *Antigone,* something like Cocteau's version would emerge.

It is always hard to approach a classic freshly. Our staleness as readers of the Bible and Shakespeare (even if we have read them very little) has already been mentioned. Cocteau felt the need of a new angle of vision.

> "It is very tempting," he writes, "to photograph Greece from the air. We find it has an entirely new and fresh appearance. I have tried to translate *Antigone* in this way. With a bird's-eye view great beauties disappear, but others arise; unexpected associations, blocks, shadows, angles, and contrasts are found. My experiment may be a means of making old masterpieces live. Through constantly living with them we become inattentive; but, because I fly over a famous text, people fancy they hear it for the first time."

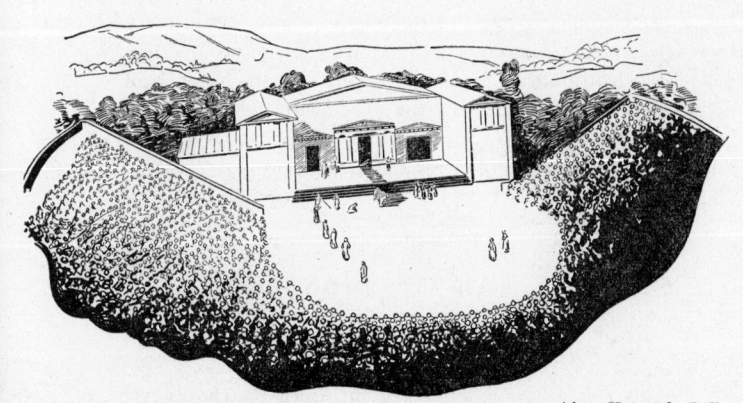

After Heinrich Bulle

RECONSTRUCTION OF THE THEATER AT ATHENS, FIFTH CENTURY

Whether or not the reader has been "constantly living with" Greek tragedy, he has here a text which he can approach without embarrassment. The language is simple and it is his own; the ideas are sharply defined. Only one idea constitutes an initial obstacle: the idea that it greatly matters whether one receives an official funeral. However, once one realizes that in Antigone's society it obviously *did* matter, one is free, without benefit of erudition, to receive the rest of the story as a very modern (i.e., perennial) thing. One can scarcely hope to become an expert on Sophocles by reading a text like the following, but this is a text with its own integrity: it can be taken for what it is. In the editor's experience it arouses more *interest* in Greek tragedy, and operates more effectively as theater, than the older versions; and, actually, it does not render any less of the original.

The reader should know that Antigone is the daughter of Oedipus. Her story, that is to say, follows the more famous story of the king of Thebes who killed his father and married his mother. When these crimes were brought to light, Oedipus blinded himself in a supreme act of self-punishment and abdicated. His sons Eteocles and Polynices then quarreled over the right to the throne. It was agreed that they would rule alternate years. After his year had elapsed, however, Eteocles refused to give up his position. Polynices, who meanwhile had married a princess of Argos, came with an Argive army to drive his brother from the Theban throne. The brothers killed each other in single combat. Creon (Oedipus' brother-in-law) became king and gave Eteocles honorable burial. But he left the rebel brother Polynices to rot on the field of battle. (We are to assume that this action is politically correct but contrary to Unwritten Laws which Sophocles' audience respected.) Polynices' sister Antigone is horrified, as we learn in the first scene.

ANTIGONE

by Sophocles

ADAPTED FROM THE GREEK
BY JEAN COCTEAU*

✷

---

* English version by Carl Wildman. Revised by E. B.

Used by permission of Carl Wildman. All rights whatsoever in this play are strictly reserved, and applications for performances, etc., should be made to Dr. Jan van Loewen, Albion House, 2 Jason's Court, 78 Wigmore Street, London, W. 1, England.

Antigone

Characters

ANTIGONE (anti'-gony) \
ISMENE (izmee'-ny) *daughters of Oedipus* \
EURYDICE (yoo-rid'-issy) *Queen of Thebes*

CREON (kree'-on) *King of Thebes* \
HAEMON (hy'-mon) *their son* \
TIRESIAS (tyree'-sias) *a sage and priest*

A Guard, A Messenger, A Chorus

THE PLACE: *Thebes. Before the palace.*

Sophocles' Antigone was first performed in Athens in 441 B.C. This shortened version was first produced in Paris at the Atelier Theatre in 1922 with scenery by Picasso, music by Honegger, and costumes by Chanel.

The extreme rapidity of the action does not prevent the actors from speaking very distinctly and moving very little. The chorus and its leader are concentrated into a single voice which speaks very loudly and quickly as if reading a newspaper article. This voice issues from a hole in the centre of the scenery.

For a revival in 1927, five monumental plaster heads of young men framed the chorus. The actors wore transparent masks after the fashion of fencing baskets; beneath the masks one could make out the actors' faces, and ethereal features were sewn on to the masks in white millinery wire. The costumes were worn over black bathing dresses, and arms and legs were covered. The general effect was suggestive of a sordid carnival of kings, a family of insects.

When the curtain rises, ANTIGONE *and* ISMENE *are standing near each other, motionless, looking straight into the auditorium.*

[J. C.]

ANTIGONE. Ismene, my sister, do you know of a single scourge in the heritage of Oedipus that Jupiter* has spared us? I think I can tell you of another. One more shame that our enemies have in store for us. Guess what it is.

ISMENE. No, Antigone. Our two brothers have died at each other's hands. The Argive horde has disappeared. And today I do not see what could make me feel more wretched—or less unhappy.

ANTIGONE. Listen. I wanted you to come out here so that no living soul should hear us.

ISMENE. What is wrong? Your look terrifies me.

ANTIGONE. You ask what is wrong? Is not Creon allowing funeral rites to one brother and denying them to the other? Eteocles will have the burial he deserves; Polynices may be neither buried nor mourned. He is to be left to the crows. Those are the orders of the noble Creon for you and me. Yes, for me too. He will come in person to this very spot and read his decree. He attaches the utmost importance to the carrying out of his orders. To infringe them is to be stoned to death by the people. I hope you will show what you are made of.

ISMENE. What can I do?

ANTIGONE. Decide if you will help me.

ISMENE. Do what?

ANTIGONE. Raise up the body.

ISMENE. You mean to bury it in defiance of the king?

ANTIGONE. I do. He is our brother. My brother—and yours. I shall bury him. No one shall say I have left him to the beasts.

ISMENE, *horrified*. Unhappy girl! Despite Creon's ban?

ANTIGONE. Has he the right to cut me off from my family?

ISMENE. Antigone! Antigone! Our poor father put out his eyes to expiate his crimes. He died in the mud. Our mother, who was *his* mother, hanged herself. Our brothers slew each other. Just think: we two are quite alone! What a sinister end will be ours if we defy our masters! Antigone, we are just women. Women unskilled in the art of subduing men. Those in command are stronger. May Polynices forgive me, but I shall acquiesce. I shall obey the powers that be. To attempt what is beyond one's strength is folly.

---

* My substitution of *Jupiter* for *Zeus* is supported by La Fontaine and Maurras. *Jupiter* sounds better in our language. [J. C.] The same is true of the Engish language. [C. W.]

ANTIGONE. I do not wish to force you. If you were to help me, your heart would not be in it. Do as you think best. I am for the burying. After that, I shall be glad to die. One sweet crime and two friends will rest side by side. For, Ismene, the time I shall have to spend pleasing the dead is far longer than the time I must spend pleasing the living. Your conduct is your affair. Despise the gods, if you must.

ISMENE. I don't despise them. I merely feel unable to fight a whole town.

ANTIGONE. Seek out excuses! I shall raise him a sort of grave.

ISMENE. This is madness! I tremble for you.

ANTIGONE. Let me alone. Think of yourself.

ISMENE. At any rate, tell no one what you intend. Keep it dark— as I shall.

ANTIGONE. Keep nothing dark. You are free to speak. I should begrudge you your silence more than your tittle-tattle.

ISMENE. Cool down. You are far too excited.

ANTIGONE. Never! I know that I please where I should.

ISMENE. Yes, if all goes well. But you are attempting the impossible.

ANTIGONE. I shall stop. When my strength fails.

ISMENE. Why try and catch the wind?

ANTIGONE. Go on like this, and I shall detest you. You will excite the hatred of the dead. Leave me alone with my plan. If it fails, I die a glorious death.

ISMENE, *mounting the steps on the left.* Very well then. Go your rash way. Your heart is your undoing. *Exit.*

ANTIGONE *remains alone, braces herself for the day ahead, and disappears in the left-hand wings.*

THE CHORUS. Under your frantic eye, O sun, the Argive troops have fled. As fast as their legs would run. They had come on the heels of Polynices and his dreams of power. Jupiter detests boasting. He has struck the plumes and armor of pride with his thunderbolt. The seven chiefs who marched against our seven gates have laid down their arms. Only two brothers of opposite camps stayed their ground.

Now victory is established in Thebes. And the people sing. But here is Creon, our new sovereign.

CREON, *at the right-hand gate.* Citizens, the gods have saved this town from ruin. I have called you together knowing your respect for the house of Laius and your loyalty to Oedipūs and to his sons. The sons have slain each other. All power passes into my hands.

Before a man has shown his worth, it is hard to know him. Personally, I condemn the man who rules without consulting those about him. Still more, the head of a state who would sacrifice the masses to the interests of a single individual. I will flatter no adversary. A just prince will not lack friends. Such are my principles.

And so I have dictated the decree concerning the sons of Oedipus. Eteocles is a soldier: let him be buried with full honors. Polynices returned from exile as an incendiary seeking to flout us and reduce us to slavery. No honors shall be paid to him. I command that his body be left to the dogs and crows. I shall never confuse virtue with crime. I have spoken.

THE CHORUS. Well said, Creon. You have a free hand. You can dispose of the dead. And of us.

CREON. Carry out my order.

THE CHORUS. Ask the young men.

CREON. Guards keep watch over the body.

THE CHORUS. What must we do then?

CREON. If laws are broken, be inflexible.

THE CHORUS. No man is so mad as to seek death.

CREON. Death would be his reward. But the hope of a purse often makes men mad.

A GUARD. *Enters, kneels, coughs nervously, and speaks.* Prince, I can't exactly say I have flown here to you. Oh, no. I stopped many times on the way. I kept saying to myself: "Don't go to him, don't go. But, on the other hand, if Creon learns about it from somewhere else, you might be in for much worse. It's not far to go." But it was. ... So you see.... You see.... I've nothing good to tell you.

CREON. What is it that's scared you out of your wits?

THE GUARD. Well, I'll tell you about number one first of all. It wasn't me. It wasn't my fault. And I don't know who it was. It wouldn't be fair of you to punish me.

CREON. You're beating about the bush. It looks to me as though you're trying to break some bad news gently.

THE GUARD. Danger kind of paralyzes you.

CREON. Speak. Then you can go.

THE GUARD. Right, I'll speak. The body has been buried.

CREON. What? Who has dared . . . ?

THE GUARD. Not the slightest idea. There's no sign of spades or picks. No footprints. No cart-tracks. Nothing to give the criminal away. By the early morning the body had disappeared under a layer of dust. Just enough to prevent sacrilege. Of course, everyone was accusing everyone else and getting worked up. We were going to fight it out. The whole guard was under suspicion because there was no proof against any one in particular. We swore we would walk on live embers without flinching and grasp red-hot irons. That's how to tell the guilty and their accomplices. In the end, we decided to make a clean breast of it. To you. We drew lots and I was the unlucky one.

THE CHORUS. Prince, I wonder if this isn't a plot hatched by the gods.

CREON. Enough nonsense from you, old man. The gods don't inter iconoclasts, incendiaries, pillagers of temples. Have you ever known the gods to favor evil? No; I should say not. But this act is an eye-opener. I knew there were traitors in this town, murmuring against my yoke. I knew of subversive activities. The culprits are in the traitors' service.

Men have invented money. Money, vile money. Money has wrought the ruin of towns, the corruption of honest men, a general demoralization. But those who have interred Polynices, bribed by a purse, have dug their own tomb. If you do not bring them to me I shall hang you. Then someone will denounce them.

THE GUARD. In any case, it wasn't me.

CREON. I wonder. You seem to me precisely the kind of fellow who would sell himself, and cheap at that!

THE GUARD. It's sad that a fair-minded prince can't see straight.

CREON. He's passing judgment on me, I do declare.

THE GUARD. I sincerely hope the guilty parties are found. I'm off.

Exit GUARD, *then* CREON.

THE CHORUS. Man is amazing. Man navigates, man ploughs, man hunts, man fishes. He tames horses. He thinks. He speaks. He invents codes, he warms himself, and roofs-in his house. He recovers from sickness. Death is the only sickness which he cannot cure. He does good and he does evil. When he listens to the laws of heaven and earth, he is a good fellow; when he does not heed them, he ceases to be so. May a criminal never be my guest. Heavens, what strange portent is this? O gods! Incredible, but true! Is it not Antigone? Antigone! Antigone, can you have disobeyed? Can you have been mad enough to cause your own undoing?

> *From the left-hand wings appears* ANTIGONE. *The hands of the* GUARD *who is pushing her forward are visible on her shoulders. Then the* GUARD *himself becomes visible.*

THE GUARD. Caught red-handed. Where's Creon?

THE CHORUS. There he is, coming out.

CREON. What is happening?

THE GUARD. Prince, chance brings me back where I had hoped not to set foot again. Question this girl. She is the guilty one.

CREON. Where and how did you take her?

THE GUARD. She was burying the body. I caught her in the act.

CREON. You swear it?

THE GUARD. Yes, I swear it. She was burying the man.

CREON. Give me some details.

THE GUARD. We were scared by your threats and got the sand off the corpse and left it naked on the earth. Then we sat down on a mound where there was a breeze—because of the stink. Then we fooled around so as not to fall asleep. Suddenly, at midday, a duststorm arose and broke the branches and blinded us. When it had passed, we saw this young woman standing near the body. Screaming her head off. She covered the body with dust, brought out a vessel from under her dress, and began libations. Psst! We pounced on her, and arrested her in half a second. We questioned her and she confessed without offering resistance. I'm sorry I had to trade one life for another, but guilt is guilt, and, when all's said and done, it's only natural I should try and save my own skin.

CREON. And you. You with the unassuming eyes, what do you say to this? Is it true?

ANTIGONE. I did it. I avow it.

CREON, *to the* GUARD. Get out. Get yourself hanged somewhere else. You're free. *To* ANTIGONE. You knew of my ban?

ANTIGONE. Yes. It was public.

CREON. And you had the audacity not to observe it.

ANTIGONE. Jupiter did not issue that decree. Nor does justice impose such laws. I was not aware that your decree could make the caprice of a man prevail over the rule of the immortals, over Unwritten Laws which nothing can efface. Such laws do not date from today or yesterday. They are for all time. No one knows when they were made. Ought I, then, for fear of a man's opinion, to disobey my gods? I knew death would follow my act. I shall die young; so much the better. The real misfortune was to have left my brother without a tomb. The rest is all the same to me.

After this you may call me mad yet in reality be yourself the madman.

THE CHORUS. By her unyielding nature we recognize the daughter of Oedipus. In the face of adversity she stands her ground.

CREON. Remember: the hardest spirits are the most easily broken. The hardest iron is the first to snap. A little curb calms an unruly horse. What pride she has, for a slave . . . a slave to duty. She deliberately insults me. She sets me at defiance and boasts about it. If I let her, she would be the man. Though I am brother to Jocasta, neither Antigone nor her sister shall escape their fate. For Ismene must be her accomplice: Let her be brought before me. A moment ago I caught sight of her in the palace, panic-stricken as a bat. The spirits of night betray themselves quickly. What I hate beyond all else is a criminal who, when caught in the act, tries to glorify his crime.

ANTIGONE. You demand more than my death?

CREON. No.

ANTIGONE and CREON stand close together as they speak to each other. Their foreheads touch.

ANTIGONE. Then why drag things out? I do not like you. You do not like me. All these people would applaud me if it were not for the fear which paralyzes their tongues. Despotism adds to its thousand privileges the right to say and hear what it likes.

CREON. You alone in Thebes are discontented.

ANTIGONE. They are all discontented but in your presence—silent.

CREON. Are you not ashamed?

ANTIGONE. Ashamed of honoring a brother?

CREON. And your brother Eteocles? Was he not also your brother? Eteocles, who died at our side?

ANTIGONE. We had the same father and mother.

CREON. Why insult him, then, by unpatriotic homage?

ANTIGONE. That is not how the dead man testifies at my trial.

CREON. What? You serve a traitor?

ANTIGONE. Dead, he is not Eteocles' enemy but his brother.

CREON. He came to attack his country. Eteocles was defending it.

ANTIGONE. Death demands a single law for all.

CREON. But invaded and invader should not be treated alike.

ANTIGONE. Who knows if your frontiers have meaning in the land of the dead?

CREON. An enemy dead never became a friend.

ANTIGONE. I was born to share love, not hatred.

CREON. Descend to the dead and love whom you please. But while I live, no woman will make the laws.

THE CHORUS. Here is poor Ismene in tears. Grief disfigures her and waters her cheeks.

CREON. Ah! there you are, viper. Come along, speak: did you or did you not know of the high treason that has been committed?

ISMENE. If my sister confesses, I confess, and wish to take the consequences.

ANTIGONE. The court forbids you to do so. You did not want to follow me. I acted alone.

ISMENE. You are unhappy. I want to follow you now. You are in trouble.

ANTIGONE. Too late, Ismene, too late. The underworld and those who live there have seen me act alone. I set little store by a sister who loves me in words.

ISMENE. Antigone, do not take from me the honor of dying with you, the honor of having buried our brother.

ANTIGONE. Do not die with me and do not boast, my dear. It is enough that *I* should die.

ISMENE. Without you, how can I enjoy life?

ANTIGONE. Ask Creon. Aren't you his puppet?

ISMENE. Why do you like to hurt me?

ANTIGONE. I laugh at you. A hollow laugh. And my mockery hurts me.

ISMENE. What can I do to help?

ANTIGONE. Spare your days. I don't envy you that good fortune.

ISMENE. Let me share your destiny.

ANTIGONE. You have chosen to live, I to die.

ISMENE. You can't say I didn't tell you often enough!

ANTIGONE. Your advice was good; I found my project better.

ISMENE. Your fault is ours.

ANTIGONE. Don't worry. You will live. My heart has been dead a long time already. It can only be of use to the dead.

CREON. These two girls are raving mad.

ISMENE. We have suffered enough to make us lose our reason.

CREON. That's what happens if you insist on sharing the criminal's punishment.

ISMENE. How do you expect me to live without Antigone?

CREON. No more of her. She is dead.

ISMENE. You will kill your son's betrothed?

CREON. He will find other wombs.

ISMENE. This is the only marriage he desires.

CREON. I will not have a bad daughter-in-law.

ANTIGONE. O, my dear Haemon, how your father speaks of you!

CREON. I begin to weary of you and your wedding.

THE CHORUS. Can you deprive your son of the one he loves?

CREON. Death shall break off their engagement.

ISMENE. Is her death certain?

CREON. Certain. Enough time wasted! Guards, arrest these women! The bravest flee when death approaches. *They go out.*

THE CHORUS. Happy are the innocent. Fatality has settled on this family. I see new misfortunes heaping up on the old for the house of Labdacus.* A god pursues them. Relentlessly. Jupiter, you never sleep: you dwell on Olympus, eternally young. But the race of man cannot enjoy unbroken peace. It runs into every disaster. For, when a god leads us to destruction, he alters the positions of good and evil. But here is Haemon. Is he coming to make complaint?

CREON. My son, you know the crime and the sentence. Do you come to us as a rebel? Or are we still as dear to you?

HAEMON. I bow to your will. After your wise counsel, there can be no question of marriage.

CREON. Well said. A son should obey. Of what good are sons if not to love our friends and inflict on our enemies the damage they deserve? In the embrace of an unworthy spouse, you would freeze. So let this young woman marry someone in the underworld. She talks of laws of Jupiter, laws of kinship! So far, so good. But if I

* Founder of the Oedipus family. Laius, son of Labdacus, was the father of Oedipus and Creon.

suffer my next of kin to rebel, what can I expect from the Thebans? Severity for all or none. I will not sing the praises of anyone who opposes my rule. Anarchy is the greatest evil. It ruins towns, breaks up families, infects the army—and a woman anarchist is the end of everything; better yield to a man. It shall not be said that a woman led *me* by the nose.

THE CHORUS. If age has not entirely disturbed my brain, it seems to me, O king, that you express yourself with exquisite wisdom.

HAEMON. You are wise, father, but others can be wise too. I am so placed that I hear what everyone thinks of you. You terrorize the people. They whisper the words you prevent them from speaking out loud. *I* can hear them. I wander about. I stumble upon secret meetings. I know how Thebes judges this noble and glorious girl whom you condemn. 'What? Is she to be killed for burying her brother? Why, she ought to be honored for it!" Such is the public rumor.

As for me, I respect your rule beyond everything else. But, father, do not persist in thinking you are always right, and you alone. The man who thinks that he alone has wisdom, eloquence, and power is exposing himself to ridicule. Intelligence allows one to contradict oneself. If a captain blindly kept his canvas stretched, he would soon capsize his ship. Lower your sail. Be calm. Believe me. I am very young, but I know I am pleading a just cause.

THE CHORUS. O king, if he is right, listen to him. If he is wrong, may he listen to you. On either side the trial is in excellent hands.

CREON. What, what? Are we to learn justice from a schoolboy?

HAEMON. Again unjust! Age does not count. Do not consider my age; consider my acts.

CREON. Is it acting well to praise anarchists?

HAEMON. I could not praise the wicked.

CREON. And is this woman not wicked? Is she not eaten up with wickedness?

HAEMON. That is not the opinion of the street.

CREON. Splendid! Now *the street* is to show me my way!

HAEMON. Now *you* have spoken like a young man, and you know it.

CREON. Am I to guide the city in one direction and my life in another?

HAEMON. No city was ever made for one man.

CREON. The city is the legitimate spouse of her lord.

HAEMON. Live in an empty city if you want to rule alone.

CREON. He seems to side with a girl!

HAEMON. That makes *you* a girl, for you are my chief concern.

CREON. Brat! You are insulting your father!

HAEMON. Because I see my father being unjust.

CREON. Is it unjust for me to uphold my prerogatives?

HAEMON. Your prerogatives! You are trampling on the will of the gods!

CREON. Soft heart! You let a woman get around you!

HAEMON. Maybe. At any rate, false proceedings will never get around me.

CREON. You are just pleading for her.

HAEMON. And for you and for me and for the infernal gods.

CREON. You shall never marry her alive!

HAEMON. Then I'll marry her dead. In the underworld!

CREON. You threaten me with suicide!

HAEMON. I threaten nothing. I am trying to combat your injustice.

CREON. You will repent, Mr. Reasoner!

HAEMON. If I were not your son, I would say you were evading the issue.

CREON. Slave to women, beware! Do not drive me crazy with your tongue-wagging!

HAEMON. *You* talk all the time and listen to no one.

CREON. Ha! Is that how things are? Soldiers, bring in the madwoman, bring in the madwoman! Quick! Quick! That she may die before the eyes of her betrothed.

HAEMON. You are mistaken. She will not die in my presence. This is the last time I speak to you. Farewell. Exercise your rage before your courtiers; they will put up with it.

THE CHORUS. O king, he is leaving. He is running. He is beside himself. At his age, despair can be dangerous.

CREON. Let him try his utmost. He will not save them.

THE CHORUS. What! Are you condemning Ismene as well as Antigone?

CREON. No. Not her who has not touched the corpse. Your remark is just.

THE CHORUS. And what kind of death have you in store for the other?

CREON. I shall wall her up alive in a desert cavern. I shall leave her some food, just enough for her expiation. She will have plenty of time to pray to Pluto. She will see if the infernal gods will protect her.*

THE CHORUS. Love that seizes all and sundry. Love that makes the rich poor and the poor rich, love that fires the maiden's cheek, love that crosses the sea and penetrates the cattle stalls—none can escape you, among the immortal gods or among short-lived men. When she unleashes desire, Venus is invincible. At this very moment, I myself, unfaithful to my prince, weep to see Antigone walking toward her tomb.

ANTIGONE *appears on the left between two* GUARDS. *She stops.*

ANTIGONE. Citizens of my country, behold me. I start out on my last journey. I look for the last time at the light of the sun. The god of Hades will take me alive. I shall not have known marriage. No wedding song will have echoed my name. Death will espouse me.

THE CHORUS. Then you will die without sickness, without a wound. You will go to Pluto free, virgin, living, renowned, alone among mortals.

ANTIGONE. I have heard how the daughter of Tantalus died. Suddenly, at the top of Sipylus, she felt the rock take her and grow around her like strong ivy. And now the snow cloaks her and its icy tears run down her body. Such will be my bed, and such the caresses that await me. *Advances.*

THE CHORUS. Ah yes, but we are just poor human beings and she was a goddess and daughter of a god. After all, for a simple mortal like you, it is a great consolation to have the fate of a divinity.

Stops.

ANTIGONE. Mock me! It is the right moment. Mock me! They do not even wait for me to disappear! My city! Thebes, the town of the fine carriages! See how they laugh as they push me towards a nameless hole.

---

* *Note*: Creon has no intention of *murdering* Antigone. Being walled up is a formal ordeal: the infernal gods may save her if they approve her conduct. (Pluto, the infernal gods, and the underworld [Hades] did not have associations like those of Satan, the minor devils, and hell.) [E.B.]

Nameless! For I am going to a dwelling place not of men, nor of shades, nor of the living, nor of the dead.

THE CHORUS. It is your own fault. You have done violence to justice. You are still paying for Oedipus.

ANTIGONE. I am a daughter of incest. That is why I die.

THE CHORUS. The cult of the dead is a fine thing. But it is not a fine thing to disobey our masters. It is pride that has undone you.

ANTIGONE. Nothing. Nothing. Nothing and no one. I go to my execution quite alone, with no one to pity me, no husband, no friend, no encouragement. Never again shall I see the light. Never see day's golden eye. Never see the sun! *Advances.*

CREON. You have said this already. If we all made such a song and dance about dying, there'd be no end to it. Quick now! Take her away! Imprison her and leave her!

As ANTIGONE *springs forward, the left-hand* GUARD *drops his lance in front of her. The right-hand* GUARD *grasps the end.* ANTIGONE *seizes the lance. She looks like a woman in a prisoner's dock between two policemen.*

ANTIGONE. Farewell. Let them steal my share of life. I go to see my father and mother again, and Eteocles. When you died I washed you and closed your eyes. I closed your eyes, too, Polynices—and—I—did —right! I should never have made that fateful effort for children or for a husband. A husband—he can be replaced. A son—another can be conceived. But, our parents being dead, I could not hope for more brothers. It was for this reason that I acted, that I am being struck down, and that Creon is denying me marriage and maternity.

What, then, have I done to the gods? They abandon me. If they approve my executioners, I shall know it tomorrow and regret my act. But, if the gods *dis*approve—let them inflict on my executioners my tortures! *Advances.*

THE CHORUS. Her spirit does not relax.

CREON. It will cost her escort dear if they insist on dawdling.

ANTIGONE. My death will not last long.

CREON. Do not imagine that the torture consists simply in frightening you.

ANTIGONE, *escorted by the* GUARDS, *comes to the lower fore-stage. One of the* GUARDS *enters the trap, the other follows pulling* ANTIGONE *lightly by the cloak. She disappears in her turn.*

ANTIGONE, *waist-deep in the trap.* My Thebes! it is finished. They bear me away. Chiefs! Theban chiefs! Your last princess is suffering outrage. See what I suffer. See what men punish me for my love.

ANTIGONE *disappears.*

THE CHORUS. Danae also was buried alive and sleeps in bronze; and yet, my child, she was of high descent and bore the golden seed of Jupiter. Bacchus turned the son of Dryas into stone. That young man much regrets having jostled the Maenades, having put out their torches and laughed at the Muses.*

TIRESIAS *enters left, guided by a* YOUNG BOY.

TIRESIAS. Theban chiefs, we are here, one in two. For I am blind and can only walk with a guide.

CREON. What news, Tiresias?

TIRESIAS. You shall hear. But obey.

CREON. I have always believed you.

TIRESIAS. And so you have governed in a straight line—but you now turn from it.

CREON. You frighten me.

TIRESIAS. This child leads me and I lead others. He has seen our altars covered with the rotting remains of Polynices. Dogs and vultures brought them. Since then, the gods reject our sacrifices and beasts, gorged with carrion, are howling everywhere.† Believe me, my son. That a man may make a mistake we can well admit, but that he should persist is a proof of stupidity. Cease striking a dead man. It is my love for you that speaks.

CREON. So! I am now an archer's target. And you all attack me in your fury. All right! Get rich! Trade away! Win all the gold of Sardis and India. Polynices shall never be buried. Were eagles to bear his carcass to Jupiter's throne, I should still refuse. A mortal cannot defile the gods. You are paid money, Tiresias: that is the sign of your downfall.

* Because they took a terrible revenge. [E.B.]
† Bad omens.

ANTIGONE 509

TIRESIAS. O for a man! A man who knows! Who would understand!

CREON. The oracle clique* is greedy for money.

TIRESIAS. And that of the kings is greedy for taxes.

CREON. You realize I am your king?

TIRESIAS. I realize it all the more since you owe your throne and the welfare of Thebes to me.

CREON. You like paradoxes.

TIRESIAS. You force me to say that which I wished to dissimulate.

CREON. Speak, but do no service to whoever it is that pays you.

TIRESIAS. Do I appear so rich?

CREON. And know that I shall not change my mind.

TIRESIAS. Know in your turn that the death of your son will pay for the crime of burying a woman alive and contending with Pluto for a corpse. Your palace will be filled with lamentations. Anger is rousing the towns against you. For men see the beasts dragging gory hunks of flesh. Lead me, little one. May this man learn in future to moderate his language and respect my age and yours. *Exit.*

THE CHORUS. Creon, his oracles are never wrong.

CREON. Alas! My mind is disturbed . . . let me see . . . it is terrible to yield . . . on the other hand it is terrible to bring on misfortune by persisting. What do you advise?

THE CHORUS. Save the girl.

CREON. That! And you want me to give way?

THE CHORUS. But you must hurry. The vengeance of the gods comes full speed.

CREON. Well, if I must. . . . *He groans* . . . it is hard . . . very hard.

THE CHORUS. Go. Go. Go. Do it yourself.

CREON. I fly. Follow with axes, picks, and crowbars. I fear it is impossible to keep to the old laws always. *Exit.*

THE CHORUS. O you who are crowned with a thousand names: Bacchus! dweller in Thebes, metropolis of Bacchantes, you make the stars dance and the night sing. Tread the mountain with your great feet as if it were grapes. Run! Fly! Help us! Leap this way with your drunken horde!

* The group of priests who guard the oracle. [E.B.]

510   ANTIGONE

*Empty stage and music.**

A MESSENGER. Fellow citizens of Cadmus,† fortune is fickle. I used to envy Creon. Now his luck is failing him. Riches and a throne: what are they without joy?

THE CHORUS. Speak.

THE MESSENGER. Haemon has committed suicide.

THE CHORUS. O Tiresias! Here is Queen Eurydice. She must have heard something.

EURYDICE, *appearing at the top of the steps, left. She speaks with difficulty*. That is . . . at least . . . I have . . . overheard a little. I was opening the door of the temple of Minerva—I nearly fainted. What has happened? I must listen. I can bear to listen to you. Go on. I am strong. I have some experience of misfortune.

THE MESSENGER. O my dear mistress, listen to a witness's tale. Having, with the help of the king, buried the remains of Polynices and prayed to the goddess of the cross-roads,‡ we were running to Antigone's cavern, when Creon thought he heard his son shouting inside. We broke in with pickaxes and saw a pitiful sight: Antigone hanging from a rope made up of her veils. Haemon was pressing the unhappy girl to his breast. At the sight of Creon, Haemon lost his head, drew his sword, and spat at his father. Creon saw the rage and disgust in his eyes, saw the danger too, and fled. Then Haemon plunged the blade into his own body. His heart bespattered Antigone. They are married in death and blood.

Having received the full force of this blow,
EURYDICE *recoils and disappears.*

THE CHORUS. Not a word from the Queen. What must we think?

Long pause.

THE MESSENGER. She does not wish to make a show of herself.

---

* In the 1927 revival, a masked prologue, a sort of living statue which preceded the play, crossed the stage during this musical interlude. [J.C.]
† Cadmus was the founder of Thebes. [E.B.]
‡ Hecate. As a goddess of the underworld she was offended by the denial of the funeral rites. [E.B.]

Long pause.

THE CHORUS. Silence is more frightening than cries.

Long pause.

THE MESSENGER. Yes. I am going to investigate.

THE MESSENGER *enters the palace.*

THE CHORUS. The king! Bearing his son.

CREON, *dragging the body on his back. He makes it roll on to the ground, kneels and caresses its hair.* My son! My son! Haemon! Oh, my son! I am a murderer. I killed you.

THE CHORUS. This is very late.

CREON. A god held me by the throat, a god pushed me in the back. The whole house of happiness collapses upon me.

THE MESSENGER. Yes, prince. One tragedy upon another.

CREON. Another tragedy! What? *He points to his son stretched out.* What more could happen?

THE MESSENGER. Your wife is dead.

CREON. My wife is dead? It is not true! Ah, Pluto, you devour all. My wife after my son. You are lying. Where is she?

THE MESSENGER. Look! The door is open. CREON *mounts the steps on the left.*

CREON. Eurydice!

THE MESSENGER. She committed suicide at the foot of the altar, calling you murderer.

CREON. I am afraid. Kill me! Kill me quickly! I am falling into a bottomless hole!

THE MESSENGER. She accused you of the murder of Haemon and of Antigone.

CREON, *stupefied.* What was it? You were saying? . . . She has killed herself? My wife has killed herself?

THE MESSENGER. I say it again.

CREON. Help! Take me away! Take me away from here! I am less than nothing, less than nothing. I do not know where to look. I do not know where to put my hands, my feet. Everything is going, slipping from under me. A thunderbolt is falling on my head.

THE CHORUS. One should beware of insulting the gods. Too late, Creon, too late.

※

IN THIS BOOK the editor has attempted to exclude general matters of dramatic theory except when a particular play brought them up. He has therefore been able to postpone any mention of Aristotle's *Poetics* (best studied as *Aristotle's Theory of Fine Art,* ed. S. H. Butcher) until the topic is Aristotle's favorite playwright, Sophocles. *Antigone* is a problematic piece of work, but certain ideas of Aristotle's help us to unravel its difficulties.

It has been suggested that *Antigone* lacks unity, since the heroine leaves the stage long before the end and we are left wondering what is the relevance of what follows. If, however, we have read Aristotle, we have been warned not to expect a play to be unified through the life of its protagonist: it may have an *action* across which the life of the main character strikes obliquely. What is an action? Clearly Aristotle is not thinking of the quantity of physical activity on stage, like people who say "this play hasn't enough action." He means something like what was meant above (pp. 283, 367) by the word *subject*: a certain grouping of events, a story seen in its dramatic shape and unity. It is this action, and not the life of the hero, that must have the integrated "beginning, middle, and end" of which Aristotle speaks. A play is an "imitation" (or image or "acting out") "not of men but of an action and of life," that is, it presents, not parallel biographies, but a unified grouping of people and the deeds of people.* The

---

* In his preface to *The Awkward Age,* Henry James described how he planned the "action" of his novel: "I drew on a sheet of paper . . . the neat figure of a circle consisting of a number of small rounds disposed at equal distance about a central object. The central object was my situation, my *subject* (my italics—E.B.) in itself, to which the thing would owe its title, and the small rounds represented so many distinct lamps, as I liked to call them, the function of each of which would be to light with all due intensity one of its aspects. . . . Each of my 'lamps' would be the light of a single 'social occasion' in the history and intercourse of the characters concerned and would bring out to the full the latent color of the scene in question and cause it to illustrate, to the last drop, its bearing on my theme."

provision "and of life" might be taken as Aristotle's veto on the kind of play that is merely a piece of clever organization, having no grip on life.

In reading Molière and Shakespeare (not to mention Rostand and Wilde) we have stressed the primacy of plot. Aristotle called it the soul of the drama. Clearly a good plot is the necessary basis of an "action." What is the plot of *Antigone?* Antigone refuses to accept Creon's decree; she buries Polynices with her own hands, and is punished for it. Her punishment leads to her death, to the death of Haemon and Eurydice, and to what might be called the "agony" of Creon. This plot, as organized by Sophocles (or Cocteau), is not a life of Antigone, is not even a story in which Antigone stands unequivocally at the center; it is a double story, that of Antigone *and Creon*. Once Sophocles' "action" is seen in this way, the "problem" of Antigone's early exit is solved and with it the problem of the play's unity.

Antigone seems to be the heroine; is Creon the villain? In other words, is this dual subject a clear balance of good and evil? At first we certainly think of Creon as a villain, but that is partly because we forget that, from Creon's standpoint, Polynices was a rebel and partly because we today are individualists to the point of sentimentality. The Greeks were more inclined than we to stress the importance of the group, as against the individual, the importance of law and its upholders. Following this line of thought, it can be maintained that Sophocles, in Antigone and Creon, has balanced, not right and wrong, but one "right" against another. Such a conflict is in some ways more subtle and human and therefore more interesting than that between good and evil, but is it really to be found in *Antigone?* The philosopher Hegel is supposed to have claimed that it is. Few Greek scholars agree, however, and at least one (C. M. Bowra) has argued that Hegel probably meant something else.

Between regarding Creon as pure villain and elevating him to the moral level of Antigone, a middle position is possible. Sophocles can be taken as presenting a ruler of more than average stature whose love of law and order passes over into fanaticism. In his love of political order Creon is apparently prepared to override the higher Unwritten Laws. In refusing to stand for this, Antigone resembles, say, Sir Thomas More, who said, "I am the king's loyal subject but

God's first." We may be sure that Creon, like Henry VIII, would have sent More to his death.

Greek ethics, as accepted by Sophocles, is at one with More and Christianity on this point, though the principle is not at bottom a theological one. It is simply the idea that one's loyalty to a ruler, to a political order, is conditional. Unconditional loyalty—being loyal at all costs—posits what we today would call the totalitarian state, a political authority which is total in the sense that there is no appeal from it to anything higher. Nontotalitarian thinkers such as Sophocles posit the possibility that the ruler may be wrong. For them, the idea of humanity is more fundamental than that of law: law, like the sabbath, was made for man, and not vice versa. Those who die rather than deny this idea are saints or heroes, champions of humanity. Antigone is one such. And the aspect which the idea of humanity presents to her is that of family devotion. In his book *Immortal Shadows*, Stark Young correctly describes Sophocles' subject-matter as "the profound and hidden ties of family devotion and its loving mystery plus the recoil from a sense of outrage done to our deepest instincts—in this particular case the reverence for the beloved dead and their souls' peace." For the Greeks, the creation of the family as a basic and stable social unit was a comparatively recent thing. They protected their creation with religious awe. Their tragedies (*Antigone* and *Oedipus the King* supremely) are solemn warnings against the violation of family piety. In the highest sense, Greek tragedy is domestic tragedy.

At least that is the view which the present editor subscribes to and puts forward for discussion. It is only fair to add that, if some make Creon a hero, others make Antigone, if not a villain, at any rate a neurotic. In his challenging essay "The Wound and the Bow," in the book of that name, Edmund Wilson portrays Sophocles as a psychologist whose greatness was to understand the depths of mental disorder without help from Freud. In his "incrimination" of Antigone, Mr. Wilson makes much of a speech which Cocteau renders thus (see above, page 507):

"I should never have made that fateful effort for children or for a husband. A husband—he can be replaced. A son—another can be conceived. But, our parents being dead, I could not hope for more brothers. It was for this principle that I acted, that I am being struck down, and that Creon is denying me marriage and maternity."

Even if this speech indicates a "brother-fixation" in Antigone, does it make the brother-fixation the subject of the play? Is not Mr. Wilson asking us to believe that Sophocles imitated men and not an action? Aristotle did not believe so.

But it would be idle to pretend that Mr. Wilson's shrewd argument can be summed up and refuted in a few sentences. His essay has to be read as a whole—and compared with more orthodox accounts of the play in, say, H. D. F. Kitto's *Greek Tragedy* and C. M. Bowra's *Sophoclean Tragedy*.

As to the form of *Antigone*—if people read the version published here and say: "How experimental!" they may be thinking of Cocteau's contribution to it: the radio announcer as chorus, the modern phrasing, and the like. Yet "experimental" nowadays often means little more than "not a Broadway play with three acts, a 'well-made' plot, a single setting, etc." In this sense, nothing could be more experimental than the ancient Greek play with its sung and danced choruses, its verse forms, its masked and fantastically dressed actors speaking through a sort of megaphone and raised off the ground by preposterous high boots. The whole occasion, retaining in part the character of a religious festival, and taking place in a setting more like a football stadium than a modern theater, is far from any theatrical experience that we are likely to have had.

But we need not be overwhelmed by the strange form of *Antigone*. Like Shakespeare, the Greeks used the alternation of scenes as their basic pattern. With them the alternation is even more clearly defined. In one scene there is dialogue—usually dialogue in the strict sense of conversation between two persons. In the next there is dancing and singing. In the one, that is to say, there are two individual actors (sometimes only one, sometimes three, seldom more).* In the other there is a group performance. Five scenes of each type played in alternation might be regarded as a five-act play with choral

---

* "The number of actors was first increased to two by Aeschylus. . . . A third actor was added by Sophocles."—Aristotle.

516   ANTIGONE

interludes. Such in fact is the origin of the five-act play, which remained the normal dramatic form until recently.

How many scenes of dialogue are there in *Antigone*? How many choral interludes? The reader might also observe how much of the action is unfolded in each scene.

A more difficult question is: what has the chorus to do with the action? It consists of a group of Thebans who are little more than onlookers. Taken literally, there is not a little absurdity in their conduct: serious human beings do not merely stand by in circumstances such as these. Historically, the chorus is a vestige of religious rites, which were all chorus until the pioneer playwrights picked out first one actor, then two, and so forth. Aesthetically, it is an artifice, on a par with other artifices that we have noted. Its function is to contribute to that definition of a subject by theatrical means which we are assuming to be the playwright's job of work.

The chorus comments on the action, but from what point of view? Naïve readers have assumed that sentiments so pontifical yet eloquent as the chorus's must be those of the author. A more sophisticated theory is that the chorus speaks the thoughts of the ideal spectator. More helpful than either of these views is a remark of Aristotle's: "the chorus too should be regarded as one of the characters." Since Cocteau has taken Aristotle at his word to the extent of reducing the chorus to a single voice, we can read his version and ask quite simply: what *kind* of a person is this chorus? We conclude, do we not? that in *Antigone* he is some sort of average Theban and thus, perhaps, average Athenian. If this is so, it is interesting how long he stays on Creon's side and against Antigone. His first rebellion comes, it seems, with the words, "Creon, his oracles are never wrong," (page 509), that is, at the point where Creon comes into conflict with Tiresias. In sum, the chorus enables the playwright to express another point of view, that of some fairly average section of society, which comes to stand for society in general. But since the chorus is to be regarded as a character, it can, like a character, *develop*. Thus, the chorus of *Antigone* comes to see that Creon is going too far: it learns a lesson.

At first it may appear that the chorus in its longer pieces goes off on a tangent. Look back at the speeches beginning "Man is amazing" (page 499), "Happy are the innocent" (page 503), and "Love that seizes all and sundry" (page 506). By looking closely at the context you can figure out why Sophocles has these very general comments made by his chorus at just these times. Incidentally, a "character" that is part of the action and yet *a*part from it, that can act the plot yet also dance and sing outside the plot, that can speak strictly to the narrative point or in broad lyric and philosophical terms, is an astonishing dramatic instrument.

For Sophocles this instrument was at once traditional and current. To the modern audience it means nothing. In search of a modern equivalent, Cocteau hit on the voice of the announcer. It is a brilliant idea, and a great piece of self-denial. If Cocteau has denied himself a good deal in telescoping the dialogue of the play, he has denied himself even more in doing without the real chorus, that is, a chorus which (*a*) is more than one person; (*b*) sings; (*c*) dances. Even if the singing has to be given up on the grounds that modern singers cannot make their words clear to an audience, or that we don't know what kind of music should be sung; even if dance is given up because there are no dancers on hand or because we don't know how a Greek chorus should be danced—we need to *see* our chorus and it needs to be a *group* of people. When there is no chorus to look at, the eye is kept too narrowly focused on the "soloists." This is a fact which the present editor noticed in actual performance. Now Sophocles did not write a narrowly focused kind of play. When the chorus speaks, the eye should not stay on the soloists: it should be led to the chorus. That the chorus is a group, as well as one of the characters in the play, should be obvious if what was said above about its social nature is half-way convincing.

If Cocteau's beautiful version is, like all adaptations, a distortion, one should note the *direction* of the distortion in order to have some inkling of what the undistorted image would be like. The direction is, so to speak, that of France—or at least that of a famous French tradition: Cocteau has gone all out for passion. He has simplified the play—by reducing it not merely in length but also in breadth, until there is nothing left but swift catastrophe. His chorus, he says, "speaks very loudly and quickly as if reading a newspaper article." The whole play speaks quickly, if not loudly, and perhaps too often we think we are listening to a newspaper article. The colloquialism that constitutes its brilliance and charm is also, perhaps, its limitation.

7. GHOSTS · 1881

IT IS NOT the aim of this book to lead the reader into general discussions of tragedy and comedy but rather to help him to experience and "possess" works which, wisely or unwisely have been *called* tragedies and comedies. When we come, as we now do, to Ibsen and Strindberg, we are faced with works which have often been said to lie outside these older categories—or between them. There is a danger here of becoming involved in disputes that are futile because purely verbal. We turn hopefully to the word *realism,* which seems nowadays to have more substance. What does it mean? We have said that Shakespeare and Molière use an unrealistic kind of vehicle yet that there is a realistic element in their plays. The modern drama is generally considered to be predominantly realistic both in vehicle and substance, form and content. This could scarcely mean that it consists of sheer chunks of life, but does mean that it adheres more closely than the pre-modern drama did to many of life's usual forms. Much greater attention is paid to the milieu, to natural details of all sorts, to psychological consistency. We have seen that Molière and Shakespeare will sacrifice verisimilitude to effect, will use highly artificial conventions to bring, as we have put it, their subject into high relief. The moderns are more reluctant to do this, or to seem to do it, and have therefore been accused of sacrificing reality to realism. Indeed it was because the reader—as a typical modern citizen—might regard modern realism as the only way of revealing reality that the present editor had to assume he would resist and resent the artifices of older drama and would have to be persuaded (see pages 515-17 above) into accepting them.

It is good to read what was written some years ago in defence of the modern realistic drama by William Archer in his book *The Old Drama and the New* and the rejoinders that were written by T. S. Eliot ("A Dialogue on Dramatic Poetry," *Selected Essays*) and E. E. Stoll ("The Drama Old and New," *Poets and Playwrights*). Archer thinks that the development of modern realism means an improvement of the dramatic art. Archer's critics seem to regard realism as largely a nuisance. One wonders if it is so necessary to take sides. Can one not respect both modern realism and the poetic drama of the Elizabethans? Can one not find much realism in the latter? And much un-realism in the former?

There follows a very celebrated example of modern realism: Ibsen's *Ghosts*. It seems doubtful whether it needs Archer's general preference for realism to defend it. Indeed the reader of the mid-twentieth century will find more artifice (or unrealism) in it than his parents

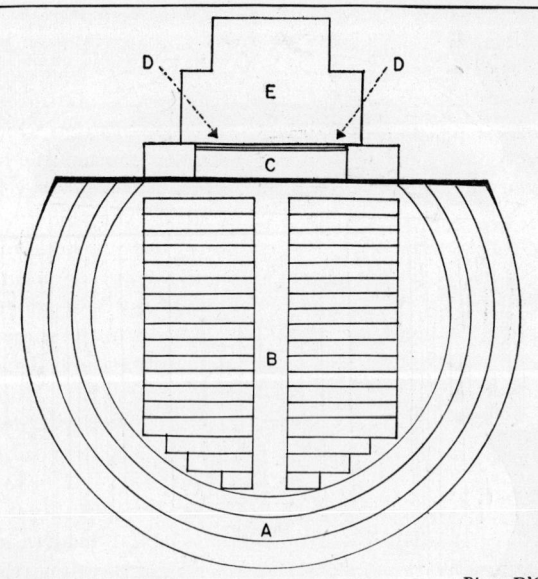

Piero D'Orazio

THE THEATER OF IBSEN

A. Upper floors of auditorium (dress circle, gallery, balcony, boxes, etc.)
B. Ground floor of auditorium ("stalls," "pit," etc.)
C. Orchestra pit: a space, sunk or walled-off, sometimes roofed-over, for musicians.
D. The proscenium arch dividing stage from auditorium. Footlights.
E. The "peepshow stage," i.e., a stage receding from the auditorium, a room seen, as it were, through a hole in one wall, a box with one side missing.

and grandparents did. At any rate, here is a play, in a nineteenth-century, middle-class setting, and written in the language of the nineteenth-century middle class, which contains material not unlike that of some classic tragedies. Let us see what a playwright can achieve in this setting, at this period of history, with these materials, with these methods.

GHOSTS

GHOSTS

by Henrik Ibsen

TRANSLATED FROM THE NORWEGIAN
BY EVA LE GALLIENNE

✶

Used by permission of Eva Le Gallienne. All rights whatsoever in this translation are strictly reserved, and applications for performances, etc., should be made to Miss Le Gallienne, Toscairn, Westport, Connecticut.

Ghosts

Characters

ENGSTRAND, *the carpenter*
REGINA, *the maid*
PASTOR MANDERS
MRS. ALVING
OSWALD, *her son*

Act I

SCENE: *A spacious garden-room, with one door to the left, and two doors to the right. In the middle of the room a round table, with chairs about it. On the table lie books, periodicals, and newspapers. In the foreground to the left a window, and by it a small sofa, with a work-table in front of it. In the background, the room is continued into a somewhat narrower conservatory, the walls of which are formed by large panes of glass. In the right-hand wall of the conservatory is a door leading down into the garden. Through the glass wall a gloomy fjord-landscape is faintly visible, veiled by steady rain.*

ENGSTRAND, *the carpenter, stands by the garden door. His left leg is somewhat bent; he has a clump of wood under the sole of his boot.* REGINA, *with an empty garden syringe in her hand, hinders him from advancing.*

REGINA. Well, what is it *you* want? No! stay where you are—you're dripping wet!

ENGSTRAND. It's only God's rain, my child.

REGINA. The devil's rain you mean!

ENGSTRAND. How you talk, Regina! *Advances into room a few steps.* But, here's what I want to tell you—

REGINA. Don't go clumping about with that foot of yours! The young master's upstairs asleep.

ENGSTRAND. Asleep at this hour—in broad daylight?

REGINA. It's none of your business.

ENGSTRAND. Now, look at *me*—I was on a bit of a spree last night.

REGINA. That's nothing new!

ENGSTRAND. Well—we're all frail creatures, my child.

REGINA. We are that!

ENGSTRAND. And temptations are manifold in this world, you see—but that didn't prevent me from going to work at half past five as usual!

REGINA. That's as it may be—and now, get out! I can't stand here having a rendezvous with you.

ENGSTRAND. What's that?

REGINA. I don't want anyone to see you here—so get out!

ENGSTRAND. Damned if I go till I've had a talk with you. Listen—I'll be through with my work at the schoolhouse this afternoon; then I'm going right back to town by the night boat—

REGINA. A pleasant journey to you!

ENGSTRAND. Thank you, my child! Tomorrow's the opening of the Orphanage, they'll all be celebrating—sure to be a lot of drinking, too—I'll prove to them that Jacob Engstrand can keep out of the way of temptation.

REGINA. Ha! . . . .

ENGSTRAND. Lots of grand people'll be here—Pastor Manders is expected from town—

REGINA. He gets here today.

ENGSTRAND. There—you see! Damned if I give *him* a chance to say anything against me!

REGINA. So that's it, is it?

ENGSTRAND. That's what?

REGINA. What are you going to try and put over on him this time?

ENGSTRAND. Are you crazy? As if I'd try and put anything over on *him!* No—Pastor Manders has been too good a friend to me—and that's just what I want to talk to you about. As I was saying, I'm going back home tonight—

REGINA. You can't go soon enough to please me!

ENGSTRAND. But I want you to come with me, Regina.

REGINA. *I,* go with you?

ENGSTRAND. Yes, I want you to come home with me.

REGINA. You'll never get me to do that!

ACT I] GHOSTS 525

ENGSTRAND. Well, we'll see.

REGINA. Yes! You'll see all right! After being brought up here by Mrs. Alving, treated almost like one of the family, do you suppose I'd ever go home with you—back to that kind of a house? You're crazy!

ENGSTRAND. What kind of talk's that! You'd defy your own father, would you?

REGINA. You've said often enough I'm no concern of yours.

ENGSTRAND. Never mind about that.

REGINA. Many's the time you've cursed at me and called me a— *Fi donc!*

ENGSTRAND. When did I ever use a foul word like that?

REGINA. I know well enough what word you used!

ENGSTRAND. Well—maybe—when I wasn't feeling quite myself— hm. Temptations are manifold in this world, Regina!

REGINA. Pah! . . . .

ENGSTRAND. And then your mother used to drive me crazy—I had to find some way to get back at her. She put on so many airs: "Let me go, Engstrand! Leave me alone! Don't forget I spent three years in Chamberlain Alving's house at Rosenvold!" *Laughs.* God Almighty! She never got over the Captain being made Chamberlain while she was working here!

REGINA. Poor mother! You certainly hounded her into her grave!

ENGSTRAND. Oh, of course! I'm to blame for everything!

REGINA. Ugh! And then that leg of yours!

ENGSTRAND. What did you say, my child?

REGINA. *Pied de mouton!*

ENGSTRAND. What's that? German?

REGINA. Yes.

ENGSTRAND. Yes—well, you've certainly got educated here—and that may come in handy too.

REGINA. Why do you want me to go back with you?

ENGSTRAND. Why wouldn't a father want his only child with him? Aren't I a lonely, deserted widower?

REGINA. Oh, don't talk rubbish to me!

ENGSTRAND. Well, I'll tell you—I'm thinking of setting up in a new line of business.

REGINA. What, again! What is it this time?

ENGSTRAND. You'll see; this time it'll be different. Christ Almighty!

REGINA. Stop your swearing! *She stamps her foot.*

ENGSTRAND. Sh! . . . You're right, my child. Well, what I wanted to say was—I've managed to save quite a bit of money from this work on the Orphanage.

REGINA. You have, have you? So much the better for you.

ENGSTRAND. There's nothing to spend your money on in this God-forsaken hole—

REGINA. Well?

ENGSTRAND. So I thought I'd invest it in a paying concern. I thought of starting a sort of tavern—for seamen.

REGINA. Ugh!

ENGSTRAND. A really high-class tavern you know, none of your cheap dives. No, by God! I'd cater to captains and first-mates—really high-class people.

REGINA. And I suppose I'd be expected to—

ENGSTRAND. Oh, you could be a great help, Regina. You wouldn't have to do anything; it wouldn't be hard on you, my child—you'd have everything your own way!

REGINA. Oh yes, of course!

ENGSTRAND. After all there must be some women in the house; that goes without saying. We'd have to have a bit of fun in the evenings, singing and dancing, and that sort of thing. You've got to remember—these poor fellows are sailors, wanderers on the seas of the world. *Comes nearer to her.* Don't be a fool and stand in your own way. What future is there for you out here? What good's all this education the missis has paid for? You're to look after the kids in the new Orphanage I hear—is that a job for you? Do you want to wear yourself to the bone looking after a lot of dirty brats?

REGINA. If things turn out as I hope—well, it could be, it could be. . . .

ENGSTRAND. What "could be"?

REGINA. You keep your nose out of that! How much money did you save?

ENGSTRAND. I'd say, in all, around seven, eight hundred dollars.

REGINA. Not so bad!

ENGSTRAND. Enough to get me started, my child.

REGINA. Do I get any of it?

ENGSTRAND. You do not!

REGINA. Not even enough to buy myself a new dress?

ENGSTRAND. You come with me—you'll get plenty of new dresses then!

REGINA. I can get them myself, if I set my mind to it.

ENGSTRAND. But a father's guiding hand is a good thing, Regina. There's a nice little house right on Harbor Street—not much money down either—it'd be like a kind of Seamen's Home, you know.

REGINA. But I don't want to live with you! I don't want to have anything to do with you! So now—get out!

ENGSTRAND. You wouldn't be with me for long, my child, I know that well enough. All you've got to do is use your wits—you've turned into a handsome wench—do you know that?

REGINA. Well, what of it?

ENGSTRAND. Before you know it, some first-mate'll come along—maybe even a captain.

REGINA. I don't intend to marry any such trash. Sailors have no *savoir vivre*.

ENGSTRAND. Well, I couldn't say about that—

REGINA. I tell you I know all about sailors. I wouldn't think of marrying one of them!

ENGSTRAND. Who says you'd have to marry? You can make it pay just the same. That Englishman, the one with the yacht, he gave three hundred dollars, he did, and she wasn't any better-looking than you are.

REGINA. Get out of here!

ENGSTRAND, *retreating*. Now, now! You wouldn't hit me, would you?

REGINA. You just say anything against mother, and you'll see whether I'd hit you or not! And don't bang the door; young Mister Alving—

ENGSTRAND. Is asleep—I know! Why should you be so worried about him? God Almighty! You don't mean to tell me that *he*—?

REGINA. You must be out of your head, you fool! Go on now, get out this minute! No, not that way—here comes Pastor Manders; the back-stairs for you!

ENGSTRAND. All right, I'll go. But listen—you have a talk with him—he'll tell you what you owe your father—for I am your father after all, you know; I can prove that by the Church Register.

He goes out by the other door and REGINA *closes it after him. She looks at herself hastily in the mirror, fans herself with her handkerchief, fixes her collar, then busies herself with the plants.* PASTOR MANDERS *in a frock-coat, carrying an umbrella and with a small traveling satchel slung over his shoulder, comes in from the garden.*

MANDERS. Good-day, Miss Engstrand.

REGINA, *turning in glad surprise.* Well! Good-day, Pastor Manders! Fancy! So the steamer's in, is it?

MANDERS. Yes, just docked. Dreadful weather we've had these last few days.

REGINA. It's a blessing for the farmers, Pastor Manders.

MANDERS. Quite right, Miss Engstrand! We city folk never think of that.

REGINA. Do let me help you! *Helps him off with his overcoat.* My goodness! It's soaking wet! I'll just hang it in the hall. And, let me take your umbrella—I'll open it up so it'll dry quicker.

She goes out with the things. MANDERS *puts his bag and hat on a chair.* REGINA *comes in again.*

MANDERS. It's very pleasant to be indoors. And how are things going here? All well, I trust?

REGINA. Yes—many thanks.

MANDERS. I expect you've been very busy with tomorrow's preparations.

REGINA. Yes, there's been so much to do!

MANDERS. And Mrs. Alving is at home, I hope?

REGINA. Oh yes, indeed. She just went upstairs to give the young master his hot chocolate.

MANDERS. Tell me—I heard down at the pier that Oswald had come home.

REGINA. He arrived the day before yesterday; we didn't expect him until today.

MANDERS. In good health and spirits, I trust?

REGINA. Yes, thank you, he seems to be—but dreadfully tired after his journey. He came straight through from Paris, without a stop. I mean, he came the whole way without a break. I think he's taking a little nap, so we must talk very quietly.

MANDERS. Sh! We'll be still as mice!

REGINA, *moving an arm-chair up to the table.* Do be so kind as to sit down, Pastor Manders, and make yourself comfortable.

He sits; she places a footstool under his feet.
There! How does that feel?

MANDERS. Most comfortable, thank you! *He looks at her.* Do you know, Miss Engstrand, I really believe you've grown since I saw you last.

REGINA. Do you think so, Pastor Manders? Mrs. Alving says I've filled out too.

MANDERS. Filled out eh? Yes, yes—perhaps a little—just suitably.
Short pause.

REGINA. Shall I tell Mrs. Alving you're here?

MANDERS. Thank you—there's no hurry, my dear child. Well—tell me, my dear Regina, how is your father getting on out here?

REGINA. Pretty well, thank you, Mr. Manders.

MANDERS. He came in to see me last time he was in town.

REGINA. Did he really? He's always so grateful for a talk with you, Mr. Manders.

MANDERS. I suppose you see him regularly, every day?

REGINA. I? .... Oh, yes .... of course. Whenever I have time—that is—

MANDERS. Your father is not a very strong character, Miss Engstrand.

REGINA. Yes, that may be so.

MANDERS. He needs someone near him—someone he can lean on—whose opinion he respects. He admitted as much, quite candidly, last time he came to see me.

REGINA. Yes, he's implied something of the sort to me. But I don't know if Mrs. Alving would want to let me go—especially now that we'll have the Orphanage to manage. And I really couldn't bear to leave Mrs. Alving—she's always been so good to me.

MANDERS. But a daughter's duty, my dear child—of course, we would first have to gain Mrs. Alving's consent.

REGINA. But would it be quite the thing, at my age, to keep house for a single man?

MANDERS. What do you mean? My dear Miss Engstrand, it's a question of your own father!

REGINA. Yes, I know—but all the same—of course, if it were a proper kind of house, belonging to a real gentleman—

MANDERS. Why, my dear Regina!

REGINA. Oh, I mean a man I could look up to—respect—become attached to—as though I were really his daughter—

MANDERS. My dear, good child—

REGINA. Under those conditions, I'd gladly live in town again, for I'm often very lonely here; and you know yourself, Mr. Manders, what it is to be all alone in the world. And I'm clever and willing, though I say it myself as shouldn't. Mr. Manders, I suppose you couldn't find me a position of that sort?

MANDERS. I? No—I'm really afraid I can't.

REGINA. But, you will think of me, dear Mr. Manders? you'll keep me in mind in case—

MANDERS. *Gets up.* Yes, yes, of course, Miss Engstrand.

REGINA. Because, you see, if I could only—

MANDERS. Would you be so kind as to tell Mrs. Alving I am here?

REGINA. I'll go and call her at once, Mr. Manders.

She exits. MANDERS *paces up and down the room a couple of times. He examines some books that are lying on the table—puts them down again disturbed by what he has seen.*

MANDERS. Hm! . . . Well—well!

MRS. ALVING *enters, followed by* REGINA, *who immediately exits by the other door.*

MRS. ALVING, *with outstretched hand.* Welcome, dear Mr. Manders!

MANDERS. Good-day, Mrs. Alving. Well, here I am, as I promised.

MRS. ALVING. Punctual as usual!

MANDERS. I had great trouble getting away. As you know, I'm chairman of so many welfare organizations, and what with my committee meetings—

MRS. ALVING. I'm all the more grateful to you for coming so promptly. Now we shall be able to get all our business settled before dinner. But where is your luggage?

MANDERS. I left my things down at the Inn—I'll put up there for the night.

MRS. ALVING. Can't I persuade you to spend the night here this time?

ACT I] GHOSTS 531

MANDERS. No, no, Mrs. Alving, thank you all the same—but I prefer to stay there as usual. It's so very convenient; right by the Pier, you know.

MRS. ALVING. Well, just as you wish! I should have thought, that perhaps, at our age—!

MANDERS. Ah yes, of course—you will have your little joke! Well, I suppose you're radiantly happy today, what with tomorrow's ceremony, and having Oswald home again.

MRS. ALVING. Yes, it's too wonderful! He hasn't been home for over two years, you know. And he's promised to spend the whole winter with me!

MANDERS. Has he really? That's a nice filial gesture, for I'm sure his life in Rome and Paris must offer many attractions.

MRS. ALVING. Yes, no doubt. But after all, he has his mother here. My darling boy—he still has a place in his heart for me.

MANDERS. It would indeed have been regrettable had he allowed separation and his interest in such a thing as art to interfere with his natural affections.

MRS. ALVING. Yes, that's true. But fortunately, there's no danger of that with him. I'll be interested to see if you know him again, after all these years; he'll be down presently, he's just having a little upstairs rest. But do sit down, Mr. Manders.

MANDERS. Thank you. You're sure I'm not disturbing you?

MRS. ALVING. *Sits by table.* Of course not!

MANDERS. Splendid—then suppose we get down to business. Now first there's this— *Breaks off.* Tell me, Mrs. Alving, what are these books doing here?

MRS. ALVING. These? They're just books I happen to be reading.

MANDERS. Do you really read that sort of thing?

MRS. ALVING. Of course I do.

MANDERS. Do you feel that this type of reading makes you any better, any happier?

MRS. ALVING. I don't know—it gives me a certain confidence.

MANDERS. Extraordinary! How do you mean?

MRS. ALVING. It seems to clarify and confirm many things I've thought myself. The strange thing is, Mr. Manders, there's really nothing new in any of these books; they deal with subjects that most of us think about and believe in; though I dare say most people don't take the trouble to look into them very deeply, or face them honestly.

MANDERS. But, good heavens, you don't seriously believe that many people—?

MRS. ALVING. Of course!

MANDERS. But, surely not our kind of people.

MRS. ALVING. Yes! "Our kind of people" too.

MANDERS. Well, I really must say!

MRS. ALVING. But, what objection have you to these books?

MANDERS. Objection? You don't imagine I waste my time delving into such subjects!

MRS. ALVING. You mean you're condemning them without knowing them?

MANDERS. I've read quite enough about these books to disapprove of them.

MRS. ALVING. But how can you form an opinion if you haven't—?

MANDERS. My dear Mrs. Alving—in some things it is wiser to depend on the opinion of others. That is the way our world functions, and it is best that it should be so. Otherwise, what would become of society?

MRS. ALVING. Well, perhaps you're right.

MANDERS. I don't deny that such books may have a certain fascination. And I don't blame you for wishing to familiarize yourself with certain intellectual trends which, I understand, are current in the sophisticated world where your son has been allowed to roam so freely. But—

MRS. ALVING. But?

MANDERS. But one doesn't discuss such things openly, Mrs. Alving. There is no reason to give an account to all and sundry of what one reads, or thinks, in the privacy of one's own room.

MRS. ALVING. Certainly—I agree with you.

MANDERS. Think of your new responsibilities towards the Orphanage. When you decided to found it, your feelings on certain subjects were decidedly at variance with those you now entertain—unless I am greatly mistaken.

MRS. ALVING. Yes, I grant you that. But let's get back to the Orphanage, Mr. Manders.

ACT I] GHOSTS 533

MANDERS. By all means; only, remember: caution, my dear Mrs. Alving! And now, to work! You see these papers?

MRS. ALVING. The Deeds?

MANDERS. Yes, all in order at last! I had great trouble to get them in time. I had to bring strong pressure to bear on the authorities; they are painfully conscientious when it comes to property settlements of any kind, but here they are at last. This is the deed of conveyance for that part of the Rosenvold estate known as the Solvik property, together with all the newly erected buildings, the school, the teacher's house and the chapel. And here is the Charter of the Institution: "Charter of the Orphanage in memory of Captain Alving."

MRS. ALVING. That all seems clear.

MANDERS. I used the title "Captain" instead of "Court Chamberlain"—it seemed less ostentatious.

MRS. ALVING. Whatever you think best.

MANDERS. Here is the bank-book controlling the invested capital— the interest on which will be used to defray the running expenses of the institution.

MRS. ALVING. Thank you—you'll take care of that, won't you?

MANDERS. Certainly, if you wish. For the time being, I think it would be wise to leave the entire sum in the bank; the interest is not very attractive it's true, but we could then take our time and later on find a good mortgage—it would of course have to be a first mortgage and on unexceptional security; we can afford to take no risks—but we can discuss that matter at a later date.

MRS. ALVING. Yes, dear Mr. Manders, I leave all that to you.

MANDERS. I'll keep a sharp look-out. Now, there's something else— I've meant to take it up with you several times.

MRS. ALVING. And what is that?

MANDERS. The question of insurance. Do you wish me to take out insurance on the Orphanage or not?

MRS. ALVING. Well, of course, it must be insured!

MANDERS. Just a moment, Mrs. Alving; let us examine the matter more carefully.

MRS. ALVING. But, everything I own is insured—my house and its contents—the livestock—everything.

MANDERS. Naturally; your personal property is another matter; all my things are insured too, of course. But the Orphanage is dedicated to a high spiritual purpose.

MRS. ALVING. Yes, but—

MANDERS. As far as I am personally concerned, I can't see the slightest objection to safe-guarding ourselves against all possible risks.

MRS. ALVING. I quite agree.

MANDERS. But what about public opinion?

MRS. ALVING. Public opinion?

MANDERS. Are there any groups of people here—people who matter, I mean—who might take exception to it?

MRS. ALVING. What do you mean by "people who matter"?

MANDERS. I mean men of wealth and influence whose opinion it might be unwise to overlook.

MRS. ALVING. I see what you mean—yes, there might be one or two people who would object.

MANDERS. There, you see! In town I think there might be a strong feeling against it—among my colleagues for instance, and some of the more influential members of their congregations. It could be implied that we hadn't sufficient faith in Divine Providence.

MRS. ALVING. But, surely, Mr. Manders, you have no such feeling.

MANDERS. Oh, as far as I am personally concerned, I have no qualms in the matter. But we might not be able to prevent our action from being interpreted in an erroneous and unfortunate light, and this in turn might reflect on the work of the Orphanage.

MRS. ALVING. Of course, if that were to be the case—

MANDERS. And I admit, I can't quite overlook the embarrassing—I might even say difficult—position I should find myself in. In town this Orphanage has been much discussed by the leading citizens. They are well aware of the benefits that would accrue to the town from such an institution; its existence would undoubtedly reduce to an important degree the yearly sums they are expected to donate to charitable works. And, since I have been your adviser in this matter—your business representative from the beginning—most of the blame and criticism would inevitably fall on me.

MRS. ALVING. I wouldn't want you to be exposed to that.

MANDERS. Not to speak of the attacks that would unquestionably be made against me by certain newspapers.

MRS. ALVING. That settles it, Mr. Manders—we'll say no more about it!

MANDERS. Then, we decide against insurance?

MRS. ALVING. Yes, most certainly.

MANDERS. But, on the other hand, Mrs. Alving, suppose there should be an accident—one never knows—would you be prepared to make good the damage?

MRS. ALVING. No, I must tell you quite frankly, that would be out of the question.

MANDERS. In that case we are assuming a very grave responsibility.

MRS. ALVING. Well, do you see anything else to do?

MANDERS. I'm afraid not—I don't really see that there's anything else we *can* do. We don't want to be placed in a false position; and it would be most unwise to arouse the antagonism of the community.

MRS. ALVING. Especially for you, as a clergyman.

MANDERS. We must simply have faith that our institution will be under the special protection of Providence.

MRS. ALVING. Let us hope so, Mr. Manders.

MANDERS. So that question is settled. *Makes a note.* No insurance.

MRS. ALVING. Strange you should bring this up today.

MANDERS. I've been meaning to discuss it with you.

MRS. ALVING. Because only yesterday we nearly had a fire down there.

MANDERS. What!

MRS. ALVING. Nothing came of it, fortunately; some wood-shavings caught fire in the carpenter's shop.

MANDERS. Where Engstrand works?

MRS. ALVING. Yes. He's often very careless with matches.

MANDERS. Poor man, he has so much on his mind—so many worries. I'm happy to say he's decided to turn over a new leaf.

MRS. ALVING. Indeed? Who told you that?

MANDERS. He assured me so himself. I'm very glad; he's such an excellent worker.

MRS. ALVING. Yes—when he's sober.

MANDERS. That unfortunate weakness! He's often in great pain with that poor leg of his. Last time he came to see me in town, he was really very touching. He was so grateful to me for getting him this work here—where he could be near Regina.

MRS. ALVING. I don't think he sees much of her.

MANDERS. Oh yes, he sees her every day—he told me so himself.

MRS. ALVING. Well, it's possible.

MANDERS. He desperately needs someone near him, to help him when temptation gets too strong for him. The other day he accused himself so bitterly; he realizes how weak he is and is so anxious to reform. Mrs. Alving, if he should feel the need of having Regina with him—

MRS. ALVING. Regina?

MANDERS. I urge you not to oppose it.

MRS. ALVING. I most certainly would oppose it! And besides—Regina is to work at the Orphanage.

MANDERS. But remember—he *is* her father.

MRS. ALVING. I know the kind of father he is! No! She shall never go back to him while I have anything to say in the matter!

MANDERS. But, my dear Mrs. Alving, why be so violent about it! It's a great pity that you misjudge Engstrand so. One would think you were actually afraid—

MRS. ALVING. That's not the point. I am looking after Regina and she will stay here with me. Sh! Let's say no more about it. Here comes Oswald—let's think of him now.

OSWALD ALVING *enters left. He has on a light overcoat and is carrying his hat. He is smoking a large Meerschaum pipe.*

OSWALD. Oh, I'm sorry; I thought you were in the library. I didn't mean to disturb you. How do you do, Mr. Manders!

MANDERS. How do you do! But, what an amazing. . . . !

MRS. ALVING. What do you think of him, Mr. Manders?

MANDERS. Can it really be?

OSWALD. Yes—it's the Prodigal Son, Mr. Manders!

MANDERS. My dear boy!

OSWALD. Or the lost sheep returned to the fold—if you prefer.

MRS. ALVING. He's only joking, Mr. Manders. He remembers your disapproval of an artist's career.

MANDERS. We are not infallible in our judgments. Certain steps may seem to us dangerous that turn out in the end to be. . . . So, welcome! Welcome home, my dear Oswald! I may call you Oswald, I trust?

OSWALD. What else should you call me, Mr. Manders?

MANDERS. Splendid! .... Don't imagine, my dear Oswald, that I unconditionally condemn the artist's life. I dare say there are many who succeed, in spite of everything, in preserving their integrity of character.

OSWALD. Let us hope so!

MRS. ALVING. Well, here's one who's managed to do so, Mr. Manders —you've only to look at him to see that!

OSWALD. There, there, mother dear; never mind!

MANDERS. Yes, fortunately, that's undeniable! And you've begun to make quite a name for yourself. I've often seen you mentioned in the papers, and always most favorably. Though recently I haven't seen so much about your work.

OSWALD. No—I haven't done much painting lately.

MRS. ALVING. Even an artist needs to rest now and then.

MANDERS. Most understandable—you need to gather new strength, for even finer work.

OSWALD. Quite so.—Will dinner be ready soon, mother?

MRS. ALVING. In half an hour, dear. There's nothing wrong with his appetite, thank God!

MANDERS. And I see he's partial to tobacco too.

OSWALD. I found this old pipe of father's up in his study.

MANDERS. Oh, so that accounts for it!

MRS. ALVING. How do you mean?

MANDERS. When Oswald came in just now—with that pipe in his mouth—he was the living image of his father.

OSWALD. Really?

MRS. ALVING. How can you say that? Oswald takes after me.

MANDERS. Yes, perhaps; but, still, there's something about his mouth—something in the expression—that reminds me very strongly of Alving.

MRS. ALVING. I don't see it at all—Oswald's mouth is much more sensitive. But put out your pipe now, Oswald dear. I don't allow smoking in this room.

OSWALD. Very well, mother. I only wanted to try it; I smoked it once before you see—when I was a child.

MRS. ALVING. *You* did?

OSWALD. Yes, I was very little at the time—I remember I went up to father's study one evening; he was in a very gay, jolly mood.

MRS. ALVING. How could you possibly remember so far back as that?

OSWALD. Oh, but I do! I remember it very distinctly; he sat me on his knee and told me to smoke his pipe. "Smoke, son," he said, "go on, son, have a good smoke." So I smoked away with all my might, until I felt deathly ill and great beads of perspiration stood out on my forehead. He thought it was very funny. I remember he roared with laughter at me.

MANDERS. What a very odd thing to do!

MRS. ALVING. It's a lot of nonsense! Oswald must have dreamed it.

OSWALD. No mother, I assure you I didn't! Don't you remember, you came in and rushed me off to the nursery. I felt very sick—and then I noticed you'd been crying. . . . I suppose it *was* rather odd . . . . did father often do things like that?

MANDERS. He was always full of fun.

OSWALD. Yet think of all that he accomplished! Although he died quite young—he achieved so much that was good and valuable.

MANDERS. Yes, you have a fine heritage, Oswald Alving. It should be a great incentive to you!

OSWALD. Yes, you're right! Indeed it should.

MANDERS. And it was good of you to come home for the ceremony tomorrow.

OSWALD. That's the least I could do for father's memory.

MRS. ALVING. But the best thing of all is that he plans to stay here for a while.

MANDERS. Yes—you intend to spend the winter here, I understand.

OSWALD. I plan to stay here indefinitely, Mr. Manders. It's so good to be home again!

MRS. ALVING. Yes, you really feel that, don't you dear?

MANDERS. You were very young when you left home, my dear Oswald.

OSWALD. A little too young, perhaps.

MRS. ALVING. What nonsense! It's good for a strong healthy boy—especially an only child—to get away from home. Much better than being petted and spoiled by doting parents!

MANDERS. I think that is open to debate, Mrs. Alving. A home and parents are still a child's best refuge.

OSWALD. I'm inclined to agree with Mr. Manders there.

MANDERS. Take your own son here as an example—there's no harm in discussing it before him—what has been the result in his case? Here he is, twenty-five or twenty-six years old, and he has never yet known what a normal, well-regulated home can be.

OSWALD. I beg your pardon, Mr. Manders, but that's not quite true.

MANDERS. Really? But, I thought you'd been living exclusively in artistic circles.

OSWALD. So I have.

MANDERS. And mostly among the younger artists, I believe.

OSWALD. Quite right.

MANDERS. But surely the majority of such people are in no position to found a home and family.

OSWALD. Most of them are in no position to get married, that's true enough.

MANDERS. That's just what I say.

OSWALD. But that doesn't necessarily mean that they can't have homes of their own—and many of them have—very comfortable and well-run homes too.

MANDERS. I'm not thinking of bachelor-establishments; when I use the word "home" I mean a family—a home where a man lives with his wife and children.

OSWALD. Or with his children—and their mother.

MANDERS. Good heavens!

OSWALD. What is it?

MANDERS. —his children's mother!

OSWALD. What would you have him do? Abandon her?

MANDERS. Then you're speaking of illegal unions—vicious and corrupt relationships!

OSWALD. I've never noticed anything especially corrupt in the lives these people lead.

MANDERS. How could any decent young man or woman degrade themselves by living in such shameful circumstances!

OSWALD. Well, what do you expect them to do? Some poor young artist, some poor girl—marriage is an expensive business. What do you expect them to do?

MANDERS. I would expect them to resist temptation, Mr. Alving—to part before it is too late.

OSWALD. That's a lot to expect of young people in love, Mr. Manders.

MRS. ALVING. Yes, I'm afraid it is!

MANDERS. And to think that such behavior should be openly tolerated. *To* MRS. ALVING. You see how right I was to be concerned about your son. Living in circles where such rampant immorality prevails, where it's taken for granted, one might say—

OSWALD. Let me tell you something, Mr. Manders—I've spent many a Sunday at some of these "illegal homes," as you call them—

MANDERS. On Sundays too. . . . !

OSWALD. Sunday happens to be a holiday—but I've never once heard a single vulgar or indecent word, nor have I ever witnessed any behavior that could possibly be called immoral. I've only seen such behavior—can you guess when?

MANDERS. I? God forbid!

OSWALD. Then I'll tell you: When some of your highly respected citizens—your model fathers and husbands from back home here—take a trip abroad to "see a bit of life." When they condescend to honor us poor artists with their presence—then you would see "rampant immorality" if you like! These respectable gentlemen could tell us about things that we had never even dreamed of!

MANDERS. What! You dare imply that honorable men. . . . ?

OSWALD. You must have heard these same "honorable men" when they get safely home again, hold forth on the outrageous immorality that prevails abroad?

MANDERS. I have indeed.

MRS. ALVING. I've heard them too.

OSWALD. Well you may take their word for it! They speak with authority. It's an outrage that we whose lives are full of truth and freedom should be slandered by such hypocrites!

MRS. ALVING. Don't get so excited, Oswald. It's not good for you.

OSWALD. You're right, mother. It's bad for me I know, but I'm so damned tired. I think I'll take a little walk before dinner. Forgive me, Mr. Manders, I shouldn't have let go like that. I know you can't possibly understand my feelings. *He goes into the garden.*

MRS. ALVING. Poor boy!

MANDERS. You may well say so! That he should have sunk to this!
MRS. ALVING *looks at him in silence.* He called himself the Prodigal Son. . . . Tragic! Tragic! MRS. ALVING *continues to look at him silently.* And what do you say to all this?

MRS. ALVING. I say Oswald was right in every word he said.

MANDERS. Right! You mean you agree to such principles?

MRS. ALVING. Living here alone all these years, I've come to the same conclusions—but I've never put my thoughts into words. Well, now my boy can speak for me.

MANDERS. You are greatly to be pitied, Mrs. Alving! I have always had your best interests at heart. For many years I have advised you in business matters. For many years I have been your friend and your late husband's friend. As your spiritual adviser I once saved you from a reckless and foolhardly action. And once again I feel it my duty to talk to you with the utmost solemnity.

MRS. ALVING. What is it you wish to say to me, Mr. Manders?

MANDERS. Look back over the years; it's appropriate that you should do so today, for tomorrow is the tenth anniversary of your husband's death and his Memorial will be unveiled. Tomorrow I shall speak to the crowd assembled in his honor, but today I must speak to you alone.

MRS. ALVING. I'm listening.

MANDERS. You had been married scarcely a year when you took the step that might have wrecked your life. You left house and home and ran away from your husband—yes, Mrs. Alving, ran away, and refused to go back to him in spite of all his entreaties.

MRS. ALVING. I was miserably unhappy that first year—don't forget that.

MANDERS. Why should we expect happiness in this life? It is the sign of a rebellious spirit—No! Mrs. Alving, we are here to do our duty, and it was your duty to stay with the man you had chosen and to whom you were bound in holy matrimony.

MRS. ALVING. You know all about the dissipated life Alving led.

MANDERS. It's true, I heard many rumors about him—and had those rumors been true, I should have been the first to condemn his conduct at that time. But it is not a wife's place to judge her husband; your duty was to resign yourself and bear your cross with true humility. But you rebelled against it and instead of giving your husband the help he needed, you left him, and by so doing jeopardized your own good name and reputation—and that of others too.

MRS. ALVING. Of "others"? Of *one* other you mean.

MANDERS. It was highly imprudent to come to me, of all people, for help.

MRS. ALVING. But why? Weren't you our "spiritual adviser" as well as our friend?

MANDERS. All the more reason. But God gave me the necessary strength to dissuade you from your reckless purpose, to guide you back to the path of duty and home to your husband.

MRS. ALVING. Yes, Mr. Manders—that was certainly your doing.

MANDERS. I was merely an instrument in God's hand. And, as I had foreseen, once you had returned to your duties, and humbled your spirit in obedience you were repaid a hundredfold. Alving reformed entirely, and remained a good and loving husband to the end of his days. He became a real benefactor to this whole community, and he allowed you to share, as his fellow-worker, in all his enterprises—and a very able fellow-worker too, I am aware of that, Mrs. Alving—I must pay you that tribute: but now I must speak of your second great mistake.

MRS. ALVING. What do you mean by that?

MANDERS. You first betrayed your duty as a wife; you later betrayed your duty as a mother.

MRS. ALVING. Ah!

MANDERS. All your life you have been possessed by a wilful, rebellious spirit. Your natural inclinations always led you towards the undisciplined and lawless. You could never tolerate the slightest restraint. Any responsibility, you carelessly and unscrupulously disregarded, as though it were a burden you had a right to cast aside. It no longer suited you to be a wife, so you left your husband. The cares of motherhood were too much for you, so you sent your child away to be brought up by strangers.

MRS. ALVING. That's true; I did do that.

MANDERS. And for that reason you are now a stranger to him.

MRS. ALVING. No! No! I'm not!

MANDERS. Of course you are! How could you be otherwise? And

now you see the result of your conduct. You have much to atone for; you failed your husband miserably—you are seeking to atone for that by raising this memorial in his honor; how are you going to atone for your failure towards your son? It may not be too late to save him: by redeeming yourself, Mrs. Alving, you may still help him to redemption!

MRS. ALVING. I have listened to you talk, Mr. Manders. Tomorrow you will be making speeches in my husband's honor. I shall not make any speeches tomorrow: but now I intend to talk to you, just as frankly, just as brutally, as you have talked to me!

MANDERS. Of course, it's natural that you should try and justify your conduct.

MRS. ALVING. No, I only want to make a few things clear to you.

MANDERS. Well?

MRS. ALVING. You've just talked a great deal about my married life after you—as you put it—"led me back to the path of duty." What do you really know about it? From that day on you never set foot inside this house—you who had been our closest friend.

MANDERS. But, you and your husband left town, almost immediately.

MRS. ALVING. And you never once came out here to see us during my husband's lifetime. It wasn't until this Orphanage business, that you felt compelled to visit me.

MANDERS, *with some embarrassment*. If that is meant as a reproach, my dear Helene, I beg you to consider—

MRS. ALVING. I know—you had to protect your reputation! After all, I was a woman who had tried to leave her husband! One can't be too careful with such females!

MANDERS. Oh, my dear!—Mrs. Alving—what a gross exaggeration!

MRS. ALVING. Well, never mind about that; the point is this: your opinions of my married life are based on nothing but hearsay.

MANDERS. That may be so; what then?

MRS. ALVING. Just this: that now, Manders, I am going to tell you the truth; I swore to myself I would tell it to you—one day.

MANDERS. And what is the truth?

MRS. ALVING. The truth is this. My husband died as he had lived: a degenerate and a drunkard!

MANDERS. What's that you said?

MRS. ALVING. After nineteen years of marriage—a degenerate and a drunkard—as he was the day you married us.

MANDERS. How can you use such dreadful words!

MRS. ALVING. They are the words our doctor used.

MANDERS. But, I don't understand—

MRS. ALVING. Why should you?

MANDERS. You mean that instead of that happy marriage, those years of comradeship we all believed in, there was only this—*abyss?*

MRS. ALVING. That is exactly what I mean; now you know it.

MANDERS. But it's inconceivable; I can't grasp it! How was it possible to? How could such a thing be hidden?

MRS. ALVING. My life became one long fight to that end. After Oswald was born, Alving seemed to me a little better—but it didn't last long! And then I had to fight for my son as well. I was determined that no living soul should ever know the kind of father my boy had. . . . As a matter of fact, you know how charming Alving could be—it was hard for people to think ill of him. He was one of those fortunate men whose private lives never seem to damage their public reputation. But then, Manders—I want you to know the whole story—then the most horrible thing of all happened.

MANDERS. How could anything be worse than. . . . ?

MRS. ALVING. I knew well enough all that was going on, and I put up with it as long as I didn't have to see it—but, when I was faced with it here—in my own home!

MANDERS. Here?

MRS. ALVING. Yes, in this very house. The first time I became aware of it, I was in there—in the dining room. I was busy with something, and the door was ajar; then I heard the maid come up from the garden with water for the plants.

MANDERS. Yes?

MRS. ALVING. In a few moments, I heard Alving come in after her; he said something to her in a low voice—and then I heard—it still rings in my ears, it was so horrible, and yet somehow so ludicrous—I heard my own servant-girl whisper: "Let me go, Mr. Alving! Leave me alone!"

MANDERS. But he couldn't have meant anything by it, Mrs. Alving; believe me, I'm sure he didn't!

MRS. ALVING. I soon found out what to believe. My husband had his way with the girl, and there were—consequences—Mr. Manders.

MANDERS. To think, that in this house!

MRS. ALVING. I had been through a lot in this house! Night after night, in order to keep him home, I sat up in his study with him—pretending to join him in his private drinking bouts. I sat there alone with him for hours on end listening to his obscene, senseless talk, and at last, by sheer brute force, when he became exhausted, I managed to drag him to bed.

MANDERS. How were you able to stand all this?

MRS. ALVING. I had to stand it; I had my little boy to think of. But when I discovered this final outrage—with a servant—in our own house! That was the end. From that day on I became master here. I took full control—over him and over everything. Alving didn't dare say a word; he knew he was in my power. It was then I decided to send Oswald away. He was nearly seven and was beginning to notice things and ask questions, as children do. I couldn't endure that, Manders. I felt the child would be poisoned in this sordid, degraded home. That's why I sent him away. Now perhaps you understand why I never let him set foot in this house as long as his father was alive. What you could never understand is what agony it was to have to do it!

MANDERS. To think of all you have been through . . . !

MRS. ALVING. I could never have stood it if I hadn't had my work. For I can honestly say I have worked! Alving received all the praise—all the credit—but don't imagine he had anything to do with it! The increase in the value of our property, the improvements, all those fine enterprises you spoke of—all that was *my* work. All he did was to sprawl on the sofa in his study reading old newspapers. In his few lucid moments I did try to spur him to some effort, but it was no use. He sank back again into his old habits and then spent days in a maudlin state of penitence and self-pity.

MANDERS. And you're building a memorial to such a man?

MRS. ALVING. That's what comes of having a bad conscience.

MANDERS. A bad—? What do you mean?

MRS. ALVING. I'll try and explain to you. . . . To begin with—of course, I feared that some day the truth would come out, so I decided to dedicate this Orphanage to Alving, in order to dispel once and for all any possible rumors, any possible doubts.

MANDERS. You've fully succeeded in that.

MRS. ALVING. But my main reason was: I didn't want my son to inherit anything whatsoever from his father.

MANDERS. I see, so you used Alving's money to—?

MRS. ALVING. Precisely. The money that has gone into the Orphanage amounts to the exact sum—I've calculated it very carefully—to the exact sum of the fortune, that once made people consider Lieutenant Alving a good match.

MANDERS. I understand you.

MRS. ALVING. I sold myself for that sum. I don't want Oswald to touch a penny of it. Everything he has will come from me—everything!

OSWALD *enters from the hall door; he has left his hat and coat outside.*

MRS. ALVING. Back already, dear?

OSWALD. Yes, what can one do out in this awful downpour? But I hear dinner's nearly ready—splendid!

REGINA *enters from the dining-room carrying a small parcel.*

REGINA. This parcel just came for you, Mrs. Alving.

MRS. ALVING, *with a glance at* MANDERS. It's a special hymn for tomorrow's ceremony, I expect.

MANDERS. Hm. . . .

REGINA. And dinner is served, Mrs. Alving.

MRS. ALVING. Good, we'll be there in a moment.

REGINA, *to* OSWALD. Would you like red or white wine, Mr. Alving?

OSWALD. Both, by all means, Miss Engstrand.

REGINA. *Bien*—Very good, Mr. Alving.   *Exits into dining-room.*

OSWALD. Let me help you uncork it. . . .

Follows her into the dining-room, half closing the door.

MRS. ALVING, *who has opened the parcel.* Yes, just as I thought, the hymn for tomorrow, Mr. Manders.

MANDERS. How I'm ever going to make my speech tomorrow!

MRS. ALVING. You'll manage, somehow.

MANDERS, *softly, so as not to be heard in the dining-room.* It would never do to arouse suspicion.

MRS. ALVING. No. . . . . And from tomorrow on, I shall be free at last; the long, hideous farce will be over; I shall forget that such a person as Alving ever lived in this house—there'll be no one here but my son and me.

The noise of a chair being overturned is heard from the dining-room—at the same time REGINA'S *voice.*

REGINA'S *voice, off stage.* Oswald! Are you mad? Let me go!

MRS. ALVING, *terrified.* Ah!

She starts towards the half-open door. The sound of OSWALD *coughing and then humming a tune; then a cork is drawn.*

MANDERS. But what is it? What's the matter, Mrs. Alving?

MRS. ALVING. Ghosts. . . . . Those two in the conservatory. . . . . Ghosts. . . . . They've come to life again!

MANDERS. You mean—? Regina—? Is *she*—?

MRS. ALVING. Yes. . . . . Let us go in. Not a word!

Act II

SCENE: *The same room a short while later.* MANDERS *and* MRS. ALVING *enter from the dining-room.* MRS. ALVING *turns and calls into dining-room.*

MRS. ALVING. Aren't you coming too, Oswald?

OSWALD, *off stage.* No, thank you, mother; I think I'll go out for a bit.

MRS. ALVING. Yes, do, dear; I think it's cleared up a little. *She closes the dining-room door, crosses to the hall door and calls:* Regina!

REGINA, *off stage.* Yes, Mrs. Alving?

MRS. ALVING. Go down to the sewing-room and help with the wreaths.

REGINA. Very well, Mrs. Alving.

MRS. ALVING *makes sure that* REGINA *has gone and then closes the door.*

MANDERS. You're quite sure he can't hear us in there?

MRS. ALVING. Not with the door shut—besides, he's going out.

MANDERS. I feel so overcome. I couldn't eat a morsal of that delicious food.

MRS. ALVING. No, neither could I. Well—what's to be done?

MANDERS. What's to be done indeed! I wish I knew what to suggest; I don't feel competent to deal with a crisis of this sort.

MRS. ALVING. One thing I'm convinced of—that, so far, there's been nothing wrong.

MANDERS. God forbid! It's a shameful business all the same.

MRS. ALVING. As for Oswald—it's only a passing whim. I'm sure of that.

MANDERS. As I said before—I have no experience in such things, but I really must say—

MRS. ALVING. One thing's clear: she must leave this house at once—before it's too late.

MANDERS. That goes without saying.

MRS. ALVING. Yes, but where can she go? We certainly wouldn't be justified in—

MANDERS. Why can't she go home with her father?

MRS. ALVING. With whom did you say?

MANDERS. With her—but of course! Engstrand isn't her—Good heavens, Mrs. Alving, all this is impossible; there must be some mistake!

MRS. ALVING. I'm afraid there is no mistake, Manders. The girl confessed to me herself. And Alving didn't deny it. So the only thing we could do was to try and hush the matter up. The girl left my service at once and was given a handsome sum to keep her mouth shut. She then took matters into her own hands—went back to town and renewed an old friendship with the carpenter, Engstrand. She hinted that she had money, told him some cock-and-bull story about a foreigner with a yacht; the outcome of all this was that they were married in great haste. You married them yourself, I believe.

MANDERS. But I can't understand it! I remember distinctly Engstrand coming to arrange about the wedding. He was overcome with confusion and shame—and kept reproaching himself bitterly for his sinful behavior.

MRS. ALVING. Well, I suppose he had to take the blame on himself.

MANDERS. I certainly never would have believed Jacob Engstrand capable of such duplicity—and to me of all people! I shall have to teach him a good lesson, I can see that. . . . A disgraceful relationship—and for money too! How much did the girl receive?

MRS. ALVING. Three hundred dollars.

MANDERS. Can you believe it? For three hundred dollars consenting to marry a—a—corrupt woman!

MRS. ALVING. After all, I married a corrupt man.

MANDERS. A corrupt—? What on earth are you talking about!

MRS. ALVING. Was Alving any better when he married me than the girl Johanna was when she married Engstrand?

MANDERS. But, good heavens—the two cases are utterly different.

MRS. ALVING. Perhaps not so very different, after all. There was a colossal difference in the price, that's true enough! A paltry three hundred dollars as against a large fortune.

MANDERS. But there *can* be no comparison in this instance! Your decision was based on the advice of relatives and friends, as well as the promptings of your heart.

MRS. ALVING. My heart, as you call it, was involved elsewhere at the time—as I thought you knew.

MANDERS. Had I known any such thing I should not have been a constant visitor in your husband's house.

MRS. ALVING. One thing is certain; I never really consulted my own feelings in the matter.

MANDERS. Perhaps not, but you consulted your mother, your two aunts, all those nearest to you—as was only right.

MRS. ALVING. Yes, those three! They were the ones that settled the whole business for me. As I look back on it, it seems incredible. They pointed out, in the most forceful terms, that it would be nothing short of folly to refuse an offer of such magnificence! Poor mother! If she only knew what that "magnificence" has led to.

MANDERS. No one can be held responsible for the outcome. The fact remains that your marriage in every way conformed to the strictest rules of law and order.

MRS. ALVING. All this talk about law and order! I often think all the suffering in the world is due to that.

MANDERS. That is a very wicked thing to say, Mrs. Alving.

MRS. ALVING. That may be. All I know is, I've had enough of it. I've had enough of all this cant—all this hypocrisy—I want the simplicity of freedom!

MANDERS. I don't understand you.

MRS. ALVING. I should never have lied about Alving, but I didn't dare do anything else at the time; and it wasn't only for Oswald's sake, it was for my own sake too. What a coward I've been!

MANDERS. A coward?

MRS. ALVING. A coward, yes. I could just hear what people would say if they found out the truth: "Poor man! One can hardly blame him with a wife like that! She tried to leave him, you know!"

MANDERS. They might perhaps have been justified in that.

MRS. ALVING. I ought to tell Oswald—God! if I only had the strength! I ought to say to him: "Listen, my son—your father was a corrupt drunkard."

MANDERS. Good God!

MRS. ALVING. And then I ought to tell him the whole story, word for word, just as I told it to you.

MANDERS. You horrify me, Mrs. Alving!

MRS. ALVING. I know—God, yes! I know!—I'm horrified myself at the thought of it! That's how much of a coward I am.

MANDERS. How can you call yourself a coward for doing what was merely your duty. Have you forgotten that a child should honor his father and mother?

MRS. ALVING. Why generalize? Why not ask: "Should Oswald love and honor Captain Alving?"

MANDERS. You're his mother—you wouldn't be so cruel as to shatter his ideals?

MRS. ALVING. Oh, ideals, ideals! What about the truth? If only I weren't such a coward!

MANDERS. You shouldn't scoff at ideals, Mrs. Alving; they have a way of avenging themselves. God knows, Oswald doesn't seem to have many, unfortunately. But his father seems to be somewhat of an ideal to him.

MRS. ALVING. Yes, that's quite true.

MANDERS. Your letters must be responsible for that feeling in him; you must have fostered it.

MRS. ALVING. Yes. I was treading the path of duty and obedience, Mr. Manders. I therefore lied to my son, religiously, year after year. What a coward—what a coward I was!

MANDERS. You have fostered a happy illusion in your son's mind, Mrs. Alving; you shouldn't underestimate its value.

MRS. ALVING. Its value may turn out to be dubious, who knows?

But he must leave Regina alone; he mustn't be allowed to get her into trouble.

MANDERS. No! That would be dreadful!

MRS. ALVING. If I thought she would really make him happy; if he were really serious about it—

MANDERS. What do you mean?

MRS. ALVING. Oh, but he couldn't be—Regina would never be enough for him.

MANDERS. What are you talking about?

MRS. ALVING. If I weren't such a miserable coward I'd say to him: "Marry her—come to any arrangement you like with her—only be honest about it!"

MANDERS. A marriage between them? You really wouldn't allow such an abominable thing!

MRS. ALVING. Abominable, you say? Why not face the truth, Manders? You know there are dozens of married couples out here in the country who are related in the same way.

MANDERS. I refuse to understand you.

MRS. ALVING. Of course you understand!

MANDERS. There may be a few instances; family-life is not always as blameless as it should be, unfortunately. But in nine cases out of ten the relationship is unsuspected, or at worst unconfirmed. Here, on the other hand— That you should be willing to allow your son!

MRS. ALVING. But I'm not willing to allow it—that's just what I'm saying—I wouldn't allow it for anything in the world.

MANDERS. Only because you're a coward, as you express it. But if you weren't a coward! Such a revolting marriage—God forgive you!

MRS. ALVING. We're all of us descended from that kind of marriage, so they say. And who was responsible for that arrangement, Mr. Manders?

MANDERS. I refuse to discuss these matters with you, Mrs. Alving; you are in no fit state to touch on such things. How you can have the effrontery to call yourself a coward for not. . . . !

MRS. ALVING. I'll tell you what I mean by that; I live in constant dread—constant terror—because I feel myself surrounded by ghosts, that I can't seem to shake off.

MANDERS. Ghosts, you say?

MRS. ALVING. Yes. Just now, when I heard Regina and Oswald in there, I felt hemmed in by ghosts. You know, Manders, the longer I live the more convinced I am that we're all haunted in this world, not only by the things we inherit from our parents, but by the ghosts of innumerable old prejudices and beliefs, half-forgotten cruelties and betrayals. We may not even be aware of them, but they're there just the same, and we can't get rid of them. The whole world is haunted by these ghosts of the dead past; you have only to pick up a newspaper to see them weaving in and out between the lines. Ah! if we only had the courage to sweep them all out and let in the light!

MANDERS. So this is the result of all this reading of yours—this detestable, pernicious, free-thinking literature!

MRS. ALVING. You're mistaken, my dear Manders. It was you who first goated me into thinking—I shall always be grateful to you for that.

MANDERS. I?

MRS. ALVING. Yes. When you forced me to obey what you called my conscience and my duty; when you hailed as right and noble what my whole soul rebelled against as false and ugly—that's when I started to analyze your teachings; that's when I first started to *think*. And one day I saw quite clearly that all that you stand for, all that you preach, is mechanical and dead; there's no life or truth in it.

MANDERS. So that's all I achieved by the hardest struggle of my life.

MRS. ALVING. I'd call it your most ignominious defeat.

MANDERS. It was a victory over myself, Helene, my greatest victory.

MRS. ALVING. It was a crime against us both.

MANDERS. The fact that I had strength for both of us—that I persuaded you to return to your husband—was that a crime?

MRS. ALVING. Yes. I think it was.

MANDERS. There's no possible understanding between us.

MRS. ALVING. Not any more, at any rate.

MANDERS. You have always been to me—even in my most secret thoughts—another man's wife.

MRS. ALVING. You don't really believe that, Manders?

MANDERS. Helene!

MRS. ALVING. It's so easy to forget one's feelings!

MANDERS. I don't forget. I am exactly the same as I always was.

MRS. ALVING. Oh, don't let's talk any more about the old days! Now you're up to your eyes in committee meetings and advisory boards, and I sit out her and battle with ghosts—invisible ghosts—and visible too.

MANDERS. I can at least help you conquer the visible ones. After the dreadful things you've said to me today, I couldn't dream of leaving a young, unprotected girl alone in your house.

MRS. ALVING. I think the best thing would be to arrange a good match for her—don't you agree?

MANDERS. Unquestionably. It would be best for her in every respect. Regina has reached the age when—of course, I know very little about these things—

MRS. ALVING. Yes, she developed early.

MANDERS. So it seemed to me. I remember thinking when I prepared her for confirmation that she was remarkably well-developed for a child of her age. For the present she had better go home, under her father's care. . . . but, of course, Engstrand isn't—I really can't understand his concealing the truth from me—

There is a knock at the hall door.

MRS. ALVING. Who can that be? Come in!

ENGSTRAND *appears in the doorway; he is in his Sunday clothes.*

ENGSTRAND. I most humbly beg pardon, but—

MRS. ALVING. Oh, it's you, Engstrand.

ENGSTRAND. None of the maids seemed to be about, so I took the liberty of knocking, ma'am. . . .

MRS. ALVING. Oh, very well, come in. Do you wish to speak to me?

ENGSTRAND. No—thank you all the same, Mrs. Alving. But if I might have a word with the Reverend—

MANDERS. With me, eh? So you want to talk to me, do you?

ENGSTRAND. I'd be most grateful.

MANDERS. Well, what is it?

ENGSTRAND. It's just this, sir: we're being paid off down there—and many thanks to you, ma'am—our work's all finished; and I thought how nice and helpful it would be to all of us who've worked together so hard and faithfully if we could have a few prayers this evening.

MANDERS. Prayers? Down at the Orphanage?

ENGSTRAND. Yes, sir; of course if it isn't convenient to you, sir. . . . .

MANDERS. Oh, it's convenient enough, but—hm. . . .

ENGSTRAND. I've taken to saying a few prayers myself down there of an evening.

MRS. ALVING. *You* have?

ENGSTRAND. Yes—now and then; we can all do with a little edification I thought; but I'm just a simple, humble fellow— I'm not much good at it, God help me! But as long as the Reverend happened to be here, I thought—

MANDERS. Look here, Engstrand, I must first ask you a question. Are you in a proper state of mind for prayer? Have you a clear conscience?

ENGSTRAND. God help me! Perhaps we'd better not talk about my conscience, Mr. Manders.

MANDERS. That is exactly what we must talk about. Well, answer me!

ENGSTRAND. Well, sir—of course, now and then, it does trouble me a bit.

MANDERS. I'm glad you admit that at least. Now, will you be so kind as to tell me honestly—what is the truth about Regina?

MRS. ALVING. Mr. Manders!

MANDERS. I'll handle this.

ENGSTRAND. Regina! Lord, how you frightened me! There's nothing wrong with Regina, is there?

MANDERS. It is to be hoped not. But what I mean is this: what is your true relationship to Regina? You pretend to be her father, do you not?

ENGSTRAND. Yes—hm—well, sir, you know all about me and poor Johanna. . . . .

MANDERS. No more prevarication, please! Your late wife confessed the whole truth to Mrs. Alving before she left her service.

ENGSTRAND. Do you mean to say she—? Oh, she did, did she?

MANDERS. Yes. So it's no use lying any longer, Engstrand.

ENGSTRAND. Well! And after her swearing up and down—

MANDERS. Swearing, you say?

ENGSTRAND. I mean, she gave me her solemn word, sir.

MANDERS. And all these years you've kept the truth from me—from me, who has always had the utmost, the utmost faith in you!

ENGSTRAND. Yes, sir, I'm afraid I have.

ACT II] GHOSTS 555

MANDERS. Have I deserved that, Engstrand? Haven't I always done everything in my power to help you? Answer me, haven't I?

ENGSTRAND. Yes, sir. Things would often have looked pretty black for me, if it hadn't been for Mr. Manders.

MANDERS. And this is how you repay me! You cause me to enter erroneous statements in the Church Register, and withhold from me for years the truth which it was your duty to impart to me. Your conduct has been inexcusable, Engstrand; from now on, I shall have nothing more to do with you.

ENGSTRAND, *with a sigh*. Yes, sir; I suppose that's how it has to be!

MANDERS. I don't see how you can possibly justify your conduct.

ENGSTRAND. We felt it better not to add to her shame by talking about it. Supposing you'd been in poor Johanna's place, Mr. Manders—

MANDERS. I!

ENGSTRAND. Lord bless me! I don't mean that the way it sounds! What I mean is: suppose you had done something you were ashamed of in the eyes of the world, as they say; we men oughtn't to judge a poor woman too hard, Mr. Manders.

MANDERS. But I don't judge her; it's you I'm accusing.

ENGSTRAND. Mr. Manders, would you allow me to ask you just one little question?

MANDERS. Very well—what is it?

ENGSTRAND. Shouldn't a decent honorable man help those who've gone astray?

MANDERS. Well, naturally. . . .

ENGSTRAND. And isn't a man bound to keep his word of honor?

MANDERS. Yes, of course, but. . . .

ENGSTRAND. Well, you see, after Johanna got into trouble with that Englishman, or maybe he was American, or one of those Russians even—anyway, she came back to town. Poor thing, she'd already refused me twice; she only had eyes for the handsome fellows; and, of course, I had this deformed leg of mine. You remember, sir, I was once rash enough to enter one of those dance-halls—one of those dives where sailors spend their time drinking and carousing, as they say—I was just trying to persuade them to try another kind of life. . . .

MRS. ALVING. Hm. . . .

MANDERS. Yes, I know, Engstrand, those dreadful men threw you downstairs. I remember your telling me of that tragic experience. You bear your deformity with honor.

ENGSTRAND. I don't mean to brag about it, sir. Well, anyway, she came to me, and confided her whole trouble to me, with tears and lamentations—it broke my heart to listen to her.

MANDERS. I can well believe it, Engstrand; well, and then—?

ENGSTRAND. Well, then I said to her, I said: "That American is wandering on the seas of the world; and you, Johanna, are a sinful fallen creature," I said. "But Jacob Engstrand," I said, "stands here on two solid legs," I said; of course I only meant that in a manner of speaking you know, sir—

MANDERS. Yes, yes, I understand; go on. . . . .

ENGSTRAND. Well then, sir, I married her—I made her an honest woman—so no one would know of her reckless behavior with that foreigner.

MANDERS. All of that was very right and good of you, Engstrand; but I don't understand how you could have accepted money.

ENGSTRAND. Money? Me? Not a penny.

MANDERS. But—?

ENGSTRAND. Oh yes—wait a bit—now I remember: Johanna did say something about some money she had, but I wouldn't hear about that! "Get Thee behind me Satan," I said, "it's Mammon's gold" (or bank-notes or whatever it was), "we'll throw it back in the American's face," I said. But, of course, he had disappeared, sir, disappeared over the vast ocean you see.

MANDERS. Yes, I see—my dear Engstrand.

ENGSTRAND. Yes, sir. And then Johanna and I agreed that every penny of that money should go to the child's upbringing; and so it was; and I can account for every cent of it, sir.

MANDERS. But this puts things in an entirely different light—

ENGSTRAND. That's the way it was, Mr. Manders. And, though I say it myself, I've tried to be a good father to Regina—to the best of my ability that is; you know what a weak man I am, unfortunately.

MANDERS. Yes, yes—I know, dear Engstrand.

ENGSTRAND. I can truly say I gave the child a decent upbringing and made poor Johanna a good and loving husband; but it never would have occurred to me to go to you, Mr. Manders, and brag about it and pat myself on the back for doing a good action; I'm not made like that. And most of the time, unfortunately, I've little enough to brag about. When I go and talk to you, sir, it's mostly to confess my sins and weaknesses. For, as I said just now, my conscience troubles me quite a bit, Mr. Manders.

MANDERS. Give me your hand, Jacob Engstrand.

ENGSTRAND. Oh— Lord, sir!

MANDERS. Come now, no nonsense! There!

ENGSTRAND. I most humbly ask you to forgive me, sir.

MANDERS. On the contrary, it's I who must ask your forgiveness.

ENGSTRAND. Oh, no, sir!

MANDERS. Most certainly—and I do so with all my heart. Forgive me, dear Engstrand, for so misjudging you. I wish I might give you some proof of my sincere regret and of the esteem in which I hold you.

ENGSTRAND. You'd really like to do that, sir?

MANDERS. With the greatest of pleasure.

ENGSTRAND. Well, it just happens, there is something you could do for me, sir. I've managed to put by a bit of money from my earnings here, and I'm thinking of opening a kind of Seaman's Home when I get back to town, sir.

MRS. ALVING. *A what?*

ENGSTRAND. It'd be like a kind of home for them you see, ma'am. These poor sailors have so many temptations when they get to port— I thought in my house, they'd find a father's care.

MANDERS. What do you say to that, Mrs. Alving?

ENGSTRAND. Of course, I haven't much capital to go on, and I thought if I could just find a helping hand—

MANDERS. I shall give it some thought. I find your schemes most interesting. But now, go and get everything ready—light the lights and prepare for our little celebration. Now I feel sure you are in a fit state for prayer, my dear Engstrand.

ENGSTRAND. Yes, I really believe I am. Well, goodbye, Mrs Alving, and thank you for everything; be sure and take good care of Regina for me. *Wipes away a tear.* Poor Johanna's child—it's strange how she's managed to creep into my heart, but she has, there's no denying it! *He bows and goes out by the hall door.*

MANDERS. Well what do you think of him now, Mrs. Alving? It certainly puts things in an entirely different light.

MRS. ALVING. It does indeed!

MANDERS. It just shows you how careful one must be in judging people. And what a satisfaction to find oneself mistaken! What do you say now?

MRS. ALVING. I say you're a great big baby, Manders!

MANDERS. *I* am?

MRS. ALVING. Yes. And I say I should like to throw my arms round your neck and give you a kiss!

MANDERS. Good heavens—what ideas you have!

MRS. ALVING. Oh, you needn't be afraid of me!

MANDERS. You have such an extravagant way of expressing yourself! I'll just gather up all these documents—there! Keep an eye on Oswald when he returns; I'll leave you for the present, but I'll come back and see you later.

He takes his hat and goes out through the hall door.

MRS. ALVING. *She sighs—looks out of the window for a moment; she goes to the dining-room door, and gives a stifled exclamation:* Oswald—are you still there?

OSWALD, *off stage*. I'm just finishing my cigar, mother.

MRS. ALVING. I thought you'd gone out for a walk.

OSWALD. In this awful weather?

Noise of a glass; MRS. ALVING *leaves the door open, and sits down on the sofa with some needlework.*

OSWALD, *off stage*. Was that Mr. Manders who went out just now?

MRS. ALVING. Yes, he went down to the Orphanage.

OSWALD. Hm. . . . *Noise of a bottle.*

MRS. ALVING, *anxiously*. Oswald dear, be careful with that liqueur—it's quite strong, you know.

OSWALD. It'll do me good, mother; I feel so chilly.

MRS. ALVING. Why don't you come in here with me?

OSWALD. You don't allow smoking in there, you said.

MRS. ALVING. I don't mind a cigar, dear.

OSWALD. Very well, then I'll come in. I'll just have another little drop—there!

He comes in smoking a cigar. Closes the door after him. A short silence.

Where's Mr. Manders?

MRS. ALVING. I just told you; he went down to the Orphanage.

OSWALD. Oh yes, of course.

MRS. ALVING. It's not good for you to sit so long at table, Oswald dear.

OSWALD. But it's so cozy, mother. You don't know what it means: to be home! To sit at my mother's table—in my mother's own room—to eat my mother's delicious food!

MRS. ALVING. My dear, dear boy!

OSWALD. *Walks up and down impatiently.* And what on earth is there to do here? I can't seem to settle anything—

MRS. ALVING. Can't you?

OSWALD. No, it's so gloomy; never a ray of sunshine—God! Not to be able to work!

MRS. ALVING. Perhaps you shouldn't have come home, Oswald.

OSWALD. I had to come, mother.

MRS. ALVING. But if you're unhappy, Oswald. You know I'd ten times rather give up the joy of having you here, than—

OSWALD. Tell me honestly, mother—is it really such a joy to you to have me home again?

MRS. ALVING. How can you ask such a thing!

OSWALD. I should have thought you didn't much care one way or the other.

MRS. ALVING. That's a cruel thing to say to me, Oswald.

OSWALD. After all, you managed to live without me all these years.

MRS. ALVING. That's true, I've managed to live without you.

A pause. Twilight is falling. OSWALD *paces up and down. He has put out his cigar. He suddenly stops in front of* MRS. ALVING.

OSWALD. May I sit beside you on the sofa, mother?

MRS. ALVING. Of course, dear.

OSWALD. There's something I must tell you, mother.

MRS. ALVING. What is it, dear?

OSWALD. I don't think I can bear it any longer.

MRS. ALVING. Bear what? What is it?

OSWALD. I've tried to write you about it, but somehow couldn't; and, since I've been home—

MRS. ALVING. Oswald—what is it?

OSWALD. I've tried to get rid of the thought, free myself of it, but I can't—

MRS. ALVING. You must be honest with me, Oswald.

OSWALD. No, don't get up! Sit still! I'll try and tell you. I've complained a lot about being tired after my journey—

MRS. ALVING. Yes—well, what of that?

OSWALD. But that isn't really what's the matter with me; it's not just that I'm tired—

MRS. ALVING. You're not ill, are you, Oswald?

OSWALD. No, don't get up, mother. Just be calm. I'm not really ill either—not in the usual sort of way. It's a kind of mental breakdown, mother; I'm destroyed; I'll never be able to work again.

He hides his face in his hands, and lets his head fall into her lap—shaking with sobs.

MRS. ALVING. Oswald! It's not true! Look at me!

OSWALD. I'll never be able to work again! Never, never! I'll be like a living corpse! Mother—can you imagine anything more frightful!

MRS. ALVING. But, my darling! How could such a dreadful thing happen to you?

OSWALD. That's just it—I don't know! I can't possibly imagine! I've never lived a dissipated life, not in any kind of way—you must believe that, mother—I haven't!

MRS. ALVING. I believe that, Oswald.

OSWALD. And yet, in spite of that, this ghastly thing has taken hold of me!

MRS. ALVING. You'll be all right, my darling. It's just overwork—believe me!

OSWALD. Yes, I thought that too at first, but it's not so.

MRS. ALVING. Tell me all about it.

OSWALD. Yes, I will.

MRS. ALVING. When did you first notice anything?

OSWALD. It was just after I went back to Paris, after my last visit here. I started to get terrible headaches—all up the back of my head —it was as if an iron band were screwed into my neck and into my head.

MRS. ALVING. And then?

OSWALD. At first I thought it was just the usual kind of headache I'd always had, since I was a child.

ACT II] GHOSTS 561

MRS. ALVING. Yes?

OSWALD. But it wasn't that—I soon found that out. I was no longer able to work. I'd start on a new picture and all my strength would suddenly fail me—it was as though I were paralyzed. I couldn't concentrate, and I felt sick and dizzy. It was the most ghastly sensation. At last I went to see a doctor—and then I found out the truth.

MRS. ALVING. What do you mean?

OSWALD. I was told he was a very great doctor. I described to him just how I felt, and then he started asking me all sorts of questions —about things that seemed to have no bearing on the case—I couldn't make out what he was driving at.

MRS. ALVING. Well?

OSWALD. At last he said: your constitution has been undermined from birth. He used the word "vermoulu."

MRS. ALVING. What did he mean by that?

OSWALD. I didn't know what he meant either. I asked him to explain. And do you know what he said—that cynical old man?

MRS. ALVING. No, what?

OSWALD. He said: "The sins of the fathers are visited upon the children."

MRS. ALVING. The sins of the fathers!

OSWALD. Yes! I could have killed him!!

MRS. ALVING. The sins of the fathers—

OSWALD. Can you believe it? Of course I assured him that such a thing was out of the question—but do you think he'd admit it? Not at all; he repeated what he'd said. I had one of your letters with me, and I had to translate to him some of the things you'd written about father.

MRS. ALVING. Yes?

OSWALD. Then he had to admit he must be on the wrong track. Then I realized the truth—the incredible truth! The sort of life I'd been leading—gay and carefree, but innocent enough I thought— had been too much for my strength; I should have been more careful. So, you see, I've brought it on myself—

MRS. ALVING. No! You mustn't believe that, Oswald!

OSWALD. There can be no other explanation. My whole life ruined, thrown away, through my own carelessness. All that I dreamt of achieving, of accomplishing—I dare not think of it—I *mustn't* think of it! If I could only live my life over again—if I could wipe it all out and start afresh! *He throws himself face downward on the couch;* MRS. ALVING *paces up and down, struggling with her thoughts.* It wouldn't be so bad if it was something I'd inherited—if it were something I couldn't help. But, deliberately, out of carelessness, out of shameful stupidity, to throw away happiness, health, everything that's worthwhile in this world, my future, my whole life—!

MRS. ALVING. No, no! It's impossible, Oswald—my darling, my boy! It's not true, it's not as serious as that!

OSWALD. Oh, mother, you don't know! And to think I should bring you such unhappiness! I've often hoped and prayed that you didn't care much about me, after all.

MRS. ALVING. Not care about you, Oswald? You're all I have in the world, you're the only thing on earth that matters to me.

OSWALD. Yes, mother, I know. When I'm home I realize that—and it makes it double hard for me. Well, now you know all about it. Don't let's discuss it any more today. I can't bear to dwell on it too long. . . . . Give me something to drink, mother.

MRS. ALVING. To drink? . . . . What do you want, Oswald?

OSWALD. Oh, it doesn't matter—anything! You must have something in the house.

MRS. ALVING. Yes, but Oswald—don't you think—?

OSWALD. Don't refuse me, mother—be a dear! I must have something to help me drown these hideous thoughts. *He goes up to the conservatory and looks out.* Oh! and it's so gloomy here!

MRS. ALVING *goes to the bell-pull and rings.* This incessant rain! It'll go on for weeks—for months! Never a ray of sunshine! I can't remember seeing any sunshine here!

MRS. ALVING. Oswald—you're not thinking of leaving me?

OSWALD. I'm not thinking of anything, mother. I'm not capable of thinking—I've had to give that up!

REGINA *comes in from the dining-room.*

REGINA. Did you ring, Mrs. Alving?
MRS. ALVING. Yes, bring in the lamp, will you?
REGINA. At once, Mrs. Alving—I have it ready.   *She goes out.*
MRS. ALVING. Don't keep anything from me, Oswald.

OSWALD. I won't, mother. It seems to me I've been very frank with you.

REGINA *brings in the lamp and puts it on the table.*

MRS. ALVING. Oh, and Regina—you might bring us a half bottle of champagne.

REGINA. Very good, Mrs. Alving. *She goes out.*

OSWALD. That's right, mother! I knew you wouldn't let me go thirsty!

MRS. ALVING. My own poor boy! As if I could refuse you anything!

OSWALD. You really mean that, mother?

MRS. ALVING. What?

OSWALD. That you can't refuse me anything?

MRS. ALVING. I don't know—

OSWALD. Sh!

REGINA *enters with a small tray on which are a bottle of champagne and two glasses.*

REGINA. Shall I open it, Mrs. Alving?

OSWALD. No—let me do it. REGINA *goes out.*

MRS. ALVING. Oswald, be honest with me—what is it you don't want me to refuse you?

OSWALD. First, let's have a glass of wine.

He opens the bottle and pours out one glass and is about to pour another.

MRS. ALVING. *Puts her hand over the glass.* Thanks—not for me.

OSWALD. For me, then!

He empties his glass, refills it and empties it again; he sits down at the table.

MRS. ALVING. Well—

OSWALD. Mother, tell me—what was the matter with you and Manders at dinner, just now? Why were you so quiet and solemn?

MRS. ALVING. Oh, did you notice that?

OSWALD. Yes. Hm. . . . *A pause.*
Mother, what do you think of Regina?

MRS. ALVING. What do you mean?

OSWALD. Don't you think she's wonderful?

MRS. ALVING. You don't know her as well as I do, Oswald. . . .

OSWALD. Well, what of that?

MRS. ALVING. I should have taken charge of her sooner—I'm afraid she spent too many years at home.

OSWALD. But, isn't she lovely, mother?

MRS. ALVING. She has many faults, Oswald.

OSWALD. As if that mattered! *He drinks.*

MRS. ALVING. But I'm fond of her all the same. I feel responsible for her. I wouldn't have anything happen to her for all the world.

OSWALD. Mother! The one thing that could save me is Regina!

MRS. ALVING. How do you mean?

OSWALD. I mean I can't endure this agony alone!

MRS. ALVING. But I'm here to help you, Oswald.

OSWALD. Yes, *I* know. I thought that would be enough—that's why I came home to you. But I see now that it isn't. My life here would be intolerable.

MRS. ALVING. Oswald!

OSWALD. I couldn't stand it. That's why I must go away again. I don't want you to see it happening to me—

MRS. ALVING. But you can't go away when you're so ill, Oswald.

OSWALD. If it were just an ordinary illness, of course I'd stay at home, mother. I know you're the best friend I have in the world—

MRS. ALVING. You do know that—don't you?

OSWALD. But it's the mental anguish—the remorse—and that constant ghastly fear—

MRS. ALVING. Fear? Fear of what?

OSWALD. Don't ask me about it! I don't know—I can't describe it.

MRS. ALVING *goes to the bell-pull and rings.* Do you want something?

MRS. ALVING. Yes. I want my boy to be happy. You'll see—I won't let you suffer here! *To* REGINA. More champagne, Regina! A whole bottle! *REGINA goes.*

OSWALD. Mother!

MRS. ALVING. I want you to be happy here.

OSWALD. Isn't she lovely, mother? So beautiful, so strong!

MRS. ALVING. Sit down, Oswald; let's talk quietly for a moment.

OSWALD. You don't know about it, mother, but I haven't been quite fair to Regina—

ACT II] GHOSTS

MRS. ALVING. Not fair?

OSWALD. No. It was just thoughtlessness on my part, nothing serious; but last time I was home—

MRS. ALVING. Yes?

OSWALD. She kept on asking questions about Paris. I told her a bit about my life there, and one day I said to her, quite casually: "Perhaps you'd like to go there and see it all for yourself, Regina."

MRS. ALVING. Well?

OSWALD. Then she blushed and got quite excited and said she'd give anything to go. Then I said something about, perhaps some day it might be arranged—

MRS. ALVING. I see.

OSWALD. Of course I'd forgotten all about it. But the other day, when I arrived, I asked her if she was glad I intended to spend such a long time here.

MRS. ALVING. Yes?

OSWALD. And then she looked at me so strangely and said: "What about my trip to Paris?"

MRS. ALVING. Her trip?

OSWALD. Yes—it seems she'd taken me quite seriously. She'd been thinking about it all this time—thinking about *me*, mother. She'd even tried to teach herself some French.

MRS. ALVING. So that was why—

OSWALD. I'd never noticed her much before, mother, but suddenly I saw her there: so beautiful, so vital, ready to come to me—

MRS. ALVING. Oswald!

OSWALD. And I thought—perhaps she could save me. That wonderful joy of life in her could save me.

MRS. ALVING. Joy of life.

REGINA *comes in with the champagne.*

REGINA. Excuse me for being so long, Mrs. Alving. I had to go down to the cellar. *Puts the bottle on the table.*

OSWALD. Fetch another glass.

REGINA. *Looks at him surprised.* Mrs. Alving has a glass, sir.

OSWALD. Yes, but fetch one for yourself, Regina.

She glances at MRS. ALVING.

Well?

REGINA. Do you wish me to, Mrs. Alving?

MRS. ALVING. Fetch the glass, Regina.

She goes into the dining-room.

OSWALD, *looking after her.* Have you noticed how wonderfully she walks, mother—so strong, so sure.

MRS. ALVING. This can't be allowed to happen, Oswald.

OSWALD. But it's all settled—you must see that—there's no use forbidding it.

REGINA comes in with a glass in her hand.

Sit down, Regina. *REGINA looks at MRS. ALVING.*

MRS. ALVING. Sit down.

REGINA *sits on a chair by the dining-room door, with the empty glass in her hand.*

What were you saying about the joy of life, Oswald?

OSWALD. Yes, the joy of life, mother. You don't know much about that here at home. I could never find it here—but you don't understand that.

MRS. ALVING. Yes, I believe I do understand it—now.

OSWALD. That, and the joy of work. They're really the same thing, you know. But of course, you wouldn't know anything about that either.

MRS. ALVING. No, you may be right. Tell me more about it.

OSWALD. Well—I simply mean that here people look on work as a curse, as a kind of punishment. They look on life as a dreary wretched business to be got through as soon as possible.

MRS. ALVING. I know—a "vale of tears"—we do our best to make it so.

OSWALD. But, you see, we don't look at it like that. We don't believe in that old-fashioned nonsense. To us the mere fact of being alive in this world is radiant and marvellous. You must have noticed, mother, everything I paint is filled with this joy of life. Always and forever the joy of life! My paintings are full of light, of sunshine, of glowing happy faces. That's why I'm afraid to stay here, mother.

MRS. ALVING. What could you possibly be afraid of—here with me?

OSWALD. I'm afraid that all the instinctive joy in my nature will become warped here, that it will become changed—into ugliness.

MRS. ALVING. You really believe that, Oswald?

OSWALD. Yes, I'm convinced of it! Even if I tried to live the same life here as I live abroad, it wouldn't *be* the same.

MRS. ALVING. Now I see it! It's all becoming clear to me.

OSWALD. What do you see?

MRS. ALVING. The whole pattern—for the first time, I see it—and now I must tell you everything.

OSWALD. But, I don't understand—

REGINA. Perhaps I'd better go.

MRS. ALVING. No, no, stay where you are. Now you must know everything, and then you can choose. Oswald! Regina!

OSWALD. Be quiet, mother! Here comes Manders.

MANDERS. *Enters from hall door.* Well, I must say, we've had a most edifying time.

OSWALD. So have we.

MANDERS. There can be no doubt about it—Engstrand must be helped to start that Seamen's Home of his. Regina must go back to town with him; she can be most useful.

REGINA. No thank you, Mr. Manders!

MANDERS, *who hadn't noticed her before*. What? Are you here? And with a glass in your hand?

REGINA. *Hastily puts down her glass.* Pardon!

OSWALD. Regina is going with me, Mr. Manders.

MANDERS. Going with you?

OSWALD. Yes; as my wife—if she insists on that.

MANDERS. But, good heavens!

REGINA. It's no fault of mine, Mr. Manders.

OSWALD. Or if I decide to stay here, she'll stay too.

REGINA. Stay here!

MANDERS. I am amazed at you, Mrs. Alving.

MRS. ALVING. None of this will happen—for now I can tell the truth at last.

MANDERS. But you won't, you can't!

MRS. ALVING. I can and I will—and nobody's ideals will be the worse for it.

OSWALD. Mother, what is all this? What are you hiding from me?

REGINA. Mrs. Alving, listen! I hear people shouting out there.

OSWALD. What's happening? What's that glare in the sky?

REGINA. It's the Orphanage—the Orphanage is on fire, Mrs. Alving!

MRS. ALVING. On fire?

MANDERS. On fire? Impossible! I've just come from there.

OSWALD. Give me my hat!—Oh never mind—God! Father's Orphanage! *He runs out into the garden.*

MRS. ALVING. My shawl, Regina! The whole place is in flames!

MANDERS. How horrible! It's a judgment, Mrs. Alving—a judgment on this house.

MRS. ALVING. I expect you're right, Manders. Come, Regina.

They go out through the hall door.

MANDERS. A judgment on this house!

He follows them as the curtain falls.

Act III

SCENE. *The room as before. All the doors stand open. The lamp is still burning on the table. It is dark out of doors; there is only a faint glow from the conflagration in the background to the left.*

AT RISE. MRS. ALVING, *with a shawl over her head, stands in the conservatory looking out.* REGINA, *also with a shawl on, stands a little behind her.*

MRS. ALVING. Nothing left—burned to the ground!

REGINA. The cellar is still in flames.

MRS. ALVING. I wonder why Oswald isn't back—there's nothing left to rescue now.

REGINA. Perhaps I'd better take his hat down to him, Mrs. Alving.

MRS. ALVING. Is he out there without it?

REGINA. Yes, it's hanging in the hall.

MRS. ALVING. No, leave it—he'll be back in a moment. I think I'll go and look for him. *Exits to the garden.*

MANDERS. *Enters from hall.* Where's Mrs. Alving?

REGINA. She just went down to the garden.

MANDERS. What a night—I've never gone through anything so ghastly!

REGINA. It's a terrible thing, Mr. Manders!

MANDERS. Don't speak of it! I can't bear the thought of it.

REGINA. How do you think it happened?

MANDERS. Oh, don't ask me, Miss Engstrand—how should I know! You're not implying—? Isn't it enough that your father should—?

REGINA. What's he been up to?

MANDERS. He's driven me half mad.

ENGSTRAND. *Enters through hall.* Oh there you are, Mr. Manders!

MANDERS. Must you follow me in here too!

ENGSTRAND. Oh, Mr. Manders! Such a terrible thing, sir!

MANDERS. Yes, yes! We know! We know! . . . .

REGINA. What are *you* after?

ENGSTRAND. It was all due to the prayer meeting, you see! *Aside to* REGINA. We've hooked the old fool now, my girl! *Aloud.* That poor Mr. Manders should be the cause of such a calamity—and through my fault too!

MANDERS. But I tell you, Engstrand—

ENGSTRAND. No one touched the lights but you, sir!

MANDERS. That's what *you* claim—but I could swear I never went *near* the lights!

ENGSTRAND. But I saw you with my own eyes, sir! I saw you snuff one of the candles and throw the wick right into a pile of shavings!

MANDERS. You say you *saw* this?

ENGSTRAND. So help me God, sir!

MANDERS. Incredible! . . . . I'm not in the habit of snuffing candles with my fingers.

ENGSTRAND. No, sir—I thought at the time it didn't look quite like you. It'll be quite a serious thing, won't it, sir?

MANDERS. Don't ask me about it!

ENGSTRAND. You hadn't insured the place, had you, sir?

MANDERS. I told you I hadn't!

ENGSTRAND. Hadn't insured it! . . . . And then to go and set the whole place on fire like that! Lord! What a bit of bad luck, sir!

MANDERS. You may well say so, Engstrand.

ENGSTRAND. A charitable institution too! A place dedicated, you might say, to the good of the community! . . . . It's likely the papers won't treat you any too kindly, Mr. Manders.

MANDERS. That's just it! That's what I'm thinking about—all those loathsome insults and accusations! That's the worst part of the whole business. I can't bear the thought of it!

MRS. ALVING. *Enters from the garden.* He won't come—he can't seem to tear himself away.

MANDERS. Oh, it's you, Mrs. Alving.

MRS. ALVING. Well, Manders! You got out of making your speech after all!

MANDERS. I'd be only too glad to make it!

MRS. ALVING. It's all for the best: that poor Orphanage could never have brought good to anyone!

MANDERS. You really feel that?

MRS. ALVING. Well—don't you?

MANDERS. All the same, it's a great tragedy.

MRS. ALVING. Nonsense! Now let's discuss it from a business point of view. Are you waiting for Mr. Manders, Engstrand?

ENGSTRAND. Yes, ma'am, I am.

MRS. ALVING. Well then, sit down.

ENGSTRAND. I'm all right standing, thank you, ma'am.

MRS. ALVING. I suppose you'll be leaving by the next boat?

MANDERS. Yes—there's one in an hour.

MRS. ALVING. Please take all the documents with you. I don't want to hear another word about it! I've other things to think about now.

MANDERS. Mrs. Alving—

MRS. ALVING. I'll arrange to send you power of attorney and you can wind things up as you think best.

MANDERS. I'll be glad to look after it for you. Of course now, the original terms of the bequest will have to be radically altered.

MRS. ALVING. Naturally.

MANDERS. I would suggest making the actual land over to the parish under the circumstances; it's not without value, and could be used for many purposes. As to the interest on the capital, I feel sure I can find some worthy project in need of support—something that would prove beneficial to the life of the community.

MRS. ALVING. Do anything you like with it; it makes no difference to me.

ENGSTRAND. You might give a thought to my Seaman's Home, Mr. Manders.

MANDERS. To be sure. A good suggestion. Well worth looking into.

ENGSTRAND, *aside.* Looking into! That's a good one!

MANDERS, *with a sigh.* Of course I may not be long in charge of these affairs. Public opinion may compel me to withdraw. There will naturally be an investigation to determine the cause of the fire. It all depends on the outcome of that.

MRS. ALVING. What *are* you talking about, Manders?

MANDERS. It's impossible to tell what that outcome will be.

ENGSTRAND. Oh no, it's not, Mr. Manders! Don't forget *me*—don't forget Jacob Engstrand!

MANDERS. But I don't see—

ENGSTRAND. I was never one to desert a friend in his hour of need —as they say!

MANDERS. But my dear man, how could you possibly—?

ENGSTRAND. Jacob Engstrand won't desert you, sir! He'll be like a guardian angel to you, sir!

MANDERS. But I could never consent—!

ENGSTRAND. You'll have nothing to do with it, sir. It wouldn't be the first time I'd taken the blame for others.

MANDERS. *Holds out his hand.* Jacob! You're a fine person! I'll see that you get funds for your Seaman's Home—I promise you!

ENGSTRAND *tries to thank him but is overcome with emotion.*

And now, let's be off. We'll travel together, of course.

ENGSTRAND. *Aside to* REGINA. You'd better come with me, hussy! You'll live like a queen!

REGINA. *Merci!* *She fetches* MANDERS' *coat from the hall.*

MANDERS. Goodbye, Mrs. Alving. May the spirit of truth and righteousness soon enter into this house.

MRS. ALVING. Goodbye, Manders.

She goes to meet OSWALD *who enters from the garden.*

ENGSTRAND. *As he and* REGINA *help* MANDERS *with his coat.* Goodbye, my dear child. If you ever need me you know where to find me. *Aside.* Harbor Street—*you* know! *To* MRS. ALVING *and* OSWALD. My home for poor seamen shall be called "Captain Alving's Haven" and if it turns out the way I want it, ma'am—I humbly hope it may prove worthy of Captain Alving's memory!

MANDERS, *in the doorway.* Hm—yes. Come along my dear Engstrand. Goodbye again—goodbye! *They exit through the hall.*

OSWALD. *Goes toward the table.* What does he mean? What "home" is he talking about?

MRS. ALVING. It's some sort of a hostel he and Manders are thinking of opening.

OSWALD. What's the use? It'll only burn down too—just like this one.

MRS. ALVING. Why do you say that?

OSWALD. Everything will be burnt. Father's memory will be wiped out. I shall soon be burnt up too.

REGINA looks at him in amazement.

MRS. ALVING. Oswald! . . . . You poor boy! You stayed down there too long.

OSWALD. You're probably right.

MRS. ALVING. Your face is all wet, Oswald, let me dry it for you.

Wipes his face with her handkerchief.

OSWALD, *indifferently*. Thanks, mother.

MRS. ALVING. You must be exhausted! You'd better get some sleep.

OSWALD. No! God, no! I don't want to sleep! I never sleep—I only pretend to. . . . I'll sleep soon enough!

MRS. ALVING. You know, you really are ill, my darling!

REGINA. Ill! . . . Is Mr. Alving ill?

OSWALD. And close the doors! . . . . I want all the doors closed! . . . . *I'm afraid!* . . . .

MRS. ALVING. Close the doors, Regina.

REGINA *closes the hall door and remains standing by it.* MRS. ALVING *takes off her shawl, and* REGINA *does likewise.*

MRS. ALVING. *Sits at the table next to* OSWALD. There! . . . . I'll sit here close to you.

OSWALD. Yes—do, mother. And Regina must stay too; she must never leave me. You'll help me, won't you, Regina? You'll save me?

REGINA. I don't understand. . . . .

MRS. ALVING. Save you?

OSWALD. Yes—when the time comes.

MRS. ALVING. Can't you trust your mother to do that?

OSWALD. You? *Smiles.* You'd never do it: you don't know what I mean by "saving me." You! *Laughs.* And yet you're the logical one to do it! *Vehemently.* Why are you always so formal with me, Regina? Why don't you call me "Oswald"?

REGINA. Mrs. Alving might not like it.

MRS. ALVING. You may soon have a right to—so sit down with us, Regina.

REGINA *hesitates then sits down quietly at the far off side of the table.* I won't have you tortured any more. I'm going to relieve your mind of all doubt, all remorse, all sense of guilt.

OSWALD. You, mother? . . . . Do you think you can do that?

MRS. ALVING. Yes, Oswald, I believe I can, now. Earlier this evening you were talking about the joy of life—and suddenly many things that for years have confused and bewildered me became clear and understandable.

OSWALD. I don't know what you mean.

MRS. ALVING. You should have known your father when he was a young lieutenant. He knew all about that "joy of life."

OSWALD. Yes—so I've heard.

MRS. ALVING. He seemed to radiate light and warmth; he was filled with a turbulent, joyous vitality.

OSWALD. Well?

MRS. ALVING. And this radiant child—for he was like a child then—was cooped up in this drab little provincial town, which could offer him no real joy, only dissipation. He had no real aim in life, no work that could stimulate his mind or feed his spirit, nothing but a dull, petty, routine job. He found no one here who understood that pure joy of life that was in him. What friends he had were idle, bored young men, bent on nothing but the lowest kind of pleasure and incessant drinking bouts.

OSWALD. Mother!

MRS. ALVING. And so the inevitable happened.

OSWALD. How do you mean?

MRS. ALVING. You told me a little while ago what would happen to you if you stayed here.

OSWALD. Do you mean to say that father—?

MRS. ALVING. Your poor father could find no outlet for that glorious joy of life that was in him—and I'm afraid I was no great help to him either.

OSWALD. Why, mother?

MRS. ALVING. All my life I'd been taught a great deal about duty—that seemed the all-important thing. Everything was reduced to a question of duty—*my* duty, *his* duty, your poor father—I'm afraid I must have made home intolerable for him, Oswald.

OSWALD. Why did you never write me about all this?

MRS. ALVING. You were his son; I felt it would be wrong to talk to you about it. You see, I didn't see things clearly then.

OSWALD. How did you see them?

MRS. ALVING. I was aware of one thing only, that your father was a broken, dissolute man, long before you were born.

OSWALD. Ah!

MRS. ALVING. And I was tormented by the thought that Regina actually had the same rights in this house that you have.

OSWALD. Regina!

REGINA. I!

MRS. ALVING. Yes. Now perhaps you understand everything—both of you.

OSWALD. Regina!!

REGINA. So mother was—that sort of woman.

MRS. ALVING. Your mother had many fine qualities, Regina.

REGINA. But that didn't prevent her from—! I might have known it! . . . . Mrs. Alving! Please allow me to leave at once.

MRS. ALVING. You really want to go, Regina?

REGINA. I certainly do, Mrs. Alving.

MRS. ALVING. Of course you must do as you wish, but—

OSWALD. Leave now? But you belong here.

REGINA. *Merci*, Mr. Alving—I suppose I can call you Oswald now—though this wasn't the way I wanted it to happen.

MRS. ALVING. Regina, I haven't been honest with you—

REGINA. No! You certainly haven't, Mrs. Alving! If I'd known that Oswald was a sick man—but, anyway, now there could never be anything serious between us— Well! I can't waste my time out here in the country looking after invalids.

OSWALD. Not even your own brother, Regina?

REGINA. I should say not! I'm poor—all I have is my youth—I can't afford to waste it. I don't want to be left stranded. I have some of that "joy of life" in me too, Mrs. Alving!

MRS. ALVING. No doubt. But don't throw yourself away, Regina.

REGINA. If I do—I *do*—that's all! If Oswald takes after his father,

I take after my mother, I suppose. May I ask, Mrs. Alving, if Mr. Manders knows about all this?

MRS. ALVING. Mr. Manders knows everything.

REGINA. Then I'd better try and catch that boat. Mr. Manders is such a kind man, he's sure to help me. It seems to me I have a right to some of that money too—a better right than that filthy old carpenter.

MRS. ALVING. You're welcome to it, Regina.

REGINA. And I must say, Mrs. Alving, it seems to me I also had a right to a decent upbringing—one suited to a gentleman's daughter. Well, what do I care! *Glances at the bottle of wine.* Some day I may be drinking champagne with the best of them—who knows?

MRS. ALVING. If you should ever need a home, Regina, come to me.

REGINA. No thank you, Mrs. Alving! Mr. Manders'll look after me I'm sure. And if the worst comes to the worst, I know of a place where I'd be quite at home.

MRS. ALVING. Where do you mean?

REGINA. In Captain Alving's Haven, of course!

MRS. ALVING. Be careful, Regina! Don't destroy yourself!

REGINA. What do I care? .... Well, goodbye! *Exit to hall.*

OSWALD, *standing at the window.* Did she go?

MRS. ALVING. Yes.

OSWALD. *Mutters to himself.* How stupid it all is!

MRS. ALVING. Dear Oswald—it's been a great blow to you, hasn't it?

OSWALD. All that about father, you mean?

MRS. ALVING. Oh—yes, your poor father! .... I'm afraid it's been too much for you.

OSWALD. Why do you say that? It was a great surprise to me, I admit. But, after all, it doesn't really matter.

MRS. ALVING. Not matter? That your father was so wretched and unhappy?

OSWALD. I feel sorry for him of course—as I would for anyone who suffered.

MRS. ALVING. Only that? .... But he was your *father,* Oswald.

OSWALD. My father! My father! I never *knew* my father. The only thing I remember about him is that he once made me sick!

MRS. ALVING. But that's dreadful, Oswald! A child surely must love his father in spite of everything.

OSWALD. Even if he owes his father nothing? Even if he never knew him? Come now, mother! You're too broadminded to believe in that superstitious nonsense!

MRS. ALVING. Superstitious nonsense—you think that's all it is?

OSWALD. Of course, mother—you must see that. It's one of those old-fashioned illusions people go on clinging to.

MRS. ALVING. Ghosts—

OSWALD. Yes—call them ghosts if you like.

MRS. ALVING. Then you don't love me either, Oswald.

OSWALD. Well, at least I know *you*.

MRS. ALVING. You know me—yes. But is that all?

OSWALD. I know how much you care for me; I should be grateful to you for that. And now I'm ill, you can be of great help to me.

MRS. ALVING. I can, can't I, Oswald? I'm almost glad you're ill—since it's brought you home to me. I understand—you don't belong to me yet—I'll have to win you.

OSWALD, *impatiently*. Oh, don't let's have a lot of phrases, mother! You must remember I'm ill. I can't be bothered with other people. I've got to think about myself.

MRS. ALVING. I'll be quiet and patient, Oswald.

OSWALD. And, for God's sake, *happy*, mother!

MRS. ALVING. Yes, my darling—you're right. And you've no more doubts, no more remorse? I've freed you of all that?

OSWALD. Yes, mother. It's just—the terror! Who's to free me of the terror?

MRS. ALVING. Terror!

OSWALD. Regina would have done it, if I'd asked her.

MRS. ALVING. I don't understand you. What is this terror—and what has Regina to do with it?

OSWALD. Mother—is it very late?

MRS. ALVING. It's dawn—it's going to be a lovely day, Oswald! In a little while you'll see the sun!

OSWALD. I'll be glad of that. Perhaps after all there are lots of things I could be glad about, mother—lots of things I'd like to live for.

MRS. ALVING. Of course there are!

OSWALD. And even if I can't work—

MRS. ALVING. You'll soon be able to work again, you'll see. Now that you're rid of all those gloomy, dreadful thoughts.

OSWALD. Yes—what a relief! Now if I could just conquer this one— *He sits on the sofa.* I want to talk to you, mother.

MRS. ALVING. Yes, Oswald.

OSWALD. Meanwhile the sun is rising. And now that you know, I don't feel so afraid any more.

MRS. ALVING. Now that I know—what?

OSWALD, *not listening.* Mother—didn't you say a little while ago that there was nothing in the world you wouldn't do for me?

MRS. ALVING. Yes, of course I did.

OSWALD. You stick by that, mother?

MRS. ALVING. You can depend on me, my darling. You're the only thing on earth I have to live for.

OSWALD. Well then, listen, mother: you have a strong, gallant spirit —I know that. I want you to sit quite still while I tell you something.

MRS. ALVING. What dreadful thing are you going to—?

OSWALD. Don't get excited, do you hear? Promise me! We'll sit here and talk it over quietly. Promise!

MRS. ALVING. Yes, yes, I promise! Tell me what it is!

OSWALD. Well then, listen: this fatigue of mine, my inability to work, all of that is not the *essence* of my illness—

MRS. ALVING. How do you mean?

OSWALD. You see, my illness is hereditary. It—*touches his forehead and speaks very quietly*—is centred *here.*

MRS. ALVING. Oswald! No—no!

OSWALD. Don't scream, mother—I can't stand it! It's lurking here, lying in wait, ready to spring at any moment.

MRS. ALVING. How horrible!

OSWALD. Quiet, mother! Now you understand the state I'm in.

MRS. ALVING. It can't be, Oswald, it's impossible!

OSWALD. I had one attack while I was abroad—it didn't last long. But when I realized the condition I'd been in, I was filled with unspeakable terror—and I could think of nothing but getting home to you.

MRS. ALVING. That's what you meant by "the terror"!

OSWALD. Yes, unspeakable, sickening terror! If it had only been an ordinary illness, even a fatal one, I wouldn't have minded so much —I'm not afraid of death, though I should like to live as long as possible.

MRS. ALVING. You will, Oswald—you must!

OSWALD. But there's something so utterly revolting about this! To become a child again—a helpless child—to have to be fed—to have to be—oh! It's too ghastly to think of!

MRS. ALVING. I'll be here to look after you, Oswald.

OSWALD. No, never; I won't stand it! I can't endure the thought of lingering on like that—of growing old like that—old and grey-haired like *that!* And you might die and I should be left alone like *that!* For the doctor said I might live for years, you see. He called it "softening of the brain" or something of the sort. Charming expression! It makes one think of bright red velvet curtains—soft and delicate to stroke. . . .

MRS. ALVING. Oswald!

OSWALD, *pacing up and down.* And now you've taken Regina away from me—if only I had her. She'd have been willing to help me I know.

MRS. ALVING. What do you mean by that, my darling? You know I'd give my life to help you. . . .

OSWALD. I recovered from that attack abroad—but the doctor said that the next time—and there's bound to be a "next time"—it would be hopeless.

MRS. ALVING. How could he be so brutal!

OSWALD. I insisted on the truth—I made him tell me. I explained that I had certain arrangements to make—and so I had. *Takes a small box from his breast-pocket.* Do you see these, mother?

MRS. ALVING. What are they?

OSWALD. Morphine tablets.

MRS. ALVING. Oswald—

OSWALD. I managed to save up twelve of them.

MRS. ALVING. Give them to me.

OSWALD. Not yet, mother.   *Puts them back in his pocket.*

MRS. ALVING. I can't bear it!

OSWALD. You must bear it, mother. If only Regina were here—I'd have explained to her how matters stood. I'd have asked her to help me put an end to it. She'd have done it, I know.

MRS. ALVING. Never!

OSWALD. Oh yes she would! She'd have seen that ghastly thing take hold of me; she'd have seen me lying there like an imbecile child—beyond help—hopelessly, irrevocably lost. . . . .

MRS. ALVING. Regina would never have done it!

OSWALD. Of course she would have! Regina has such a magnificently light and buoyant nature. She wouldn't have put up long with an invalid like me!

MRS. ALVING. Then I can only thank God Regina is not here!

OSWALD. Yes, but then you'll have to help me, mother.

MRS. ALVING. I!

OSWALD. Who has a better right?

MRS. ALVING. I—your own mother!

OSWALD. For that very reason.

MRS. ALVING. I, who gave you life!

OSWALD. I didn't ask you for life—and what kind of a life did you give me? I don't want it—take it back again!

MRS. ALVING. *Runs to the door.* Help—help!

OSWALD. Don't leave me! Where are you going?

MRS. ALVING. I must fetch a doctor, Oswald—let me go!

OSWALD. You're not going out—and no one is to come here!

He locks the door.

MRS. ALVING. Oswald, Oswald! My little one!

OSWALD. Mother—if you love me—how can you bear to see me suffer this agony of fear!

MRS. ALVING, *after a silence.* I give you my word, Oswald.

OSWALD. Then, you will?

MRS. ALVING. Yes—if ever it should be necessary; but it won't be, it can't be—it's impossible!

OSWALD. Let us hope you're right! . . . Meanwhile we'll stay together as long as we can. Thank you, mother.

He sits in the armchair. Day breaks.

MRS. ALVING. Do you feel calmer now?

OSWALD. Yes.

MRS. ALVING. All this has been a ghastly nightmare, Oswald—a bad dream. Now you must rest; the strain has been too much for you; you're home now and I'll look after you. I'll spoil you as I did when you were a tiny boy—you shall have everything you want. . . . .

There! You see? You feel better now—it's not so serious—I was sure it couldn't be! . . . . And what a lovely day it is—bright sunshine! You'll really be able to enjoy your home! . . . .

She puts out the lamp.

OSWALD. *Immovable in his arm-chair.* Mother—give me the sun.

MRS. ALVING. What did you say?

OSWALD. The sun. . . . the sun.

MRS. ALVING. Oswald—what's the matter with you?

He is slumped down in the chair; his face expressionless—his eyes vacant and staring.

Oswald—Oswald! What is it? *She shakes him.* Look at me! Don't you know me?

OSWALD. The sun. . . . the sun.

MRS. ALVING. No—no! I can't bear it—I *can't! Suddenly.* What did he do with them? *Searches in his pocket.* Here! . . . . But I can't do it—no, no! Never! . . . . My promise. . . . But I can't—I *can't!*

OSWALD. The sun. . . . the sun.

*

WHAT IS artificial or "unrealistic" about *Ghosts*? A critic who finds it very unrealistic indeed writes as follows:

"How unrealistic and romantic is the fate motif which dominates the play! Coincidences are skilfully given the appearance of consequences. The sins of the fathers are visited on the children in the most irrational manner. Regina, who is Oswald's sister, has opportunely escaped inheriting the venereal disease from which Oswald suffers. The incestuous love of brother and sister is a time-honoured ingredient of romantic fate-tragedy, and the rest of the devices are equally traditional. In the same room, in the same circumstances as her mother with Oswald's father, Regina reproves Oswald for his advances with exactly the same words. Nothing could, finally, be more unrealistic than Oswald's sudden physical decomposition. . . ." *

---

* From P. F. D. Tennant's *Ibsen's Dramatic Technique.*

Not all of this is convincing. Regina's being a healthier child might be put down to the fact that she had a sturdy, working-class mother. The incest motif may be "a time-honoured ingredient of romantic fate-tragedy," but, as Freud has shown, it is also a time-honoured ingredient of actual life. And the *kind* of fate that is at work in *Ghosts,* involving the guilt of a whole civilization, is surely to be distinguished from the hocus-pocus of fate in melodrama. . . . What Mr. Tennant has shown is that Ibsenite realism has its conventions too, and to that extent is unrealistic. Though it differs from classic drama in paying more attention to milieu, to natural detail, to psychological causation, it is a kind of drama and not a kind (or slice) of life. We have already granted that the mere fact of stage presentation involves artifice. Such an ardent Ibsenite as William Archer would never have dreamt of denying it. Archer's position is that he prefers Ibsen's artifices (or his use of them) to those of earlier playwrights.

Ibsen was Archer's favorite playwright as Sophocles was Aristotle's; in each case we turn to the disciple for an explanation of the master's technique. In his manual *Playmaking,* Archer explains that a leading feature of this technique is the retrospective method of exposition. "Exposition" means the presentation of the facts to the audience—those antecedent facts which it needs to know before it can comprehend the situation shown in the play itself. The simplest kind of modern play has a structure somewhat as follows. Act One is devoted to Exposition, Act Two to the Subsequent Situation, and Act Three to the Outcome. (The playwright probably starts with the situation which is to become Act Two. He then writes Act One to explain how the situation came about. Finally, he must deduce the outcome and write his last Act.) Ibsen differs from the simpler playwright in that he does not devote a special Act, or other opening section, to exposition alone. He lets the exposition and the action of the play itself interpenetrate. *Ghosts* is an extreme case of such "analytic exposition": we are still finding out vital antecedent facts during the last half-hour of the play. One can almost say that the exposition *is* the play. Once the exposition is completed, there occurs one event—and one which is already "on the cards"—and the play is over.

Archer thought Ibsen overreached himself here. He preferred plays in which there was a little more present action to offset the tale of past troubles. Nonetheless, there is a powerful interplay of past and present in *Ghosts;* and, in general, it might be said to be the chief aim of the retrospective method to set up such an interplay. It helped Ibsen to show the interaction of past and present in the lives of his characters. The past pours in through cracks in the walls of the present, and, in the end, the present is inundated. An Ibsen play is a sort of time bomb or series of time bombs. Initial mystery and subsequent surprise: there are many devices to secure these ends, and Ibsen learned to use them. But his technique is curbed and controlled by a moral awareness. What interests Ibsen is moral continuity and discontinuity in people's lives. He observes that our past may smolder long and then erupt.

Those who have been interested in Ibsen's technique alone—whether in praise or blame—have done him great injustice. "Ibsen abolished the soliloquy and the aside." "Exposition by innuendo." "Ibsen gives you the facts of the exposition without your knowing it." There is nothing in such phrases and comments to *congratulate* Ibsen on: when one playwright is congratulated for abolishing the aside, the next will be congratulated for re-creating it. An aside is not good or bad in itself. Like all technical devices, it is good when it serves a purpose, bad when it doesn't. An interest in Ibsen's technique, divorced from all interest in its very special function in Ibsen's work, accounts for the barren Ibsenism of a generation of playwrights. The heresy was to assume that Ibsen's technique was a way of by-passing technique and of rendering sheer reality. A critic like Mr. Tennant writes as if Ibsen were attempting complete verisimilitude and failing. The Ibsenites assume that he succeeds. But did he make the attempt at all? There is little reason to think that Ibsen's attitude to technique, to conventions and devices, was different from that of the other playwrights we have read. He is prepared to use artifice in order (to repeat our usual phrases) to bring his subject into high relief, to define it.

What is *Ghosts* about? Sixty years ago people were so surprised at the fact that syphilis is mentioned (though never by name!) in the play that they took syphilis to be at once the author's theme and natural element. At best Ibsen was put down as a resolute exposer of social evils. Subsequently critics pooh-poohed him as less a playwright than a propagandist.

The question of propaganda in art is complex. Some people claim to be against it, but it usually turns out that they are only against left-wing propaganda. In relation to his time Ibsen was certainly a radical thinker. His speeches and letters show him to be pretty much of an anarchist, in the strict sense that he called for the abolition of the state. But he tried to keep his political opinions out of his plays and succeeded to an unusual extent. If many people still think him a blunt political propagandist, that is partly because they do not know how to read and partly because they tend to shout Propaganda every time they meet a liberal mind. In any event, what an author says in his letters and speeches is one thing; what he says in his plays may be another. *Ghosts* requires no explanation from outside. What do we find *in* it?

The title, in Norwegian, means "spirits that return"—like the French word *revenants*. Adopting the English word *ghosts* as a very rough equivalent, we find it used by Ibsen in threefold symbolism. First, in a fairly literal sense: overheard in the next room by Mrs. Alving, Oswald and Regina sound like *ghosts* of Captain Alving and Regina's mother. Second, in a figurative yet physiological sense: Oswald's illness is the *ghost* of his father. Third, in a figurative and ideological sense: the ideas of our fathers linger on as *ghosts*.

The first of these three uses is limited to the one small incident. It is the second and third that constitute a symbolism which energizes the action as a whole. The second is incarnated in Oswald, the third in Mrs. Alving. Yet the play is not a double tragedy, the story of a mother and son, balanced the one by the other, like Antigone and Creon or Antony and Cleopatra. Ibsen subordinates the story of the son to that of the mother. The son's story is given to us as something seen by the mother. At the end, she literally witnesses his collapse. The mere act of witnessing is here a more horrible experience than that of *living* the ideological tragedy (i.e., the tragedy of a woman in whom the philosophy of the fathers is lingering).

Some think that the latter motif is weak in itself. They feel that Ibsen's play has "dated" insofar as it deals with the nineteenth-century fight for enlightenment. "Oswald's friends can live with their children's mothers for all we care. As for Alving, he should have consulted a doctor. And Manders shouldn't have sent Mrs. Alving back to her husband. So what?" It is true that Ibsen had more sympathy with liberal causes than some of his critics have. But is it true that

Ghosts is chiefly a tract in favor of those causes? You can't quote Oswald or Mrs. Alving as if they were Ibsen; that is Error Number 1 (see p. 367). And if Ibsen had wanted to pit convincing progressives against the conservatives, couldn't he have chosen more ingratiating and single-minded examples? In a note on another play, Ibsen tells us what interests him, *qua* dramatist, in the struggles between liberals and conservatives. Envisaging a person brought up (like Mrs. Alving) as a conservative, he notes the difficulty such a one would encounter in acquiring the new moral ideas:

> . . . . the play . . . deals with the struggle which all serious-minded human beings have to wage with themselves in order to bring their lives into harmony with their convictions. For the different spiritual functions do not develop evenly and abreast of each other in any one human being. The instinct of intellectual acquisition hurries on from gain to gain. The moral consciousness—what we call conscience—is, on the other hand, very conservative. It has its deep roots in traditions and the past generally. Hence the conflict. (But the play is of course first and foremost a drama of human beings and human fates.)

All of this applies, surely, to Mrs. Alving and *Ghosts*. It is true that Ibsen assumes the enlightened ideas of the books she reads to be superior to the ideas of Manders, but the play is not *about* these ideas any more than *Othello* is about marriage. It is a drama of "human beings," not in principle different from the older plays in this book.

Take the standard dramatic theme of illusion and reality. Ibsen's characters live with their illusions as long as reality will let them. The illusions that Manders and Engstrand live on are evident and gross enough. But Mrs. Alving is not immune. Not strong enough to face reality and fully to practice the liberal ideas her head has accepted, she continues to deceive not only Oswald but herself. Only in her last talk with her son does she admit even to herself that she made Alving a bad wife and thus shared the responsibility for his dissipations. (It is barely possible to believe that she is lying in order not to shake Oswald's reverence for his father. But are we given any hint that this is the case?)

Mr. Tennant sees the play dominated by a vague, romantic fatality, but are the causes of the catastrophe preternatural or otherwise intangible? They are *multiple*—which is a very different thing. Manders is partly to blame; so is Mrs. Alving, as has just been noted; so, obviously, is Captain Alving. If Ibsen suggests a common source for all their failings, it is not fate or "human nature" but something very concrete—the world, the society, in which they all live.

Now there is a school of modern writing in which all moral responsibility is laid at society's door, the individual being seen as innocent victim. Does Ibsen belong to this school? It was the little Norwegian town that gave Mrs. Alving her inadequate conservative ideas and that bored her husband and refused him a healthy outlet for his abundant passions. On the other hand, society did not prevent Mrs. Alving from getting on the track of a better theory and a better practice. If in the end she failed, the responsibility seems to be a shared one: shared between her and the other individuals concerned, shared between them all and society at large.

These are of course debatable matters, and the debate leads away from the play. One must constantly return to it, or one will forget its particularities, its significant details. Since the play is a tissue of significant details, carefully arranged as contrasts and parallels, one should not leave it without noting one or two.

An ironical contrast. Rain is mentioned several times, and the characters reveal themselves by the different things they say about it. The opposite of rainy weather is sunshine. Oswald has been in southern Europe, where the sun shines oftener. Thus Ibsen brings us to associate Paris with the joy of life, Norway with gloom. In the end Oswald gets the sun back again—but at what a price! Instead of saying, "give me the tablets," he says, "give me the sun," and this is the first time the sun has shone during the action of the play.

Ironical parallels. It is an ironical parallel that gives us our meaning number one for the word *ghosts* as discussed above.

Like the older playwrights, Ibsen uses minor episodes and minor characters as parallels of the major ones. A minor character (as in the classics) lives out the same drama as a major character, but on a lower plane. Engstrand is a religious humbug on a low plane, Manders on a high. One parallel leads to another: if Manders is promoting the idea of a home to perpetuate the memory of Captain Alving, so is Engstrand. The two homes are different yet alike! What is perhaps more important: Manders' home is burnt down, Engstrand's has a future.

The critic who has worked over the details of this complicated "action" most carefully is Hermann Weigand, in his book *The Modern Ibsen*. Also of great value in the study of Ibsen's plays are the playwright's own notes and first drafts, translated and edited by Archer in *From Ibsen's Workshop*. The draft of *Ghosts* is unfortunately a small fragment, but Ibsen did leave behind the following jottings, in which we can see the play taking shape in his mind:

> The play is to be like a picture of life. Belief undermined. But it does not do to say so. "The Orphanage"—for the sake of others. They are to be happy—but this too is only an appearance— Everything is ghosts.—
>
> A leading point: She has been a believer and romantic—this is not entirely obliterated by the standpoint reached later— "Everything is ghosts."
>
> Marriage for external reasons, even when these are religious or moral, brings a Nemesis upon the offspring.
>
> She, the illegitimate child, can be saved by being married to—the son—but then—?
>
> He was dissipated and his health was shattered in his youth; then she appeared, the religious enthusiast; she saved him; she was rich. He was going to marry a girl who was considered worthy. He had a son by his wife, then he went back to the girl; a daughter.—
>
> These women of the present day, ill-used as daughters, as sisters, as wives, not educated according to their gifts, prevented from following their inclination, deprived of their inheritance, embittered in temper—it is these who furnish the mothers of the new generation. What is the result?
>
> The key-note to be: The prolific growth of our intellectual life, in literature, art, etc.—and in contrast to this: the whole of mankind gone astray.

The complete human being is no longer a product of nature, he is an artificial product like corn, and fruit-trees, and the Creole race, and thoroughbred horses and dogs, the vine, etc.—

The fault lies in that all mankind has failed. If a man claims to live and develop in a human way, it is megalomania. All mankind, and especially the Christian part of it, suffers from megalomania.

Among us, monuments are erected to the *dead,* since we have a duty towards them; we allow lepers to marry; but their offspring—? The unborn—?

8. THE GHOST SONATA · 1907

Ghosts has been called a realistic play, yet its realism is, perhaps, not quite what we expected. *The Ghost Sonata* is a fantasy; but what is a fantasy?

The question will go unanswered even after *The Ghost Sonata* has been read. This is not a play that yields up its meaning at first acquaintance. It is rather bewildering. But is it as chaotic as it seems? As the reader will guess, the question is rhetorical: he is being invited to find hidden clues.

This is another place to recall the importance of visualizing a play's action, of reading it more than once. (Letter to the Reader, page 8.) *The Ghost Sonata* is especially difficult to grasp even at a second reading—not only because it is a religious fantasy involving some fairly abstruse thought, but because it relies very heavily on nonverbal effects, upon what is *seen* on the stage. One does not *read* a play like this: one works over it, taking one's time, and asking: how would this look? how could this be done? how are we to figure that?

THE GHOST SONATA

by August Strindberg

TRANSLATED FROM THE SWEDISH
BY ELIZABETH SPRIGGE

✽

Used by permission of Elizabeth Sprigge. All rights whatsoever in this play are strictly reserved, and applications for performances, etc., should be made to Messrs. A. P. Watt & Son, 10 Norfolk Street, London W.C. 2, England.

The Ghost Sonata

Characters

THE OLD MAN, *Hummel, a Company Director*
THE STUDENT, *Arkenholtz*
THE MILKMAID, *an apparition*
THE CARETAKER'S WIFE
THE CARETAKER
THE LADY IN BLACK, *the daughter of the Caretaker's Wife and the Dead Man. Also referred to as the Dark Lady*
THE COLONEL
THE MUMMY, *the Colonel's wife*
THE GIRL, *the Colonel's daughter, actually the daughter of the Old Man*
THE ARISTOCRAT, *Baron Skanskorg. Engaged to the Lady in Black.*
JOHANSSON, *the Old Man's servant*
BENGTSSON, *the Colonel's servant*
THE FIANCÉE, *a white-haired old woman, once betrothed to the Old Man*
THE COOK
A MAIDSERVANT
BEGGARS

Scene I

Outside the house.

The corner of the façade of a modern house, showing the ground floor, the floor above, and the street in front. The ground floor terminates on the right in the Round Room, above which, on the first floor, is a balcony with a flagstaff. The windows of the Round Room face the street in front of the house, and at the corner look on to the suggestion of a side-street running towards the back.

At the beginning of the scene the blinds of the Round Room are down. When, later, they are raised, the white marble statue of a young woman can be seen, surrounded with palms and brightly lighted by rays of sunshine.

To the left of the Round Room is the Hyacinth Room; its window filled with pots of hyacinths, blue, white and pink. Further left, at the back, is an imposing double front door with laurels in tubs on either side of it. The doors are wide open, showing a staircase of white marble with a banister of mahogany and brass. To the left of the front door is another ground-floor window, with a window-mirror.* On the balcony rail in the corner above the Round Room are a blue silk quilt and two white pillows. The windows to the left of this are hung with white sheets.†

In the foreground, in front of the house, is a green bench; to the right a street drinking-fountain, to the left an advertisement column.

It is a bright Sunday morning, and as the curtain rises the bells of several churches, some near, some far away, are ringing.

The front door is open. Inside on the stairs the LADY IN BLACK *stands motionless.*

The CARETAKER'S WIFE *sweeps the doorstep, then polishes the brass on the door and waters the laurels.*

In a wheel-chair by the advertisement column sits the OLD MAN, *reading a newspaper. His hair and beard are white and he wears spectacles.*

The MILKMAID‡ *comes round the corner on the right, carrying milk bottles in a wire basket. She is wearing a summer dress with brown shoes, black stockings and a white cap. She takes off her cap and hangs it on the fountain, wipes the perspiration from her forehead, washes her hands and arranges her hair, using the water as a mirror.*

---

* This window-mirror is set at an angle inside the window, so that by looking in it a person can see what is going on in the street. They used to be quite common in Sweden, and are mentioned in several of Strindberg's plays.

† White sheets in the windows is an old Swedish sign of mourning.

‡ The MILKMAID is simply a delivery girl, not a picturesque figure.

A steamship bell is heard, and now and then the silence is broken by the deep notes of an organ in a nearby church.

After a few moments, when all is silent and the MILKMAID *has finished her toilet, the* STUDENT *enters from the left. He has had a sleepless night and is unshaven. He goes straight up to the fountain. There is a pause before he speaks.*

STUDENT. May I have the cup? *The* MILKMAID *clutches the cup to her.* Haven't you about done with it?

The MILKMAID *looks at him with horror.*

OLD MAN, *to himself.* Who's he talking to? I don't see anybody. Is he crazy?

He goes on watching them in great astonishment.

STUDENT, *to the* MILKMAID. What are you staring at? Do I look so terrible? Well, I've had no sleep, and of course you think I've been making a night of it . . . *The* MILKMAID *stays just as she is.* You think I've been drinking, eh? Do I smell of liquor? *The* MILKMAID *does not change.* I haven't shaved, I know. Give me a drink of water, girl. I've earned it. *Pause.* Oh well, I suppose I'll have to tell you. I spent the whole night dressing wounds and looking after the injured. You see, I was there when that house collapsed last night. Now you know. *The* MILKMAID *rinses the cup and gives him a drink.* Thanks. *The* MILKMAID *stands motionless. Slowly.* Will you do me a great favor? *Pause.* The thing is, my eyes, as you can see, are inflamed, but my hands have been touching wounds and corpses, so it would be dangerous to put them near my eyes. Will you take my handkerchief—it's quite clean—and dip it in the fresh water and bathe my eyes? Will you do this? Will you play the good Samaritan? *The* MILKMAID *hesitates, but does as he bids.* Thank you, my dear. *He takes out his purse. She makes a gesture of refusal.* Forgive my stupidity, but I'm only half-awake. . . . *The* MILKMAID *disappears.*

OLD MAN, *to the* STUDENT. Excuse me speaking to you, but I heard you say you were at the scene of the accident last night. I was just reading about it in the paper.

STUDENT. Is it in the paper already?

OLD MAN. The whole thing, including your portrait. But they regret that they have been unable to find out the name of the splendid young student. . . .

STUDENT. Really? *Glances at the paper.* Yes, that's me. Well I never!

OLD MAN. Who was it you were talking to just now?

STUDENT. Didn't you see? *Pause.*

OLD MAN. Would it be impertinent to inquire—what in fact your name is?

STUDENT. What would be the point? I don't care for publicity. If you get any praise, there's always disapproval too. The art of running people down has been developed to such a pitch. . . . Besides, I don't want any reward.

OLD MAN. You're well off, perhaps.

STUDENT. No, indeed. On the contrary, I'm very poor.

OLD MAN. Do you know, it seems to me I've heard your voice before. When I was young I had a friend who pronounced certain words just as you do. I've never met anyone else with quite that pronunciation. Only him—and you. Are you by any chance related to Mr. Arkenholtz, the merchant?

STUDENT. He was my father.

OLD MAN. Strange are the paths of fate. I saw you when you were an infant, under very painful circumstances.

STUDENT. Yes, I understand I came into the world in the middle of a bankruptcy.

OLD MAN. Just that.

STUDENT. Perhaps I might ask your name?

OLD MAN. I am Mr. Hummel.

STUDENT. Are you the. . . . I remember that. . . .

OLD MAN. Have you often heard my name mentioned in your family?

STUDENT. Yes.

OLD MAN. And mentioned perhaps with a certain aversion? *The* STUDENT *is silent.* Yes, I can imagine it. You were told, I suppose, that I was the man who ruined your father? All who ruin themselves through foolish speculations consider they were ruined by those they couldn't fool. *Pause.* Now these are the facts. Your father robbed me of seventeen thousand crowns—the whole of my savings at that time.

STUDENT. It's queer that the same story can be told in two such different ways.

OLD MAN. You surely don't believe I'm telling you what isn't true?

STUDENT. What am I to believe? My father didn't lie.

OLD MAN. That is so true. A father never lies. But I too am a father, and so it follows. . . .

STUDENT. What are you driving at?

OLD MAN. I saved your father from disaster, and he repaid me with all the frightful hatred that is born of an obligation to be grateful. He taught his family to speak ill of me.

STUDENT. Perhaps you made him ungrateful by poisoning your help with unnecessary humiliation.

OLD MAN. All help is humiliating, sir.

STUDENT. What do you want from me?

OLD MAN. I'm not asking for the money, but if you will render me a few small services, I shall consider myself well paid. You see that I am a cripple. Some say it is my own fault; others lay the blame on my parents. I prefer to blame life itself, with its pitfalls. For if you escape one snare, you fall headlong into another. In any case, I am unable to climb stairs or ring doorbells, and that is why I am asking you to help me.

STUDENT. What can I do?

OLD MAN. To begin with, push my chair so that I can read those playbills. I want to see what is on tonight.

STUDENT, *pushing the chair*. Haven't you got an attendant?

OLD MAN. Yes, but he has gone on an errand. He'll be back soon. Are you a medical student?

STUDENT. No, I am studying languages, but I don't know at all what I'm going to do.

OLD MAN. Aha! Are you good at mathematics?

STUDENT. Yes, fairly.

OLD MAN. Good. Perhaps you would like a job.

STUDENT. Yes, why not?

OLD MAN. Splendid. *He studies the playbills*. They are doing *The Valkyrie* for the matinée. That means the Colonel will be there with his daughter, and as he always sits at the end of the sixth row, I'll put you next to him. Go to that telephone kiosk please and order a ticket for seat eighty-two in the sixth row.

STUDENT. Am I to go to the Opera in the middle of the day?

OLD MAN. Yes. Do as I tell you and things will go well with you. I want to see you happy, rich, and honored. Your début last night as the brave rescuer will make you famous by tomorrow and then your name will be worth something.

STUDENT, *going to the telephone kiosk*. What an odd adventure!

OLD MAN. Are you a gambler?

STUDENT. Yes, unfortunately.

OLD MAN. We'll make it fortunately. Go on now, telephone. *The* STUDENT *goes. The* OLD MAN *reads his paper. The* LADY IN BLACK *comes out on to the pavement and talks to the* CARETAKER'S WIFE. *The* OLD MAN *listens, but the audience hears nothing. The* STUDENT *returns.* Did you fix it up?

STUDENT. It's done.

OLD MAN. You see that house?

STUDENT. Yes, I've been looking at it a lot. I passed it yesterday when the sun was shining on the windowpanes, and I imagined all the beauty and elegance there must be inside. I said to my companion: "Think of living up there in the top flat, with a beautiful young wife, two pretty little children and an income of twenty thousand crowns a year."

OLD MAN. So that's what you said. That's what you said. Well, well! I too am very fond of this house.

STUDENT. Do you speculate in houses?

OLD MAN. Mm—yes. But not in the way you mean.

STUDENT. Do you know the people who live here?

OLD MAN. Every one of them. At my age one knows everybody, and their parents and grandparents too, and one's always related to them in some way or other. I am just eighty, but no one knows me— not really. I take an interest in human destiny. *The blinds of the Round Room are drawn up. The* COLONEL *is seen, wearing mufti. He looks at the thermometer outside one of the windows, then turns back into the room and stands in front of the marble statue.* Look, that's the Colonel, whom you will sit next to this afternoon.

STUDENT. Is he—the Colonel? I don't understand any of this, but it's like a fairy story.

OLD MAN. My whole life's like a book of fairy stories, sir. And although the stories are different, they are held together by one thread, and the main theme constantly recurs.

STUDENT. Who is that marble statue of?

OLD MAN. That, naturally, is his wife.

STUDENT. Was she such a wonderful person?

OLD MAN. Er. . . . yes.

STUDENT. Tell me.

OLD MAN. We can't judge people, young man. If I were to tell you that she left him, that he beat her, that she returned to him and married him a second time, and that now she is sitting inside there like a mummy, worshipping her own statue—then you would think me crazy.

STUDENT. I don't understand.

OLD MAN. I didn't think you would. Well, then we have the window with the hyacinths. His daughter lives there. She has gone out for a ride, but she will be home soon.

STUDENT. And who is the dark lady talking to the caretaker?

OLD MAN. Well, that's a bit complicated, but it is connected with the dead man, up there where you see the white sheets.

STUDENT. Why, who was he?

OLD MAN. A human being like you or me, but the most conspicuous thing about him was his vanity. If you were a Sunday child, you would see him presently come out of that door to look at the Consulate flag flying at half-mast. He was, you understand, a Consul, and he reveled in coronets and lions and plumed hats and colored ribbons.

STUDENT. Sunday child, you say? I'm told I was born on a Sunday.

OLD MAN. No, were you really? I might have known it. I saw it from the color of your eyes. Then you can see what others can't. Have you noticed that?

STUDENT. I don't know what others do see, but at times. . . . Oh, but one doesn't talk of such things!

OLD MAN. I was almost sure of it. But you can talk to me, because I understand such things.

STUDENT. Yesterday, for instance. . . . I was drawn to that obscure little street where later on the house collapsed. I went there and stopped in front of that building which I had never seen before. Then I noticed a crack in the wall. . . . I heard the floor boards snapping. . . . I dashed over and picked up a child that was passing under the wall. . . . The next moment the house collapsed. I was saved, but in my arms, which I thought held the child, was nothing at all.

OLD MAN. Yes, yes, just as I thought. Tell me something. Why were you gesticulating that way just now by the fountain? And why were you talking to yourself?

STUDENT. Didn't you see the milkmaid I was talking to?

OLD MAN, *in horror*. Milkmaid?

STUDENT. Surely. The girl who handed me the cup.

OLD MAN. Really? So that's what was going on. Ah well, I haven't second sight, but there are things I can do. THE FIANCÉE *is now seen to sit down by the window which has the window-mirror*. Look at that old woman in the window. Do you see her? Well, she was my fiancée once, sixty years ago. I was twenty. Don't be alarmed. She doesn't recognize me. We see one another every day, and it makes no impression on me, although once we vowed to love one another eternally. Eternally!

STUDENT. How foolish you were in those days! We never talk to our girls like that.

OLD MAN. Forgive us, young man. We didn't know any better. But can you see that that old woman was once young and beautiful?

STUDENT. It doesn't show. And yet there's some charm in her looks. I can't see her eyes.

The CARETAKER'S WIFE *comes out with a basket of chopped fir branches.**

OLD MAN. Ah, the caretaker's wife! That dark lady is her daughter by the dead man. That's why her husband was given the job of caretaker. But the dark lady has a suitor, who is an aristocrat with great expectations. He is in the process of getting a divorce—from his present wife, you understand. She's presenting him with a stone mansion in order to be rid of him. This aristocratic suitor is the son-in-law of the dead man, and you can see his bedclothes being aired on the balcony upstairs. It is complicated, I must say.

STUDENT. It's fearfully complicated.

OLD MAN. Yes, that it is, internally and externally, although it looks quite simple.

---

* It was customary in Sweden to strew the ground with these for a funeral.

SCENE I]   THE GHOST SONATA   599

STUDENT. But then who was the dead man?

OLD MAN. You asked me that just now, and I answered. If you were to look round the corner, where the tradesmen's entrance is, you would see a lot of poor people whom he used to help—when it suited him.

STUDENT. He was a kind man then.

OLD MAN. Yes—sometimes.

STUDENT. Not always?

OLD MAN. No-o. That's the way of people. Now, sir, will you push my chair a little, so that it gets into the sun. I'm horribly cold. When you're never able to move about, the blood congeals. I'm going to die soon, I know that, but I have a few things to do first. Take my hand and feel how cold I am.

STUDENT, *taking it*. Yes, inconceivably. *He shrinks back, trying in vain to free his hand.*

OLD MAN. Don't leave me. I am tired now and lonely, but I haven't always been like this, you know. I have an enormously long life behind me, enormously long. I have made people unhappy and people have made me unhappy—the one cancels out the other—but before I die I want to see you happy. Our fates are entwined through your father—and other things.

STUDENT. Let go of my hand. You are taking all my strength. You are freezing me. What do you want with me?

OLD MAN, *letting go*. Be patient and you shall see and understand. Here comes the young lady.

They watch the GIRL *approaching, though the audience cannot yet see her.*

STUDENT. The Colonel's daughter?

OLD MAN. His daughter—yes. Look at her. Have you ever seen such a masterpiece?

STUDENT. She is like the marble statue in there.

OLD MAN. That's her mother, you know.

STUDENT. You are right. Never have I seen such a woman of woman born. Happy the man who may lead her to the altar and his home.

OLD MAN. You can see it. Not everyone recognizes her beauty. So, then, it is written.

The GIRL *enters, wearing an English riding habit. Without noticing anyone she walks slowly to the door, where she stops to say a few words to the* CARETAKER'S WIFE. *Then she goes into the house.*

The STUDENT *covers his eyes with his hand.*

OLD MAN. Are you weeping?

STUDENT. In the face of what's hopeless there can be nothing but despair.

OLD MAN. I can open doors and hearts, if only I find an arm to do my will. Serve me and you shall have power.

STUDENT. Is it a bargain? Am I to sell my soul?

OLD MAN. Sell nothing. Listen. All my life I have *taken*. Now I have a craving to give—give. But no one will accept. I am rich, very rich, but I have no heirs, except for a good-for-nothing who torments the life out of me. Become my son. Inherit me while I am still alive. Enjoy life so that I can watch, at least from a distance.

STUDENT. What am I to do?

OLD MAN. First go to *The Valkyrie*.

STUDENT. That's settled. What else?

OLD MAN. This evening you must be in there—in the Round Room.

STUDENT. How am I to get there?

OLD MAN. By way of *The Valkyrie*.

STUDENT. Why have you chosen me as your medium? Did you know me before?

OLD MAN. Yes, of course. I have had my eye on you for a long time. But now look up there at the balcony. The maid is hoisting the flag to half-mast for the Consul. And now she is turning the bed clothes. Do you see that blue quilt? It was made for two to sleep under, but now it covers only one. *The* GIRL, *having changed her dress, appears in the window and waters the hyacinths.* There is my little girl. Look at her, look! She is talking to the flowers. Is she not like that blue hyacinth herself? She gives them drink—nothing but pure water, and they transform the water into color and fragrance. Now here comes the Colónel with the newspaper. He is showing her the bit about the house that collapsed. Now he's pointing to your portrait. She's not indifferent. She's reading of your brave deed. . . .

I believe it's clouding over. If it turns to rain I shall be in a pretty fix, unless Johansson comes back soon. *It grows cloudy and dark. The* FIANCÉE *at the window-mirror closes her window.* Now my fiancée is closing the window. Seventy-nine years old. The window-mirror is the only mirror she uses, because in it she sees not herself, but the world outside—in two directions. But the world can see her; she hasn't thought of that. Anyhow she's a handsome old woman.

Now the DEAD MAN, *wrapped in a winding sheet, comes out of the door.*

STUDENT. Good God, what do I see?

OLD MAN. What do you see?

STUDENT. Don't *you* see? There, in the doorway, the dead man?

OLD MAN. I see nothing, but I expected this. Tell me.

STUDENT. He is coming out into the street. *Pause.* Now he is turning his head and looking up at the flag.

OLD MAN. What did I tell you? You may be sure he'll count the wreaths and read the visiting cards. Woe to him who's missing.

STUDENT. Now he's turning the corner.

OLD MAN. He's gone to count the poor at the back door. The poor are in the nature of a decoration, you see. "Followed by the blessings of many." Well, he's not going to have my blessing. Between ourselves he was a great scoundrel.

STUDENT. But charitable.

OLD MAN. A charitable scoundrel, always thinking of his grand funeral. When he knew his end was near, he cheated the State out of fifty thousand crowns. Now his daughter has relations with another woman's husband and is wondering about the Will. Yes, the scoundrel can hear every word we're saying, and he's welcome to it. Ah, here comes Johansson! JOHANSSON *enters.* Report! JOHANSSON *speaks, but the audience does not hear.* Not at home, eh? You are an ass. And the telegram? Nothing? Go on. . . . At six this evening? That's good. Special edition, you say? With his name in full. Arkenholtz, a student, born. . . . parents. . . . That's splendid. . . . I think it's beginning to rain. . . . What did he say about it? So—so. He wouldn't? Well, he must. Here comes the aristocrat. Push me round the corner, Johansson, so I can hear what the poor are saying. And, Arkenholtz, you wait for me here. Understand? *To* JOHANSSON. Hurry up now, hurry up.

JOHANSSON *wheels the chair round the corner. The* STUDENT *remains watching the* GIRL, *who is now loosening the earth round the hy-*

acinths. The ARISTOCRAT, *wearing mourning, comes in and speaks to the* DARK LADY, *who has been walking to and fro on the pavement.*

ARISTOCRAT. But what can we do about it? We shall have to wait.

LADY. I can't wait.

ARISTOCRAT. You can't? Well then, go into the country.

LADY. I don't want to do that.

ARISTOCRAT. Come over here or they will hear what we are saying. *They move towards the advertisement column and continue their conversation inaudibly.* JOHANSSON *returns.*

JOHANSSON, *to the* STUDENT. My master asks you not to forget that other thing, sir.

STUDENT, *hesitating.* Look here. . . . first of all tell me. . . . who is your master?

JOHANSSON. Well, he's so many things, and he has been everything.

STUDENT. Is he a wise man?

JOHANSSON. Depends what that is. He says all his life he's been looking for a Sunday child, but that may not be true.

STUDENT. What does he want? He's grasping, isn't he?

JOHANSSON. It's power he wants. The whole day long he rides round in his chariot like the god Thor himself. He looks at houses, pulls them down, opens up new streets, builds squares. . . . But he breaks into houses too, sneaks through windows, plays havoc with human destinies, kills his enemies—and never forgives. Can you imagine it, sir? This miserable cripple was once a Don Juan—although he always lost his women.

STUDENT. How do you account for that?

JOHANSSON. You see he's so cunning he makes the women leave him when he's tired of them. But what he's most like now is a horse-thief in the human market. He steals human beings in all sorts of different ways. He literally stole me out of the hands of the law. Well, as a matter of fact I'd made a slip—hm, yes—and only he knew about it. Instead of getting me put in gaol, he turned me into a slave. I slave—for my food alone, and that's none of the best.

STUDENT. Then what is it he means to do in this house?

JOHANSSON. I'm not going to talk about that. It's too complicated.

STUDENT. I think I'd better get away from it all.

The GIRL *drops a bracelet out the window.*

JOHANSSON. Look! The young lady has dropped her bracelet out of the window. *The* STUDENT *goes slowly over, picks up the bracelet and returns it to the* GIRL, *who thanks him stiffly. The* STUDENT *goes back to* JOHANSSON. So you mean to get away. That's not so easy as you think, once he's got you in his net. And he's afraid of nothing between heaven and earth—yes, of one thing he is—of one person rather. . . .

STUDENT. Don't tell me. I think perhaps I know.

JOHANSSON. How can you know?

STUDENT. I'm guessing. Is it a little milkmaid he's afraid of?

JOHANSSON. He turns his head the other way whenever he meets a milk cart. Besides, he talks in his sleep. It seems he was once in Hamburg. . . .

STUDENT. Can one trust this man?

JOHANSSON. You can trust him—to do anything.

STUDENT. What's he doing now round the corner?

JOHANSSON. Listening to the poor. Sowing a little word, loosening one stone at a time, till the house falls down—metaphorically speaking. You see I'm an educated man. I was once a book-seller. . . . Do you still mean to go away?

STUDENT. I don't like to be ungrateful. He saved my father once, and now he only asks a small service in return.

JOHANSSON. What is that?

STUDENT. I am to go to *The Valkyrie*.

JOHANSSON. That's beyond me. But he's always up to new tricks. Look at him now, talking to that policeman. He is always thick with the police. He uses them, gets them involved in his interests, holds them with false promises and expectations, while all the time he's pumping them. You'll see that before the day is over he'll be received in the Round Room.

STUDENT. What does he want there? What connection has he with the Colonel?

JOHANSSON. I think I can guess, but I'm not sure. You'll see for yourself once you're in there.

STUDENT. I shall never be in there.

JOHANSSON. That depends on yourself. Go to *The Valkyrie*.

STUDENT. Is that the way?

JOHANSSON. Yes, if he said so. Look. Look at him in his war chariot, drawn in triumph by the beggars, who get nothing for their pains but the hint of a treat at his funeral.

The OLD MAN *appears standing up in his wheel-chair, drawn by one of the beggars and followed by the rest.*

OLD MAN. Hail the noble youth who, at the risk of his own life, saved so many others in yesterday's accident. Three cheers for Arkenholtz! *The* BEGGARS *bare their heads but do not cheer. The* GIRL *at the window waves her handkerchief. The* COLONEL *gazes from the window of the Round Room. The* OLD WOMAN *rises at her window. The* MAID *on the balcony hoists the flag to the top.* Clap your hands, citizens. True, it is Sunday, but the ass in the pit and the ear in the corn field will absolve us. And although I am not a Sunday child, I have the gift of prophecy and also that of healing. Once I brought a drowned person back to life. That was in Hamburg on a Sunday morning just like this. . . . *The* MILKMAID *enters, seen only by the* STUDENT *and the* OLD MAN. *She raises her arms like one who is drowning and gazes fixedly at the* OLD MAN. *He sits down, then crumples up, stricken with horror.* Johansson! Take me away! Quick! . . . . Arkenholtz, don't forget *The Valkyrie.*

STUDENT. What is all this?

JOHANSSON. We shall see. We shall see.

Scene II

Inside the Round Room.

At the back is a white porcelain stove. On either side of it are a mirror, a pendulum clock and candelabra. On the right of the stove is the entrance to the hall beyond which is a glimpse of a room furnished in green and mahogany. On the left of the stove is the door to a cupboard, papered like the wall. The statue, shaded by palms has a curtain which can be drawn to conceal it.

A door on the left leads into the Hyacinth Room, where the GIRL *sits reading.*

The back of the COLONEL *can be seen, as he sits in the Green Room, writing.*

BENGTSSON, *the Colonel's servant, comes in from the hall. He is wearing livery, and is followed by* JOHANSSON, *dressed as a waiter.*

BENGTSSON. Now you'll have to serve the tea, Johansson, while I take the coats. Have you ever done it before?

JOHANSSON. It's true I push a war chariot in the daytime, as you know, but in the evenings I go as a waiter to receptions and so forth. It's always been my dream to get into this house. They're queer people here, aren't they?

BENGTSSON. Ye-es. A bit out of the ordinary anyhow.

JOHANSSON. Is it to be a musical party or what?

BENGTSSON. The usual ghost supper, as we call it. They drink tea and don't say a word—or else the Colonel does all the talking. And they crunch their biscuits, all at the same time. It sounds like rats in an attic.

JOHANSSON. Why do you call it the ghost supper?

BENGTSSON. They look like ghosts. And they've kept this up for twenty years, always the same people saying the same things or saying nothing at all for fear of being found out.

JOHANSSON. Isn't there a mistress of the house?

BENGTSSON. Oh yes, but she's crazy. She sits in a cupboard* because her eyes can't bear the light. *He points to the papered door.* She sits in there.

JOHANSSON. In there?

BENGTSSON. Well, I told you they were a bit out of the ordinary.

JOHANSSON. But then—what does she look like?

BENGTSSON. Like a mummy. Do you want to have a look at her? *He opens the door.* There she is.

The figure of the COLONEL'S WIFE *is seen, white and shrivelled into a* MUMMY.

JOHANSSON. Oh my God!

MUMMY, *babbling.* Why do you open the door? Haven't I told you to keep it closed?

BENGTSSON, *in a wheedling tone.* Ta, ta, ta, ta. Be a good girl now, then you'll get something nice. Pretty Polly.

MUMMY, *parrot-like.* Pretty Polly. Are you there, Jacob? Currrrr!

---

* i.e., in American usage, a closet.

BENGTSSON. She thinks she's a parrot, and maybe she's right. *To the* MUMMY. Whistle for us, Polly. *The* MUMMY *whistles.*

JOHANSSON. Well, I've seen a few things in my day, but this beats everything.

BENGTSSON. You see, when a house gets old, it grows moldy, and when people stay a long time together and torment each other they go mad. The mistress of the house—shut up, Polly—that mummy there, has been living here for forty years—same husband, same furniture, same relatives, same friends. *He closes the papered door.* And the goings-on in this house—well, they're beyond me. Look at that statue—that's her when she was young.

JOHANSSON. Good Lord! Is that the mummy?

BENGTSSON. Yes. It's enough to make you weep. And somehow, carried away by her own imagination or something, she's got to be a bit like a parrot—the way she talks and the way she can't stand cripples or sick people. She can't stand the sight of her own daughter, because she's sick.

JOHANSSON. Is the young lady sick?

BENGTSSON. Didn't you know that?

JOHANSSON. No. And the Colonel, who is he?

BENGTSSON. You'll see.

JOHANSSON, *looking at the statue.* It's horrible to think that. . . . How old is she now?

BENGTSSON. Nobody knows. But it's said that when she was thirty-five she looked like nineteen, and that's what she made the Colonel believe she was—here in this very house. Do you know what that black Japanese screen by the couch is for? They call it the death-screen, and when someone's going to die, they put it round—same as in a hospital.

JOHANSSON. What a horrible house! And the student was longing to get in, as if it were paradise.

BENGTSSON. What student? Oh, I know. The one who's coming here this evening. The Colonel and the young lady happened to meet him at the Opera, and both of them took a fancy to him. Hm. Now it's my turn to ask questions. Who is your master—the man in the wheel-chair?

JOHANSSON. Well, he er. . . . Is he coming here too?

BENGTSSON. He hasn't been invited.

JOHANSSON. He'll come uninvited—if need be.

The OLD MAN *appears in the hall on crutches, wearing a frock-coat and top-hat. He steals forward and listens.*

BENGTSSON. He's a regular old devil, isn't he?

JOHANSSON. Up to the ears.

BENGTSSON. He looks like old Nick himself.

JOHANSSON. And he must be a wizard too, for he goes through locked doors.

The OLD MAN *comes forward and takes hold of* JOHANSSON *by the ear.*

OLD MAN. Rascal—take care! *To* BENGTSSON. Tell the Colonel I am here.

BENGTSSON. But we are expecting guests.

OLD MAN. I know. But my visit is as good as expected, if not exactly looked forward to.

BENGTSSON. I see. What name shall I say? Mr. Hummel?

OLD MAN. Exactly. Yes. BENGTSSON *crosses the hall to the Green Room, the door of which he closes behind him. To* JOHANSSON. Get out! JOHANSSON *hesitates.* Get out! JOHANSSON *disappears into the hall. The* OLD MAN *inspects the room and stops in front of the statue in much astonishment.* Amelia! It is she—she!

MUMMY, *from the cupboard.* Prrr-etty Polly. *The* OLD MAN *starts.*

OLD MAN. What was that? Is there a parrot in the room? I don't see it.

MUMMY. Are you there, Jacob?

OLD MAN. The house is haunted.

MUMMY. Jacob!

OLD MAN. I'm scared. So these are the kind of secrets they guard in this house. *With his back turned to the cupboard he stands looking at a portrait.* There he is—he!

The MUMMY *comes out behind the* OLD MAN *and gives a pull at his wig.*

MUMMY. Currrrr! Is it . . . ? Currrrr!

OLD MAN, *jumping out of his skin.* God in heaven! Who is it?

MUMMY, *in a natural voice.* Is it Jacob?

OLD MAN. Yes, my name is Jacob.

MUMMY, *with emotion.* And my name is Amelia.

OLD MAN. No, no, no. . . . Oh my God!

MUMMY. That's how I look. Yes. *Pointing to the statue.* And that's how I *did* look. Life opens one's eyes, does it not? I live mostly in the cupboard to avoid seeing and being seen. . . . But, Jacob, what do you want here?

OLD MAN. My child. Our child.

MUMMY. There she is.

OLD MAN. Where?

MUMMY. There—in the Hyacinth Room.

OLD MAN, *looking at the* GIRL. Yes, that is she. *Pause.* And what about her father—the Colonel, I mean—your husband?

MUMMY. Once, when I was angry with him, I told him everything.

OLD MAN. Well. . . . ?

MUMMY. He didn't believe me. He just said: "That's what all wives say when they want to murder their husbands." It was a terrible crime none the less. It has falsified his whole life—his family tree too. Sometimes I take a look in the Peerage, and then I say to myself: Here she is, going about with a false birth certificate like some servant girl, and for such things people are sent to the reformatory.

OLD MAN. Many do it. I seem to remember your own date of birth was given incorrectly.

MUMMY. My mother made me do that. I was not to blame. And in our crime, *you* played the biggest part.

OLD MAN. No. Your husband caused that crime, when he took my fiancée from me. I was born one who cannot forgive until he has punished. That was to me an imperative duty—and is so still.

MUMMY. What are you expecting to find in this house? What do you want? How did you get in? Is it to do with my daughter? If you touch her, you shall die.

OLD MAN. I mean well by her.

MUMMY. Then you must spare her father.

OLD MAN. No.

MUMMY. Then you shall die. In this room, behind that screen.

OLD MAN. That may be. But I can't let go once I've got my teeth into a thing.

MUMMY. You want to marry her to that student. Why? He is nothing and has nothing.

OLD MAN. He will be rich, through me.

MUMMY. Have you been invited here tonight?

OLD MAN. No, but I propose to get myself an invitation to this ghost supper.

MUMMY. Do you know who is coming?

OLD MAN. Not exactly.

MUMMY. The Baron. The man who lives up above—whose father-in-law was buried this afternoon.

OLD MAN. The man who is getting a divorce in order to marry the daughter of the Caretaker's wife. . . . The man who used to be—your lover.

MUMMY. Another guest will be your former fiancée, who was seduced by my husband.

OLD MAN. A select gathering.

MUMMY. Oh God, if only we might die, might die!

OLD MAN. Then why have you stayed together?

MUMMY. Crime and secrets and guilt bind us together. We have broken our bonds and gone our own ways, times without number, but we are always drawn together again.

OLD MAN. I think the Colonel is coming.

MUMMY. Then I will go in to Adèle. *Pause.* Jacob, mind what you do. Spare him.

Pause. She goes into the Hyacinth Room and disappears. The COLONEL *enters, cold and reserved, with a letter in his hand.*

COLONEL. Be seated, please. *Slowly the* OLD MAN *sits down. Pause. The* COLONEL *stares at him.* You wrote this letter, sir?

OLD MAN. I did.

COLONEL. Your name is Hummel?

OLD MAN. It is. *Pause.*

COLONEL. As I understand you have bought in all my unpaid promissory notes, I can only conclude that I am in your hands. What do you want?

OLD MAN. I want payment, in one way or another.

COLONEL. In what way?

OLD MAN. A very simple one. Let us not mention the money. Just bear with me in your house as a guest.

COLONEL. If so little will satisfy you. . . .

OLD MAN. Thank you.

COLONEL. What else?

OLD MAN. Dismiss Bengtsson.

COLONEL. Why should I do that? My devoted servant, who has been with me a lifetime, who has the national medal for long and faithful service—why should I do that?

OLD MAN. That's how you see him—full of excellent qualities. He is not the man he appears to be.

COLONEL. Who is?

OLD MAN, *taken aback*. True. But Bengtsson must go.

COLONEL. Are you going to run my house?

OLD MAN. Yes. Since everything here belongs to me—furniture, curtains, dinner service, linen. . . . and more too.

COLONEL. How do you mean—more?

OLD MAN. Everything. I own everything here. It is mine.

COLONEL. Very well, it is yours. But my family escutcheon and my good name remain my own.

OLD MAN. No, not even those. *Pause*. You are not a nobleman.

COLONEL. How dare you!

OLD MAN, *producing a document*. If you read this extract from *The Armorial Gazette,* you will see that the family whose name you are using has been extinct for a hundred years.

COLONEL. I have heard rumors to this effect, but I inherited the name from my father. *Reads*. It is true. You are right. I am not a nobleman. Then I must take off my signet ring. It is true, it belongs to you. *Gives it to him*. There you are.

OLD MAN, *pocketing the ring*. Now we will continue. You are not a Colonel either.

COLONEL. I am not. . . . ?

OLD MAN. No. You once held the temporary rank of Colonel in the American Volunteer Force, but after the war in Cuba and the reorganization of the Army, all such titles were abolished.

COLONEL. Is this true?

OLD MAN, *indicating his pocket*. Do you want to read it?

COLONEL. No, that's not necessary. Who are you, and what right have you to sit there stripping me in this fashion?

OLD MAN. You will see. But as far as stripping you goes. . . . do you know who you are?

COLONEL. How dare you?

OLD MAN. Take off that wig and have a look at yourself in the mirror. But take your teeth out at the same time and shave off your moustache. Let Bengtsson unlace your metal stays and perhaps a certain X.Y.Z., a lackey, will recognize himself. The fellow who was a cupboard lover in a certain kitchen . . . *The* COLONEL *reaches for the bell on the table, but* HUMMEL *checks him.* Don't touch that bell, and don't call Bengtsson. If you do, I'll have him arrested. *Pause.* And now the guests are beginning to arrive. Keep your composure and we will continue to play our old parts for a while.

COLONEL. Who are you? I recognize your voice and eyes.

OLD MAN. Don't try to find out. Keep silent and obey.

The STUDENT *enters and bows to the* COLONEL.

STUDENT. How do you do, sir.

COLONEL. Welcome to my house, young man. Your splendid behavior at that great disaster has brought your name to everybody's lips, and I count it an honor to receive you in my home.

STUDENT. My humble descent, sir. . . . Your illustrious name and noble birth. . . .

COLONEL. May I introduce Mr. Arkenholtz—Mr. Hummel. If you will join the ladies in here, Mr. Arkenholtz—I must conclude my conversation with Mr. Hummel. *He shows the* STUDENT *into the Hyacinth Room, where he remains visible, talking shyly to the* GIRL. A splendid young man, musical, sings, writes poetry. If he only had blue blood in him, if he were of the same station, I don't think I should object. . . .

OLD MAN. To what?

COLONEL. To my daughter. . . .

OLD MAN. *Your* daughter! But apropos of that, why does she spend all her time in there?

COLONEL. She insists on being in the Hyacinth Room except when she is out-of-doors. It's a peculiarity of hers. Ah, here comes Miss Beatrice von Holsteinkrona—a charming woman, a pillar of the Church, with just enough money of her own to suit her birth and position.

OLD MAN, *to himself.* My fiancée.

The FIANCÉE *enters, looking a little crazy.*

COLONEL. Miss Holsteinkrona—Mr. Hummel. *The* FIANCÉE *curtseys and takes a seat. The* ARISTOCRAT *enters and seats himself. He wears mourning and looks mysterious.* Baron Skanskorg . . .

OLD MAN, *aside, without rising*. That's the jewel-thief, I think. *To the* COLONEL. If you bring in the Mummy, the party will be complete.

COLONEL, *at the door of the Hyacinth Room*. Polly!

MUMMY, *entering*. Currrrr . . . !

COLONEL. Are the young people to come in too?

OLD MAN. No, not the young people. They shall be spared.

They all sit silent in a circle.

COLONEL. Shall we have the tea brought in?

OLD MAN. What's the use? No one wants tea. Why should we pretend about it?

COLONEL. Then shall we talk?

OLD MAN. Talk of the weather, which we know? Inquire about each other's health, which we know just as well. I prefer silence—then one can hear thoughts and see the past. Silence cannot hide anything—but words can. I read the other day that differences of language originated among savages for the purpose of keeping one tribe's secrets hidden from another. Every language therefore is a code, and he who finds the key can understand every language in the world. But this does not prevent secrets from being exposed without a key, specially when there is a question of paternity to be proved. Proof in a Court of Law is another matter. Two false witnesses suffice to prove anything about which they are agreed, but one does not take witnesses along on the kind of explorations I have in mind. Nature herself has instilled in human beings a sense of modesty which tries to hide what should be hidden, but we slip into situations unintentionally, and by chance sometimes the deepest secret is divulged—the mask torn from the imposter, the villain exposed. . . . *Pause. All look at each other in silence.* What a silence there is now! *Long silence.* Here, for instance, in this honorable house, in this elegant home, where beauty, wealth and culture are united. . . . *Long silence.* All of us now sitting here know who we are—do we not? There's no need for me to tell you. And you know me, although you pretend ignorance. *He indicates the Hyacinth Room.* In there is my daughter. *Mine*—you know that too. She had lost the desire to live, without knowing why. The fact is she was withering away in this air charged with crime and deceit and falseness of every kind. That is why I looked for a friend for her in whose company she might enjoy the light and warmth of noble deeds. *Long silence.* That was my mission in this house: to pull up the weeds, to expose the crimes, to settle all accounts, so that those young people might start afresh in this home, which is my gift to them. *Long silence.* Now I am going to grant safe-conduct, to each of you in his and her proper time and turn. Whoever stays I shall have arrested. *Long silence.* Do you hear the clock ticking like a death-watch beetle in the wall? Do you hear what it says? "It's time, it's time, it's time." When it strikes, in a few moments, your time will be up. Then you can go, but not before. It's raising its arm against you before it strikes. Listen! It is warning you. "The clock can strike." And I can strike too. *He strikes the table with one of his crutches.* Do you hear? *Silence. The* MUMMY *goes up to the clock and stops it, then speaks in a normal and serious voice.*

MUMMY. But I can stop time in its course. I can wipe out the past and undo what is done. But not with bribes, not with threats—only through suffering and repentance. *She goes up to the* OLD MAN. We are miserable human beings, that we know. We have erred and we have sinned, we like all the rest. We are not what we seem, because at bottom we are better than ourselves, since we detest our sins. But when you, Jacob Hummel, with your false name, choose to sit in judgment over us, you prove yourself worse than us miserable sinners. For you are not the one you appear to be. You are a thief of human souls. You stole me once with false promises. You murdered the Consul who was buried today; you strangled him with debts. You have stolen the student, binding him by the pretence of a claim on his father, who never owed you a farthing. *Having tried to rise and speak, the* OLD MAN *sinks back in his chair and crumples up more and more as she goes on.* But there is one dark spot in your life which I am not quite sure about, although I have my suspicions. I think Bengtsson knows. *She rings the bell on the table.*

OLD MAN. No, not Bengtsson, not him.

MUMMY. So he does know. *She rings again. The* MILKMAID *appears in the hallway door, unseen by all but the* OLD MAN, *who shrinks back in horror. The* MILKMAID *vanishes as* BENGTSSON *enters.* Do you know this man, Bengtsson?

BENGTSSON. Yes, I know him and he knows me. Life, as you are aware, has its ups and downs. I have been in his service; another time he was in mine. For two whole years he was a sponger in my kitchen. As he had to be away by three, the dinner was got ready at two, and the family had to eat the warmed-up leavings of that brute. He drank the soup stock, which the cook then filled up with water. He sat out there like a vampire, sucking the marrow out of the house, so that we became like skeletons. And he nearly got us put in prison when we called the cook a thief. Later I met this man in Hamburg under another name. He was a usurer then, a blood-sucker. But while he was there he was charged with having lured a young girl out on to the ice so as to drown her, because she had seen him commit a crime he was afraid would be discovered. . . .

The MUMMY *passes her hand over the* OLD MAN'S *face.*

MUMMY. *This* is you. Now give up the notes and the Will. JOHANSSON *appears in the hallway door and watches the scene with great interest, knowing he is now to be freed from slavery. The* OLD MAN *produces a bundle of papers and throws it on the table. The* MUMMY *goes over and strokes his back.* Parrot. Are you there, Jacob?

OLD MAN, *like a parrot.* Jacob is here. Pretty Polly. Currrrr!

MUMMY. May the clock strike?

OLD MAN, *with a clucking sound.* The clock may strike. *Imitating a cuckoo clock.* Cuckoo, cuckoo, cuckoo. . . .

The MUMMY *opens the cupboard door.*

MUMMY. Now the clock has struck. Rise, and enter the cupboard where I have spent twenty years repenting our crime. A rope is hanging there, which you can take as the one with which you strangled the Consul, and with which you meant to strangle your benefactor. . . . Go! *The* OLD MAN *goes in to the cupboard. The* MUMMY *closes the door.* Bengtsson! Put up the screen—the death-screen. BENGTSSON *places the screen in front of the door.* It is finished. God have mercy on his soul.

ALL. Amen. *Long silence.*

The GIRL *and the* STUDENT *appear in the Hyacinth Room. She has a harp, on which he plays a prelude, and then accompanies the* STUDENT'S *recitation.*

STUDENT. I saw the sun. To me it seemed
    that I beheld the Hidden.
    Men must reap what they have sown;
    blest is he whose deeds are good.
    Deeds which you have wrought in fury,
    cannot in evil find redress.
    Comfort him you have distressed
    with loving-kindness—this will heal.
    No fear has he who does no ill.
    Sweet is innocence.

Scene III

Inside the Hyacinth Room. The general effect of the room is exotic and oriental. There are hyacinths everywhere, of every color, some in pots, some with the bulbs in glass vases and the roots going down into the water.

On top of the tiled stove is a large seated Buddha, in whose lap rests a bulb from which rises the stem of a shallot (Allium ascalonicum), bearing its globular cluster of white, starlike flowers.

On the right is an open door, leading into the Round Room, where the COLONEL *and the* MUMMY *are seated, inactive and silent. A part of the death-screen is also visible.*

On the left is a door to the pantry and kitchen.

The STUDENT *and the* GIRL *(Adèle) are beside the table; he standing, she seated with her harp.*

THE GIRL. Now sing to my flowers.
STUDENT. Is this the flower of your soul?
GIRL. The one and only. Do you too love the hyacinth?
STUDENT. I love it above all other flowers—its virginal shape rising straight and slender out of the bulb, resting on the water and sending its pure white roots down into the colorless fluid. I love its colors: the snow-white, pure as innocence, the yellow honey-sweet, the youth-

ful pink, the ripe red, but best of all the blue—the dewy blue, deep-eyed and full of faith. I love them all, more than gold or pearls. I have loved them ever since I was a child, have worshipped them because they have all the fine qualities I lack. . . . And yet. . . .

GIRL. Go on.

STUDENT. My love is not returned, for these beautiful blossoms hate me.

GIRL. How do you mean?

STUDENT. Their fragrance, strong and pure as the early winds of spring which have passed over melting snows, confuses my senses, deafens me, blinds me, thrusts me out of the room, bombards me with poisoned arrows that wound my heart and set my head on fire. Do you know the legend of that flower?

GIRL. Tell it to me.

STUDENT. First its meaning. The bulb is the earth, resting on the water or buried in the soil. Then the stalk rises, straight as the axis of the world, and at the top are the six-pointed star-flowers.

GIRL. Above the earth—the stars. Oh, that is wonderful! Where did you learn this? How did you find it out?

STUDENT. Let me think. . . . In your eyes. And so, you see, it is an image of the Cosmos. This is why Buddha sits holding the earth-bulb, his eyes brooding as he watches it grow, outward and upward, transforming itself into a heaven. This poor earth will become a heaven. It is for this that Buddha waits.

GIRL. I see it now. Is not the snowflake six-pointed too like the hyacinth flower?

STUDENT. You are right. The snowflakes must be falling stars.

GIRL. And the snowdrop is a snow-star, grown out of snow.

STUDENT. But the largest and most beautiful of all the stars in the firmament, the golden-red Sirius, is the narcissus with its gold and red chalice and its six white rays.

GIRL. Have you seen the shallot in bloom?

STUDENT. Indeed I have. It bears its blossoms within a ball, a globe like the celestial one, strewn with white stars.

GIRL. Oh how glorious! Whose thought was that?

STUDENT. Yours.

GIRL. Yours.

STUDENT. Ours. We have given birth to it together. We are wedded.

GIRL. Not yet.

STUDENT. What's still to do?

GIRL. Waiting, ordeals, patience.

STUDENT. Very well. Put me to the test. *Pause.* Tell me. Why do your parents sit in there so silently, not saying a single word?

GIRL. Because they have nothing to say to each other, and because neither believes what the other says. This is how my father puts it: What's the point of talking, when neither of us can fool the other?

STUDENT. What a horrible thing to hear!

GIRL. Here comes the Cook. Look at her, how big and fat she is. *They watch the* COOK, *although the audience cannot yet see her.*

STUDENT. What does she want?

GIRL. To ask me about the dinner. I have to do the housekeeping as my mother's ill.

STUDENT. What have we to do with the kitchen?

GIRL. We must eat. Look at the Cook. I can't bear the sight of her.

STUDENT. Who is that ogress?

GIRL. She belongs to the Hummel family of vampires. She is eating us.

STUDENT. Why don't you dismiss her?

GIRL. She won't go. We have no control over her. We've got her because of our sins. Can't you see that we are pining and wasting away?

STUDENT. Don't you get enough to eat?

GIRL. Yes, we get many dishes, but all the strength has gone. She boils the nourishment out of the meat and gives us the fibre and water, while she drinks the stock herself. And when there's a roast, she first boils out the marrow, eats the gravy and drinks the juices herself. Everything she touches loses its savor. It's as if she sucked with her eyes. We get the grounds when she has drunk the coffee. She drinks the wine and fills the bottles up with water.

STUDENT. Send her packing.

GIRL. We can't.

STUDENT. Why not?

GIRL. We don't know. She won't go. No one has any control over her. She has taken all our strength from us.

STUDENT. May I get rid of her?

GIRL. No. It must be as it is. Here she is. She will ask me what is to be for dinner. I shall tell her. She will make objections and get her own way.

STUDENT. Let her do the ordering herself then.

GIRL. She won't do that.

STUDENT. What an extraordinary house! It is bewitched.

GIRL. Yes. But now she is turning back, because she has seen you.

THE COOK, *in the doorway.* No, that wasn't the reason.

She grins, showing all her teeth.

STUDENT. Get out!

COOK. When it suits me. *Pause.* It does suit me now.

She disappears.

GIRL. Don't lose your temper. Practise patience. She is one of the ordeals we have to go through in this house. You see, we have a housemaid too, whom we have to clean up after.

STUDENT. I am done for. *Cor in æthere.* Music!

GIRL. Wait.

STUDENT. Music!

GIRL. Patience. This room is called the room of ordeals. It looks beautiful, but it is full of defects.

STUDENT. Really? Well, such things must be seen to. It is very beautiful, but a little cold. Why don't you have a fire?

GIRL. Because it smokes.

STUDENT. Can't you have the chimney swept?

GIRL. It doesn't help. You see that writing-desk there?

STUDENT. An unusually fine piece.

GIRL. But it wobbles. Every day I put a piece of cork under that leg, and every day the housemaid takes it away when she sweeps and I have to cut a new piece. The penholder is covered with ink every morning and so is the inkstand. I have to clean them up every morning after that woman, as sure as the sun rises. *Pause.* What's the worst job you can think of?

STUDENT. To count the washing. Ugh!

GIRL. That I have to do. Ugh!

STUDENT. What else?

GIRL. To be waked in the middle of the night and have to get up and see to the window, which the housemaid has left banging.

STUDENT. What else?

SCENE III] THE GHOST SONATA 619

GIRL. To get up on a ladder and tie the cord on the damper* which the housemaid has torn off.

STUDENT. What else?

GIRL. To sweep after her, to dust after her, to light the fire in the stove when all she's done is throw in some wood. To see to the damper, to wipe the glasses, to lay the table over again, to open the bottles, to see that the rooms are aired, to remake my bed, to rinse the water-bottle when it's green with sediment, to buy matches and soap which are always lacking, to wipe the chimneys and trim the wicks to keep the lamps from smoking—and so that they don't go out when we have company, I have to fill them myself. . . .

STUDENT. Music!

GIRL. Wait. The labor comes first. The labor of keeping the dirt of life at a distance.

STUDENT. But you are wealthy and have two servants.

GIRL. It doesn't help. Even if we had three. Living is hard work, and sometimes I grow tired. *Pause.* Think then if there were a nursery as well.

STUDENT. The greatest of joys.

GIRL. And the costliest. Is life worth so much hardship?

STUDENT. That must depend on the reward you expect for your labors. I would not shrink from anything to win your hand.

GIRL. Don't say that. You can never have me.

STUDENT. Why not?

GIRL. You mustn't ask. *Pause.*

STUDENT. You dropped your bracelet out of the window. . . .

GIRL. Because my hand has grown so thin. *Pause. The* COOK *appears with a Japanese bottle in her hand.* There she is—the one who devours me and all of us.

STUDENT. What has she in her hand?

GIRL. It is the bottle of coloring matter that has letters like scorpions on it. It is the soy which turns water into soup and takes the place of gravy. She makes cabbage soup with it—and mock-turtle soup too.

STUDENT, *to* COOK. Get out!

COOK. You drain us of sap, and we drain you. We take the blood

* Damper to the big stove.

and leave you the water, but colored . . . colored. I am going now, but all the same I shall stay, as long as I please. *She goes out.*

STUDENT. Why did Bengtsson get a medal?

GIRL. For his great merits.

STUDENT. Has he no defects?

GIRL. Yes, great ones. But you don't get a medal for them.

They smile.

STUDENT. You have many secrets in this house.

GIRL. As in all others. Permit us to keep ours.

STUDENT. Don't you approve of candor?

GIRL. Yes—within reason.

STUDENT. Sometimes I'm seized with a raging desire to say all I think. But I know the world would go to pieces if one were completely candid. *Pause.* I went to a funeral the other day . . . in church. It was very solemn and beautiful.

GIRL. Was it Mr. Hummel's?

STUDENT. My false benefactor's—yes. At the head of the coffin stood an old friend of the deceased. He carried the mace. I was deeply impressed by the dignified manner and moving words of the clergyman. I cried. We all cried. Afterwards we went to a tavern, and there I learned that the man with the mace had been in love with the dead man's son. . . . *The* GIRL *stares at him, trying to understand.* And that the dead man had borrowed money from his son's admirer. *Pause.* Next day the clergyman was arrested for embezzling the church funds. A pretty story.

GIRL. Oh . . . ! *Pause.*

STUDENT. Do you know how I am thinking about you now?

GIRL. Don't tell me, or I shall die.

STUDENT. I must, or I shall die.

GIRL. It is in asylums that people say everything they think.

STUDENT. Exactly. My father finished up in an asylum.

GIRL. Was he ill?

STUDENT. No, he was well, but he was mad. You see, he broke out once—in these circumstances. Like all of us, he was surrounded with a circle of acquaintances; he called them friends for short. They were a lot of rotters, of course, as most people are, but he had to have some society—he couldn't get on all alone. Well, as you know, in everyday life no one tells people what he thinks of them, and he didn't either. He knew perfectly well what frauds they were—he'd sounded the depths of their deceit—but as he was a wise and well-bred man, he was always courteous to them. Then one day he gave a big party. It was in the evening and he was tired by the day's work and by the strain of holding his tongue and at the same time talking rubbish with his guests. . . . *The* GIRL *is frightened.* Well, at the dinner table he rapped for silence, raised his glass, and began to speak. Then something loosed the trigger. He made an enormous speech in which he stripped the whole company naked, one after the other, and told them of all their treachery. Then, tired out, he sat down on the table and told them all to go to hell.

GIRL. Oh!

STUDENT. I was there, and I shall never forget what happened then. Father and Mother came to blows, the guests rushed for the door . . . and my father was taken to a madhouse, where he died. *Pause.* Water that is still too long stagnates, and so it is in this house too. There is something stagnating here. And yet I thought it was paradise itself that first time I saw you coming in here. There I stood that Sunday morning, gazing in. I saw a Colonel who was no Colonel. I had a benefactor who was a thief and had to hang himself. I saw a mummy who was not a mummy and an old maid—what of the maidenhood, by the way? Where is beauty to be found? In nature, and in my own mind, when it is in its Sunday clothes. Where are honor and faith? In fairy-tales and children's fancies. Where is anything that fulfills its promise? In my imagination. Now your flowers have poisoned me and I have given the poison back to you. I asked you to become my wife in a home full of poetry and song and music. Then the Cook came. . . . *Sursum Corda!* * Try once more to strike fire and glory out of the golden harp. Try, I beg you, I implore you on my knees. *Pause.* Then I will do it myself. *He picks up the harp, but the strings give no sound.* It is dumb and deaf. To think that the most beautiful flowers are so poisonous, are the most poisonous. The curse lies over the whole of creation, over life itself. Why will you not be my bride? Because the very life-spring within you is sick . . . now I can feel that vampire in the kitchen beginning to suck me. I believe she is a Lamia, one of those that suck the blood of children. It is always in the kitchen quarters that the seed-

* Courage!

leaves of the children are nipped, if it has not already happened in the bedroom. There are poisons that destroy the sight and poisons that open the eyes. I seem to have been born with the latter kind, for I cannot see what is ugly as beautiful, or call evil good. I cannot. Jesus Christ descended into hell. That was His pilgrimage on earth—to this madhouse, this prison, this charnel-house, this earth. And the madmen killed Him when He wanted to set them free; but the robber they let go. The robber always gets the sympathy. Woe! Woe to us all. Saviour of the world, save us! We perish.

And now the GIRL *has drooped, and it is seen that she is dying. She rings.* BENGTSSON *enters.*

GIRL. Bring the screen. Quick. I am dying.

BENGTSSON *comes back with the screen, opens it and arranges it in front of the* GIRL.

STUDENT. The Liberator is coming. Welcome, pale and gentle one. Sleep, you lovely, innocent, doomed creature, suffering for no fault of your own. Sleep without dreaming, and when you wake again . . . may you be greeted by a sun that does not burn, in a home without dust, by friends without stain, by a love without flaw. You wise and gentle Buddha, sitting there waiting for a Heaven to sprout from the earth, grant us patience in our ordeal and purity of will, so that this hope may not be confounded.

The strings of the harp hum softly and a white light fills the room.

> I saw the sun. To me it seemed
> that I beheld the Hidden.
> Men must reap what they have sown,
> blest is he whose deeds are good.
> Deeds which you have wrought in fury,
> cannot in evil find redress.
> Comfort him you have distressed
> with loving-kindness—this will heal.
> No fear has he who does no ill.
> Sweet is innocence.

A faint moaning is heard behind the screen. You poor little child, child of this world of illusion, guilt, suffering and death, this world of endless change, disappointment, and pain. May the Lord of Heaven be merciful to you upon your journey.

The room disappears. Bœcklin's picture The Island of the Dead *is seen in the distance, and from the island comes music, soft, sweet, and melancholy.*

*

THERE ARE three scenes. They constitute a statement, a counter-statement, and a conclusion. In Scene I an old man tells a young man about the series of events that has brought him to the wheelchair, a spectator on the scene of life. Despite certain warnings (e.g., page 602), we are prepared to view the old man sympathetically throughout Scene I and part of the way through Scene II, for he is an effective advocate of his own cause. But when he is arraigned on the very charges he himself has been making against another, we are not sad or surprised that he hangs himself. Scene III is a dialogue between our young man and a young lady. Will youth succeed where age has failed? Probably not. For the wicked old man has a successor in the Cook. Evil is much the same today as yesterday. The young lady dies. The young man recommends religious resignation.

Strindberg has filled in this outline with a good deal of narrative matter. There are two "eternal triangles," and an illegitimate daughter has been born of each. Strindberg links his personages by these and several other amorous episodes of a past which is not at rest. In other words, his conception of ghosts is the same as Ibsen's. A character in another Strindberg play cries: "Everything is dug up! Everything comes back!" In the *Sonata*, ghosts appear on the stage, but more formidable are the still living older people who are but ghosts of their former selves. The old man's one-time lover is now a crazed old mummy in a closet. She thinks she is a parrot except when, with the lucid license of nightmare, she becomes sane for a moment in order to denounce her man. She is mocked by the presence of a statue of herself as she was in the days of her youth. The old man's one-time fiancée is a white-haired old lady now, but, lest we form too ideal a conception of her, we learn that she was seduced by the Colonel (whom, for that matter, our old man had cuckolded). The knots of legitimate and illegitimate relationship are tied and re-tied by Strindberg until we have a group of persons resembling a European royal family. The mummy comments: "Crime and secrets and guilt bind us together."

People have gone off, Strindberg is saying, on various journeys through life, yet they are tied to their past, to their actions, to the house where they were born. (This last item also carries us back to Ibsen and beyond.) "We have broken our bonds," says the mummy, "and gone apart innumerable times but we are always drawn together again." Guilt hangs in the air, and the crimes that lie behind it are crimes of tyrannous possession, which Strindberg represents in two recurring images—a musician might call them leitmotifs: the creditor using his power over the debtor and the vampire sucking his victim's blood:

> You murdered the Consul, who was buried today; you strangled him with debts. You have stolen the student, binding him by the pretence of a claim on his father, who never owed you a farthing. (Scene II, page 613.)

> He drank the soup stock, which the cook then filled up with water. He sat out there like a vampire, sucking the marrow out of the house . . . (Scene II, page 614.)

> She belongs to the Hummel family of vampires. She is eating us. (Scene III, page 617.)

> You drain us of sap and we drain you. (Scene III, page 619.)

> I believe she is a Lamia, one of those who suck the blood of children. (Scene III, page 621.)

Such is Strindberg's picture of life in this play. The conclusion he reaches is clear. Even the hyacinth is poisoned: there is no joy without sorrow, no life without death. The natural situation is hopeless: only supernatural mercy can save us. The play ends with what the ancients called a *deus ex machina*—a god who suddenly descends and puts everything to rights. In Strindberg it is the Christian God in the guise of poetry, soft music, and a famous painting.

If we find this ending stuck on, rather than growing out of the action, there is still much in the play to admire. The action is very clearly *seen*. It is a myth presented in terms of place. In the first scene we see the façade of the building which is our human habitation; we are outside, but we can see a little way inside. In the second scene we are in the Round Room. In the third, we are even further inside: in the Hyacinth Room. Then the whole natural world dissolves in the supernatural.

The first scene poses the question: what is behind the façade? The second scene answers the question for the old man, who dies, having got no further than the Round Room. He is a man of this world, a man of power. Power exists in time only, and stops when the clock strikes. The third scene answers the question for the young man. He gets through to the Hyacinth Room and learns of the dual nature of life, of the universality of guilt, of the hope of salvation. While in the Round Room a clock stands for time, in the Hyacinth Room a Buddha stands for eternity. The young man is not irredeemably a man of this world; he is Sunday's child; he is a seeker, a poet; he has glimpses of reality, and there is hope for him. The third scene has a double formal relationship to the previous scenes. It looks directly back to Scene I in answering the young man's query. It also directly continues the inward movement—*into* the house, *into* reality—of Scenes I and II.

What is a fantasy? *The Ghost Sonata* is a play of startling originality. Yet it is doubtful whether Strindberg regarded it as primarily a technical experiment. He was not so much trying to startle us with heterodoxy of form as to follow out his religious ideas and fancies in an appropriate way. The technical originality is a by-product of a spiritual quest. Since we have already found Ibsen's technical originality to be the by-product of a moral quest, there is food for thought here as to technique in general.

In *The Ghost Sonata* Strindberg followed out the dream, the religious vision, into some formal consequences. He was also guided, to a lesser degree, by the idea of music. The play is called a sonata. Though analogies between music and drama are never very exact, we have found them useful in connection with Shakespeare, and Strindberg compels us—by using the word *sonata*—to hear that he worked out his play in terms of changing tempo and volume. Perhaps he meant us to think of the three scenes as three "movements." He included the play in a group of "chamber plays" with opus numbers. Like chamber music, this sort of art was designed for the small auditorium, the group of connoisseurs, the intimate occasion.

We have seen that Shakespeare anchored a romance in common life by introducing a realistic subplot. The main substance of Strindberg's dream is a straightforward realism. We have already noted many similarities between *The Ghost Sonata* and *Ghosts*. Ibsen and Strindberg are treating a very similar subject-matter, and their way of seeing it is not nearly as different as we at first think. We see middle-class civilization haunted by guilt. The portrait of the old man in *The Ghost Sonata* is not less realistic than that of Manders in *Ghosts*. The Cook is not a less realistic version of malignity than Engstrand. Scene II opens with one of those revealing conversations between servants that we associate with very humdrum Ibsenite plays. And so forth.

On the other hand, though the play is pieced together from realistic particulars, the piecing is done upon "fantastic" principle. The milkmaid is an ordinary delivery girl, but she appears and disappears like a sprite. Events succeed one another with no more orderly a progression than the events of dreams. In fact, this combination of clear natural detail with unnatural sequences and juxtapositions *is* dream. In a program note to an earlier work entitled *The Dream Play,* Strindberg had written:

> In this play. . . . the author has tried to imitate the disjointed but apparently logical form of a dream. Anything may happen: everything is possible and probable. Time and space do not exist; on an insignificant groundwork of reality, imagination spins and weaves new patterns: a mixture of memories, experiences, unfettered fancies, absurdities, and improvisation.
>
> The characters are split, doubled, and multiplied: they evaporate and are condensed, are diffused and concentrated. . . .

Not all this, perhaps, applies to *The Ghost Sonata,* but knowing that Strindberg talks this way, the reader will not expect to arrive at a definitive interpretation of every detail in the play. It is not even clear (and this can be urged as an adverse criticism of Strindberg) what kind of interpretation holds. What are we entitled to take as symbolic and to what extent? Some sort of analogy is probably intended between Brynhild the Valkyrie and the young woman in the play. The young man is Siegfried? The old man Wotan?

Unless we intend to follow Strindberg into his Swedenborgian researches, we shall probably not unravel his symbols. His dream-forms will be of largely technical interest (to us if not to him). They are an attempt to break the rigid structure of plays like *Ghosts*. Their fluidity reveals to us very interesting theatrical possibilities. Consider for instance the transition from the Amen to the poem at the end of Scene II. Such a thing is inconceivable within the framework of the conventional play. Of such is the kingdom of Strindberg. . . .

However this may be, the whole discussion should make us tread warily among terms. The term *realism* may today have more in it than the term *tragedy,* but it is no easier to use. In speaking of art, we have always to make sure that we are using our terms—and not being used by them. That we cannot give a cut-and-dried definition of tragedy or even of realism is very well, provided we always remember the fact and do not fall into the habit of regarding our pet terms as realities prior to the works of art they are supposed to help us describe. If we must have a formula, let it be: when confused by descriptions and denominations, return to the facts—to the plays—themselves.

DEATH OF A SALESMAN

Drawn by Robert Mackintosh from the setting by Jo Mielziner

9. DEATH OF A SALESMAN · 1949

WITH *The Ghost Sonata* this little course in drama ends. But the reader may want to take stock, to see whether he seems to have made any progress in understanding dramatic art. To the cycle of plays ancient and modern which have made up the course is now added a specimen of native American drama. Here is the kind of thing which the reader may expect to be confronted with if he leaves his room and actually goes to the theater in America. In a way, we are now returning to our starting-point, to drama which is fairly close to our own experience, which presupposes no special knowledge, which makes no special demands. Can we cope with it better than we could have at the outset? Does our analysis of other plays help us analyze this one? Can we point to any particular merits the play may possess? To any shortcomings or faults? It is suggested that the play be read twice, that the reader then constitute himself a drama critic and write a notice of the play as if he had just witnessed a performance. Afterwards he should compare his notice with the others hereafter appended—the notices which the New York production actually received—and discuss with friends or with himself the rights and wrongs of the case. Since the critics are so much at odds, the reader will find himself forced into judging independently. The criterion of this whole course will be whether he prove equal to the situation.

Admittedly, if he is unsure whether he has proved equal to the occasion or not, there are no acknowledged authorities or generally accepted standards for him to appeal to. The critics printed below are at odds not only as to *Death of a Salesman* but also as to drama—and the arts—generally, a fact which leads us beyond the frontiers of the present course. To ask how such a situation has come into being, and what consequences it has brought in its train, is to begin to analyze all modern culture.

Short of embarking on such an analysis, we can content ourselves with an observation and a query which directly concern our present study. Some of our critics, it can scarcely be doubted, would find the method and presuppositions of this book quite erroneous. At any rate the demands they make on *Death of a Salesman* are not those we have been making on the eight preceding plays. Who is right? What are the pertinent questions to ask of a play? Have we been on the wrong track all this while? Or . . . ?

DEATH OF A SALESMAN

by Arthur Miller

∗

Copyright 1949 by Arthur Miller. Reprinted by permission of The Viking Press, Inc. All rights reserved: no public or private performance of the play, professional or amateur, may be given; no film, radio or television use or public reading, without authorization from the author's representative, MCA Management, Ltd., 444 Madison Ave., New York 22. For permission to reprint excerpts from the play, address The Viking Press, Inc., 18 E. 48th St., New York 17.

Death of a Salesman

Characters

WILLY LOMAN	UNCLE BEN
LINDA	HOWARD WAGNER
BIFF	JENNY
HAPPY	STANLEY
BERNARD	MISS FORSYTHE
THE WOMAN	LETTA
CHARLEY	

THE PLACE: *Willy Loman's house and yard and various places he visits in the New York and Boston of today.*

Throughout the play, in the stage directions, left and right mean stage left and stage right.

Act I

A melody is heard, played upon a flute. It is small and fine, telling of grass and trees and the horizon. The curtain rises.

Before us is the Salesman's house. We are aware of towering, angular shapes behind it, surrounding it on all sides. Only the blue light of the sky falls upon the house and forestage; the surrounding area shows an angry glow of orange. As more light appears, we see a solid vault of apartment houses around the small, fragile-seeming home. An air of the dream clings to the place, a dream rising out of reality. The kitchen at center seems actual enough, for there is a kitchen table with three chairs, and a refrigerator. But no other fixtures are seen. At the back of the kitchen there is a draped entrance, which leads to the living-room. To the right of the kitchen, on a level raised two feet, is a bedroom furnished only with a brass bedstead and a straight chair. On a shelf over the bed a silver athletic trophy stands. A window opens onto the apartment house at the side.

Behind the kitchen, on a level raised six and a half feet, is the boys' bedroom, at present barely visible. Two beds are dimly seen, and at the back of the room a dormer window. (This bedroom is above the unseen living-room.) At the left a stairway curves up to it from the kitchen.

The entire setting is wholly or, in some places, partially transparent. The roof-line of the house is one-dimensional; under and over it we see the apartment buildings. Before the house lies an apron, curving beyond the forestage into the orchestra. This forward area serves as the back yard as well as the locale of all WILLY'S *imaginings and of his city scenes. Whenever the action is in the present the actors observe the imaginary wall-lines, entering the house only through its door at the left. But in the scenes of the past these boundaries are broken, and characters enter or leave a room by stepping "through" a wall onto the forestage.*

From the right, WILLY LOMAN, *the Salesman, enters, carrying two large sample cases. The flute plays on. He hears but is not aware of it. He is past sixty years of age, dressed quietly. Even as he crosses the stage to the doorway of the house, his exhaustion is apparent. He unlocks the door, comes into the kitchen, and thankfully lets his burden down, feeling the soreness of his palms. A word-sigh escapes his lips —it might be "Oh, boy, oh, boy." He closes the door, then carries his cases out into the living-room, through the draped kitchen doorway.*

LINDA, *his wife, has stirred in her bed at the right. She gets out and puts on a robe, listening. Most often jovial, she has developed an iron repression of her exceptions to* WILLY'S *behavior—she more than loves him, she admires him, as though his mercurial nature, his temper, his massive dreams and little cruelties, served her only as sharp reminders of the turbulent longings within him, longings which she shares but lacks the temperament to utter and follow to their end.*

LINDA, *hearing* WILLY *outside the bedroom, calls with some trepidation.* Willy!

ACT I] DEATH OF A SALESMAN 635

WILLY. It's all right. I came back.

LINDA. Why? What happened? *Slight pause.* Did something happen, Willy?

WILLY. No, nothing happened.

LINDA. You didn't smash the car, did you?

WILLY, *with casual irritation.* I said nothing happened. Didn't you hear me?

LINDA. Don't you feel well?

WILLY. I'm tired to the death. *The flute has faded away. He sits on the bed beside her, a little numb.* I couldn't make it. I just couldn't make it, Linda.

LINDA, *very carefully, delicately.* Where were you all day? You look terrible.

WILLY. I got as far as a little above Yonkers. I stopped for a cup of coffee. Maybe it was the coffee.

LINDA. What?

WILLY, *after a pause.* I suddenly couldn't drive any more. The car kept going off onto the shoulder, y'know?

LINDA, *helpfully.* Oh. Maybe it was the steering again. I don't think Angelo knows the Studebaker.

WILLY. No, it's me, it's me. Suddenly I realize I'm goin' sixty miles an hour and I don't remember the last five minutes. I'm—I can't seem to—keep my mind to it.

LINDA. Maybe it's your glasses. You never went for your new glasses.

WILLY. No, I see everything. I came back ten miles an hour. It took me nearly four hours from Yonkers.

LINDA, *resigned.* Well, you'll just have to take a rest, Willy, you can't continue this way.

WILLY. I just got back from Florida.

LINDA. But you didn't rest your mind. Your mind is overactive, and the mind is what counts, dear.

WILLY. I'll start out in the morning. Maybe I'll feel better in the morning. *She is taking off his shoes.* These goddam arch supports are killing me.

LINDA. Take an aspirin. Should I get you an aspirin? It'll soothe you.

WILLY, *with wonder.* I was driving along, you understand? And I was fine. I was even observing the scenery. You can imagine, me looking at scenery, on the road every week of my life. But it's so beautiful up there, Linda, the trees are so thick, and the sun is warm. I opened the windshield and just let the warm air bathe over me. And then all of a sudden I'm goin' off the road! I'm tellin' ya, I absolutely forgot I was driving. If I'd've gone the other way over the white line I might've killed somebody. So I went on again—and five minutes later I'm dreamin' again, and I nearly— *He presses two fingers against his eyes.* I have such thoughts, I have such strange thoughts.

LINDA. Willy, dear. Talk to them again. There's no reason why you can't work in New York.

WILLY. They don't need me in New York. I'm the New England man. I'm vital in New England.

LINDA. But you're sixty years old. They can't expect you to keep traveling every week.

WILLY. I'll have to send a wire to Portland. I'm supposed to see Brown and Morrison tomorrow morning at ten o'clock to show the line. Goddammit, I could sell them! *He starts putting on his jacket.*

LINDA, *taking the jacket from him.* Why don't you go down to the place tomorrow and tell Howard you've simply got to work in New York? You're too accommodating, dear.

WILLY. If old man Wagner was alive I'd a been in charge of New York now! That man was a prince, he was a masterful man. But that boy of his, that Howard, he don't appreciate. When I went north the first time, the Wagner Company didn't know where New England was!

LINDA. Why don't you tell those things to Howard, dear?

WILLY, *encouraged.* I will, I definitely will. Is there any cheese?

LINDA. I'll make you a sandwich.

WILLY. No, go to sleep. I'll take some milk. I'll be up right away. The boys in?

LINDA. They're sleeping. Happy took Biff on a date tonight.

WILLY, *interested.* That so?

LINDA. It was so nice to see them shaving together, one behind the other, in the bathroom. And going out together. You notice? The whole house smells of shaving lotion.

WILLY. Figure it out. Work a lifetime to pay off a house. You finally own it, and there's nobody to live in it.

LINDA. Well, dear, life is a casting off. It's always that way.

WILLY. No, no, some people—some people accomplish something. Did Biff say anything after I went this morning?

LINDA. You shouldn't have criticized him, Willy, especially after he just got off the train. You mustn't lose your temper with him.

WILLY. When the hell did I lose my temper? I simply asked him if he was making any money. Is that a criticism?

LINDA. But, dear, how could he make any money?

WILLY, *worried and angered*. There's such an undercurrent in him. He became a moody man. Did he apologize when I left this morning?

LINDA. He was crestfallen, Willy. You know how he admires you. I think if he finds himself, then you'll both be happier and not fight any more.

WILLY. How can he find himself on a farm? Is that a life? A farmhand? In the beginning, when he was young, I thought, well, a young man, it's good for him to tramp around, take a lot of different jobs. But it's more than ten years now and he has yet to make thirty-five dollars a week!

LINDA. He's finding himself, Willy.

WILLY. Not finding yourself at the age of thirty-four is a disgrace!

LINDA. Shh!

WILLY. The trouble is he's lazy, goddammit!

LINDA. Willy, please!

WILLY. Biff is a lazy bum!

LINDA. They're sleeping. Get something to eat. Go on down.

WILLY. Why did he come home? I would like to know what brought him home.

LINDA. I don't know. I think he's still lost, Willy. I think he's very lost.

WILLY. Biff Loman is lost. In the greatest country in the world a young man with such—personal attractiveness, gets lost. And such a hard worker. There's one thing about Biff—he's not lazy.

LINDA. Never.

WILLY, *with pity and resolve*. I'll see him in the morning; I'll have a nice talk with him. I'll get him a job selling. He could be big in no time. My God! Remember how they used to follow him around in high school? When he smiled at one of them their faces lit up. When he walked down the street. . . . *He loses himself in reminiscences.*

LINDA, *trying to bring him out of it.* Willy, dear, I got a new kind of American-type cheese today. It's whipped.

WILLY. Why do you get American when I like Swiss?

LINDA. I just thought you'd like a change—

WILLY. I don't want a change! I want Swiss cheese. Why am I always being contradicted?

LINDA, *with a covering laugh.* I thought it would be a surprise.

WILLY. Why don't you open a window in here, for God's sake?

LINDA, *with infinite patience.* They're all open, dear.

WILLY. The way they boxed us in here. Bricks and windows, windows and bricks.

LINDA. We should've bought the land next door.

WILLY. The street is lined with cars. There's not a breath of fresh air in the neighborhood. The grass don't grow any more, you can't raise a carrot in the back yard. They should've had a law against apartment houses. Remember those two beautiful elm trees out there? When I and Biff hung the swing between them?

LINDA. Yeah, like being a million miles from the city.

WILLY. They should've arrested the builder for cutting those down. They massacred the neighborhood. *Lost.* More and more I think of those days, Linda. This time of year it was lilac and wisteria. And then the peonies would come out, and the daffodils. What fragrance in this room!

LINDA. Well, after all, people had to move somewhere.

WILLY. No, there's more people now.

LINDA. I don't think there's more people. I think—

WILLY. There's more people! That's what's ruining this country! Population is getting out of control. The competition is maddening! Smell the stink from that apartment house! And another one on the other side . . . How can they whip cheese?

On WILLY's *last line,* BIFF *and* HAPPY *raise themselves up in their beds, listening.*

LINDA. Go down, try it. And be quiet.

WILLY, *turning to* LINDA, *guiltily.* You're not worried about me, are you, sweetheart?

BIFF. What's the matter?

HAPPY. Listen!

LINDA. You've got too much on the ball to worry about.

WILLY. You're my foundation and my support, Linda.

LINDA. Just try to relax, dear. You make mountains out of molehills.

WILLY. I won't fight with him any more. If he wants to go back to Texas, let him go.

LINDA. He'll find his way.

WILLY. Sure. Certain men just don't get started till later in life. Like Thomas Edison, I think. Or B. F. Goodrich. One of them was deaf. *He starts for the bedroom doorway.* I'll put my money on Biff.

LINDA. And Willy—if it's warm Sunday we'll drive in the country. And we'll open the windshield, and take lunch.

WILLY. No, the windshields don't open on the new cars.

LINDA. But you opened it today.

WILLY. Me? I didn't. *He stops.* Now isn't that peculiar! Isn't that a remarkable— *He breaks off in amazement and fright as the flute is heard distantly.*

LINDA. What, darling?

WILLY. That is the most remarkable thing.

LINDA. What, dear?

WILLY. I was thinking of the Chevvy. *Slight pause.* Nineteen twenty-eight . . . when I had that red Chevvy— *Breaks off.* That funny? I coulda sworn I was driving that Chevvy today.

LINDA. Well, that's nothing. Something must've reminded you.

WILLY. Remarkable. Ts. Remember those days? The way Biff used to simonize that car? The dealer refused to believe there was eighty thousand miles on it. *He shakes his head.* Heh! *To Linda.* Close your eyes, I'll be right up. *He walks out of the bedroom.*

HAPPY, *to* BIFF. Jesus, maybe he smashed up the car again!

LINDA, *calling after* WILLY. Be careful on the stairs, dear! The cheese is on the middle shelf! *She turns, goes over to the bed, takes his jacket, and goes out of the bedroom.*

Light has risen on the boys' room. Unseen, WILLY *is heard talking to himself,* "Eighty thousand miles," *and a little laugh.* BIFF *gets out of bed, comes downstage a bit, and stands attentively.* BIFF *is two years older than his brother* HAPPY, *well built, but in these days bears a worn air and seems less self-assured. He has succeeded less, and his dreams are stronger and less acceptable than* HAPPY'S. HAPPY *is tall, powerfully made. Sexuality is like a visible color on him, or a scent that many women have discovered. He, like his brother, is lost, but in a different way, for he has never allowed himself to turn his face toward defeat and is thus more confused and hard-skinned, although seemingly more content.*

HAPPY, *getting out of bed.* He's going to get his license taken away if he keeps that up. I'm getting nervous about him, y'know, Biff?

BIFF. His eyes are going.

HAPPY. No, I've driven with him. He sees all right. He just doesn't keep his mind on it. I drove into the city with him last week. He stops at a green light and then it turns red and he goes. *He laughs.*

BIFF. Maybe he's color-blind.

HAPPY. Pop? Why he's got the finest eye for color in the business. You know that.

BIFF, *sitting down on his bed.* I'm going to sleep.

HAPPY. You're not still sour on Dad, are you, Biff?

BIFF. He's all right, I guess.

WILLY, *underneath them, in the living-room.* Yes, sir, eighty thousand miles—eighty-two thousand!

BIFF. You smoking?

HAPPY, *holding out a pack of cigarettes.* Want one?

BIFF, *taking a cigarette.* I can never sleep when I smell it.

WILLY. What a simonizing job, heh!

HAPPY, *with deep sentiment.* Funny, Biff, y'know? Us sleeping in here again? The old beds. *He pats his bed affectionately.* All the talk that went across those two beds, huh? Our whole lives.

BIFF. Yeah. Lotta dreams and plans.

HAPPY, *with a deep and masculine laugh.* About five hundred women would like to know what was said in this room.

They share a soft laugh.

BIFF. Remember that big Betsy something—what the hell was her name—over on Bushwick Avenue?

HAPPY, *combing his hair.* With the collie dog!

BIFF. That's the one. I got you in there, remember?

HAPPY. Yeah, that was my first time—I think. Boy, there was a pig! *They laugh, almost crudely.* You taught me everything I know about women. Don't forget that.

BIFF. I bet you forgot how bashful you used to be. Especially with girls.

HAPPY. Oh, I still am, Biff.

BIFF. Oh, go on.

HAPPY. I just control it, that's all. I think I got less bashful and you got more so. What happened, Biff? Where's the old humor, the old confidence? *He shakes* BIFF's *knee.* BIFF *gets up and moves restlessly about the room.* What's the matter?

BIFF. Why does Dad mock me all the time?

HAPPY. He's not mocking you, he—

BIFF. Everything I say there's a twist of mockery on his face. I can't get near him.

HAPPY. He just wants you to make good, that's all. I wanted to talk to you about Dad for a long time, Biff. Something's—happening to him. He—talks to himself.

BIFF. I noticed that this morning. But he always mumbled.

HAPPY. But not so noticeable. It got so embarrassing I sent him to Florida. And you know something? Most of the time he's talking to you.

BIFF. What's he say about me?

HAPPY. I can't make it out.

BIFF. What's he say about me?

HAPPY. I think the fact that you're not settled, that you're still kind of up in the air . . .

BIFF. There's one or two other things depressing him, Happy.

HAPPY. What do you mean?

BIFF. Never mind. Just don't lay it all to me.

HAPPY. But I think if you just got started—I mean—is there any future for you out there?

BIFF. I tell ya, Hap, I don't know what the future is. I don't know —what I'm supposed to want.

HAPPY. What do you mean?

BIFF. Well, I spent six or seven years after high school trying to work myself up. Shipping clerk, salesman, business of one kind or another. And it's a measly manner of existence. To get on that subway on the hot mornings in summer. To devote your whole life to keeping stock, or making phone calls, or selling or buying. To suffer fifty weeks of the year for the sake of a two-week vacation, when all you really desire is to be outdoors, with your shirt off. And always to have to get ahead of the next fella. And still—that's how you build a future.

HAPPY. Well, you really enjoy it on a farm? Are you content out there?

BIFF, *with rising agitation*. Hap, I've had twenty or thirty different kinds of jobs since I left home before the war, and it always turns out the same. I just realized it lately. In Nebraska when I herded cattle, and the Dakotas, and Arizona, and now in Texas. It's why I came home now, I guess, because I realized it. This farm I work on, it's spring there now, see? And they've got about fifteen new colts. There's nothing more inspiring or—beautiful than the sight of a mare and a new colt. And it's cool there now, see? Texas is cool now, and it's spring. And whenever spring comes to where I am, I suddenly get the feeling, my God, I'm not gettin' anywhere! What the hell am I doing, playing around with horses, twenty-eight dollars a week! I'm thirty-four years old, I oughta be makin' my future. That's when I come running home. And now, I get here, and I don't know what to do with myself. *After a pause*. I've always made a point of not wasting my life, and everytime I come back here I know that all I've done is to waste my life.

HAPPY. You're a poet, you know that, Biff? You're a—you're an idealist!

BIFF. No, I'm mixed up very bad. Maybe I oughta get married. Maybe I oughta get stuck into something. Maybe that's my trouble. I'm like a boy. I'm not married, I'm not in business, I just—I'm like a boy. Are you content, Hap? You're a success, aren't you? Are you content?

HAPPY. Hell, no!

BIFF. Why? You're making money, aren't you?

HAPPY, *moving about with energy, expressiveness*. All I can do now is wait for the merchandise manager to die. And suppose I get to be merchandise manager? He's a good friend of mine, and he just built a terrific estate on Long Island. And he lived there about two months and sold it, and now he's building another one. He can't enjoy it once it's finished. And I know that's just what I would do. I don't know what the hell I'm workin' for. Sometimes I sit in my apartment—all alone. And I think of the rent I'm paying. And it's crazy. But then, it's what I always wanted. My own apartment, a car, and plenty of women. And still, goddammit, I'm lonely.

BIFF, *with enthusiasm*. Listen, why don't you come out West with me?

HAPPY. You and I, heh?

BIFF. Sure, maybe we could buy a ranch. Raise cattle, use our muscles. Men built like we are should be working out in the open.

HAPPY, *avidly*. The Loman Brothers, heh?

BIFF, *with vast affection*. Sure, we'd be known all over the counties!

HAPPY, *enthralled*. That's what I dream about, Biff. Sometimes I want to just rip my clothes off in the middle of the store and outbox that goddam merchandise manager. I mean I can outbox, outrun, and outlift anybody in that store, and I have to take orders from those common, petty sons-of-bitches till I can't stand it any more.

BIFF. I'm tellin' you, kid, if you were with me I'd be happy out there.

HAPPY, *enthused*. See, Biff, everybody around me is so false that I'm constantly lowering my ideals. . . .

BIFF. Baby, together we'd stand up for one another, we'd have someone to trust.

HAPPY. If I were around you—

BIFF. Hap, the trouble is we weren't brought up to grub for money. I don't know how to do it.

HAPPY. Neither can I!

BIFF. Then let's go!

HAPPY. The only thing is—what can you make out there?

BIFF. But look at your friend. Builds an estate and then hasn't the peace of mind to live in it.

HAPPY. Yeah, but when he walks into the store the waves part in front of him. That's fifty-two thousand dollars a year coming through the revolving door, and I got more in my pinky finger than he's got in his head.

BIFF. Yeah, but you just said—

HAPPY. I gotta show some of those pompous, self-important executives over there that Hap Loman can make the grade. I want to walk into the store the way he walks in. Then I'll go with you, Biff. We'll be together yet, I swear. But take those two we had tonight. Now weren't they gorgeous creatures?

BIFF. Yeah, yeah, most gorgeous I've had in years.

HAPPY. I get that any time I want, Biff. Whenever I feel disgusted. The only trouble is, it gets like bowling or something. I just keep knockin' them over and it doesn't mean anything. You still run around a lot?

BIFF. Naa. I'd like to find a girl—steady, somebody with substance.

HAPPY. That's what I long for.

BIFF. Go on! You'd never come home.

HAPPY. I would! Somebody with character, with resistance! Like Mom, y'know? You're gonna call me a bastard when I tell you this. That girl Charlotte I was with tonight is engaged to be married in five weeks. *He tries on his new hat.*

BIFF. No kiddin'!

HAPPY. Sure, the guy's in line for the vice-presidency of the store. I don't know what gets into me, maybe I just have an overdeveloped sense of competition or something, but I went and ruined her, and furthermore I can't get rid of her. And he's the third executive I've done that to. Isn't that a crummy characteristic? And to top it all, I go to their weddings! *Indignantly, but laughing.* Like I'm not supposed to take bribes. Manufacturers offer me a hundred-dollar bill now and then to throw an order their way. You know how honest I am, but it's like this girl, see. I hate myself for it. Because I don't want the girl, and, still, I take it and—I love it!

BIFF. Let's go to sleep.

HAPPY. I guess we didn't settle anything, heh?

BIFF. I just got one idea that I think I'm going to try.

HAPPY. What's that?

BIFF. Remember Bill Oliver?

HAPPY. Sure, Oliver is very big now. You want to work for him again?

BIFF. No, but when I quit he said something to me. He put his arm on my shoulder, and he said, "Biff, if you ever need anything, come to me."

HAPPY. I remember that. That sounds good.

BIFF. I think I'll go to see him. If I could get ten thousand or even seven or eight thousand dollars I could buy a beautiful ranch.

HAPPY. I bet he'd back you. 'Cause he thought highly of you, Biff. I mean, they all do. You're well liked, Biff. That's why I say to come back here, and we both have the apartment. And I'm tellin' you, Biff, any babe you want. . . .

BIFF. No, with a ranch I could do the work I like and still be something. I just wonder though. I wonder if Oliver still thinks I stole that carton of basketballs.

HAPPY. Oh, he probably forgot that long ago. It's almost ten years. You're too sensitive. Anyway, he didn't really fire you.

BIFF. Well, I think he was going to. I think that's why I quit. I was never sure whether he knew or not. I know he thought the world of me, though. I was the only one he'd let lock up the place.

WILLY, *below*. You gonna wash the engine, Biff?

HAPPY. Shh!

BIFF *looks at* HAPPY, *who is gazing down, listening.* WILLY *is mumbling in the parlor.*

HAPPY. You hear that?

They listen. WILLY *laughs warmly.*

BIFF, *growing angry*. Doesn't he know Mom can hear that?

WILLY. Don't get your sweater dirty, Biff!

A look of pain crosses BIFF'S *face.*

HAPPY. Isn't that terrible? Don't leave again, will you? You'll find a job here. You gotta stick around. I don't know what to do about him, it's getting embarrassing.

WILLY. What a simonizing job!

BIFF. Mom's hearing that!

WILLY. No kiddin', Biff, you got a date? Wonderful!

HAPPY. Go on to sleep. But talk to him in the morning, will you?

BIFF, *reluctantly getting into bed*. With her in the house. Brother!

HAPPY, *getting into bed*. I wish you'd have a good talk with him.

The light on their room begins to fade.

BIFF, *to himself in bed.* That selfish, stupid . . .

HAPPY. Sh . . . Sleep, Biff.

Their light is out. Well before they have finished speaking, WILLY's form is dimly seen below in the darkened kitchen. He opens the refrigerator, searches in there, and takes out a bottle of milk. The apartment houses are fading out, and the entire house and surroundings become covered with leaves. Music insinuates itself as the leaves appear.

WILLY. Just wanna be careful with those girls, Biff, that's all. Don't make any promises. No promises of any kind. Because a girl, y'know, they always believe what you tell 'em, and you're very young, Biff, you're too young to be talking seriously to girls.

Light rises on the kitchen. WILLY, talking, shuts the refrigerator door and comes downstage to the kitchen table. He pours milk into a glass. He is totally immersed in himself, smiling faintly.

WILLY. Too young entirely, Biff. You want to watch your schooling first. Then when you're all set, there'll be plenty of girls for a boy like you. *He smiles broadly at a kitchen chair.* That so? The girls pay for you? *He laughs.* Boy, you must really be makin' a hit.

WILLY *is gradually addressing—physically—a point offstage, speaking through the wall of the kitchen, and his voice has been rising in volume to that of a normal conversation.*

WILLY. I been wondering why you polish the car so careful. Ha! Don't leave the hubcaps, boys. Get the chamois to the hubcaps. Happy, use newspaper on the windows, it's the easiest thing. Show him how to do it, Biff! You see, Happy? Pad it up, use it like a pad. That's it, that's it, good work. You're doin' all right, Hap. *He pauses, then nods in approbation for a few seconds, then looks upward.* Biff, first thing we gotta do when we get time is clip that big branch over the house. Afraid it's gonna fall in a storm and hit the roof. Tell you what. We get a rope and sling her around, and then we climb up there with a couple of saws and take her down. Soon as you finish the car, boys, I wanna see ya. I got a surprise for you, boys.

BIFF, *offstage.* Whatta ya got, Dad?

WILLY. No, you finish first. Never leave a job till you're finished—

ACT I] DEATH OF A SALESMAN 647

remember that. *Looking toward the "big trees."* Biff, up in Albany I saw a beautiful hammock. I think I'll buy it next trip, and we'll hang it right between those two elms. Wouldn't that be something? Just swingin' there under those branches. Boy, that would be. . . .

Young BIFF *and Young* HAPPY *appear from the direction* WILLY *was addressing.* HAPPY *carries rags and a pail of water.* BIFF, *wearing a sweater with a block "S," carries a football.*

BIFF, *pointing in the direction of the car offstage.* How's that, Pop, professional?

WILLY. Terrific. Terrific job, boys. Good work, Biff.

HAPPY. Where's the surprise, Pop?

WILLY. In the back seat of the car.

HAPPY. Boy! *He runs off.*

BIFF. What is it, Dad? Tell me, what'd you buy?

WILLY, *laughing, cuffs him.* Never mind, something I want you to have.

BIFF, *turns and starts off.* What is it, Hap?

HAPPY, *offstage.* It's a punching bag!

BIFF. Oh, Pop!

WILLY. It's got Gene Tunney's signature on it!

HAPPY *runs onstage with a punching bag.*

BIFF. Gee, how'd you know we wanted a punching bag?

WILLY. Well, it's the finest thing for the timing.

HAPPY, *lies down on his back and pedals with his feet.* I'm losing weight, you notice, Pop?

WILLY, *to* HAPPY. Jumping rope is good too.

BIFF. Did you see the new football I got?

WILLY, *examining the ball.* Where'd you get a new ball?

BIFF. The coach told me to practice my passing.

WILLY. That so? And he gave you the ball, heh?

BIFF. Well, I borrowed it from the locker room. *He laughs confidentially.*

WILLY, *laughing with him at the theft.* I want you to return that.

HAPPY. I told you he wouldn't like it!

BIFF, *angrily.* Well, I'm bringing it back!

WILLY, *stopping the incipient argument, to* HAPPY. Sure, he's gotta practice with a regulation ball, doesn't he? *To* BIFF. Coach'll probably congratulate you on your initiative!

BIFF. Oh, he keeps congratulating my initiative all the time, Pop.

WILLY. That's because he likes you. If somebody else took that ball there'd be an uproar. So what's the report, boys, what's the report?

BIFF. Where'd you go this time, Dad? Gee we were lonesome for you.

WILLY, *pleased, puts an arm around each boy and they come down to the apron.* Lonesome, heh?

BIFF. Missed you every minute.

WILLY. Don't say? Tell you a secret, boys. Don't breathe it to a soul. Someday I'll have my own business, and I'll never have to leave home any more.

HAPPY. Like Uncle Charley, heh?

WILLY. Bigger than Uncle Charley! Because Charley is not—liked. He's liked, but he's not—well liked.

BIFF. Where'd you go this time, Dad?

WILLY. Well, I got on the road, and I went north to Providence. Met the Mayor.

BIFF. The Mayor of Providence!

WILLY. He was sitting in the hotel lobby.

BIFF. What'd he say?

WILLY. He said, "Morning!" And I said, "You got a fine city here, Mayor." And then he had coffee with me. And then I went to Waterbury. Waterbury is a fine city. Big clock city, the famous Waterbury clock. Sold a nice bill there. And then Boston—Boston is the cradle of the Revolution. A fine city. And a couple of other towns in Mass., and on to Portland and Bangor and straight home!

BIFF. Gee, I'd love to go with you sometime, Dad.

WILLY. Soon as summer comes.

HAPPY. Promise?

WILLY. You and Hap and I, and I'll show you all the towns. America is full of beautiful towns and fine, upstanding people. And they know me, boys, they know me up and down New England. The finest people. And when I bring you fellas up, there'll be open sesame for all of us, 'cause one thing, boys: I have friends. I can park my car in any street in New England, and the cops protect it like their own. This summer, heh?

BIFF *and* HAPPY, *together*. Yeah! You bet!

WILLY. We'll take our bathing suits.

HAPPY. We'll carry your bags, Pop!

WILLY. Oh, won't that be something! Me comin' into the Boston stores with you boys carryin' my bags. What a sensation!

BIFF *is prancing around, practicing passing the ball.*

WILLY. You nervous, Biff, about the game?

BIFF. Not if you're gonna be there.

WILLY. What do they say about you in school, now that they made you captain?

HAPPY. There's a crowd of girls behind him everytime the classes change.

BIFF, *taking* WILLY's *hand*. This Saturday, Pop, this Saturday—just for you, I'm going to break through for a touchdown.

HAPPY. You're supposed to pass.

BIFF. I'm takin' one play for Pop. You watch me, Pop, and when I take off my helmet, that means I'm breakin' out. Then you watch me crash through that line!

WILLY, *kisses* BIFF. Oh, wait'll I tell this in Boston!

BERNARD *enters in knickers. He is younger than* BIFF, *earnest and loyal, a worried boy.*

BERNARD. Biff, where are you? You're supposed to study with me today.

WILLY. Hey, looka Bernard. What're you lookin' so anemic about, Bernard?

BERNARD. He's gotta study, Uncle Willy. He's got Regents next week.

HAPPY, *tauntingly, spinning* BERNARD *around*. Let's box, Bernard!

BERNARD. Biff! *He gets away from* HAPPY. Listen, Biff, I heard Mr. Birnbaum say that if you don't start studyin' math he's gonna flunk you, and you won't graduate. I heard him!

WILLY. You better study with him, Biff. Go ahead now.

BERNARD. I heard him!

BIFF. Oh, Pop, you didn't see my sneakers! *He holds up a foot for* WILLY *to look at.*

WILLY. Hey, that's a beautiful job of printing!

BERNARD, *wiping his glasses*. Just because he printed University of Virginia on his sneakers doesn't mean they've got to graduate him, Uncle Willy!

WILLY, *angrily*. What're you talking about? With scholarships to three universities they're gonna flunk him?

BERNARD. But I heard Mr. Birnbaum say—

WILLY. Don't be a pest, Bernard! *To his boys*. What an anemic!

BERNARD. Okay, I'm waiting for you in my house, Biff.

BERNARD goes off. The Lomans laugh.

WILLY. Bernard is not well liked, is he?

BIFF. He's liked, but he's not well liked.

HAPPY. That's right, Pop.

WILLY. That's just what I mean. Bernard can get the best marks in school, y'understand, but when he gets out in the business world, y'understand, you are going to be five times ahead of him. That's why I thank Almighty God you're both built like Adonises. Because the man who makes an appearance in the business world, the man who creates personal interest, is the man who gets ahead. Be liked and you will never want. You take me, for instance. I never have to wait in line to see a buyer. "Willy Loman is here!" That's all they have to know, and I go right through.

BIFF. Did you knock them dead, Pop?

WILLY. Knocked 'em cold in Providence, slaughtered 'em in Boston.

HAPPY, *on his back, pedaling again*. I'm losing weight, you notice, Pop?

LINDA enters, as of old, a ribbon in her hair, carrying a basket of washing.

LINDA, *with youthful energy*. Hello, dear!

WILLY. Sweetheart!

LINDA. How'd the Chevvy run?

WILLY. Chevrolet, Linda, is the greatest car ever built. *To the boys*. Since when do you let your mother carry wash up the stairs?

BIFF. Grab hold there, boy!

HAPPY. Where to, Mom?

LINDA. Hang them up on the line. And you better go down to your friends, Biff. The cellar is full of boys. They don't know what to do with themselves.

BIFF. Ah, when Pop comes home they can wait!

WILLY, *laughs appreciatively.* You better go down and tell them what to do, Biff.

BIFF. I think I'll have them sweep out the furnace room.

WILLY. Good work, Biff.

BIFF, *goes through wall-line of kitchen to doorway at back and calls down.* Fellas! Everybody sweep out the furnace room! I'll be right down!

VOICES. All right! Okay, Biff.

BIFF. George and Sam and Frank, come out back! We're hangin' up the wash! Come on, Hap, on the double! *He and* HAPPY *carry out the basket.*

LINDA. The way they obey him!

WILLY. Well, that's training, the training. I'm tellin' you, I was sellin' thousands and thousands, but I had to come home.

LINDA. Oh, the whole block'll be at that game. Did you sell anything?

WILLY. I did five hundred gross in Providence and seven hundred gross in Boston.

LINDA. No! Wait a minute, I've got a pencil. *She pulls pencil and paper out of her apron pocket.* That makes your commission. . . . Two hundred—my God! Two hundred and twelve dollars!

WILLY. Well, I didn't figure it yet, but. . . .

LINDA. How much did you do?

WILLY. Well, I—I did—about a hundred and eighty gross in Providence. Well, no—it came to—roughly two hundred gross on the whole trip.

LINDA, *without hesitation.* Two hundred gross. That's. . . . *She figures.*

WILLY. The trouble was that three of the stores were half closed for inventory in Boston. Otherwise I woulda broke records.

LINDA. Well, it makes seventy dollars and some pennies. That's very good.

WILLY. What do we owe?

LINDA. Well, on the first there's sixteen dollars on the refrigerator—

WILLY. Why sixteen?

LINDA. Well, the fan belt broke, so it was a dollar eighty.

WILLY. But it's brand new.

LINDA. Well, the man said that's the way it is. Till they work themselves in, y'know.

They move through the wall-line into the kitchen.

WILLY. I hope we didn't get stuck on that machine.

LINDA. They got the biggest ads of any of them!

WILLY. I know, it's a fine machine. What else?

LINDA. Well, there's nine-sixty for the washing machine. And for the vacuum cleaner there's three and a half due on the fifteenth. Then the roof, you got twenty-one dollars remaining.

WILLY. It don't leak, does it?

LINDA. No, they did a wonderful job. Then you owe Frank for the carburetor.

WILLY. I'm not going to pay that man! That goddam Chevrolet, they ought to prohibit the manufacture of that car!

LINDA. Well, you owe him three and a half. And odds and ends, comes to around a hundred and twenty dollars by the fifteenth.

WILLY. A hundred and twenty dollars! My God, if business don't pick up I don't know what I'm gonna do!

LINDA. Well, next week you'll do better.

WILLY. Oh, I'll knock 'em dead next week. I'll go to Hartford. I'm very well liked in Hartford. You know, the trouble is, Linda, people don't seem to take to me.

They move onto the forestage.

LINDA. Oh, don't be foolish.

WILLY. I know it when I walk in. They seem to laugh at me.

LINDA. Why? Why would they laugh at you? Don't talk that way, Willy.

WILLY *moves to the edge of the stage.* LINDA *goes into the kitchen and starts to darn stockings.*

WILLY. I don't know the reason for it, but they just pass me by. I'm not noticed.

LINDA. But you're doing wonderful, dear. You're making seventy to a hundred dollars a week.

WILLY. But I gotta be at it ten, twelve hours a day. Other men—I don't know—they do it easier. I don't know why—I can't stop myself—I talk too much. A man oughta come in with a few words. One thing about Charley. He's a man of few words, and they respect him.

LINDA. You don't talk too much, you're just lively.

WILLY, *smiling*. Well, I figure, what the hell, life is short, a couple of jokes. *To himself*. I joke too much! *The smile goes*.

LINDA. Why? You're—

WILLY. I'm fat. I'm very—foolish to look at, Linda. I didn't tell you, but Christmas time I happened to be calling on F. H. Stewarts, and a salesman I know, as I was going in to see the buyer I heard him say something about—walrus. And I—I cracked him right across the face. I won't take that. I simply will not take that. But they do laugh at me. I know that.

LINDA. Darling. . . .

WILLY. I gotta overcome it. I know I gotta overcome it. I'm not dressing to advantage, maybe.

LINDA. Willy, darling, you're the handsomest man in the world—

WILLY. Oh, no, Linda.

LINDA. To me you are. *Slight pause*. The handsomest.

From the darkness is heard the laughter of a woman. WILLY *doesn't turn to it, but it continues through* LINDA'S *lines*.

LINDA. And the boys, Willy. Few men are idolized by their children the way you are.

Music is heard as behind a scrim, to the left of the house, THE WOMAN, *dimly seen, is dressing.*

WILLY, *with great feeling*. You're the best there is, Linda, you're a pal, you know that? On the road—on the road I want to grab you sometimes and just kiss the life outa you.

The laughter is loud now, and he moves into a brightening area at the left, where THE WOMAN *has come from behind the scrim and is standing, putting on her hat, looking into a "mirror" and laughing.*

WILLY. 'Cause I get so lonely—especially when business is bad and there's nobody to talk to. I get the feeling that I'll never sell anything again, that I won't make a living for you, or a business, a business for the boys. *He talks through* THE WOMAN's *subsiding laughter;* THE WOMAN *primps at the "mirror."* There's so much I want to make for—

THE WOMAN. Me? You didn't make me, Willy. I picked you.

WILLY, *pleased*. You picked me?

THE WOMAN, *who is quite proper-looking,* WILLY's *age*. I did. I've been sitting at that desk watching all the salesmen go by, day in, day out. But you've got such a sense of humor, and we do have such a good time together, don't we?

WILLY. Sure, sure. *He takes her in his arms.* Why do you have to go now?

THE WOMAN. It's two o'clock. . . .

WILLY. No, come on in! *He pulls her.*

THE WOMAN. . . . . my sisters'll be scandalized. When'll you be back?

WILLY. Oh, two weeks about. Will you come up again?

THE WOMAN. Sure thing. You do make me laugh. It's good for me. *She squeezes his arm, kisses him.* And I think you're a wonderful man.

WILLY. You picked me, heh?

THE WOMAN. Sure. Because you're so sweet. And such a kidder.

WILLY. Well, I'll see you next time I'm in Boston.

THE WOMAN. I'll put you right through to the buyers.

WILLY, *slapping her bottom*. Right. Well, bottoms up!

THE WOMAN, *slaps him gently and laughs*. You just kill me, Willy. *He suddenly grabs her and kisses her roughly.* You kill me. And thanks for the stockings. I love a lot of stockings. Well, good night.

WILLY. Good night. And keep your pores open!

THE WOMAN. Oh, Willy!

THE WOMAN *bursts out laughing, and* LINDA's *laughter blends in.* THE WOMAN *disappears into the dark. Now the area at the kitchen table brightens.* LINDA *is sitting where she was at the kitchen table, but now is mending a pair of her silk stockings.*

LINDA. You are, Willy. The handsomest man. You've got no reason to feel that—

WILLY, *coming out of* THE WOMAN'S *dimming area and going over to* LINDA. I'll make it all up to you, Linda, I'll—

LINDA. There's nothing to make up, dear. You're doing fine, better than—

WILLY, *noticing her mending.* What's that?

LINDA. Just mending my stockings. They're so expensive—

WILLY, *angrily, taking them from her.* I won't have you mending stockings in this house! Now throw them out!

LINDA *puts the stockings in her pocket.*

BERNARD, *entering on the run.* Where is he? If he doesn't study!

WILLY, *moving to the forestage, with great agitation.* You'll give him the answers!

BERNARD. I do, but I can't on a Regents! That's a state exam! They're liable to arrest me!

WILLY. Where is he? I'll whip him, I'll whip him!

LINDA. And he'd better give back that football, Willy, it's not nice.

WILLY. Biff! Where is he? Why is he taking everything?

LINDA. He's too rough with the girls, Willy. All the mothers are afraid of him!

WILLY. I'll whip him!

BERNARD. He's driving the car without a license!

THE WOMAN'S *laugh is heard.*

WILLY. Shut up!

LINDA. All the mothers—

WILLY. Shut up!

BERNARD, *backing quietly away and out.* Mr. Birnbaum says he's stuck up.

WILLY. Get outa here!

BERNARD. If he doesn't buckle down he'll flunk math! *He goes off.*

LINDA. He's right, Willy, you've gotta—

WILLY, *exploding at her.* There's nothing the matter with him! You want him to be a worm like Bernard? He's got spirit, personality. . . .

As he speaks, LINDA, *almost in tears, exits into the living-room.* WILLY *is alone in the kitchen, wilting and staring. The leaves are gone. It is night again, and the apartment houses look down from behind.*

WILLY. Loaded with it. Loaded! What is he stealing? He's giving it back, isn't he? Why is he stealing? What did I tell him? I never in my life told him anything but decent things.

HAPPY *in pajamas has come down the stairs;* WILLY *suddenly becomes aware of* HAPPY'S *presence.*

HAPPY. Let's go now, come on.

WILLY, *sitting down at the kitchen table.* Huh! Why did she have to wax the floors herself? Everytime she waxes the floors she keels over. She knows that!

HAPPY. Shh! Take it easy. What brought you back tonight?

WILLY. I got an awful scare. Nearly hit a kid in Yonkers. God! Why didn't I go to Alaska with my brother Ben that time! Ben! That man was a genius, that man was success incarnate! What a mistake! He begged me to go.

HAPPY. Well, there's no use in—

WILLY. You guys! There was a man started with the clothes on his back and ended up with diamond mines!

HAPPY. Boy, someday I'd like to know how he did it.

WILLY. What's the mystery? The man knew what he wanted and went out and got it! Walked into a jungle, and comes out, the age of twenty-one, and he's rich! The world is an oyster, but you don't crack it open on a mattress!

HAPPY. Pop, I told you I'm gonna retire you for life.

WILLY. You'll retire me for life on seventy goddam dollars a week? And your women and your car and your apartment, and you'll retire me for life! Christ's sake, I couldn't get past Yonkers today! Where are you guys, where are you? The woods are burning! I can't drive a car!

CHARLEY *has appeared in the doorway. He is a large man, slow of speech, laconic, immovable. In all he says, despite what he says, there is pity, and, now, trepidation. He has a robe over pajamas, slippers on his feet. He enters the kitchen.*

CHARLEY. Everything all right?

HAPPY. Yeah, Charley, everything's . . .

WILLY. What's the matter?

CHARLEY. I heard some noise. I thought something happened. Can't we do something about the walls? You sneeze in here, and in my house hats blow off.

HAPPY. Let's go to bed, Dad. Come on.

CHARLEY signals to HAPPY to go.

WILLY. You go ahead, I'm not tired at the moment.

HAPPY, *to* WILLY. Take it easy, huh? *He exits.*

WILLY. What're you doin' up?

CHARLEY, *sitting down at the kitchen table opposite* WILLY. Couldn't sleep good. I had a heartburn.

WILLY. Well, you don't know how to eat.

CHARLEY. I eat with my mouth.

WILLY. No, you're ignorant. You gotta know about vitamins and things like that.

CHARLEY. Come on, let's shoot. Tire you out a little.

WILLY, *hesitantly*. All right. You got cards?

CHARLEY, *taking a deck from his pocket*. Yeah, I got them. Someplace. What is it with those vitamins?

WILLY, *dealing*. They build up your bones. Chemistry.

CHARLEY. Yeah, but there's no bones in a heartburn.

WILLY. What are you talkin' about? Do you know the first thing about it?

CHARLEY. Don't get insulted.

WILLY. Don't talk about something you don't know anything about.

They are playing. Pause.

CHARLEY. What're you doin' home?

WILLY. A little trouble with the car.

CHARLEY. Oh. *Pause.* I'd like to take a trip to California.

WILLY. Don't say.

CHARLEY. You want a job?

WILLY. I got a job, I told you that. *After a slight pause.* What the hell are you offering me a job for?

CHARLEY. Don't get insulted.

WILLY. Don't insult me.

CHARLEY. I don't see no sense in it. You don't have to go on this way.

WILLY. I got a good job. *Slight pause.* What do you keep comin' in here for?

CHARLEY. You want me to go?

WILLY, *after a pause, withering.* I can't understand it. He's going back to Texas again. What the hell is that?

CHARLEY. Let him go.

WILLY. I got nothin' to give him, Charley, I'm clean, I'm clean.

CHARLEY. He won't starve. None a them starve. Forget about him.

WILLY. Then what have I got to remember?

CHARLEY. You take it too hard. To hell with it. When a deposit bottle is broken you don't get your nickel back.

WILLY. That's easy enough for you to say.

CHARLEY. That ain't easy for me to say.

WILLY. Did you see the ceiling I put up in the living-room?

CHARLEY. Yeah, that's a piece of work. To put up a ceiling is a mystery to me. How do you do it?

WILLY. What's the difference?

CHARLEY. Well, talk about it.

WILLY. You gonna put up a ceiling?

CHARLEY. How could I put up a ceiling?

WILLY. Then what the hell are you bothering me for?

CHARLEY. You're insulted again.

WILLY. A man who can't handle tools is not a man. You're disgusting.

CHARLEY. Don't call me disgusting, Willy.

UNCLE BEN, *carrying a valise and an umbrella, enters the forestage from around the right corner of the house. He is a stolid man, in his sixties, with a mustache and an authoritative air. He is utterly certain of his destiny, and there is an aura of far places about him.*
He enters exactly as WILLY *speaks.*

WILLY. I'm getting awfully tired, Ben.

BEN'S *music is heard.* BEN *looks around at everything.*

ACT I] DEATH OF A SALESMAN 659

CHARLEY. Good, keep playing; you'll sleep better. Did you call me Ben?

BEN *looks at his watch.*

WILLY. That's funny. For a second there you reminded me of my brother Ben.

BEN. I only have a few minutes. *He strolls, inspecting the place.* WILLY *and* CHARLEY *continue playing.*

CHARLEY. You never heard from him again, heh? Since that time?

WILLY. Didn't Linda tell you? Couple of weeks ago we got a letter from his wife in Africa. He died.

CHARLEY. That so.

BEN, *chuckling.* So this is Brooklyn, eh?

CHARLEY. Maybe you're in for some of his money.

WILLY. Naa, he had seven sons. There's just one opportunity I had with that man. . . .

BEN. I must make a train, William. There are several properties I'm looking at in Alaska.

WILLY. Sure, sure! If I'd gone with him to Alaska that time, everything would've been totally different.

CHARLEY. Go on, you'd froze to death up there.

WILLY. What're you talking about?

BEN. Opportunity is tremendous in Alaska, William. Surprised you're not up there.

WILLY. Sure, tremendous.

CHARLEY. Heh?

WILLY. There was the only man I ever met who knew the answers.

CHARLEY. Who?

BEN. How are you all?

WILLY, *taking a pot, smiling.* Fine, fine.

CHARLEY. Pretty sharp tonight.

BEN. Is Mother living with you?

WILLY. No, she died a long time ago.

CHARLEY. Who?

BEN. That's too bad. Fine specimen of a lady, Mother.

WILLY, *to* CHARLEY. Heh?

BEN. I'd hoped to see the old girl.

CHARLEY. Who died?

BEN. Heard anything from Father, have you?

WILLY, *unnerved.* What do you mean, who died?

CHARLEY, *taking a pot.* What're you talkin' about?

BEN, *looking at his watch.* William, it's half-past eight!

WILLY, *as though to dispel his confusion he angrily stops* CHARLEY's *hand.* That's my build!

CHARLEY. I put the ace—

WILLY. If you don't know how to play the game I'm not gonna throw my money away on you!

CHARLEY, *rising.* It was my ace, for God's sake!

WILLY. I'm through, I'm through!

BEN. When did Mother die?

WILLY. Long ago. Since the beginning you never knew how to play cards.

CHARLEY, *picks up the cards and goes to the door.* All right! Next time I'll bring a deck with five aces.

WILLY. I don't play that kind of game!

CHARLEY, *turning to him.* You ought to be ashamed of yourself!

WILLY. Yeah?

CHARLEY. Yeah! *He goes out.*

WILLY, *slamming the door after him.* Ignoramus!

BEN, *as* WILLY *comes toward him through the wall-line of the kitchen.* So you're William.

WILLY, *shaking* BEN's *hand.* Ben! I've been waiting for you so long! What's the answer? How did you do it?

BEN. Oh, there's a story in that.

LINDA *enters the forestage, as of old, carrying the wash basket.*

LINDA. Is this Ben?

BEN, *gallantly.* How do you do, my dear.

LINDA. Where've you been all these years? Willy's always wondered why you—

WILLY, *pulling* BEN *away from her impatiently.* Where is Dad? Didn't you follow him? How did you get started?

BEN. Well, I don't know how much you remember.

WILLY. Well, I was just a baby, of course, only three or four years old—

BEN. Three years and eleven months.

WILLY. What a memory, Ben!

BEN. I have many enterprises, William, and I have never kept books.

WILLY. I remember I was sitting under the wagon in—was it Nebraska?

BEN. It was South Dakota, and I gave you a bunch of wild flowers.

WILLY. I remember you walking away down some open road.

BEN, *laughing*. I was going to find Father in Alaska.

WILLY. Where is he?

BEN. At that age I had a very faulty view of geography, William. I discovered after a few days that I was heading due south, so instead of Alaska, I ended up in Africa.

LINDA. Africa!

WILLY. The Gold Coast!

BEN. Principally diamond mines.

LINDA. Diamond mines!

BEN. Yes, my dear. But I've only a few minutes—

WILLY. No! Boys! Boys! *Young* BIFF *and* HAPPY *appear*. Listen to this. This is your Uncle Ben, a great man! Tell my boys, Ben!

BEN. Why, boys, when I was seventeen I walked into the jungle, and when I was twenty-one I walked out. *He laughs*. And by God I was rich.

WILLY, *to the boys*. You see what I been talking about? The greatest things can happen!

BEN, *glancing at his watch*. I have an appointment in Ketchikan Tuesday week.

WILLY. No, Ben! Please tell about Dad. I want my boys to hear. I want them to know the kind of stock they spring from. All I remember is a man with a big beard, and I was in Mamma's lap, sitting around a fire, and some kind of high music.

BEN. His flute. He played the flute.

WILLY. Sure, the flute, that's right!

New music is heard, a high, rollicking tune.

BEN. Father was a very great and a very wild-hearted man. We would start in Boston, and he'd toss the whole family into the wagon, and then he'd drive the team right across the country; through Ohio, and Indiana, Michigan, Illinois, and all the Western states. And we'd stop in the towns and sell the flutes that he'd made on the way. Great inventor, Father. With one gadget he made more in a week than a man like you could make in a lifetime.

WILLY. That's just the way I'm bringing them up, Ben—rugged, well liked, all-around.

BEN. Yeah? *To* BIFF. Hit that, boy—hard as you can. *He pounds his stomach.*

BIFF. Oh, no, sir!

BEN, *taking boxing stance.* Come on, get to me! *He laughs.*

WILLY. Go to it, Biff! Go ahead, show him!

BIFF. Okay! *He cocks his fists and starts in.*

LINDA, *to* WILLY. Why must he fight, dear?

BEN, *sparring with* BIFF. Good boy! Good boy!

WILLY. How's that, Ben, heh?

HAPPY. Give him the left, Biff!

LINDA. Why are you fighting?

BEN. Good boy! *Suddenly comes in, trips* BIFF, *and stands over him, the point of his umbrella poised over* BIFF's *eye.*

LINDA. Look out, Biff!

BIFF. Gee!

BEN, *patting* BIFF's *knee.* Never fight fair with a stranger, boy. You'll never get out of the jungle that way. *Taking* LINDA's *hand and bowing.* It was an honor and a pleasure to meet you, Linda.

LINDA, *withdrawing her hand coldly, frightened.* Have a nice—trip.

BEN, *to* WILLY. And good luck with your—what do you do?

WILLY. Selling.

BEN. Yes. Well . . . *He raises his hand in farewell to all.*

WILLY. No, Ben, I don't want you to think . . . *He takes* BEN's *arm to show him.* It's Brooklyn, I know, but we hunt too.

BEN. Really, now.

WILLY. Oh, sure, there's snakes and rabbits and—that's why I moved out here. Why, Biff can fell any one of these trees in no time! Boys! Go right over to where they're building the apartment house and get some sand. We're gonna rebuild the entire front stoop right now! Watch this, Ben!

BIFF. Yes, sir! On the double, Hap!

HAPPY, *as he and* BIFF *run off.* I lost weight, Pop, you notice?

CHARLEY *enters in knickers, even before the boys are gone.*

CHARLEY. Listen, if they steal any more from that building the watchman'll put the cops on them!

LINDA, *to* WILLY. Don't let Biff . . .

BEN *laughs lustily.*

WILLY. You shoulda seen the lumber they brought home last week. At least a dozen six-by-tens worth all kinds a money.

CHARLEY. Listen, if that watchman—

WILLY. I gave them hell, understand. But I got a couple of fearless characters there.

CHARLEY. Willy, the jails are full of fearless characters.

BEN, *clapping* WILLY *on the back, with a laugh at* CHARLEY. And the stock exchange, friend!

WILLY, *joining in* BEN'S *laughter.* Where are the rest of your pants?

CHARLEY. My wife bought them.

WILLY. Now all you need is a golf club and you can go upstairs and go to sleep. *To* BEN. Great athlete! Between him and his son Bernard they can't hammer a nail!

BERNARD, *rushing in.* The watchman's chasing Biff!

WILLY, *angrily.* Shut up! He's not stealing anything!

LINDA, *alarmed, hurrying off left.* Where is he? Biff, dear! *She exits.*

WILLY, *moving toward the left, away from* BEN. There's nothing wrong. What's the matter with you?

BEN. Nervy boy. Good!

WILLY, *laughing.* Oh, nerves of iron, that Biff!

CHARLEY. Don't know what it is. My New England man comes back and he's bleedin', they murdered him up there.

WILLY. It's contacts, Charley, I got important contacts!

CHARLEY, *sarcastically.* Glad to hear it, Willy. Come in later, we'll shoot a little casino. I'll take some of your Portland money. *He laughs at* WILLY *and exits.*

WILLY, *turning to* BEN. Business is bad, it's murderous. But not for me, of course.

BEN. I'll stop by on my way back to Africa.

WILLY, *longingly*. Can't you stay a few days? You're just what I need, Ben, because I—I have a fine position here, but I—well, Dad left when I was such a baby and I never had a chance to talk to him and I still feel—kind of temporary about myself.

BEN. I'll be late for my train.

They are at opposite ends of the stage.

WILLY. Ben, my boys—can't we talk? They'd go into the jaws of hell for me, see, but I—

BEN. William, you're being first-rate with your boys. Outstanding, manly chaps!

WILLY, *hanging on to his words*. Oh, Ben, that's good to hear! Because sometimes I'm afraid that I'm not teaching them the right kind of— Ben, how should I teach them?

BEN, *giving great weight to each word, and with a certain vicious audacity*. William, when I walked into the jungle, I was seventeen. When I walked out I was twenty-one. And, by God, I was rich! *He goes off into darkness around the right corner of the house.*

WILLY. . . . .was rich! That's just the spirit I want to imbue them with! To walk into a jungle! I was right! I was right! I was right!

BEN *is gone, but* WILLY *is still speaking to him as* LINDA, *in nightgown and robe, enters the kitchen, glances around for* WILLY, *then goes to the door of the house, looks out and sees him. Comes down to his left. He looks at her.*

LINDA. Willy, dear? Willy?

WILLY. I was right!

LINDA. Did you have some cheese? *He can't answer.* It's very late, darling. Come to bed, heh?

WILLY, *looking straight up*. Gotta break your neck to see a star in this yard.

LINDA. You coming in?

WILLY. Whatever happened to that diamond watch fob? Remember? When Ben came from Africa that time? Didn't he give me a watch fob with a diamond in it?

LINDA. You pawned it, dear. Twelve, thirteen years ago. For Biff's radio correspondence course.

WILLY. Gee, that was a beautiful thing. I'll take a walk.

LINDA. But you're in your slippers.

WILLY, *starting to go around the house at the left.* I was right! I was! *Half to* LINDA, *as he goes, shaking his head.* What a man! There was a man worth talking to. I was right!

LINDA, *calling after* WILLY. But in your slippers, Willy!

WILLY *is almost gone when* BIFF, *in his pajamas, comes down the stairs and enters the kitchen.*

BIFF. What is he doing out there?

LINDA. Sh!

BIFF. God Almighty, Mom, how long has he been doing this?

LINDA. Don't, he'll hear you.

BIFF. What the hell is the matter with him?

LINDA. It'll pass by morning.

BIFF. Shouldn't we do anything?

LINDA. Oh, my dear, you should do a lot of things, but there's nothing to do, so go to sleep.

HAPPY *comes down the stair and sits on the steps.*

HAPPY. I never heard him so loud, Mom.

LINDA. Well, come around more often; you'll hear him. *She sits down at the table and mends the lining of* WILLY'S *jacket.*

BIFF. Why didn't you ever write me about this, Mom?

LINDA. How would I write to you? For over three months you had no address.

BIFF. I was on the move. But you know I thought of you all the time. You know that, don't you, pal?

LINDA. I know, dear, I know. But he likes to have a letter. Just to know that there's still a possibility for better things.

BIFF. He's not like this all the time, is he?

LINDA. It's when you come home he's always the worst.

BIFF. When I come home?

LINDA. When you write you're coming, he's all smiles, and talks about the future, and—he's just wonderful. And then the closer you seem to come, the more shaky he gets, and then, by the time you get here, he's arguing, and he seems angry at you. I think it's just that maybe he can't bring himself to—to open up to you. Why are you so hateful to each other? Why is that?

BIFF, *evasively*. I'm not hateful, Mom.

LINDA. But you no sooner come in the door than you're fighting!

BIFF. I don't know why. I mean to change. I'm tryin', Mom, you understand?

LINDA. Are you home to stay now?

BIFF. I don't know. I want to look around, see what's doin'.

LINDA. Biff, you can't look around all your life, can you?

BIFF. I just can't take hold, Mom. I can't take hold of some kind of a life.

LINDA. Biff, a man is not a bird, to come and go with the springtime.

BIFF. Your hair. . . . *He touches her hair.* Your hair got so gray.

LINDA. Oh, it's been gray since you were in high school. I just stopped dyeing it, that's all.

BIFF. Dye it again, will ya? I don't want my pal looking old. *He smiles.*

LINDA. You're such a boy! You think you can go away for a year and. . . . You've got to get it into your head now that one day you'll knock on this door and there'll be strange people here—

BIFF. What are you talking about? You're not even sixty, Mom.

LINDA. But what about your father?

BIFF, *lamely*. Well, I meant him too.

HAPPY. He admires Pop.

LINDA. Biff, dear, if you don't have any feeling for him, then you can't have any feeling for me.

BIFF. Sure I can, Mom.

LINDA. No. You can't just come to see me, because I love him. *With a threat, but only a threat, of tears.* He's the dearest man in the world to me, and I won't have anyone making him feel unwanted and low and blue. You've got to make up your mind now, darling, there's no leeway any more. Either he's your father and you pay him that respect, or else you're not to come here. I know he's not easy to get along with—nobody knows that better than me—but. . . .

WILLY, *from the left, with a laugh*. Hey, hey, Biffo!

BIFF, *starting to go out after* WILLY. What the hell is the matter with him? HAPPY *stops him.*

LINDA. Don't—don't go near him!

BIFF. Stop making excuses for him! He always, always wiped the floor with you. Never had an ounce of respect for you.

HAPPY. He's always had respect for—

BIFF. What the hell do you know about it?

HAPPY, *surlily*. Just don't call him crazy!

BIFF. He's got no character— Charley wouldn't do this. Not in his own house—spewing out that vomit from his mind.

HAPPY. Charley never had to cope with what he's got to.

BIFF. People are worse off than Willy Loman. Believe me, I've seen them.

LINDA. Then make Charley your father, Biff. You can't do that, can you? I don't say he's a great man. Willy Loman never made a lot of money. His name was never in the paper. He's not the finest character that ever lived. But he's a human being, and a terrible thing is happening to him. So attention must be paid. He's not to be allowed to fall into his grave like an old dog. Attention, attention must be finally paid to such a person. You called him crazy—

BIFF. I didn't mean—

LINDA. No, a lot of people think he's lost his—balance. But you don't have to be very smart to know what his trouble is. The man is exhausted.

HAPPY. Sure!

LINDA. A small man can be just as exhausted as a great man. He works for a company thirty-six years this March, opens up unheard-of territories to their trademark, and now in his old age they take his salary away.

HAPPY, *indignantly*. I didn't know that, Mom.

LINDA. You never asked, my dear! Now that you get your spending money someplace else you don't trouble your mind with him.

HAPPY. But I gave you money last—

LINDA. Christmas time, fifty dollars! To fix the hot water it cost ninety-seven fifty! For five weeks he's been on straight commission, like a beginner, an unknown!

BIFF. Those ungrateful bastards!

LINDA. Are they any worse than his sons? When he brought them business, when he was young, they were glad to see him. But now his old friends, the old buyers that loved him so and always found some order to hand him in a pinch—they're all dead, retired. He used to be able to make six, seven calls a day in Boston. Now he takes his valises out of the car and puts them back and takes them out again and he's exhausted. Instead of walking he talks now. He drives seven hundred miles, and when he gets there no one knows him any more, no one welcomes him. And what goes through a man's mind, driving seven hundred miles home without having earned a cent? Why shouldn't he talk to himself? Why? When he has to go to Charley and borrow fifty dollars a week and pretend to me that it's his pay? How long can that go on? How long? You see what I'm sitting here and waiting for? And you tell me he has no character? The man who never worked a day but for your benefit? When does he get the medal for that? Is this his reward—to turn around at the age of sixty-three and find his sons, who he loved better than his life, one a philandering bum—

HAPPY. Mom!

LINDA. That's all you are, my baby! *To* BIFF. And you! What happened to the love you had for him? You were such pals! How you used to talk to him on the phone every night! How lonely he was till he could come home to you!

BIFF. All right, Mom. I'll live here in my room, and I'll get a job. I'll keep away from him, that's all.

LINDA. No, Biff. You can't stay here and fight all the time.

BIFF. He threw me out of this house, remember that.

LINDA. Why did he do that? I never knew why.

BIFF. Because I know he's a fake and he doesn't like anybody around who knows!

LINDA. Why a fake? In what way? What do you mean?

BIFF. Just don't lay it all at my feet. It's between me and him—that's all I have to say. I'll chip in from now on. He'll settle for half my pay check. He'll be all right. I'm going to bed. *He starts for the stairs.*

LINDA. He won't be all right.

BIFF, *turning on the stairs, furiously.* I hate this city and I'll stay here. Now what do you want?

LINDA. He's dying, Biff.

HAPPY *turns quickly to her, shocked.*

ACT I]   DEATH OF A SALESMAN   669

BIFF, *after a pause.* Why is he dying?

LINDA. He's been trying to kill himself.

BIFF, *with great horror.* How?

LINDA. I live from day to day.

BIFF. What're you talking about?

LINDA. Remember I wrote you that he smashed up the car again? In February?

BIFF. Well?

LINDA. The insurance inspector came. He said that they have evidence. That all these accidents in the last year—weren't—weren't—accidents.

HAPPY. How can they tell that? That's a lie.

LINDA. It seems there's a woman. . . . *She takes a breath as*

{ BIFF, *sharply but contained.* What woman?
{ LINDA, *simultaneously.* . . . and this woman . . .

LINDA. What?

BIFF. Nothing. Go ahead.

LINDA. What did you say?

BIFF. Nothing. I just said what woman?

HAPPY. What about her?

LINDA. Well, it seems she was walking down the road and saw his car. She says that he wasn't driving fast at all, and that he didn't skid. She says he came to that little bridge, and then deliberately smashed into the railing, and it was only the shallowness of the water that saved him.

BIFF. Oh, no, he probably just fell asleep again.

LINDA. I don't think he fell asleep.

BIFF. Why not?

LINDA. Last month. . . . *With great difficulty.* Oh, boys, it's so hard to say a thing like this! He's just a big stupid man to you, but I tell you there's more good in him than in many other people. *She chokes, wipes her eyes.* I was looking for a fuse. The lights blew out, and I went down the cellar. And behind the fuse box—it happened to fall out—was a length of rubber pipe—just short.

HAPPY. No kidding?

LINDA. There's a little attachment on the end of it. I knew right away. And sure enough, on the bottom of the water heater there's a new little nipple on the gas pipe.

HAPPY, *angrily*. That—jerk.

BIFF. Did you have it taken off?

LINDA. I'm—I'm ashamed to. How can I mention it to him? Every day I go down and take away that little rubber pipe. But, when he comes home, I put it back where it was. How can I insult him that way? I don't know what to do. I live from day to day, boys. I tell you, I know every thought in his mind. It sounds so old-fashioned and silly, but I tell you he put his whole life into you and you've turned your backs on him. *She is bent over in the chair, weeping, her face in her hands.* Biff, I swear to God! Biff, his life is in your hands!

HAPPY, *to* BIFF. How do you like that damned fool!

BIFF, *kissing her*. All right, pal, all right. It's all settled now. I've been remiss. I know that, Mom. But now I'll stay, and I swear to you, I'll apply myself. *Kneeling in front of her, in a fever of self-reproach.* It's just—you see, Mom, I don't fit in business. Not that I won't try. I'll try, and I'll make good.

HAPPY. Sure you will. The trouble with you in business was you never tried to please people.

BIFF. I know, I—

HAPPY. Like when you worked for Harrison's. Bob Harrison said you were tops, and then you go and do some damn fool thing like whistling whole songs in the elevator like a comedian.

BIFF, *against* HAPPY. So what? I like to whistle sometimes.

HAPPY. You don't raise a guy to a responsible job who whistles in the elevator!

LINDA. Well, don't argue about it now.

HAPPY. Like when you'd go off and swim in the middle of the day instead of taking the line around.

BIFF, *his resentment rising*. Well, don't you run off? You take off sometimes, don't you? On a nice summer day?

HAPPY. Yeah, but I cover myself!

LINDA. Boys!

HAPPY. If I'm going to take a fade the boss can call any number where I'm supposed to be and they'll swear to him that I just left. I'll tell you something that I hate to say, Biff, but in the business world some of them think you're crazy.

BIFF, *angered*. Screw the business world!

HAPPY. All right, screw it! Great, but cover yourself!

LINDA. Hap, Hap!

BIFF. I don't care what they think! They've laughed at Dad for years, and you know why? Because we don't belong in this nuthouse of a city! We should be mixing cement on some open plain, or—or carpenters. A carpenter is allowed to whistle!

WILLY *walks in from the entrance of the house, at left.*

WILLY. Even your grandfather was better than a carpenter. *Pause. They watch him.* You never grew up. Bernard does not whistle in the elevator, I assure you.

BIFF, *as though to laugh* WILLY *out of it.* Yeah, but you do, Pop.

WILLY. I never in my life whistled in an elevator! And who in the business world thinks I'm crazy?

BIFF. I didn't mean it like that, Pop. Now don't make a whole thing out of it, will ya?

WILLY. Go back to the West! Be a carpenter, a cowboy, enjoy yourself!

LINDA. Willy, he was just saying—

WILLY. I heard what he said!

HAPPY, *trying to quiet* WILLY. Hey, Pop, come on now . . .

WILLY, *continuing over* HAPPY's *line.* They laugh at me, heh? Go to Filene's, go to the Hub, go to Slattery's, Boston. Call out the name Willy Loman and see what happens! Big shot!

BIFF. All right, Pop.

WILLY. Big!

BIFF. All right!

WILLY. Why do you always insult me?

BIFF. I didn't say a word. *To* LINDA. Did I say a word?

LINDA. He didn't say anything, Willy.

WILLY, *going to the doorway of the living-room.* All right, good night, good night.

LINDA. Willy, dear, he just decided. . . .

WILLY, *to* BIFF. If you get tired hanging around tomorrow, paint the ceiling I put up in the living-room.

BIFF. I'm leaving early tomorrow.

HAPPY. He's going to see Bill Oliver, Pop.

WILLY, *interestedly.* Oliver? For what?

BIFF, *with reserve, but trying, trying.* He always said he'd stake me. I'd like to go into business, so maybe I can take him up on it.

LINDA. Isn't that wonderful?

WILLY. Don't interrupt. What's wonderful about it? There's fifty men in the City of New York who'd stake him. *To* BIFF. Sporting goods?

BIFF. I guess so. I know something about it and—

WILLY. He knows something about it! You know sporting goods better than Spalding, for God's sake! How much is he giving you?

BIFF. I don't know, I didn't even see him yet, but—

WILLY. Then what're you talkin' about?

BIFF, *getting angry.* Well, all I said was I'm gonna see him, that's all!

WILLY, *turning away.* Ah, you're counting your chickens again.

BIFF, *starting left for the stairs.* Oh, Jesus, I'm going to sleep!

WILLY, *calling after him.* Don't curse in this house!

BIFF, *turning.* Since when did you get so clean?

HAPPY, *trying to stop them.* Wait a . . . .

WILLY. Don't use that language to me! I won't have it!

HAPPY, *grabbing* BIFF, *shouts.* Wait a minute! I got an idea. I got a feasible idea. Come here, Biff, let's talk this over now, let's talk some sense here. When I was down in Florida last time, I thought of a great idea to sell sporting goods. It just came back to me. You and I, Biff—we have a line, the Loman Line. We train a couple of weeks, and put on a couple of exhibitions, see?

WILLY. That's an idea!

HAPPY. Wait! We form two basketball teams, see? Two water-polo teams. We play each other. It's a million dollars' worth of publicity. Two brothers, see? The Loman Brothers. Displays in the Royal Palms—all the hotels. And banners over the ring and the basketball court: "Loman Brothers." Baby, we could sell sporting goods!

WILLY. That is a one-million-dollar idea!

LINDA. Marvelous!

BIFF. I'm in great shape as far as that's concerned.

HAPPY. And the beauty of it is, Biff, it wouldn't be like a business. We'd be out playin' ball again. . . .

BIFF, *enthused.* Yeah, that's. . . .

WILLY. Million-dollar. . . .

HAPPY. And you wouldn't get fed up with it, Biff. It'd be the family again. There'd be the old honor, and comradeship, and if you wanted to go off for a swim or somethin'—well, you'd do it! Without some smart cooky gettin' up ahead of you!

WILLY. Lick the world! You guys together could absolutely lick the civilized world.

BIFF. I'll see Oliver tomorrow. Hap, if we could work that out. . . .

LINDA. Maybe things are beginning to—

WILLY, *wildly enthused, to* LINDA. Stop interrupting! *To* BIFF. But don't wear sport jacket and slacks when you see Oliver.

BIFF. No, I'll—

WILLY. A business suit, and talk as little as possible, and don't crack any jokes.

BIFF. He did like me. Always liked me.

LINDA. He loved you!

WILLY, *to* LINDA. Will you stop! *To* BIFF. Walk in very serious. You are not applying for a boy's job. Money is to pass. Be quiet, fine, and serious. Everybody likes a kidder, but nobody lends him money.

HAPPY. I'll try to get some myself, Biff. I'm sure I can.

WILLY. I see great things for you kids, I think your troubles are over. But remember, start big and you'll end big. Ask for fifteen. How much you gonna ask for?

BIFF. Gee, I don't know—

WILLY. And don't say "Gee." "Gee" is a boy's word. A man walking in for fifteen thousand dollars does not say "Gee!"

BIFF. Ten, I think, would be top though.

WILLY. Don't be so modest. You always started too low. Walk in with a big laugh. Don't look worried. Start off with a couple of your good stories to lighten things up. It's not what you say, it's how you say it—because personality always wins the day.

LINDA. Oliver always thought the highest of him—

WILLY. Will you let me talk?

BIFF. Don't yell at her, Pop, will ya?

WILLY, *angrily*. I was talking, wasn't I?

BIFF. I don't like you yelling at her all the time, and I'm tellin' you, that's all.

WILLY. What're you, takin' over this house?

LINDA. Willy—

WILLY, *turning on her*. Don't take his side all the time, goddammit!

BIFF, *furiously*. Stop yelling at her!

WILLY, *suddenly pulling on his cheek, beaten down, guilt ridden*. Give my best to Bill Oliver—he may remember me. *He exits through the living-room doorway.*

LINDA, *her voice subdued*. What'd you have to start that for? BIFF *turns away*. You see how sweet he was as soon as you talked hopefully? *She goes over to* BIFF. Come up and say good night to him. Don't let him go to bed that way.

HAPPY. Come on, Biff, let's buck him up.

LINDA. Please, dear. Just say good night. It takes so little to make him happy. Come. *She goes through the living-room doorway, calling upstairs from within the living-room.* Your pajamas are hanging in the bathroom, Willy!

HAPPY, *looking toward where* LINDA *went out*. What a woman! They broke the mold when they made her. You know that, Biff?

BIFF. He's off salary. My God, working on commission!

HAPPY. Well, let's face it: he's no hot-shot selling man. Except that sometimes, you have to admit, he's a sweet personality.

BIFF, *deciding*. Lend me ten bucks, will ya? I want to buy some new ties.

HAPPY. I'll take you to a place I know. Beautiful stuff. Wear one of my striped shirts tomorrow.

BIFF. She got gray. Mom got awful old. Gee, I'm gonna go in to Oliver tomorrow and knock him for a—

HAPPY. Come on up. Tell that to Dad. Let's give him a whirl. Come on.

BIFF, *steamed up*. You know, with ten thousand bucks, boy!

HAPPY, *as they go into the living-room*. That's the talk, Biff, that's the first time I've heard the old confidence out of you! *From within the living-room, fading off.* You're gonna live with me, kid, and any babe you want just say the word. . . . *The last lines are hardly heard. They are mounting the stairs to their parents' bedroom.*

LINDA, *entering her bedroom and addressing* WILLY, *who is in the*

ACT I] DEATH OF A SALESMAN 675

bathroom. She is straightening the bed for him. Can you do anything about the shower? It drips.

WILLY, *from the bathroom.* All of a sudden everything falls to pieces! Goddam plumbing, oughta be sued, those people. I hardly finished putting it in and the thing. . . . *His words rumble off.*

LINDA. I'm just wondering if Oliver will remember him. You think he might?

WILLY, *coming out of the bathroom in his pajamas.* Remember him? What's the matter with you, you crazy? If he'd've stayed with Oliver he'd be on top by now! Wait'll Oliver gets a look at him. You don't know the average caliber any more. The average young man today—*he is getting into bed*—is got a caliber of zero. Greatest thing in the world for him was to bum around.

BIFF *and* HAPPY *enter the bedroom. Slight pause.*

WILLY, *stops short, looking at* BIFF. Glad to hear it, boy.

HAPPY. He wanted to say good night to you, sport.

WILLY, *to* BIFF. Yeah. Knock him dead, boy. What'd you want to tell me?

BIFF. Just take it easy, Pop. Good night. *He turns to go.*

WILLY, *unable to resist.* And if anything falls off the desk while you're talking to him—like a package or something—don't you pick it up. They have office boys for that.

LINDA. I'll make a big breakfast—

WILLY. Will you let me finish? *To* BIFF. Tell him you were in the business in the West. Not farm work.

BIFF. All right, Dad.

LINDA. I think everything—

WILLY, *going right through her speech.* And don't undersell yourself. No less than fifteen thousand dollars.

BIFF, *unable to bear him.* Okay. Good night, Mom. *He starts moving.*

WILLY. Because you got a greatness in you, Biff, remember that. You got all kinds a greatness. . . . *He lies back, exhausted.* BIFF *walks out.*

LINDA, *calling after* BIFF. Sleep well, darling!

HAPPY. I'm gonna get married, Mom. I wanted to tell you.

LINDA. Go to sleep, dear.

HAPPY, *going*. I just wanted to tell you.

WILLY. Keep up the good work. HAPPY *exits*. God. . . . remember that Ebbets Field game? The championship of the city?

LINDA. Just rest. Should I sing to you?

WILLY. Yeah. Sing to me. LINDA *hums a soft lullaby*. When that team came out—he was the tallest, remember?

LINDA. Oh, yes. And in gold.

BIFF *enters the darkened kitchen, takes a cigarette, and leaves the house. He comes downstage into a golden pool of light. He smokes, staring at the night.*

WILLY. Like a young god. Hercules—something like that. And the sun, the sun all around him. Remember how he waved to me? Right up from the field, with the representatives of three colleges standing by? And the buyers I brought, and the cheers when he came out—Loman, Loman, Loman! God Almighty, he'll be great yet. A star like that, magnificent, can never really fade away!

The light on WILLY *is fading. The gas heater begins to glow through the kitchen wall, near the stairs, a blue flame beneath red coils.*

LINDA, *timidly*. Willy dear, what has he got against you?

WILLY. I'm so tired. Don't talk any more.

BIFF *slowly returns to the kitchen. He stops, stares toward the heater.*

LINDA. Will you ask Howard to let you work in New York?

WILLY. First thing in the morning. Everything'll be all right.

BIFF *reaches behind the heater and draws out a length of rubber tubing. He is horrified and turns his head toward* WILLY'S *room, still dimly lit, from which the strains of* LINDA'S *desperate but monotonous humming rise.*

WILLY, *staring through the window into the moonlight*. Gee, look at the moon moving between the buildings!

BIFF *wraps the tubing around his hand and quickly goes up the stairs.*

Act II

Music is heard, gay and bright. The curtain rises as the music fades away. WILLY, *in shirt sleeves, is sitting at the kitchen table, sipping coffee, his hat in his lap.* LINDA *is filling his cup when she can.*

WILLY. Wonderful coffee. Meal in itself.

LINDA. Can I make you some eggs?

WILLY. No. Take a breath.

LINDA. You look so rested, dear.

WILLY. I slept like a dead one. First time in months. Imagine, sleeping till ten on a Tuesday morning. Boys left nice and early, heh?

LINDA. They were out of here by eight o'clock.

WILLY. Good work!

LINDA. It was so thrilling to see them leaving together. I can't get over the shaving lotion in this house!

WILLY, *smiling.* Mmm—

LINDA. Biff was very changed this morning. His whole attitude seemed to be hopeful. He couldn't wait to get downtown to see Oliver.

WILLY. He's heading for a change. There's no question, there simply are certain men that take longer to get—solidified. How did he dress?

LINDA. His blue suit. He's so handsome in that suit. He could be a—anything in that suit!

WILLY gets up from the table. LINDA *holds his jacket for him.*

WILLY. There's no question, no question at all. Gee, on the way home tonight I'd like to buy some seeds.

LINDA, *laughing.* That'd be wonderful. But not enough sun gets back there. Nothing'll grow any more.

WILLY. You wait, kid, before it's all over we're gonna get a little place out in the country, and I'll raise some vegetables, a couple of chickens. . . .

LINDA. You'll do it yet, dear.

WILLY *walks out of his jacket.* LINDA *follows him.*

WILLY. And they'll get married, and come for a weekend. I'd build a little guest house. 'Cause I got so many fine tools, all I'd need would be a little lumber and some peace of mind.

LINDA, *joyfully.* I sewed the lining. . . .

WILLY. I could build two guest houses, so they'd both come. Did he decide how much he's going to ask Oliver for?

LINDA, *getting him into the jacket.* He didn't mention it, but I imagine ten or fifteen thousand. You going to talk to Howard today?

WILLY. Yeah. I'll put it to him straight and simple. He'll just have to take me off the road.

LINDA. And Willy, don't forget to ask for a little advance, because we've got the insurance premium. It's the grace period now.

WILLY. That's a hundred. . . . ?

LINDA. A hundred and eight, sixty-eight. Because we're a little short again.

WILLY. Why are we short?

LINDA. Well, you had the motor job on the car . . .

WILLY. That goddam Studebaker!

LINDA. And you got one more payment on the refrigerator . . .

WILLY. But it just broke again!

LINDA. Well, it's old, dear.

WILLY. I told you we should've bought a well-advertised machine. Charley bought a General Electric and it's twenty years old and it's still good, that son-of-a-bitch.

LINDA. But, Willy—

WILLY. Whoever heard of a Hastings refrigerator? Once in my life I would like to own something outright before it's broken! I'm always in a race with the junkyard! I just finished paying for the car and it's on its last legs. The refrigerator consumes belts like a goddam maniac. They time those things. They time them so when you finally paid for them, they're used up.

LINDA, *buttoning up his jacket as he unbuttons it.* All told, about two hundred dollars would carry us, dear. But that includes the last payment on the mortgage. After this payment, Willy, the house belongs to us.

WILLY. It's twenty-five years!

LINDA. Biff was nine years old when we bought it.

ACT II] DEATH OF A SALESMAN 679

WILLY. Well, that's a great thing. To weather a twenty-five year mortgage is—

LINDA. It's an accomplishment.

WILLY. All the cement, the lumber, the reconstruction I put in this house! There ain't a crack to be found in it any more.

LINDA. Well, it served its purpose.

WILLY. What purpose? Some stranger'll come along, move in, and that's that. If only Biff would take this house, and raise a family. . . . *He starts to go.* Good-by, I'm late.

LINDA, *suddenly remembering.* Oh, I forgot! You're supposed to meet them for dinner.

WILLY. Me?

LINDA. At Frank's Chop House on Forty-eighth near Sixth Avenue.

WILLY. Is that so! How about you?

LINDA. No, just the three of you. They're gonna blow you to a big meal!

WILLY. Don't say! Who thought of that?

LINDA. Biff came to me this morning, Willy, and he said, "Tell Dad, we want to blow him to a big meal." Be there six o'clock. You and your two boys are going to have dinner.

WILLY. Gee whiz! That's really somethin'. I'm gonna knock Howard for a loop, kid. I'll get an advance, and I'll come home with a New York job. Goddammit, now I'm gonna do it!

LINDA. Oh, that's the spirit, Willy!

WILLY. I will never get behind a wheel the rest of my life!

LINDA. It's changing, Willy, I can feel it changing!

WILLY. Beyond a question. G'by, I'm late. *He starts to go again.*

LINDA, *calling after him as she runs to the kitchen table for a handkerchief.* You got your glasses?

WILLY, *feels for them, then comes back in.* Yeah, yeah, got my glasses.

LINDA, *giving him the handkerchief.* And a handkerchief.

WILLY. Yeah, handkerchief.

LINDA. And your saccharine?

WILLY. Yeah, my saccharine.

LINDA. Be careful on the subway stairs.

She kisses him, and a silk stocking is seen hanging from her hand.
WILLY *notices it.*

WILLY. Will you stop mending stockings? At least while I'm in the house. It gets me nervous. I can't tell you. Please.

LINDA *hides the stocking in her hand as she follows* WILLY *across the forestage in front of the house.*

LINDA. Remember, Frank's Chop House.
WILLY, *passing the apron.* Maybe beets would grow out there.
LINDA, *laughing.* But you tried so many times.
WILLY. Yeah. Well, don't work hard today. *He disappears around the right corner of the house.*
LINDA. Be careful!

As WILLY *vanishes,* LINDA *waves to him. Suddenly the phone rings. She runs across the stage and into the kitchen and lifts it.*

LINDA. Hello? Oh, Biff! I'm so glad you called, I just. . . . Yes, sure, I just told him. Yes, he'll be there for dinner at six o'clock, I didn't forget. Listen, I was just dying to tell you. You know that little rubber pipe I told you about? That he connected to the gas heater? I finally decided to go down the cellar this morning and take it away and destroy it. But it's gone! Imagine? He took it away himself, it isn't there! *She listens.* When? Oh, then you took it. Oh—nothing, it's just that I'd hoped he'd taken it away himself. Oh, I'm not worried, darling, because this morning he left in such high spirits, it was like the old days! I'm not afraid any more. Did Mr. Oliver see you? . . . . Well, you wait there then. And make a nice impression on him, darling. Just don't perspire too much before you see him. And have a nice time with Dad. He may have big news too! . . . . That's right, a New York job. And be sweet to him tonight, dear. Be loving to him. Because he's only a little boat looking for a harbor. *She is trembling with sorrow and joy.* Oh, that's wonderful, Biff, you'll save his life. Thanks, darling. Just put your arm around him when he comes into the restaurant. Give him a smile. That's the boy. . . . Good-by, dear. . . . You got your comb? . . . That's fine. Good-by, Biff dear.

In the middle of her speech, HOWARD WAGNER, *thirty-six, wheels on a small typewriter table on which is a wire-recording machine and proceeds to plug it in. This is on the left forestage. Light slowly fades*

ACT II] DEATH OF A SALESMAN 681

on LINDA *as it rises on* HOWARD. HOWARD *is intent on threading the machine and only glances over his shoulder as* WILLY *appears.*

WILLY. Pst! Pst!
HOWARD. Hello, Willy, come in.
WILLY. Like to have a little talk with you, Howard.
HOWARD. Sorry to keep you waiting. I'll be with you in a minute.
WILLY. What's that, Howard?
HOWARD. Didn't you ever see one of these? Wire recorder.
WILLY. Oh. Can we talk a minute?
HOWARD. Records things. Just got delivery yesterday. Been driving me crazy, the most terrific machine I ever saw in my life. I was up all night with it.
WILLY. What do you do with it?
HOWARD. I bought it for dictation, but you can do anything with it. Listen to this. I had it home last night. Listen to what I picked up. The first one is my daughter. Get this. *He flicks the switch and "Roll out the Barrel" is heard being whistled.* Listen to that kid whistle.
WILLY. That is lifelike, isn't it?
HOWARD. Seven years old. Get that tone.
WILLY. Ts, ts. Like to ask a little favor if you . . .

The whistling breaks off, and the voice of HOWARD's *daughter is heard.*

HIS DAUGHTER. "Now you, Daddy."
HOWARD. She's crazy for me! *Again the same song is whistled.* That's me! Ha! *He winks.*
WILLY. You're very good!

The whistling breaks off again. The machine runs silent for a moment.

HOWARD. Sh! Get this now, this is my son.
HIS SON. "The capital of Alabama is Montgomery; the capital of Arizona is Phoenix; the capital of Arkansas is Little Rock; the capital of California is Sacramento. . . ." *and on, and on.*
HOWARD, *holding up five fingers.* Five years old, Willy!
WILLY. He'll make an announcer some day!
HIS SON, *continuing.* "The capital. . . ."

HOWARD. Get that—alphabetical order! *The machine breaks off suddenly.* Wait a minute. The maid kicked the plug out.

WILLY. It certainly is a—

HOWARD. Sh, for God's sake!

HIS SON. "It's nine o'clock, Bulova watch time. So I have to go to sleep."

WILLY. That really is—

HOWARD. Wait a minute! The next is my wife.

They wait.

HOWARD'S VOICE. "Go on, say something." *Pause.* "Well, you gonna talk?"

HIS WIFE. "I can't think of anything."

HOWARD'S VOICE. "Well, talk—it's turning."

HIS WIFE, *shyly, beaten.* "Hello." *Silence.* "Oh, Howard, I can't talk into this . . ."

HOWARD, *snapping the machine off.* That was my wife.

WILLY. That is a wonderful machine. Can we—

HOWARD. I tell you, Willy, I'm gonna take my camera, and my bandsaw, and all my hobbies, and out they go. This is the most fascinating relaxation I ever found.

WILLY. I think I'll get one myself.

HOWARD. Sure, they're only a hundred and a half. You can't do without it. Supposing you wanna hear Jack Benny, see? But you can't be at home at that hour. So you tell the maid to turn the radio on when Jack Benny comes on, and this automatically goes on with the radio . . . .

WILLY. And when you come home you. . . .

HOWARD. You can come home twelve o'clock, one o'clock, any time you like, and you get yourself a Coke and sit yourself down, throw the switch, and there's Jack Benny's program in the middle of the night!

WILLY. I'm definitely going to get one. Because lots of time I'm on the road, and I think to myself, what I must be missing on the radio!

HOWARD. Don't you have a radio in the car?

WILLY. Well, yeah, but who ever thinks of turning it on?

HOWARD. Say, aren't you supposed to be in Boston?

WILLY. That's what I want to talk to you about, Howard. You got a minute? *He draws a chair in from the wing.*

HOWARD. What happened? What're you doing here?

WILLY. Well . . . .

HOWARD. You didn't crack up again, did you?

WILLY. Oh, no. No . . . .

HOWARD. Geez, you had me worried there for a minute. What's the trouble?

WILLY. Well, tell you the truth, Howard. I've come to the decision that I'd rather not travel any more.

HOWARD. Not travel! Well, what'll you do?

WILLY. Remember, Christmas time, when you had the party here? You said you'd try to think of some spot for me here in town.

HOWARD. With us?

WILLY. Well, sure.

HOWARD. Oh, yeah, yeah. I remember. Well, I couldn't think of anything for you, Willy.

WILLY. I tell ya, Howard. The kids are all grown up, y'know. I don't need much any more. If I could take home—well, sixty-five dollars a week, I could swing it.

HOWARD. Yeah, but Willy, see I—

WILLY. I tell ya why, Howard. Speaking frankly and between the two of us, y'know—I'm just a little tired.

HOWARD. Oh, I could understand that, Willy. But you're a road man, Willy, and we do a road business. We've only got a half-dozen salesmen on the floor here.

WILLY. God knows, Howard, I never asked a favor of any man. But I was with the firm when your father used to carry you in here in his arms.

HOWARD. I know that, Willy, but—

WILLY. Your father came to me the day you were born and asked me what I thought of the name of Howard, may he rest in peace.

HOWARD. I appreciate that, Willy, but there just is no spot here for you. If I had a spot I'd slam you right in, but I just don't have a single solitary spot.

He looks for his lighter. Willy has picked it up and gives it to him. Pause.

WILLY, *with increasing anger.* Howard, all I need to set my table is fifty dollars a week.

HOWARD. But where am I going to put you, kid?

WILLY. Look, it isn't a question of whether I can sell merchandise, is it?

HOWARD. No, but it's a business, kid, and everybody's gotta pull his own weight.

WILLY, *desperately.* Just let me tell you a story, Howard—

HOWARD. 'Cause you gotta admit, business is business.

WILLY, *angrily.* Business is definitely business, but just listen for a minute. You don't understand this. When I was a boy—eighteen, nineteen—I was already on the road. And there was a question in my mind as to whether selling had a future for me. Because in those days I had a yearning to go to Alaska. See, there were three gold strikes in one month in Alaska, and I felt like going out. Just for the ride, you might say.

HOWARD, *barely interested.* Don't say.

WILLY. Oh, yeah, my father lived many years in Alaska. He was an adventurous man. We've got quite a little streak of self-reliance in our family. I thought I'd go out with my older brother and try to locate him, and maybe settle in the North with the old man. And I was almost decided to go, when I met a salesman in the Parker House. His name was Dave Singleman. And he was eighty-four years old, and he'd drummed merchandise in thirty-one states. And old Dave, he'd go up to his room, y'understand, put on his green velvet slippers—I'll never forget—and pick up his phone and call the buyers, and without ever leaving his room, at the age of eighty-four, he made his living. And when I saw that, I realized that selling was the greatest career a man could want. 'Cause what could be more satisfying than to be able to go, at the age of eighty-four, into twenty or thirty different cities, and pick up a phone, and be remembered and loved and helped by so many different people? Do you know? when he died—and by the way he died the death of a salesman, in his green velvet slippers in the smoker of the New York, New Haven and Hartford, going into Boston—when he died, hundreds of salesmen and buyers were at his funeral. Things were sad on a lotta trains for months after that. *He stands up. Howard has not looked at him.* In those days

ACT II] DEATH OF A SALESMAN 685

there was personality in it, Howard. There was respect, and comradeship, and gratitude in it. Today, it's all cut and dried, and there's no chance for bringing friendship to bear—or personality. You see what I mean? They don't know me any more.

HOWARD, *moving away, to the right.* That's just the thing, Willy.

WILLY. If I had forty dollars a week—that's all I'd need. Forty dollars, Howard.

HOWARD. Kid, I can't take blood from a stone, I—

WILLY, *desperation is on him now.* Howard, the year Al Smith was nominated, your father came to me and—

HOWARD, *starting to go off.* I've got to see some people, kid.

WILLY, *stopping him.* I'm talking about your father! There were promises made across this desk! You mustn't tell me you've got people to see—I put thirty-four years into this firm, Howard, and now I can't pay my insurance! You can't eat the orange and throw the peel away—a man is not a piece of fruit! *After a pause.* Now pay attention. Your father—in 1928 I had a big year. I averaged a hundred and seventy dollars a week in commissions.

HOWARD, *impatiently.* Now, Willy, you never averaged—

WILLY, *banging his hand on the desk.* I averaged a hundred and seventy dollars a week in the year of 1928! And your father came to me—or rather, I was in the office here—it was right over this desk— and he put his hand on my shoulder—

HOWARD, *getting up.* You'll have to excuse me, Willy, I gotta see some people. Pull yourself together. *Going out.* I'll be back in a little while.

On Howard's exit, the light on his chair grows very bright and strange.

WILLY. Pull myself together! What the hell did I say to him! My God, I was yelling at him! How could I! *Willy breaks off, staring at the light, which occupies the chair, animating it. He approaches this chair, standing across the desk from it.* Frank, Frank, don't you remember what you told me that time? How you put your hand on my shoulder, and Frank. . . . *He leans on the desk and as he speaks the dead man's name he accidentally switches on the recorder, and instantly*

HOWARD'S SON. ". . . . of New York is Albany. The capital of Ohio is Cincinnati, the capital of Rhode Island is. . . ." *The recitation continues.*

WILLY, *leaping away with fright, shouting.* Ha! Howard! Howard! Howard!

HOWARD, *rushing in.* What happened?

WILLY, *pointing at the machine, which continues nasally, childishly, with the capital cities.* Shut it off! Shut it off!

HOWARD, *pulling the plug out.* Look, Willy . . . .

WILLY, *pressing his hands to his eyes.* I gotta get myself some coffee. I'll get some coffee . . . .

WILLY starts to walk out. HOWARD stops him.

HOWARD, *rolling up the cord.* Willy, look . . . .

WILLY. I'll go to Boston.

HOWARD. Willy, you can't go to Boston for us.

WILLY. Why can't I go?

HOWARD. I don't want you to represent us. I've been meaning to tell you for a long time now.

WILLY. Howard, are you firing me?

HOWARD. I think you need a good long rest, Willy.

WILLY. Howard—

HOWARD. And when you feel better, come back, and we'll see if we can work something out.

WILLY. But I gotta earn money, Howard. I'm in no position to—

HOWARD. Where are your sons? Why don't your sons give you a hand?

WILLY. They're working on a very big deal.

HOWARD. This is no time for false pride, Willy. You go to your sons and you tell them that you're tired. You've got two great boys, haven't you?

WILLY. Oh, no question, no question, but in the meantime . . . .

HOWARD. Then that's that, heh?

WILLY. All right, I'll go to Boston tomorrow.

HOWARD. No, no.

WILLY. I can't throw myself on my sons. I'm not a cripple!

HOWARD. Look, kid, I'm busy this morning.

ACT II] DEATH OF A SALESMAN 687

WILLY, *grasping Howard's arm.* Howard, you've got to let me go to Boston!

HOWARD, *hard, keeping himself under control.* I've got a line of people to see this morning. Sit down, take five minutes, and pull yourself together, and then go home, will ya? I need the office, Willy. *He starts to go, turns, remembering the recorder, starts to push off the table holding the recorder.* Oh, yeah. Whenever you can this week, stop by and drop off the samples. You'll feel better, Willy, and then come back and we'll talk. Pull yourself together, kid, there's people outside.

HOWARD *exits, pushing the table off left.* WILLY *stares into space, exhausted. Now the music is heard—*BEN'S *music—first distantly, then closer, closer. As* WILLY *speaks,* BEN *enters from the right. He carries valise and umbrella.*

WILLY. Oh, Ben, how did you do it? What is the answer? Did you wind up the Alaska deal already?

BEN. Doesn't take much time if you know what you're doing. Just a short business trip. Boarding ship in an hour. Wanted to say good-by.

WILLY. Ben, I've got to talk to you.

BEN, *glancing at his watch.* Haven't the time, William.

WILLY, *crossing the apron to* BEN. Ben, nothing's working out. I don't know what to do.

BEN. Now, look here, William. I've bought timberland in Alaska and I need a man to look after things for me.

WILLY. God, timberland! Me and my boys in those grand outdoors!

BEN. You've a new continent at your doorstep, William. Get out of these cities, they're full of talk and time payments and courts of law. Screw on your fists and you can fight for a fortune up there.

WILLY. Yes, yes! Linda, Linda!

LINDA *enters as of old, with the wash.*

LINDA. Oh, you're back?

BEN. I haven't much time.

WILLY. No, wait! Linda, he's got a proposition for me in Alaska.

LINDA. But you've got— *To* BEN. He's got a beautiful job here.

WILLY. But in Alaska, kid, I could—

LINDA. You're doing well enough, Willy!

BEN, *to* LINDA. Enough for what, my dear?

LINDA, *frightened of* BEN *and angry at him*. Don't say those things to him! Enough to be happy right here, right now. *To* WILLY, *while* BEN *laughs*. Why must everybody conquer the world? You're well liked, and the boys love you, and someday—*to* BEN—why, old man Wagner told him just the other day that if he keeps it up he'll be a member of the firm, didn't he, Willy?

WILLY. Sure, sure. I am building something with this firm, Ben, and if a man is building something he must be on the right track, mustn't he?

BEN. What are you building? Lay your hand on it. Where is it?

WILLY, *hesitantly*. That's true, Linda, there's nothing.

LINDA. Why? *To* BEN. There's a man eighty-four years old—

WILLY. That's right, Ben, that's right. When I look at that man I say, what is there to worry about?

BEN. Bah!

WILLY. It's true, Ben. All he has to do is go into any city, pick up the phone, and he's making his living and you know why?

BEN, *picking up his valise*. I've got to go.

WILLY, *holding* BEN *back*. Look at this boy!

BIFF, *in his high school sweater, enters carrying suitcase*. HAPPY *carries* BIFF's *shoulder guards, gold helmet, and football pants*.

WILLY. Without a penny to his name, three great universities are begging for him, and from there the sky's the limit, because it's not what you do, Ben. It's who you know and the smile on your face! It's contacts, Ben, contacts! The whole wealth of Alaska passes over the lunch table at the Commodore Hotel, and that's the wonder, the wonder of this country, that a man can end with diamonds here on the basis of being liked! *He turns to* BIFF. And that's why when you get out on that field today it's important. Because thousands of people will be rooting for you and loving you. *To* BEN, *who has again begun to leave*. And Ben! when he walks into a business office his name will sound out like a bell and all the doors will open to him! I've seen it, Ben, I've seen it a thousand times! You can't feel it with your hand like timber, but it's there!

BEN. Good-by, William.

ACT II] DEATH OF A SALESMAN 689

WILLY. Ben, am I right? Don't you think I'm right? I value your advice.

BEN. There's a new continent at your doorstep, William. You could walk out rich. Rich! *He is gone.*

WILLY. We'll do it here, Ben! You hear me? We're gonna do it here!

Young BERNARD *rushes in. The gay music of the Boys is heard.*

BERNARD. Oh, gee, I was afraid you left already!

WILLY. Why? What time is it?

BERNARD. It's half-past one!

WILLY. Well, come on, everybody! Ebbets Field next stop! Where's the pennants? *He rushes through the wall-line of the kitchen and out into the living-room.*

LINDA, *to* BIFF. Did you pack fresh underwear?

BIFF, *who has been limbering up*. I want to go!

BERNARD. Biff, I'm carrying your helmet, ain't I?

HAPPY. No, I'm carrying the helmet.

BERNARD. Oh, Biff, you promised me.

HAPPY. I'm carrying the helmet.

BERNARD. How am I going to get in the locker room?

LINDA. Let him carry the shoulder guards. *She puts her coat and hat on in the kitchen.*

BERNARD. Can I, Biff? 'Cause I told everybody I'm going to be in the locker room.

HAPPY. In Ebbets Field it's the clubhouse.

BERNARD. I meant the clubhouse. Biff!

HAPPY. Biff!

BIFF, *grandly, after a slight pause*. Let him carry the shoulder guards.

HAPPY, *as he gives* BERNARD *the shoulder guards*. Stay close to us now.

WILLY *rushes in with the pennants.*

WILLY, *handing them out*. Everybody wave when Biff comes out on the field. HAPPY *and* BERNARD *run off*. You set now, boy?

The music has died away.

BIFF. Ready to go, Pop. Every muscle is ready.

WILLY, *at the edge of the apron.* You realize what this means?

BIFF. That's right, Pop.

WILLY, *feeling* BIFF's *muscles.* You're comin' home this afternoon captain of the All-Scholastic Championship Team of the City of New York.

BIFF. I got it, Pop. And remember, pal, when I take off my helmet, that touchdown is for you.

WILLY. Let's go! *He is starting out, with his arm around* BIFF, *when* CHARLEY *enters, as of old, in knickers.* I got no room for you, Charley.

CHARLEY. Room? For what?

WILLY. In the car.

CHARLEY. You goin' for a ride? I wanted to shoot some casino.

WILLY, *furiously.* Casino! *Incredulously.* Don't you realize what today is?

LINDA. Oh, he knows, Willy. He's just kidding you.

WILLY. That's nothing to kid about!

CHARLEY. No, Linda, what's goin' on?

LINDA. He's playing in Ebbets Field.

CHARLEY. Baseball in this weather?

WILLY. Don't talk to him. Come on, come on! *He is pushing them out.*

CHARLEY. Wait a minute, didn't you hear the news?

WILLY. What?

CHARLEY. Don't you listen to the radio? Ebbets Field just blew up.

WILLY. You go to hell! CHARLEY *laughs. Pushing them out.* Come on, come on! We're late.

CHARLEY, *as they go.* Knock a homer, Biff, knock a homer!

WILLY, *the last to leave, turning to* CHARLEY. I don't think that was funny, Charley. This is the greatest day of his life.

CHARLEY. Willy, when are you going to grow up?

WILLY. Yeah, heh? When this game is over, Charley, you'll be laughing out of the other side of your face. They'll be calling him another Red Grange. Twenty-five thousand a year.

CHARLEY, *kidding.* Is that so?

WILLY. Yeah, that's so.

CHARLEY. Well, then, I'm sorry, Willy. But tell me something.

WILLY. What?
CHARLEY. Who is Red Grange?
WILLY. Put up your hands. Goddam you, put up your hands!

CHARLEY, *chuckling, shakes his head and walks away, around the left corner of the stage.* WILLY *follows him. The music rises to a mocking frenzy.*

WILLY. Who the hell do you think you are, better than everybody else? You don't know everything, you big, ignorant, stupid. . . . Put up your hands!

Light rises, on the right side of the forestage, on a small table in the reception room of CHARLEY'S *office. Traffic sounds are heard.* BERNARD, *now mature, sits whistling to himself. A pair of tennis rackets and an overnight bag are on the floor beside him.*

WILLY, *offstage*. What are you walking away for? Don't walk away! If you're going to say something say it to my face! I know you laugh at me behind my back. You'll laugh out of the other side of your goddam face after this game. Touchdown! Touchdown! Eighty thousand people! Touchdown! Right between the goal posts.

BERNARD *is a quiet, earnest, but self-assured young man.* WILLY'S *voice is coming from right upstage now.* BERNARD *lowers his feet off the table and listens.* JENNY, *his father's secretary, enters.*

JENNY, *distressed*. Say, Bernard, will you go out in the hall?
BERNARD. What is that noise? Who is it?
JENNY. Mr. Loman. He just got off the elevator.
BERNARD, *getting up*. Who's he arguing with?
JENNY. Nobody. There's nobody with him. I can't deal with him any more, and your father gets all upset everytime he comes. I've got a lot of typing to do, and your father's waiting to sign it. Will you see him?
WILLY, *entering*. Touchdown! Touch— *He sees* JENNY. Jenny, Jenny, good to see you. How're ya? Workin'? Or still honest?
JENNY. Fine. How've you been feeling?
WILLY. Not much any more, Jenny. Ha, ha! *He is surprised to see the rackets.*

BERNARD. Hello, Uncle Willy.

WILLY, *almost shocked.* Bernard! Well, look who's here! *He comes quickly, guiltily, to* BERNARD *and warmly shakes his hand.*

BERNARD. How are you? Good to see you.

WILLY. What are you doing here?

BERNARD. Oh, just stopped by to see Pop. Get off my feet till my train leaves. I'm going to Washington in a few minutes.

WILLY. Is he in?

BERNARD. Yes, he's in his office with the accountant. Sit down.

WILLY, *sitting down.* What're you going to do in Washington?

BERNARD. Oh, just a case I've got there, Willy.

WILLY. That so? *Indicating the rackets.* You going to play tennis there?

BERNARD. I'm staying with a friend who's got a court.

WILLY. Don't say. His own tennis court. Must be fine people, I bet.

WILLY, *with a big smile.* Yeah, Biff's in. Working on a very big deal,

BERNARD. They are, very nice. Dad tells me Biff's in town. Bernard.

BERNARD. What's Biff doing?

WILLY. Well, he's been doing very big things in the West. But he decided to establish himself here. Very big. We're having dinner. Did I hear your wife had a boy?

BERNARD. That's right. Our second.

WILLY. Two boys! What do you know!

BERNARD. What kind of a deal has Biff got?

WILLY. Well, Bill Oliver—very big sporting-goods man—he wants Biff very badly. Called him in from the West. Long distance, carte blanche, special deliveries. Your friends have their own private tennis court?

BERNARD. You still with the old firm, Willy?

WILLY, *after a pause.* I'm—I'm overjoyed to see how you made the grade, Bernard, overjoyed. It's an encouraging thing to see a young man really—really— Looks very good for Biff—very— *He breaks off, then.* Bernard— *He is so full of emotion, he breaks off again.*

BERNARD. What is it, Willy?

WILLY, *small and alone.* What—what's the secret?

BERNARD. What secret?

WILLY. How—how did you? Why didn't he ever catch on?

ACT II] DEATH OF A SALESMAN 693

BERNARD. I wouldn't know that, Willy.

WILLY, *confidentially, desperately*. You were his friend, his boyhood friend. There's something I don't understand about it. His life ended after that Ebbets Field game. From the age of seventeen nothing good ever happened to him.

BERNARD. He never trained himself for anything.

WILLY. But he did, he did. After high school he took so many correspondence courses. Radio mechanics; television; God knows what, and never made the slightest mark.

BERNARD, *taking off his glasses*. Willy, do you want to talk candidly?

WILLY, *rising, faces* BERNARD. I regard you as a very brilliant man, Bernard. I value your advice.

BERNARD. Oh, the hell with the advice, Willy. I couldn't advise you. There's just one thing I've always wanted to ask you. When he was supposed to graduate, and the math teacher flunked him—

WILLY. Oh, that son-of-a-bitch ruined his life.

BERNARD. Yeah, but, Willy, all he had to do was go to summer school and make up that subject.

WILLY. That's right, that's right.

BERNARD. Did you tell him not to go to summer school?

WILLY. Me? I begged him to go. I ordered him to go!

BERNARD. Then why wouldn't he go?

WILLY. Why? Why! Bernard, that question has been trailing me like a ghost for the last fifteen years. He flunked the subject, and laid down and died like a hammer hit him!

BERNARD. Take it easy, kid.

WILLY. Let me talk to you—I got nobody to talk to. Bernard, Bernard, was it my fault? Y'see? It keeps going around in my mind, maybe I did something to him. I got nothing to give him.

BERNARD. Don't take it so hard.

WILLY. Why did he lay down? What is the story there? You were his friend!

BERNARD. Willy, I remember, it was June, and our grades came out. And he'd flunked math.

WILLY. That son-of-a-bitch!

BERNARD. No, it wasn't right then. Biff just got very angry, I remember, and he was ready to enroll in summer school.

WILLY, *surprised*. He was?

BERNARD. He wasn't beaten by it at all. But then, Willy, he disappeared from the block for almost a month. And I got the idea that he'd gone up to New England to see you. Did he have a talk with you then?

WILLY *stares in silence.*

BERNARD. Willy?

WILLY, *with a strong edge of resentment in his voice.* Yeah, he came to Boston. What about it?

BERNARD. Well, just that when he came back—I'll never forget this, it always mystifies me. Because I'd thought so well of Biff, even though he'd always taken advantage of me. I loved him, Willy, y'know? And he came back after that month and took his sneakers—remember those sneakers with "University of Virginia" printed on them? He was so proud of those, wore them every day. And he took them down in the cellar, and burned them up in the furnace. We had a fist fight. It lasted at least half an hour. Just the two of us, punching each other down the cellar, and crying right through it. I've often thought of how strange it was that I knew he'd given up his life. What happened in Boston, Willy?

WILLY *looks at him as at an intruder.*

BERNARD. I just bring it up because you asked me.

WILLY, *angrily.* Nothing. What do you mean, "What happened?" What's that got to do with anything?

BERNARD. Well, don't get sore.

WILLY. What are you trying to do, blame it on me? If a boy lays down is that my fault?

BERNARD. Now, Willy, don't get—

WILLY. Well, don't—don't talk to me that way! What does that mean, "What happened?"

CHARLEY *enters. He is in his vest, and he carries a bottle of bourbon.*

CHARLEY. Hey, you're going to miss that train. *He waves the bottle.*

BERNARD. Yeah, I'm going. *He takes the bottle.* Thanks, Pop. *He picks up his rackets and bag.* Good-by, Willy, and don't worry about it. You know, "If at first you don't succeed. . . ."

WILLY. Yes, I believe in that.

ACT II] DEATH OF A SALESMAN 695

BERNARD. But sometimes, Willy, it's better for a man just to walk away.

WILLY. Walk away?

BERNARD. That's right.

WILLY. But if you can't walk away?

BERNARD, *after a slight pause.* I guess that's when it's tough. *Extending his hand.* Good-by, Willy.

WILLY, *shaking* BERNARD's *hand.* Good-by, boy.

CHARLEY, *an arm on* BERNARD's *shoulder.* How do you like this kid? Gonna argue a case in front of the Supreme Court.

BERNARD, *protesting.* Pop!

WILLY, *genuinely shocked, pained, and happy.* No! The Supreme Court!

BERNARD. I gotta run. 'By, Dad!

CHARLEY. Knock 'em dead, Bernard!

BERNARD *goes off.*

WILLY, *as* CHARLEY *takes out his wallet.* The Supreme Court! And he didn't even mention it!

CHARLEY, *counting out money on the desk.* He don't have to—he's gonna do it.

WILLY. And you never told him what to do, did you? You never took any interest in him.

CHARLEY. My salvation is that I never took any interest in anything. There's some money—fifty dollars. I got an accountant inside.

WILLY. Charley, look. . . . *With difficulty.* I got my insurance to pay. If you can manage it—I need a hundred and ten dollars.

CHARLEY *doesn't reply for a moment; merely stops moving.*

WILLY. I'd draw it from my bank but Linda would know, and I. . . .

CHARLEY. Sit down, Willy.

WILLY, *moving toward the chair.* I'm keeping an account of everything, remember. I'll pay every penny back. *He sits.*

CHARLEY. Now listen to me, Willy.

WILLY. I want you to know I appreciate . . .

CHARLEY, *sitting down on the table.* Willy, what're you doin'? What the hell is goin' on in your head?

WILLY. Why? I'm simply. . . .

CHARLEY. I offered you a job. You can make fifty dollars a week. And I won't send you on the road.

WILLY. I've got a job.

CHARLEY. Without pay? What kind of a job is a job without pay? *He rises.* Now, look, kid, enough is enough. I'm no genius but I know when I'm being insulted.

WILLY. Insulted!

CHARLEY. Why don't you want to work for me?

WILLY. What's the matter with you? I've got a job.

CHARLEY. Then what're you walkin' in here every week for?

WILLY, *getting up.* Well, if you don't want me to walk in here—

CHARLEY. I am offering you a job.

WILLY. I don't want your goddam job!

CHARLEY. When the hell are you going to grow up?

WILLY, *furiously.* You big ignoramus, if you say that to me again I'll rap you one! I don't care how big you are! *He's ready to fight.*

Pause.

CHARLEY, *kindly, going to him.* How much do you need, Willy?

WILLY. Charley, I'm strapped. I'm strapped. I don't know what to do. I was just fired.

CHARLEY. Howard fired you?

WILLY. That snotnose. Imagine that? I named him. I named him Howard.

CHARLEY. Willy, when're you gonna realize that them things don't mean anything? You named him Howard, but you can't sell that. The only thing you got in this world is what you can sell. And the funny thing is that you're a salesman, and you don't know that.

WILLY. I've always tried to think otherwise, I guess. I always felt that if a man was impressive, and well liked, that nothing—

CHARLEY. Why must everybody like you? Who liked J. P. Morgan? Was he impressive? In a Turkish bath he'd look like a butcher. But with his pockets on he was very well liked. Now listen, Willy, I know you don't like me, and nobody can say I'm in love with you, but I'll give you a job because—just for the hell of it, put it that way. Now what do you say?

WILLY. I—I just can't work for you, Charley.

CHARLEY. What're you, jealous of me?

WILLY. I can't work for you, that's all, don't ask me why.

CHARLEY, *angered, takes out more bills.* You been jealous of me all your life, you damned fool! Here, pay your insurance. *He puts the money in Willy's hand.*

WILLY. I'm keeping strict accounts.

CHARLEY. I've got some work to do. Take care of yourself. And pay your insurance.

WILLY, *moving to the right.* Funny, y'know? After all the highways, and the trains, and the appointments, and the years, you end up worth more dead than alive.

CHARLEY. Willy, nobody's worth nothin' dead. *After a slight pause.* Did you hear what I said?

WILLY stands still, dreaming.

CHARLEY. Willy!

WILLY. Apologize to Bernard for me when you see him. I didn't mean to argue with him. He's a fine boy. They're all fine boys, and they'll end up big—all of them. Someday they'll all play tennis together. Wish me luck, Charley. He saw Bill Oliver today.

CHARLEY. Good luck.

WILLY, *on the verge of tears.* Charley, you're the only friend I got. Isn't that a remarkable thing? *He goes out.*

CHARLEY. Jesus!

CHARLEY *stares after him a moment and follows. All light blacks out. Suddenly raucous music is heard, and a red glow rises behind the screen at right.* STANLEY, *a young waiter, appears, carrying a table, followed by* HAPPY, *who is carrying two chairs.*

STANLEY, *putting the table down.* That's all right, Mr. Loman, I can handle it myself. *He turns and takes the chairs from* HAPPY *and places them at the table.*

HAPPY, *glancing around.* Oh, this is better.

STANLEY. Sure, in the front there you're in the middle of all kinds a noise. Whenever you got a party, Mr. Loman, you just tell me and I'll put you back here. Y'know, there's a lotta people they don't like it private, because when they go out they like to see a lotta action around them because they're sick and tired to stay in the house by theirself. But I know you, you ain't from Hackensack. You know what I mean?

HAPPY, *sitting down*. So how's it coming, Stanley?

STANLEY. Ah, it's a dog's life. I only wish during the war they'd a took me in the Army. I coulda been dead by now.

HAPPY. My brother's back, Stanley.

STANLEY. Oh, he come back, heh? From the Far West.

HAPPY. Yeah, big cattle man, my brother, so treat him right. And my father's coming too.

STANLEY. Oh, your father too!

HAPPY. You got a couple of nice lobsters?

STANLEY. Hundred per cent, big.

HAPPY. I want them with the claws.

STANLEY. Don't worry, I don't give you no mice. HAPPY *laughs*. How about some wine? It'll put a head on the meal.

HAPPY. No. You remember, Stanley, that recipe I brought you from overseas? With the champagne in it?

STANLEY. Oh, yeah, sure. I still got it tacked up yet in the kitchen. But that'll have to cost a buck apiece anyways.

HAPPY. That's all right.

STANLEY. What'd you, hit a number or somethin'?

HAPPY. No, it's a little celebration. My brother is—I think he pulled off a big deal today. I think we're going into business together.

STANLEY. Great! That's the best for you. Because a family business, you know what I mean?—that's the best.

HAPPY. That's what I think.

STANLEY. 'Cause what's the difference? Somebody steals? It's in the family. Know what I mean? *Sotto voce*. Like this bartender here. The boss is goin' crazy what kinda leak he's got in the cash register. You put it in but it don't come out.

HAPPY, *raising his head*. Sh!

STANLEY. What?

HAPPY. You notice I wasn't lookin' right or left, was I?

STANLEY. No.

HAPPY. And my eyes are closed.

STANLEY. So what's the—?

HAPPY. Strudel's comin'.

STANLEY, *catching on, looks around*. Ah, no, there's no—

ACT II] DEATH OF A SALESMAN

He breaks off as a furred, lavishly dressed girl enters and sits at the next table. Both follow her with their eyes.

STANLEY. Geez, how'd ya know?
HAPPY. I got radar or something. *Staring directly at her profile.* Oooooooo. . . . Stanley.
STANLEY. I think that's for you, Mr. Loman.
HAPPY. Look at that mouth. Oh, God. And the binoculars.
STANLEY. Geez, you got a life, Mr. Loman.
HAPPY. Wait on her.
STANLEY, *going to the girl's table*. Would you like a menu, ma'am?
GIRL. I'm expecting someone, but I'd like a—
HAPPY. Why don't you bring her—excuse me, miss, do you mind? I sell champagne, and I'd like you to try my brand. Bring her a champagne, Stanley.
GIRL. That's awfully nice of you.
HAPPY. Don't mention it. It's all company money. *He laughs.*
GIRL. That's a charming product to be selling, isn't it?
HAPPY. Oh, gets to be like everything else. Selling is selling, y'know.
GIRL. I suppose.
HAPPY. You don't happen to sell, do you?
GIRL. No, I don't sell.
HAPPY. Would you object to a compliment from a stranger? You ought to be on a magazine cover.
GIRL, *looking at him a little archly*. I have been.

STANLEY *comes in with a glass of champagne.*

HAPPY. What'd I say before, Stanley? You see? She's a cover girl.
STANLEY. Oh, I could see, I could see.
HAPPY, *to the* GIRL. What magazine?
GIRL. Oh, a lot of them. *She takes the drink.* Thank you.
HAPPY. You know what they say in France, don't you? "Champagne is the drink of the complexion"—Hya, Biff!

BIFF *has entered and sits with* HAPPY.

BIFF. Hello, kid. Sorry I'm late.
HAPPY. I just got here. Uh, Miss—?
GIRL. Forsythe.

HAPPY. Miss Forsythe, this is my brother.

BIFF. Is Dad here?

HAPPY. His name is Biff. You might've heard of him. Great football player.

GIRL. Really? What team?

HAPPY. Are you familiar with football?

GIRL. No, I'm afraid I'm not.

HAPPY. Biff is quarterback with the New York Giants.

GIRL. Well, that is nice, isn't it? *She drinks.*

HAPPY. Good health.

GIRL. I'm happy to meet you.

HAPPY. That's my name. Hap. It's really Harold, but at West Point they called me Happy.

GIRL, *now really impressed*. Oh, I see. How do you do? *She turns her profile.*

BIFF. Isn't Dad coming?

HAPPY. You want her?

BIFF. Oh, I could never make that.

HAPPY. I remember the time that idea would never come into your head. Where's the old confidence, Biff?

BIFF. I just saw Oliver—

HAPPY. Wait a minute. I've got to see that old confidence again. Do you want her? She's on call.

BIFF. Oh, no. *He turns to look at the* GIRL.

HAPPY. I'm telling you. Watch this. *Turning to the* GIRL. Honey? *She turns to him.* Are you busy?

GIRL. Well, I am. . . . but I could make a phone call.

HAPPY. Do that, will you, honey? And see if you can get a friend. We'll be here for a while. Biff is one of the greatest football players in the country.

GIRL, *standing up*. Well, I'm certainly happy to meet you.

HAPPY. Come back soon.

GIRL. I'll try.

HAPPY. Don't try, honey, try hard.

The GIRL *exits.* STANLEY *follows, shaking his head in bewildered admiration.*

HAPPY. Isn't that a shame now? A beautiful girl like that? That's why I can't get married. There's not a good woman in a thousand. New York is loaded with them, kid!

BIFF. Hap, look—

HAPPY. I told you she was on call!

BIFF, *strangely unnerved*. Cut it out, will ya? I want to say something to you.

HAPPY. Did you see Oliver?

BIFF. I saw him all right. Now look, I want to tell Dad a couple of things and I want you to help me.

HAPPY. What? Is he going to back you?

BIFF. Are you crazy? You're out of your goddam head, you know that?

HAPPY. Why? What happened?

BIFF, *breathlessly*. I did a terrible thing today, Hap. It's been the strangest day I ever went through. I'm all numb, I swear.

HAPPY. You mean he wouldn't see you?

BIFF. Well, I waited six hours for him, see? All day. Kept sending my name in. Even tried to date his secretary so she'd get me to him, but no soap.

HAPPY. Because you're not showin' the old confidence, Biff. He remembered you, didn't he?

BIFF, *stopping* HAPPY *with a gesture*. Finally, about five o'clock, he comes out. Didn't remember who I was or anything. I felt like such an idiot, Hap.

HAPPY. Did you tell him my Florida idea?

BIFF. He walked away. I saw him for one minute. I got so mad I could've torn the walls down! How the hell did I ever get the idea I was a salesman there? I even believed myself that I'd been a salesman for him! And then he gave me one look and—I realized what a ridiculous lie my whole life has been! We've been talking in a dream for fifteen years. I was a shipping clerk.

HAPPY. What'd you do?

BIFF, *with great tension and wonder*. Well, he left, see. And the secretary went out. I was all alone in the waiting-room. I don't know what came over me, Hap. The next thing I know I'm in his office—paneled walls, everything. I can't explain it. I—Hap, I took his fountain pen.

HAPPY. Geez, did he catch you?

BIFF. I ran out. I ran down all eleven flights. I ran and ran and ran.

HAPPY. That was an awful dumb—what'd you do that for?

BIFF, *agonized*. I don't know, I just—wanted to take something, I don't know. You gotta help me, Hap, I'm gonna tell Pop.

HAPPY. You crazy? What for?

BIFF. Hap, he's got to understand that I'm not the man somebody lends that kind of money to. He thinks I've been spiting him all these years and it's eating him up.

HAPPY. That's just it. You tell him something nice.

BIFF. I can't.

HAPPY. Say you got a lunch date with Oliver tomorrow.

BIFF. So what do I do tomorrow?

HAPPY. You leave the house tomorrow and come back at night and say Oliver is thinking it over. And he thinks it over for a couple of weeks, and gradually it fades away and nobody's the worse.

BIFF. But it'll go on forever!

HAPPY. Dad is never so happy as when he's looking forward to something!

WILLY *enters*.

HAPPY. Hello, scout!

WILLY. Gee, I haven't been here in years!

STANLEY *has followed* WILLY *in and sets a chair for him.* STANLEY *starts off but* HAPPY *stops him.*

HAPPY. Stanley!

STANLEY *stands by, waiting for an order.*

BIFF, *going to* WILLY *with guilt, as to an invalid.* Sit down, Pop. You want a drink?

WILLY. Sure, I don't mind.

BIFF. Let's get a load on.

WILLY. You look worried.

BIFF. N-no. *To* STANLEY. Scotch all around. Make it doubles.

STANLEY. Doubles, right. *He goes.*

WILLY. You had a couple already, didn't you?

BIFF. Just a couple, yeah.

WILLY. Well, what happened, boy? *Nodding affirmatively, with a smile.* Everything go all right?

BIFF, *takes a breath, then reaches out and grasps* WILLY'S *hand.* Pal. . . . *He is smiling bravely, and* WILLY *is smiling too.* I had an experience today.

HAPPY. Terrific, Pop.

WILLY. That so? What happened?

BIFF, *high, slightly alcoholic, above the earth.* I'm going to tell you everything from first to last. It's been a strange day. *Silence. He looks around, composes himself as best he can, but his breath keeps breaking the rhythm of his voice.* I had to wait quite a while for him, and—

WILLY. Oliver?

BIFF. Yeah, Oliver. All day, as a matter of cold fact. And a lot of —instances—facts, Pop, facts about my life came back to me. Who was it, Pop? Who ever said I was a salesman with Oliver?

WILLY. Well, you were.

BIFF. No, Dad, I was a shipping clerk.

WILLY. But you were practically—

BIFF, *with determination.* Dad, I don't know who said it first, but I was never a salesman for Bill Oliver.

WILLY. What're you talking about?

BIFF. Let's hold on to the facts tonight, Pop. We're not going to get anywhere bullin' around. I was a shipping clerk.

WILLY, *angrily.* All right, now listen to me—

BIFF. Why don't you let me finish?

WILLY. I'm not interested in stories about the past or any crap of that kind because the woods are burning, boys, you understand? There's a big blaze going on all around. I was fired today.

BIFF, *shocked.* How could you be?

WILLY. I was fired, and I'm looking for a little good news to tell your mother, because the woman has waited and the woman has suffered. The gist of it is that I haven't got a story left in my head, Biff. So don't give me a lecture about facts and aspects. I am not interested. Now what've you got to say to me?

STANLEY *enters with three drinks. They wait until he leaves.*

WILLY. Did you see Oliver?

BIFF. Jesus, Dad!

WILLY. You mean you didn't go up there?

HAPPY. Sure he went up there.

BIFF. I did. I—saw him. How could they fire you?

WILLY, *on the edge of his chair*. What kind of a welcome did he give you?

BIFF. He won't even let you work on commission?

WILLY. I'm out! *Driving*. So tell me, he gave you a warm welcome?

HAPPY. Sure, Pop, sure!

BIFF, *driven*. Well, it was kind of—

WILLY. I was wondering if he'd remember you. *To* HAPPY. Imagine, man doesn't see him for ten, twelve years and gives him that kind of a welcome!

HAPPY. Damn right!

BIFF, *trying to return to the offensive*. Pop, look—

WILLY. You know why he remembered you, don't you? Because you impressed him in those days.

BIFF. Let's talk quietly and get this down to the facts, huh?

WILLY, *as though* BIFF *had been interrupting*. Well, what happened? It's great news, Biff. Did he take you into his office or'd you talk in the waiting-room?

BIFF. Well, he came in, see, and—

WILLY, *with a big smile*. What'd he say? Betcha he threw his arm around you.

BIFF. Well, he kinda—

WILLY. He's a fine man. *To* HAPPY. Very hard man to see, y'know.

HAPPY, *agreeing*. Oh, I know.

WILLY, *to* BIFF. Is that where you had the drinks?

BIFF. Yeah, he gave me a couple of—no, no!

HAPPY, *cutting in*. He told him my Florida idea.

WILLY. Don't interrupt. *To* BIFF. How'd he react to the Florida idea?

BIFF. Dad, will you give me a minute to explain?

WILLY. I've been waiting for you to explain since I sat down here! What happened? He took you into his office and what?

BIFF. Well—I talked. And—and he listened, see.

WILLY. Famous for the way he listens, y'know. What was his answer?

BIFF. His answer was— *He breaks off, suddenly angry.* Dad, you're not letting me tell you what I want to tell you!

WILLY, *accusing, angered.* You didn't see him, did you?

BIFF. I did see him!

WILLY. What'd you insult him or something? You insulted him, didn't you?

BIFF. Listen, will you let me out of it, will you just let me out of it!

HAPPY. What the hell!

WILLY. Tell me what happened!

BIFF, *to* HAPPY. I can't talk to him!

A single trumpet note jars the ear. The light of green leaves stains the house, which holds the air of night and a dream. YOUNG BERNARD *enters and knocks on the door of the house.*

YOUNG BERNARD, *frantically.* Mrs. Loman, Mrs. Loman!

HAPPY. Tell him what happened!

BIFF, *to* HAPPY. Shut up and leave me alone!

WILLY. No, no! You had to go and flunk math!

BIFF. What math? What're you talking about?

YOUNG BERNARD. Mrs. Loman, Mrs. Loman!

LINDA *appears in the house, as of old.*

WILLY, *wildly.* Math, math, math!

BIFF. Take it easy, Pop!

YOUNG BERNARD. Mrs. Loman!

WILLY, *furiously.* If you hadn't flunked you'd've been set by now!

BIFF. Now, look, I'm gonna tell you what happened, and you're going to listen to me.

YOUNG BERNARD. Mrs. Loman!

BIFF. I waited six hours—

HAPPY. What the hell are you saying?

BIFF. I kept sending in my name but he wouldn't see me. So finally he. . . . *He continues unheard as light fades low on the restaurant.*

YOUNG BERNARD. Biff flunked math!

LINDA. No!

YOUNG BERNARD. Birnbaum flunked him! They won't graduate him!

LINDA. But they have to. He's gotta go to the university. Where is he? Biff! Biff!

YOUNG BERNARD. No, he left. He went to Grand Central.

LINDA. Grand— You mean he went to Boston!

YOUNG BERNARD. Is Uncle Willy in Boston?

LINDA. Oh, maybe Willy can talk to the teacher. Oh, the poor, poor boy!

Light on house area snaps out.

BIFF, *at the table, now audible, holding up a gold fountain pen* . . . so I'm washed up with Oliver, you understand? Are you listening to me?

WILLY, *at a loss.* Yeah, sure. If you hadn't flunked—

BIFF. Flunked what? What're you talking about?

WILLY. Don't blame everything on me! I didn't flunk math—you did! What pen?

HAPPY. That was awful dumb, Biff, a pen like that is worth—

WILLY, *seeing the pen for the first time.* You took Oliver's pen?

BIFF, *weakening.* Dad, I just explained it to you.

WILLY. You stole Bill Oliver's fountain pen!

BIFF. I didn't exactly steal it! That's just what I've been explaining to you!

HAPPY. He had it in his hand and just then Oliver walked in, so he got nervous and stuck it in his pocket!

WILLY. My God, Biff!

BIFF. I never intended to do it, Dad!

OPERATOR'S VOICE. Standish Arms, good evening!

WILLY, *shouting.* I'm not in my room!

BIFF, *frightened.* Dad, what's the matter? *He and* HAPPY *stand up.*

OPERATOR. Ringing Mr. Loman for you!

WILLY. I'm not there, stop it!

BIFF, *horrified, gets down on one knee before* WILLY. Dad, I'll make good, I'll make good. WILLY *tries to get to his feet.* BIFF *holds him down.* Sit down now.

WILLY. No, you're no good, you're no good for anything.

BIFF. I am, Dad, I'll find something else, you understand? Now don't worry about anything. *He holds up* WILLY's *face.* Talk to me, Dad.

OPERATOR. Mr. Loman does not answer. Shall I page him?

WILLY, *attempting to stand, as though to rush and silence the* OPERATOR. No, no, no!

HAPPY. He'll strike something, Pop.

WILLY. No, no. . . .

BIFF, *desperately, standing over* WILLY. Pop, listen! Listen to me! I'm telling you something good. Oliver talked to his partner about the Florida idea. You listening? He—he talked to his partner, and he came to me. . . . I'm going to be all right, you hear? Dad, listen to me, he said it was just a question of the amount!

WILLY. Then you . . . got it?

HAPPY. He's gonna be terrific, Pop!

WILLY, *trying to stand.* Then you got it, haven't you? You got it! You got it!

BIFF, *agonized, holds* WILLY *down.* No, no. Look, Pop. I'm supposed to have lunch with them tomorrow. I'm just telling you this so you'll know that I can still make an impression, Pop. And I'll make good somewhere, but I can't go tomorrow, see?

WILLY. Why not? You simply—

BIFF. But the pen, Pop!

WILLY. You give it to him and tell him it was an oversight!

HAPPY. Sure, have lunch tomorrow!

BIFF. I can't say that—

WILLY. You were doing a crossword puzzle and accidentally used his pen!

BIFF. Listen, kid, I took those balls years ago, now I walk in with his fountain pen? That clinches it, don't you see? I can't face him like that! I'll try elsewhere.

PAGE'S VOICE. Paging Mr. Loman!

WILLY. Don't you want to be anything?

BIFF. Pop, how can I go back?

WILLY. You don't want to be anything, is that what's behind it?

BIFF, *now angry at* WILLY *for not crediting his sympathy.* Don't take it that way! You think it was easy walking into that office after what I'd done to him? A team of horses couldn't have dragged me back to Bill Oliver!

WILLY. Then why'd you go?

BIFF. Why did I go? Why did I go! Look at you! Look at what's become of you!

Off left, THE WOMAN *laughs.*

WILLY. Biff, you're going to go to that lunch tomorrow, or—

BIFF. I can't go. I've got no appointment!

HAPPY. Biff, for . . . !

WILLY. Are you spiting me?

BIFF. Don't take it that way! Goddammit!

WILLY, *strikes* BIFF *and falters away from the table.* You rotten little louse! Are you spiting me?

THE WOMAN. Someone's at the door, Willy!

BIFF. I'm no good, can't you see what I am?

HAPPY, *separating them.* Hey, you're in a restaurant! Now cut it out, both of you! *The girls enter.* Hello, girls, sit down.

THE WOMAN *laughs, off left.*

MISS FORSYTHE. I guess we might as well. This is Letta.

THE WOMAN. Willy, are you going to wake up?

BIFF, *ignoring* WILLY. How're ya, miss, sit down. What do you drink?

MISS FORSYTHE. Letta might not be able to stay long.

LETTA. I gotta get up very early tomorrow. I got jury duty. I'm so excited! Were you fellows ever on a jury?

BIFF. No, but I been in front of them! *The girls laugh.* This is my father.

LETTA. Isn't he cute? Sit down with us, Pop.

HAPPY. Sit him down, Biff!

BIFF, *going to him.* Come on, slugger, drink us under the table. To hell with it! Come on, sit down, pal.

On BIFF's *last insistence,* WILLY *is about to sit.*

THE WOMAN, *now urgently.* Willy, are you going to answer the door!

THE WOMAN's *call pulls* WILLY *back. He starts right, befuddled.*

BIFF. Hey, where are you going?
WILLY. Open the door.
BIFF. The door?
WILLY. The washroom. . . . the door. . . . where's the door?
BIFF, *leading* WILLY *to the left.* Just go straight down.

WILLY *moves left.*

THE WOMAN. Willy, Willy, are you going to get up, get up, get up, get up?

WILLY *exits left.*

LETTA. I think it's sweet you bring your daddy along.
MISS FORSYTHE. Oh, he isn't really your father!
BIFF, *at left, turning to her resentfully.* Miss Forsythe, you've just seen a prince walk by. A fine, troubled prince. A hard-working, unappreciated prince. A pal, you understand? A good companion. Always for his boys.
LETTA. That's so sweet.
HAPPY. Well, girls, what's the program? We're wasting time. Come on, Biff. Gather round. Where would you like to go?
BIFF. Why don't you do something for him?
HAPPY. Me!
BIFF. Don't you give a damn for him, Hap?
HAPPY. What're you talking about? I'm the one who—
BIFF. I sense it, you don't give a good goddam about him. *He takes the rolled-up hose from his pocket and puts it on the table in front of* HAPPY. Look what I found in the cellar, for Christ's sake. How can you bear to let it go on?
HAPPY. Me? Who goes away? Who runs off and—
BIFF. Yeah, but he doesn't mean anything to you. You could help him—I can't! Don't you understand what I'm talking about? He's going to kill himself, don't you know that?
HAPPY. Don't I know it! Me!
BIFF. Hap, help him! Jesus . . . help him. . . . Help me, help me, I can't bear to look at his face! *Ready to weep, he hurries out, up right.*
HAPPY, *starting after him.* Where are you going?

MISS FORSYTHE. What's he so mad about?

HAPPY. Come on, girls, we'll catch up with him.

MISS FORSYTHE, *as* HAPPY *pushes her out*. Say, I don't like that temper of his!

HAPPY. He's just a little overstrung, he'll be all right!

WILLY, *off left, as* THE WOMAN *laughs*. Don't answer! Don't answer!

LETTA. Don't you want to tell your father—

HAPPY. No, that's not my father. He's just a guy. Come on, we'll catch Biff, and, honey, we're going to paint this town! Stanley, where's the check! Hey, Stanley!

They exit. STANLEY *looks toward left.*

STANLEY, *calling to* HAPPY *indignantly*. Mr. Loman! Mr. Loman!

STANLEY *picks up a chair and follows them off. Knocking is heard off left.* THE WOMAN *enters, laughing.* WILLY *follows her. She is in a black slip; he is buttoning his shirt. Raw, sensuous music accompanies their speech.*

WILLY. Will you stop laughing? Will you stop?

THE WOMAN. Aren't you going to answer the door? He'll wake the whole hotel.

WILLY. I'm not expecting anybody.

THE WOMAN. Whyn't you have another drink, honey, and stop being so damn self-centered?

WILLY. I'm so lonely.

THE WOMAN. You know you ruined me, Willy? From now on, whenever you come to the office, I'll see that you go right through to the buyers. No waiting at my desk any more, Willy. You ruined me.

WILLY. That's nice of you to say that.

THE WOMAN. Gee, you are self-centered! Why so sad? You are the saddest, self-centeredest soul I ever did see-saw. *She laughs. He kisses her.* Come on inside, drummer boy. It's silly to be dressing in the middle of the night. *As knocking is heard.* Aren't you going to answer the door?

WILLY. They're knocking on the wrong door.

THE WOMAN. But I felt the knocking. And he heard us talking in here. Maybe the hotel's on fire!

WILLY, *his terror rising*. It's a mistake.

THE WOMAN. Then tell him to go away!

WILLY. There's nobody there.

THE WOMAN. It's getting on my nerves, Willy. There's somebody standing out there and it's getting on my nerves!

WILLY, *pushing her away from him.* All right, stay in the bathroom here, and don't come out. I think there's a law in Massachusetts about it, so don't come out. It may be that new room clerk. He looked very mean. So don't come out. It's a mistake, there's no fire.

The knocking is heard again. He takes a few steps away from her, and she vanishes into the wing. The light follows him, and now he is facing YOUNG BIFF, *who carries a suitcase.* BIFF *steps toward him. The music is gone.*

BIFF. Why didn't you answer?

WILLY. Biff! What are you doing in Boston?

BIFF. Why didn't you answer? I've been knocking for five minutes, I called you on the phone—

WILLY. I just heard you. I was in the bathroom and had the door shut. Did anything happen home?

BIFF. Dad—I let you down.

WILLY. What do you mean?

BIFF. Dad. . . .

WILLY. Biffo, what's this about? *Putting his arm around* BIFF. Come on, let's go downstairs and get you a malted.

BIFF. Dad, I flunked math.

WILLY. Not for the term?

BIFF. The term. I haven't got enough credits to graduate.

WILLY. You mean to say Bernard wouldn't give you the answers?

BIFF. He did, he tried, but I only got a sixty-one.

WILLY. And they wouldn't give you four points?

BIFF. Birnbaum refused absolutely. I begged him, Pop, but he won't give me those points. You gotta talk to him before they close the school. Because if he saw the kind of man you are, and you just talked to him in your way, I'm sure he'd come through for me. The class came right before practice, see, and I didn't go enough. Would you talk to him? He'd like you, Pop. You know the way you could talk.

WILLY. You're on. We'll drive right back.

BIFF. Oh, Dad, good work! I'm sure he'll change it for you!

WILLY. Go downstairs and tell the clerk I'm checkin' out. Go right down.

BIFF. Yes, sir! See, the reason he hates me, Pop—one day he was late for class so I got up at the blackboard and imitated him. I crossed my eyes and talked with a lithp.

WILLY, *laughing.* You did? The kids like it?

BIFF. They nearly died laughing!

WILLY. Yeah? What'd you do?

BIFF. The thquare root of thixthy twee is. . . . WILLY *bursts out laughing;* BIFF *joins him.* And in the middle of it he walked in!

WILLY *laughs and* THE WOMAN *joins in offstage.*

WILLY, *without hesitation.* Hurry downstairs and—

BIFF. Somebody in there?

WILLY. No, that was next door.

THE WOMAN *laughs offstage.*

BIFF. Somebody got in your bathroom!

WILLY. No, it's the next room, there's a party—

THE WOMAN, *enters, laughing. She lisps this.* Can I come in? There's something in the bathtub, Willy, and it's moving!

WILLY *looks at* BIFF, *who is staring open-mouthed and horrified at* THE WOMAN.

WILLY. Ah—you better go back to your room. They must be finished painting by now. They're painting her room so I let her take a shower here. Go back, go back. . . . *He pushes her.*

THE WOMAN, *resisting.* But I've got to get dressed, Willy, I can't—

WILLY. Get out of here! Go back, go back. . . . *Suddenly striving for the ordinary.* This is Miss Francis, Biff, she's a buyer. They're painting her room. Go back, Miss Francis, go back. . . .

THE WOMAN. But my clothes, I can't go out naked in the hall!

WILLY, *pushing her offstage.* Get outa here! Go back, go back!

BIFF *slowly sits down on his suitcase as the argument continues offstage.*

ACT II] DEATH OF A SALESMAN 713

THE WOMAN. Where's my stockings? You promised me stockings, Willy!

WILLY. I have no stockings here!

THE WOMAN. You had two boxes of size nine sheers for me, and I want them!

WILLY. Here, for God's sake, will you get outa here!

THE WOMAN, *enters holding a box of stockings.* I just hope there's nobody in the hall. That's all I hope. *To* BIFF. Are you football or baseball?

BIFF. Football.

THE WOMAN, *angry, humiliated.* That's me too. G'night. *She snatches her clothes from* WILLY, *and walks out.*

WILLY, *after a pause.* Well, better get going. I want to get to the school first thing in the morning. Get my suits out of the closet. I'll get my valise. BIFF *doesn't move.* What's the matter? BIFF *remains motionless, tears falling.* She's a buyer. Buys for J. H. Simmons. She lives down the hall—they're painting. You don't imagine— *He breaks off. After a pause.* Now listen, pal, she's just a buyer. She sees merchandise in her room and they have to keep it looking just so. . . . *Pause. Assuming command.* All right, get my suits. BIFF *doesn't move.* Now stop crying and do as I say. I gave you an order. Biff, I gave you an order! Is that what you do when I give you an order? How dare you cry! *Putting his arm around* BIFF. Now look, Biff, when you grow up you'll understand about these things. You mustn't —you mustn't overemphasize a thing like this. I'll see Birnbaum first thing in the morning.

BIFF. Never mind.

WILLY, *getting down beside* BIFF. Never mind! He's going to give you those points. I'll see to it.

BIFF. He wouldn't listen to you.

WILLY. He certainly will listen to me. You need those points for the U. of Virginia.

BIFF. I'm not going there.

WILLY. Heh? If I can't get him to change that mark you'll make it up in summer school. You've got all summer to—

BIFF, *his weeping breaking from him.* Dad. . . .

WILLY, *infected by it.* Oh, my boy. . . .

BIFF. Dad. . . .

WILLY. She's nothing to me, Biff. I was lonely, I was terribly lonely.

BIFF. You—you gave her Mama's stockings! *His tears break through and he rises to go.*

WILLY, *grabbing for* BIFF. I gave you an order!

BIFF. Don't touch me, you—liar!

WILLY. Apologize for that!

BIFF. You fake! You phony little fake! You fake! *Overcome, he turns quickly and weeping fully goes out with his suitcase.* WILLY *is left on the floor on his knees.*

WILLY. I gave you an order! Biff, come back here or I'll beat you! Come back here! I'll whip you!

STANLEY *comes quickly in from the right and stands in front of* WILLY.

WILLY, *shouts at* STANLEY. I gave you an order. . . .

STANLEY. Hey, let's pick it up, pick it up, Mr. Loman. *He helps* WILLY *to his feet.* Your boys left with the chippies. They said they'll see you home.

A second waiter watches some distance away.

WILLY. But we were supposed to have dinner together.

Music is heard, WILLY's *theme.*

STANLEY. Can you make it?

WILLY. I'll—sure, I can make it. *Suddenly concerned about his clothes.* Do I—I look all right?

STANLEY. Sure, you look all right. *He flicks a speck off* WILLY's *lapel.*

WILLY. Here—here's a dollar.

STANLEY. Oh, your son paid me. It's all right.

WILLY, *putting it in* STANLEY's *hand.* No, take it. You're a good boy.

STANLEY. Oh, no, you don't have to. . . .

WILLY. Here—here's some more, I don't need it any more. *After a slight pause.* Tell me—is there a seed store in the neighborhood?

STANLEY. Seeds? You mean like to plant?

As WILLY *turns,* STANLEY *slips the money back into his jacket pocket.*

ACT II] DEATH OF A SALESMAN 715

WILLY. Yes. Carrots, peas. . . .

STANLEY. Well, there's hardware stores on Sixth Avenue, but it may be too late now.

WILLY, *anxiously*. Oh, I'd better hurry. I've got to get some seeds. *He starts off to the right.* I've got to get some seeds, right away. Nothing's planted. I don't have a thing in the ground.

WILLY *hurries out as the light goes down.* STANLEY *moves over to the right after him, watches him off. The other waiter has been staring at* WILLY.

STANLEY, *to the waiter*. Well, whatta you looking at?

The waiter picks up the chairs and moves off right. STANLEY *takes the table and follows him. The light fades on this area. There is a long pause, the sound of the flute coming over. The light gradually rises on the kitchen, which is empty.* HAPPY *appears at the door of the house, followed by* BIFF. HAPPY *is carrying a large bunch of long-stemmed roses. He enters the kitchen, looks around for* LINDA. *Not seeing her, he turns to* BIFF, *who is just outside the house door, and makes a gesture with his hands, indicating "Not here, I guess." He looks into the living-room and freezes. Inside,* LINDA, *unseen, is seated,* WILLY'S *coat on her lap. She rises ominously and quietly and moves toward* HAPPY, *who backs up into the kitchen, afraid.*

HAPPY. Hey, what're you doing up? LINDA *says nothing but moves toward him implacably.* Where's Pop? *He keeps backing to the right, and now* LINDA *is in full view in the doorway to the living-room.* Is he sleeping?

LINDA. Where were you?

HAPPY, *trying to laugh it off*. We met two girls, Mom, very fine types. Here, we brought you some flowers. *Offering them to her.* Put them in your room, Ma.

She knocks them to the floor at BIFF'S *feet. He has now come inside and closed the door behind him. She stares at* BIFF, *silent.*

HAPPY. Now what'd you do that for? Mom, I want you to have some flowers—

LINDA, *cutting* HAPPY *off, violently to* BIFF. Don't you care whether he lives or dies?

HAPPY, *going to the stairs.* Come upstairs, Biff.

BIFF, *with a flare of disgust, to* HAPPY. Go away from me! *To* LINDA. What do you mean, lives or dies? Nobody's dying around here, pal.

LINDA. Get out of my sight! Get out of here!

BIFF. I wanna see the boss.

LINDA. You're not going near him!

BIFF. Where is he? *He moves into the living-room and* LINDA *follows.*

LINDA, *shouting after* BIFF. You invite him for dinner. He looks forward to it all day—BIFF *appears in his parents' bedroom, looks around, and exits*—and then you desert him there. There's no stranger you'd do that to!

HAPPY. Why? He had a swell time with us. Listen, when I—LINDA *comes back into the kitchen*—desert him I hope I don't outlive the day!

LINDA. Get out of here!

HAPPY. Now look, Mom . . .

LINDA. Did you have to go to women tonight? You and your lousy rotten whores!

BIFF *re-enters the kitchen.*

HAPPY. Mom, all we did was follow Biff around trying to cheer him up! *To* BIFF. Boy, what a night you gave me!

LINDA. Get out of here, both of you, and don't come back! I don't want you tormenting him any more. Go on now, get your things together! *To* BIFF. You can sleep in his apartment. *She starts to pick up the flowers and stops herself.* Pick up this stuff, I'm not your maid any more. Pick it up, you bum, you!

HAPPY *turns his back to her in refusal.* BIFF *slowly moves over and gets down on his knees, picking up the flowers.*

LINDA. You're a pair of animals! Not one, not another living soul would have had the cruelty to walk out on that man in a restaurant!

BIFF, *not looking at her.* Is that what he said?

LINDA. He didn't have to say anything. He was so humiliated he nearly limped when he came in.

HAPPY. But, Mom, he had a great time with us—

BIFF, *cutting him off violently.* Shut up!

ACT II] DEATH OF A SALESMAN 717

Without another word, HAPPY *goes upstairs.*

LINDA. You! You didn't even go in to see if he was all right!

BIFF, *still on the floor in front of* LINDA, *the flowers in his hand; with self-loathing.* No. Didn't. Didn't do a damned thing. How do you like that, heh? Left him babbling in a toilet.

LINDA. You louse. You. . . .

BIFF. Now you hit it on the nose! *He gets up, throws the flowers in the wastebasket.* The scum of the earth, and you're looking at him!

LINDA. Get out of here!

BIFF. I gotta talk to the boss, Mom. Where is he?

LINDA. You're not going near him. Get out of this house!

BIFF, *with absolute assurance, determination.* No. We're gonna have an abrupt conversation, him and me.

LINDA. You're not talking to him!

Hammering is heard from outside the house, off right. BIFF *turns toward the noise.*

LINDA, *suddenly pleading.* Will you please leave him alone?

BIFF. What's he doing out there?

LINDA. He's planting the garden!

BIFF, *quietly.* Now? Oh, my God!

BIFF *moves outside,* LINDA *following. The light dies down on them and comes up on the center of the apron as* WILLY *walks into it. He is carrying a flashlight, a hoe, and a handful of seed packets. He raps the top of the hoe sharply to fix it firmly, and then moves to the left, measuring off the distance with his foot. He holds the flashlight to look at the seed packets, reading off the instructions. He is in the blue of night.*

WILLY. Carrots. . . . quarter-inch apart. Rows. . . . one-foot rows. *He measures it off.* One foot. *He puts down a package and measures off.* Beets. *He puts down another package and measures again.* Lettuce. *He reads the package, puts it down.* One foot— *He breaks off as* BEN *appears at the right and moves slowly down to him.* What a proposition, ts, ts. Terrific, terrific. 'Cause she's suffered, Ben, the woman has suffered. You understand me? A man can't go out the way he came in, Ben, a man has got to add up to something. You can't, you can't— BEN *moves toward him as though to interrupt.* You gotta consider, now. Don't answer so quick. Remember, it's a guaranteed twenty-thousand-dollar proposition. Now look, Ben, I want you to go through the ins and outs of this thing with me. I've got nobody to talk to, Ben, and the woman has suffered, you hear me?

BEN, *standing still, considering.* What's the proposition?

WILLY. It's twenty thousand dollars on the barrelhead. Guaranteed, gilt-edged, you understand?

BEN. You don't want to make a fool of yourself. They might not honor the policy.

WILLY. How can they dare refuse? Didn't I work like a coolie to meet every premium on the nose? And now they don't pay off? Impossible!

BEN. It's called a cowardly thing, William.

WILLY. Why? Does it take more guts to stand here the rest of my life ringing up a zero?

BEN, *yielding.* That's a point, William. *He moves, thinking, turns.* And twenty thousand—that *is* something one can feel with the hand, it is there.

WILLY, *now assured, with rising power.* Oh, Ben, that's the whole beauty of it! I see it like a diamond, shining in the dark, hard and rough, that I can pick up and touch in my hand. Not like—like an appointment! This would not be another damned-fool appointment, Ben, and it changes all the aspects. Because he thinks I'm nothing, see, and so he spites me. But the funeral— *Straightening up.* Ben, that funeral will be massive! They'll come from Maine, Massachusetts, Vermont, New Hampshire! All the old-timers with the strange license plates—that boy will be thunder-struck, Ben, because he never realized—I am known! Rhode Island, New York, New Jersey—I am known, Ben, and he'll see it with his eyes once and for all. He'll see what I am, Ben! He's in for a shock, that boy!

BEN, *coming down to the edge of the garden.* He'll call you a coward.

WILLY, *suddenly fearful.* No, that would be terrible.

BEN. Yes. And a damned fool.

WILLY. No, no, he mustn't, I won't have that! *He is broken and desperate.*

BEN. He'll hate you, William.

The gay music of the Boys is heard.

WILLY. Oh, Ben, how do we get back to all the great times? Used to be so full of light, and comradeship, the sleigh-riding in winter, and the ruddiness on his cheeks. And always some kind of good news coming up, always something nice coming up ahead. And never even let me carry the valises in the house, and simonizing, simonizing that little red car! Why, why can't I give him something and not have him hate me?

BEN. Let me think about it. *He glances at his watch.* I still have a little time. Remarkable proposition, but you've got to be sure you're not making a fool of yourself.

BEN *drifts off upstage and goes out of sight.* BIFF *comes down from the left.*

WILLY, *suddenly conscious of* BIFF, *turns and looks up at him, then begins picking up the packages of seeds in confusion.* Where the hell is that seed? *Indignantly.* You can't see nothing out here! They boxed in the whole goddam neighborhood!

BIFF. There are people all around here. Don't you realize that?

WILLY. I'm busy. Don't bother me.

BIFF, *taking the hoe from* WILLY. I'm saying good-by to you, Pop. WILLY *looks at him, silent, unable to move.* I'm not coming back any more.

WILLY. You're not going to see Oliver tomorrow?

BIFF. I've got no appointment, Dad.

WILLY. He put his arm around you, and you've got no appointment?

BIFF. Pop, get this now, will you? Everytime I've left it's been a fight that sent me out of here. Today I realized something about myself and I tried to explain it to you and I—I think I'm just not smart enough to make any sense out of it for you. To hell with whose fault it is or anything like that. *He takes* WILLY's *arm.* Let's just wrap it up, heh? Come on in, we'll tell Mom. *He gently tries to pull* WILLY *to left.*

WILLY, *frozen, immobile, with guilt in his voice.* No, I don't want to see her.

BIFF. Come on! *He pulls again, and* WILLY *tries to pull away.*

WILLY, *highly nervous.* No, no, I don't want to see her.

BIFF, *tries to look into* WILLY's *face, as if to find the answer there.* Why don't you want to see her?

WILLY, *more harshly now.* Don't bother me, will you?

BIFF. What do you mean, you don't want to see her? You don't want them calling you yellow, do you? This isn't your fault; it's me, I'm a bum. Now come inside! WILLY *strains to get away.* Did you hear what I said to you?

WILLY *pulls away and quickly goes by himself into the house.* BIFF *follows.*

LINDA, *to* WILLY. Did you plant, dear?

BIFF, *at the door, to* LINDA. All right, we had it out. I'm going and I'm not writing any more.

LINDA, *going to* WILLY *in the kitchen.* I think that's the best way, dear. 'Cause there's no use drawing it out, you'll just never get along.

WILLY *doesn't respond.*

BIFF. People ask where I am and what I'm doing, you don't know, and you don't care. That way it'll be off your mind and you can start brightening up again. All right? That clears it, doesn't it? WILLY *is silent, and* BIFF *goes to him.* You gonna wish me luck, scout? *He extends his hand.* What do you say?

LINDA. Shake his hand, Willy.

WILLY, *turning to her, seething with hurt.* There's no necessity to mention the pen at all, y'know.

BIFF, *gently.* I've got no appointment, Dad.

WILLY, *erupting fiercely.* He put his arm around . . . ?

BIFF. Dad, you're never going to see what I am, so what's the use of arguing? If I strike oil I'll send you a check. Meantime forget I'm alive.

WILLY, *to* LINDA. Spite, see?

BIFF. Shake hands, Dad.

WILLY. Not my hand.

BIFF. I was hoping not to go this way.

WILLY. Well, this is the way you're going. Good-by.

BIFF *looks at him a moment, then turns sharply and goes to the stairs.*

WILLY, *stops him with* May you rot in hell if you leave this house!

BIFF, *turning.* Exactly what is it that you want from me?

WILLY. I want you to know, on the train, in the mountains, in the valleys, wherever you go, that you cut down your life for spite!

BIFF. No, no.

WILLY. Spite, spite, is the word of your undoing! And when you're down and out, remember what did it. When you're rotting somewhere beside the railroad tracks, remember, and don't you dare blame it on me!

BIFF. I'm not blaming it on you!

WILLY. I won't take the rap for this, you hear?

HAPPY *comes down the stairs and stands on the bottom step, watching.*

BIFF. That's just what I'm telling you!

WILLY, *sinking into a chair at the table, with full accusation.* You're trying to put a knife in me—don't think I don't know what you're doing!

BIFF. All right, phony! Then let's lay it on the line. *He whips the rubber tube out of his pocket and puts it on the table.*

HAPPY. You crazy—

LINDA. Biff! *She moves to grab the hose, but* BIFF *holds it down with his hand.*

BIFF. Leave it there! Don't move it!

WILLY, *not looking at it.* What is that?

BIFF. You know goddam well what that is.

WILLY, *caged, wanting to escape.* I never saw that.

BIFF. You saw it. The mice didn't bring it into the cellar! What is this supposed to do, make a hero out of you? This supposed to make me sorry for you?

WILLY. Never heard of it.

BIFF. There'll be no pity for you, you hear it? No pity!

WILLY, *to* LINDA. You hear the spite!

BIFF. No, you're going to hear the truth—what you are and what I am!

LINDA. Stop it!

WILLY. Spite!

HAPPY, *coming down toward* BIFF. You cut it now!

BIFF, *to* HAPPY. The man don't know who we are! The man is gonna know! *To* WILLY. We never told the truth for ten minutes in this house!

HAPPY. We always told the truth!

BIFF, *turning on him.* You big blow, are you the assistant buyer? You're one of the two assistants to the assistant, aren't you?

HAPPY. Well, I'm practically—

BIFF. You're practically full of it! We all are! And I'm through with it. *To* WILLY. Now hear this, Willy, this is me.

WILLY. I know you!

BIFF. You know why I had no address for three months? I stole a suit in Kansas City and I was in jail. *To* LINDA, *who is sobbing.* Stop crying. I'm through with it.

Linda turns away from them, her hands covering her face.

WILLY. I suppose that's my fault!

BIFF. I stole myself out of every good job since high school!

WILLY. And whose fault is that?

BIFF. And I never got anywhere because you blew me so full of hot air I could never stand taking orders from anybody! That's whose fault it is!

WILLY. I hear that!

LINDA. Don't, Biff!

BIFF. It's goddam time you heard that! I had to be boss big shot in two weeks, and I'm through with it!

WILLY. Then hang yourself! For spite, hang yourself!

BIFF. No! Nobody's hanging himself, Willy! I ran down eleven flights with a pen in my hand today. And suddenly I stopped, you hear me? And in the middle of that office building, do you hear this? I stopped in the middle of that building and I saw—the sky. I saw the things that I love in this world. The work and the food and time to sit and smoke. And I looked at the pen and said to myself, what the hell am I grabbing this for? Why am I trying to become what I don't want to be? What am I doing in an office, making a contemptuous, begging fool of myself, when all I want is out there, waiting for me the minute I say I know who I am! Why can't I say that, Willy? *He tries to make* WILLY *face him, but* WILLY *pulls away and moves to the left.*

WILLY, *with hatred, threateningly.* The door of your life is wide open!

BIFF. Pop! I'm a dime a dozen, and so are you!

WILLY, *turning on him now in an uncontrolled outburst.* I am **not** a dime a dozen! I am Willy Loman, and you are Biff Loman!

BIFF *starts for* WILLY, *but is blocked by* HAPPY. *In his fury,* BIFF *seems on the verge of attacking his father.*

BIFF. I am not a leader of men, Willy, and neither are you. You were never anything but a hard-working drummer who landed in the ash can like all the rest of them! I'm one dollar an hour, Willy! I tried seven states and couldn't raise it. A buck an hour! Do you gather my meaning? I'm not bringing home any prizes any more, and you're going to stop waiting for me to bring them home!

WILLY, *directly to* BIFF. You vengeful, spiteful mutt!

BIFF *breaks from* HAPPY. WILLY, *in fright, starts up the stairs.* BIFF *grabs him.*

BIFF, *at the peak of his fury.* Pop, I'm nothing! I'm nothing, Pop. Can't you understand that? There's no spite in it any more. I'm just what I am, that's all.

BIFF's *fury has spent itself, and he breaks down, sobbing, holding on to* WILLY, *who dumbly fumbles for* BIFF's *face.*

WILLY, *astonished.* What're you doing? What're you doing? *To* LINDA. Why is he crying?

BIFF, *crying, broken.* Will you let me go, for Christ's sake? Will you take that phony dream and burn it before something happens? *Struggling to contain himself, he pulls away and moves to the stairs.* I'll go in the morning. Put him—put him to bed. *Exhausted,* BIFF *moves up the stairs to his room.*

WILLY, *after a long pause, astonished, elevated.* Isn't that—isn't that remarkable? Biff—he likes me!

LINDA. He loves you, Willy!

HAPPY, *deeply moved.* Always did, Pop.

WILLY. Oh, Biff! *Staring wildly.* He cried! Cried to me. *He is choking with his love, and now cries out his promise.* That boy—that boy is going to be magnificent!

BEN *appears in the light just outside the kitchen.*

BEN. Yes, outstanding, with twenty thousand behind him.

LINDA, *sensing the racing of his mind, fearfully, carefully.* Now come to bed, Willy. It's all settled now.

WILLY, *finding it difficult not to rush out of the house.* Yes, we'll sleep. Come on. Go to sleep, Hap.

BEN. And it does take a great kind of a man to crack the jungle.

In accents of dread, BEN's *idyllic music starts up.*

HAPPY, *his arm around* LINDA. I'm getting married, Pop, don't forget it. I'm changing everything. I'm gonna run that department before the year is up. You'll see, Mom. *He kisses her.*

BEN. The jungle is dark but full of diamonds, Willy.

WILLY *turns, moves, listening to* BEN.

LINDA. Be good. You're both good boys, just act that way, that's all.

HAPPY. 'Night, Pop. *He goes upstairs.*

LINDA, *to* WILLY. Come, dear.

BEN, *with greater force.* One must go in to fetch a diamond out.

WILLY, *to* LINDA, *as he moves slowly along the edge of the kitchen, toward the door.* I just want to get settled down, Linda. Let me sit alone for a little.

LINDA, *almost uttering her fear.* I want you upstairs.

WILLY, *taking her in his arms.* In a few minutes, Linda. I couldn't sleep right now. Go on, you look awful tired. *He kisses her.*

BEN. Not like an appointment at all. A diamond is rough and hard to the touch.

WILLY. Go on now. I'll be right up.

LINDA. I think this is the only way, Willy.

WILLY. Sure, it's the best thing.

BEN. Best thing!

ACT II] DEATH OF A SALESMAN 725

WILLY. The only way. Everything is gonna be—go on, kid, get to bed. You look so tired.

LINDA. Come right up.

WILLY. Two minutes.

LINDA *goes into the living-room, then reappears in her bedroom.* WILLY *moves just outside the kitchen door.*

WILLY. Loves me. *Wonderingly.* Always loved me. Isn't that a remarkable thing? Ben, he'll worship me for it!

BEN, *with promise.* It's dark there, but full of diamonds.

WILLY. Can you imagine that magnificence with twenty thousand dollars in his pocket?

LINDA, *calling from her room.* Willy! Come up!

WILLY, *calling into the kitchen.* Yes! Yes. Coming! It's very smart, you realize that, don't you, sweetheart? Even Ben sees it. I gotta go, baby. 'By! 'By! *Going over to* BEN, *almost dancing.* Imagine? When the mail comes he'll be ahead of Bernard again!

BEN. A perfect proposition all around.

WILLY. Did you see how he cried to me? Oh, if I could kiss him, Ben!

BEN. Time, William, time!

WILLY. Oh, Ben, I always knew one way or another we were gonna make it, Biff and I!

BEN, *looking at his watch.* The boat. We'll be late. *He moves slowly off into the darkness.*

WILLY, *elegiacally, turning to the house.* Now when you kick off, boy, I want a seventy-yard boot, and get right down the field under the ball, and when you hit, hit low and hit hard, because it's important, boy. *He swings around and faces the audience.* There's all kinds of important people in the stands, and the first thing you know.... *Suddenly realizing he is alone.* Ben! Ben, where do I....? *He makes a sudden movement of search.* Ben, how do I....?

LINDA, *calling.* Willy, you coming up?

WILLY, *uttering a gasp of fear, whirling about as if to quiet her.* Sh!

He turns around as if to find his way; sounds, faces, voices, seem to be swarming in upon him and he flicks at them, crying, Sh! Sh!

Suddenly music, faint and high, stops him. It rises in intensity, almost to an unbearable scream. He goes up and down on his toes, and rushes off around the house. Shhh!

LINDA. Willy?

There is no answer. LINDA *waits.* BIFF *gets up off his bed. He is still in his clothes.* HAPPY *sits up.* BIFF *stands listening.*

LINDA, *with real fear.* Willy, answer me! Willy!

There is the sound of a car starting and moving away at full speed.

LINDA. No!
BIFF, *rushing down the stairs.* Pop!

As the car speeds off, the music crashes down in a frenzy of sound, which becomes the soft pulsation of a single cello string. BIFF *slowly returns to his bedroom. He and* HAPPY *gravely don their jackets.* LINDA *slowly walks out of her room. The music has developed into a dead march. The leaves of day are appearing over everything.* CHARLEY *and* BERNARD, *somberly dressed, appear and knock on the kitchen door.* BIFF *and* HAPPY *slowly descend the stairs to the kitchen as* CHARLEY *and* BERNARD *enter. All stop a moment when* LINDA, *in clothes of mourning, bearing a little bunch of roses, comes through the draped doorway into the kitchen. She goes to* CHARLEY *and takes his arm. Now all move toward the audience, through the wall-line of the kitchen. At the limit of the apron,* LINDA *lays down the flowers, kneels, and sits back on her heels. All stare down at the grave.*

Requiem

CHARLEY. It's getting dark, Linda.

LINDA *doesn't react. She stares at the grave.*

BIFF. How about it, Mom? Better get some rest, heh? They'll be closing the gate soon.

LINDA *makes no move. Pause.*

HAPPY, *deeply angered.* He had no right to do that. There was no necessity for it. We would've helped him.

CHARLEY, *grunting.* Hmmm.

BIFF. Come along, Mom.

LINDA. Why didn't anybody come?

CHARLEY. It was a very nice funeral.

LINDA. But where are all the people he knew? Maybe they blame him.

CHARLEY. Naa. It's a rough world, Linda. They wouldn't blame him.

LINDA. I can't understand it. At this time especially. First time in thirty-five years we were just about free and clear. He only needed a little salary. He was even finished with the dentist.

CHARLEY. No man only needs a little salary.

LINDA. I can't understand it.

BIFF. There were a lot of nice days. When he'd come home from a trip; or on Sundays, making the stoop; finishing the cellar; putting on the new porch; when he built the extra bathroom; and put up the garage. You know something, Charley, there's more of him in that front stoop than in all the sales he ever made.

CHARLEY. Yeah. He was a happy man with a batch of cement.

LINDA. He was so wonderful with his hands.

BIFF. He had the wrong dreams. All, all, wrong.

HAPPY, *almost ready to fight* BIFF. Don't say that!

BIFF. He never knew who he was.

CHARLEY, *stopping* HAPPY's *movement and reply. To* BIFF. Nobody dast blame this man. You don't understand: Willy was a salesman. And for a salesman, there is no rock bottom to the life. He don't put a bolt to a nut, he don't tell you the law or give you medicine. He's a man way out there in the blue, riding on a smile and a shoeshine. And when they start not smiling back—that's an earthquake. And then you get yourself a couple of spots on your hat, and you're finished. Nobody dast blame this man. A salesman is got to dream, boy. It comes with the territory.

BIFF. Charley, the man didn't know who he was.

HAPPY, *infuriated.* Don't say that!

BIFF. Why don't you come with me, Happy?

HAPPY. I'm not licked that easily. I'm staying right in this city, and I'm gonna beat this racket! *He looks at* BIFF, *his chin set.* The Loman Brothers!

BIFF. I know who I am, kid.

HAPPY. All right, boy. I'm gonna show you and everybody else that Willy Loman did not die in vain. He had a good dream. It's the only dream you can have—to come out number-one man. He fought it out here, and this is where I'm gonna win it for him.

BIFF, *with a hopeless glance at* HAPPY, *bends toward his mother.* Let's go, Mom.

LINDA. I'll be with you in a minute. Go on, Charley. *He hesitates.* I want to, just for a minute. I never had a chance to say good-by.

CHARLEY *moves away, followed by* HAPPY. BIFF *remains a slight distance up and left of* LINDA. *She sits there, summoning herself. The flute begins, not far away, playing behind her speech.*

LINDA. Forgive me, dear. I can't cry. I don't know what it is, but I can't cry. I don't understand it. Why did you ever do that? Help me, Willy, I can't cry. It seems to me that you're just on another trip. I keep expecting you. Willy, dear, I can't cry. Why did you do it? I search and search and I search, and I can't understand it, Willy. I made the last payment on the house today. Today, dear. And there'll be nobody home. *A sob rises in her throat.* We're free and clear. *Sobbing more fully, released.* We're free. BIFF *comes slowly toward her.* We're free . . . We're free . . .

BIFF *lifts her to her feet and moves out up right with her in his arms.* LINDA *sobs quietly.* BERNARD *and* CHARLEY *come together and follow them, followed by* HAPPY. *Only the music of the flute is left on the darkening stage as over the house the hard towers of the apartment buildings rise into sharp focus, and*

The Curtain Falls

REVIEWS

Brooks Atkinson*

EVEN THE PEOPLE who have had nothing to do with the production of Arthur Miller's *Death of a Salesman* take a kind of platonic pride in it. What Mr. Miller has achieved somehow seems to belong to everybody. For he is writing as an American with an affectionate understanding of American family people and their family problems; and everybody recognizes in his tragic play things that they know are poignantly true. Although Mr. Miller is the author, he does not dissociate himself from his simple story of an ordinary family. He participates by recording it with compassion.

Discarded in his old age from the only world he knows, Willy Loman, the worn-out salesman, crawls into his grave where he thinks he is worth more to his family than he would be if he were still tinkering around the house. But Mr. Miller does not blame Willy, his sons, his boss or the system, and he draws no moral conclusions. In the space of one somber evening in the theatre he has caught the life and death of a traveling salesman and told it tenderly with a decent respect for Willy's dignity as a man.

In *All My Sons* two seasons ago Mr. Miller was arguing a moral point; like an efficient craftsman, he constructed his drama to reach a conclusion. That was a first-rate piece of work by an author of high convictions. But without being precious or self-conscious, *Death of a Salesman* is a creative work of art in which the form is so completely blended with the theme that you are scarcely aware of the writing. You accept it as a whole—play, acting, directing and scene designing fused into a unit of expression.

From the technical point of view Mr. Miller has accomplished some remarkable things in this drama. Without moving scenery, he has

* *The New York Times*, February 11, 1949. Used by permission of the author.

covered the past and present of Willy's itinerant career in Brooklyn, New York and Boston, recorded the separate careers of his two sons and the neighbors, touched on the problems and personality of Willy's boss and introduced some imagery from Willy's separate dream-world.

At one time, this would have been highly daring and experimental in the theatre. We once had a jargon for things like these—"expressionistic," "constructivist," "centrifugal." But *Death of a Salesman* belongs in none of the categories. It is a fresh creation in a style of its own. Mr. Miller has mastered his material and turned it directly into the grievous life of an affable man.

Strictly speaking there is a moral basis for the catastrophe in the last act. Willy has always believed in something that is unsound. He has assumed that success comes to those who are "well liked," as he puts it. He does not seem to be much concerned about the quality of the product he is selling. His customers buy, he thinks, because they like him—because he is hale and hearty and a good man with jokes.

Out of sheer physical exuberance he rears his son, Biff, in the same tradition. Biff is popular, too. Willy indulgently overlooks Biff's easy going cheating in school and petty pilfering from the contractor next door. So long as Biff plays good football, wins games, gets his name in the newspapers and makes friends Willy thinks that he will succeed in life and carry on the jovial Loman tradition.

But these are the most unsubstantial things in a life. Although Biff is well liked, he is flunked out of school because he is not interested in studying. Although he is as good hearted as his father, he never gets over his habit of stealing, which finally lands him in jail. Willy has staked his whole happiness on Biff's success, but Biff is a failure.

And the unsubstantial quality of his own success catches up with Willy in his old age. The formula of personal popularity no longer works. The competition of chain stores has eliminated the personal element. Willy's friends are old or dead. Willy is old himself. He no longer has the physical gusto for slapping people on the back and breaking down resistance with good fellowship. He cannot stand the nervous strain of driving his car. Willy has lost his usefulness to the business world because he has founded a career on things that are ephemeral. He and Biff are good fellows and good animals—strong, full of fun and carefree. But they live in a world of golden illusion and they founder on reality in the end.

Not that Mr. Miller is holding them up as bad examples. On the contrary he knows that they are good men—especially Willy, who has never had a mean thought in his life. Out of sheer good nature he has gone cheerfully down a dead end street, always devoted to his family and carelessly sure of himself. Although his two boys do not understand him, they love him. His wife not only loves him but understands him thoroughly. Mr. Miller is not writing about ideas but about human beings, whom he is sufficiently modest to be able to value properly. And the tragedy of *Death of a Salesman* is almost unbearable in the last act because Mr. Miller has drawn the portrait of a good man who represents the homely, decent, kindly virtues of a middle-class society.

By common consent, this is one of the finest dramas in the whole range of the American theatre. Humane in its point of view, it has stature and insight, awareness of life, respect for people and knowledge of American manners and of modern folkways. From the technical point of view, it is virtuoso theatre. It brings the whole theatre alive.

Although Elia Kazan has done some memorable jobs of direction in the past few years, he has never equaled the selfless but vibrant expression of this epic drama which has force, clarity, rhythm and order in the performing. Without being fastidious, the performance has taste. Jo Mielziner's skeletonized setting is a brilliant design, tragic in mood, but also selfless and practical. Alex North has composed a stirring interpretive score which, like the direction and scenery, has the grace to melt unobtrusively into the work as a whole.

The acting is superb, particularly in Mildred Dunnock's warmly devoted portrait of the wife and Arthur Kennedy's turbulent, anxious playing of Biff. Although the part of the bewildered salesman is fully developed in Mr. Miller's writing, Lee J. Cobb brings a touch of human grandeur to the acting. He keeps it on the high plane of tragic acting—larger than the specific life it is describing. Willy is not a great man, but his tragedy is great, partly because of the power and range of Mr. Cobb's acting. When Willy's life collapses, a whole world crashes because Mr. Cobb fills the play with so much solid humanity. In terms of the business world Willy is insignificant. But in terms of life he is a hero. Like Mr. Miller, Mr. Cobb knows what Willy is worth, and so do all of us.

Ivor Brown[*]

Before the production of *Death of a Salesman* there was considerable publicity about this smashing New York success. One critic, writing after the opening—as critics usually do—remarked that he seemed to be the only person who had not reviewed the play in advance. Roughly, the story was that New Yorkers were so overwhelmed by Arthur Miller's tragedy of the defeated salesman that they sat sniffling and even sobbing and staggered into the street with tear-streaked faces.

I understand there was a certain amount of ballyhoo in all this. New York was certainly hard hit by the piece and accepted it as a tremendous and typical tragedy of a typical national figure; but that the flooded floors of the theatre had to be mopped up after tearful sessions is not true. It is a pity that so much was written in advance and such exaggeration used.

From the box-office point of view I doubt whether the insistently repeated information that a play has knocked the audience all of a heap in another metropolis is prudent. The recipients of the news are apt to say grimly, "Now let them show us," thus seeming to imply, "We're not simpletons or cry-babies. They won't get us fainting in the stalls."

When *Death of a Salesman* was given in London it was received with fair ovation and mainly respectful, appreciative notices. But I saw no signs of emotional collapse in the audience; nor have I heard of any since. What was praised was the imaginative staging and performance of a moving play about a poor, flashy, self-deceiving little man. Moving—but not overwhelming.

There were cheers for Paul Muni but no tears for Willy Loman, central figure of the play. I doubt whether one extra handkerchief has been sold by the haberdashers of the neighborhood.

Why the astonishing impact of this play upon Broadway? One point that has been made is that Americans can identify themselves with Willy because his outlook is so largely theirs, whatever his faults may have been. This matter of self-identification with the person or the story is, I think, very important in establishing success.

[*] *The New York Times Magazine Section*, August 28, 1949. Used by permission of the author.

In Britain we notice it particularly in the case of radio characters. There are several family sagas which are given regular space on the air—"The McFlannels" in Scotland and Dr. Dale and his family of "Mrs. Dale's Diary" in England. Mrs. Dale comes on in the afternoons and there is dead silence for the "ordinary adventures of herself and her family" in myriads of parlors, kitchens and workshops.

Let one of these chronicles be long enough established and public opinion will not allow it to be stopped. It just has to go on and on. Myriads of women are identifying themselves with Mrs. Dale. One proof of this close affection is that presents arrive at BBC marked for Mrs. Dale, not for the actress playing the part.

In Arthur Miller's character study, Willy Loman is carefully labeled a salesman. The word has more value in the United States than in Britain. Remember that Britain since 1939 has needed workers and buyers rather than drummers. Now, of course, it needs as never before salesmanship abroad. But at home the supply of goods was still so short until a year ago that little competitive salesmanship was needed. Rivalry is getting keen again but the commercial traveler, as we call the drummer, has never been the figure in English life that he has been in America. So this title, "Death of a Salesman," strikes home less strongly. There is not the same sense of a national type.

Then Willy has a pathetic faith in being liked. Here again Arthur Miller seems to have seized on an essential feature of American psychology. You cannot sell a book by the million in Britain by giving advice on how to make friends and so gain influence. Willy, in the play, reflects over and over again his belief that he is beloved of buyers and that to be beloved is to be a success. "The wonder of this country is that a man can end with diamonds on the basis of being liked."

Whether this is true of the United States, it is certainly untrue of England. We regard the very likable fellow as one who will end in the way he began: Not starving, not a plutocrat, just making do. The diamond-set class are the unlikable—or at least so people think. We're suspicious of popularity hunters, the man with a fixed smile and a quip always ready. In the North especially a salesman would do much better if he were regarded as "Jannock" (i.e., genuine) than as "the life of the party."

Not that we austerely avoid or snub the good companion; we just don't think that he will get very far unless he's a good deal more than that.

This throws some light on the failure of Willy Loman to draw tears by the gallon from British eyes. The British are likely to despise Loman for an outlook on life (smiles into diamonds) which other nations regard as quite natural. And if you despise a man you naturally don't become frantically upset by his downfall.

Willy's fatal adulation of his supposedly wonderful sons is also outside British sympathy. Of course, there are doting parents who spoil their children everywhere. But Loman's silly encouragement of his boys to be "sports," which turns one of them into a seedy seducer and the other into a drifting lawbreaker, is perhaps less intelligible in England than elsewhere, despite our national taste for games.

At certain social levels, Britain may be called sport crazy. But the majority keep their sense of values.

Again Loman's hunger for success through popularity makes less appeal to British compassion since the way of life in Britain is obviously less competitive. That Britain has gone too far in its search for equality at the expense of liberty is my own opinion and that of millions of others, too. But whether right or wrong, the fact is that while British parents like their boys and girls to do well, they are chiefly eager to seek security for them by finding jobs at the bottom of the ladder in big business or in teaching or in civil service —a ladder up which it will be easy to climb gradually if no silly mistakes are made.

This preoccupation with security is doubtless a natural weakness. But there it is, and those who value steady plodding instead of success hunting by the good-at-games and smile-on-your-buddy methods of Lomanism will hardly be struck with horror when the little man is finally ruined by a tough employer. This fellow applies the tests of success without mercy to Loman's own inadequate performance as an aging salesman.

I take from my American friends the information that New York has a very large and hard core of unhappiness at the heart of it. This is attributed to the immense drive of a vast nation, a great many of whose more ambitious members want to get to Manhattan. Since everybody in New York cannot have the best jobs or even good ones, and since pressure from the outside continues unabated, many of the incomers must experience frustration and disappointment.

Loman of Brooklyn is a typical New Yorker of the Failure Fringe.

He hasn't "made it" and he has bluffed and dodged to pretend that he has. His wife sees through him, his brother-in-law gives him doles, and still he bluffs. Still he masquerades as a success. Pathetic? Yes, but its pathos is more easily recognizable in Brooklyn than in Balham. Loman cannot fill the British playgoer with the compassion due a next door neighbor because he is not a Londoner's neighbor at all. He is just the subject of an efficient and well-acted play which one goes to see dispassionately, praises and before long forgets.

What has puzzled me about these Broadway tears for Willy Loman is the fact that the average shedder of those tears over a stage figure couldn't be bothered for one minute with Willy Loman if the poor little man came round in real life to beg a small loan. I don't say that he would grudge Loman the money, for Americans are uncommonly generous, but he would grudge him sympathy for Americans are quite ready to be tough. After all, there is almost nothing to be said for Loman, who lies to himself as to others, has no creed or philosophy of life beyond that of making money by making buddies, and cannot even be faithful to his helpful and long-suffering wife.

It occurred to me that New York's emotional response to the salesman whose leaving of life (modestly to enrich his family with insurance money) is his lonely piece of good conduct, may be due to a wide subconscious feeling that the fate of failure is too hard. The large, hard core of unhappiness is made to seem actual by the fictitious personage of Loman. So those who in their offices would brush him aside as just one more shabby and ineffective nuisance among a million may be sitting in their expensive seats to pay him the tribute of a sigh, even of a tear, since he is the symbol of all those failures on which alone success can be built.

Though some London critics declared themselves unmoved by "Death of a Salesman," it is certainly a skillful piece of stagecraft, and the production deserves unreserved applause. It suits the mood of the time, both here and in America, because it makes the little man the hero. In that respect both publics are alike.

There are many points of psychological detail in which Loman is a stranger to British playgoers. But now the little man is everywhere the center of attraction and of sympathy. Thus news interest and a good production have been filling the Phoenix Theatre constantly.

Both nations accept the change of taste about suitable characters for tragedy. The classic hero, the Elizabethan hero, had to be a man of might, power and position. He fell because of some flaw in his character. The fall was greater because he was himself great. He was not a clown tumbling off his chair: he was a king crashing tremendously from his throne.

But now on both sides of the Atlantic we have stool tragedies, not throne tragedies. It is the clerk, not the king, who inspires the tragedian, Loman not Highman who throws Broadway into compassionate lamentation.

London too will like that. We recently had from the all-conquering Terence Rattigan a tragedy about the globe-trotting Alexander the Great. It was not one of his box-office victories. Alexander the Great touches few hearts nowadays. But Loman the Little? There I think Britain and the United States are on common ground.

For that reason London support for the play has been abundant so far. The Age of the Common Man is the Age of the Shrimp, and Loman, because he pretends to be a prawn,* is really just a little shrimp. And nowadays we all are a dish of shrimps. The nations, not united on much, are at least united on that.

John Mason Brown†

George Jean Nathan once described a certain actress's Camille as being the first Camille he had ever seen who had died of catarrh. This reduction in scale of a major disease to an unpleasant annoyance is symptomatic of more than the acting practice of the contemporary stage. Even our dramatists, at least most of them, tend in their writing, so to speak, to turn t.b. into a sniffle. They seem ashamed of the big things; embarrassed by the raw emotions; afraid of the naked passions; and unaware of life's brutalities and tolls.

Of understatement they make a fetish. They have all the reticences and timidities of the over-civilized and undemonstrative. They pride themselves upon writing around a scene rather than from or to it; upon what they hold back instead of upon what they release. They paint with pastels, not oils, and dodge the primary anguishes as they would the primary colors.

Their characters belong to an anemic brood. Lacking blood, they lack

* In American usage: shrimp. What the British call shrimp is much smaller.

† From "Seeing Things," *Saturday Review of Literature*, February 26, 1949. Used by permission of the author.

not only violence but humanity. They are the puppets of contrivance, not the victims of circumstance or themselves. They are apt to be shadows without substance, surfaces without depths. They can be found in the *dramatis personae* but not in the telephone book. If they have hearts, their murmurings are seldom audible. They neither hear nor allow us to hear those inner whisperings of hope, fear, despair, or joy, which are the true accompaniment to spoken words. Life may hurt them, but they do not suffer from the wounds it gives them so that we, watching them, are wounded ourselves and suffer with them.

This willingness, this ability, to strike unflinchingly upon the anvil of human sorrow is one of the reasons for O'Neill's pre-eminence and for the respect in which we hold the best work of Clifford Odets and Tennessee Williams. It is also the source of Arthur Miller's unique strength and explains why his fine new play, *Death of a Salesman*, is an experience at once pulverizing and welcome.

Mr. Miller is, of course, remembered as the author of *Focus*, a vigorous and terrifying novel about anti-Semitism, and best known for *All My Sons*, which won the New York Critics Award two seasons back. Although that earlier play lacked the simplicity, hence the muscularity, of Mr. Miller's novel, it was notable for its force. Overelaborate as it may have been, it introduced a new and unmistakable talent. If as a young man's script it took advantage of its right to betray influences, these at least were of the best. They were Ibsen and Chekhov. The doctor who wandered in from next door might have been extradited from *The Three Sisters*. The symbolical use to which the apple tree was put was pure Ibsen. So, too, was the manner in which the action was maneuvered from the present back into the past in order to rush forward. Even so, Mr. Miller's own voice could be heard in *All My Sons*, rising strong and clear above those other voices. It was a voice that deserved the attention and admiration it won. It was not afraid of being raised. It spoke with heat, fervor, and compassion. Moreover, it had something to say.

In *Death of a Salesman* this same voice can be heard again. It has deepened in tone, developed wonderfully in modulation, and gained in carrying power. Its authority has become full-grown. Relying on no borrowed accents, it now speaks in terms of complete accomplishment rather than exciting promise. Indeed, it is released in a drama which is not only by all odds the best play to have been written by an American this season, but a play which provides one of the modern theatre's most overpowering evenings.

How good the writing of this or that of Mr. Miller's individual scenes may be, I do not know. Nor do I really care. When hit in the face, you do not bother to count the knuckles which strike you. All that matters, all you remember, is the staggering impact of the blow.

Mr. Miller's is a terrific wallop, as furious in its onslaught on the heart as on the head. His play is the most poignant statement of man as he must face himself to have come out of our theatre. It finds the stuffs of life so mixed with the stuffs of the stage that they become one and indivisible.

If the proper study of mankind is man, man's inescapable problem is himself—what he would like to be, what he is, what he is not, and yet what he must live and die with. These are the moving, everyday, all-inclusive subjects with which Mr. Miller deals in *Death of a Salesman*. He handles them unflinchingly, with enormous sympathy, with genuine imagination, and in a mood which neither the prose of his dialogue nor the reality of his probing can rob of its poetry. Moreover, he has the wisdom and the insight not to blame the "system," in Mr. Odets's fashion, for what are the inner frailties and shortcomings of the individual. His rightful concern is with the dilemmas which are timeless in the drama because they are timeless in life.

Mr. Miller's play is a tragedy modern and personal, not classic and heroic. Its central figure is a little man sentenced to discover his smallness rather than a big man undone by his greatness. Although he happens to be a salesman tested and found wanting by his own very special crises, all of us sitting out front are bound to be shaken, long before the evening is over, by finding something of ourselves in him.

Mr. Miller's Willy Loman is a family man, father of two sons. He is sixty-three and has grubbed hard all his life. He has never possessed either the daring or the gold-winning luck of his prospector brother, who wanders through the play as a somewhat shadowy symbol of success but a necessary contrast. Stupid, limited, and confused as Willy Loman may have been, however, no one could have questioned his industry or his loyalty to his family and his firm. He has loved his sons and, when they were growing up, been rewarded by the warmth of their returned love. He loves his wife, too, and has been unfaithful to her only because of his acute, aching loneliness when on the road.

He has lived on his smile and on his hopes; survived from sale to sale; been sustained by the illusion that he has countless friends in his territory, that everything will be all right, that he is a success, and that his boys will be successes also. His misfortune is that he has gone through his life as an eternal adolescent, as someone who has not dared to take stock, as someone who never knew who he was. His personality has been his profession; his energy, his protection. His major ambition has been not only to be liked, but well liked. His ideal for himself and for his sons has stopped with an easy, back-slapping, sports-loving, locker-room popularity. More than ruining his sons so that one has become a woman chaser and the other a thief, his standards have turned both boys against their father.

When Mr. Miller's play begins, Willy Loman has reached the ebb-tide years. He is too old and worn out to continue traveling. His back aches when he stoops to lift the heavy sample cases that were once his pride. His tired, wandering mind makes it unsafe for him to drive the car which has carried him from one town and sale to the next. His sons see through him and despise him. His wife sees through him and defends him, knowing him to be better than most and, at any rate, well-intentioned. What is far worse, when he is fired from his job he begins to see through himself. He realizes he is, and has been, a failure. Hence his deliberate smash-up in his car, in order to bring in some money for his family and make the final payment on his home when there is almost no one left who wants to live in it.

Although *Death of a Salesman* is set in the present, it also finds time and space to include the past. It plays the agonies of the moment of collapse against the pleasures and sorrows of recollected episodes. Mr. Miller is interested in more than the life and fate of his central character. His scene seems to be Willy Loman's mind and heart no less than his home. What we see might just as well be what Willy Loman thinks, feels, fears, or remembers, as what we see him doing. This gives the play a double and successful exposure in time. It makes possible the constant fusion of what has been and what is. It also enables it to achieve a greater reality by having been freed from the fetters of realism.

Once again Mr. Miller shows how fearless and perceptive an emotionalist he is. He writes boldly and brilliantly about the way in which we disappoint those we love by having disappointed ourselves. He knows the torment of family tensions, the compensations of friendship, and the heartbreak that goes with broken pride and lost confidence. He is aware of the loyalties, not blind but open-eyed, which are needed to support mortals in their loneliness. The anatomy of failure, the pathos of age, and the tragedy of those years when a life begins to slip down the hill it has labored to climb are subjects at which he excels.

The quality and intensity of his writing can perhaps best be suggested by letting Mr. Miller speak for himself, or rather by allowing his characters to speak for him, in a single scene; in fact, in the concluding one. It is then that Willy's wife, his two sons, and his old friend move away from Jo Mielziner's brilliantly simple and imaginative multiple setting, and advance to the footlights. It is then that Mr. Miller's words supply a scenery of their own. Willy Loman, the failure and suicide, has supposedly just been buried, and all of us are at his grave, including his wife who wants to cry but cannot and who keeps thinking that it is just as if he were off on another trip.

"You don't understand," says Willy's friend, defending Willy from one of his sons. "Willy was a salesman; and for a salesman, there is no rock bottom to the life. He don't put a bolt to a nut, he don't tell you the law, or give you medicine. He's a man way out there in the blue, ridin' on a smile and a shoeshine; and when they start not smilin' back—boys, that's an earthquake. And then you get yourself a couple a spots on your hat, and you're finished. Nobody dast blame this man. A salesman is got to dream, boys; it comes with the territory."

The production of *Death of a Salesman* is as sensitive, human, and powerful as the writing. Elia Kazan has solved, and solved superbly, what must have been a difficult and challenging problem. He captures to the full the mood and heartbreak of the script. He does this without ever surrendering to sentimentality. He manages to mingle the present and the past, the moment and the memory, so that their intertwining raises no questions and causes no confusions. His direction, so glorious in its vigor, is no less considerate of those small details which can be both mountainous and momentous in daily living.

It would be hard to name a play more fortunate in its casting than *Death of a Salesman*. All of its actors—especially Arthur Kennedy and Cameron Mitchell as the two sons, and Howard Smith as the friend—act with such skill and conviction that the line of demarcation between being and pretending seems abolished. The script's humanity has taken possession of their playing and is an integral part of their performances.

Special mention must be made of Lee J. Cobb and Mildred Dunnock as the salesman, Willy Loman, and his wife, Linda. Miss Dunnock is all heart, devotion, simplicity. She is unfooled but unfailing. She is the smiling, mothering, hardworked, good wife, the victim of her husband's budget. She is the nourisher of his dreams, even when she knows they are only dreams; the feeder of his self-esteem. If she is beyond whining or nagging, she is above self-pity. She is the marriage vow—"for better for worse, for richer for poorer, in sickness and in health"—made flesh; slight of body but strong of faith.

Mr. Cobb's Willy Loman is irresistibly touching and wonderfully unsparing. He is a great shaggy bison of a man seen at that moment of defeat when he is deserted by the herd and can no longer run with it. Mr. Cobb makes clear the pathetic extent to which the herd has been Willy's life. He also communicates the fatigue of Willy's mind and body and that boyish hope and buoyancy which his heart still retains. Age, however, is his enemy. He is condemned by it. He can no more escape from it than he can from himself. The confusions, the weakness, the goodness, the stupidity, and the self-sustaining illusions which are Willy—all of these are established by Mr. Cobb. Seldom has an average man at the moment of his breaking been characterized with such exceptional skill.

Did Willy Loman, so happy with a batch of cement, when puttering around the house, or when acquaintances on the road smiled back at him, fail to find out who he was? Did this man, who worked so hard and meant so well, dream the wrong dream? At least he was willing to die by that dream, even when it had collapsed for him. He was a breadwinner almost to the end, and a breadwinner even in his death. Did the world walk out on him, and his sons see through him? At any rate he could boast one friend who believed in him and thought his had been a good dream, "the only dream you can have." Who knows? Who can say? One thing is certain. No one could have raised the question more movingly or compassionately than Arthur Miller.

Eleanor Clark*

IT WOULD SEEM that the success of Arthur Miller's, or Elia Kazan's, *Death of a Salesman* has been due largely to the feeling of depression with which one makes for the exit. The idea is that anything that can make you feel that glum must be good, true and above all important—and publicity aside, it must be admitted that this cul-

* *Partisan Review*, Vol. XVI, No. 6 (June 1949). Reprinted by permission of the author and *Partisan Review*.

turally lace-curtain notion has a few things to support it these days at the Morosco. These are, notably, a superb performance by Lee Cobb as the salesman, a beautifully flexible and elegant stylization of a small Brooklyn house by Jo Mielziner, and a production so slick and fast that you have hardly the time or the presumption to question it. Unfortunately, however, it becomes necessary to question just what it is that gives the play its brilliant down-in-the-mouth effect, since it would surely be hard for any but its most insensitive admirers to deny that although they came out from it stuffed full of gloom, they were strangely lacking in a sense either of pity or of illumination.

They have seen a good, or good enough, man driven to suicide, a family in despair, an illusion shattered, and a portrayal of American life that should, it seems, have given them the sharpest pang of all; they have been expressly invited to indulge the tragic sense and to carry away a conception of man's fate as though from a production of *Oedipus Rex*, and what they have carried away instead is just that curious, rankling gloom. As the salesman's wife puts it after he has thrown himself under a train: "I can't cry. I want to cry, but I can't." If an honest poll could be taken it might well turn out that a large majority of these admirers, including the critics, had been secretly telling themselves not only after the play but during it that they were not really bored, just a little tired that night. Or was it perhaps that the tragic sense with all it has undergone from the facts of recent times needs now some entirely different, some unimaginably new appeal, and this was too much to ask of a play?—better be grateful for this. But of course there is no reason to be grateful for something that pretends to be what it is not, and the fact of the matter is that these secret whisperings, if they occurred, were well justified. The play, with its peculiar hodge-podge of dated materials and facile new ones, is not tragedy at all but an ambitious piece of confusionism, such as in any other sphere would probably be called a hoax, and which has been put across by purely technical skills not unlike those of a magician or an acrobat.

Up to a point this might be considered no more than the usual operation of the second-rate mind as glamorized by Broadway. But there is a particular twist to the matter this time, which helps to explain how a subject that in its general lines was run ragged fifteen or twenty years ago should be able to turn up now as a vehicle for such large claims and such ponderous emotionalizing.

Certainly as representing the false dream aspect of American society Mr. Miller's salesman offers nothing very original. The old gag about the installment-plan frigidaire ("Once in my life I'd like to own something outright before it's broke") are evidently still good for a laugh, and there is always a pocket of pathos reserved for the mortgage, but things have been sadder and funnier before. A slightly fresher breeze does blow at moments. Willy Loman calls for a genuine smile or two with his distinction between being "liked" and being "well-liked," and the perception behind this is accurate enough, even though in context it becomes one of the half-truths typical of the play. Willy's rock-bottom faith has been in the capacity to get along with people, to "make a good impression"; it is with this faith that he slides to old age and ruin while his brother Ben, who appears in some well-staged flashbacks, piles up a fortune in Alaska, and because of it at the end he is still pushing his favorite son Biff toward a failure worse than his own, the irony, as presented, lying not so much in the failure as in the denial of the man's true nature and talents along the way. Willy liked to work with his hands and had been happy when he was making a cement porch; and Biff, who had been happy as a ranch-hand in the West, has at the time of the play restlessly driven himself back home. In the end, after the suicide, it is the flashy son Hap, content with cheap success and easy women, who speaks of the salesman's dream as having been "good." Biff knows better—the dream was rotten though he speaks of his father nevertheless as a "prince"—and the wife knows better still; Willy was as good "as many other people." In short, he is the common man, and something or other has gone terribly wrong. The point is, what and why.

At first blush the answer seems fairly simple. Willy has a fatal flaw. He lives in a dream world; he can't face reality; he has always had excuses for his own failures ("the shop was closed for inventory") and has ruined Biff's life by indulging him all through his childhood in any whim including theft. It is a good theme. But it turns out not only that the author is saying a good deal more than this, but that he is also either very unclear as to his further meanings, or very anxious to present them and evade responsibility for them at the same time. It is, of course, the capitalist system that has done Willy in; the scene in which he is brutally fired after some forty years with the firm comes straight from the party line literature of the 'thirties, and the idea emerges lucidly enough through all the confused motivations of the play that it is our particular form of money economy that has bred the absurdly false ideals of both father and sons. It emerges, however, like a succession of shots from a duck-blind. Immediately after every crack the playwright withdraws behind an air of pseudo-universality, and hurries to present some cruelty or misfortune due either to Willy's own weakness, as when he refuses his friend's offer of a job after he has been fired, or gratuitously from some other source, as in the quite unbelievable scene of the two sons walking out on their father in the restaurant. In the end, after so much heaping of insult on injury, all one really knows about Willy Loman is that if the system doesn't kick him in the teeth he will do it himself—a well-known if wearisome tendency, that in itself might have dramatic possibilities, but that is neither particularly associated with salesmen nor adapted to the purposes of this play.

What it does lend itself to in this case is an intellectual muddle and a lack of candor that regardless of Mr. Miller's conscious intent are the main earmark of contemporary fellow-traveling. What used to be a roar has become a whine, and this particular piece of whining has been so expertly put over that it has been able to pass for something else, but behind all the fancy staging the old basic clumsiness and lack of humor are there. To be sure there are a few moments of ordinary Broadway sprightliness, as in the matter of the ice-box, or Hap's little performance with the girls in the restaurant, but these are in passing.

The crucial scenes, like the general conception, are all heavily deadpan, to an extent that floors the talents of every actor in the play but Mr. Cobb; Cameron Mitchell and Arthur Kennedy as the two sons do as well as possible with the script but both are driven by it at various points to over-act, and Mildred Dunnock in the part of the wife is obliged to keep up a tension of high-pitched nobility that would wear out one's tragic sense long before the end even if nothing else did. As for the clumsiness, it shows not only in the large aspects of the play but, rather surprisingly considering the general technical excellence of the job, in a number of small ones too. That the much-stressed point of Willy's being deprived of working with his hands, and of his pride in that, is not a specific reflection on the money standards which are central to the play's action, but as remarked on by many writers over the last hundred years, has to do with modern mechanized society in whatever form, could perhaps be passed over. But nothing excuses the triteness and pseudo-psychoanalytic nature of the Boston scene, dragged in to explain Biff's failures, though he would have been far better perceived as a contemporary character without it. It is also annoying not to know what the salesman sells, and whether or not the insurance is going to be paid after his death, and to have the wife say in her final speech that they were just getting out of debt, with no previous explanation of how, and when in fact we have just seen Willy getting further into debt.

These are details, but they indicate something of the speciousness of the play, which manages at every point to obscure both the real tragedy and the real comedy of the material. Willy is presumed to be losing his mind because he talks to himself, which permits the long series of flashbacks that give the play its illusion of liveliness, a form of madness that can at least, in the case, be called convenient; but all of us have seen and probably most of us have experienced delusions wilder and more illuminating than this. In the picture of Biff's unhappy restlessness Mr. Miller gives an impression of contemporaneity, but that is all; the true malaise of men of thirty now is a great deal more terrible than what happens to anyone in this play, and would not be a subject for a Broadway success. And so on. The play is made of such semi-perceptions, as can easily be appreciated by a glance at Eudora Welty's story, "Death of a Traveling Salesman," published some years ago.*

There are of course many possible approaches to the character of the salesman, and Miss Welty was humble in hers, but she succeeded nevertheless in some twenty pages in creating a figure of loneliness and haunting futility that conveys a truly tragic sense, and remains as a clear, echoing symbol in the mind. The story makes no claims, it says only what it has to say, at its own sure quiet pace, and its limitations are never violated, but it strikes deep and has been deeply felt and so they become irrelevant. If one chooses to take it that way, this is as strong a condemnation as one could wish of one of the abnormal, humanly

* And republished in *The Story: A Critical Anthology*, edited by Mark Schorer, Prentice-Hall, Inc., 1950.

stultifying aspects of our society, as represented by one of its most victimized as well as victimizing characters; and yet the effect, with all its continuing vibrations of meaning, has been achieved by nothing but a simple juxtaposition of a moment of the salesman's life with a pattern of simple, almost primitive love. There is no sound of whining here. It may be that this salesman too would have enjoyed working with his hands, but he is incapable of it; when his car rolls into a ditch another man has to haul it out for him, and he goes to his death in a dumb despair at the thought of that other man's life.

As against as strong and unpretentious a piece as this, Mr. Miller's use of his material seems even more unpleasantly pompous, and above all, flat. It can hardly have occurred to anyone to use such a word as, for instance, suggestiveness in connection with it. Everything is stated, two or three times over, all with a great air of something like poetry about it but actually with no remove, no moment of departure from the literal whatever; through scene after snappy scene the action ploughs along on a level of naturalism that has not even the virtue of being natural. A jumble of styles is maintained, with borrowings from the movies, the ballet and the Greeks, and at moments of particular significance the colloquial but unimagized language of the play becomes a trifle more genteel—"I search, and I search, and I search, and I can't understand," Willy's wife says after his suicide, though she has been foreseeing it and explaining it from the beginning of the play. But such tricks, however skillfully worked, are no substitute for real impact, and can only momentarily hide the fact that this is a very dull business, which departs in no way that is to its credit from the general mediocrity of our commercial theater. . . .

Frederick Morgan*

Arthur Miller's *Death of a Salesman* has received, this year, most of the prizes, plaudits and acclamations that inevitably attend the doings on Broadway. It is, not surprisingly, a miserable affair; and it would be unfair to single it out here from among the many Broad-

* From "Notes on the Theater," *The Hudson Review* Vol. II, No. 2 (Summer 1949), copyright 1949 by The Hudson Review, Inc. Reprinted by permission of the author and *The Hudson Review*.

way productions which are completely devoid of merit, were it not for just this excessive publicity which it has received. The action outlines the mental and moral collapse, leading to suicide, of an aging traveling salesman, who comes to realize that he had based his life on false ideals. Miller had the makings of some sort of play; but he was unfortunately unable to bring a single spark of dramatic intelligence to bear on his material. The terms in which he conceived of his theme are so trite and clumsy as to invalidate the entire play and render offensive its continual demand for the sympathy and indulgence of the audience. It proceeds, with unrelieved vulgarity, from cliché to stereotype. The language is entirely undistinguished (the personages are continually grunting, groaning and vehemently repeating the tritest colloquialisms); the tone of the play can best be described as a sustained snivel. With Tennessee Williams, one can at least maintain that he was "cut out to be" a playwright rather than a poet. But one would be justified in suspecting that the author of *Death of a Salesman* would have attained the same level of untalented and conscientious dullness if he had decided to write an epic poem or a novel instead of a play. On the basis of certain of his newspaper articles I presume that Miller considers his new play to be the Tragedy of a Common Man. It is not a tragedy; nor is it, rightly speaking, about any man, common or uncommon. It is, however, pure Broadway, Broadway in a self-pitying mood; and this no doubt accounts for its success, and for the esteem in which it is held by the newspaper reviewers. . . .

APPENDIX

*

APPENDIX

IF THE READER now knows something about dramatic art, he is in a position to compare the art of the stage with the most popular art of our time, that of the motion picture. Perhaps the boldest attempt to define the art of the motion picture (largely in contradistinction to the art of the stage) is an essay by Professor Erwin Panofsky here reprinted in its entirety.

STYLE AND MEDIUM IN THE MOTION PICTURES

FILM ART is the only art the development of which men now living have witnessed from the very beginnings; and this development is all the more interesting as it took place under conditions contrary to precedent. It was not an artistic urge that gave rise to the discovery and gradual perfection of a new technique; it was a technical invention that gave rise to the discovery and gradual perfection of a new art.

From this we understand two fundamental facts. First, that the primordial basis of the enjoyment of moving pictures was not an objective interest in a specific subject matter, much less an aesthetic interest in the formal presentation of subject matter, but the sheer delight in the fact that things seemed to move, no matter what things they were. Second, that films—first exhibited in "kinetoscopes," viz., cinematographic peep-shows, but projectable to a screen since as early as 1894—are, originally, a product of genuine folk art (whereas,

Critique (New York), I, No. 3 (January-February, 1947), pp. 5-28. Used by permission of the author. The first version of this essay was published in 1934 by the Department of Archaeology of Princeton University, a second one in transition, No. 26 (1937), and in *Preface to Our Day*, New York, 1940.

as a rule, folk art derives from what is known as "higher art"). At the very beginning of things we find the simple recording of movements: galloping horses, railroad trains, fire engines, sporting events, street scenes. And when it had come to the making of narrative films these were produced by photographers who were anything but "producers" or "directors," performed by people who were anything but actors, and enjoyed by people who would have been much offended had anyone called them "art lovers."

The casts of these archaic films were usually collected in a "café" where unemployed supers or ordinary citizens possessed of a suitable exterior were wont to assemble at a given hour. An enterprising photographer would walk in, hire four or five convenient characters and make the picture while carefully instructing them what to do: "Now, you pretend to hit this lady over the head"; and (to the lady): "And you pretend to fall down in a heap." Productions like these were shown, together with those purely factual recordings of "movement for movement's sake," in a few small and dingy cinemas mostly frequented by the "lower classes" and a sprinkling of youngsters in quest of adventure (about 1905, I happen to remember, there was only one obscure and faintly disreputable *kino* in the whole city of Berlin, bearing, for some unfathomable reason, the English name of "The Meeting Room"). Small wonder that the "better classes," when they slowly began to venture into these early picture theaters, did so, not by way of seeking normal and possibly serious entertainment, but with that characteristic sensation of self-conscious condescension with which we may plunge, in gay company, into the folkloristic depths of Coney Island or a European Kermis; even a few years ago it was the regulation attitude of the socially or intellectually prominent that one could confess to enjoying such austerely educational films as "The Sex Life of the Starfish" or films with "beautiful scenery," but never to a serious liking for narratives.

Today there is no denying that narrative films are not only "art" —not often good art, to be sure, but this applies to other media as well—but also, besides architecture, cartooning, and "commercial design," the only visual art entirely alive. The "movies" have re-established that dynamic contact between art production and art consumption which, for reasons too complex to be considered here, is sorely attenuated, if not entirely interrupted, in many other fields of artistic endeavor. Whether we like it or not, it is the movies that mold, more than any other single force, the opinions, the taste, the language, the dress, the behavior, and even the physical appearance of a public comprising more than 60% of the population of the earth. If all the serious lyrical poets, composers, painters and sculptors were forced by law to stop their activities, a rather small fraction of the general public would become aware of the fact and a still smaller fraction would seriously regret it. If the same thing were to happen with the movies the social consequences would be catastrophic.

* * * * *

In the beginning, then, there were the straight recordings of movement no matter what moved, viz., the prehistoric ancestors of our "documentaries"; and, soon after, the early narratives, viz., the prehistoric ancestors of our "feature films." The craving for a narrative element could be satisfied only by borrowing from older arts, and one should expect that the natural thing would have been to borrow from the theatre, a theatre play being apparently the *genus proximum* to a narrative film in that it consists of a narrative enacted by persons that move. But in reality the imitation of stage performances was a comparatively late and thoroughly frustrated development. What happened at the start was a very different thing: instead of imitating a theatrical performance already endowed with a certain amount of motion, the earliest films added movement to works of art originally stationary, so that the dazzling technical invention might achieve a triumph of its own without intruding upon the sphere of higher culture. The living language, which is always right, has endorsed this sensible choice when it still speaks of a "moving picture" or, simply, a "picture," instead of accepting the pretentious and fundamentally erroneous "screen play."

The stationary works enlivened in the earliest movies were indeed pictures: bad nineteenth-century paintings and postcards (or wax works *à la* Madame Tussaud's), supplemented by the comic strips— a most important root of cinematic art—and the subject matter of popular songs, pulp magazines and dime novels; and the films descending from this ancestry appealed directly and very intensely to a folk art mentality. They gratified—often simultaneously—first: a primitive sense of justice and decorum when virtue and industry were rewarded while vice and laziness were punished; second, plain sentimentality when "the thin trickle of a fictive love interest" took its course "through somewhat serpentine channels," or when, father, dear father, returned from the saloon to find his child dying of diphtheria; third, a primordial instinct for bloodshed and cruelty when Andreas Hofer faced the firing squad, or when (in a film of 1893/94) the head of Mary Queen of Scots actually came off; fourth, a taste for mild pornography (I remember with great pleasure a French film of *ca.* 1900 wherein a seemingly but not really well-rounded lady as well as a seemingly but not really slender one were shown changing to bathing suits—an honest, straightforward *porcheria* much less objectionable than the now extinct Betty Boop films and, I am sorry to say, some of the more recent Walt Disney productions); and, finally, that crude sense of humor, graphically described as "slapstick," which feeds upon the sadistic and the pornographic instinct, either singly or in combination.

Not until as late as *ca.* 1905 was a film adaptation of "Faust" ventured upon (cast still "unknown," characteristically enough), and not until 1911 did Sarah Bernhardt lend her prestige to an unbelievably funny film tragedy *Queen Elizabeth of England*. These films represent the first conscious attempt at transplanting the movies from the folk art level to that of "real art"; but they also bear witness to the fact that this commendable goal could not be reached in so simple a manner. It was soon realized that the imitation of a theatre performance with a set stage, fixed entries and exits, and distinctly literary ambitions is the one thing the film must avoid.

The legitimate paths of evolution were opened, not by running away from the folk art character of the primitive film but by developing it within the limits of its own possibilities. Those primordial archetypes of film productions on the folk art level—success or retribution, sentiment, sensation, pornography, and crude humor—could blossom forth into genuine history, tragedy and romance, crime and adventure, and comedy, as soon as it was realized that they could be transfigured: not by an artificial injection of literary values but by the exploitation of the unique and specific possibilities of the new medium. Significantly, the beginnings of this legitimate development antedate the attempts at endowing the film with higher values of a foreign order (the crucial period being the years from 1902 to *ca.*

1905), and the decisive steps were taken by people who were laymen or outsiders from the view-point of the serious stage.

*　　*　　*　　*　　*

These unique and specific possibilities can be defined as *dynamization of space* and, accordingly, *spatialization of time*. This statement is self-evident to the point of triviality but it belongs to that kind of truths which, just because of their triviality, are easily forgotten or neglected: all that which exists in space, even the walls of a room or the Rock of Gibraltar, can and should be invested with a semblance of movement, while all that which happens in time, even the thoughts and feelings in the souls of men, can and should be made visible.

In a theatre, space is static, that is, the space represented on the stage, as well as the spatial relation of the beholder to the spectacle, are unalterably fixed. The spectator cannot leave his seat, and the setting of the stage cannot change, during one act (except for such incidentals as rising moons or gathering clouds and such illegitimate re-borrowings from the film as turning wings or gliding backdrops). But, in return for this restriction, the theatre has the advantage that time, the medium of emotion and thought conveyable by speech, is free and independent of anything that may happen in visible space. Hamlet may deliver his famous monologue lying on a couch in the middle distance, doing nothing and only dimly discernible to the spectator and listener, and yet by his mere words enthrall him with a feeling of intensest emotional action.

With the movies the situation is reversed. Here, too, the spectator occupies a fixed seat, but only physically, not as the subject of an aesthetic experience. Aesthetically, he is in permanent motion as his eye identifies itself with the lens of the camera which permanently shifts in distance and direction. And as movable as the spectator is, as movable is, for the same reason, the space presented to him. Not only bodies move in space, but space itself does, approaching, receding, turning, dissolving and recrystallizing as it appears through the controlled locomotion and focussing of the camera and through the cutting and editing of the various shots—not to mention such special effects as visions, transformations, disappearances, slow-motion and fast-motion shots, reversals and trick films. This opens up a world of possibilities of which the stage can never dream. Quite apart from such photographic tricks as the participation of disembodied spirits in the action of the *Topper* series, or the more effective wonders wrought by Roland Young in *The Man Who Could Work Miracles*, there is, on the purely factual level, an untold wealth of themes as inaccessible to the "legitimate" stage as a fog or a snowstorm is to the sculptor; all sorts of violent elemental phenomena and, conversely, events too microscopic to be visible under normal conditions (such as the life-saving injection with the serum flown in at the very last moment, or the fatal bite of the yellow fever mosquito); full-scale battle scenes; all kinds of operations, not only in the surgical sense but also in the sense of any actual construction, destruction or experimentation, as in *Louis Pasteur* or *Madame Curie;* a really grand party, moving through many rooms of a mansion or palace. Features like these, even the mere shifting of the scene from one place to another by means of a car perilously negotiating heavy traffic or a motor-boat steered through a nocturnal harbour, will not only always retain their primitive cinematic appeal but also remain enormously effective as a means of stirring the emotions and creating suspense. In addition, the movies have the power, entirely denied to the theatre, to convey psychological experiences by directly projecting their content to the screen, substituting, as it were, the eye of the beholder for the consciousness of the character (as when the imaginings and hallucinations of the drunkard in the otherwise overrated *Lost Weekend* appear as stark realities instead of being described by mere words). But any attempt to convey thought and feelings exclusively, or even primarily, by speech leaves us with a feeling of embarrassment, boredom, or both.

What I mean by thoughts and feelings "conveyed exclusively, or even primarily, by speech" is simply this: contrary to naive expectation, the invention of the sound track in 1928 has been unable to change the basic fact that a moving picture, even when it has learned to talk, remains a picture that moves, and does not convert itself into a piece of writing that is enacted. Its substance remains a series of visual sequences held together by an uninterrupted flow of movement in space (except, of course, for such checks and pauses as have the same compositional value as a rest in music), and not a sustained study in human character and destiny transmitted by effective, let alone "beautiful," diction. I cannot remember a more misleading statement about the movies than Mr. Eric Bentley's in *The Playwright as Thinker*, p. 289: "[The potentialities of the talking screen] differ from those of the silent screen in adding the dimension of dialogue —which, potentially, is poetry." I would suggest: "The potentialities of the talking screen differ from those of the silent screen in integrating visible movement with dialogue which, therefore, had better not be poetry."

All of us, if we are old enough to remember the period prior to 1928, recall the old-time pianist who, with his eyes glued on the screen, would accompany the events with music adapted to their mood and rhythm; and we also recall the weird and spectral feeling overtaking us when this pianist left his post for a few minutes and the film was allowed to run by itself, the darkness haunted by the monotonous rattle of the machinery. Even the silent film, then, was never mute. The visible spectacle always required, and received, an audible accompaniment which, from the very beginning, distinguished the film from simple pantomime and rather classed it— *mutatis mutandis*—with the ballet. The advent of the talkie meant, not so much an "addition" as a transformation: the transformation of musical sound into articulate speech and, therefore, of quasi-pantomime into an entirely new species of spectacle which differs from the ballet, and agrees with the stage play, in that its acoustic component consists of intelligible words, but differs from the stage play and agrees with the ballet in that this acoustic component is not detachable from the visual. In a film, that which we hear remains, for good or worse, inextricably fused with that which we see; the sound, articulate or not, cannot express any more than is expressed, at the same time, by visible movement; and in a good film it does not even attempt to do so. To put it briefly: the play—or, as it is very properly called, the "script"—of a moving picture is subject to what might be termed the *principle of coexpressibility*.

Empirical proof of this principle is furnished by the fact that, wherever the dialogical or monological element gains temporary prominence there appears, with the inevitability of a natural law, the "close-up." What does the close-up achieve? In showing us, in magnification, either the face of the speaker or the face of the listeners or both in alternation, the camera transforms the human physiognomy into a huge field of action where—given the qualification of the performers—every subtle movement of the features, almost imperceptible from a natural distance, becomes an expressive event in visible space and thereby completely integrates itself with the expressive content of the spoken word; whereas, on the stage, the spoken word makes a stronger rather than a weaker impression if we are not permitted to count the hairs in Romeo's moustache.

This does not mean that the scenario is a negligible factor in the making of a moving picture. It only means that its artistic intention differs in kind from that of a stage play, and much more from that of a novel or a piece of poetry. As the success of a Gothic jamb figure depends, not only upon its quality as a piece of sculpture but also, or even more so, upon its integrability with the architecture of the portal, so does the success of a movie script—not unlike that of an opera libretto—depend, not only upon its quality as a piece of literature but also, or even more so, upon its integrability with the events on the screen.

As a result—another empirical proof of the coexpressibility principle—good movie scripts are unlikely to make good reading and have seldom been published in book form; whereas, conversely, good stage plays have to be severely altered, cut, and, on the other hand, enriched by interpolations to make good movie scripts. In Shaw's *Pygmalion,* for instance, the actual process of Eliza's phonetic education and, still more important, her final triumph at the grand party, are wisely omitted; we see—or, rather, hear—some samples of her gradual linguistic improvement and finally encounter her, upon her return from the reception, victorious and splendidly arrayed but deeply hurt for want of recognition and sympathy. In the film adaptation, precisely these two scenes are not only supplied but also strongly emphasized; we witness the fascinating activities in the laboratory with its array of spinning disks and mirrors, organ pipes and dancing flames, and we participate in the ambassadorial party, with many moments of impending catastrophe and a little counter-intrigue thrown in for suspense. Unquestionably these two scenes, entirely absent from the play, and indeed unachievable upon the stage, were the highlights of the film; whereas the Shavian dialogue, however severely cut, turned out to fall a little flat in certain moments. And wherever, as in so many other films, a poetic emotion, a musical outburst, or a literary conceit (even, I am grieved to say, some of the wisecracks of Groucho Marx) entirely lose contact with visible movement, they strike the sensitive spectator as, literally, out of place. It is certainly terrible when a soft-boiled He-Man, after the suicide of his mistress, casts a twelve-foot glance upon her photograph and says something less-than-coexpressible to the effect that he would never forget her. But when he recites, instead, a piece of poetry as sublimely more-than-coexpressible as Romeo's monologue at the bier of Juliet, it is still worse. Reinhardt's *Midsummer Night's Dream* is probably the most unfortunate major film ever produced; and Olivier's *Henry V* owes its comparative success, apart from the all but providential adaptability of this particular play, to so many *tours de force* that it will remain, God willing, an exception rather than set a pattern. It combines "judicious pruning" with the interpolation of pageantry, non-verbal comedy and melodrama; it uses a device perhaps best designated as "oblique close-up" (Mr. Olivier's beautiful face inwardly listening to but not pronouncing the great soliloquy); and, most notably, it shifts between three levels of archaeological reality: a reconstruction of Elizabethan London, a reconstruction of the events of 1415 as laid down in Shakespeare's play, and the reconstruction of a performance of this play on Shakespeare's own stage. All this is perfectly legitimate; but, even so, the highest praise of the film will always come from those who, like the critics of the *New Yorker,* are not quite in sympathy with either the movies *au naturel* or Shakespeare *au naturel.*

* * * * *

As the writings of Conan Doyle potentially contain all modern mystery stories (except for the tough specimens of the Dashiell Hammett school), so do the films produced between 1900 and 1910 preestablish the subject matter and methods of the moving picture as we know it. This period produced the incunabula of the Western and the crime film (Edwin S. Porter's amazing *Great Train Robbery* of 1903) from which developed the modern Gangster, Adventure, and Mystery pictures (the latter, if well done, is still one of the most honest and genuine forms of film entertainment, space being doubly charged with time as the beholder asks himself, not only "what is going to happen?" but also "what has happened before?"). The same period saw the emergence of the fantastically imaginative film (Méliès) which was to lead to the expressionist and surrealist experiments (*The Cabinet of Dr. Caligari, Sang d'un Poète,* etc.), on the one hand, and to the more superficial and spectacular fairy tales à la Arabian Nights, on the other. Comedy, later to triumph in Charlie Chaplin, the still insufficiently appreciated Buster Keaton, the Marx Brothers, and the pre-Hollywood creations of René Clair, reached a respectable level in Max Linder and others. In historical and melodramatic films the foundations were laid for movie iconography and movie symbolism, and in the early work of D. W. Griffith we find, not only remarkable attempts at psychological analysis (*Edgar Allen Poe*) and social criticism (*A Corner in Wheat*) but also such basic technical innovations as the long-shot, the flashback and the close-up. And modest trick-films and cartoons paved the way to Felix the Cat, Pop-Eye the Sailor, and Felix's prodigious offspring, Mickey Mouse.

Within their self-imposed limitations the earlier Disney films, and certain sequences in the later ones,[1] represent, as it were, a chemi-

---

[1] I make this distinction because it was, in my opinion, a fall from grace when *Snow-White* introduced the human figure and when *Fantasia* attempted to picturalize The World's Great Music. The very virtue of the animated cartoon is to animate, that is to say, endow lifeless things with life, or living things with a different kind of life. It effects a metamorphosis, and such a metamorphosis is wonderfully present in Disney's animals, plants, thunderclouds and railroad trains. Whereas his dwarfs, glamorized princesses, hillbillies, baseball players, rouged centaurs and *amigos* from South America are not transformations but caricatures at best, and fakes or vulgarities at worst. Concerning music, however, it should be borne in mind that its cinematic use is no less predicated upon the principle of co-expressibility than is the cinematic use of the spoken word. There is music permitting or even requiring the accompaniment of visible action (such as dances, ballet music and any kind of operatic compositions) and music of which the opposite is true; and this is, again, not a question of quality (most of us rightly prefer a waltz by Johann Strauss to a symphony by Sibelius) but one of intention. In *Fantasia* the hippopotamus ballet was wonderful, and the Pastoral Symphony and Ave Maria sequences were deplorable, not because the cartooning in the first case was infinitely better than in the two others (*cf. above*), and certainly not because Beethoven and Schubert are too sacred for picturalization, but simply because Ponchielli's Dance of the Hours is coexpressible while the Pastoral Symphony and the Ave Maria are not. In cases like these even the best imaginable music and the best imaginable cartoon will impair rather than enhance each other's effectiveness.

cally pure distillation of cinematic possibilities. They retain the most important folkloristic elements—sadism, pornography, the humor engendered by both, and moral justice—almost without dilution and often fuse these elements into a variation on the primitive and inexhaustible David-and-Goliath motif, the triumph of the seemingly weak over the seemingly strong; and their fantastic independence of the natural laws gives them the power to integrate space with time to such perfection that the spatial and temporal experiences of sight and hearing come to be almost interconvertible. A series of soap bubbles, successively punctured, emits a series of sounds exactly corresponding in pitch and volume to the size of the bubbles; the three uvulae of Willie the Whale—small, large and medium—vibrate in consonance with tenor, bass and baritone notes; and the very concept of stationary existence is completely abolished. No object in creation, whether it be a house, a piano, a tree, or an alarm clock, lacks the faculties of organic, in fact anthropomorphic, movement, facial expression and phonetic articulation. Incidentally, even in normal, "realistic" films the inanimate object, provided that it is dynamizable, can play the role of a leading character as do the ancient railroad engines in Buster Keaton's *General* and *Niagara Falls*. How the earlier Russian films exploited the possibility of heroizing all sorts of machinery lives in everybody's memory; and it is perhaps more than an accident that the two films which will go down in history as the great comical and the great serious masterpiece of the silent period bear the names and immortalize the personalities of two big ships: Keaton's *Navigator* (1924) and Eisenstein's *Potemkin* (1925).

* * * * *

The evolution from the jerky beginnings to this grand climax offers the fascinating spectacle of a new artistic medium gradually becoming conscious of its legitimate, that is, exclusive, possibilities and limitations—a spectacle not unlike the development of the mo-

---

Experimental proof of all this was furnished by Disney's more recent *Make Mine Music* where The World's Great Music was fortunately restricted to Prokofieff. Even among the other sequences the most successful ones were those in which the human element was either absent or reduced to a minimum; Willie the Whale, the Ballad of Johnny Fedora and Alice Blue-Bonnet, and, above all, the truly magnificent Goodman Quartet.

saic, which started out with transposing illusionistic genre pictures into a more durable material and culminated in the hieratic supernaturalism of Ravenna; or the development of line engraving, which started out as a cheap and handy substitute for book illumination and culminated in the purely "graphic" style of Dürer.

Just so the silent movies developed a definite style of their own, adapted to the specific conditions of the medium. A hitherto unknown language was forced upon a public not yet capable of reading it, and the more proficient the public became the more refinement could develop in the language. For a Saxon peasant of around 800 it was not easy to understand the meaning of a picture showing a man as he pours water over the head of another man, and even later many people found it difficult to grasp the significance of two ladies standing behind the throne of an emperor. For the public of around 1910 it was no less difficult to understand the meaning of the speechless action in a moving picture, and the producers employed means of clarification similar to those we find in mediaeval art. One of these were printed titles or letters, striking equivalents of the mediaeval *tituli* and scrolls (at a still earlier date there even used to be explainers who would say, *viva voce:* "Now he thinks his wife is dead but she isn't" or: "I don't wish to offend the ladies in the audience but I doubt that any of them would have done that much for her child"). Another, less obtrusive method of explanation was the introduction of a fixed iconography which from the outset informed the spectator about the basic facts and characters, much as the two ladies behind the emperor, when carrying a sword and a cross, respectively, were uniquely determined as Fortitude and Faith. There arose, identifiable by standardized appearance, behavior, and attributes, the well-remembered types of the Vamp and the Straight Girl (perhaps the most convincing modern equivalents of the mediaeval personifications of the Vices and Virtues), the Family Man, and the Villain, the latter marked by a black moustache and walking stick. Nocturnal scenes were printed on blue or green film. A checkered table cloth meant, once for all, a "poor but honest" milieu; a happy marriage, soon to be endangered by the shadows from the past, was symbolized by the young wife's pouring the breakfast coffee for her husband; the first kiss was invariably announced by the lady's gently playing with her partner's necktie and was invariably accompanied by her kicking out with her left foot. The conduct of the characters was predetermined accordingly. The poor but honest laborer who, after leaving his little house with the checkered table cloth, came upon an abandoned baby could not but take it to his home and bring it up as best he could; the Family Man could not but yield, however temporarily, to the temptations of the Vamp. As a result these early melodramas had a highly gratifying and soothing quality in that events took shape, without the complications of individual psychology, according to a pure Aristotelian logic so badly missed in real life.

Devices like these became gradually less necessary as the public grew accustomed to interpret the action by itself and were virtually abolished by the invention of the talking film. But even now there survive—quite legitimately, I think—the remnants of a "fixed attitude and attribute" principle and, more basic, a primitive or folkloristic concept of plot construction. Even today we take it for granted that the diphtheria of a baby tends to occur when the parents are out, and, having occurred, solves all their matrimonial problems. Even today we demand of a decent mystery film that the butler, though he may be anything from an agent of the British Secret Service to the real father of the daughter of the house, must not turn out to be the murderer. Even today we love to see Pasteur, Zola, or Ehrlich win out against stupidity and wickedness, with their respective wives trusting and trusting all the time. Even today we much prefer a happy finale to a gloomy one, and insist, at the very least, on the observance of the Aristotelian rule that the story have a beginning, a middle, and an ending—a rule the abrogation of which has done so much to estrange the general public from the more elevated spheres of modern writing. Primitive symbolism, too, survives in such amusing details as the last sequence of *Casablanca* where the delightfully crooked and right-minded *Préfet de Police* casts an empty bottle of Vichy water into the wastepaper basket; and in such telling symbols of the supernatural as Sir Cedric Hardwicke's Death in the guise of a "gentleman in a dustcoat trying" (*On Borrowed Time*) or Claude Rains' Hermes Psychopompos in the striped trousers of an airline manager (*Here Comes Mister Jordan*).

The most conspicuous advances were made in directing, lighting, camera work, cutting, and acting proper. But while in most of these fields the evolution proceeded continuously—though, of course, not without detours, breakdowns and archaic relapses—the development of acting suffered a sudden interruption by the invention of the talking film; so that the style of acting in the silents can already be evaluated in retrospect, as a lost art not unlike the painting technique of Jan van Eyck or, to take up our previous simile, the burin technique of Dürer. It was soon realized that acting in a silent film neither meant a pantomimic exaggeration of stage acting (as was generally and erroneously assumed by professional stage actors who more and more frequently condescended to perform in the movies), nor could dispense with stylization altogether; a man photographed while walking down a gangway in ordinary, every-day-life fashion looked like anything but a man walking down a gangway when the result appeared on the screen. If the picture was to look both natural and meaningful the acting had to be done in a manner equally different from the style of the stage and the reality of ordinary life; speech had to be made dispensable by establishing an organic relation between the acting and the technical procedure of cine-photography—much as in Dürer's prints color had been made dispensable by establishing an organic relation between the design and the technical procedure of line engraving.

This was precisely what the great actors of the silent period accomplished, and it is a significant fact that the best of them did not come from the stage, whose crystallized tradition prevented Duse's only film, *Cenere,* from being more than a priceless record of Duse. They came instead from the circus or the variety, as was the case of Chaplin, Keaton and Will Rogers; from nothing in particular, as was the case of Theda Bara, of her greater European parallel, the Danish actress Asta Nielsen, and of Garbo; or from everything under the sun, as was the case of Douglas Fairbanks. The style of these "old masters" was indeed comparable to the style of line engraving in that it was, and had to be, exaggerated in comparison with stage acting (just as the sharply incised and vigorously curved *tailles* of the burin are exaggerated in comparison with pencil strokes or brushwork), but richer, subtler and infinitely more precise. The advent of the talkies, reducing if not abolishing this difference between acting and stage acting, thus confronted the actors and actresses of the silent screen with a serious problem. Buster Keaton yielded to temptation and fell. Chaplin first tried to stand his ground and to remain an exquisite archaist but finally gave in, with only moderate success (*The Dictator*). Only the glorious Harpo has thus far successfully refused to utter a single articulate sound; and only Greta Garbo succeeded, in a measure, in transforming her style in principle. But even in her case one cannot help feeling that her first talking picture, *Anna Christie,* where she could ensconce herself, most of the time, in mute or monosyllabic sullenness, was better than her later performances; and in the second, talking version of *Anna Karenina,* the weakest moment is certainly when she delivers a big Ibsenian speech to her husband, and the strongest when she silently moves along the platform of the railroad station while her despair takes shape in the consonance of her movement (and expression) with the movement of the nocturnal space around her, filled with the real noises of the trains and the imaginary sound of the "little men with the iron hammers" that drives her, relentlessly and almost without her realizing it, under the wheels.

Small wonder that there is sometimes felt a kind of nostalgia for the silent period and that devices have been worked out to combine the virtues of sound and speech with those of silent acting, such as the "oblique close-up" already mentioned in connection with *Henry V;* the dance behind glass doors in *Sous les Toits de Paris;* or, in the *Histoire d'un Tricheur,* Sacha Guitry's recital of the events of his youth while the events themselves are "silently" enacted on the screen. However, this nostalgic feeling is no argument against the talkies as such. Their evolution has shown that, in art, every gain entails a certain loss on the other side of the ledger; but that the gain remains a gain, provided that the basic nature of the medium is realized and respected. One can imagine that, when the cave-men of Altamira began to paint their buffaloes in natural colors instead of merely incising the contours, the more conservative cave-men foretold the end of palaeolithic art. But palaeolithic art went on, and so will the movies. New technical inventions always tend to dwarf the values already attained, especially in a medium that owes its very existence to technical experimentation. The earliest talkies were infinitely inferior to the then mature silents, and most of the present technicolor films are still inferior to the now mature talkies in black and white. But even if Aldous Huxley's nightmare should come true and the experiences of taste, smell and touch should be added to those of sight and hearing, even then we may say with the Apostle, as we have said when first confronted with the sound track and the technicolor film: "We are troubled on every side, yet not distressed; we are perplexed, but not in despair."

* * * * *

From the law of time-charged space and space-bound time, there follows the fact that the *"screen play,"* in contrast to the theater play, *has no aesthetic existence independent of its performance, and that its characters have no aesthetic existence outside the actors.*

The playwright writes in the fond hope that his work will be an imperishable jewel in the treasure house of civilization and will be presented in hundreds of performances that are but transient variations on a "work" that is constant. The script writer, on the other hand, writes for one producer, one director and one cast. Their work achieves the same degree of permanence as does his; and should the same or a similar scenario ever be filmed by a different director and a different cast there will result an altogether different "play."

Othello and Nora are definite, substantial figures created by the playwright. They can be played well or badly, and they can be "interpreted" in one way or another; but they most definitely exist, no matter who plays them or even whether they are played at all. The character in a film, however, lives and dies with the actor. It is not the entity "Othello" interpreted by Robeson or the entity "Nora" interpreted by Duse; it is the entity "Greta Garbo" incarnate in a figure called Anna Christie or the entity "Robert Montgomery" incarnate in a murderer who, for all we know or care to know, may forever remain anonymous but will never cease to haunt our memories. Even when the names of the characters happen to be Henry VIII or Anna Karenina, the King who ruled England from 1509 to 1547 and the woman created by Tolstoi do not exist outside the being of Garbo and Laughton. They are but empty and incorporeal outlines like the shadows in Homer's Hades, assuming the character of reality only when filled with the life blood of an actor. Conversely, if a movie role is badly played there remains literally nothing of it, no matter how interesting the character's psychology or how elaborate the words.

What applies to the actor applies, *mutatis mutandis,* to most of the other artists, or artisans, who contribute to the making of a film: the director, the sound man, the enormously important camera man, even the make-up man. A stage production is rehearsed until everything is ready, and then it is repeatedly performed in three consecutive hours. At each performance everybody has to be on hand and does his work; and afterwards he goes home and to bed. The work of the stage actor may thus be likened to that of a musician, and that of the stage director to that of a conductor. Like these, they have a certain répertoire which they have studied and present in a number of complete but transitory performances, be it "Hamlet" today and "Ghosts" tomorrow, or "Life with Father" *per saecula saeculorum.* The activities of the film actor and the film director, however, are comparable, respectively, to those of the plastic artist and the architect, rather than to those of the musician and conductor. Stage work is continuous but transitory; film work is discontinuous but permanent. Individual sequences are done piecemeal and out of order according to the most efficient use of sets and personnel. Each bit is done over and over again until it stands; and when the whole has been cut and composed everyone is through with it forever. Needless to say that this very procedure cannot but emphasize the curious consubstantiality that exists between the person of the movie actor and his role. Coming into existence piece by piece, regardless of the natural sequence of events, the "character" can grow into a unified whole only if the actor manages to be, not merely to play, Henry VIII or Anna Karenina throughout the entire wearisome period of shooting. I have it on the best of authorities that Laughton was really difficult to live with in the particular six or eight weeks during which he was doing—or rather being—Captain Bligh.

It might be said that a film, called into being by a cooperative effort in which all contributions have the same degree of permanence, is the nearest modern equivalent of a mediaeval cathedral; the role of the producer corresponding, more or less, to that of the bishop or archbishop; that of the director to that of the architect-in-chief; that of the scenario writers to that of the scholastic advisers, establishing the iconographical program; and that of the actors, camera men, cutters, sound men, make-up men and the divers technicians to that of those whose work provided the physical entity of the finished product, from the sculptors, glass painters, bronze casters, carpenters and skilled masons down to the quarry men and woodsmen. And if you speak to any one of these collaborators he will tell you, with perfect *bona fides,* that his is really the most important job—which is quite true to the extent that it is indispensable.

This comparison may seem sacrilegious, not only because there are, proportionally, fewer good films than there are good cathedrals, but also because the movies are commercial. However, if commercial art be defined as all art not primarily produced in order to gratify the creative urge of its maker but primarily intended to meet the requirements of a patron or a buying public, it must be said that non-commercial art is the exception rather than the rule, and a fairly recent and not always felicitous exception at that. While it is true that commercial art is always in danger of ending up as a prostitute, it is equally true that non-commercial art is always in danger of ending up as an old maid. Non-commercial art has given us Seurat's *Grande Jatte* and Shakespeare's Sonnets, but also much that is esoteric to the point of incommunicability. Conversely, commercial art has given us much that is vulgar or snobbish (two aspects of the same thing) to the point of loathsomeness, but also Dürer's prints and Shakespeare's plays. For, we must not forget that Dürer's prints were partly made on commission and partly intended to be sold in the open market; and that Shakespeare's plays—in contrast to the earlier masques and *intermezzi* which were produced at court by aristocratic amateurs and could afford to be so incomprehensible that even those who described them in printed monographs occasionally failed to grasp their intended significance—were meant to appeal, and did appeal, not only to the select few but also to everyone who was prepared to pay a shilling for admission.

It is this requirement of communicability that makes commercial art more vital than non-commercial, and therefore potentially much more effective for better or for worse. The commercial producer can both educate and pervert the general public, and can allow the general public—or rather his idea of the general public—both to educate and to pervert himself. As is demonstrated by a number of excellent films that proved to be great box office successes, the public does not refuse to accept good products if it gets them. That it does not get them very often is caused, not so much by commercialism as such as by too little discernment and, paradoxical though it may seem, too much timidity in its application. Hollywood believes that it must produce "what the public wants" while the public would take whatever Hollywood produces. If Hollywood were to decide for itself what it wants it would get away with it—even if it should decide to "depart from evil and do good." For, to revert to whence we started: in modern life the movies are what most other forms of art have ceased to be, not an adornment but a necessity.

That this should be so is understandable, not only from a sociological but also from an art-historical point of view. The processes of all the earlier representational arts conform, in a higher or lesser degree, to an idealistic conception of the world. These arts operate from top to bottom, so to speak, and not from bottom to top; they start with an idea to be projected into shapeless matter and not with the objects that constitute the physical world. The painter works on a blank wall or canvas which he organizes into a likeness of things and persons according to his idea (however much this idea may have been nourished by reality); he does not work with the things and persons themselves even if he works "from the model." The same is true of the sculptor with his shapeless mass of clay or his untooled block of stone or wood; of the writer with his sheet of paper or his dictaphone; and even of the stage designer with his empty and sorely limited section of space. It is the movies, and only the movies, that do justice to that materialistic interpretation of the universe which, whether we like it or not, pervades contemporary civilization. Excepting the very special case of the animated cartoon, the movies organize material things and persons, not a neutral medium, into a composition that receives its style, and may even become fantastic or pretervoluntarily symbolic,[2] not so much by an interpretation in the artist's mind as by the actual manipulation of physical objects and

[2] I cannot help feeling that the final sequence of the Marx Brothers film *Night in Casablanca*—where Harpo unaccountably usurps the pilot's seat of a big airplane, causes incalculable havoc by flicking one tiny little control after another, and waxes the more insane with joy the greater the disproportion between the smallness of his effort and the magnitude of the disaster—is a magnificent and terrifying symbol of man's behavior in the "atomic age." No doubt the Marx Brothers would vigorously reject this interpretation; but so would Dürer have done had anyone told him that his Apocalypse foreshadowed the cataclysm of the Reformation.

recording machinery. The medium of the movies is physical reality as such: the physical reality of eighteenth-century Versailles—no matter whether it be the original or a Hollywood facsimile indistinguishable therefrom for all aesthetic intents and purposes—or of a suburban home in Westchester; the physical reality of the Rue de Lappe in Paris or of the Gobi Desert, of Paul Ehrlich's apartment in Frankfurt or of the streets of New York in the rain; the physical reality of engines and animals, of Edward G. Robinson and Jimmy Cagney. All these objects and persons must be organized into a work of art. They can be arranged in all sorts of ways ("arrangement" comprising, of course, such things as make-up, lighting and camera work); but there is no running away from them. From this point of view it becomes evident that an attempt at subjecting the world to artistic pre-stylization, as in the expressionist settings of *The Cabinet of Doctor Caligari* (1919), could be no more than an exciting experiment that could exert but little influence upon the general course of events. To pre-stylize reality prior to tackling it amounts to dodging the problem. The problem is to manipulate and shoot unstylized reality in such a way that the result has style. This is a proposition no less legitimate and no less difficult than any proposition in the older arts.

★

PROFESSOR PANOFSKY indicates that his view of the movies is different from that of the present editor. The latter has the following questions to ask:

1. Mr. Panofsky argues that the proper style for the film is realism, yet he argues also in favor of Disney. What is the logic here?
2. A movie, says Mr. Panofsky, exists only as performed: there is no play-script. Isn't this misleading? Couldn't one equally say: "Music exists only as performed: there is no score"?
3. Is it true that the movie actor *necessarily* "is" the rôle in a way that the stage actor is not? Or is Mr. Panofsky here (as elsewhere) assuming that something *must* be so because at

present it *happens* to be so? Thus present-day studio procedures are elevated to the rank of divine ordinance.

4. Is the view that the actor "is" the rôle compatible with Mr. Panofsky's remarks on movie acting on page 768?

5. Could not Mr. Panofsky's point about close-ups (pp. 761-62) be used to support an opposite conclusion, namely, that the close-up does enable the screen to present drama that is mainly psychological?

6. Is sound in talking pictures just an extension of the piano accompaniment to silents? How would one prove this? (In *Film Technique,* the great film director Pudovkin writes: "Music must in sound film *never be the accompaniment*. It must retain its own line.")

7. Is space as unimportant on the stage as Mr. Panofsky seems to assume? After all not many plays just present a young man in black making soliloquies from his sofa.

8. In presenting space there are admittedly many things the camera can do which the stage cannot do. But has not the stage, for its part, certain advantages—in regard to space?

9. Has the principle of co-expressibility no application to the stage?

10. Mr. Panofsky regards the play as primarily something heard, the film as primarily something seen. Is this a satisfactory statement? Or might it be said that, in principle, Mr. Panofsky is talking about *radio* plays and *silent* films?

11. Mr. Panofsky assumes that a medium, such as film, has a "basic nature" and that an artist's job is to exploit "the unique and specific possibilities of [his] medium." Thus Mr. Panofsky speaks on the one hand of the "legitimate paths of evolution" in which an art may run and, on the other, of "illegitimate" borrowings from other arts. It might, however, be argued that an art can be just as effective on territory which it has in common with another art as on its own unique and separate ground. Thus a good scene in a movie might be pretty close to theater and vice versa. Or not?

21. Mr. Panofsky assumes (a) that the nature of a machine—the camera—determines the nature of the film art; (b) that art produced commercially and approved by the general public is

more real than any other; and (c) that, in general, the arts are governed by known or knowable laws. These laws turn out to be either Mr. Panofsky's theories raised to the rank of dogma (e.g., the law of time-charged space) or are a result of confusing the *origin* of a thing with the *nature* of a thing: film began as a miraculous mechanism which appealed to the masses, therefore the nature of film is to be, now and always, a miraculous mechanism which appeals to masses. Are not all these propositions highly questionable?

Answers to questions 7 and 8—very different answers from Mr. Panofsky's—are to be found in the essays of Adolphe Appia, excerpts from which were printed in *Theatre Arts Monthly*, August 1932: in Appia's opinion *space* and *movement* are basic categories of the theatrical art. A characteristic statement of his position occurs in his book *The Living Work of Art* (as cited in *Theatre Arts*): "The body, the living, moving body of the actor represents movement in space. Its rôle is therefore of capital importance. Without the text (with or without music) dramatic art ceases to exist. The actor is the bearer of the text. Without movement the other arts cannot take part in the action. The actor holds the text with one hand, with the other he grasps, as in a sheaf, the arts of space. Then, irresistibly, he brings his two hands together and creates, by movement, the integrated work of art. The living body is thus the creator of that art. . . ."

The Panofskyan tradition, on the other hand, is upheld by many serious critics of film, such as George Barbarow in the magazine *Politics* (1946-8) and *The Hudson Review* (1948-).

For an attempt to write an Aristotelian poetics of the film, see Mortimer J. Adler's *Art and Prudence*. For an imaginative account of the film as a new—or, in part, very old—kind of drama, see Arthur Mizener's essay "The Elizabethan Art of Our Movies," *The Kenyon Review*, Spring, 1942. Among books by actual makers of film, probably the best are *Film Technique and Film Acting*, by V. I. Pudovkin, and *The Film Sense* and *Film Form*, both by Sergei Eisenstein.

SUGGESTIONS FOR READING

BY FAR the most readable collection of Greek plays in English is *Greek Plays in Modern Translation* (Dial Press and Dryden Press), edited by Dudley Fitts. Shakespeare's plays are most pleasant to read in separate volumes, as in the Penguin Shakespeare, the New Temple Shakespeare, or even the more classroom-ish Kittredge (Ginn & Co.) and Yale Shakespeares. The most attractive one-volume Shakespeares are probably the Shakespeare Head Edition (Blackwell and Oxford University), the Neilson-Hill Edition (Houghton, Mifflin), and *Shakespeare: 23 Plays and the Sonnets* (Harcourt, Brace & Co.). The last contains fascinating pictorial material. The handiest and handsomest Molière in French is the two-volume Pléiade Edition (Gallimard). The reader whose French is weak will do better with *Ten Masterpieces of Molière,* edited by H. W. Church (Harper & Brothers.) The reader whose French is non-existent can choose between the Molière collections in the Modern and Everyman's Libraries; neither is very satisfactory. Ibsen is most readily available to the American public in *Three Plays* (Rinehart Editions) and two Modern Library volumes. Two Strindberg collections are in print at the moment of writing (1949). They are *Plays* in three volumes (J. W. Luce, Boston) and *Eight Famous Plays* (Scribner's).

Among general anthologies of modern drama, perhaps the most useful are: *Twenty-Five Modern Plays,* edited by S. Marion Tucker and Alan S. Downer (Harper & Brothers) and the three-volume anthology edited by Harlan Hatcher—*Modern Continental Dramas, Modern British Dramas, Modern American Dramas* (Harcourt, Brace & Co.).

Among separate editions of plays in the present anthology, two are of special interest: *Stanislavsky Produces Othello* (Geoffrey Bles, London), which is Stanislavsky's edition of *Othello*—or rather of its first three acts—and *L'avare* in the Editions Mises en Scène, Paris, edited by Charles Dullin. Since neither *Twelfth Night* nor the "willow" scene of Othello can be understood without music, the reader is recommended to obtain either *Shakespeare Music* (2nd. ed. 1928), edited by E. W. Naylor, or any phonograph recording of the songs concerned.

Among books similar in intention to the present volume, *Understanding Drama,* edited by Cleanth Brooks and Robert Heilman (Henry Holt & Co.), is outstanding.

Beyond this, the best reading list could be compiled from the chapter headings, indexes, and bibliographies of such books as John Gassner's *Masters of the Drama* (Dover Publications) and Allardyce Nicoll's *World Drama* (Harcourt, Brace & Co.)